The

MIDNIGHT CRY

★ ★ ★ ★ ★ ★ ★ ★

A DEFENSE OF THE CHARACTER AND CONDUCT
OF WILLIAM MILLER AND THE MILLERITES,
WHO MISTAKENLY BELIEVED THAT THE
SECOND COMING OF CHRIST WOULD TAKE
PLACE IN THE YEAR 1844

BY

FRANCIS D. NICHOL

★

TEACH Services, Inc.
PUBLISHING
www.TEACHServices.com • (800) 367-1844

World rights reserved. This book or any portion thereof may not be copied or reproduced in any form or manner whatever, except as provided by law, without the written permission of the publisher, except by a reviewer who may quote brief passages in a review.

This book was written to provide truthful information in regard to the subject matter covered. The author assumes full responsibility for the accuracy of all facts and quotations as cited in this book. The opinions expressed in this book are the author's personal views and interpretation of the Bible, Spirit of Prophecy, and/or contemporary authors and do not necessarily reflect those of TEACH Services, Inc.

This book is sold with the understanding that the publisher is not engaged in giving spiritual, legal, medical, or other professional advice. If authoritative advice is needed, the reader should seek the counsel of a competent professional.

Facsimile Reproduction

As this book play a formative role in the development of Christian thought and the publisher feels that this book, with its candor and depth, still holds significance for the church today. Therefore, the publisher has chosen to reproduce this historical classic from an original copy. Frequent variations in the quality of the print are unavoidable due to the condition of the original. Thus the print may look darker or lighter or appear to missing detail, more in some places than in others.

Copyright © 2000, 2005, 2013 TEACH Services, Inc.
ISBN-13: 978-1-4796-0235-3
Library of Congress Control Number: 2013942081

Published by

WILLIAM MILLER, LEADER OF THE MILLERITE MOVEMENT

To My Mother, Who Taught Me in Childhood the Blessed Hope of the Advent; and to My Father, Who Daily Prayed at the Family Altar for the Speedy Coming of Our Lord, This Book Is Affectionately Dedicated.

THE MIDNIGHT CRY

This phrase, which the Millerites used to describe their message to the world, is adapted from the words of Christ's parable regarding the wise and foolish virgins who were waiting for the bridegroom to come forth that they might go "with him to the marriage." During the long wait they "all slumbered and slept. And at midnight there was a cry made, Behold, the bridegroom cometh; go ye out to meet him." The wise virgins had taken oil in their lamps. All arose when the cry went forth at midnight. The foolish went to buy oil; the wise went in with the bridegroom to the marriage celebration, and "the door was shut." The lesson Christ drew was this: "Watch therefore, for ye know neither the day nor the hour wherein the Son of man cometh." Matthew 25:1-13. The language of this parable is woven all through Millerite literature. They believed they fulfilled this parable.

Contents

	From the Author to the Reader of This Book	9
1.	From Cradle to Army Camp	17
2.	From Doubt to Faith	26
3.	From Farmer to Preacher	41
4.	Laying the Groundwork of the Movement	57
5.	Millerism Spreads to the Great Cities	70
6.	The Movement Takes Definite Shape	85
7.	The First Millerite Camp Meeting	104
8.	The Great Tent is Raised	114
9.	Interest and Opposition Increase	126
10.	The Year of the End of the World	135
11.	The First Disappointment	158
12.	The Millerite Leaders—Courageous Individualists	174
13.	Other Millerite Spokesmen	191
14.	"Behold the Bridegroom Cometh"	206
15.	Hastening on to the Climax	217
16.	The Great Day of Hope	228
17.	The Great Disappointment	247
18.	Confident in Defeat	261
19.	The Movement Called Millerism Draws to Its Close	274
20.	The Kind of World in Which Millerism Flourished	288
21.	Did the Millerites Indulge in Fanatical Practices?	303
22.	Was Fanaticism Rampant in October, 1844?	321
23.	Did Millerism Cause Insanity, Suicide, and Murder?	337
24.	Old Asylum Records Offer Further Testimony	349
25.	Did the Millerites Wear Ascension Robes?	370
26.	Tracing the Robe Story Through the Years	399
27.	The Robe Story in Twentieth Century Dress	414
28.	Did the Millerites Set Forth Strange, New Beliefs?	427

29. Did the Advent Faith Miller Kindled, Die with Him? 454
30. The Case for the Defense Summed Up 470
    Acknowledgments 475
    Appendices 477
       A. Miller Family Genealogy....................... 477
       B. Clemons' Letter on Millerite Activities in October, 1844 478
       C. The So-Called Trial of Joshua V. Himes 480
       D. Miller's Accusation of Fanaticism 481
       E. Himes' Comment on Gorgas Incident 484
       F. Certain Cases in the New Hampshire Asylum 488
       G. Hereditary and Periodical Insanity in Relation to So-Called Religion-Induced Insanity 493
       H. An Ascension Robe Affidavit 496
       I. Further Comments on the Book *Days of Delusion* 498
       J. How Did the Ascension Robe Story Start? 502
       K. Miller's Interpretation of Major Prophecies 505
       L. Miller's Secondary Proofs for the 1843 Date 507
       M. The Idea of Gradual World Improvement Heavily Discounted Today 511
       N. "Gabriel, Blow That Horn!" 513
    Bibliography 519
    Index 549

From the Author

To the Reader of This Book

A LITTLE OVER A CENTURY AGO, in that mysterious way known only to God, devout men in different lands were simultaneously quickened to search the Scriptures on the subject of the second advent of Christ. The results of that study may rightly be described as an advent awakening of hope and belief that the great day of Christ's coming was drawing on apace. In no land was that awakening more clear cut, more definitely organized, or more dramatically brought to a climax than in America. In this country the most prominent spokesman was William Miller, and thus the advent movement in the Western Hemisphere is generally known as Millerism.

The purpose of this book is twofold: (1) to present the story of the life of Miller and the activities of the Millerite movement; and (2) to examine a series of charges against the Millerites. To present the first without the second would leave a number of questions unanswered, for virtually all well-read persons are acquainted with various charges of fanaticism that have been leveled at the movement. The very fact that the subject is controversial makes it difficult to present the story of the Millerites in proper perspective. Heat warps everything it touches, particularly the heat of controversy. The task of straightening out the record is the one we have here set for ourselves.

We traveled New England three times to visit historic places, to examine the records in historical society offices and libraries, and even to check case history records in asylums. On another trip (to Aurora College, Illinois), we had the opportunity of reading the correspondence of William Miller, a collection of more than eight hundred letters to and from him, and also other manuscripts of Miller. Most of this material has lain unused and quite forgotten since Sylvester Bliss wrote his biography of Miller, in 1853.

We thought, at first, of attempting to write a history. But according to the canons of history writing, which theoretically seem sweetly reasonable and easy to conform to, we would be expected to write in a detached style. We would be supposed to reveal only in the closing chapter, if at all, our personal judgment on the merits of the conflicting evidence. We finally decided not to attempt this, and for the following reasons:

1. We have spiritual kinship with the Millerites; we belong to a religious body (Seventh-day Adventists) whose roots go down into the soil of Millerism. Long-established judicial rules require a judge to disqualify himself from sitting on a case in which he has any personal interest. He may honorably act as an advocate for one side, but not as a judge between disputants.

We believe the same principle holds for an author. It is not necessarily a question of his sincerity, for even the most sincere person may be quite unconsciously affected by submerged premises fixed in his mind through long years. Particularly is this true in the field of religion, where our deepest feelings almost defy analysis. This handicap may be partly overcome by setting down the bare facts with studied objectivity. But such writing is likely to be more insipid than impartial.

2. We doubt whether it is possible even for trained writers to deal in a wholly dispassionate way with any subject that involves human passions and prejudices. We have read the story of the Revolutionary War, by able chroniclers who differed considerably in their accounts. Yet these divergent historians would doubtless insist that they were students of the objective school of history writing. Their thinking was unconsciously affected by whether they were writing at Harvard or at Oxford.*

Some keen students of the science of history writing declare that there is no truly impartial writing, or at least that few are capable of it. One of them observes: "Probably the recording

---

* Unfortunately, there are numerous factors besides geography and race that unconsciously affect our thinking and thus our conclusions. Experience has taught the courts through the

angel is the only example of an historian who is both impartial and objective." [1] * He gives the names of certain men long known as great historians, and declares they were far from impartial, and quite possibly would have spoiled such historical and literary abilities as they possessed if they had tried to attain to the rare heights of absolute detachment. This leads him to remark, immediately, that "minds capable of this task" of writing impartially "are few." His counsel, therefore, is this:

"The beginner, who aims at impartiality and objectivity, will assuredly hamper himself and fail to achieve them; it is far better for him to put all such ideals on one side, and let his mind work freely on its own natural lines. Let him take lower levels and train himself to be an advocate before he attempts to play the part of the recording angel." [2]

Certainly the historians who have included in their encyclopedias or histories a discussion of Millerism have not written impartially. That, we believe, will be evident as the reader examines the charges in the latter part of this book. Whether this illustrates how difficult is the feat of impartial writing, or merely how befogged is the subject of Millerism, we shall let the reader judge. In either case it helps, at least, to

---

centuries that the most diligent attention must be given to the selection of a jury to weigh evidence. And anyone who has listened even to the classic series of questions asked of a prospective juror, to say nothing of special questions applicable to the particular case, will be slow to feel that he is prepared to weigh evidence impartially on any subject.

It is not sufficient for a writer to say in support of his claim to have written impartially and objectively that he has simply set down the facts as he found them. Such a statement is naive. In the first place, personal judgment must often decide whether a fact or a fancy is before the writer's eye. In the second place, all facts do not have the same intrinsic weight, and the writer must use his personal judgment in determining the weight. Even writers who use the modern objective technique differ widely in their decision as to what are facts, how much each fact should weigh, and the meaning of all the facts put together. This is strikingly illustrated by two manuscripts on the Millerite movement that are on file in the archives of two great universities. These are doctoral dissertations accepted by the respective universities for the degree of doctor of philosophy. The writer of one of these concludes from his investigation that Millerism is to be explained in terms of the unrest generated by the economic troubles that afflicted the country in the 1830's. The most restrained way we can describe that interpretation is to call it fanciful. We would expect Karl Marx to reason thus, but not a dispassionate candidate for a university degree. The other thesis reaches an entirely different conclusion!

[1] C. G. Crump, *History and Historical Research*, p. 10.
[2] *Ibid.*, pp. 10, 11.

* Other writers are equally outspoken. One of these declares that a historian "should divest himself of prejudices and predilections, so far as he can, and approach his material with open mind and a desire only to know what the facts teach." But he adds immediately: "Admirable as this attitude is in theory, it is psychologically untenable . . . A mind devoid of prepossessions is likely to be devoid of all mental furniture. And the historian who thinks that

reveal how bold and ambitious we would be to claim to set forth a wholly dispassionate account of Millerism.

3. We are not certain that a detached, delicately balanced presentation is needed at this juncture. To borrow a homely illustration from the playground: When a teeterboard has seated on it a child at each end, then someone may be needed to stand in the middle, to throw his weight, first on one side and then on the other. But if one child after another sits down at the same end, the only hope of bringing the board into line is for someone to throw all his weight on the other end. Now during a hundred years a host of writers—one after another—have added their weight to one end of the board that constitutes the record of Millerism. They have rested heavily on a few eccentric incidents, and where they lacked any factual data they have been aided by hearsay and rumor, which have a way of growing weightier with the years. The result is that the reputation of the unfortunate Millerites has been quite literally up in the air for long years. Under such circumstances we believe that a heroic move must be made by someone in order to bring things into balance. It would never have occurred to us to stress certain of the facts in the record as we vigorously do, were it not that these facts deal with matters long emphasized in an opposite way. If the reader thinks we have walked far out to one end in our emphasis of the evidence for the Millerites, we invite him to remember the teeterboard.

---

he can clean his mind as he would a slate with a wet sponge, is ignorant of the simplest facts of mental life."—*Allen Johnson, The Historian and Historical Evidence, pp. 159, 160.*

Another writer in the field of historiography declares: "Ancient and modern historians have been affected equally by an influence of which neither the one nor the other has been fully conscious. . . . Every generation, Mark Pattison said, requires the facts to be recast in its own mold, and demands that history be rewritten from its own point of view. This is not because the facts are continually accumulating, because criticism is growing more rigid, or even because style varies. The reason is that ideas change, and that the whole mode and manner of looking at things alters in every age."—*Frederick J. Teggart, Theory and Process of History, pp. 15, 16.*

Both Johnson and Teggart quote from Merz in illustration of their statements. Says Merz: "Most of the great historians whom our age has produced will, centuries hence, probably be more interesting as exhibiting special methods of research, special views on political, social, and literary progress, than as faithful and reliable chroniclers of events; and the objectivity on which some of them pride themselves will be looked upon not as freedom from but as unconsciousness on their part of the preconceived notions which have governed them."—*J. T. Merz, A History of European Thought in the Nineteenth Century, Vol. I, p. 7.*

Comment on these quotations seems unnecessary.

For these three reasons we have not attempted to write an objective history of Millerism. Instead, as the subtitle declares, this is "A Defense of William Miller and the Millerites." We think such a declaration has at least this much to be said in its favor: it is forthright and honest. However, some readers may be tempted to conclude that this must therefore be a biased work, so hopelessly prejudiced that it gives a grossly distorted picture. We think this conclusion does not necessarily follow. Contrary to the mistaken idea of some, a lawyer may plead for his client and still conform to the highest standards of fairness and honesty. The author we quoted as declaring that a writer in the field of history should "train himself to be an advocate before he attempts to play the part of the recording angel," adds:

"To do this he must possess the virtues of an advocate, including above all the virtues of fairness and honesty. The task of passing final judgment he may leave to those who essay it, and to the advocates of the other side. It is his part to practice honesty and fearlessness in expressing such opinions as he may form or possess; and for this purpose he will do well to observe two rules of conduct. The first rule is that the evidence for all conclusions must be stated as it exists in the source from which it is taken, avoiding any method of statement that may alter or impair its meaning or its emphasis. The second rule is that the writer must distinguish clearly between the evidence and any criticisms or inferences made by himself." [3]

In our writing we have sought to be governed, and are now willing to be judged, by these obviously fair rules. We have endeavored to give the charges and the arguments against the Millerites in the very language of the prosecution and at sufficient length to enable the full force of those charges to be felt. Likewise, we have given the reply of the Millerites in their own words, whenever they replied directly to a charge.

As an advocate we have invoked in behalf of the defendants a few of the most elementary rules employed for long generations in the courts to ensure a fair trial to an accused person. We are thinking particularly of such rules as these:

The accused is to be considered innocent until proved guilty

---

[3] *Ibid.*, p. 11.

beyond a reasonable doubt. He has the right to bring in character witnesses. If the testimony of these witnesses clearly shows him to be a man of good character and reputation in the community in which he resides, that fact may rightly be stressed by counsel for the defense as a piece of presumptive evidence bearing upon his innocence. The accused has a right to be heard in his own defense, and if his character witnesses have established his standing as a reputable citizen, his personal testimony is entitled to great weight. Hearsay and rumor are inadmissible as evidence.

We believe that the writer in a controversial field such as Millerism will be more safely guided in penning a historical sketch if he follows rigidly such judicial rules as these than if he trusts wholly to his own powers of objectivity and impartiality. At least we are sure of this, that much of what has appeared in history books, encyclopedias, and similar works, regarding the Millerites, would never have been penned if these simple rules had been employed. We are thinking particularly of the rule that forbids the introduction of hearsay and rumor in the testimony of any witness. The reader of this book will be struck, we believe, with the frequency of such irresponsible phrases as "it is said," "it is reported," and even "it is rumored," in the introductions of newspaper stories of the 1840's regarding the Millerites. And yet it is on such stories that most of the charges against the Millerites rest and most of the colorful descriptions of them have been built.*

---

* For illustration, one very well-known historian unblushingly builds his sketch of Millerism from such newspaper items, without even giving the reader an inkling that these items are quite uniformly prefaced, in the irresponsible newspaper style of a century ago, with such disqualifying phrases as "it is said," etc. See at the close of this work a bibliographical note on John B. McMaster's *A History of the People of the United States.*

We believe that the most charitable way to explain the supercilious attitude of sober historians who have discussed Millerism, and their readiness to accept the most fanciful reports regarding the movement, is as follows: These historians knew that Miller believed that the second advent of Christ was at hand. To them this seemed prima-facie evidence that he, and all who followed him, must have been at least mildly demented. Hence the cautious, critical attitude that should characterize historians has been relaxed, with the result that they have given ready credence to the most farfetched stories concerning the Millerites that were invented by writers at that time.

This relaxation of critical caution is understandable, but unpardonable. Our historians ought to know that in past centuries any man with a distinctive idea has been almost invariably handled in shabby fashion by the writers who lived at the time. In most instances these

We have invoked fully the judicial rule that the accused has a right to be heard in his own defense. That is why we have quoted at length from Millerite writings. In fact, we believe their own testimony is their best defense. However, we have not invoked as fully as we might the judicial ban on hearsay and rumor, even though this is one of the most rigid of all rules regarding testimony. If we had, there would have been few charges to consider, and someone would complain that we were seeking to win the case by a legal technicality.*

Occasionally we have refused to dignify an absurd rumor with a serious refutation. Rumors and toy balloons have three things in common: both are mostly air, both can suffer heavy blows without permanently losing their original shape, but both collapse completely if given merely a sharp pinprick. Our English language, we believe, may properly be used at times to give a pinprick as well as a heavy blow.†

We began the study of this subject with the feeling that there was doubtless some truth to the array of charges against the Millerites—how much, we wished to discover. We ended our study fully convinced that these people, though imperfect as are other men, were so largely the victims of religious prejudice and fanciful rumor that we decided to write a defense.

We heartily subscribe to the principle that no matter what may be the writer's personal interest, he should diligently seek to have an open mind while investigating a matter, in order to

---

writers never deigned to examine carefully the "queer" ideas of the disturbing person they were contemptuously discussing. In the present instance, if writers had taken time to study carefully Miller's views, they would have found them not so queer after all. This we think will be evident to the reader as he examines Chapter 28.

* We are aware that no matter how strong may be the evidence we present in this book in refutation of rumors and charges, there will always lurk in some readers' minds the feeling that perhaps there *was* something to the stories. Against such mental reactions we have no argument. We would only reply that if such readers ever find themselves the objects of conscienceless rumors, they will have to resign themselves to the unhappy fact that no matter how vigorously they expose the rumors, there will still be people—good people—who will feel there must be something to the stories.

† In this connection a word might be said regarding our occasional use of a whimsical or perhaps even humorous phrase in what is obviously intended to be a serious work. Some would frown upon any such digression as alien to the spirit of true research. Perhaps they are right. However, the great Spurgeon observed in the preface to one of his works, in which he defended his use of humor: "There is no particular virtue in being seriously unreadable."
—*C. H. Spurgeon, John Ploughman's Talks, page ix.*

gather everything that bears on the subject. But we believe that the moment should come when he finally closes his mind on a conclusion and takes up his pen. Robust old Chesterton was right when he said that the only excuse for an open mind is the same as that for an open mouth, to close again on something solid.

We believe that the best biographies are generally written by the children of the great men. Their writings may be tinctured with prejudiced thinking in favor of their own fathers; but despite this, the children seem best able to interpret the real viewpoint, purposes, and ideals of the characters being sketched. Even the most fair-minded stranger can hardly hope to enter the inner sanctum of motives and objectives as can a member of the family. And certainly an unfriendly writer can never catch the pulse of the great man. The same principle, we believe, applies in writing the record of a religious leader and the movement he raises up. One of his spiritual children can understand his motives, sympathize with his hopes, and follow his reasoning in theological areas in a way that a stranger never can. The sympathetic approach has much to commend it as a technique for discovering the real truth regarding a man or a movement.

We have stated that this work does not pose as a history. Perhaps it may best be described as simply a sympathetic approach to the people called Millerites. We willingly leave to the "few" "minds capable of" it, and to "the recording angel," the task of writing a history "both impartial and objective."

Washington, D. C.
October 22, 1944.

CHAPTER 1

From Cradle to Army Camp

IF YOU HAD LIVED IN THE UNITED STATES in the early 1840's you would have heard the startling news that the world was soon to come to a fiery end. From the rostrum and through the printed page the awesome announcement was made that the personal second coming of Christ would take place "about the year 1843." A well-defined religious movement was created through this preaching of the "advent near," as the distinctive teaching was described.

The movement was launched by William Miller, whose name became a household term in most of America. Those who believed his views were soon known as Millerites. The comment offered by skeptical onlookers was generally critical, sometimes even defamatory. Strange were the stories told about the preachers and laity who constituted this religious movement. They were pictured as fit for the asylum and as sending many there by their preaching. They were accused of strange, fanatical acts. People today are even more sure than was the public a hundred years ago that the Millerites were guilty of every kind of irrational act, for stories have a way of growing with the years.

Who was this man Miller that stirred all America and beyond with his preaching? And what kind of religious movement did he create?

William Miller was born in Pittsfield, Massachusetts, February 15, 1782.* When he was a small child his parents moved to the hamlet of Low Hampton, in Washington County, New York, almost on the Vermont line. He was reared in a religious

---

* See Appendix A for genealogical note on Miller family.

atmosphere, for his pious mother had obediently woven into her life the religious instruction received in a minister's home.

Thus early William came under the potent influence of religion. But he was no queer lad with strange experiences or abnormal reactions to life. He grew up as a healthy young American, living in what were then the western edges of civilization.

Young William, in those early years, lived up to the best American traditions of an ambitious boy undaunted by pioneer hardships. He was determined, despite all handicaps, to better his lot and to secure a training of mind as well as of body. School facilities in the sparsely settled community of his childhood were very limited. He enjoyed the luxury of three months' formal education in a schoolhouse each winter. We have no records of how he performed in reading and writing, but we do have his arithmetic notebook. The pages are foolscap size. The handwriting is clear and of a much better grade than that of the average grammar school child who grows up in our modern educational institutions.

In common with most early settlers, Miller lived in a home blessed with poverty. Every dollar that could be secured must be placed against the mortgage. There was no money for books. They might be desirable, but they were luxuries. Even candles could be used only in a sparing way. If the eldest son of the house had been content, along with the other children, to believe that something accomplished, something done, had earned him his night's repose and nothing more, we would not be writing this story today.

But William had an unquenchable desire for knowledge. He collected a store of pine knots to provide illumination. When all the family were asleep he would silently make his way to the fireside, stir the embers, light a pine knot, and begin his reading. One night his father, awakening from slumber and seeing the cabin aglow, thought it was on fire. Whatever lurking admiration he may have had for his son's ambition was lost in that first great fear that fire was about to devour their home. He chased

William to bed with the threat, "Bill, if you don't go to bed, I'll horsewhip you!" There is no reason to believe, however, that this one outburst of paternal wrath retarded for long William's studious inclination.

In his teens he began to keep a diary. This simple fact in itself is revealing. What farmer's son in those frontier days would set himself to the task of keeping a diary? Here is one of the earliest indications not only of Miller's methodical mind but also of his bent toward writing. This diary, to be sure, is brief and rather spotty. The date on the title page is "July 10th, 1797." In obviously boyish handwriting, for he was only fifteen, we find this heading to the diary, "The History of My Life."

That first page contains the statement: "I was early educated and taught to pray the Lord." That is the only descriptive statement that he gave concerning himself in the introduction. Evidently he thought it important and quite the most distinguishing statement that he could make.

The first of his day-by-day entries is dated "11th day of March, 1798." The entry is brief but revealing: "Sunday—grandfather preached at our house from Psalms 23, 4th verse, from Colossians 3, 1st verse. I lay at home. Rainy day."

Grandfather, Elnathan Phelps, brought religion home to William in the most literal sense of the word. Evidently it made an impression on his youthful mind, for he records chapter and verse of the Scriptural passages on the subject of the sermon.

As William grew, his thirst for knowledge increased, and the few books that the meager funds of the family permitted were not sufficient to satisfy that thirst. Combining resourcefulness and courage he went out to see some prominent citizens near by to ask for the loan of books. Thus did this resourceful youth seek to store his restless mind with the treasures that ever have been found in books.

William's literary leanings did not find sufficient expression in keeping a diary and reading borrowed books. He soon became a kind of community scribe. Sylvester Bliss, who wrote a biography of him in 1853 and to whom we are greatly indebted for a number of the incidents in Miller's early life, calls him a "scribbler-general." Bliss states that if anyone wished "verses made," a letter written, "or anything which required extra taste and fancy in the use of the pen, it was pretty sure to be planned, if not executed, by him." [1]

A youth who possessed the initiative and resourcefulness William Miller displayed even in his teens, might easily be expected to have early success in the field of matrimony. In the near-by village of Poultney, Vermont, lived a young woman, Lucy P. Smith. In his diary, under date of "January second, 1803," Miller wrote:

"Be it remembered that on this day, it being a Sunday in the afternoon of the aforesaid day, I did bind myself and was bound to be, the partner of Miss Lucy Smith, of Poultney. And by these presents do agree to be hers and only hers till death shall part us (provided she is of the same mind). Whereunto I here set my hand and seal."

January 2, 1803, was a high day in William Miller's life. It appears that on that day he pledged his troth to Miss Lucy. His reading must have included some law books, for this diary entry has a distinctly legal flavor. Miller sought to make the diary record of this high moment in his life sure and certain, and legal language seemed most impressive. He may have been desperately in love, but he did not lose his head or his balance. He remembered the simple principle that a marriage is a contract and that it takes two to make a bargain. Hence his parenthetical clause, for our delighted reading today: "Provided she is of the same mind."

She *was* of the same mind, for his diary states that they were married on Wednesday, the twenty-ninth of June. And they continued of the same mind for almost fifty years, until death broke the contract.

Upon his marriage he moved about six miles to Poultney, Vermont, his wife's home town. There he soon became known in the village as one who spent his spare hours at the little library

---

[1] Sylvester Bliss, *Memoirs of William Miller*, p. 16.

in the community. He naturally sought out those kindred spirits who also liked to pore over books. Evidently within the first few years in his new home, he joined some kind of literary or cultural society, for he has left on record in his handwriting a manuscript which opens thus: "Mr. Chairman and Gentlemen: Though I feel myself inadequate to the task; yet I will endeavor to surmount all difficulties and give the society a short dissertation on calumny." *

Little did Miller realize when he delivered that address in his twenties, within the circle of warm and trusting friends, that he was forecasting his own distressing experiences with calumny. He was to live to see the day when his name would be maligned, or at least held up to ridicule, by enemies in every part of the country.

Miller's reading of books and his discussions with literary friends were not confined to such fields as history, poetry, and the like. Philosophy in its most subtle, skeptical form soon made its appeal to his mind. Deism, that halfway station on the road to atheism, which viewed God as a sort of absentee landlord far removed from and wholly uninterested in His created works, had been a blight on the religious life of England in the eighteenth century. The infection had been brought across the waters by skeptical books and papers, and among Miller's friends were several prominent citizens who were deists.

Miller, who up to this time had evidently lived on the spiritual momentum of his pious mother and other churchly relatives, soon found himself in this new community and among these new and impressive friends, with no firsthand personal conviction to immunize him against the virus of infidelity. The youth who had inscribed on the title page of his diary that he was "early educated and taught to pray the Lord," and who noted in his first entry in that diary his listening to Grandfather Phelps

---

* Though the manuscript is undated, internal evidence reveals that it was prepared during the Presidency of Thomas Jefferson, who was in office from 1801 to 1809. The "dissertation" was well written. While it might not be called a literary masterpiece in form or content, it is above the level of many a modern college student's production.

preach, had become an avowed skeptic. Those who before had been objects of respect and veneration, became, instead, objects of mirth. To the delight of his skeptical friends he would caricature the tones of voice and the actions of the pious in the community, including among them his own clerical grandfather.

Miller entered public life in the capacity of a deputy sheriff in the year 1809. Soon after he added the duties of a military officer, following closely the steps of his fathers before him. In 1810 he was appointed a lieutenant in the militia of the State of Vermont. The formal order was signed by Governor Jonas Galusha, July 21, 1810. If the international relations of the United States had remained peaceful, this military office would probably have meant little in Miller's life. But in 1812 war was again declared between the United States and Great Britain. On November 7, 1812, Lieutenant Miller was made a captain of militia.

No draft system, no selective service, was in operation in 1812 in the United States. The country relied on volunteers, and the officer who could, by his personality and standing in the eyes of those who knew him, succeed in enlisting volunteers for the Army, was a man of great value and importance. Miller was such a man. Framed in the law office of a great-grandson* of Miller's in Fair Haven, Vermont, is a faded but important military document that bears eloquent testimony to the standing of William Miller in his own community. This document was signed at "Poultney, November 16, 1812." In the very legible handwriting of William Miller it reads:

"We, the undersigners, feeling it an indispensable duty for us, in the present situation of our national concerns, to step forward in the defense of our rights, our country, and friends, do voluntarily tender our services to the President of the United States agreeable to an act passed by the legislature of the State of Vermont, November 6, 1812, and do therefore enlist ourselves into a company of infantry to be commanded by William Miller, to hold ourselves in readiness to march at a moment's warning until the first day of May next 1813."

---

* Philip M. M. Phelps.

The remainder of the document consists of two parallel columns of signatures of the men who enlisted, with the "place of abode" and the date of enlistment following. There is a total of forty-seven names, most of them from near-by communities such as Fair Haven.

William Miller did not long remain an officer in the Vermont State militia. In the spring of 1813 he was appointed a lieutenant in the United States Army.*

The military history of his ancestors might be considered a sufficient explanation of why he accepted a commission as an officer in the Army. But there was another reason also. It may have been the chief one. Years afterward, in writing a very brief sketch of his early life, Miller told of his descent into the dismal swamps of deism, and of the hopelessly pessimistic view of mankind and of history that fastened upon him:

"I could discern no bright spot in the history of the past. Those conquerors of the world, and heroes of history, were apparently but demons in human form. All the sorrow, suffering, and misery in the world, seemed to be increased in proportion to the power they obtained over their fellows. I began to feel very distrustful of all men. In this state of mind I entered the service of my country; I fondly cherished the idea, that I should find one bright spot at least in the human character, as a star of hope, a love of *country*—PATRIOTISM." [2]

An insight into Miller's feeling at this time is found in a letter he wrote in the spring of 1814 to "Friend Robins," an officer in the United States Navy in the area of Lake Champlain. Miller told his friend how his spirits were depressed by the way the war was going:

"Could I be as certain of [our] conquering the land forces; could I see that busy industry, bravery, and skill in our commanders as we do among our naval heroes (could I believe our Government was determined on the taking of the Canadas); that unanimity and patriotism among our citizens

---

[2] *The Midnight Cry*, Nov. 17, 1842, p. 1.

* A letter dated April 10, 1813, and signed by Elias Fasset, "Colonel 30th regiment infantry," conveys this notification of appointment to William Miller. On the back of the letter is this memorandum in Miller's hand: "Rec'd April 20, 1813. Accepted appointment 21st, 1813."

which is necessary to reap advantages from our successes—then I should be satisfied, and willingly would I devote the remainder part of my life for the Government that I wish to leave uncontaminated by the finger of aristocracy or hand of monarchy." [3]

This letter shows how deeply and personally Miller viewed the whole subject of service to his country, and how his disillusionment regarding mankind, that had come to him through deism, now seemed to be well substantiated. Here was no soldier of fortune speaking, not even a professional soldier, but an ardent citizen with a deep love of country. He was really hoping against hope that the world was not quite as bad as his skeptical philosophy would lead him to believe.

In the early part of 1814 Miller was raised to the rank of captain in the United States Army. In August of that year we find him with his regiment, the 30th Infantry, at Plattsburg on the west bank of Lake Champlain, where an important army camp had been set up.*

On the lake and in sight of the fort where he was stationed was soon to be fought the decisive Battle of Plattsburg. The United States forces might well be apprehensive as they anticipated the engagement. They were outnumbered on land and sea. The battle was joined by an engagement between the opposing naval forces September 11, 1814. In writing of this experience in connection with a sketch of his life and beliefs, Miller declared, "At the commencement of the battle, we looked upon our own defeat as almost certain, and yet we were victorious." [4]

Lying before us as we write is a faded letter dated "Fort Scott, September 11, 1814. Twenty minutes past two o'clock, P. M." † It gives an eyewitness's account of the engagement,

---

[3] Manuscript letter, April 27, 1814.
[4] William Miller, *Apology and Defence*, p. 4.

* Most of the source material on Miller's military life, including the "Friend Robins" letter, is in the library of the Vermont Historical Society. This military material, however, throws little light on the man or his activities and consists largely of weekly and monthly reports of "Captain Miller's Company, 30th Infantry."

† This is the earliest of a collection of more than eight hundred letters either to or from Miller, from which we shall draw as our story progresses. The collection is in the library of Aurora College, Illinois.

written by a man whose ears were ringing with the sounds of exploding shells. It opens in a staccato tempo. Wrote Miller:

"Sir: It is over, it is done. The British fleet has struck to the American flag. Great slaughter on both sides—they are in plain view where I am now writing. . . . The sight was majestic, it was noble, it was grand. This morning at 10 o'clock the British opened a very heavy and destructive fire upon us, both by water and land. Their congreve rockets flew like hailstones about us, and round shot and grape from every quarter. You have no idea of the battle. Our force was small, but how bravely they fought. . . . I have no time to write any more. You must conceive what we feel, for I cannot describe it. I am satisfied that I can fight. I know I am no coward. Therefore call on Mr. Loomis and drink my health, and I will pay the shot. Three of my men are wounded by a shell which burst within two feet of me. The boat from the fleet which has just landed under our fort says the British commodore is killed; out of 300 on board their ship 25 remain alive. . . .

"Yours forever,
"Wm. Miller.

"Give my compliments to all and send this to my wife." [5] *

In spite of his skeptical views, which left no room for a superintending God with His providences, much less a future life, Miller was deeply impressed that the victory of the United States troops and fleet against overwhelming odds could be explained only as an act of Providence. Said he:

"It seemed to me that the Supreme Being must have watched over the interests of this country in an especial manner, and delivered us from the hands of our enemies. . . . So surprising a result against such odds, did seem to me like the work of a mightier power than man." [6]

His release from the Army came on June 18, 1815. Thus ended an exciting chapter in William Miller's life. But more stirring days lay ahead.

---

[5] Manuscript letter to John Stanley, Esquire, Poultney, Vt., Sept. 11, 1814.
[6] William Miller, *Apology and Defence*, p. 4.
* In a letter written to his wife at seven o'clock the next morning Miller related in general the same story. Though he may not have realized it at the moment, for he was too close to the fighting, he had just witnessed one of the final, deciding battles of the War of 1812.

CHAPTER 2

From Doubt to Faith

AFTER TWO YEARS OF ACTIVE MILITARY SERVICE the close of the war found William Miller, like any other normal man, happy to forget battlefield and army camp and to return to the quiet of home. He moved his family back to Low Hampton once more. There he built for himself a two-story frame house. The building still stands and is occupied after nearly one hundred and thirty years. William Miller now found himself in the center of the little community he knew so well and in which he hoped to live quietly as a farmer through his remaining years. But this was not to be.

There were restless stirrings in the soul of this man that cannot be fitted into the typical picture of the peaceful farmer cultivating his crops by day, sitting contented by the fireside after supper, and retiring early to a well-deserved rest. The inquiring, questioning, restless mind which had begun to reveal itself in early youth was as active as ever. By his own testimony he entered the Army with the hope of finding in patriotism one bright spot in a seamy, sinister world. "But," said he, "two years in the service was enough to convince me that I was in error in this thing also. When I left the service I had become completely disgusted with man's public character." [1]

Of course, the trouble lay primarily in himself. A man who has acquired a skeptical outlook on life sees everything in the wrong light. This has ever been so. The Good Book declares that as a man thinks in his heart so is he. Miller was paying a dear price for his deism. Into the depths of his

---

[1] *The Midnight Cry*, Nov. 17, 1842, p. 1.

naturally restless and inquiring spirit he had poured this disturbing ferment of skeptical discontent. Normally he had every reason to be at peace with the world. But peace with the world outside seems largely to be dependent on whether there is peace within. And Miller was not at peace with himself. He did not realize it, but he was really at heart a deeply religious man. He belonged to that class—too rare in the world —who can find no inner calm until they have thought through to a satisfactory conclusion in their own mind the problem of the mysterious ways of God toward man.

Though he had caricatured religion for a time, and though in two years of army life he must certainly have heard almost every brand of profanity, he gives this revealing incident that stands in sharp contrast:

"One day in May, 1816, I detected myself in the act of taking the name of God in vain, a habit I had acquired in the service; and I was instantly convicted of its sinfulness." [2]

But this thought and conviction forced him, whether he would or no, to the next step in his thinking:

"I was then led to inquire how a just Being could consistently save those who should violate the laws of justice. The works of Nature or of Providence, could give no answer to this question; and I was almost led to despair. In this state of mind, I continued for some months." [3]

Though conscience-smitten by the sound of his own voice in blasphemy, he could not easily shake off skeptical thoughts. He had heard the still small voice speak to his conscience in rebuke, but it was while he was standing confused in the fogs of doubt and cynicism. He had quite resigned himself to the idea that man is "no more than a brute," that the idea of the hereafter is "a dream."

"Annihilation was a cold and chilling thought, and accountability was sure destruction to all. The heavens were as brass over my head, and the

---
[2] William Miller, *Apology and Defence,* pp. 4, 5.
[3] *Ibid.,* p. 5.

earth as iron under my feet. ETERNITY! *What was it? And death, why was it?* The more I reasoned, the further I was from demonstration. The more I thought, the more scattered were my conclusions." [4]

Up to this point in thinking many a man has come, but too often men never go beyond it. They find the thought too troublesome or too deep for them. They decide that such questions must be left to the preachers and a few saints, and proceed to quiet their minds by immersing themselves more actively in business or pleasure, or both. But Miller, as we have remarked, belonged to that rare group who think through to a conclusion.

"I tried to stop thinking, but my thoughts would not be controlled. I was truly wretched, but did not understand the cause. I murmured and complained, but knew not of whom. I felt that there was a wrong, but knew not how, or where to find the right. I mourned, but without hope." [5]

This sounds not unlike the account of Christian in Bunyan's *Pilgrim's Progress;* in fact, not unlike the experience of many good men in the flesh who have left revealing records of their struggles of spirit and their gropings of soul before they moved out onto a high tableland to walk in the light of heaven.

The inner tension was rapidly coming to the breaking point. Some release had to be found. Miller described that release in simple yet mysterious language. Though he knew it not, he was really borrowing the language men have used through long centuries to describe that singular experience called conversion, by which a man turns about, as the word literally means, to see all life from a new angle, and to travel a new road. "At length," said he, "when brought almost to despair, God by His Holy Spirit opened my eyes. I saw Jesus as a friend, and my only help, and the Word of God as the *perfect rule* of duty." [6]

That is how he described the experience of transition when he was writing many years later, in 1842. In the summer of 1845 he described it thus:

---

[4] *The Midnight Cry,* Nov. 17, 1842, p. 1.
[5] *Ibid.*
[6] *Ibid.*

"Suddenly the character of a Saviour was vividly impressed upon my mind. It seemed that there might be a Being so good and compassionate as to Himself atone for our transgressions, and thereby save us from suffering the penalty of sin. I immediately felt how lovely such a Being must be; and imagined that I could cast myself into the arms of, and trust in the mercy of such an One." [7]

The average student of religious experience who has read the records men have left of their conversions would say with little hesitation that the conflict in Miller's soul was resolved, that he had entered the fraternity of those who may genuinely be called Christians. Probably the tension in his soul *was* ended at that moment of spiritual insight when "the character of a Saviour was vividly impressed" upon his mind. But Miller was the kind of man who wanted to support his feelings with facts, his intuitions with evidence.

In a moment of spiritual exaltation there had been pictured in his mind the Saviour, gracious and forgiving. The natural response of his heart and of his will was to turn to such a being. "But the question arose," said he, in analyzing his own thoughts in connection with that experience, "How can it be proved that such a Being does exist?" [8]

Here was no emotionalist speaking. Here was a man calmly and analytically looking at the whole subject of the Christian religion, and asking the most pertinent question that any man could ever ask who examines the claims of Christianity.

Miller immediately followed his question, as to how it can be proved that such a being exists, with this conclusion: "Aside from the Bible, I found that I could get no evidence of the existence of such a Saviour, or even of a future state." [9] In that conclusion he was absolutely right. Christian leaders through all the centuries have held that the Bible is the revealed will of God to man, and that in it is to be found the one great revelation of God through Jesus Christ. Wrote Miller:

---
[7] William Miller, *Apology and Defence*, p. 5.
[8] *Ibid.*
[9] *Ibid.*

"I felt that to believe in such a Saviour without evidence, would be visionary in the extreme. I saw that the Bible did bring to view just such a Saviour as I needed; and I was perplexed to find how an uninspired book should develop principles so perfectly adapted to the wants of a fallen world. I was constrained to admit that the Scriptures must be a revelation from God; they became my delight, and in Jesus I found a friend." [10]

But Miller was not to be allowed to enjoy his peace of mind, his Saviour, and his newly found inspired book without challenge. He still had his skeptical friends in the neighborhood, and the news of his conversion immediately became a subject of discussion. The very arguments which he himself had so recently employed against the Scriptures were now turned against him. He was placed in that most perplexing of all situations—he was called upon to refute the very things he once affirmed, and to answer questions which he had declared were unanswerable. Let him describe his embarrassing situation in his own words. We quote, beginning at the very next sentence after the one in which he told of how the Scriptures became his delight and Jesus, his friend:

"Soon after this, in the fall of 1816, I was conversing with a friend respecting my hope of a glorious eternity through the merits and intercessions of the Saviour, and he asked me how I knew there was a Saviour? I replied that He was revealed in the Bible. He then asked me how I knew the Bible was true? and advanced my former deistical arguments on the inconsistencies, the contradictions, and the mysticisms in which I had claimed it was shrouded. I replied that if the Bible was the word of God, everything contained therein might be understood, and all its parts be made to harmonize; and I said to him that if he would give me time, I would harmonize all these apparent contradictions, to my own satisfaction, or I would be a deist still." [11]

The task Miller set for himself was rather breathtaking. He could hardly have known in advance what any careful student of the Bible soon discovers, that certain things in the Scriptures are "hard to be understood." But we must honor the trans-

---
[10] *Ibid.*
[11] *Ibid.*, pp. 5, 6.

parent honesty of the man and his resolute decision to go forward in sincerity to justify his new-found faith. In this very statement he made to his deist friend is found one of the best insights into the character of Miller. So far from being a man with an emotional temperament, or one given to jumping to conclusions and hurrying off to broadcast them to the world, he was the kind of man who asks for time, that he may study, examine, and prove. We may not agree with all the conclusions he reached. Even great theologians and great saints have differed widely—and sometimes in unsaintly fashion—over the meaning of the Scriptures. But any unprejudiced mind will surely agree on this, that in his search for truth and in his endeavor to find a rational basis for his faith, he proceeded on the sound principle of searching the Scriptures.

He leaves us in no doubt as to the specific methods he employed in his examination of the Scriptures.

"I then devoted myself to prayer and to the reading of the word. I determined to lay aside all my prepossessions, to thoroughly compare Scripture with Scripture, and to pursue its study in a regular and methodical manner. I commenced with Genesis, and read verse by verse, proceeding no faster than the meaning of the several passages should be so unfolded, as to leave me free from embarrassment respecting any mysticism or contradictions. Whenever I found anything obscure, my practice was to compare it with all collateral passages; and by the help of Cruden [a concordance], I examined all the texts of Scripture in which were found any of the prominent words contained in any obscure portion. Then by letting every word have its proper bearing on the subject of the text, if my view of it harmonized with every collateral passage in the Bible, it ceased to be a difficulty." [12]

Miller explained that he thus pursued the study of the Bible "for about two years," with the result that he was "satisfied that it is its own interpreter." This was no new, strange conclusion he reached; rather it was a conclusion that all conservative Bible students have reached through the centuries. It is true that reaching such a conclusion, and proceeding upon it, is no guarantee that the finite mind will always interpret

---

[12] *Ibid.*, p. 6.

rightly each passage of scripture. But this much is certain, that only by proceeding on the conclusion that the Bible is its own best interpreter, is there any hope of finding our way safely through the deeper or more obscure passages of the Scriptures.

Miller also concluded from his study of the Bible that it should be understood literally unless there is clear proof that figurative language is being employed by the inspired writer. That is, the words of Scripture ought to be understood in their ordinary historical and grammatical sense, even as with secular writing, except in those instances where the writer used figurative language. In thus viewing the Scriptures literally Miller was simply following the path of conservative theologians from the very beginnings of Protestantism. He was announcing no new arbitrary rule for understanding the Bible. The Protestant Reformers declared that the medieval practice of giving mysterious and varied spiritual meanings to Scripture texts, really gave to the Bible a nose of wax by which it could be turned in any direction that the unbridled fancy and spiritual imagination of the theologian might wish to turn it. Now, the employment of the rule that the Scriptures should be viewed literally unless an obviously figurative language is employed, will not in itself assure us fallible mortals a correct understanding of the Holy Word. But of this we can be sure, that only by following faithfully this rule can we hope to walk in the path that leads toward a correct understanding. Miller chose at the very outset to walk that path.

As Miller concentrated month after month for those two years in his reading and comparing of scriptures, he made a further discovery. He noted that while prophecies are generally couched in figurative language, they are fulfilled literally. He observed this not only by comparing scripture with scripture but also by comparing scripture with history. With this conclusion any conservative theologian agrees. Unquestionably the Bible prophecies regarding the first advent of Christ were most literally fulfilled, even though those prophecies themselves were framed in symbolic language.

The first part of a recruiting document which gives the names of forty-seven men who volunteered to fight in the War of 1812 under Miller's command. (See pages 22, 23.)

The opening sentences of a letter from Miller to a friend in Poultney, Vermont, in which he describes the Battle of Plattsburg. (See pages 24, 25.)

© 1944, REVIEW AND HERALD PUB. ASSN. HARRY ANDERSON, ARTIST

For fourteen years, from 1816 to 1831, Miller diligently studied his Bible before going forth to promote his views on prophecy.

This house, built by Miller in 1815, at Low Hampton, New York, is still standing. The northeast corner room, which is mentioned in Millerite literature as his study, is on the lower left-hand side in this picture.

FROM DOUBT TO FAITH 33

From this deduction he moved logically to a final conclusion which was to launch him ultimately on his lifework. He reasoned that if the prophecies which have been fulfilled in the past provide a key to understanding those yet to be fulfilled, then we should look for a literal second advent of Christ.

He argued cogently that if the Bible is truly a revelation of God's will to man, it is not presumptuous to seek to understand the prophecies that are a part of the revelation. He explained that in his study of the prophecies he examined one line of prophetic statement after another, reaching each time the conclusion that the prophets pointed to his day as the very last period of earth's history. To phrase it in his own words:

> "Finding all the signs of the times and the present condition of the world, to compare harmoniously with the prophetic descriptions of the last days, I was compelled to believe that this world had about reached the limits of the period allotted for its continuance. As I regarded the evidence, I could arrive at no other conclusion." [13]

Specifically, he put his first and greatest emphasis on the prophetic declaration, "Unto two thousand and three hundred days; then shall the sanctuary be cleansed." Daniel 8:14. Believing that the "cleansing" of the sanctuary involved the purging of this earth by fire, that "days" in symbolic prophecy stand for years, and that this time prophecy began about 457 B. C., he reached this final conclusion:

> "I was thus brought, in 1818, at the close of my two years' study of the Scriptures, to the solemn conclusion, that in about twenty-five years from that time all the affairs of our present state would be wound up." [14]

Now, "about twenty-five years from" 1818 would be "about the year 1843." Let Miller tell in his own language of the effect produced upon him, an effect that was to be reproduced in many thousands of others in the years to come:

> "I need not speak of the joy that filled my heart in view of the delightful prospect, nor of the ardent longings of my soul, for a participation in the joys of the redeemed. The Bible was now to me a new book. It was indeed

---
[13] *Ibid.*, p. 9.
[14] *Ibid.*, pp. 11, 12.

a feast of reason: all that was dark, mystical, or obscure to me in its teachings, had been dissipated from my mind, before the clear light that now dawned from its sacred pages; and O how bright and glorious the truth appeared. . . . I became nearly settled in my conclusions, and began to wait, and watch, and pray for my Saviour's coming." [15]

Did Miller immediately rush forth from that northeast front room of his house, which had been his study for two years, to announce to the world his conclusions? If he had been a notoriety-seeking adventurer who wished to make money from prophesying, as was so often charged in the public press in later years, any delay in going forth to capitalize on such a discovery would seem inexplicable. Why delay? Even if we eliminate the idea of mercenary adventure and think of Miller simply as an excitable fanatic—as some of his critics indulgently described him—we are equally puzzled to know why he should not have hastened from his home in 1818 to begin proclaiming to all the world his conclusions about the second advent of Christ. Miller actually waited thirteen years. And why? To the person who wishes to find the true measure of the man the answer to this question is of great importance. Let him speak for himself:

"With the solemn conviction that such momentous events were predicted in the Scriptures to be fulfilled in so short a space of time, the question came home to me with mighty power regarding my duty to the world in view of the evidence that had affected my own mind. If the end was so near, it was important that the world should know it. I supposed that it would call forth the opposition of the ungodly; but it never came into my mind that any Christian would oppose it. I supposed that all such would be so rejoiced in view of the glorious prospect, that it would only be necessary to present it, for them to receive it. My great fear was, that in their joy at the hope of a glorious inheritance so soon to be revealed, they would receive the doctrine without sufficiently examining the Scriptures in demonstration of its truth. I therefore feared to present it, lest by some possibility I should be in error, and be the means of misleading any." [16]

How carefully he sought to criticize his own beliefs and conclusions is revealed in the next sentence:

---
[15] *Ibid.*, pp. 12, 13.
[16] *Ibid.*, p. 13.

"Various difficulties and objections would arise in my mind, from time to time; certain texts would occur to me, which seemed to weigh against my conclusions; and I would not present a view to others, while any difficulty appeared to militate against it. I therefore continued the study of the Bible, to see if I could sustain any of these objections. My object was not merely to remove them, but I wished to see if they were valid." [17]

In thus examining and re-examining the arguments for and against his belief, he "was occupied for five years."

"I was then fully settled in the conclusions which seven years previously had begun to bear with such impressive force upon my mind; and the duty of presenting the evidence of the nearness of the advent to others—which I had managed to evade while I could find the shadow of an objection remaining against its truth—again came home to me with great force." [18]

Up to this time, he explained, he had thrown out only occasional hints of his views. He "then began to speak more clearly" his opinions to "neighbors, to ministers, and others." He was astonished to find "very few who listened with any interest." How could this combination of farmer and soldier, who possessed no theological training, have any ideas worth serious attention in the field of religion? This probably was the way the neighbors reasoned. Had they not known William since he was a small boy on the farm?

Though disappointed in this response, he "continued to study the Scriptures" with the increasing conviction settling upon him that he had "a personal duty to perform respecting this matter." He wrote that when he was about his business there was continually ringing in his ears the command, "Go and tell the world of their danger."

And why did he delay still longer after having spent more than seven years in intensive study and critical examination of his conclusions? We read:

"I tried to excuse myself to the Lord for not going out and proclaiming it to the world. I told the Lord that I was not used to public speaking, that

---
[17] *Ibid.*
[18] *Ibid.*, p. 15.

I had not the necessary qualifications to gain the attention of an audience, that I was very diffident and feared to go before the world." [19]

Thus we have the full answer to why he waited thirteen years before going out to preach. Here was no cocksure enthusiast making a snap judgment or jumping to a conclusion; rather, the opposite. Keenly aware of the limitations of the mind, of the dangers of error in reasoning, he gave to all these dangers great weight. Far from being an irrepressible person seeking an excuse to stand in the limelight, he was so diffident about assuming the role of public lecturer that it took eight years for him to bring himself to the point of speaking publicly even after he had reached a final and fixed conclusion as to the validity of his beliefs. Captain Miller who had stood bravely at Fort Scott while men fell close beside him, quailed at the thought of becoming Preacher Miller who would have to stand before the public. More than one brave man has had a sinking of heart at the thought of looking into a sea of faces.

Miller's study of the Bible, which is best remembered for the arresting conclusion he reached regarding the time of the end of the world, was not confined to this one line of thought. He evidently studied the Scriptures with a view to formulating for himself a clear-cut belief on every Bible doctrine that affected his salvation. In a small notebook, still preserved, is found a statement of belief in his own handwriting. It is dated "Hampton, September 5th, 1822." There is nothing startling about most of the articles in this creed.* Any Calvinistic Baptist would probably subscribe to all except one of them, with scarcely a change of a word. In fact, if we eliminate from his creed Calvin's dour doctrine of predestination, and the Baptist statement on the mode of baptism, virtually all conservative Protestant bodies would subscribe to the views he set down. He had no theological training and had sat down alone with the Bible in one hand and

---

[19] *Ibid.*, p. 16.

* The twentieth article stands unfinished. Probably interrupted at his task, he laid it aside for a more convenient season, which never came.

the concordance in the other. But the results of his years of study, as revealed in his creed and in his basic rules of interpretation, speak eloquently of the straightness of his thinking.

The one article of his faith which not even a Calvinistic Baptist would have been ready to accept was that numbered fifteen. It reads, "I believe that the second coming of Jesus Christ is near, even at the door, even within twenty-one years, or on or before 1843."

Of his life during this period of study we know little. In fact, we have been able to find only one letter written during that time. This letter was written in 1824. It is addressed to Elisha Ashley, Esq., of Poultney, Vermont. He told "Brother Ashley" about the "fractured arm" he had suffered, and how he was detained in Newhaven and thus would be unable to attend a missionary meeting at which Brother Ashley was to be present. The fervent missionary zeal that controlled Miller is revealed in this letter:

"While the Lord gives me breath I hope I shall feel anxious for the cause and willing to do all that our duty requires. Do try to raise a missionary spirit in our brethren. Oh! that they might feel the importance of being co-workers with God—for the time is at hand when the captivity of Zion shall return and her walls will be built up." [20]

Miller's biographer has preserved for us a letter he wrote to his sister and brother-in-law in the summer of 1825, in which he reveals the same ardent religious feelings and exhorts his sister to live a life acceptable to God. This letter contains an interesting postscript dated June 30. It tells of his having gone to Whitehall, about five miles from Low Hampton, to see Marquis de Lafayette, who had endeared himself to America at the time of the Revolution. Lafayette was making a tour of the States in his old age. Here is Miller's firsthand comment on the marquis:

"He has suffered much; yet he retains a good constitution. He goes a little lame, occasioned by wounds he received in the Revolution. He deserves

---

[20] Manuscript letter, Oct. 3, 1824.

the thanks of Americans, and he has received a general burst of gratitude from Maine to the Mississippi. He has visited every State in the Union and almost every important town. I had the pleasure of dining with him; and after dinner he took a passage for New York." [21]

Captain Miller must have been considered a leading citizen in the area in which he lived. It was no small honor to dine with Marquis de Lafayette.

During his postwar, studious years Miller was busy with the many tasks that belonged to the farmer. Most of the time, however, he held also the office of justice of the peace.*

If during the week Miller was busy with his farm, or with jotting down the important matters concerning the cases that came before him, he also took time on Sunday to record important statements he heard in sermons. How long he followed this practice is not known. There is preserved a small book in which he wrote out briefly the salient facts of the weekly sermons with the names of the ministers who spoke.† Sometimes the outline of a sermon is quite lengthy. Miller must have paid very close attention in order to write so specifically. Probably he did not then realize that he was taking a very practical course in sermon preparation. His own sermon outlines in later years reveal that he had profited well by this course.

The time was drawing near when Miller would no longer be the worshiper in the pew but the preacher in the pulpit. An Elder Andrus, whose sermons Miller outlined in his "Text Book," as he called it, quite possibly was one of those to whom Miller spoke of the soon coming of Christ. At least we have in Miller's handwriting a statement of certain of his beliefs addressed to Andrus, which begins—

---

[21] Sylvester Bliss, *Memoirs of William Miller*, p. 84.

* His commission bears date of February 28, 1821. In his methodical style Miller wrote on the margin, "Received March 10th, 1821," and signed his name. The book that he kept while holding the office of justice reveals the usual array of small cases that came before a justice's court. How long he served in this capacity we do not know. So far as we have been able to determine, the latest date on any legal document signed by him while justice is February 13, 1834. This document is a summons empowering any constable to bring before him a Benjamin Eastman.

† The first entry is dated January 14, 1829.

"The first proof we have, as it respects Christ's second coming as to time, is in Daniel 8:14: 'Unto two thousand three hundred days; then shall the sanctuary be cleansed.' By days we are to understand years, sanctuary we understand the church, cleansed we may reasonably suppose means that complete redemption from sin, both soul and body, after the resurrection when Christ comes the second time 'without sin unto salvation.' " [22]

Into the details of his explanation of this prophetic statement we need not here go. The manuscript fills eight closely packed pages and moves from one line of evidence to another in the series of reasons which, according to Miller, established the belief that the Lord would come "about the year 1843."

But writing even an extended statement like this to a ministerial friend did not quiet the clamorous command that kept ringing in his ears: "Go and tell the world of their danger." He could not free his mind from that impelling sense of duty. If he remained silent, the blood of the lost would be on his garments. Thus he reasoned.

His conviction, his sense of duty, was real, constant, and insistent. But the reader would be mistaken if he now pictured Miller as a man with a strange glint in his eye, so completely obsessed with a sense of duty and destiny that he was no longer quite human like the rest of us. The evidence is clear that this man, who was soon to mount the public platform, always kept his feet on the ground, and strange as it may seem to some who think of a crusading religionist as being rather devoid of normal emotions, Miller actually displayed a delightful sense of humor. God gave us that sense; we did not acquire it with the forbidden fruit. Its judicious, wholesome use has saved more than one man from tense nerves and helped him to maintain his balance. We would not be presenting a full picture of Miller if we failed to quote from a letter he wrote to "Dear Brother and Sisters, Emily and all," in 1831. A few lines down in the letter we read these solicitous words to Emily:

"Emily, I thank you for writing, and if it was possible for me to find

---

[22] Manuscript, *A Few Evidences of the Time of the Second Coming of Christ, to Elder Andrus by William Miller*, dated "Feb. 15, 1831."

you a husband I would do it. But that is doubtful you know. But my prayers are that you may not be an old maid. Therefore you see I have your welfare at heart." [23]

In a later paragraph he returns to this sensitive subject:

"Emily, I must tell you some news. The gossips say Pardy is going to be married to an old maid that keeps house for him. Her name is McCotter. She is about your age and not half as handsome. . . . I beg of you, Emily, not to be an old maid if you can buy a *man* for love or money. And if there is none that will be sold or given for love, do beg one, old or young, big or little, . . . and take off the curse."

This was William Miller speaking in 1831, only a few months before he began his life's work. The counsel he gave is whimsical, perhaps even banal, but it shows better than any reasoned argument ever could that Miller's fervent conviction of religious duty had not made him less human. Within the circle of his family—and the letter was written only for their eyes—there was no doubt that he was considered a very normal man.

But "Brother and Sisters, Emily and all," were not left with a one-sided humorous view of him, pardonable as that might be in a family letter. In the very next sentence after he had pleaded with Emily to "take off the curse," Miller declared with simple fervor, and with no apology for the swift transition in thought, "The Lord is pouring out His Spirit in this region in a miraculous manner." Then follows in detail a description of revivals being held in that area. This was William Miller—both fervent and human. This was the man whose voice was so soon to be heard in the pulpit, proclaiming the second coming of Christ "about the year 1843."

---

[23] Manuscript letter to Joseph Attwood (also spelled Atwood), May 31, 1831.

CHAPTER 3

From Farmer to Preacher

IT WAS A SUMMER'S MORNING IN 1831. Breakfast was finished, and Miller went to his study to "examine some point." There was only one subject of all-consuming interest to him. True, he was a farmer interested in his crops, and a justice of the peace interested in the lawful handling of community affairs; but he was above all else a Bible student absorbed in his investigation of Scripture, particularly of prophecy.

Suddenly he was overwhelmed with the conviction that he should go out and tell the world what he had learned. The conviction was deep, but his objections and protests were as real as ever, even though the year was now 1831 and his knowledge was more full than when the impression first came to him that he should go out. But all the excuses he could muster failed to silence the voice that so clamorously demanded, "Go and tell it to the world." Said he, in relating the experience:

"My distress became so great, I entered into a solemn covenant with God, that if He would open the way, I would go and perform my duty to the world. 'What do you mean by opening the way?' seemed to come to me. Why, said I, if I should have an invitation to speak publicly in any place, I will go and tell them what I find in the Bible about the Lord's coming. Instantly all my burden was gone; and I rejoiced that I should not probably be thus called upon; for I had never had such an invitation: my trials were not known, and I had but little expectation of being invited to any field of labor." [1]

Miller simply did what more than one good man before him had done—tried to strike a compact with God on such terms

---

[1] William Miller, *Apology and Defence*, pp. 17, 18.

as he thought would protect him against carrying out a distasteful task. What he did not know was that even as he was making such apparently safe terms with the Lord, there was traveling down the highway from the near-by town of Dresden a young man bearing an invitation to him to preach the following day, for this was a Saturday morning.

The youth entered Miller's study and announced that there was to be no preaching in the church at Dresden on the morrow, and that his father wanted him to come and talk to the people on the second advent of Christ. Miller was too astonished even to reply. He walked out of the room "angry with myself," said he, "for having made the covenant I had; I rebelled at once against the Lord, and determined not to go."[2] Through the house and out the back door he went. Following close behind was six-year-old Lucy Ann. Lucy was father's favorite child. When he started out of the house in the morning, it was her custom to run along with him. But little did she know of the tumult in his soul, or that he was headed, not for the barn or the field for routine labor, but for a near-by grove where he could pray. The inner conflict was so great that it was soon evident on his countenance and in his walk. Lucy did not have to be told that all was not well; it was evident. Hurrying back into the house, she announced in frightened tones to her mother, "Something's the matter with daddy."

There was. He was at the great turning point in his life. There went into that grove a farmer; there came out a preacher. No man makes so mighty a change suddenly in his life without a tremendous upheaval. In the quietness of the grove his conscience insistently demanded, "Will you make a covenant with God and break it so soon?" There was only one answer that a man of Miller's character could return to such a question. Could an army officer who came of a family of fighting men go back on his word? He promised the Lord that if He would give him words to say and stand by him, he would go out and speak. When

---

[2] *Ibid.*, p. 18.

FROM FARMER TO PREACHER

he returned to the house the youth was still waiting for his answer. After dinner Miller left with him for Dresden. It was probably the longest sixteen miles he had ever traveled.

The next morning, Sunday, he found a well-filled house of attentive people waiting for his message.* His experience he recorded thus:

> "As soon as I commenced speaking, all my diffidence and embarrassment were gone, and I felt impressed only with the greatness of the subject, which, by the providence of God, I was enabled to present." [3]

Evidently his maiden speech, or lecture, as he described it, must have made a real impression on those in charge of the service, for he was invited to remain during the week and lecture. People gathered from near-by towns. Miller found himself engaged in a revival. He had not planned it that way, but the preaching of prophecy, he discovered, produced a profound effect upon the listeners. The preaching of the doctrine of the soon coming of Christ seemed naturally and inevitably to lead men to seek to make ready for that solemn event. This experience was to be repeated many times.

When Miller returned home from his week of lectures he found a letter waiting for him from Elder Fuller of Poultney, Vermont, asking him to come and talk to his church on the second advent. The old adage about a prophet's not being without honor save in his own country found an exception here. Miller traveled the six miles to the town where he had lived for years, and delivered a series of lectures.

Miller wrote later that Elder Fuller was the first convert he

---

[3] *Ibid.*

* Miller, in his *Apology and Defence,* written in 1845, stated that this Sunday, "as nearly as I can remember, was about the first Sabbath in August, 1833."—*Page 18.* This is evidently a slip of memory. His biographer, Bliss, refers to this error as to the year and also as to the day being the *"first* Sabbath in August." The first Sunday was the seventh. Bliss reasons that because Miller made no mention of the Dresden meeting in his letter to Hendryx on August 9, this silence proves he did not hold his first public service till at least the second Sunday. (See *Memoirs of William Miller,* p. 98, footnote.) The evidence for its being at least the fourteenth is stronger than simply Miller's silence in this letter. He stayed in Dresden a week. But he wrote Hendryx from his home in Low Hampton on the ninth! A delightful, yet true, story of this Dresden meeting, which was held at the Silas Guilford home—Mrs. Guilford was Miller's sister, Sylvia—is found in *Pioneer Stories,* by A. W. Spalding, pages 40-49.

made to his prophetic views from the ranks of the ministry. He did not have to go far afield among strangers in order to secure a hearing or to gain converts. That in itself is significant. Whether it was the character of the man or the cogency and fervor of his preaching that produced immediate results, no one can now say with certainty. Probably it was a combination of both. A reading of the lectures which he finally put in print reveals that there was both force and fire in the man, and that he presented his views of prophecy in a manner exceedingly persuasive.

But Dresden and Poultney were not the beginning and the end of his public life. They were only the introduction. He was soon to find himself in the position of having to turn down more requests than he filled simply because he could not be in more than one place at once, or because he had to spend some time on the farm. In his own brief summary of his life he covered the decade from 1830 to 1840 in about three pages. Fortunately, we are not confined to this terse record, nor even to the more extended story that his biographer left for us in 1853. Miller carried on a considerable correspondence. In one series of letters particularly—those to a fellow minister, Truman Hendryx—is found a rather clear picture of his expanding activities, interests, and views.

Miller's first letter to Hendryx was written in the summer of 1831. At the top margin in Miller's bold handwriting is a notation: "No. 1." It was written in reply to a letter received from Hendryx the day before. After an introductory paragraph Miller came to the point of his letter:

"You say, Brother Hendryx, you want 'more light.' I wish that you might receive it, and I shall be willing to assist you with what little I have at every convenient opportunity. Do not be discouraged. When you have studied fourteen years, if you do not find 'more light,' then you may complain." [4]

Miller, of course, was alluding to the fact that he had been studying for that length of time himself. The remainder of the

---

[4] Manuscript letter, Aug. 9, 1831.

letter consists wholly of an exposition of prophecy as Miller understood it, the "light" which he believed he had both for Hendryx and for the world. Unquestionably the very act of writing out his views, as he did for Hendryx and for others, explains in no small degree the immediate and unexpected ease with which he found himself orally expounding his views at Dresden and elsewhere. This particular letter was written only a few days before the Dresden meeting.

The friendship between these men, born of a mutual interest in Bible study, grew rapidly. Early in 1832 Miller addressed Hendryx in this direct fashion:

"I want to know how you progress in Scripture, and what you preach. You promised me a visit this winter. Do not forget. At any rate you can write." [5]

He wrote of a "Brother Sawyer" who had adopted some of his views, but who had "not improved so much in Bible knowledge as he might" because, added Miller, he "was afraid of being 'a Millerite.'" Here is the first reference to the idea of converts as followers of a particular man. The word "Millerite" was soon to be heard over the whole land, and was generally employed by the user as a term of contempt.*

Miller remarked to Hendryx concerning Brother Sawyer, "I pity him, for he has some fetters on." Also in this letter Miller mentioned for the first time, so far as we have been able to discover, his having written for publication "a few numbers on the coming of Christ." They were written in the form of "letters to Elder Smith of Poultney," to whom Miller had given "liberty to publish." He thought that they "may appear in the *Vermont Telegraph*, if not in pamphlet form." †

---

[5] Manuscript letter, Jan. 25, 1832.

* We may remark in passing that after the lapse of a hundred years we shall use the term "Millerite" without in any way implying contempt or ridicule, but merely as the simplest way to describe that group of people who believed the preaching of Miller.

† The *Vermont Telegraph* was a weekly Baptist paper, published in Brandon, Vermont. Miller's biographer said: "The articles referred to were sent as anonymous to the editor of the *Telegraph*, who declined their publication unless informed of the name of the writer. This being communicated to him, they appeared, in a series of sixteen articles, over the initials of W. M. The first article was published in the paper of May 15, 1832."—*Sylvester Bliss,*

Miller continued, with this fervent praise of the Book of God:

"I am more and more astonished at the harmony and strength of the Word of God, and the more I read, the more I see the folly of the infidel in rejecting this Word."

Then, fearing that perhaps Hendryx had become afraid of being known as "a Millerite," though he evidently had nothing on which to base his fear, he thus ended his letter:

"But, Brother Hendryx, have you been ridiculed out of your belief or not? Tell me, kind sir, and believe me ever yours in the bond of Christ."

Hendryx was not the only one who had heard of Miller's unusual views of Scripture. In a letter to him two months later, Miller told Hendryx that he would have replied earlier to his letter, but he had been occupied at home for several days in deep study with a young preacher who had come to his home. He said that this youthful minister came "on purpose to learn these strange notions of 'crazy Miller's' or at least to save Brother Miller if possible from going down to the grave with such an error." Miller explained that his visitor was a stranger to him. What happened "after he introduced himself," Miller described in this vigorous language:

"We went to work, night and day, and he has just left me, Monday, 3 o'clock P. M. He has got his load, and as he says, he never was so loaded before. You may say this is boasting. *No, No,* Brother Hendryx. You know better. I only made him read Bible and I held the concordance.

Memoirs of William Miller, pp. 99, 100. A letter from Henry Jones to Miller implies that the "first eight numbers" may have been published as a complete series. (See manuscript letter, Jones to Miller, Dec. 27, 1832.)

There is preserved the manuscript of Miller's first eight articles to the *Telegraph.* The first number of this series of eight begins thus: "Mr. Editor: A number of your subscribers have requested me to give my views, of the times spoken of in Daniel's and John's prophecies, when the latter-day glory will commence, and the 'beast shall be destroyed and his body given to the burning flames.'" Compare this language with Miller's statement to Hendryx: "I have written a few numbers on the coming of Christ and the final destruction of the beast when his 'body shall be given to the burning flame.' It [they] may appear in the *Vermont Telegraph."*

Bliss's statement implies that the editor held the articles until informed as to the author, and then published them over the initials, "W. M." But the manuscript of the first eight articles reveals the initials "W. M." in Miller's own handwriting at the bottom of seven of them. The eighth has no identifying initial at the close. Miller wrote articles for the *Telegraph* at least as late as March 12, 1833. The files of this paper are too incomplete to permit of our securing exact information as to the number and the dates of publication of all his articles.

No praise to me; give God the glory. At any rate he will find it hard to resist the truth. He wants me to let him come and board with me two or three months to study BIBLE. He is a young man of brilliant talents." [6]

Here is William Miller in action in terms of personal ministry for an audience of one. You can feel the vigor of the man, the drive, the earnestness. You see him seated close beside his inquirer, in whose hand he has placed the Bible. In Miller's hand is the concordance with all its connected references to any particular word, classified for ready reference. We do not have to accept all Miller's beliefs regarding the Bible in order to agree that here was no airy speculator dreamily sitting on a mountaintop and out of the fullness of his own mystical speculations spinning a philosophy of things that were and are and are to be. Instead, Miller turned his mind and all his thoughts to searching the one Book which all Christendom has declared is the true source of knowledge and revelation.

The visit of this young preacher was not a lone instance of interested inquiry by someone. Miller went on to tell Hendryx:

"I have somebody to labor with almost daily. I have been into Poultney, and some other places to lecture on the coming of Christ, and in every case I have had large assemblies. There is an increasing anxiety on the subject in this quarter."

Then he offered a little counsel to his preacher friend, counsel that might properly have come from a seasoned instructor in pastoral training. In speaking of some of the problems of preaching to those with differing views on salvation, he counseled:

"I would therefore advise you to lead your hearers by slow and sure steps to Jesus Christ. I say *slow* because I expect they are not strong enough to run yet, *sure* because the Bible is a sure word. And where your hearers are not well doctrinated, you must preach *Bible*. You must prove all things by *Bible*. You must talk *Bible,* you must exhort *Bible,* you must pray *Bible,* and love *Bible,* and do all in your power to make others love *Bible* too. One great means to do good is to make your parishioners sensible that you are in earnest and fully and solemnly believe what you preach. If you wish your people to feel, feel yourself. If you wish them to believe

---

[6] Manuscript letter, March 26, 1832.

as you do, show them by your constant assiduity in teaching, that you sincerely wish it. You can do more good by the fireside and in your conference circles than in the pulpit."

No truer observation was ever made on the fine art of bringing spiritual conviction to others. He immediately explained his statement more fully by remarking that pulpit preaching "has long been no more considered than a trade," and that people remark, "Why, he is hired to preach." But when a man goes out of his way to use his time in private conference, seeking to expound the Word, people "will say he expects nothing for this, surely our salvation is his anxious desire."

At this point the letter was laid aside and the remainder written under date of May 20. Miller started this second section of his epistle by remarking, "I ought to make some apology for my long neglect. But I hate apologies, for we never tell the whole truth." Quite direct, quite frank. That was typical of William Miller.

He told Hendryx that he would probably see even before he received this letter, "two numbers in the *Telegraph*," and explained that "a number more will soon follow." He anticipated that they would start "some queries if nothing more." Then comes this ominous line: "There is much opposition expressed, by some who ought to have taught the same things." Here is a report on the first stirrings of that opposition that was finally to display itself in a veritable flood of opposing arguments, both oral and written, some serious, many scurrilous.

Six months later he wrote to Hendryx, expressing an ardent desire to see him. And why? "So that we can sit down and have a good dish of Bible together." Though Miller brought all his study to a focus in the doctrine of the second advent, he saw it properly as a climax to a plan God had devised for the salvation of men. Listen to the next line of his letter:

"The light is continually breaking in, and I am more and more confirmed in those things of which I told you, when you were here; to wit, redemption by grace, the efficacy of Christ's blood, justification by His righteousness imputed to us, sanctification through the operation of the Divine Spirit, and glorification by our gathering together unto Him at His coming and His appearing." [7]

The series of steps in salvation here set forth sounds very orthodox. It is.

The next month he again wrote to Hendryx, and told of hearing a certain minister preach on the second coming of Christ: "He is a 'Millerite' and knows it not. But from what I could learn Brother Hendryx made him a 'Millerite,' and will have to answer for it, to the craft (the modern ministry)." [8]

By this time Miller was meeting with sufficient opposition from certain ministers to lead him to caution Hendryx in whimsical fashion. He warned him that he did not realize how much he was "to blame, for endangering the sale of the modern shrines of Diana. Take care of your head."

The Baptist church at Low Hampton at the time was needing a minister. A young preacher located near Hendryx had been suggested for the place. Miller asked for Hendryx' comment on him and proceeded to express his own views on the proper qualifications for a good pastor:

"You had better hear him yourself, and then if you think he will be the one for us, send him on. We do not want one who thinks much of his own gifts and is lifted up with pride. Neither do we want a novice, I mean a fool, one who knows nothing about the gospel of Christ. We want one good to stir up our minds, to visit, etc. And one who is good to learn, apt to teach, modest, unassuming, pious, devotional, and faithful to his calling. If his natural talents are brilliant, with these qualifications they would not hurt him. If they are only middling they may do well enough for us. But you can tell better than I can write. Some of our people want a quick gab. But I had rather a quick understanding."

It would be difficult to disagree with Miller's analysis of what makes a good preacher. And that analysis gives an insight into the mind of Miller as to his sense of values in spiritual things.

Miller's traveling, preaching, and correspondence were rapidly increasing, even though it was little more than a year

---
[7] Manuscript letter, Oct. 1, 1832.
[8] Manuscript letter, Nov. 17, 1832.

since he had delivered his first public lecture and only about eight months since his initial article had appeared in print. Probably the first letter he received in the opening days of 1833 was one signed by a stranger, Henry Jones. Miller was to receive many letters from him in the future, for Henry Jones became a rather important figure in the Millerite movement. Because he was a total stranger he introduced himself by stating that when he was traveling in New York State the previous June, he fell in company with a minister, and "heard him converse on the subject of the millennium." He explained that this minister had "been led to a particular and careful inquiry on the subject from peculiar views which he had heard advanced by yourself in private conversation, some of which," he said, "you had published in the *Vermont Telegraph* over the signature 'W. M.'" Jones continued:

"After this, in my travels as agent for the circulation of temperance newspapers, by inquiry I found and purchased the several *Telegraph* papers which contain your first eight numbers on the subject or subjects now mentioned, and read them with much interest."[9]

Then follow pages of discussion of prophetic passages, with this frank comment in the closing paragraph:

"I am aware that most of our Bible men would consider you very visionary or fanatical were they to be informed of your views. And though I know not but you are truly so, and running wild, I should be very glad to see you and talk with you several hours, as I was told that you had made the subject your great study for many years and now stand ready to talk upon it and to defend it against all plausible objections."

The letter ends with a request that Miller write him a letter explaining certain points of his belief. We do not have Miller's reply. From Jones' further letters we can discover that he was increasingly coming to the same viewpoint that Miller held. We will have more to say about him in a later chapter devoted to Miller's associates. We refer to this letter here only to show that very early in his public life Miller was attracting the serious

---

[9] Manuscript letter, Dec. 27, 1832.

attention and interest of fellow ministers—for Jones was a minister.

A little later, in writing to Hendryx, Miller referred to his correspondence with Henry Jones and remarked:

"So you see, my brother, the Lord is scattering the seed. I can now reckon eight ministers that preach this doctrine more or less besides yourself, and whether you do or not, your letter does not state. I know of more than one hundred private brethren that say they have adopted my views as their belief. Be that as it may, 'truth is mighty and will prevail.'" [10]

We may rightly conclude that Miller really believed Hendryx agreed with his teaching, for he inquired in the next sentence, "If I should get my views printed, how many can you dispose of in pamphlet form, say between thirty and forty pages?" *

Miller seemed to take a matter-of-fact attitude, sometimes even a slightly humorous one, toward his critics. In this same letter he referred to two men who had apparently made some rather noisy, boastful thrusts at him. "But do not be alarmed on my account Brother Hendryx," he said, "I have heard lions *roar,* and jackasses *bray,* and I am yet alive."

Miller's reputation as a preacher must have been growing in his own community as well as abroad, for he informed Hendryx, "Our people are about giving me a license to lecture."

The thought of this troubled him greatly. "I hardly know what to do," said he. "I am too old, too wicked, and too proud. I want your advice; be plain and tell me the whole truth."

---

[10] Manuscript letter, Feb. 8, 1833.

* It was not long after this that there was published under the imprint of the *Vermont Telegraph* office, at Brandon, 1833, a sixty-four-page pamphlet, entitled *Evidences From Scripture & History of the Second Coming of Christ about the Year* A. D. *1843, and of His Personal Reign of 1,000 Years,* by Wm. Miller.

Underneath this title and name is printed the appropriate text of Scripture: "Prove all things; hold fast that which is good." 1 Thessalonians 5:21.

This was the beginning of a wide array of published works in behalf of Miller's views.

Miller opened his "Introduction" in the pamphlet with the rather modest declaration: "The writer does not claim the title of a Theologist, nor of infallibility, and only presents himself in common with other writers on the same, or other subjects of like import, to be tried by the infallible touchstone of Divine truth."—*Page 3.* He closes the "Introduction" thus: "I do most solemnly believe that assiduity, patience, perseverance and prayer, assisted by the grace of God, will overcome more obstacles than all the learning one man could contain without these, to understand the Bible. And yet of how great help would erudition be accompanied with the before-mentioned graces, for Daniel says, 'the wise shall understand.' Which wisdom may you obtain, my dear reader, is the earnest prayer of your humble servant." —*Page 6.*

In between these various letters written from his home Miller was making one trip after another to lecture on the prophecies. One day on a steamboat on the Hudson he was thrown in company with a group of men who were discussing the marvelous discoveries and inventions of their day, expressing wonder at what the future might hold, for in 1833 the steamboat was still considered quite marvelous. Miller remarked that the discussion made him think of the prophetic statement, "Many shall run to and fro, and knowledge shall be increased." Daniel 12:4.

He then proceeded to discuss at some length the prophecies of the Bible in their relation to the last days of earth's history. After rather extended presentation he excused himself and withdrew to the other end of the boat, not wishing to impose his ideas further on a company of strangers. But the whole group followed and requested that he continue. As the boat made its way mile after mile down the Hudson, he proceeded from one chapter to another in the book of the prophet Daniel and gave them what he believed was the true interpretation. He had with him copies of his recently published sixty-four-page pamphlet to hand out to them in response to their inquiry for something to read on the prophecies.[11]

In the spring of 1833 Low Hampton was still without a Baptist preacher. Miller had been called upon to occupy the pulpit. Here is the way he described himself and his preaching:

"We have no preacher as yet, except the *old man* with his *Concordance*. And he is so shunned, with his cold, dull and lifeless performance, that I have strong doubts whether he will attempt again. But hush—not a word of what I tell you. Send us a minister if you can." [12]

He mourns because he does not feel gifted:

"I wish I had the tongue of an Apollos, the powers of mind of a Paul; what a field might I not explore, and what powerful arguments might not be brought to prove the authenticity of the Scriptures, but I want one thing, more than either, the Spirit of Christ and of God, for He is able to take *worms* and thrash *mountains*."

---

[11] See Sylvester Bliss, *Memoirs of William Miller*, p. 106.
[12] Manuscript letter to Hendryx, April 10, 1833.

The letter closes with an extended eulogy of the Scriptures.

Miller had been correct in his forecast, in a letter to Hendryx a few months previously, that his church was about to give him a license to preach. The original license is still preserved and is dated September 14, 1833. It gives evidence of being well worn. Presumably it was carried around by Miller for years.

This was only two years and one month from that Saturday in August, 1831, when Miller struggled with his own soul in prayer in that grove near his home and came forth a preacher. The church may not have known it, but they were simply giving formal ratification to the transaction Miller had made with his God in that grove.

From various references in his letters, and other sources, we are to conclude that in the twelve months following his receipt of a license Miller simply continued doing what he had been doing for two years previous, traveling here and there as he could find the time. He had not yet turned over the operation of his farm to his growing family, which finally numbered eight, nor had he yet resigned his office as a justice of the peace. We have records that show him serving as a justice as late as February, 1834. Though not poor, Miller was not a rich man. He had to provide for his family with the labors of his own hands and head.

Early in 1834, in another of his letters to Brother Hendryx, he wrote that he had been very busily engaged in preaching:

"I have forgotten whether I answered your last letter or not. I have been so much engaged for a few months past, that I have had no time to keep up a correspondence with the best friend on earth. This must be my apology. . . . You laugh, Brother Hendryx, to think old Brother Miller is preaching. But laugh on. You are not the only one that laughs, and it is all right. I deserve it. But if I could preach the truth, it is all I could ask. Can you tell me how old Noah was when he began to preach? And Lot, Moses, etc.?" [13]

Perhaps it was Miller's rather poor health that made him unusually conscious of his years, for he referred to his age quite

---
[13] Manuscript letter, Feb. 25, 1834.

frequently. At the time of writing this particular letter he was only fifty-two years old. He actually began to preach when he was not quite fifty. Though hardly old in terms of a lifetime, fifty is rather a ripe age at which to begin preaching. The ease with which he moved into this new field, the ability which he soon displayed in holding audiences spellbound—an ability which even his enemies freely admitted—reveals a rather remarkable adaptability.

This letter deals largely with Miller's views concerning the Negro and the abolitionist movement that had recently been formed, and which was meeting with the most violent opposition and misrepresentation. If we were setting out to write a story of Miller that was as hopelessly one-sided on the good side as enemies' stories have been on the bad, we would pass by this letter. His remarks are complimentary neither to the abolitionist nor to the Negro. He wrote on this subject with the same vigor as he wrote on everything else. To a greater or lesser extent we are all creatures of our age and of our times, and our minds are clothed in the fashions of thought of our particular day, even as our bodies are robed in the dress of the times. The great majority of people thought abolitionists were dangerous disturbers of the peace and likewise believed that the Negro ought rightly to be kept in bondage because he was little, if anything, better than the beast.

Miller held what was then considered a very charitable view. He believed, with others, that the Negro should be sent back to Africa. The letter reveals, however, that he is not quite sure that his view of the whole matter is correct. He wants Hendryx to help him clarify his thinking and fortify him in his position against the disturbing abolitionists. Here is the vigorous way in which he wrote his closing paragraph:

"Do write and help me, brother, for as long as I have one shot I will fight: for these fire-skulled, visionary, fanatical, treasonable, suicidal, demoralizing, hot-headed set of abolitionists are worse, if possible, than Antimasonry, and if they go on in this way they will set our world on fire, before the time."

There was nothing halfway about Miller. He reminds one a little of the apostle Paul. He thought and acted intensely. He used in abundance those handmaidens of the fervid—colorful adjectives and superlatives.

But we must not turn aside further to discuss abolitionism or any other of the forces that were working on the body politic. We shall later devote a chapter to the discussion of the kind of world in which the Millerite movement lived.

Although we are most fortunate in having a series of letters that Miller wrote to his bosom friend, Hendryx, we do not have the letters that Hendryx wrote in reply. It seems that when Hendryx wrote to Miller after he had received his license he addressed him as the Reverend William Miller. This provoked from Miller a protest in the first lines of his letter:

"I wish you would look into your Bible and see if you can find the word 'Rev.' applied to a sinful mortal as myself and govern yourself accordingly. Otherwise, I received your friendly epistle and hasten to answer." [14]

There is no reason to believe that this was feigned humility. There was no smirking, simpering pretense of piety, rather a forthright expression of an innermost feeling; it was simply William Miller speaking from his heart. It is interesting, however, to note that the address on the letters which Miller wrote to Hendryx both before and after this date begins thus: "Rev. Truman Hendryx." Some may consider this inconsistent. In a sense it probably was; yet Miller doubtless reasoned that while he himself could not honestly accept the title he would not deny it to others who did feel free to use it.

Miller was busy during the summer of 1834. This is evident from a letter to Hendryx which tells of various trips he had taken, in which he said: "After haying and harvesting are over, I shall go again." [15]

In the autumn he wrote to this fellow preacher, opening his letter with this play on words:

---

[14] Manuscript letter, March 22, 1834.
[15] Manuscript letter, Aug. 17, 1834.

"I now have seated myself at the northeast part of my room, at the *old* desk, to answer a new letter from an *old* friend. . . . It is an *old* man who is writing and the good *old* Book that he is writing about, and an *old* way of expressing himself. . . .

"I have had good success since I wrote you before. The Lord has been with me. I have been into a number of towns in Vermont. Some old hardened rebels have been brought to plead for mercy, even before I got through a course of my lectures. Blessed be the holy name of God; He has given me even more than I should have dared to ask. How good, my brother, it is to preach, having God for paymaster. Oh, I would not be a hireling to the *sheep* and *the world*. . . . He pays down; He pays in souls." [16]

He cannot assure Hendryx of "coming into your country, for I find doors opening in this vicinity to last one year at least."

He then added this postscript:

"I devote my whole time lecturing, spend about a week in a place, have very crowded assemblies, generally more last day than preceding. Many say it looks rational and go to reading; some scoff and ridicule; others believe it is true. Ministers generally are the hardest to be convinced; yet they say 'they can bring no argument but what the *old* man will remove.' You know Estee. He happened in one evening where I was lecturing (though he laughed and jeered before); next day sent me an invitation. Case, of Cornwall, laughed and ridiculed. I went and lectured four nights, five ministers present. Case was first to believe."

Here is a brief, staccato record of the groundwork Miller was beginning to lay, that provides the real explanation for the rather impressive monument of a movement that was reared in the early 1840's. Estee and Case were just two of an increasing number who listened to the *"old* man" and were convicted.

---

[16] Manuscript letter, Nov. 28, 1834.

CHAPTER 4

Laying the Groundwork of the Movement

"I DEVOTE MY WHOLE TIME, LECTURING." These words to his friend Hendryx near the close of 1834 reveal the rising tempo of Miller's program. Preaching was no longer an avocation. A diary he kept of his travels for a period of years carries this line at the top of the first page: "Beginning October 1st, 1834." The diary records the date and place of each lecture for a period of four years and eight months, and gives the book, chapter, and verse that he used in each lecture. He calls this little diary a "Text Book."

The early months of 1835 showed an expansion of Miller's activity and success. Writing to Hendryx in the spring, he said:

"In every place I have visited, the Lord has given me some fruits. Oh! Brother Hendryx, this is marvelous in our eyes that He should take such an old 'dry stick' as I am, and bring down the proud and haughty infidel. Yet blessed be His name, He can and will work by whom He will. Pray for me, my brother, that I may be kept humble, for I am exceeding jealous of my proud heart. . . . I now have four or five ministers to hear me in every place I lecture. I tell you it is making no small stir in these regions." [1]

Then he added this news item: "Old Elder Fuller is preaching this same doctrine in Connecticut and writes me that it has a powerful effect." This is perhaps the first record of definite activity in the preaching of Miller's views of the prophecies on the part of any other minister, with definite results.

The edition of the sixty-four-page pamphlet printed in 1833 must have been exhausted early in 1835, for the publisher, Isaac Wescott, wrote that he had decided to get out another edition.

---
[1] Manuscript letter, March 6, 1835.

"I shall get 1,000 copies for myself which can be done for $100. If you want 500 copies I can get 1,500 for $135. Do you wish to revise the work or make any addition? If so, write or come and see me immediately. The latter would be best." [2]

We do not know the exact size of any of these early editions. But even an edition of 1,500 may be considered quite impressive when it is remembered that up to this time practically the only stimulus to the sale and circulation of this literature was the preaching of one man. And most of that preaching was done in villages and small towns.

We pick up the thread of Miller's travels again in a letter written to Hendryx at the end of the summer of 1835. He opened his letter with this comment on his delay in writing:

"More than two months and my letter not answered, you will say. Yes, and if I did not hate apologies abominably I would make one; but as they always contain lies and are the child of vanity or pride, I shall only say, I have now sat down to my old-fashioned desk, in my east room, to have a few minutes' conversation with Brother Truman. . . . I am yet engaged in my occupation in warning the inhabitants to be prepared for the great day of God Almighty, and am endeavoring to prove by the Scriptures that that day is near 'even at the door.' . . . Then I pray God to direct the arrow to the heart, the seat of life. But in the first place I ask God through Jesus Christ to nerve the arm that pulls the bow, to sharpen the arrow that twangs from it." [3]

Miller, fearing that such speaking might sound too vain, added immediately that he thought he heard his friend Hendryx saying, "Brother Miller smells a little of egotism, great I." A true revelation of his heart is disclosed in the next sentence:

"But I will confess more. I sometimes feel as though I can do all things 'through Christ strengthening me,' and sometimes the shaking of a leaf is terror to me. Now laugh as much as you please, if it does you any good, my brother; it will do me no hurt."

Even a brave soldier has to admit fear at times, and Miller by his own testimony was not always the bold, poised, confident man that his listeners may have thought him to be.

---

[2] Manuscript letter, March 12, 1835.
[3] Manuscript letter, Aug. 27, 1835.

He gave a long recital of the different cities in which he had recently lectured, and ended on this hurried note: "Shall be under the necessity of starting in a few minutes. I shall be absent until about the first of October."

The year 1836 saw a further significant development in his work. Up to now he had had only his sixty-four page pamphlet to leave with those who requested reading matter. But increasingly he was asked why he did not put his lectures in a permanent book form. Writing to Hendryx in the spring, he said: "I have, when at home, been engaged in writing and preparing for the press eighteen lectures on the second coming, . . . as I have been strongly solicited for a copy of the lectures for publication."[4] He stated that the book would be about 200 pages in length and sell for about fifty cents, and that it would "be much more full than the pamphlet."[*] He also remarked that another edition of the pamphlet had been brought out, "but by whom I cannot tell." In those days it was quite a common thing for a not too scrupulous publisher to bring out an edition of a work without the knowledge of the author or the first publisher. However, no publisher would engage in this morally doubtful procedure unless he was certain that the publication would have a good sale. This is simply another way of saying that the interest in Millerism must have become quite real and evident by then.

Miller told his Baptist preacher friend, Hendryx, of eight Baptist ministers who "are now preaching" his views. He gave the name of each and added, "Many others believe but dare not preach it." On this point he was very specific, for he named

---

[4] Manuscript letter, April 2, 1836.

[*] The book to which he referred is *Evidence From Scripture and History of the Second Coming of Christ, About the Year 1843: Exhibited in a Course of Lectures.* This was brought out sometime in 1836. However, it did not contain "eighteen lectures," but sixteen. The "about 200 pages" became 223. This book became commonly known as Miller's Lectures. Note the similarity between the title of this book and the title of the 1833 pamphlet. Miller's ideas on writing had not yet gone beyond the pamphlet stage even in 1836, for he began his "Introduction" to his book of lectures thus: "In presenting this pamphlet to the public . . . ." —*Page 3.* Evidently, by the time he brought out a revised edition in 1838, he had gone beyond the pamphlet stage. His "Introduction" opens thus: "In presenting these Lectures to the public . . . ."—*Page iii.*

ten preachers, concluding the series with this rather pointed remark: "And may I say Hendryx belongs to this class."

While Miller may have had rugged speech, he did not have a rugged constitution. The labors of his later years were to be greatly hampered by periods of illness. One of the first mentions we have of sickness is in a letter to Hendryx in the summer of 1836. Miller wrote of having been "confined at home for three weeks past by a bilious complaint."[5] The doctors today might diagnose the case differently, but the important point is that Miller was already beginning to be troubled with those spells of illness that broke into the cycle of his lecturing. He related that he was "taken unwell while lecturing." "Yet I finished my course of lectures," he added. There was a stimulus to keep him going in the fact that the meeting place was "filled to overflowing for eight days in succession."

There were many clergymen attending. They seemed not to be confined to any one denomination, for he mentioned Baptists, Methodists, Congregationalists, Presbyterians, and Universalists. That such men came out night after night, listening attentively, never failed to astonish Miller. Said he:

"I can only account for it by supposing that God is supporting the *old man,* weak, wicked, imperfect, and ignorant as he is, to confound the wise and mighty. . . . It makes me feel like a worm, a poor feeble creature, for it is God only that could produce such an effect on such audiences."

Remember that this statement, in common with similar ones already quoted, is not the platform utterance of a man who is seeking to create the effect of humility before an audience of strangers. These are the quiet, confidential thoughts expressed by one intimate friend to another.

There is a good reason for calling particular attention to different statements in Miller's correspondence at this period of his life. In the first place, it is during this period that we have the best collection of personal letters that reveal his character. From 1840 onward Millerism was no longer the activity of one

---

[5] Manuscript letter, July 21, 1836.

man primarily, but of a very great and increasing group of men. The distinctive features of his character are then not so clearly evident, nor do we have so many of his letters from which to draw. Second, in those later years the Millerite movement, and most particularly Miller, came under heavy fire from every kind of critic. Much of the criticism impugned the personal motives of Miller and his close associates. It will help us later in evaluating these numerous character indictments if we keep in mind what his personal letters reveal in this decade from 1830 to 1840.

At the close of the year he was able to tell Hendryx that the book of lectures had been published and that there was already a large market for it. "I sold 300 in three towns in St. Lawrence County this fall." [6] He had spent eight weeks in that area and had delivered "82 lectures" during the fall. He expected the next week to leave home again for another tour. His "Text Book" shows that he lectured some in every month of the year 1836 except November and December. This little "Text Book" contains something else very interesting. Beside the entry for June 20, 1836, is this notation in the margin, "$4." Someone had given him four dollars to pay his transportation to Lansingburgh, New York. This, along with a "$2" entry of September 3, 1835, apparently represented the total of gifts he had received since he began his public labors in 1831.* In the margin of his entry for October 3 is found the notation ".50," and then under October 16 is the notation "$3." After that there is no further financial item recorded until February 10, 1837, which carries the notation "$1.50." Thus the record reads in small change,

---

[6] Manuscript letter, Dec. 23, 1836.

* We say "apparently represented." An absolute statement cannot be made. But his methodical way of recording items would suggest strongly that if he had received other monies than those here mentioned, he would have listed them. This presumption seems to be supported by the statement of his biographer, who was intimately acquainted with him. Referring to the Lansingburgh trip on the nineteenth of June, 1836, Bliss said, "To pay his stage fare he received, on this occasion, four dollars, which, with the two half dollars received in Canada, was all the remuneration he had thus far received for his expenses."—*Memoirs of William Miller, p. 125.* There is a discrepancy, however, between Bliss' statement about the "two half dollars" and the "Text Book" record, which contains, previous to the Lansingburgh trip, only one financial entry, the "$2" item. However, this does not affect the main point, the smallness of the contributions received,

scattered sparsely over the months and years. As a financial venture Millerism was not paying large dividends.

When Miller wrote to Hendryx early in 1837 he had something new to tell of successes attending his lectures. He had just delivered a series of sixteen lectures on the second coming. As usual there were ministers present, but in this case one of the ministers arose to confess his belief in Miller's preaching. Here is the way he describes it in his letter:

"Elder Mattison got up at the close of my last discourse, and in a most solemn and impressive manner told the congregation that he 'had been convicted, confounded and converted,' and confessed he had written and said things against the speaker of which he was now ashamed. He had called him 'the end of the world man' and 'the old visionary,' 'dreamer,' 'fanatic,' etc. 'And,' said he, 'I came to meeting with a determination to not believe, and to expose him and his folly to the people who should be present. And have therefore watched with a close attention and a jealous eye.' " [7]

But he found no occasion to object. "If you will believe me, brother," continued Miller, "this honest confession was like a thunderbolt in the assembly."

So the number of those who accepted his teachings grew. Not simply unlettered laymen but ministers were being steadily added to the total. What manner of man was this William Miller who could persuade preachers of various denominations to accept his teachings? Preachers are not in the habit of changing their religious views. Laymen may and do change beliefs at times, but ministers rarely. This is a simple statement of fact and only gives point to the question, What manner of man was this William Miller that he could persuade even ministers to believe teachings that could result only in their being called visionaries and fanatics, even as Miller was being called? The answer cannot be found in the personality of the man. He was anything but prepossessing. Even his friends painted a rather modest picture of him as regards his platform ability. His language was often colloquial and occasionally ungrammatical.

---

[7] Manuscript letter, Feb. 21, 1837.

His word pictures help to explain why he could hold an audience for an hour or two at a time. But even such oratory does not fully explain his success. We believe it does not even go to the heart of the matter. While an emotional fraction of the population can unthinkingly be carried away by colorful adjectives and dramatic perorations, the clergy are not thus swept off their feet. The ministers who came to listen to him were accustomed to using adjectives and dramatics themselves.

There must have been a certain force and appeal not only in the earnestness of the man but in the logical way in which he marshaled his arguments. True, there was patently an error somewhere in his reasoning. Christ did not come "about the year 1843," but that error was not immediately discernible to the ministry who came to listen. Later we shall devote a chapter to a discussion of the controversy that raged between Miller and certain of the ministry who sought to demolish his teachings. For the present we need only remark that the force and effectiveness of Miller's preaching lay in the kind of argument and evidence that he brought forth in support of his teachings, and not in any dramatics or tricks of publicity.

This conclusion finds strong support in the fact that many became converts to Miller's views without ever having met him. They simply read what he wrote. Take this letter, for example, that was written to him from Boston early in 1838:

"I am a stranger to you, but I trust that through the free sovereign grace of God I am not altogether a stranger to Jesus Christ, whom you serve. I am the pastor of an orthodox Congregational church in this city. A few weeks since, your lectures on the second coming of Christ were put into my hands. I sat down to read the work, knowing nothing of the views which it contained. I have *studied* it with an overwhelming interest, such as I never felt in any other book except the Bible. I have compared it with Scripture and history, and I find nothing on which to rest a single doubt respecting the correctness of your views. . . .

"There is a meeting of our ministerial association tomorrow, and as I am appointed to read an essay, I design to bring up this whole subject for discussion, and trust that I may thereby do something to spread the truth." [8]

---
[8] Manuscript letter, March 5, 1838.

Here is no illiterate layman expressing himself under the spell of Miller's preaching. This is a minister who had studied at Brown University telling of the effect produced on him by merely reading Miller's book of lectures. His name is Charles Fitch. We shall hear more of him later as a prominent spokesman of the Millerite movement in the early 1840's.

In midsummer of 1838 Miller wrote to Hendryx: "I have been absent from home more than three fourths of my time." Hendryx had written, urging Miller to come over into Pennsylvania to his church. Miller replied:

"You speak of my coming there, and the house being crammed. I need not go there to see a house, not only crammed, but jammed. Last Sabbath I preached in Benson and saw the house jammed full, lobby and all. But, my brother, there is no pleasure to me particularly in that. The multitude may today cry Hosanna, and tomorrow 'Crucify him.' Lord, what is man?" [9]

He told of having received a letter from an Elder West, who had charged him in vigorous language with holding certain wrong views on salvation, and of having received a letter from an Elder Claflin, charging him with holding exactly the opposite views on salvation. Observed Miller: "They both quote Bible."

Miller felt hopeful, however, that something could be done for these two preachers who assailed him on different sides and in such an unchristian spirit. Here is the picturesque way he believed they could be helped:

"I think if we could take Elder West and Elder Claflin and boil them well over the fire of persecution, stir them well together with the rod of Christian experience, cool them off in the kettle of practical godliness, and strain them both through the sieve of electing love, then stir in a little leaven of Christian piety, then let them stand in a by place until suppertime, when the blessed Saviour should come they would be fit for use."

The reading of the West and Claflin letters with their opposite theological views and their equal appeal to Scripture aroused a serious line of thought in Miller's mind, hardly the line of thought that any irrevocably fixed fanatic would entertain:

---

[9] Manuscript letter, July 27, 1838.

"Since I read Father West's letter, I have had some strong jealousy of old Brother Miller. Thinks I to myself: If as good a man as you say Father West is, can twist the Scriptures to accommodate his views, as he does the parable of the ten virgins, why may not old Brother Miller do the same and neither of us know it? He thinks he had got the truth on one point, and therefore bends all the Scriptures to his point. When in fact and truth, there are more points than one in Scripture. Brother Claflin has a different point, and does the same. And who knows but that old Brother Miller has the same fault? He sees, he thinks, clearly both of them in this fault, but not his own fault. So do they. 'Lord, what is man.'"

Could anyone be asked to make a more penetrating criticism of himself than that? Or could any man find a more reasonable way out of the dilemma that such musings generate, than the forthright plan Miller suggested when he wrote the next sentence?

"I have finally come to this conclusion that I must read the Bible for myself, try all that in me lies to divest myself of prejudice, judge with candor, get rid of self, preach what I believe to be truth, try to please God more than man, and then leave all in the hand of my divine Master and wait for His decision."

Addressing himself to his friend, he asked, "Will this do, Brother Hendryx? or can you give me some better advice? If you will, I will listen."

In November, Miller wrote to his son from Montpelier, where he was holding a series of lectures. He told his firstborn, William S., of the "solemn and interesting meeting" being conducted. "The minister has come out on my side. He is a good man."

Even in this personal letter to his own son Miller could not refrain from expressing a tremendous sense of duty to preach a message:

"Oh may God help me to give the truth! I think God has helped me thus far. I am more and more convinced that God is speaking through me. I know my own weakness, and I do know that I have neither power of body or mind to do what the Lord is doing by me as an instrument. It is the Lord's doings and marvelous in our eyes. The world do not know how weak I am. They think more, much more, of the old man than I think of him. Therefore I know it is God that is warning men of their danger.

How often I think of Hampton—of the people—of my children. Why will they not believe? Why will they not hear! Why not be wise? O God do awake the people of God in Hampton, and those who are sleeping over the volcano of God's wrath. Do, my Father, convert my children!" [10]

His "Text Book" shows 1838 bristling with a record of appointments, many of them, in every month of the year. And with rare exceptions, when on a speaking trip, the record shows two lectures delivered daily.

The year 1839 found Miller lecturing in Rochester, Vermont. With the exception of the seventh of January he preached every day that month. There were two lectures each day, and as if to make up for his failure to lecture on the seventh, for he had been traveling to a new place on that day, the "Text Book" shows that he preached three times on the fourteenth. One sermon must have been before breakfast in the morning, because on the fourteenth he not only lectured three times but traveled to a new place. Of the difficulties of travel he wrote this home to his son William:

"There has been a great freshet in this place [Gaysville] and vicinity, so much as to sweep off almost all the bridges, and of course I shall not be able to come home until next Thursday. I will if God permit be at Castleton [a town near Low Hampton] on Thursday evening in the Rutland stage, and if I can be met there I shall be glad." [11]

However, despite inclement weather, success had attended his efforts throughout the month:

"I received the box of books [on January 18 his son had written saying he was sending a box of sixty books as requested], and they were all sold in two hours. If I had as many more I could dispose of them immediately."

No advance agents had preceded him to create a stir in each community. He traveled as any other mortal. From the stagecoach or the train stepped "the old man with his concordance," who had a series of lectures to deliver. That was all. There might not even be anyone at the station to meet him. How unimpressive he appeared is revealed in an incident

---
[10] Manuscript letter, Nov. 17, 1838.
[11] Manuscript letter, Jan. 28, 1839.

LAYING THE GROUNDWORK 67

recorded by his biographer, Bliss. Before Miller went down to Massachusetts in the spring of 1839 on his first trip to that State, Timothy Cole, who knew of Miller only by reputation, had written inviting him to lecture in his church in Lowell. The arrangement was that on a certain evening Miller would arrive at the railway station. Cole knew only that Miller "wore a camlet cloak and white hat, but expected to see a fashionably dressed gentleman." Let Bliss tell the story from this point onward:

"On the arrival of the [railway] cars, he went to the depot to meet him. He watched closely the appearance of all the passengers as they left the cars, but saw no one who corresponded with his expectations of Mr. M. Soon he saw an old man, shaking with the palsy, with a white hat and camlet cloak, alight from the cars. Fearing that this one might prove to be the man, and, if so, regretting that he had invited him to lecture in *his* church, he stepped up to him, and whispered in his ear,

" 'Is your name Miller?'

"Mr. M. nodded assent.

" 'Well,' said he, 'follow me.'

"He led the way, walking on ahead, and Mr. M. keeping as near as he could, till he reached his house. He was much chagrined that he had written for a man of Mr. M's appearance, who, he concluded, could know nothing respecting the Bible, but would confine his discourse to visions and fancies of his own.

"After tea, he told Mr. M. he supposed it was about time to attend church; and again led the way, Mr. M. bringing up the rear. He showed Mr. M. into the desk, but took a seat himself among the congregation. Mr. M. read a hymn; after it was sung he prayed, and read another hymn, which was also sung. He felt unpleasant at being left in the pulpit alone, but took for his text: 'Looking for that blessed hope, and the glorious appearing of the great God and our Saviour Jesus Christ.' This he sustained and illustrated by apposite quotations of Scripture, proving a second personal and glorious appearing of Christ. Elder C. listened for about fifteen minutes, when, seeing that he presented nothing but the word of God, and that he opened the Scriptures in a manner that did honor to the occasion, like a workman who needeth not to be ashamed, he walked up into the pulpit, and took his seat. Mr. M. lectured there from the 14th to the 22d of May, and again from the 29th to the 4th * of June. A glorious

---

* Reference to Miller's "Text Book" reveals that the "4th" is an error. He ended his Lowell series on the 2d and began lecturing in Lynn on the 3d. Bliss himself states on page 137 that the Lynn meetings began on the 3d.

revival followed, and Elder C. embraced his views in full, continuing for six years a devoted advocate of them." [12]

It was in connection with these meetings at Lowell, so Bliss recorded, that Miller first met Josiah Litch, a minister who had recently accepted his views on prophecy and was soon to join him in a greatly enlarged work of preaching.

The aftereffect of Miller's preaching in Lowell was set down by Cole in a letter to Miller the next month:

"We have seen a good day here in the things of the kingdom. Since you left us I have baptized about forty, and sixty in all have joined the church, and there are yet some who are seeking the Lord. Our brethren most of them stand fast in the faith which they have received and are looking for the blessed hope and glorious appearing." [13]

Then follows an item of rumor which by itself might have meant little:

"Brother Miller, there is rumor here that you have published to the world that you had made a mistake of 100 years in your calculation and that Christ will not come till 1943 or thereabouts. Now, I do not believe it, but I want you to write me on this subject immediately and let me know, for our enemies are busy in circulating the report that you have acknowledged your mistake."

This was only one of many rumors that soon were in circulation regarding Miller's teachings and the Millerite movement. One reason why it was difficult even for well-meaning people to see the movement in the right light was the heavy fog of rumor and false stories—a synthetic fog generated by the hot breath of gossip and ridicule condensing in the chilly atmosphere that increasingly enveloped the Millerites.

This particular hundred-year error story was repeatedly denied and as repeatedly arose again, for a "good" story need not be true in order to survive denial—it need only be "good." That story grew, as all "good" stories grow, so that it was not long before the word was abroad that Miller had admitted an error of a thousand years in his reckoning. This is not the only instance,

---
[12] Sylvester Bliss, *Memoirs of William Miller*, pp. 135, 136.
[13] Manuscript letter, July 25, 1839.

LAYING THE GROUNDWORK 69

as we shall discover, where stories quickly grew to ten times their original size.

However, so far as Cole's church was concerned, the rumor seemed not to have proved very disastrous to the convictions of the members, for he said this in a closing line:

"Your son sent me eighty books. I sold them all in a week and could have sold eighty more."

A further light on the growth of Millerism in terms of the circulation of his book of lectures, is indicated in a letter from the publisher, Isaac Wescott, to Miller's son: "Saturday evening I received your letter saying that your father would take the 1,000 Miller's lectures provided 600 could be sent to Boston in 15 days from date of your letter." [14] Wescott assured the son that the books would be sent.

Miller's first * "Text Book" ends with June 9, 1839, carrying this line near the bottom of the page: "Here ends my tour into Massachusetts."

Immediately below is a summary: "Making 800 lectures from October 1, 1834, to June 9, 1839, four years, six [eight?] months, nine days." This summary speaks for itself as to the time and nervous energy spent by Miller to promote the doctrine of the "advent near" in those few brief years.

---
[14] Manuscript letter, Nov. 12, 1839.
* A second "Text Book" carries the record down to 1844. Together they provide a silent but weighty testimony to the indefatigable labor he put forth in public for a decade.

CHAPTER 5

Millerism Spreads to the Great Cities

FOR MORE THAN EIGHT YEARS the "old farmer," as Miller picturesquely called himself, carried on his preaching mostly in small towns and villages in northern New England. He had gone from place to place wholly in response to direct invitations. He was a good preacher but not a good promoter. The idea of renting a large hall in a great city and employing the standard publicity methods for drawing a crowd, had probably never occurred to him. When he made the compact with God in the grove by his house that August day in 1831, he had agreed to go and tell the world. He was giving increasingly of his time and of his means to reach as many as desired to hear him. What more could he be expected to do? That was probably the way he reasoned. It is nothing against the man that his vision was limited. We marvel, not that he failed to do more, but that he accomplished what he did singlehanded at his own charges, and with no theological training. He had never lived in or near large cities. He was part of frontier America.

But the seed that he had sown during those eight years was soon to spring forth in a hundred places. The discussion of Miller's views had extended far beyond the literal range of his voice. Many ministers who might be skeptical of his particular views about the time of the advent were at least interested to hear him, particularly because his preaching uniformly resulted in a revival of religion, with all the stimulus of church life and activities that revival meant.

While traveling and lecturing in Massachusetts in October of 1839, Miller received an invitation to speak at the Chardon

Street Chapel in Boston. The letter was signed by Joshua V. Himes, the pastor. Coming events may cast their shadows before, but there was nothing in this invitation that seemed different from scores of others Miller had been receiving. In fact, it was so routine, perhaps beyond his limit to accept, that it seems he had not even replied to the request when a few weeks later he met Himes, as one of a group of ministers who had come to hear him lecture at Exeter, New Hampshire. Though Himes had only a brief contact with him, he was sufficiently impressed to renew his invitation. Miller accepted, and on the eighth of December, 1839, he began his first preaching in the cultural center called Boston.

Little did Miller realize that as Himes listened day by day to the lectures, great thoughts were stirring in his mind. Miller did not know that this pastor was in some respects different from any other preacher whose church he had visited. Here was a man of action, a born promoter, a man whose name was soon to be linked with his in every discussion of Millerism throughout the country. It was Himes who made the Boston visit important. The quality of importance ever resides in personalities, in people. It is not multitudes in the abstract, nor buildings, nor organizations that accomplish great things, but men, individual men with vision, conviction, faith, and ardor. Himes was in the spiritual succession of those who long ago were accused of turning the world upside down.

So far as Himes was concerned, Miller's preaching was either true or false. He squarely confronted Miller with the question: "Do you really believe this doctrine?" That question was no sooner answered than it was followed with this: "What are you doing to spread or diffuse it through the world?"

In that initial question is found a true insight into the man Himes. For him there was only one question of importance. If this message was really true, then what steps should be taken to blazon it over the whole land? Action, and on a large scale and without delay—that was the spirit of Joshua V. Himes.

Miller assured him that he was doing all that was within

his limited powers. Himes did not dispute this, but insisted that despite all Miller's faithful efforts, his great message for the world was hardly known over the land. To which Miller replied:

> "What can an old farmer do? I was never used to public speaking: I stand quite alone; and, though I have labored much, and seen many converted to God and the truth, yet *no one,* as yet, seems to enter into the *object* and *spirit of my mission,* so as to render me much aid. They like to have me preach and build up their churches; and there it ends, with most of the ministers, as yet. I have been looking for help—I want help."

For Himes, who had now accepted Miller's views, there was only one response he could make: "I laid myself, family, society, reputation, all, upon the altar of God, to help him, to the extent of my power, to the end."

Himes could not understand why Miller had not been in the large cities before. Miller explained that he had gone only to those places where he had been invited. Himes inquired whether he would be willing to go with him "where doors are opened." Miller assured him he would. "I then told him he might prepare for the campaign," said Himes; "for doors should be opened in every city in the Union, and the warning should go to the ends of the earth! Here I began to 'help' Father Miller." [1]

An audacious declaration, indeed, for a young pastor scarcely thirty-five years of age to make. What resources, what connections, did he possess? What powers were his that enabled him to make so bold a promise? There is no answer to such a question, except as it may be found in those mysterious qualities of the human spirit—faith, courage, and an irresistible sense of duty—qualities which ever have been more valuable than gold or princely connections in enabling a man to accomplish a great work.

Some readers no doubt will see in all this, not a display of high faith by a courageous man, but simply the foolhardy decision of a deluded fanatic. We shall not here argue that point. The degree of truth and error in the Millerite preaching we shall

---

[1] See Sylvester Bliss, *Memoirs of William Miller,* pp. 140, 141.

consider later. Even if we were to agree that the whole cause to which he dedicated his life was a mistake, consistency would not necessarily call for us to dismiss him with a pitying look. Have not some very great men been identified with lost causes—causes which now stand revealed as having been reared on altogether false premises?

We would here remark only that the true appraisal of a man must be made in terms of the sincerity, moral courage, and sacrificial ardor with which he seeks to promote a cause he truly believes to be good. If the reader is willing to keep this simple criterion of values in the forefront of his thinking, he will be better able to understand Miller and the group of ministers and others who cast in their lot with him.

Himes did not take long to give concrete proof of the genuineness of his interest in the prophetic views preached by Miller. One of the matters discussed by them almost immediately was the need of a paper of some kind for a more rapid, widespread presentation of the prophetic message. On more than one occasion Miller had wished that he might begin a paper, but he had "never been able to find a man who was willing to run the risk of his reputation and the pecuniary expense, in such a publication." [2]

There was a further reason why he desired a paper: "For a long time previous to this, the papers had been filled with abusive stories respecting my labors, and they had refused to publish anything from me in reply." [3]

In the light of what was to follow in the next few years in this respect, the "abusive stories" that had thus far appeared were very tame. But at least they were very effective in confusing the minds of a great many people who otherwise might have been willing to listen to what Miller had to say. He wanted an organ through which he might present the truth concerning these false charges.

---

[2] William Miller, *Apology and Defence*, p. 21.
[3] *Ibid.*

Hardly had he described to Himes the need of a publication for the movement when this born promoter proceeded "without a subscriber or any promise of assistance" to issue the first number of a publication called the *Signs of the Times*. This paper was started early in 1840. It was published in Boston and continued uninterruptedly throughout the history of the movement as a representative and powerful organ. Frequent references are found in the newspapers of the day to the *Signs of the Times* and to *The Advent Herald,* the name it assumed early in 1844.

How very real and scandalous was the abuse heaped upon Miller is evidenced from this item that appeared in the first issue:

"Rev. Parsons Cook of Lynn (Mass.) asserts in the *Puritan,* that Mr. Miller's lectures are more demoralizing than the theater!!!

"We should be pleased to hear from those societies with whom Mr. Miller has lectured. Will they tell us whether this charge is *true?* What has been the effect of Mr. Miller's labors among them? Brethren, please let us hear soon." [4]

Here is plain speaking; here is a display of a forthright endeavor to get to the roots of a libelous story. But this is only the beginning, a rather mild sample of what was to engage the attention of the *Signs of the Times* and other Millerite publications in their endeavor not only to present truth as they saw it but to meet the attacks of their adversaries. Anyone who may have been under the impression that the Millerites were simply a company of shouting enthusiasts who let amens substitute for arguments and warm exhortation for cold logic, ought to read the Millerite papers. Not infrequently these papers quoted in full the outrageous yet often plausible stories, and then cut them to pieces with logic, sharp and often unanswerable. But we must not run ahead of our story.

It may seem incredible to some that Himes, in the first issue of the paper he was publishing because he wished to help Miller, should even by inference be willing to admit there was truth in

---

[4] *Signs of the Times,* March 20, 1840, p. 8.

the charge made by Parsons Cook. But one who has read extensively in the Millerite papers finds nothing incredible in the inquiry Himes appends to Cook's charge. The freest kind of discussion characterized these papers. Millerite leaders were so confident the various charges made against the movement were false, or at best half-truths, that they consistently followed the daring policy of publishing the charges and asking friend or foe for comments, if the editors were not prepared to dispose of the charge at once with a few vigorous strokes.

About this time a prominent Boston publisher brought out a new edition of Miller's lectures. His preaching must have been producing some effect upon the public that was discernible to businessmen, for this publisher was willing to risk an edition of 5,000 copies.

After lecturing for a brief period in Boston and near-by cities Miller went to Watertown, Massachusetts, to lecture there for the first week in March, 1840. We pick up the thread of our story in a letter he wrote to his son from Medford immediately afterward.

"We are now in this town on our way to Portland, Maine. I closed my course of lectures in Watertown last evening. I have never seen so great an effect in one place as there. I preached from Gen. 19:17, last lecture. Between 1,500 and 1,800 present. More than 100 under conviction."[5]

He added this on the personal subject of his health: "My health is some better than when I wrote last. My lungs are yet affected."

Miller lectured for thirteen days at the Casco Street Christian church in Portland. How great was the interest aroused among the thoughtless and ungodly as well as among the pious, is well illustrated by the following incident:

"A young man, hardly out of his teens, residing in the city, heard of Mr. M's lecturing, and though unconverted he was so awakened he determined to hear for himself. He entered a rumshop, where he found twelve of his acquaintances playing cards. Said he, 'Friends, there is a man in the

---

[5] Manuscript letter to William S. Miller, March 9, 1840.

city preaching at the Casco Street church that the Lord is coming in 1843. I think you better leave your gambling and go and hear him.' They at once stopped their gambling, gathered up their cards and money, and accompanied the young man to the meeting. The result was that the entire company was converted; and this man lives today to testify to the saving grace of God in rescuing him through the influence of Mr. Miller's preaching." [6]

The powerful effect produced by Miller's lectures is further revealed in a letter the pastor, L. D. Fleming, wrote him the next month:

"Since you left, the good work has been progressing firmly. I should think somewhere near 200 have professed conversion in our meetings since you left and the good work is spreading all over the city and in the country all around the city. Such a time was never known here. A number of grogshops have been broken up and converted into little meetinghouses. One or two gambling establishments have been also broken up. Little prayer meetings have been set up in almost every part of the city. . . .

"Many opposers begin to acknowledge that there is a work of God here. But some of them hate to own that Miller had any hand as an instrument in the matter." [7]

Enclosed with Fleming's letter was one from Thomas F. Barry, another minister who had accepted Miller's views, and who had seen some of the results of his preaching. Barry informed Miller that the same kind of results reported by Fleming were continuing also in Portsmouth, Rye, Exeter, and other places. But, added Barry:

"The Congregationalists through this section report that Mr. Miller has by his lectures prompted many to read the Bible and thus have been led to embrace religion. But say they, he has done nothing to commence or to aid the *unusual* revivals of religion among us. This appears to be strange and inconsistent reasoning!" [8]

It would seem that good men a hundred years ago found it as hard as do good men today to admit even an evident fact when it goes counter to their prejudices.

There were notable exceptions, however. Specifically, there

---
[6] W. H. Mitchell, *History of the Second Advent Church in Portland, Maine*, p. 7.
[7] Manuscript letter, April 11, 1840.
[8] Manuscript letter, April 11, 1840.

was the striking exception represented by the editor of the *Maine Wesleyan Journal,* who wrote in his paper a report of Miller's visit to Portland. We quote at some length because it is written, not by a friend of Miller, but simply by an onlooker:

"Mr. Miller has been in Portland, lecturing to crowded congregations in Casco Street church, on his favorite theme, the end of the world, or literal reign of Christ for 1,000 years. As faithful chroniclers of passing events, it will be expected of us that we say something of the man, and his peculiar views.

"Mr. Miller is about sixty years of age; a plain farmer from Hampton, in the State of New York. He is a member of the Baptist church in that place, from which he brings satisfactory testimonials of good standing, and a license to improve publicly. He has, we understand, numerous testimonials also from clergymen of different denominations favorable to his general character. We should think him a man of but common-school education; evidently possessing strong powers of mind, which for about fourteen years have been almost exclusively bent to the investigation of Scripture prophecies. The last eight years of his life have been devoted to lecturing on this favorite subject.

"In his public discourses he is self-possessed and ready; distinct in his utterance, and frequently quaint in his expressions. He succeeds in chaining the attention of his auditory for an hour and a half to two hours; and in the management of his subject discovers much tact, holding frequent colloquies with the objector and inquirer, supplying the questions and answers himself in a very natural manner; and although grave himself, sometimes producing a smile from a portion of his auditors.

"Mr. Miller is a great stickler for literal interpretations; never admitting the figurative, unless absolutely required to make correct sense or meet the event which is intended to be pointed out. He doubtless believes, most unwaveringly, all he teaches to others. His lectures are interspersed with powerful admonitions to the wicked, and he handles Universalism with gloves of steel.

"He is evidently disposed to make but little allowance for those who think differently from him on the millennium; dealing often in terrible denunciations against such as oppose his peculiar views on this point; as he fully believes they are crying peace and safety when sudden destruction cometh. Judging from what we see and hear, we should think his lectures are making a decided impression on many minds, favorable to his theory." [9]

---

[9] Quoted by Joshua V. Himes, in *Views of the Prophecies and Prophetic Chronology, Selected From Manuscripts of William Miller, With a Memoir of His Life,* pp. 15, 16.

Himes reported that when Miller read this story he exclaimed, "I have found *one* honest editor!" [10]

A letter from Fleming to Himes throws further light on the effect of Miller's meetings in Portland:

"Being down in the business part of our city, on the fourth inst., I was conducted into a room over one of the banks, where I found about thirty or forty men of different denominations, engaged with one accord in prayer, at about 11 o'clock in the daytime! . . . There is nothing like extravagant excitement, but an almost universal solemnity on the minds of all the people. One of the principal booksellers informed me that he had sold more Bibles in *one month* (since Brother Miller came here) than he had in any four months previous." [11]

Even when Miller returned home from a series of lectures, he did not throw off the role of preacher. With him the earnest, fervent appeal made audible on the platform was but the outward expression of a deep conviction that was always with him. When he returned from Portland he wrote to Himes:

"Those souls whom I have addressed in my six months' tour are continually before me, sleeping or waking; I can see them perishing by thousands; and when I reflect on the accountability of their teachers, who say 'peace and safety,' I am in pain for them." [12]

Even Miller's bitterest enemies among the clergy were willing to admit that he was a powerful speaker, drew great crowds, and made a deep impression. For example, there is the comment on his tour of the Boston area that was made by the *Trumpet,* an organ of the Universalists. The editor explained to his readers who lived far from Boston why he was taking time to discuss "so wild a vagary" as that of Miller's views. He said that while "William Miller is a weak-minded, vain, and self-confident old man," nevertheless he is making sufficient impression to demand some consideration. The editor charged that "certain societies and clergymen in different parts of New England have seen fit to make a tool of the old man, for the purpose of getting

---
[10] *Ibid.,* p. 16.
[11] Letter, April 6, 1840, in *Signs of the Times,* April 15, 1840, p. 14.
[12] Letter, March 31, 1840, in *Signs of the Times,* April 15, 1840, p. 14.

Opening lines of the manuscript of Miller's first article for the press. This article appeared in the *Vermont Telegraph* on May 15, 1832. (See page 45.)

Opening lines of the manuscript of Miller's first published work, a 64-page pamphlet, printed in 1833. (See page 51, footnote.)

This license to preach, dated September 12, 1833, gave Miller his first ministerial standing.

Opening and closing lines of Miller's first diary of his travels. He called this his "Text Book." A record of the sermons preached, with sermon text, is recorded. In many instances there were two sermons a day.

up excitements, and gaining converts for their churches.... Miller has been in the vicinity of Boston, some two or three months. He is constantly giving lectures, on his theory, which are attended by immense crowds." [13]

This and similar attacks quoted in the *Signs* appeared under the department head, "Refuge of Scoffers."

During the spring and summer of 1840 Miller continued his ceaseless round of lecturing. In May of that year he delivered his first series in New York City. The record is very meager. Occasionally there appear the names of ministers who have accepted his views, and were beginning to make themselves felt either in their own churches or from the lecture platform elsewhere. The opposition was growing. There began to take shape in Miller's mind the realization that he was not simply a lone preacher filling individual appointments, but was the leader of a movement for which he must speak, and against whose traducers, in either the realm of character or doctrine, he must wield his sword. Near the close of the summer he wrote to Himes:

"Day after tomorrow I begin a course of lectures at Fort Ann. The next week I go north, where I have three places, which will take three weeks at least. I do not know what to say to you about coming to Massachusetts again. I have more business on hand than two men like me could perform. I must lecture twice every day. I must converse with many—answer a host of questions—write answers to letters from all points of the compass, from Canada to Florida, from Maine to Missouri. I must read all the candid arguments, (which I confess are not many,) that are urged against me. I must read all the 'slang' of the drunken and the sober.... The polar Star must be kept in view,—the Chart consulted,—the compass watched,—the reckoning kept,—the sails set,—the rudder managed,—the ship cleaned,—the sailors fed,—the voyage prosecuted,—the port of rest to which we are destined, understood,—the watchman to answer the call, 'Watchman, what of the night?' " [14]

The very fact that others besides Miller were beginning to preach the doctrine of the soon coming of Christ seemed naturally

---

[13] Quoted in *Signs of the Times,* May 1, 1840, p. 23.
[14] Letter, Aug. 12, 1840, in *Signs of the Times,* Sept. 1, 1840, p. 81.

to call for a conference of some sort where they could exchange ideas and harmonize as far as possible any differences they might have in their views. No movement can develop very far without some kind of exchange of ideas and co-ordination of activity. Up to this point there had been no real need of co-ordination, for Miller had been virtually the whole movement. The activity of any other preachers who had accepted his views had been rather sporadic and almost wholly limited to the particular churches over which they presided.

In the late summer a group of ministers headed by William Miller signed their names to a call for "a general conference on the second coming of the Lord Jesus Christ." The meeting was announced to open October 13 at Boston. Said they:

"The object of the conference will not be to form a new organization in the faith of Christ; nor to assail others of our brethren who differ from us in regard to the period and manner of the advent; but to discuss the whole subject faithfully and fairly, in the exercise of that spirit of Christ in which it will be safe immediately to meet Him at the judgment seat.

"By so doing we may accomplish much in the rapid, general, and powerful spread of 'the everlasting gospel of the kingdom at hand,' that the way of the Lord may be speedily prepared, whatever may be the precise period of His coming." [15]

In an editorial that followed this announcement in the *Signs of the Times,* Himes remarked:

"The proposed conference is a new thing, and those who are concerned in calling it, intend to make it a holy convocation, a blessed meeting of humble, faithful, pious souls, who fear God and devoutly cherish the glorious hope of His soon appearing, to make this earth which He has redeemed both 'pure and holy, the land of the living and not of the dead.' " [16]

Miller started for this meeting, but he had traveled only a few miles when it became evident that a fever had overtaken him, and he was brought back home. He was suffering from what is now a relatively rare malady in America, typhoid fever. His inability to be present at this important conference brought

---
[15] *Signs of the Times,* Sept. 1, 1840, p. 84.
[16] *Ibid.*

him a disappointment that may well be imagined. His preaching for nine years was now ready to bear fruit on a large scale, and he must languish at home. How a man meets disappointment of cherished hopes, how he faces the painfully intimate problem of sickness, provides a real measure of the man. Miller's feelings and thoughts because of his sickness and disappointment are reflected in the message he sent to the conference, which reads in part:

"Why was I deprived of meeting those congenial minds in this good, this glorious cause of light and truth? Why am I to bear this last affliction, and not enjoy this one pleasure of meeting fellow laborers in a cause so big with prospects, so glorious in its results, so honoring to God, and so safe to man? Why are the providences of God so mysterious? I have often inquired. Am I never to have *my will?* No, never, until my will shall harmonize with Thine, O Father! Yes, God is right; His providence is right; His ways are just and true; and I am foolish to murmur or complain....

"O, I had vainly hoped to see you all, to breathe and feel that sacred flame of love, of heavenly fire; to hear and speak of that dear blessed Saviour's near approach!... But here I am, a weak, a feeble, toil-worn old man, upon a bed of sickness, with feeble nerves, and, worse than all, a heart, I fear, in part unreconciled to God. But bless the Lord, O my soul! I have great blessings yet, more than I can number." [17]

The conference was held in Chardon Street Chapel in Boston, of which Joshua V. Himes was the pastor. Among the presiding officers and committee members of this conference are found the names of such men as Henry Dana Ward, Henry Jones, Joshua V. Himes, Josiah Litch, and Joseph Bates. We shall hear more of these men later in our narrative.

The printed report of the proceedings, which consists mostly of the addresses that were prepared and read, fills nearly two hundred pages. The publication of the report was made possible because Himes set out to raise five hundred dollars to defray publication costs. We are not informed how much actually was raised, but evidently it was sufficient to make possible the publication.

---
[17] Sylvester Bliss, *Memoirs of William Miller*, p. 153.

The really important resolution that was passed was the empowering of a committee "to call another general conference, as soon, and at such place, as they may deem expedient." [18]

During the next two years many sessions of the general conference were held in different cities. These served a very real purpose, co-ordinating the planning and thinking of what was otherwise a rather loosely knit movement. In our modern language we would probably describe it as an interchurch movement. Those who made the call for the first session of the general conference were very specific, as we noted, in announcing that they had no intention to set up a new sect.

The very fact that this movement did not immediately crystallize into a close-knit organization, with precise doctrinal formulas and strong disciplinary powers over its ministry and members, makes it difficult at times for a writer on Millerism to be absolutely sure he is following the main stream and not some eddying swirl or stagnant backwater when he is discussing the movement. Some of the markers that enable us to know where the main channel lies are the reports of the session of the general conference. Not infrequently at these meetings a broad declaration of beliefs and views was formulated for the advent believers and the public at large. This first general conference addressed a message to "all that in every place call upon the name of Jesus Christ our Lord, both theirs and ours." We quote briefly from this pronouncement:

"*Our object* in assembling at this time, our object in addressing you, and our object in other efforts, separate and combined, on the subject of 'the kingdom of heaven at hand,' is to revive and restore this ancient faith, to renew ancient landmarks, to 'stand in the ways, and see and ask for the old paths, where is the good way' in which our fathers walked and the martyrs 'found rest for their souls.' We have no purpose to distract the churches with any new inventions, or to get to ourselves a name by starting another sect among the followers of the Lamb. We neither condemn, nor rudely assail, others of a faith different from our own, nor dictate in matters of conscience for our brethren, nor seek to demolish their organizations, nor

---

[18] *The First Report of the General Conference of Christians Expecting the Advent of Our Lord Jesus Christ,* sec., "Proceedings of the Conference," p. 12.

build new ones of our own; but simply to express our convictions like Christians, with the reasons for entertaining them which have persuaded us to understand the word and promises, the prophecies and the gospel, of our Lord, as the first Christians, the primitive ages of the church, and the profoundly learned and intelligent Reformers, have unanimously done, in the faith and hope that the Lord will 'come quickly,' 'in His glory,' to fulfill all His promises in the resurrection of the dead. . . .

"Though in some of the less important views of this momentous subject we are not ourselves agreed, particularly in regard to fixing the year of Christ's second advent, yet we are unanimously agreed and established in this all-absorbing point, that the coming of the Lord to judge the world is now specially 'nigh at hand.' " [19]

Thus spoke the Millerite leaders in their first formal gathering.

It is not necessary to record the details of Miller's travels from one place to another in the months immediately following his recovery from the fever that had kept him from this first session of the general conference. In the very nature of the case there is a certain sameness to the reports of lectures in first one place and then another as he continued on his unremitting task of preaching the soon coming of Christ.

In the spring of '41 he explained in a letter to Hendryx why he had been slow in writing to him, and in this explanation is found a vivid summary of his labors during the preceding year:

"Could you see the applications made for me to lecture, and the distances I have to travel, you would make an excuse for me. I will just state for your edification, that for one year up to the first of October, 1840, I traveled 4,560 miles, preached 627 lectures—each lecture would average as much as 1½ hours long. To sum up the number hopefully converted perhaps would be not an easy task; but from letters and other sources of information I speak within bounds to say 5,000. . . . The majority are men between the ages of 30 and 50." [20]

This same letter also gives us Miller's idea of how to bring conviction and conversion to the hearts of men. Remember he lived in a day when it was not uncommon for preachers to make

---

[19] *Ibid.*, pp. 14, 15.
[20] Manuscript letter, May 19, 1841.

a major appeal to the emotions, employing the mourners' bench and "anxious seats" to set off from the main assembly those who were in various stages of conviction. But, said Miller, "I make no use of anxious seats." He did not seem to feel the need of "this machinery." He preferred to rely rather on "the naked Word." Then follows his picturesque description of how to proceed in winning a battle for God in the hearts of men:

"Depend wholly on the power of the Spirit. Keep your sword the right side up, the edge to the heart, and your arm well nerved. Bring home the blow with an intent to kill. Be not afraid of hurting your hearers, wind no silk handkerchiefs around your blade, nor withhold one moiety of power when you make a thrust. Some are in the habit of hiding a part of the sword, for fear the enemy will dodge the blow; but this will never do. The moment your enemy discovers your cowardice or fear, they despise you. They rouse to action with redoubled vigor and ten to one if you are not overthrown. Never show any discouragement, or unbelief in the strength or power of your Commander. Let His name be your watchword, His armor your shield, and His cause your field. If the enemy roar and make a noise, take courage, double your diligence; it is a certain sign that your blows are telling home."

Here is the church militant; here is a blending of the captain and the preacher. It is not hard to see how Miller made headway and gained thousands of converts despite the increasing opposition and misrepresentation on every side, and despite the fact that he did not employ the technique of "anxious seats" in his public ministry.

The fact that he did not appeal primarily to the emotions but to the intellect through a reading of the Word, does not mean that there was no emotion in connection with his meetings. The records of the public meetings indicate that there were often strong cryings and tears, and men coming forward to kneel in contrition. If there had not been, we might well question the spirit in which Miller wielded the sword. The important point, however, is that he sought to bring the conviction through a forthright preaching and exposition of the Scriptures, and not by a maudlin appeal to the emotions.

CHAPTER 6

The Movement Takes Definite Shape

DURING THE WHOLE SUMMER of 1841 Miller was confined to his home by illness. Once more he was called upon to contemplate the mysterious ways of God toward man and to learn patience in the face of disappointment. It was during this summer that the second session of the general conference was held. This was called to meet in Lowell, Massachusetts, on the morning of June 15, 1841.[1]

At this second session a resolution was passed calling on the friends of the movement to "take measures for procuring for circulation in their neighborhoods and towns the *Second Advent Library;* * that none need be in darkness on the doctrine who will take the pains to read these valuable works." [2]

The list of the members of the conference, with their addresses, reveals a representation from Massachusetts, New Hampshire, Maine, Vermont, and New York. Approximately two hundred names are recorded. When we think of the difficulties and costs of travel in those days we may rightly describe a conference of two hundred meeting for several days as a significant event. Millerism was making headway.

This second session of the general conference drafted an address directed to "all who love the Lord Jesus and His glorious kingdom." The address expresses, first, the profound conviction that the day of the Lord is near, and that because of

---

[1] See *Signs of the Times,* April 15, 1841, p. 12.
[2] *Ibid.,* July 15, 1841, p. 62.

* This Second Advent Library was a general title for an extended series of pamphlets, some of them containing more than two hundred pages, which began to be published about this time, and which were widely used in the following years in promoting the teachings of the movement.

this there is a tremendous responsibility resting on the believers in this truth to publish it abroad. The address presents nine specific suggestions as to the procedures to follow in order to accomplish successfully the solemn task. Set forth early in the history of the now more or less well-defined movement, these suggestions laid down the strategy of warfare that was to be employed with increasing vigor in the days to come.

"1. The work of personal consecration to God. Little or nothing can be done without this. But this point will not be attained nor maintained without labor and sacrifice. . . . Watchfulness and prayer is the great secret of a holy life. . . .

"2. The work of personal conversation with others on religion, and especially on the near coming of our Lord Jesus Christ. But, says one, I have no talent for doing this, I do not sufficiently understand it myself to enter into it. Then there is the more need of applying yourself diligently to the study of it, until you can do something in that way. . . . Let the testimony of the Holy Scriptures but be applied, although it may be in ever so feeble a manner, if it be done in a right spirit, and from a heart overflowing with the love of Christ, and it will produce its effect.

"3. We recommend the formation of Bible classes for the mutual study of this great question. . . .

"4. Social meetings for prayer and exhortation have been established in several places since our former conference, and have been found to be of special service in strengthening the faith of believers, and cheering on their way the lovers of the Lord Jesus Christ and His appearing. They should be held in every place where there are a sufficient number of believers to sustain them. . . .

"5. We recommend the practice of questioning your ministers on the subject. Propose to them texts of Scripture for their explanation. They are set for the defense of the gospel, and *have* or *should have* the keys of knowledge, so as to be able to open to the people of their charge the Word of God. . . . We know of no better way than this, to bring them to an examination of the points.

"6. Another part of our work, and not an unimportant part either, is the circulation of books. We have them, but to do good with them they must be circulated. Multitudes would read and be benefited if the works were put into their hands, who will not take the pains to procure a book themselves."

[Then follows a discussion of how much time and resources should be put into this work of circulating the literature. It was feared that some might conclude that the conference was "recommending an entire abandonment of business, because we believe the coming of the Lord draweth nigh. Far from it. The command is as binding now as it ever was, to 'be diligent in business, fervent in spirit, serving the Lord.' " At the same time the conference warned against the opposite extreme of being so filled up with "the cares of this life" as to neglect the work of God. "There is no necessity of going to either extreme," continued the address. "Be diligent; but be sure to take time for religious duties and an entire preparation for the kingdom of heaven."]

"7. There are some who feel themselves burdened because the church with which they are connected not only do not fall in with their views of the coming of the Saviour but actually oppose them on that ground. What shall we do? they ask; shall we remain with them or is it our duty to go somewhere else? We answer, it is impossible for us to give any general advice which will be appropriate in all cases. Circumstances will alter cases. But as a general rule we think it best for persons in such circumstances to abide where they are and endeavor to do what they can to bring the church to a better mind. . . .

"8. *The spirit with which we should labor and suffer.* That we shall meet with opposition, scorn, reproach, and many other things hard to be endured by nature, is to be expected. But we should never murmur nor be impatient under them. . . .

"9. We also would say a word on a subject introduced in a resolution. The establishment of Second Advent Libraries.* Let no town or village be destitute of one of these auxiliaries of our cause: and let it be free for all who will take, read, and return, the books. No time should be lost in starting this enterprise; great good may and will be the result." [3]

Shortly after the Lowell conference Himes wrote to Miller expressing the hope that he would be sending along from his sickbed two lectures and "a good letter to the brethren of the conference to be published in the report." [4] Himes assured him that "the brethren in this vicinity are firm and much engaged. One thing is manifest *in regard to the time:* they are *more confirmed* as the time draws *near.*"

---

[3] *Signs of the Times,* Aug. 2, 1841, pp. 69, 70.
[4] Manuscript letter, June 26, 1841.
* The phrase, Second Advent Library, was used to describe both the series of booklets published by the movement and the organization or center created in a city or town for a circulating of the library. Later reports in the Millerite papers speak of such libraries being opened in certain places.

He added that "Brother Litch has now entered the field. God will give him success I doubt not. He is a strong man." Litch's own published works reveal that as far back as 1838 he had been sufficiently impressed on the nearness of the second advent to write on the subject. But with him as with most others there was a lag between the time of believing and the time of actually entering the field, as Himes expressed it.

When Josiah Litch "entered the field," it was as a "general agent" of the movement. In a report of the "Doings of the Committee of Publication" held on July 15, 1841, we read:

"The Committee will depend upon the friends of the cause to supply the wants of their agent, wherever he may work. 'The laborer is worthy of his hire.' " [5]

This was another definite step in giving substance and stability to the movement. It was the custom of religious bodies in those days to employ ministers to travel in behalf of the publications of that body. Such persons were known as general agents. Thus the Committee of Publication of the Millerite movement was following a well-established practice. While it was true he was to devote his time lecturing, he was being sent forth by the Committee of Publication, evidently to foster very particularly that phase of the movement. Litch was one of the first of the really prominent men of the movement who went wholeheartedly into the promotion of it.

Himes, in the same letter from which we have been quoting, told Miller of the plans for literature distribution:

"We shall distribute $1,000 worth of the 'reports' and publications this year. You may ask where we expect to get it? Answer. We have got about $700 now; and the rest will be forthcoming when needed. We have resolved to establish a library in every town, where it is practicable." [6]

Then employing a mixed metaphor, he added with vigor, "These libraries will make some noise about town, but we must let the light shine."

---

[5] *Signs of the Times,* Aug. 2, 1841, p. 72.
[6] Manuscript letter, June 26, 1841.

Himes assured Miller that he had done such a good job answering attacks made by two religious papers named in the letter that he ought to try his hand on a third one that had been attacking them. The story of the running fight—that is precisely the word to use—carried on between the Millerites and their opponents of the religious and secular press would fill a volume in itself. And for the lovers of polemics it would provide stimulating reading. Debate a hundred years ago, whether conducted orally or in print, did not employ vague phrases. Even the short, ugly words "lie" and "liar" are often found in the controversial literature of those robust times, both secular and religious.

The charge that the leaders of the Millerite movement were adventurers, that the preaching of Millerism was resulting in insanity and murder, were charges already being sounded, and in language that left little to the imagination. These charges will be examined in later chapters. We refer to them now only to indicate the increasingly bleak climate in which the Millerites found themselves.

This intensifying opposition put a very great strain upon the patience and poise of Miller and his associates. They were men of like passions as we are. Take, for example, the retort Miller made to a false accuser. A minister who opposed Millerism preached a sermon against it in which, among other things, he read a signed statement from a man who impressively began with the words, "This certifies," and went on to declare that he had heard Miller state in a certain church in the month of May, 1839, that "there would not be any more rain on the earth or any marriages" after a certain date.

The facts were that Miller had never given a lecture in the church named, nor had he ever made such forecasts. But he was not content with a simple denial. He could not resist the temptation to add a vigorous thrust for good measure. We quote in part:

"I never predicted there would be no *rain* on earth, at any time or place since I have believed my Bible. For I do solemnly and firmly believe that when Christ comes, He will rain hail, fire, and brimstone upon all *liars*, and will sweep away the refuge of lies." [7]

We would not respond to an attack in that way today; at least, we would try not to make such thoughts audible, and that would be well. But Miller was employing a style common to his day, and even his adversaries had to admit that he wielded the sword with deadly force. So effectively, indeed, did he and his close associates strike down false accusations, that rarely, if ever, did an opponent return to the attack with alleged further proof in support of his original charge. Perhaps this does not so much prove the skill of the Millerites in debate as it does the utter groundlessness of the charges made against them. Opponents followed the path of least resistance—when one charge was refuted they simply trumped up another.

In the light of such disputes we can better understand the letter Henry Dana Ward wrote to William Miller. Ward had presided at the first session of the general conference. Though he was active in the movement, believing that the second advent of Christ was near, he did not accept Miller's forecast that sought to name the year. Wrote Ward:

"I write you without ceremony as a brother called to suffer reproach for Christ's sake. . . . Your confidence in the *time* of the Lord's coming I understand, and yet I am far from *feeling:* but that does not hinder me from uniting in the cry: 'The Lord is at hand!' . . . The enunciation of the date also subjects you and those who act with you, to great reproach and obloquy: and one great and moving consideration of this letter is to persuade you to bear it (reproach) meekly. . . .

"I think you wrong in urging the matter of the date; but I honor your zeal, your fidelity, your learning, your industry; and I desire to preserve you from the hurt of those wounds which the malice of the enemy inflicts. . . . I know you think and feel right upon this subject, and I wish heartily that you would exert your great influence in subduing the passions and restraining the vexed spirits of others, whose feelings are smarting under the undeserved wounds of their friends." [8]

By the close of the summer of 1841 the movement had made

---
[7] *Signs of the Times,* June 1, 1841, p. 37.
[8] Manuscript letter, Oct. 29, 1841.

THE MOVEMENT TAKES DEFINITE SHAPE

a further concrete development in the city of Boston, as the following item in the *Signs of the Times* reveals:

"The friends of the cause in this city have procured a spacious and convenient room within one minute's walk of the Post Office, where a Library and Reading Room, as a place of resort for our citizens who are interested in the cause; and for strangers in the country who may wish information, aid, or publications on the subject of the advent near.

"It will afford to inquirers all necessary information on the state, and progress of the cause. American and English periodicals will be furnished having any bearing on the subject of the advent near, and signs of the times: a rich collection also of ancient and modern works on the predictions of the holy prophets.

"It will be sustained by the voluntary contributions of those who appreciate the measure as a profitable auxiliary to the cause." [9]

An examination of Millerite correspondence shows that they knew how to promote in season and out of season with the printed page. Letters in those days were not sent in envelopes. They were simply folded to what would be approximately the size of our envelopes today, and then sealed with a drop of wax or a small sticker of some kind. Himes, who had promised Miller that he would publish the truth of the second coming to every corner of the land and beyond, offered to the ardent members of the movement stickers about two thirds the size of our United States postage stamp, on which was printed "an appropriate passage of Scripture, or a striking sentiment" on the second advent, that the writer could use for sealing his letters. They were called "monitory wafers." [10]

The third session of the "General Conference, Expecting the Advent of the Lord," was held in Portland, Maine, October 12-14, 1841. A round of other appointments prevented Miller from attending. In his letter to the conference he dwelt on the importance of promoting the beliefs they held dear, and offered certain suggestions by which they could effectively do this.[11] He saw the danger to the cause of being misrepresented on the public

---
[9] *Signs of the Times,* Sept. 1, 1841, p. 88.
[10] See *Signs of the Times,* Sept. 15, 1841, p. 96.
[11] See *Signs of the Times,* Nov. 1, 1841, p. 117.

platform by those who had a zeal to speak, but were not qualified. He recommended that a "committee be appointed for the express purpose of examining, advising and recommending" such persons as the committee felt were qualified to lecture.

Since Millerism was a movement and not a church body with disciplinary powers, such committee action regarding qualification of lecturers could have only the power of recommendation. There was nothing to prevent a man's rising up anywhere as a lecturer and declaring that he was a preacher of the doctrines of Miller. While it is remarkable that the movement held as closely together as it did and presented such a large measure of unanimity in views in different parts of the country, there were inevitably instances where men wholly on their own presumed to speak for the teachings of Miller without truly representing those teachings either in doctrine or in life. The embarrassment and confusion that may result from this are merely part of the price that any new religious movement in the world must pay in its formative years.

In suggesting the creation of a committee to examine prospective lecturers, Miller displayed keen insight. He foresaw the potential dangers in connection with a religious movement that was rapidly developing on all sides, and sought to protect against the dangers. He called for unity. In the very next paragraph following his recommendation of a committee, he declared, "Union is strength." He expressed the fear that "all of us [are] so liable to be prejudiced in our own favor, that it becomes a matter of some difficulty to know, and keep the place in the vineyard, which God calls us to fill"—in other words, some who think they are called to be lecturers are not. But, he added, there "is a field for usefulness, in which we can all work." He reminded the members of the conference that many of them were probably first awakened to consider the subject of the advent by means of the printed page. Therefore, if God "has blessed this means, to the good of our souls, why may we not reasonably suppose He will bless the same means to the good of others?" Hence he felt safe in encouraging all to distribute literature.

THE MOVEMENT TAKES DEFINITE SHAPE   93

He encouraged those who were able to write "useful and interesting articles" on the subject of the advent, to write them, and "if any have important questions which they wish to have solved, let them not be backward in asking: for light is our object, and what may be hid unto us, may be made clear unto another. Let us interchange our views one with the other in a Christian spirit, by so doing, we may receive, as well as give much good."

It would be hard to take exception to this forthright formula for making progress in Scriptural knowledge. Miller referred to the difference of viewpoint within the movement as to the matter of the time of the end. He referred to those who believed simply "in the advent near" and to those who believed "with the writer, that 1843 will close our period of probation." He considered both as parts of one whole, together constituting a movement whose prime object was to make men ready to meet their God.

So real was the unity of heart of the conference members, so lifted were they above sectarian levels, that they held a communion service together. In a day when sectarian controversies raged bitterly, this was no small achievement.

Not only were the general conference sessions models of propriety, but the theological views they expounded, with the exception of the controversial question of the *time* of the advent, could easily have passed for orthodox views in most denominations.

If Miller could not come to the general conference—thus far he had been present only in spirit and by letter—the general conference would finally come to him. The fifth session was held in Low Hampton, November 2-5, 1841.*

---

* The fourth session of the general conference was held in New York City late in October. While en route to the fifth session of the general conference, on the steamboat from New York to Albany Litch fell into conversation with the passengers on the subject of prophecy. They invited him to lecture. The spread of Millerism cannot be accurately described as something altogether spontaneous, securing an ever-increasing momentum simply from the startling quality of the message. The record reveals that at least part of the reason for the expansion of the movement was the consistent and audacious endeavors made by its proponents to discover or create opportunities for preaching it. Why not use the deck of a steamer for a lecture room? Were not judgment-bound men and women traveling on that steamer? Then why not speak to them? That is the way the Millerite preachers reasoned. (See *Signs of the Times*, Nov. 15, 1841, p. 124.)

One of the resolutions passed at this session specifically named "Brethren Miller, Himes, Litch, Jones, and Ward, together with those according with them in sentiment, and associate with them in effort" as being "entitled to the confidence, prayers, and co-operation" of all the believers in the advent near.[12] It would seem a reasonable deduction that an endeavor was here being made to place the movement on record as to who might rightly be considered as representing it. A prudent move indeed!

While Himes could say in his letter of June 26, 1841, that in the Boston area, at least, "the brethren" are "more confirmed" in "regard to the time" of the advent, there were some, as already observed, who were not confirmed. Near the close of 1841 more than a page of an issue of the *Signs of the Times* is filled with a letter to the editors from Henry Dana Ward, setting forth his reasons why he could not accept that part of Miller's teachings which forecast the advent in 1843. It is a model of restraint in presentation of a differing viewpoint, for the editors of the *Signs of the Times* believed with Miller on the matter of time. Said Ward, in his closing paragraph:

"This is the length and breadth of our opinion relative to fixed times. It is not forwarded to you, Messrs. Editors, in a controversial spirit, but with the desire, humble and honest, to be held personally responsible, only for that I personally hold; and to be instructed in any matter on which I may seem to differ without reason. It is one of the blessed fruits of the doctrine of our Lord's near coming, that men can walk together, who differ on other points, while they accord in *'that blessed hope.'* I wish to encourage your circulation, and to multiply the number of your readers, and I ask the insertion of this, not for debate, but for the liberty of opinion to hold with our Lord. 'It is not for you to *know* the times, *or the seasons,* which the Father has put in His own power,' while I am with you expectant of His coming and kingdom." [13]

If the reader is startled at the fact that the chairman of the first advent conference failed to accept Miller's view on time,

---
[12] See *Signs of the Times,* Dec. 1, 1841, p. 131.
[13] Letter, Nov 15. 1841, in *Signs of the Times,* Dec. 1, 1841, p. 136.

he will also be surprised to know that Henry Jones, the secretary of that first conference, likewise demurred on this point. Nor were these two the only prominent men who had a vital part in promoting the movement called Millerism without accepting what many mistakenly have thought was the one and only teaching that characterized Millerism, the teaching that the Lord would come "about the year 1843." If such men as Ward, Jones, and others could devote their time and reputation in promoting Millerism, it must have been something larger than this one teaching on *time*. It was. How much larger, we shall seek to discover in a closing chapter, where we shall consider more particularly the religious teachings that distinguished the Millerite movement.

In an earlier chapter we quoted from a letter written by a minister, Charles Fitch, to Miller in 1838, telling of having read Miller's book of lectures and being persuaded of the truth of them. A news note in the *Signs* at the close of 1841 states briefly concerning Fitch: "This dear brother has come into the full faith of the second advent." [14] And so the ranks of the spokesmen for the movement were rapidly filling. Fitch was to prove to be one of the most prominent of Miller's associates.

At the sixth session of the general conference, which opened November 30 at Himes' Chardon Street Chapel in Boston, an appeal was made for additional funds for the publication and distribution of literature. About a thousand dollars was raised. When it is remembered that men often worked for from fifty cents to a dollar a day in those times, and that those attending the conference were not rich, this thousand dollars begins to assume large size.* And when it is further remembered that this was not the first thousand that had been raised, nor the last

---

[14] *Signs of the Times,* Dec. 15, 1841, p. 144.

* It is very difficult to make accurate comparisons between money values of one era and those of another. There are too many factors involved. For the student who wishes to read on this subject, the following is probably the best treatise: *History of Wages in the United States From Colonial Times to 1928,* (Bulletin of the United States Bureau of Labor Statistics, No. 604). This is an exhaustive treatment of the subject, with extensive tables of rates for different trades, and covers 574 pages.

that was to be raised, it takes on even larger dimensions. These conference members who were the very center of the movement, gave rather concrete proof of the genuineness of their interest and belief.[15]

Thus far the preachers of the movement had met only verbal opposition. Something more concrete than this was soon to add to their troubles in various places. One of the first omens of it is found in a letter written in December, telling of a series of lectures in Nashua, New Hampshire, that were "well-nigh broken up by some twelve or fifteen fellows of the baser sort." [16] The revival meetings of John Wesley and others in past years had often been disturbed by mobs. Now, in turn, the Millerites were to be confronted with this test to their patience and their resourcefulness.

The year 1842 opened with sessions of the general conference held in rapid succession in Connecticut, New York State, Vermont, and New Hampshire. The session in Sandy Hill, a town in the same county as Low Hampton, held its closing service at the courthouse. Among others who arose to speak near the close of the service, was a prominent lawyer of the county. He told of having stood many times to address the jury in that very room, and of how he had come to the lectures "predisposed to reject the doctrine, and exceedingly skeptical." But he now wished to confess that his mind was changed. He was not prepared to say that the event would take place in 1843, but that certainly according to the Bible the event was near.[17]

Those Millerite preachers must have been persuasive men whose line of reasoning was not quite so thin or irrational as critics have thought!

How earnest were becoming the requests from various places for firsthand knowledge on the teachings of Miller is illustrated by a letter written to Miller early in 1842 from Charles W. Stewart, postmaster in Morristown, Vermont. This was the

---

[15] See *Signs of the Times,* Jan. 1, 1842, p. 150.
[16] Letter from T. M. Preble, Dec. 22, 1841, in *Signs of the Times,* Jan. 15, 1842, p. 159.
[17] See *Signs of the Times,* Feb. 15, 1842, pp. 172, 173.

second letter he wrote to Miller urging him to come to lecture:

"The minds of the people are strongly fixed on *you* and there is an impression on the minds of many that some *great event* is about to transpire. . . . Many are deeply solicitous to have you come, while others manifest not a little uneasiness about your coming." [18]

Stewart assured Miller that the one inquiry of the people in his town and in the adjoining towns was this: "Is Mr. Miller a coming?" The time was drawing near when the fateful year of the end of the world would begin. This was in Stewart's mind when he repeated once more in his letter his urgent request for Miller to come: "We cannot refrain from beseeching you to come down ere we die."

About the same time Miller received a letter from a Sarah M. Marsh, who explained that she was writing from the "*Palladium* office" for her husband, Joseph Marsh. The *Christian Palladium* was an organ of the Christian Church, and Joseph Marsh was one of the editors. Mrs. Marsh explained that her husband had been wanting to write to Miller, but a revival service that "has been going on in this, and the adjacent neighborhoods since you left us," together with his editorial work, had hindered him. He had requested her to write in his stead.

She told Miller of her changing feelings after hearing his preaching:

"At the first, when I examined the subject I was convinced the testimony was weighty and altogether in favor of the speedy return of our Lord, but I could not (strange as it may appear) wish it true. But of late, I have felt to *rejoice* in the exceeding great and precious promises of God, and to pray that He would 'come quickly.' My soul grows happy when I contemplate the glorious appearing of the dear Saviour." [19]

She stated also that after Miller had left their town, "Elder Marsh commenced a critical examination of the Scriptures." And what was the effect?

---
[18] Manuscript letter, Feb. 21, 1842.
[19] Manuscript letter, Feb. 24, 1842.

"After *much* study and *prayerful examination* of the matter, he fearlessly asserted some things in favor of the doctrine in the *Palladium* and called for a candid and careful *investigation* of this important subject. *You* will anticipate the result. It has raised *much opposition* from some of our dear and good brethren. Some feared the evil consequences of a failure; some advise that it be thrown out of the *Palladium* immediately. . . .

"It is true, Elder Marsh is taking a bold stand and fearlessly presents his views in favor of the doctrine you preach, but is unwilling to admit *anything* on this point which he has not *himself* investigated, and compared with the Word of God. With regard to the *time* his mind is not *fully* settled, save that it is *near* even at the door. And *never* did I see him so much engaged in preaching and laboring for the salvation of an ungodly world as now."

The sequel to this is a letter to Miller from Joseph Marsh himself two months later. Marsh wrote of preaching to a "crowded house" on the subject of the millennium. "I have not yet lectured on the *time*," he continued, "but shall before I close. I am *fully* convinced that the glorious advent is *near*. And if I *define* the time I shall be compelled to say A. D. 1843." [20]

Marsh's difficulty in giving free expression to his new-found belief on the advent, while still holding his editorial position, is revealed in this line: "I am bound here and sigh to be free, and mean to have my liberty as soon as circumstances will admit."

In the 1840's a harmless humbug known as phrenology had considerable vogue. Students of phrenology believed, among other things, that the various faculties of the mind were situated in different areas of the brain, and that the relative development of these faculties was revealed, in part at least, by the shape of the skull. It was quite the thing to have one's head examined by a phrenologist. In the spring of 1842, while Miller was lecturing in the vicinity of Boston, a man who had espoused Miller's views on the advent, till he was rather generally known as a Millerite, persuaded Miller to go with him to a phrenologist in the city. The phrenologist was personally acquainted with Miller's convert —knew him as a Millerite—but not with Miller, nor was he

---

[20] Manuscript letter, April 22, 1842.

THE MOVEMENT TAKES DEFINITE SHAPE 99

informed whose head it was he was about to examine. As he proceeded, he turned sarcastically to Miller's convert:

"'I tell you what it is, Mr. Miller could not easily make a convert of *this* man to his hare-brained theory. He has too much good sense.'

"Thus he proceeded, making comparisons between the head he was examining and the head of Mr. Miller, as he fancied it would be. 'Oh, how I should like to examine Mr. Miller's head,' said he; 'I would give it one squeezing.'

"The phrenologist, knowing that the gentleman was a particular friend of Mr. Miller, spared no pains in going out of the way to make remarks upon him. Putting his hand upon the organ of fanaticism, as it is sometimes called, or the organ of marvelousness, he said, 'There, I'll bet you anything that old Miller has got a bump on his head there as big as my fist,' at the same time doubling up his fist as a sample. Others laughed at the perfection of the joke, and he heartily joined them, supposing they were laughing at his dry jokes on Mr. Miller. . . .

"He got through, made out his chart, and politely asked Mr. Miller for his name. Mr. M. remarked, that it was of no consequence about putting his name upon the chart, but the phrenologist insisted. 'Very well,' said Mr. M., 'you may call it Miller, if you choose.'

"'Miller, Miller,' said he, 'what is your first name?'

"'Well, they call me *William* Miller.'

"'What, the gentleman who is lecturing in Boston?'

"'Yes, sir, the same.'

"At this, the phrenologist, filled with astonishment and dismay, settled back into his chair, pale and trembling, and spake not a word while the company remained. The reader may judge of the poor fellow's feelings." [21]

This much can be said for the embarrassed man: he was no more mistaken in his preconceived ideas of what Miller was like than were thousands of others.

While Miller and others were increasing their activities from the pulpit and lecture platform, Himes was busily engaged in expanding the publishing side of the movement. The eight-page *Signs of the Times* which had been begun early in 1840 and had been published for two years as a semimonthly, was now changed to a weekly. It was no small undertaking to conduct a paper of any kind as the organ of a movement no more closely organized

---

[21] *The Midnight Cry,* Nov. 23, 1842, p. 2

than Millerism. But doubling the issues of the *Signs of the Times* was only one step in the expanding literature program of Millerism. New volumes of the Second Advent Library were being published by Himes in increasing numbers. The authors represented a wide range of men.

Though by this time the name of Miller was sufficiently well known, so that the simple announcement that he was to conduct a series of lectures in a city was generally sufficient to bring out a large crowd, this was not always the case. In the spring of 1842 Miller and Himes went down to New York City and hired the large, expensive Apollo Hall on Broadway for a series of lectures. New York was different from most places where lectures had been held. There were too many attractions in that metropolis to make Miller's preaching of sufficient interest to draw the multitudes. Besides, the bad press reports that Miller was generally receiving, produced a particularly effective prejudice in New York. Writing of this two years later Josiah Litch recorded:

"An impression had gone abroad in reference to the Adventists, that they were monsters, or almost anything but civilized beings. So strong was this impression, and so general, that a number of days had passed and scarcely a lady dared to make her appearance in the meetings." [22]

In this great city there were few, if any, friends of the movement. No one invited Miller or Himes even for a meal or a night's lodging. Their funds were too limited, they felt, to warrant taking rooms in a hotel; so they lived and slept for a time in an anteroom just off the lecture hall. Their bed was the floor. Finally someone brought them a cot. The story has a happy ending. Those who did attend the lectures began to tell others, and before the close of the series the hall was filled.[23]

The lectures in New York closed with a three-day general conference session beginning May 10. The "sentiments" set forth by this conference dealt almost exclusively with matters of

---
[22] *The Advent Shield and Review*, May, 1844, p. 67.
[23] See letters of Joshua V. Himes to Josiah Litch, April 23, 25, 1842, in *Signs of the Times*, May 4, 1842; and letter to Litch, in *Signs of the Times*, May 11, 1842, p. 41.

> Portland April 11th 1840
>
> Dear Bro Miller
>
> I shall take the liberty of addressing you thro' your Son, the P. M.
>
> Since you left, the good work has been progressing finely. I should think somewhere near 200 have professed conversion in our meetings since you left & the good work is spreading all over the city, & in the country all around the city. Such a time was never known here. A number of grog shops have been broken up, & converted into little meeting houses. One or two gambling establishments have been also broken up. Little prayer meetings have been set up in almost every part of the city...

L. D. Fleming, pastor of the Casco Street Christian church of Portland, Maine, describes the effects produced by Miller's preaching. (See page 76.)

The Great Tent, as pictured in the New York *Herald*, November 14, 1842, in connection with a series of articles reporting the Millerite tent meetings at Newark, New Jersey.

A typical camp meeting scene in mid-nineteenth century.

HARPER'S MAGAZINE, 1859

THE MOVEMENT TAKES DEFINITE SHAPE 101

theology, and to these we shall refer later. The conference report contained this one item of news: "The brethren in New York intend to form an association, and open a depository for publications." [24]

This association was formed on May 18. Those who joined it "were to pay a sum monthly, to defray expenses of forwarding the message of Christ's immediate coming." [25]

But more important in the rapid expansion of the movement than any local association or any session of the general conference, significant as these meetings were, was the holding of camp meetings. The decision to hold such meetings was reached at a session of the general conference held in Boston in the spring of 1842. The conference opened on May 24, presided over by Joseph Bates. In this conference the significance of the time element in the preaching of the advent came definitely to the front as indicated in this resolution that was passed:

"*Resolved,* That in the opinion of this conference, there are most serious and important reasons for believing that God has revealed the time of the end of the world and that that time is 1843." [26]

However, a person did not need to be a believer in the precise time to be enrolled as a member of the conference. So long as he rejected certain false teachings about the advent, and believed that Christ's personal coming and the first resurrection were "the next great events of prophetic history" he could be a member, and in good standing.

The very fact that an increasing emphasis was being placed on the time element meant that all who accepted this phase of the teaching felt an increasing sense of urgency in discharging their responsibility to warn the world. They believed that the time had come to proclaim with vigor what they described as "the midnight cry." *

---

[24] *Signs of the Times,* May 25, 1842, p. 62.
[25] Isaac C. Wellcome, *History of the Second Advent Message,* p. 231.
[26] *Signs of the Times,* June 1, 1842, p. 69.

* This language is adapted from Christ's parable regarding the wise and foolish virgins who were waiting for the bridegroom to come forth that they might go "with him to the marriage." During the long wait they "all slumbered and slept. And at midnight there was

Looking about them in the religious world, the Millerites saw the effective way in which camp meetings were being employed for disseminating religious teachings and awakening religious conviction. So they reasoned:

"These means have been eminently owned and blessed of God to the awakening and salvation of souls. Why, then, should we not seize upon them as one of the most efficient means of giving the midnight cry? We believe we should be criminally negligent not to do so." [27]

A formal resolution was therefore passed that in view of the fact that "our time for giving the *midnight cry* is short," a series of camp meetings be held.

How deep and how vivid now was the sense of urgency is revealed in this resolution:

"*Resolved,* That we should keep it distinctly in mind, that we are this year to do our last praying, and make our last efforts, and shed our last tears for a perishing world." [28]

Important as was the camp meeting action taken by this general conference, there was another of equal significance. The Millerites were great believers in the promotion value of the printed page. Describing the action of the conference regarding the printing of charts to visualize the prophecies, Joseph Bates, who was chairman, wrote a few years later:

"At the opening of this meeting Brethren Charles Fitch and A. Hale of Haverhill, presented us the Visions of Daniel and John which they had painted on cloth, with the prophetic numbers and ending of the vision, which they called a chart. Brother Fitch, in explaining the subject said in substance as follows: he had been turning it over in his mind, and felt that if something of this kind could be done, it would simplify the subject, and make it much easier for him to present it to the people. Here new light seemed to spring up. These brethren had fulfilled a prophecy given by

---

a cry made, Behold, the bridegroom cometh; go ye out to meet him." The wise virgins had taken oil in their lamps. All arose when the cry went forth at midnight. The foolish went to buy oil; the wise went in with the bridegroom to the marriage celebration, and "the door was shut." The lesson Christ drew was this: "Watch therefore, for ye know neither the day nor the hour wherein the Son of man cometh." Matthew 25:1-13. The language of this parable is woven all through the literature of the Millerites. They believed they were fulfilling this parable.

[27] *Ibid.*, p. 68.
[28] *Ibid.*, p. 69.

THE MOVEMENT TAKES DEFINITE SHAPE   103

Habakkuk 2,468 years before, where it says, 'And the Lord answered me and said, *write the vision and make it plain upon tables, that he may run that readeth it.*' This thing now became so plain to all, that it was unanimously voted to have three hundred of these charts lithographed forthwith, that those who felt the message may read and run with it." ²⁹ *

In the very same issue of the *Signs of the Times* that contained the report of the Boston conference is a letter from one of the Millerite preachers, telling of meetings he had been holding in a Methodist church and of the good results. The same sense of urgency that controlled the conference was controlling the writer of this letter, for after telling of the meeting he added:

"But with so short a time to awake the slumbering virgins, and save souls, we must *work; work* night and day. God has thrust us out in haste, to give the *last* invitation, and we must labor in earnest, and *compel* them to come in, that His house may be filled. Why, I expect that God will shake the world with a moral earthquake, before the close of '43. Strong men in Israel are rallying to our help. The midnight cry must yet be made to ring, and ring through every valley and over every hilltop and plain. An awful trembling must yet seize upon sinners in Zion, a crisis *must come,* before the door of mercy is everlastingly shut against them. They must be made to feel that it is *now or never*. And they will." ³⁰

This is increasingly the tempo of the Millerite movement as it entered the summer of 1842.

---

²⁹ Joseph Bates, *Second Advent Way Marks and High Heaps,* pp. 10, 11.
³⁰ Letter of L. C. Collins to Himes and Litch, May 23, 1842, in *Signs of the Times,* June 1, 1842, p. 69.

* One of these charts, well preserved, is to be found in the library of the Ellen G. White Publications, Washington, D. C.

CHAPTER 7

The First Millerite Camp Meeting

IN THE VERDANT, ROLLING COUNTRY of southern New Hampshire lies the village of East Kingston, a small group of farmhouses spread out on a green carpet of grazing ground and farmland. The quietness and tranquillity are disturbed only occasionally by the rumble of a hurrying train.

Move back a hundred years. The same village is there, serene and inviting, far removed from the madding throng, yet easy of access by the cars, as the railroads were called. A mile north, and on the west side of the railroad stood a grove of tall hemlocks, a part of the forest primeval. What more ideal spot could be found for communion with God, for a camp meeting. So thought Ezekiel Hale, Jr., who was chairman of the committee created by the Boston conference to make plans for a camp meeting. Hale lived only a few miles south of East Kingston in Haverhill, Massachusetts.

He and his committee were ready to report without delay. They were men of action. That was a characteristic of the men of the Millerite movement. It is no mere play on words to say that a new movement arises in the world only when there are men of action who are determined to set something in motion. And a movement truly continues as such only so long as men of action constitute it and control it. After that it becomes simply one more static organization in the world. The committee created in the last week of May had a report ready on the ninth of June. We quote in part from that report:

"The principal object of the meeting is to awake sinners and purify Christians by giving the midnight cry, viz., to hold up the immediate coming of Christ to judge the world.

THE FIRST MILLERITE CAMP MEETING 105

"We therefore inform all our Christian friends, by the permission of Divine Providence, that the meeting will be held at East Kingston, N. H., in a fine grove near the railroad, leading to Exeter. Commencing Tuesday, June 28, and continuing to July 5th, brethren and friends of the cause are affectionately invited to come and participate with us in this great feast of tabernacles, and bring their families and unconverted friends, with them.

"The object of the meeting is not controversy, the brethren and friends will understand that none will take part in public speaking except those who are believers in the second coming of Christ, near, even at the door."[1]

The notice of the camp meeting stated that those who were coming to stay on the grounds should bring their own bedding, that the cost of "board and lodging in tents" would be "$2 per week." However, the committee "recommended to churches and brethren to club together and provide for themselves."[2]

Special rates had been secured from the railroad. This may have reflected the business connections of Hale, the chairman. The fare from Boston or Lowell, each forty-four miles from East Kingston, was reduced to ninety cents. We wonder what the regular fare must have been, for those rates were high in terms of dollar values a hundred years ago. A man would need to work about a day in order to find the fare to go to the camp meeting from either of those cities.

The Millerites themselves fully realized that they were making an audacious move in calling a camp meeting. They had some misgivings whether it would be a success. The matter of the cost of transportation was only one factor, though a real one in those days when money was always scarce. But the sense of urgency that controlled these men made them ready to risk something in an endeavor to promote the movement.

But with all their faith and vision they scarcely could have pictured what actually happened. By stage, by horse and buggy, but mostly by train, people poured in literally by thousands. It is impossible to give an accurate figure, for the reports reveal that a hundred years ago there seemed to be about as wide a diver-

---
[1] *Signs of the Times*, June 15, 1842, p. 88.
[2] *Ibid.*, June 22, 1842, p. 92.

gence of estimates of attendance as there are today when a great meeting is reported. The estimates ranged all the way from seven thousand to fifteen thousand, according to the reports in the papers. The *Signs of the Times* itself estimated "probably ten or fifteen thousand." [3]

It is true that the camp meeting idea was not a new one in 1842. Methodists and others had been conducting them for forty years, and the public was camp meeting minded. But those camp meetings had behind them the momentum of large, well-organized denominations. Millerism had behind it only the driving fervor of a small group of men.

A great many of those who attended returned to their own homes at night, for there were no accommodations to care for any such outpouring of the population. There were twenty-six large family tents pitched. Apparently it was the custom in those days at camp meetings for a church or for a group of families to use jointly a large tent. This could be conveniently subdivided as needed. The public services of those early camp meetings were generally conducted in the open. A rude platform was constructed for the speakers and benches for the congregation. Around the meeting area stood the wide circle of tents.

This, as nearly as we can reconstruct the picture, is the way in which the first Millerite camp meeting was held. What could be more inspiring than to listen to an exposition of the Word of God amid the solemn and silent forest, with the hemlock spires as nature's architectural contribution to a worshipful atmosphere? Overhead was the blue sky, the vast expanse of the heavens which the Millerite preachers devoutly believed was soon to be rolled back at the majestic appearing of our Lord and Saviour Jesus Christ. In front of the speaker sat, for hours, the thousands who had come to hear Millerism preached.

The principal speaker was Miller himself, who gave the main course of lectures, though he was assisted by a large group of Millerite preachers. For eight days, from June 28 to July 5,

---
[3] See *Signs of the Times,* July 13, 1842, pp. 114, 116.

the meetings were held. All New England was represented, and some were there from Canada. All the creeds were represented, too. In the report written by the secretary of this camp meeting, as is true of virtually all reports of Millerite meetings, special mention is made of the number converted to Christ. While New England in the 1840's was in many respects religious, yet there was also a very widespread skeptical element. There were many deists and infidels. From the ranks of these the Millerites always rejoiced to see conversions to God. Special mention is made of one man in attendance at the camp meeting who was a traveling agent for the leading infidel weekly, the *Investigator*. The secretary's report stated:

> "He was convinced of the divine origin and truth of the Bible by reading William Miller's lectures, and soon brought to submit his heart to God. He is now a member of a Congregational church, and employed in lecturing on the coming of Christ in '43." [4]

It is not difficult to imagine how even a few such ardent converts mingled with the multitude at the camp meeting, would have a leavening influence in behalf of Millerism.

Nor was this traveling agent for the *Investigator* the only one present who had been converted by reading Millerite literature, for the secretary of the camp meeting remarked:

> "Various and singular, in some cases, were the means by which individuals were brought to believe in the second advent doctrine; in one case an individual, with others, I believe, was led to embrace it by reading a part of a copy of the *Signs of the Times,* in which a parcel of tea was sent from the store." [5]

But while there was rejoicing over the conversion of the ungodly and of the infidel, the secretary records that the camp meeting had even a greater value than this: "The great amount of good was among the ministers and members of the church. Such searching of heart—such humiliation—such confessions the writer of this article never before witnessed." In other

---
[4] *Ibid.*, p. 116.
[5] *Ibid.*

words, there was a revival among those who were professed members of various churches. We must not forget that while this was a Millerite camp meeting, Millerism was still very definitely an interchurch movement. Those who spoke from the platform had not divorced themselves from their pastoral or other connections with various denominations.

But the leaders of the movement were not content simply with one great gathering. This camp meeting had not ended before plans were laid for further meetings. They envisioned camp meetings being held all over New England, and beyond. And they envisioned something more—a great tent under which thousands could be seated, safely protected from the undue heat of the sun or from rain or storm. They saw that such a tent would have great possibilities as a place for holding a series of lectures in various cities where it might be difficult to secure a hall.

That would take a great deal of money, and truly loyal members of the movement were still relatively few in numbers and very far from rich. But it seems ever to be the case that for men possessed of a sense of duty to God, for men possessed of daring and faith, obstacles and difficulties are only a challenge to action. An offering was taken. The total was one thousand dollars. Viewing that as comparable to several thousand in our day, we have something of the measure of the genuineness of the interest and belief that the Millerites had in promoting their message to all men. The great tent was assured.

Apollos Hale well remarked in recording the East Kingston meeting, and particularly the large offering, that "the desire for the riches of this world gives place to the stronger desire to secure a title to the better country,—worldly hopes all fade under the brighter 'hope of the glory of God' soon to be revealed."

On the last morning of the camp meeting a singular and impressive service was held. Gathered in a large circle, each clasping the hand of the one beside him, stood the campers; in their midst a minister, reading a series of resolutions. These resolutions reaffirmed the conviction that the great day of the Lord might be expected in 1843, "that other meetings of the same character should be encouraged," "that the numerous and urgent calls from all parts of the land for lecturers demand that we should furnish such means as may be needed to sustain" such workers, and that wide circulation should be given to the second advent publications. The resolutions were fervently voted. Then Himes, who was superintendent of the meeting, made a few remarks, "and the circle dispersed to take breakfast."

Thus ended the first Millerite camp meeting. Well might the secretary say in writing up the report: "The holding of second advent camp meetings may be regarded as the commencement of a new era in the second advent cause."

Interchurch movements, which in our day have had such meager success in their endeavor to lift divergent groups to a higher plane of unity, might well ponder the phenomenon of Millerism. The gathering glory of the advent blinded the eyes of those men and women to sectarian differences. The confident belief that they were soon to be taken literally into the circle of heaven and the fellowship of the saints produced a spontaneous desire for fellowship here and immediately with all whom they believed would soon be with them in that better world.

The meeting was also a success in that it proved the value of the prophetic charts that had just been printed for the use of Millerite lecturers. The idea of the value of visual education is not new. The Millerites believed that they should carry out the inspired command: "Write the vision, and make it plain upon tables, that he may run that readeth it." Habakkuk 2:2.

Visitors to the camp meeting might forget much of what the speaker said, but they could hardly forget the vivid pictures that the chart presented. Here was visual education of the most graphic character. In the days ahead these charts were to be a distinguishing mark of the Millerite lecturers. They needed to do little more than hang up the chart in order to grip the interest of the audience and hold it throughout a lecture that might last anywhere from one to two hours.

A description of this first camp meeting would not be complete without the comment of the poet Whittier:

"Three or four years ago, on my way eastward, I spent an hour or two at a campground of the second advent in East Kingston. The spot was well chosen. A tall growth of pine and hemlock threw its melancholy shadow over the multitude, who were arranged upon rough seats of boards and logs. Several hundred—perhaps a thousand people—were present, and more were rapidly coming. Drawn about in a circle, forming a background of snowy whiteness to the dark masses of men and foliage, were the white tents, and back of them the provision stalls and cook shops. When I reached the ground, a hymn, the words of which I could not distinguish, was pealing through the dim aisles of the forest. I could readily perceive that it had its effect upon the multitude before me, kindling to higher intensity their already excited enthusiasm. The preachers were placed in a rude pulpit of rough boards, carpeted only by the dead forest leaves and flowers, and tasselled, not with silk and velvet, but with the green boughs of the sombre hemlocks around it. One of them followed the music in an earnest exhortation on the duty of preparing for the great event. Occasionally he was really eloquent, and his description of the last day had the ghastly distinctness of Anelli's painting of the End of the World. Suspended from the front of the rude pulpit were two broad sheets of canvas, upon one of which was the figure of a man, the head of gold, the breast and arms of silver, the belly of brass, the legs of iron, and feet of clay,—the dream of Nebuchadnezzar. On the other were depicted the wonders of the Apocalyptic vision—the beasts, the dragons, the scarlet woman seen by the seer of Patmos, Oriental types, figures, and mystic symbols, translated into staring Yankee realities, and exhibited like the beasts of a traveling menagerie. One horrible image, with its hideous heads and scaly caudal extremity, reminded me of the tremendous line of Milton, who, in speaking of the same evil dragon describes him as

" 'Swindging the scaly horrors of his folded tail.' *-

"To an imaginative mind the scene was full of novel interest. The white circle of tents; the dim wood arches; the upturned, earnest faces; the loud voices of the speakers, burdened with the awful symbolic language of the Bible; the smoke from the fires, rising like incense,—carried me back to those days of primitive worship which tradition faintly whispers of, when on hilltops and in the shade of old woods Religion had her first altars, with every man for her priest and the whole universe for her temple." [6]

---

[6] John Greenleaf Whittier, *Prose Works*, Vol. 1, pp. 425, 426.

* Whittier gives a loose quotation. Milton's original line in "Ode on the Morning of Christ's Nativity" reads thus:
"Swindges the scaly horrour of his foulded tail."

THE FIRST MILLERITE CAMP MEETING

This camp meeting was not the first held by the Millerites in America. On June 21 in Hatley, Lower Canada—as the southern portion of Canada was then described—a camp meeting was begun which lasted for a week.* Josiah Litch described the interest of the public as follows:

"Waves on waves of people have flowed in upon us, day after day, until our arena within the circle of the tents has been almost crowded with a living mass of beings, eagerly inquiring 'Watchman, what of the night?' ... The mighty tide of influence in reference to this great question which I have spoken of in a former letter, is in no degree abated, but is rather increasing from day to day." [7]

It was at the time of these first camp meetings that Himes placed in the *Signs of the Times* the notice that those wishing lecturers to visit them to talk on the prophecies should send in their request to the editor. He explained that there are "new lecturers now entering the field, and we hope to be able to supply more of the numerous calls in future, than we have been able in time past. The South and West also must be visited." [8]

Two weeks later appeared a news item in the *Signs* to the effect that Charles Fitch was expected to go soon to Oberlin, Ohio, to give a course of lectures. Thus the movement was spreading to the West.[9]

Even lonely lighthouse keepers were not left without the light on the prophecies. A Joseph Howland, who was employed by the Government to carry oil to the lighthouses along the Atlantic coast, was a fervent Millerite who carried with him not only oil but Millerite literature. With every lighthouse keeper he left something to read.[10]

The strenuous program under which Miller himself was working at this time is best revealed in a letter he wrote to Himes from Low Hampton in midsummer:

---

[7] *Signs of the Times,* July 13, 1842, p. 117.
[8] *Ibid.,* June 29, 1842, p. 101.
[9] *Ibid.,* July 13, 1842, p. 117.
[10] See letter, June 29, 1842, in *Signs of the Times,* July 20, 1842, p. 127.

* However, the East Kingston meeting is generally and rather properly described as the first Millerite camp meeting. It was the first of the series of such gatherings authorized by general conference action.

"I am now at home, and my health is as good as I could expect, after so long and wearisome a tour as my last; not having enjoyed one day's repose since the first of March last. How the old frame has been supported I cannot tell, unless God by His special providence has interposed, as in the case of Moses. And it looks to me as astonishing that God should select so unworthy an instrument as myself to give the midnight cry." [11]

His growing confidence in the time element of his preaching and his longing to be ready for that great day are revealed further on in his letter:

"I am more and more confident in my expectation of beholding my Saviour face to face, if I am His, in 1843. . . . I see by faith a smiling Son of God, in whom I have redemption by His blood, remittance of the past by grace. How can I fear? I love. Is this what our dear friends call perfection? I have it then; but not enough. I long, I hunger yet for more. . . . Oh, I need much, to keep off anger, malice and revenge, and drive those hateful passions from my mind."

Miller's desire to drive anger and kindred passions from his breast, reflects the increasing conflicts in which he found himself with enemies of every kind, some of them wholly unscrupulous, who would defame both him and the movement.

While Miller was turning homeward for a much-deserved rest, Himes was journeying far northward to Bangor, Maine, for a second advent conference. During the time of the conference a number of ships put into the port. What an excellent opportunity to send to the four corners of the earth a knowledge of the prophecies! Loaded down with several thousand papers and tracts, those in attendance at the conference "visited every vessel." On one boat they were invited to give a discourse. The next "Sunday morning at 5 o'clock," Himes preached "on the deck of the schooner *Martha Wood,* from the second and seventh chapter of Daniel." His comment was, "I never preached to a more attentive audience." [12]

Five o'clock is a little early to be up preaching, but the

---

[11] Letter, July 19, 1842, in *Signs of the Times,* Aug. 3, 1842, p. 137.
[12] See letter by Joshua V. Himes, July 19, 1842, in *Signs of the Times,* July 27, 1842, p. 132.

THE FIRST MILLERITE CAMP MEETING 113

Millerites took very literally the command that they should labor for God not only in season but out of season.

Returning from Bangor, Himes traveled by boat. "Although a little seasick," he put up his chart and discoursed on the prophecies for "an hour or two." Why should a man consult his feelings if he truly believed that he was a bearer of the last message to men, and they were willing to listen? So Himes reasoned.

No religious movement can hope to give full expression to its beliefs, its hopes, its feelings, without hymns. The Millerites realized this, and in the summer of 1842 the *Signs of the Times* carried this announcement:

"*The Millennial Harp* is now out, and will be published in a few days. Music of 72 pages, and the *Millennial Musings,* of 144 pages added, makes 216 pages."[13] These hymns are dominantly second advent hymns. Here is a typical stanza from one of them:

> "How long, O Lord our Saviour,
> Wilt Thou remain away?
> Our hearts are growing weary
> Of Thy so long delay.
> O when shall come the moment
> When, brighter far than morn,
> The sunshine of Thy glory
> Shall on Thy people dawn?"

Thus the Millerites poured forth in song their hopes and their longings for the advent as they looked forward to the bright day that they thought was almost upon them.

---
[13] *Signs of the Times,* July 27, 1842, p. 136.

CHAPTER 8

The Great Tent Is Raised

MILLERITE MINISTERS AND LECTURERS were not the only ones who were busily occupied during midsummer of 1842. A tentmaker had been working against time to provide the large tent made possible by the East Kingston camp meeting fund, so that it could be used extensively before inclement weather set in. It was first raised in Concord, New Hampshire, about the beginning of August. No one in those parts probably had ever seen so large a tent. It was 120 feet in diameter, about 50 feet high in the center, and was variously reported as able to seat between 3,000 and 4,000 persons. Millerism was now under canvas. This was the first time the Millerites had provided their own auditorium. The Concord meeting was a combination of camp meeting and series of lectures, such as might ordinarily have been carried on in a hall.[1]

Nothing better reveals the sense of urgency under which the Millerites labored than the speed with which they moved the great tent from one place to another. The Concord meeting closed about four o'clock Monday afternoon, August 8. The people of Albany, New York, saw the great tent reared on Wednesday morning, the tenth, on a hill not far from the main part of the city. If the record were not so clear and specific we would question it.* The great tent had the advantage of novelty. Thousands poured out from the city; the tent was filled. So great was the stir that some warped mind sent two

---

[1] See *Signs of the Times*, Aug. 17, 1842, p. 157.

* There must have been no lost motion, and very close connections from Concord to Boston to Albany. That was apparently the only train route in those days, as a railway map of the time reveals.

THE GREAT TENT IS RAISED

anonymous letters to the mayor of Albany, uttering dire threatenings against him if he did not order the meetings closed. Then came a third letter threatening the life of Mr. Himes and of his family if he did not "immediately leave this city." [2]

About four miles from Springfield, Massachusetts, stood the little village of Chicopee Falls. Here it was decided to hold the next camp meeting, beginning August 25. From the chairman of the camp meeting committee, H. P. Stebbins, went a letter to William Miller, urging him to come, and saying that they would "expect a course of lectures from Father Miller in good *melting mood* (not of body but of soul)." He ended his letter thus: "Yours in hope of the speedy fulfillment of all the prophecies." [3] Miller was able to attend for the last four days of the camp meeting, which ran for ten days.

When the morning of parting came, campers marched in joyful ranks around the encampment, singing an advent hymn. Then came the farewell handclasp, symbolic of the deep sense of fellowship and the submerging of "sectarian prejudices," and another impressive camp meeting had ended.[4]

One of the Springfield papers wrote a lurid story declaring baldly that "the sole object of the managers of this stupendous humbug, is to fill their pockets with *money* at the expense of the credulity of the people." The article went on to say that from $3,000 to $5,000 in cash and property was collected. The real facts, declared the editor of *Signs of the Times,* were these: "About five hundred dollars was pledged, and some was paid in, for the distribution of tracts, etc." "The money and jewelry sent to this office will amount to about one hundred and fifty dollars, when all [is] disposed of to the best advantage." Then with vigor the editor added, *"These are the facts in the case. Now read the 'Liar's Department,' in another part of this paper."*

Elsewhere in the issue is found the article from the Springfield

---

[2] See *Signs of the Times,* Aug. 17, 1842, pp. 156, 157; Aug. 24, 1842, p. 164.
[3] Manuscript letter, July 23, 1842.
[4] See *Signs of the Times,* Sept. 21, 1842, pp. 4, 5; Hiram Munger, *Life and Religious Experience,* pp. 34-40.

newspaper, to which we have referred. It is published under the "Liar's Department." In explanation of this new department, the editor said:

"The times seem to demand a new department in our paper. The spirit of lying is so prevalent, especially among many of the conductors of the public press, that we shall hereafter devote a portion of our sheet to chronicle the deeds of our opponents who have no arguments to urge against the truth but *lying and scoffing*. We shall publish their shame in their own words, in general, without note or comment. We commence with the *Springfield Democrat*." [5]

In small type under the department heading is the text of Scripture: "All liars shall have their part in the lake that burneth with fire and brimstone, which is the second death."

This was bald language to be sure, but it was the style of the day, and no more robust than that used by the press in general.

Camp meetings, lectures, literature—all these were being used in increasing measure as the year 1842 drew toward its close. The *Signs of the Times* bristles with reports of activity East, West, North, and South. Take this letter to the editors, for example; it is typical of the effectiveness of the Millerite literature in winning adherents and inspiring them with the same fervor that controlled those who had given them the literature:

"In passing through Rochester, a short time since, I chanced to come across a copy of Fitch's letter [published as a pamphlet and setting forth Fitch's reasons for accepting Miller's views], which I examined, and have been led diligently to search the Scriptures to see if these things are so—praying to God for understanding, and I rejoice in belief of the truth that Jesus will come quickly, and that the redemption of the saints draweth nigh.

"Shortly after reading Mr. Fitch's letter, I sent for a quantity, and obtained 160 copies; and scarcely a day passes but some are issuing from the drugstore of which I am proprietor, medicine and truth going out together. I resolved, long ago, not to live for myself, and not to lay up treasure for this world—and I am anxious to scatter truth, and ready to do according to my ability to promote its advancement and triumph." [6]

---

[5] *Signs of the Times*, Sept. 21, 1842, p. 8.
[6] Letter from Edward Canfield to Himes and Litch, Sept. 27, 1842, in *Signs of the Times*, Oct. 12, 1842, p. 32.

The writer of the letter asked for further information about publications and their price. He was writing from western New York, and added in conclusion, "We want light in western New York, and truth to silence the mouths of scoffers."

The last time the great tent was pitched in the 1842 season was at Newark, New Jersey, November 3. It is possible to present a very detailed picture of this meeting because the New York *Herald,* James Gordon Bennett's paper, sent a reporter to cover in detail the happenings of each day.*

Because the Newark meeting was typical of Millerite camp meeting technique we quote at some length from this reporter's story,[7] which begins Thursday, November 3, As the tent began to rise the Millerites became the one subject of conversation in the town. The reporter wrote:

"You can form no idea of the excitement this camp meeting has created in this very orderly and sober little town, or city. It is the universal subject discussed here."

The reporter's story for Saturday, the fifth, opens thus:

"The excitement is gradually but surely increasing in this place in relation to the second advent. . . .

"Those who think that one of these Millerite meetings resembles a Methodist camp meeting are greatly mistaken; there is much more order, decorum, and argument in these Miller meetings. Up to the present time there has not been a disorderly person upon the ground; all has been quiet and decorous."

The order of the services for the day was first "the ordinary prayer meeting in the morning," the regular preaching service at which Josiah Litch spoke, then the noonday meal, then certain special prayer groups at one o'clock, followed later in the afternoon by "Father Miller's sermon."

---

[7] These reports, which first appeared in the New York *Herald,* Nov. 4-15, 1842, were finally published as an eight-page Extra about the size of our present-day tabloid newspapers. Our quotations are from the Extra.

* After making due allowance for some flippant and occasionally sacrilegious comment, the news story bears on the whole the clear proofs of serious reporting. At least it gives us the firsthand impressions of a man who was reporting what he had seen and heard, in contrast to the usual practice of the newspapers of reporting merely hearsay and rumor regarding Millerism.

Sunday, as naturally would be expected, was a very important day. The reporter estimates that "at one time there were over

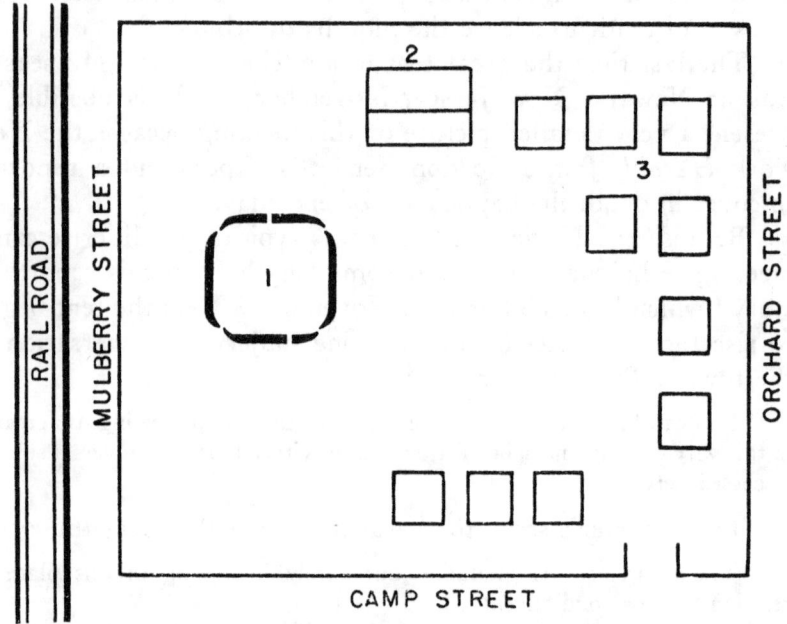

The New York *Herald* Reporter's Diagram of the Newark Campground
"1. The Great Tent. 2. Mr. Miller's Tent and Headquarters of the Preachers. 3. Great Cooking Tent and Headquarters for Eating and Drinking."

six thousand people on the campground today. . . . There was no riot, no confusion, no disturbance on the campground."

In his report for Monday, the seventh, he wrote:

"The excitement in regard to this camp meeting increases with every succeeding day. . . . At any rate, the excitement is so great, that at all the churches here yesterday, the respective ministers preached against it. Some . . . denounced Mr. Miller as a great humbug."

At this point the reporter made his personal observation on Miller: "He appears to be very sincere, although he is a Yankee."

The reporter made a few critical comments on the way some of the people prayed in their little groups in the prayer tent between the general meetings, but he added immediately:

"Now, I have not a word to say against all this; I repeat, there is no doubt of the piety and sincerity of these people, and that they have as keen a sense of propriety as anybody else, and as much or more morality, but this *is* a queer way of showing it."

Though it was a Monday, "there were six thousand people here today," said the reporter.

He told of a prominent minister who was coming to Newark within the next day or two to speak against Millerism. That seemed to be a more or less common practice where Millerite services were held. It always added to the interest in the meetings.

On Tuesday, the eighth, on account of "a terrible storm of wind and rain" no service was held in the tent, and "Mr. Miller preached a sermon in the afternoon in one of the regular churches here." Then follows a summary of the sermon, with a concluding note: "This sermon was attended by many ladies of the first standing, and preachers of all denominations, and made a great impression."

On Wednesday the great tent was raised once more, but the place was still too damp for meeting, and "Mr. Miller preached again in the church in town." The reporter added:

"As he has already converted three ministers in this place, and secured a footing in one of the churches, I think it highly advisable that the learned theologians of New York should be made fully acquainted with his movements and his statements, in order that they may prepare themselves as the ministers of this place and Doctor Brownlee are doing, to controvert him. . . . I sincerely hope that next Sunday they will all preach upon it. Bear in mind, that I am no believer in or convert to his doctrines, but he has produced a tremendous impression among the people of this city and the country round about."

In his report for Thursday, the tenth, the newsman told of the sermon preached against Millerism by Doctor Brownlee the preceding evening and of the great crowds who sought admittance to his meeting.

The write-up for the eleventh consists almost wholly of a summary of the sermon preached by Miller.

On Saturday a heavy rain prevented the holding of meetings in the tent. "A large iron foundry," with a capacity of 5,000, was hired. By this time the reporter was rather used up by the strenuous program of attending all the services, for he remarked:

"I have to attend their meetings, morning, noon and night until I feel completely fagged out. Some days I have scarcely had time to get my meals, and write out the report between the acts. I thought the Methodists were pretty indefatigable at camp meetings, but these people can beat 'em hollow."

Though the camp meeting had come virtually to a close, the reporter remarked with apparent surprise: "I haven't heard the old gentleman [Miller] allude to money matters or contributions at all yet, nor any of his regular preachers."

If they were such avaricious, mercenary adventurers as their critics were increasingly declaring, then these Millerites were letting many valuable days go by in which they could have been pleading for contributions morning, afternoon, and evening at the services.

The services on Sunday morning were conducted in Mechanics Hall in the city, the tents having all been taken down the day before. On Sunday afternoon Miller "preached on the steps of the courthouse . . . to a large crowd of country people," estimated at "near 5,000 people."

The closing service was held Monday morning in the Presbyterian church. The most distinctive feature of this meeting was the denying of various wild rumors afloat regarding Miller and his associates. This prompted one after another in the congregation to rise up and tell of the rumor he had heard and to ask for the facts in the case. Himes made a statement which presented in vivid and specific fashion the kind of opposition that confronted the Millerites as they neared the end of 1842:

"We have been classed, by the clergy, with Joe Smith, Matthias, and others, as base fanatics; but we have sought to spread the truth, not by fanatical prophecies arising out of our own hearts, but by the light of the Scriptures, history, and by sober argument. We appeal only to the Bible, and give you our rules of interpretation. The veriest villains on earth would

THE GREAT TENT IS RAISED

be saints compared to us, if we were not sincere. We sacrifice time, health, money, personal comfort, and all earthly prospects, to the cause. We have continual calls to give lectures all over the country; as we can't do this, we publish books to speak for us. This they call a speculation, and they say Brother Miller has made a fortune by his writings. Why he hasn't made enough to pay for the paper and ink on which his books were written. ... We have pitched our great tent eight times, in places 500 miles apart." [8]

It was no small task to set up the great tent, and with transportation facilities poor, it was even a greater task to move it from one place to another. They did this eight times from the twenty-seventh of July to the third of November. This reveals something of the industry and indefatigable zeal of these Millerite leaders.

But that is only part of the picture. A little further on in his statement he declared, "We have held 30 camp meetings within the last four months." At the Boston conference in May there was doubt whether the movement was large enough or strong enough to conduct *one* camp meeting. It is certain that if they had been governed by their fears and their limitations, there never would have been any camp meetings. But these men believed that they must preach a certain message for God, and within a limited time. Their faith offset their fears, and whenever that takes place, great things happen. The Millerites provide another heartening illustration that it is neither money, numbers, nor influence that finally counts. Men may lack all these and still do amazing things. Thirty camp meetings within four months was nothing short of amazing. The bitterest enemies of Millerism were very willing to admit that.

Himes climaxed his remarks with an appeal to his hearers to form a Second Advent Association in Newark:

"And now you must get up an association here, to be as a depot. The whole State must be waked up. Love your church, your minister, your Bible, but don't let your mouth be gagged. Pray, read, circulate pamphlets, form Bible classes; get your ministers to join them. Be kind and good to all."

---

[8] *The Midnight Cry*, Nov. 17, 1842, p. 3.

After the close of the Newark meeting Miller "got into a plain wagon, drove down to the boat, and put off for New York amid the prayers and singing of many who accompanied him." The last of the 1842 camp meetings had ended.

In connection with his day-by-day story the reporter gave this word picture of Miller:

"In person he is about five feet seven inches in height, very thick set, broad shoulders; lightish brown hair, a little bald, a benevolent countenance, full of wrinkles, and his head shakes as though he was slightly afflicted with the palsy. His manners are very much in his favor; he is not a very well-educated man; but he has read and studied history and prophecy very closely; has much strong common sense, and is evidently sincere in his belief." [9]

Speaking of pen pictures of Miller, a number have been left for us by newspaper reporters and others. Some of them, as may be presumed, were not wholly complimentary. When Miller was in Bennington, Vermont, shortly after his Newark meeting, a reporter thus described him in the *State Banner,* published in that city:

"He is earnest and vehement in his delivery, and frequently intersperses his argument with epithets in which he sometime puts in 'the rich licks' against the clergy who oppose his system, and sometimes administers some very wholesome exhortations to sinners and unbelievers, in general. He is afflicted with a shaking or trembling which is so considerable that the motion of his head and hands can be observed across the house. . . . The old gentleman has a good fund of historical and Biblical information, and a very retentive memory." [10]

When Miller was in Philadelphia the month following, a writer in the *Pennsylvania Inquirer,* guessing him about eleven years younger than he was, wrote this:

"He is apparently about fifty years of age, of robust and healthy appearance, and he speaks with energy. He utters his opinions in a somewhat positive tone, and occasionally appeals to his audience in language of earnest persuasion. He is by no means choice of epithets when alluding to the prominent religious persuasions of the day, and the clergy are anything

---

[9] New York *Herald* Extra.
[10] Quoted in *Massachusetts Spy* (Worcester), Feb. 22, 1843.

but complimented. His style of argument is not remarkable either for grace or eloquence." [11]

And here is a picture of Miller drawn from memory about fifty years later by Jane Marsh Parker, daughter of Joseph Marsh, a Millerite preacher. This is a child's memory, for Mrs. Parker was about eight years old at the time described in the article from which we quote. Despite the connection her father once had with the movement, Mrs. Parker always described it in her writings as simply a delusion. Said she:

" 'Father Miller' he was called by his followers. He had aged prematurely from a stroke of palsy, which made him tremulous. He had a rosy, kindly face, shrewd, twinkling blue eyes, which could read character unerringly. The many cranks and impostors that were the barnacles of the delusion did not deceive him. His power was in his strong mellow voice and earnest manner, making his most cultivated hearers to forget his homely phraseology and provincial pronunciation." [12]

The inclement weather that had now brought the camp meeting season to a close did not dampen the ardor of the Millerites. Papers could be circulated even in cold, rainy weather. Himes, who had started the *Signs of the Times* in Boston early in 1840, now started *The Midnight Cry* in New York. The first issue bears date of November 17, 1842, and carries the announcement:

"We intend by this little sheet to lay before the public in a cheap and popular form, some of the principal reasons for our faith in the second coming of Christ in 1843. It is an apostolic injunction, that we be always prepared to give a reason of the hope we have within us. Conformable to this command, we hold ourselves in readiness to give, not only our *reasons* for such a glorious hope, but to lay the claims of this great, this overwhelming truth before the people. We esteem it not only our right and our privilege, but our *duty* to do so. Were we to hold our peace in the assuring prospect we have of such an event, it would be a cowardly betrayal of our trust." [13]

---

[11] Quoted in *Providence Daily Journal* (R. I.), Feb. 10, 1843.
[12] Jane Marsh Parker, "A Spiritual Cyclone: The Millerite Delusion," *Magazine of Christian Literature*, September, 1891, p. 325.
[13] *The Midnight Cry*, Nov. 17, 1842, p. 2.

Himes added that this paper "will also labor to disabuse the public mind of the one thousand and one false reports that have been put in circulation, and heralded by the press through the length and breadth of the land." [14]

At the outset the plan was simply to publish one volume of twenty-four numbers, and to do this in the brief space of four weeks. In other words, a daily paper, Sundays excepted. Even though these daily issues were only four pages each, this was no small undertaking. Ten thousand copies of each number were printed, or a total of about a quarter of a million papers in four weeks' time. Most of these were intended for free circulation.

It seems only natural to exclaim frequently as one reads the story of these men: Why such ardor, such sacrifice? One of the best answers found in all the Millerite writings is the editor's statement in the first issue of *The Midnight Cry*. Said Himes:

"OUR WORK—is one of unutterable magnitude. It is a mission and an enterprise, unlike, in some respects, anything that has ever awakened the energies of man. It is not a subserviency to human institutions.—It is not a conflict on a political arena.—It is not the operation of a distinct religious sect. But it is an *alarm,* and a CRY, uttered by those who, from among all Protestant sects, as watchmen standing upon the walls of the moral world, believe the WORLD'S CRISIS IS COME—and who, under the influence of this faith, are united in proclaiming to the world, 'Behold the Bridegroom cometh, go ye out to meet Him!' It is an enterprise that swallows up all the petty peculiarities of sectarianism, and unites us upon an elevation so far above those mercenary undulations, that they are utterly lost to our view below." [15]

Though the editor made no promise that there would be issues of the paper beyond the first twenty-four, the facts are that *The Midnight Cry* was continued as one of the most influential Millerite publications to the end of 1844.

It was frequently the practice of the Millerites to found a paper for a few weeks or months in connection with a special series of lectures in a city. For example, the *Philadelphia Alarm*

---
[14] *Ibid.*
[15] *Ibid.*

was started early in 1843, as an adjunct to a series of lectures. Thirteen numbers were issued. Thus a local color could be given to the literature in any city while an initial endeavor was being made there. Afterward the more permanently established publications could be used for promotion and for educating the believers in the movement.

The influence of these papers was not confined to America. Mention has already been made of the Millerites at Bangor, Maine, who distributed thousands of copies of their papers to sailors who would soon be on their way to the four corners of the earth. This sending of literature abroad was a definite part of Millerite promotion. It could hardly fail to arouse interest in the subject of the advent in various lands. At the close of 1842 the *Signs of the Times* could say:

"The expectation of the second advent in 1843, is becoming general in all parts of the world. We are informed by a gentleman from New Bedford, that the sailors who go out to sea from that port, are writing home from all parts of the world respecting it. These sailors have carried out from that port second advent publications, and are scattering them in all lands, and are telling of these things wherever they go, from port to port, and from coast to coast." [16]

About the same time *The Midnight Cry* ran the following news note under the title "Faith in Scotland":

"A young lady, lately from that country, states that in one small town in Scotland the people generally are in the church every day in the week, preparing for the coming of the Lord in 1843. They distribute what they have among them, and do not dream of a failure." [17]

Thus the movement approached the fateful year 1843.

---

[16] *Signs of the Times*, Jan. 4, 1843, p. 128.
[17] *The Midnight Cry*, Nov. 30, 1842, p. 3.

CHAPTER 9

Interest and Opposition Increase

UNTIL THE VERY YEAR 1843 was ready to open, Miller had continued to use only the general phrase, "about the year 1843," to describe his belief as to the time of the advent. On January 1, 1843, Miller published a synopsis of his belief, and in a closing article, No. 14, set forth his view on the time:

"I believe the time can be known by all who desire to understand and to be ready for His coming. And I am fully convinced that sometime between March 21st, 1843, and March 21st, 1844, according to the Jewish mode of computation of time, Christ will come, and bring all His saints with Him; and that then He will reward every man as his work shall be." [1]

Miller set no date or day within this period. The leaders who were associated with him likewise refused to name a specific date. In the first issue of January, 1843, the *Signs of the Times* declared, in refutation of a widely circulated charge that the Millerites had set on a certain day in April:

"The fact is, that the believers of the second advent in 1843, have *fixed* NO TIME *in the year* for the event. And Brethren Miller, Himes, Litch, Hale, Fitch, Hawley, and other prominent lecturers, most decidedly protest against . . . fixing the day or hour of the event. This we have done over and over again, in our paper." [2]

It is true that individual preachers or limited groups here and there sought to find in a Scriptural analogy or by a certain reading of the prophecy a warrant for predicting the advent on some particular day during the year. But there was no general

---

[1] *Signs of the Times*, Jan. 25, 1843, p. 147.
[2] *Ibid.*, Jan. 4, 1843, p. 121. See also issue of Jan. 18, 1843, p. 141, in which George Storrs, another Millerite minister, protests against the fixing of any day; also issue of April 5, 1843, pp. 33-35, 37.

INTEREST AND OPPOSITION INCREASE

acceptance of any of these views, and they received no publicity in the Millerite papers during that year. We must wait until the summer of 1844 for the setting of a definite day.*

In anticipation of the great year of 1843 that was just ahead, Miller addressed a letter to all the believers, "A New Year's Address." He called on the believers to "remember":

"The world will watch for our halting. They cannot think we believe what we speak, for they count our faith a strange faith, and now beware and not give them any advantage of ground over us. They will perhaps look for the halting and falling away of many. But I hope none who are looking for the glorious appearing, will let their faith waver, keep cool, let patience have its perfect work, and after ye have done the will of God, ye may receive the promises." ³

He also has a warning for them, a warning that shows how well he understood human nature, and perhaps how well he had read church history:

"I beseech you my dear brethren, be careful that Satan get no advantage over you, by scattering coals of wild fire among you; for if he cannot drive you into unbelief and doubt, he will then try his wild fire of fanaticism, and speculation, to get us off from the Word of God. . . .

"Then let me advise a continual searching for the truth, both for faith and practice, and wherever we have wandered from the Word of God, let us come back to the primitive simplicity of the gospel." ⁴

The increasing interest in Millerism on the part of the public was revealed early in 1843 in Washington, D. C., in a most

---

³ *Signs of the Times,* Jan. 25, 1843, p. 150.
⁴ *Ibid.*

* Josiah Litch, in his summary of Millerite activity, written in the spring of 1844, tells of various dates which were viewed with special anticipation by varying numbers of Millerites. (See *The Advent Shield and Review,* May, 1844, pp. 73, 74.) However, neither the *Signs of the Times* nor *The Midnight Cry* gave any endorsement; in fact, they made scarcely any reference to such dates. It seems reasonable, therefore, to conclude that no particular date or dates during the year 1843 could have had much standing with the leadership of the movement as a possible specific day of the advent. After the great disappointment on October 22, 1844, the Millerites made an official statement of their previous course in relation to particular days when the advent might have been expected. We quote in part: "There were never any set days in that year [1843], as our opponents have repeatedly asserted, upon which the Adventists were united in their expectations, as the day which would be honored by the Lord's advent. There were, however, several days in that year, which were looked to with great interest; but while some had their eye upon one day, others had their minds directed to other days, so that there was no unanimity of expectation respecting them. In the *year* we were all united, and believed that sometime between March 21st, 1843, and March 21st, 1844, the Lord would come."—*The Advent Herald, Nov. 13, 1844, p. 108.*

unexpected way. Handbills scattered over the city and placed on prominent corners announced that William Miller was to speak from the steps of the Patent Office the next day, Sunday, the twenty-second. The public did not know that this was a hoax perpetrated probably by some practical jokesters. Out came the crowds, filling the streets for two blocks, their number "estimated from five to ten thousand." [5]

Even the writers of advertising copy were now beginning to take notice of Millerism. One advertisement that ran for months in the newspapers pictured an angel flying, carrying a banner with the inscription "The Time Has Come," obviously a burlesque on the flying angel of Revelation 14:6. The reader was then informed that the time had come to take a certain patent medicine.

There were advertisements carrying the startling heading "End of the World" or "The Second Advent," as eye stoppers to call the reader's attention to some manufacturer's lozenges or cigars, for example, suggesting to the reader that he ought to enjoy these while the world lasted.[6]

Even those who dealt in the field of geology began to join in the discussion. In one of the Boston churches a lecturer discussed the theme: "Duration and Destruction of the World, as Inferred from the Records of Geology." He argued that the present world which we see is the result of long, slow changes, and that we must look for the same slow process of change in the future. The idea of a sudden transition could not be admitted. Even the ancient rocks were being asked to bear testimony against the Millerites.[7]

Early in 1843 Miller wrote for publication a letter answering various stories that involved him personally, such as that he claimed to be a prophet and made money out of his public work. His letter very tersely describes his personal affairs. After declaring that he was "not a prophet" but was sent simply to "read, believe, and publish, what God has inspired the ancient

---
[5] See *Signs of the Times,* Feb. 1, 1843, p. 157.
[6] *Ibid.,* p. 156.
[7] *Ibid.,* Feb. 8, 1843, p. 168.

prophets to administer unto us," he gave this intimate view of his affairs:

> "As to worldly cares, I have had but very few for twelve years past. I have a wife, and eight children; I have great reason to believe they are all the children of God, and believers in the same doctrine with myself. I own a small farm in Low Hampton, New York, my family support themselves upon it. . . . 'I owe no man anything;' I have expended more than 2,000 dollars of my property in twelve years, besides what God has given me through the dear friends, in this cause." [8]

This letter was sent out to the daily press and widely printed.[9]

It seems to be part of the price of being in public life, especially as the exponent of unpopular views, that a man must open the doors of his home to the public as it were, and invite them to look within, even to look into his pocketbook. Miller did not fear what men would see when he opened the door.

How deeply he was distressed by the increasing attacks upon him is revealed in a letter he wrote to his eldest son from Philadelphia early in 1843. He explained that he was going to begin a course of lectures in that city the next day. He observed that it was known as the city of brotherly love, but he added, "Here, as in all other places, the D. D's., and priests, the clergy and editors, are out upon us with all their ribaldry and lies." [10]

He sought to keep calm over it, declaring that "God converts it all to His glory, and their shame. I rejoice that I am counted worthy to receive persecution and slander for the truth's sake."

Miller referred only to the attacks that had been made upon him by pulpit and press. He might have added the attacks that were made by letter, including that most cowardly form, the anonymous letter. For example, there was the letter signed only "R. D.," and consisting of one sentence: "Please inform the public how much you have made by your speculation." [11]

---

[8] Letter to Himes, Feb. 4, 1843, in *Signs of the Times,* Feb. 15, 1843, p. 173.
[9] See, for example, *New York Daily Tribune,* Feb. 11, 1843; *Hampshire Gazette* (Northampton, Mass.), Feb. 21, 1843; *Kennebec Journal* (Augusta, Maine), March 10, 1843; *Connecticut Courant* (Hartford), Feb. 25, 1843.
[10] Manuscript letter, Feb. 2, 1843.
[11] Manuscript letter from R. D., Aug. 15, 1842.

When Miller wrote his son, the lectures at the Chinese Museum—one of the large auditoriums of Philadelphia—were due to begin the next day. He did not know that an incident happening near the close of this series would be a further occasion for slander against him. In the midst of one of the lectures a mischievous fellow shouted "fire," and stampeded the assembly. The next morning, someone else disturbed the meeting, and the owner of the building declared that the lectures must close.[12]

Various papers were not slow to pick up the story and distort it into a charge that the Millerites conducted wild gatherings that were against law and order. Here is what a widely circulated news weekly of the time said about the lectures, coupled with a false charge about a proposed Millerite building in Boston:

"The Millerites have very properly been shut out of the buildings in which they have for some time been holding their orgies in Philadelphia, and we are happy to learn that the grand jury of the Boston municipal court has presented the great temple itself as a dangerous structure. After some half dozen more deaths occur and a few more men and women are sent to madhouses by this miserable fanaticism perhaps some grand jury may think it worth while to indict the vagabonds who are the cause of so much mischief."[13]

However, a local Philadelphia newspaper, which on more than one occasion had printed slurs on Miller, was fair enough to give this report of Miller's lectures:

"It is generally known that the Rev. Mr. Miller, sometimes known as 'End of the World' Miller, came into our city on Friday last, and rented the Chinese Museum for thirteen days and nights, for $300. He has since three times a day and evening, held meetings which have been numerously attended. Last night he had an audience of between four and five thousand persons, all of whom listened with great decorum to a sermon from him of more than an hour and half's length."[14]

The news weekly describes Miller's meetings in Philadelphia as "wild orgies." The other paper, right on the ground, speaks of the "great decorum" of the audience.

---
[12] See *Signs of the Times*, March 1, 1843, p. 189.
[13] *Brother Jonathan*, Feb. 18, 1843.
[14] *Philadelphia Public Ledger*, Feb. 8, 1843.

INTEREST AND OPPOSITION INCREASE

The charge briefly mentioned in the news weekly, that Millerism caused insanity, soon became one of the major indictments against the movement. We shall examine that charge fully in later chapters.

Miller had hardly ended his series when a Philadelphia theater opened a play entitled "Miller, Or the End of the World." The part of Miller was played by a comedian.[15]

On leaving Philadelphia, Miller was invited by the mayor of Trenton, New Jersey, to deliver a series of lectures in that city. That fact in itself speaks well for him. But it did not speak well enough to protect him against this story's being put into circulation in the papers:

"Mr. Miller has been holding forth on his narrow-minded humbug at Trenton to large audiences.... This Miller does not appear to be a knave, but simply a fool, or more properly a monomaniac. If the Almighty intended to give due notice of the world's destruction, He would not do it by sending a fat, illiterate old fellow to preach bad grammar and worse sense, down in Jersey!" [16]

The scurrilous attacks made upon Miller went so far beyond bounds as to provoke occasionally from a fair-minded editor a stinging rebuke. The editor of the Sandy Hill *Herald,* who lived in the same county, wrote the following under the heading "Father Miller":

"While we are not prepared to subscribe to the doctrine promulgated by this gentleman, we have been surprised at the means made use of by its opponents to put it down. Certainly all who have ever heard him lecture, or have read his works, must acknowledge that he is a sound reasoner, and as such is entitled to fair arguments from those who differ with him. Yet his opposers do not see fit to exert their reasoning powers, but content themselves by denouncing the old gentleman, as a 'fanatic,' a 'liar,' 'deluded old fool,' 'speculator,' etc., etc. Mr. Miller is now, and has been for many years a resident of this county, and as a citizen, a man and a Christian, stands high in the estimation of all who know him, and we have been pained to hear the gray-headed, trembling old man denounced as a 'speculating knave.' Speculating, forsooth. Why need he speculate? He has enough

---
[15] See *Lowell Courier* (Mass.), Feb. 23, 1843.
[16] New York *Plebeian,* quoted in *Maine Inquirer* (Bath), March 1, 1843.

of the good things of this world to last him through the few days which at longest may be his on earth, without traveling from city to city, from town to village, laboring night and day, like a galley-slave, to add to a store which is already abundant. Who, that has witnessed his earnestness in the pulpit, and listened to the uncultivated eloquence of nature which falls in such rich profusion from his lips, dare say that he is an impostor? We answer, without fear of contradiction from any candid mind, none!" [17]

Another editor had a kind word to say for the Millerites. In a newspaper is found the account of a convert to Millerism living near Concord, New Hampshire, who traveled thirty miles on one of the coldest days of the season to confess to a man that thirteen years before he had stolen $13 from him. The writer of the news item then remarked:

"If all men could become the Millerites of this fashion, and be prompted to like acts of justice—what a revolution would be effected throughout this entire country." [18]

With the year of the end of the world so near at hand, there were probably some among the Millerites who were beginning to ask whether they ought not to forsake their trade or their farms and devote themselves wholly to making ready for the end. In the *Signs of the Times* appeared an editorial entitled "Occupy Till I Come." Borrowing in part the language and arguments of one of the early sessions of the general conference, the editorial expressed emphatically the belief that while in certain instances believers would be justified in turning their whole attention to visiting friends and neighbors, this would not be true in the great majority of cases. We quote:

"To conclude that we have nothing to do by way of laboring for the souls of others or providing for our temporal wants, and therefore spend our time in idleness, is to disobey God and bring dishonor on the cause we have espoused. Let everyone therefore 'be diligent in business, fervent in spirit serving the Lord.' Let him visit the sick, feed the hungry, clothe the naked, administer to the afflicted, relieve the wants of the destitute, and do good as he may have opportunity.

---

[17] Sandy Hill *Herald*, quoted in *Signs of the Times*, March 1, 1843, p. 186.
[18] *Connecticut Courant* (Hartford), Feb. 4, 1843.

"Let him also continue to sow his field and gather the fruits of the earth while seedtime and harvest may continue, neglecting none of the duties of this life. But watch, stand fast in the faith, lead holy lives, showing to the world that this is not our home, that our affections are not set on the things of this world." [19]

From time to time religious papers, the organs of different denominations, that realized how rapidly Millerism was spreading, sought to find satisfaction in the claim that at least in their particular denomination Millerism had made no headway. For example, a Congregationalist paper is quoted in the *Signs of the Times* as making such a claim in behalf of its denomination. To which the Millerite paper replied:

"The junior editor of this paper is now of that order, and was never in connection with any other, and a good proportion of our lecturers are of that denomination." [20]

The facts are that Millerism was drawing from all denominations. As already remarked, it was truly an interchurch movement. Laymen and ministers were allying themselves with the movement while still retaining, in varying degrees of good standing, their membership in their particular denominations.

So widespread had the interest in Millerism become that, as the year of the end of the world approached, one of the leading dailies of New York City published an Extra that pictorially presented the symbolic image of Nebuchadnezar's dream and the beasts seen in vision by Daniel and John. Accompanying this is a long article, which is described as a "clear and complete refutation of Mr. Miller's interpretation of the prophecies," "written by Rev. Mr. Dowling, a Baptist clergyman of Providence." [21]

Early in 1843 the editors of the *Signs of the Times* gave a brief sketch of the progress of the movement up to that time. They were able to say that now "numerous, able and devoted advocates have been raised up" to preach the "advent near."

---
[19] *Signs of the Times,* Feb. 22, 1843, p. 180.
[20] *Ibid.,* p. 182.
[21] See *New York Daily Tribune,* Extra, March 2, 1843.

"Publications . . . [have] found their way not only into nearly every section and district of our own land, but are being read and believed in the islands of the sea, and at all the missionary stations, of which we have any knowledge, on the face of the globe." [22]

On the financial state of the movement they could report:

"We have been enabled thus far, by the sums received for publications, together with the free offerings of the friends of the cause, to defray the expenses of printing, binding, etc., as also to increase in amount and variety such publications as have a salutary bearing, upon the great truths we are laboring to inculcate and enforce. We have established, with the means thus afforded, a depot for the sale and circulation of these publications, in New York." [23]

In this sketch certain of the leaders are named and the places of their activities, such as Pennsylvania, "and other portions of the South." There had been special efforts, in New York, Albany, Utica; and over in Ohio, Charles Fitch had settled to carry on his steadily enlarging work. Depots for publications had been established in Boston and in Philadelphia.

Laymen were as active as the ministers. When they wrote letters they often used a special stationery which had printed on one of the four pages a small chart of the prophetic symbols and time prophecies.[24]

The Millerites were not sitting down in a corner to await the year of the end of the world. They intended that even the last hours of earthly probation should ring with their message.

---

[22] *Signs of the Times,* March 8, 1843, p. 4.
[23] *Ibid.*
[24] See *The Midnight Cry,* Dec. 5, 1842, p. 2.

CHAPTER 10

The Year of the End of the World

MARCH WAS TO OPEN THE YEAR of the end of the world. Farmers, merchants, housewives—everyone knew it. Men might not believe Miller's preaching, and yet have a strange feeling of uneasiness. They may have even looked furtively at the sky betimes as the fateful year drew near.

Suddenly in the cold twilight of late February there appeared, blazoned across the southwestern sky, a flaming comet. A seemingly aimless wanderer from the chill depths of interstellar space, this celestial visitor appeared unannounced. It was apparently a new comet. No astronomer's forecast of its arrival had prepared the public for the arresting spectacle. In a day when men were more given to reading a meaning into unusual events, the appearance of such an object in the skies could hardly fail to arouse comment, questioning, and, in some instances, fear. But this was no ordinary time and this no ordinary comet.* Nature herself seemed to be conspiring with the Millerites to turn men's eyes toward the skies.

Nor did nature confine herself to this one dazzling phenomenon which was to last for some time. The newspapers of 1843 contain a considerable number of news items of strange sights seen by men here and there as they looked at the heavens by day

---

* Following is the letter written by Captain J. F. Hellweg, superintendent of the U. S. Naval Observatory, in response to our inquiry regarding this comet: "The great comet of 1843 was easily visible in broad daylight. It was first seen about 11 A. M. on February 27, 1843, by people in the Southern Hemisphere. . . . On the next day, February 28, the comet was seen by a multitude of people on both the Northern and Southern Hemispheres. For a month it was a brilliant object, seen in the southwestern sky in the evening. It began to fade about the first of April. . . . The comet of 1843 was the most brilliant of the century. The head of the comet was about a degree in width and the tail was nearly 60 degrees in length."
—*Letter dated Feb. 21, 1944.*

or by night. Some of these stories seem to have been well attested and were reported to the newspapers by men who were not Millerites. It is very difficult today to evaluate these reports. Undoubtedly there was an element of truth in the comment of the *Kennebec Journal,* that "signs and wonders are becoming very common in the sky since the advent of Millerism. Every meteor that flashes in the heavens is imagined to have some portentous meaning and seen to take some extraordinary form." After relating several of the current stories regarding heavenly phenomena, the paper adds, "Large allowances must be made for stories of this kind." [1]

While some Millerite leaders were ready to attach a certain weight to these phenomena, believing them to be part of the signs in the heavens foretold by Bible prophets, it is remarkable how restrained was the attitude of the Millerite spokesmen in general. The very fact that so limited a space in Millerite papers is given over to a discussion of these phenomena, when the temptation might be considered almost overwhelming to play them up to the last degree, provides a valuable commentary on the true character of the movement.

At the height of the interest in the great comet, an editorial appeared in the *Signs of the Times* commenting on this phenomenon. Said the editor:

"While the community were evidently excited with varied forebodings, those who are looking for the blessed hope of the glorious appearing of the great God and our Saviour Jesus Christ, have looked on unmoved, with nought to arouse their fears." [2]

And then in matter-of-fact language the editor remarked, "Having established that it is a comet, the present great question is as to its probable course." "Advent believers," said he, "care but little" about the comet's course.

"They believe the Lord is coming, and that right speedily; and whether He sends this as the messenger of His fury, is immaterial, knowing that

---
[1] *Kennebec Journal* (Augusta, Maine), April 28, 1843.
[2] *Signs of the Times,* March 29, 1843, p. 28.

whether so or not, He will be revealed in flaming fire, taking vengeance on them that know not God; and that a fiery stream will issue and come forth before Him." [3]

A few weeks later another Millerite weekly devoted a page to quotations from various papers that describe current phenomena in the heavens. The editor prefaced these clippings with this matter of fact statement:

"We have been looking on in silence, for several weeks, while the newspapers have teemed with descriptions of wonderful sights. We now publish some of them as specimens. . . . Our faith rests on the Word of God, and such things are not needed to confirm it; but we are willing our readers should see the sort of statements which are spread before so many minds by the press." [4]

However, there *was* a matter of real concern to the Millerites at this time. The increasing membership of the movement, especially in a great city like Boston, made ever more acute the problem of finding a satisfactory meeting place for general gatherings. These believers, though still in good standing in their own churches, and worshiping there weekly, wished at the same time to meet with others of like faith to hear the preaching distinctive of Millerism. Time was short, they believed, but that was only an added reason why it was important to have a central rallying place to which they might come from time to time to receive inspiration and guidance, and to lay plans for the successful promotion of their work. The result was a decision to erect a building in Boston.

This proposed structure, which quickly became known as the Millerite tabernacle, was the occasion for an almost unbelievable amount of comment in the newspapers. There were stories that the building under erection was condemned by the mayor as unsafe, that the walls were cracking, and that the Millerites were taking out a seven-year fire insurance policy on the building and thus denying their faith. If rumors could ruin construction, the building would never have been erected. The seven-year

---
[3] *Ibid.*
[4] *The Midnight Cry*, April 13, 1843, p. 9.

insurance story proved to have been blown up to seven times the size of the facts; only a one-year policy had been taken out. A reporter for the *Christian Herald* gave the following description of the finished tabernacle. His account differs very sharply from the strange stories that were written up in most of the newspapers while the building was under construction.

"This building erected by the '43 brethren in Boston, is one of the most spacious, convenient, and pleasant houses of worship I was ever in. On entering it I was greatly disappointed. I expected to see a rough, uncouth affair, which would end whether the world did or not, with the exciting cause to which it owes its existence. But not so. I beheld a neat, spacious room, capable of seating over 3,000 persons, so constructed as to be easy to speak in, and to be so substantial in its structure as to promise to vie with Marlborough Chapel, (should the world stand,) as a lecture room and house of prayer, for at least one generation. It is indeed a model of neatness, simplicity, comfort and frugality. It cost, exclusive of the land, I am informed, about $4,000. Those brethren who are in want of chapels, and have but little money, will do well to visit the tabernacle—learn a good lesson and go home and build on the same plan." [5]

The dedication of the tabernacle on May 4, 1843, was a high day in the history of Millerism. The place was filled to capacity, with an estimated 3,500 persons present. Included in the audience were "a large number of the clergy of this vicinity." Silas Hawley, a Presbyterian minister who had accepted Miller's views, preached the dedicatory sermon.

One newspaper made this frank admission regarding the services of the day:

"The spacious building, which is certainly a very pleasant one inside, and very convenient withal, was completely filled with a very solemn attentive and apparently intelligent audience. The whole proceedings were conducted with great regularity and good order and broke up quietly between 5 and 6 o'clock." [6] *

---

[5] *Christian Herald,* quoted in *Signs of the Times,* June 14, 1843, p. 119.
[6] *Massachusetts Spy* (Worcester), May 10, 1843.

* The Tabernacle passed out of the hands of the Millerites in 1845 and became the Howard Athenaeum. It was destroyed by fire on February 23, 1846. Commenting on the fire, *The Advent Herald* said, "It [the Tabernacle] now lies a heap of ruins—a fit, but faint picture of the great conflagration which now awaits the world that 'now is'; a truth which has been so faithfully and ably proclaimed within its walls."—*March 4, 1846, p. 32.*

In connection with the dedicatory services the "tabernacle committee" read a report which set forth at some length the theological positions taken by the Millerites and concluded with warnings against certain dangers confronting them. This committee report is one of the important documents in the history of the movement. The report, like the statement issued by the sessions of the general conference, is of primary value in marking out the main channel of the stream of Millerite thinking and action.

We shall consider here only what the committee described as "dangers which believers in the doctrine of the second advent should avoid." Nine dangers were listed in order:

"1. We should avoid a censorious spirit towards those who cannot see all things in the same light that we do. . . . If others are honest in their views, and are candid, they are entitled to the utmost charity. . . .

"2. Second advent believers are from all religious denominations; and to act in unison, it is necessary to meet on common ground; to so meet it is necessary to lay aside all sectarian views. . . .

"3. We should avoid bringing in connection with the second advent, and a preparation therefor, any doctrines not necessarily connected therewith. . . .

"4. We should avoid all extravagant notions, and everything which may tend to fanaticism. God is not the author of confusion. . . .

"5. We should avoid placing too much reliance upon *impressions*. . . .

"6. Judge no man. . . .

"7. We should avoid setting up one's own experience as the standard by which to test the experience of others. Men's experience will differ, as did those of the apostles. . . .

"8. 'Let him that thinketh he standeth take heed lest he fall.' . . . Our adversary is continually on the watch, that he may overcome us at our least guarded point. He likes to whisper in the ear of man that he has attained the victory, and become so holy, that do what he will, it is not sin. . . .

"9. We are commanded to occupy till Christ comes. We are to sow our seed, and gather our harvest, so long as God gives us seedtime and harvest." [7]

This must make very dull and disappointing reading to those who have always been led to believe that Millerism was a synonym

---

[7] *Signs of the Times,* May 10, 1843, pp. 74, 75.

for unbridled fanaticism. But here is the record. The official statements and committee reports of the movement are models of restraint and good counsel.

Miller had little part in the activities of the opening months of this year of the end of the world. En route to Albany to speak he was taken ill. Erysipelas had fastened on him again.* He was troubled also with what he describes as "carbuncle boils." For a time his life was despaired of. It was while he was lying ill that he received an anonymous letter which referred to him on the cover as "Great End of the World Man" and carried the notation to the postmaster, "To be delivered before the 23d of April." We have already referred to the unfounded charge, which rapidly gained circulation in the newspapers, that the Millerites had set April 23, 1843, as the date for the end of the world, and that repeatedly the Millerite papers had denied the charge. But denials never kill a "good" story, nor silence a charge, no matter how well the denial may be supported by evidence. The letter is one sentence long. The only justification for quoting this inane, anonymous note is that it illustrates so well the constant and increasing attacks made upon Millerism in general and Miller in particular:

"Daddy Miller: Do you intend to wait the end of the world or go off prematurely? Bah!!!" [8]

By the first week in May, Miller had recovered sufficiently to write to Himes:

"My health is on the gain, as my folks would say. I have now only twenty-two boils, from the bigness of a grape to a walnut, on my shoulder, side, back and arms. I am truly afflicted like Job. And about as many comforters—only they do not come to see me as did Job's, and their arguments are not near so rational." [9]

Although Miller continued slowly to recover, he was not able to be out lecturing again until the fall. But the movement was

---

[8] Manuscript letter, postmarked Philadelphia, April 22.
[9] Letter, May 3, 1843, in *Signs of the Times*, May 17, 1843, p. 85.
* This malady must have been very prevalent in those times, judging by the numerous patent medicine cures advertised in the newspapers.

now much larger than one man. As the summer season drew near again, there was renewed activity on the part of ministers, lecturers, and all. The great tent was made ready for a round of camp meetings. Second advent conferences were planned for strategic centers. And of course the great tabernacle in Boston became increasingly a center of interest and preaching. The range of Millerite promotion in North America was from the lower reaches of Canada on the north to Virginia and Kentucky on the south, and westward as far as Ohio. An occasional letter printed in Millerite papers from ministers and others in Indiana, Illinois, and the territory that is now Wisconsin, suggests that Millerism had reached almost as far west as civilization.

How the movement spread to what were then the western outposts of the country is suggested by the incidents Fitch related when he came to Boston to attend an advent conference, the last few days of May, 1843. He told of one man who had been known for his great desire to accumulate wealth, but who upon his conversion to the advent doctrine "immediately sent for $100 worth of books, which he scattered" in his neighborhood.

A young businessman in Cleveland had planned to spend the winter vacationing, and had purchased a horse and buggy so that he would be able to "travel wherever inclination might prompt him." But he attended some Millerite lectures and was converted. Immediately he put himself at Fitch's disposal to carry him to his lectures. In telling the story Fitch added that the young man had "made his plans to enjoy himself, but he had no expectation of enjoying himself half so well." Fitch told also of finding a printer in Cleveland who was stirred in his heart to do something for "the cause." The result was that he "commenced publishing a paper, 4,000 copies for $40 per week, which was but little more than enough to pay expenses." [10]

A preacher in Michigan wrote to say: "In connection with my other engagements, I have given the warning in sixteen different settlements, at the distance of one hundred miles, and

---

[10] See *Signs of the Times*, June 7, 1843, p. 107.

to large and crowded audiences." He had never heard a Millerite lecture. Someone had sent him literature on the subject, and from reading it he became convinced of the "advent near." [11]

About the same time came a letter from England written by Robert Winter, who had accepted Millerism at the East Kingston camp meeting the previous summer. He told of having met many who were "ready to receive the truth." He stated that he was operating a press in London and had printed 15,000 copies of certain Millerite books. Then he added:

"We are at work all the time, and many preachers have received the truth by reading these works. I preach about the streets with my chart hoisted up on a pole. Another preacher and myself are passing all through the country. Others are proclaiming the cry. Methodists, Baptists, and Independent preachers have embraced the doctrine, and are at work. We intend to hold a second advent camp meeting in May, if time continues; but if the Lord comes, we will hold it in the new earth. The way is now prepared for any of you to come over if the time is not too short. They will more readily receive this doctrine in England, than in America. I have preached about the streets of London, our books are flying about, and are making quite a stir in this great city." [12]

One of the first and most important of the camp meetings held in the summer of 1843 was that in Rochester, New York. The great tent was pitched on the twenty-third of June. Himes and Fitch and other Millerite speakers were in attendance. The next day a heavy wind and rain storm collapsed the tent.*

The following day was Sunday, which ordinarily would have been a time of heavily attended meetings at the tent. Did they sit down to bemoan their fate? No. The record states:

"Brother Himes addressed the people three times in the market, where it was supposed several thousand persons assembled to hear the Word.

---

[11] Letter, S. Barnes to Himes, May 4, 1843, in *Signs of the Times*, May 31, 1843, p. 99.
[12] *The Midnight Cry*, May 18, 1843, p. 65.

* "The heavy squall which struck the tent, parted fifteen of the guy chains, and several inch ropes. It was done in an instant. The windward side of the tent was pressed in toward the audience, and by the pressure of the wind, the leeward side was raised up so that the audience passed out without an exception unharmed. The tent itself was but little injured."
—*Joshua V. Himes in Signs of the Times, July 19, 1843, p. 156.*

THE YEAR OF THE END OF THE WORLD

Multitudes came in from the surrounding country who could not find the place of meeting, and returned disappointed. The attention of the audience was most profound. . . . The time occupied in the three lectures was not much short of eight hours; and the people were not tired of hearing, though nearly all had to stand up." [13]

Monday morning all the citizens interested in seeing the tent erected again were invited to attend meeting. The result was that sufficient funds were raised to repair and erect the tent again. Two days later one of the daily papers of Rochester wrote this:

"The misfortune which befell the great Miller tent on Saturday, has awakened the active benevolence of many of our most respected citizens, who have determined that the tent shall once more arise, and our citizens beneath the shelter of its shade hear the doctrines of Millerism fairly expounded. This is as it should be. We ought at all events to listen, and calmly and dispassionately balance in the mind the arguments adduced in support of their peculiar points of doctrine. . . .

"The professors of the Miller interpretation of the Scriptures, are evidently gentlemen well versed in the subject—thoroughly conversant with theology—have given deep study to this particular branch, and collected the opinions of the most learned commentators on Scriptural prophecy." [14]

The collapse of the tent had actually won friends and financial aid for the movement. The old adage proved true, that it is an ill wind that blows no good.

The collapse of the tent was not the only sensational thing that happened at Rochester. A woman, quickened in her conscience by the preaching she had heard, confessed that she had committed a murder several years before in Great Britain and expressed her wish to be sent back to pay the penalty of the law. Commenting on this, a Boston newspaper observed: "Millerism seems likely to prove not the *worst* of the isms with which this country at present abounds." [15]

To reinforce the tent meeting and to provide a follow-up program for those citizens of Rochester who had accepted

---

[13] *Signs of the Times*, July 12, 1843, p. 152.
[14] *Evening Post* (Rochester, N. Y.), June 26, 1843, quoted in *Signs of the Times*, July 5, 1843, p. 144; see also *Signs of the Times*, July 12, 1843, p. 152, July 19, 1843, p. 156.
[15] *Daily Evening Transcript* (Boston), July 10, 1843.

Millerism, a paper called *The Glad Tidings* was started. It was published weekly for a period of thirteen weeks and was scattered widely over the city, the surrounding area, and also on canal boats. It was filled largely with articles that had been published in *Signs of the Times* and *The Midnight Cry*.* A book depository was also opened. Here certain literature could be sold, but generally it was given gratuitously to the inquirer who came in to read.

The techniques of evangelistic promotion that the Millerites had developed and proved effective in their tent and camp meetings the preceding year were used even more effectively and widely in the summer of '43.

From Rochester the great tent was moved to Buffalo early in August and from there to Ohio. Writing from Rochester on July 28, regarding these proposed moves, Himes declared that he intended "to distribute four or five hundred dollars' worth of books" in Buffalo. "We mean that the West shall have light, if we spend the last farthing we possess." Of the plans for Ohio he predicted:

"We intend, if permitted, to meet our brethren in that part of the country, to distribute about $2,000 worth of publications, in that portion of the Union. We shall supply every town with a [Second Advent] Library, as far as practicable. We intend also to furnish all the ministers, *who will read on the subject,* with publications. If they cannot furnish themselves, *we will furnish them.* They shall be left without excuse. We hope and expect to see one mighty gathering in the west." [16]

Himes had lost none of the fervor that had been created in his soul in December, 1839, when, sitting in his church in Boston, he heard Miller expound the prophecies, and promised him that the message would be carried to every corner of the land.

While the great tent was stirring large interest in the West, other open air meetings were being held on the Atlantic seaboard.

---

[16] *Signs of the Times,* Aug. 9, 1843, p. 181.

* The publishing of a local Millerite paper for a period of weeks, to reinforce the lectures, was a rather common practice with the Millerites. With rare exceptions, no files of any of these short-term papers are to be found today.

The Millerite papers during the summer of '43 are filled with notices of camp meetings. Many of these, of course, were not large, and in cases where the prejudice was great, there were even instances of limited attendance, though this was the exception. At the Hempstead, Long Island, camp meeting, for example, there "was not a person on the seats, and but few in the vicinity" when the hour came to open the meeting, but the preacher announced his text and began. By the time he closed, from "fifty to one hundred were present." These must have taken back a good report, for "a still larger number came in the evening." Before the camp meeting ended, the attendance had increased very gratifyingly. [17]

Commenting on this camp meeting, the Hempstead *Inquirer* said:

"Many of our editorial brethren are disposed to ridicule this doctrine and its propagators, although not one of them has endeavored to prove that it is not true. . . . If ridiculing a doctrine proves its falsity, then none are true. Even the Word of God itself has not been exempt from the shafts of ridicule. . . .

"That those who recently held a camp meeting near this village, were true and sincere Christians, we have good reason to believe. . . . They appeared to be well acquainted with the Scriptures, and urged their hearers to search for themselves, to see whether their doctrine was true or not. If then these men were Christians, and in the discharge of what they conceive to be their duty, are they the proper subjects for sarcasm and ridicule?" [18]

In addition to camp meetings, grove meetings were held. Someone conceived the idea that a short rally could be held in a grove near a city or town. A Millerite minister describes one such meeting near Utica, New York:

"No house could be obtained for the presentation of the subject. But we went to a sanctuary of the Lord's own erection, composed of butternuts of a tall and thrifty growth, spreading their long and ample branches over our heads, and forming a vast arch of great beauty and grandeur. Under that, in a lumber wagon, surrounded by a large number of persons, I preached

---

[17] See *The Midnight Cry,* June 22, 1843, p. 121.
[18] Hempstead *Inquirer,* June 24, 1843, quoted in *The Midnight Cry,* July 13, 1843, p. 160.

two discourses, both occupying nearly *five* hours. God was there—a deep impression was produced. Some of the first men in the place, as to piety, intelligence and influence, were there, to hear candidly; and went away favorably disposed. Sinners were there, to tremble and turn pale." [19]

In New York City, where neither camp meeting nor grove meetings were possible, a newly constructed building that had evidently been intended for a theater was leased by "the Second Advent Association for the City of New York." Easy of access in Chatham Square, it provided for the Millerites in New York what the tabernacle was providing for them in Boston, a meeting place they could call their own.[20]

One distinctive feature of the public meetings held by the Millerites was the great interest stirred up in the reading of the Bible. Booksellers found themselves selling more Bibles in a week's time than they had been accustomed to selling in months. The editor of *The Midnight Cry*, reporting on one of the camp meetings in the summer of '43, remarked:

"The great eagerness of the people for Bibles, was a very cheering illustration of the effect of the Lectures. Two lots were sold, and we sent to Philadelphia for a bundle of two dozen more, of which fifteen were sold in a few hours." [21]

The real problem that began to perplex the movement in 1843 was not fanaticism, that age-old affliction of all religions.* The problem was of a different kind. There comes a time in the history of almost every religious movement when the distinctive teachings or convictions that set it in motion, result in friction and opposition in the church or churches from which it sprang. The founders may have started the movement with no idea of a separate organization, but they generally end up as a distinct

---

[19] Letter from Silas Hawley, Aug. 15, 1843, in *The Midnight Cry*, Aug. 24, 1843, p. 6.
[20] See *The Midnight Cry*, Sept. 7, 1843, p. 17.
[21] *Signs of the Times*, Aug. 16, 1843, p. 191.

* The newspaper reports of Millerite camp meetings in 1843 contain little in the way of specific charges of fanaticism, with one clear-cut exception. Both the public press and the Millerite papers had much to say about fanatical acts at a trio of camp meetings held in Connecticut. But rather than break the main thread of our story by an investigation of these incidents here, we are reserving discussion of them for a later chapter. In that chapter we shall examine very fully the various incidents in Millerite history on which critics of the movement have based their charges of fanaticism.

THE YEAR OF THE END OF THE WORLD

body. Wesley, for example, did not start his revivals with the thought of creating a new denomination, but the movement finally became a separate religious body. The Millerites in their formal pronouncement at the time of the first session of the general conference in October, 1840, very explicitly stated that the movement had no sectarian designs. And that position they restated in obvious sincerity from time to time.

However, various of the clergy soon began to display a real hostility to the distinctive preaching of the "advent near." In many instances the believers in Miller's teachings were not permitted to express themselves on the subject in any way in their own churches. They felt repressed and spiritually suffocated. In the Millerite meetings they had found their hearts strangely warmed and their spiritual natures quickened as they listened to the prophecies expounded, and pictured in their minds the stimulating thought of the soon coming of Christ. To go from such a series of meetings back to their own churches and find there an atmosphere of coldness toward the whole subject of the advent, could not fail to lead many to question the wisdom of remaining in those churches. Some felt that to stay in their church would really be to deny their faith. Others were not quite sure.

By the summer of 1843 the discussion of the question reached the pages of the Millerite papers in a definite way. It could hardly be otherwise. For example, Silas Hawley, who preached the dedicatory sermon at the Boston tabernacle in May, wrote three months later of his evangelistic labors, and of the nearly 200 "hopeless and hardened cases" that had been converted:

"There is one thing, in reference to these converts, that should be noticed. The great mass of them have not joined any of the existing sects: they stand by themselves. Nearly all such are living, *thriving* Christians, and strong in the belief of the speedy advent. But most of those who have connected themselves with any of the sects, are dying in religion, and are giving up the doctrine of the speedy appearing. They have the *spiritual asthma*; it is hard for them to breathe." [22]

---

[22] Letter from Silas Hawley, Aug. 15, 1843, in *The Midnight Cry,* Aug. 24, 1843, p. 7.

This might be considered typical of the feeling and temper of some of the Millerite ministry that was beginning to express itself spontaneously.

About the same time that Hawley was expressing himself in this way, Charles Fitch, one of the most prominent of the Millerite leaders, was writing a sermon entitled "Come Out of Her, My People." The title of his sermon was taken from the figurative language of the eighteenth chapter of the Revelation. This presents a mighty angel crying, "Babylon the great is fallen," followed by the warning voice, "Come out of her, My people, that ye be not partakers of her sins, and that ye receive not of her plagues." This sermon set forth the view that "Babylon" refers not only to the "Catholic Church," as Protestantism had taught since Reformation times, but also to the great body of "Protestant Christendom." Fitch reasoned that both Catholic and Protestant branches of Christendom had fallen from the high spiritual state of pure Christianity. He contended that the Protestant world, in responding so coldly to the doctrine of a literal coming of Christ, or in spiritualizing it away, revealed that they did not truly love His appearing. This led him to declare:

"To come out of Babylon, is to be converted to the true Scriptural doctrine of the personal coming and kingdom of Christ: to receive the truth on this subject with all readiness of mind, as you find it plainly written out on the pages of the Bible, to love Christ's appearing and rejoice in it, and fully and faithfully to avow to the world your unshrinking belief in God's Word touching this momentous subject, and to do all in your power to open the eyes of others, and influence them to a similar course, that they may be ready to meet their Lord. . . .

"If you are a Christian, *come out of Babylon.* If you intend to be found a Christian when Christ appears, *come out of Babylon,* and come out *now.* Throw away that miserable medley of ridiculous spiritualizing nonsense, with which multitudes have so long been making the Word of God of none effect, and dare to believe the Bible." [23]

The growing conviction of various of the Millerite preachers

---

[23] *The Second Advent of Christ,* July 26, 1843, p. 2.

THE YEAR OF THE END OF THE WORLD   149

and laity that they should no longer stay in their respective churches, now was reinforced by a solemn Scriptural command: "Come out of her, My people." Fitch's view quickly took hold of many minds. His sermon was published first in the Millerite paper in Cleveland, of which he was the editor. It was soon republished as a pamphlet. A little later the prominent Millerite publication in New York printed the sermon in full, explaining that the "call for it has been so great that we have inserted it in the [*Midnight*] *Cry*." [24]

But there was no immediate, united acceptance of Fitch's interpretation of symbolic "Babylon" to include Protestantism. The editorial note, which states that the sermon is being reprinted in *The Midnight Cry*, concludes thus: "We should make a different application of the Scriptures relating to the fall of Babylon."

The editor may have thought he was safely dismissing the subject with such comment. But we shall discover, as the story of Millerism unfolds, that this subject would not down. The Millerites became more fervent in their beliefs, the church more cold toward them. And had not the Bible prophet commanded them to "come out"? Slowly but certainly the movement was beginning to take shape as a distinct entity in the religious world.

The Millerite papers, which so largely were devoted to theological discussion and reports of activities, occasionally printed a letter that revealed the more human side of the man who most of all was the guiding head of the movement, William Miller. One of the few intimate sketches of him published in the extensive writings of the movement, is the letter written by the editor of *The Midnight Cry*, N. Southard, after he had visited Miller in his home in October of '43. [25]

Southard said that what surprised him at the very outset was the number of visitors who came to see Miller. The next day after his arrival was very stormy, the editor related, but that

---
[24] *The Midnight Cry,* Sept. 21, 1843, p. 33.
[25] See letter, Oct. 23, 1843, in *The Midnight Cry,* Oct. 26, 1843, p. 88.

did not prevent five visitors from arriving, one from as far away as Iowa. Ten children had been born in Miller's home, seven sons and three daughters. Eight were then living.* Four of them were under the parental roof at that time. The eldest son was postmaster of Low Hampton.†

Southard examined the old family Bible‡ and the copy of Cruden's Concordance and then related the story of a clergyman who once paid a visit to the home. Miller was away. The clergyman sought to ease his disappointment by at least the sight of Miller's library. One of the daughters took him to the northeast room, and pointing to the Bible and the Concordance upon Miller's writing desk, said, "That is his library." Southard added:

"Her remark was strictly true, as far as theological writings were concerned. He never had a commentary in his house, and did not remember reading any work upon the prophecies, except Newton and Faber, about 30 years ago." §

One of the very widely circulated stories about Miller was that he had recently built an imposing stone wall around his large farm. The inference was that he really did not believe what he was preaching, because he was substantially improving his property for the long years ahead. Southard saw a stone wall on the property. "But," he added, "the moss-grown, weather-beaten stones unanimously contradict the foolish and malicious lies which have been told about its recent origin."

---

* One had died on the day of its birth, the other at the age of three. The remaining eight children grew to adulthood and married.

† This was the name for the post office that served the little cluster of farmhouses located about four miles north of Hampton.

‡ There are today a number of Bibles which are said to be Miller's Bible or Miller's family Bible. Perhaps they were all in the family at some time or other. The Bible that has best claim, we believe, to the title of Miller's family Bible is one that is now in the possession of Philip M. M. Phelps, of Fair Haven, Vermont, a great-grandson. This Bible contains the most detailed record of births, deaths, and marriages of the Miller family for three generations.

§ This is the most specific statement we have found as to Miller's indebtedness to others in the matter of his interpretation of Bible prophecy. While it is true that he repeatedly declared that his prophetic views were not new and strange—and a later chapter will present evidence in support of this claim—he insisted that he came to his conclusions quite exclusively through a study of the Bible and reference to a concordance. In various letters he mentioned this Bible-concordance combination in describing his method of study. The "Newton" mentioned by Southard could have been either Sir Isaac or Bishop Newton, both of whom wrote works on prophecy.

Miller kept closely in touch with the activities of the movement. "He is a diligent reader of second advent papers," continued Southard. "After he has received one, he seldom lays it aside, till he has become acquainted with all its contents. The rest of his reading is nearly confined to the Scriptures."

Miller received not only many visitors but also many letters. A collection of more than eight hundred of them, most of them letters *to* Miller, which are still preserved, are mute testimony to the truth of Southard's statement that "it requires no small share of his [Miller's] time to attend to the numerous letters he receives." Then as a good editor, who is always on the lookout for worth-while contributions, he added immediately: "We hope the readers of the [*Midnight*] *Cry* will hear from him soon."

Another visitor to Miller's home contributed this to the picture:

"Brother Miller occupies one of the lower front rooms, where he has his bed, a few common chairs, his old bookcase and clock. In the other room is a portrait, painted some twenty years ago; a large diagram of the visions of Daniel and John, painted on canvas, some like the miniature one in the last part of his book. The most elegant article in the house was a Bible, presented by a friend in Boston." [26]

Miller's long absence from the lecture platform, because of illness, had not decreased the interest of various churches to hear him. No other lecturer could take his place. In Miller's correspondence is found a letter from Lockport, New York, written in the autumn of 1843, which opens thus:

"We the undersigned are very desirous of having you deliver a course of lectures here on the subject of the second advent. *You* have been much maligned and misrepresented, as well as the sentiments which you inculcate. And it would be very grateful to us to hear you for ourselves, to know *what* and *wherefore* you affirm." [27]

The letter carries more than sixty signatures, headed by that

---
[26] A. Spaulding in *The Midnight Cry*, July 6, 1843, p. 145.
[27] Manuscript letter from Elon Galusha, *et al.*, Oct. 2, 1843.

of "Elon Galusha, the Pastor of the Baptist church of Lockport." *

Up to the time of his writing this letter Galusha had not committed himself to the Millerite teaching. It is evident, then, that in spite of the increasing tension between church organizations and the Millerite movement, there were still churches whose members were ready to go on record with their signatures by the score, urging Miller to come and preach. He responded to this request the following month—November. When the series of lectures was concluded, Galusha was a confirmed Millerite. And from that time onward he was an active preacher in the movement.[28]

All during the year the interest in Millerism had been steadily rising. Newspaper and other references were increasing. It is doubtful that any other religious movement in the nineteenth century received so much free publicity in so short a time as did the Millerites. And even though the publicity was generally hostile, the Millerites wisely reasoned that any publicity was good publicity, though they phrased the thought in the Scriptural words, "We can do nothing against the truth, but for the truth."

Speaking of hostile publicity, the year 1843 witnessed a new variety. The Millerite papers refer repeatedly to "caricature prints." These were often in the form of broadsides presenting large cartoonlike caricatures of the Millerite teachings. They could scarcely escape being sacrilegious, for they pictured in ludicrous form the prophetic symbols found in the Bible. Then there were caricatures of Miller himself.

"There is one caricature going the rounds representing Mr. Miller ascending to heaven with all the Millerites—so called—hanging on to him. It is adorned with various cuts, among which is an enormous key, called 'the key to the great tent of salvation.' . . . There is another sheet just issued, No. 1, Vol. 1, called the 'Vial of Wrath, and Junk Bottle of Destruction.' In this sheet the most sacred truths are the most wickedly scoffed at. The

---

[28] See *The Advent Shield and Review*, May, 1844, p. 78.

* Elon Galusha was the son of Jonas Galusha, who was governor of Vermont during the War of 1812, and from whom Miller received his commission as an officer in the State militia.

resurrection of the dead is ridiculed, and caricatured by a cut of a skeleton rising half way out of his coffin, and throwing his shin bone at a croaking toad that sits on the foot of the coffin. The ascension of the saints to meet their Lord in the air, is shown in a ludicrous light, in various attitudes of ascension, while the fat ones are described as being drawn up with hooks by angels." [29]

These caricature prints, as they were called by the Millerites, seemed to be a feature of the opposition until the climax of the movement the following year. It must have taken courage for a person to accept the teachings of Miller, and even more courage to be one of that steadily growing number who were actively promoting the movement.

But the press was not unitedly scurrilous during this fateful year. We have already given one or two illustrations of favorable mention by newspapers. Strange as it seems, the most complimentary comment on the Millerites during the summer of '43 was by a religious monthly, the organ of Alexander Campbell, principal founder of the Disciples of Christ Church (sometimes known as the Christian Church). Religious papers were generally the most hostile of all. But Campbell, though he stated frankly that he did not believe Miller's teachings, and thought them "destitute of rational arguments," waxed oratorical in his eulogy of the men who constituted the movement:

"Many sincere and conscientious spirits are already enrolled amongst its advocates, and some of them are not only sincere, but pure, and noble, and amiable Christians. These are the great Apostles of the theory, to whose virtues and excellencies the cause is mainly indebted for its comparative success. Its temples are festooned with Christian charity. Its altars are covered with the garlands and wreaths of piety and humanity. Its priests wear the coronal of elevated sanctity, and its votaries are from necessity all more learned in the symbols of prophecy than those who oppose them. It is true that amongst them are found the 'ring-streaked, speckled, and spotted kine' of every denominational peculiarity; and it is said that in their solemnities even hypocrites and knaves, as among other sects and professions, have made their appearance." [30]

---

[29] *Signs of the Times,* March 29, 1843, p. 29; see also issue of March 22, 1843, p. 20.
[30] Alexander Campbell, "The Coming of the Lord," *Millennial Harbinger,* July, 1843, p. 289.

He observed, regarding the growth of the movement, that "as time advances the doctrine of the second advent in 1843 gains new interest, and grasps with a stronger hold the minds of all who assent to its strong probability." There was, of course, no way of telling with accuracy the number of adherents to Millerism at this time, or at any time, for that matter. However, we have this interesting side light on the growth of the movement from a writer in a Methodist paper:

"They who limit the influence of Millerism to those who have adopted its chronology, form a very inadequate estimate of its effects. It has affected the whole public mind of New England." [31]

When Miller came home from a lecture tour in November, 1843, he wrote:

"What a great change since I went to Massachusetts a few years ago. Then I had not a minister to stand by me except Brother Cole of Lowell—God bless him—and a few brethren in Randolph.... In my last tour to Boston through Vermont, New Hampshire and Massachusetts, I was introduced to, and saw more than one hundred servants of Christ, who are giving the midnight cry, all of whom are better able to present, and defend the blessed truth than myself." [32]

If in that one tour Miller personally met one hundred men who were preaching the advent near, it is evident that the total number over the country must have been very much larger.

Late in the fall Litch gave this brief summary of the activities of the movement and its expansion:

"Camp meetings and conferences have been held in all parts of the country.... We have our depots for publications in most of the cities, especially in the Eastern, Northern and Western States, and to a limited extent in the South. There are second advent meetings held regularly in most of our cities, and hundreds of men devoting their whole time to the work of giving the cry. Within the past year God has raised up men of learning and talents to defend the cause, and that too, at a time when it was most desperately assailed both from pulpit and press." [33]

---

[31] *Zion's Herald*, Nov. 22, 1843, quoted in *Signs of the Times*, Dec. 27, 1843, p. 158.
[32] Letter, Nov. 3, 1843, in *The Midnight Cry*, Dec. 7, 1843, p. 139.
[33] Letter, Oct. 24, 1843, in *The Midnight Cry*, Nov. 2, 1843, p. 94.

THE YEAR OF THE END OF THE WORLD 155

Even a brief summary of the spread of Millerism in other lands during the year reveals that the movement made a definite impression far beyond the bounds of the United States. The Millerite captain of a canal boat running between Albany and Buffalo discussed the subject of the advent with some emigrants from Norway, and inquired whether they had ever heard of it in their own land. Said the captain:

"They asked if it was Mr. Miller's prophecy. I told them it was so called. They then said that almost every paper among them, last fall and winter had more or less to say on the subject. I then showed them the chart I have on board. The moment they saw it, they said that they had seen it in their own country." [34]

A letter from a missionary in the Sandwich Islands told of having received a Millerite publication, and of the effect it produced on him: "I have *studied* the Bible more within a fortnight past, than I have before, since I came to the Islands." [35]

Late in 1843 Robert Winter, a Millerite convert who had returned to England, describes the progress of Miller's teachings in that country:

"The Advent doctrine is chiefly the talk in this country now,—the newspapers often contain sketches about the people in America, especially Mr. Miller. Various reports have been circulated about this country in reference to him,—some say he is in prison—some say he is dead—some say he has denied his doctrine, and altered his calculations—some say he and many others have turned infidels. . . .

"Thousands are now looking for the coming of the Lord, and believe it is at the door—and preachers of all denominations are now giving the midnight cry. . . . The midnight cry has produced such powerful effects in some parts of this country, that nearly whole villages have turned to the Lord.

"Our London mission is doing well—the Lord has raised up several good laborers, and two or three are now lecturing on this subject in London in different chapels—and many of our friends are holding Bible meetings, and reading our second advent books to the people. . . .

"Our Norfolk mission is doing exceedingly well. Near one thousand

---
[34] *The Midnight Cry,* Sept. 21, 1843, p. 37.
[35] See *Signs of the Times,* Oct. 4, 1843, pp. 54, 55.

have embraced this doctrine in Norfolk of late. We had one of the largest and most powerful camp meetings at Litchar, of any in this country." [36]

In the *Signs of the Times,* in November, the Millerite spokesman, Litch, asked the question, "Is this *everlasting glad tidings* now preached in all the world for a witness to all nations?" Here is his answer in part:

"So far as we have the means of knowing, it is. Within the last few years, there has been a continuous effort by the believers in the speedy coming of the Lord, to send light on this subject to the whole world. And so far as the opportunity has offered, publications have been sent to every English and American mission in the world. These publications have gone to the various parts of the four quarters of the earth and various islands of the sea." [37]

He told of a whaling vessel that touched at a port on the coast of Chile, South America. There the people were not only acquainted with Millerism in general, they had also heard the false rumor that the end of the world was set for the "23d of April." From a "hundred miles back in the country" people had come to the port city for the allegedly fateful day.*

Litch mentioned "the English Adventists," a group entirely independent of the Millerites, who for years had also been preaching the soon coming of Christ. He referred also to Joseph Wolff, who a few years earlier "went through the interior and southern parts of Asia, proclaiming the coming kingdom of the Lord."

The limits of this book do not permit our turning aside to relate the activity of the English Adventists, or Wolff, or others who might be named. But it is a remarkable fact that at the very time Millerism was capturing the attention of America, more or less similar endeavors were being carried on in other

---

[36] Letter, Nov. 6, 1843, in *The Midnight Cry,* Jan. 4, 1844, p. 189.
[37] *Signs of the Times,* Nov. 15, 1843, p. 109.
* The charge that Miller had fixed upon April 23, 1843, was a falsehood made out of whole cloth. It had been repeatedly repudiated by the Millerites almost from the day it was first made, which was months before April 23. But this false story traveled over mountain, valley, and ocean to the west coast of South America. The truth on the matter had not reached them. As the proverb declares, a lie can travel around the world while truth is getting its boots on!

parts of the civilized world, to say nothing of the Millerite promotion overseas. The early decades of the nineteenth century witnessed a great awakening in the study of prophecy, particularly the study of the doctrine of the second advent of Christ, which is the subject of so much Bible prophecy.

When we turn from a survey of Millerite activity abroad, to look into the office of *The Midnight Cry*, we find that 3,500 letters had been written to that office alone during the calendar year. No wonder Himes could feel justified in believing that the interest was very great and growing. He realized that it would not be long before the prophetic year of the end of the world would close. If Millerite preaching were correct, the Lord would come within the next few months. All this was in his mind when he wrote in the last issue of *The Midnight Cry* for 1843:

"The advent of the Lord is right upon us. All our efforts now should tend to prepare for this solemn event. To this end I propose to issue a *million* or more of little tracts of a practical character, to cost from *two cents* to *one mill a piece*. These will be furnished to all our depots, where brethren wishing to aid in the circulation can get them. . . .

"The Lord in His providence favoring us with the means, we intend to fill the land with these swift messengers of truth. Who will help in this work? What we do must be done quickly!" [38]

---

[38] *The Midnight Cry*, Dec. 28, 1843, p. 172.

CHAPTER 11

The First Disappointment

THE OPENING DAYS OF 1844 found William Miller at home resting from a strenuous tour of eight weeks, during which he gave eighty-five lectures. He was almost sixty-two and had been in poor health for a number of years. Even in the best of weather and with the best of accommodations, travel a century ago could scarcely be called a pleasure. Traveling by stagecoach or drafty trains in winter was a program no man would set out for himself for weeks at a time unless there was an urgent reason. Miller had that urgent reason. The year of the end of the world was drawing to its close. He must hasten abroad to give the last warning to sinners and to strengthen the faith of believers.

"To second advent believers," he wrote a letter of comfort, counsel, and warning which began thus:

"Time rolls on his resistless course. We are one more year down its rapid stream towards the ocean of eternity. We have passed what the world calls the last round of 1843; and already they begin to shout victory over us. Does your heart begin to quail? Are you ready to give up your blessed hope in the glorious appearing of Jesus Christ? or are you waiting for it, although it seems to us that it tarries? Let me say to you in the language of the blessed Book of God, 'Although it tarry, wait for it; it will surely come, it will not tarry.' Never has my faith been stronger than at this very moment." [1]

Though Miller had set the bounds of the prophetical Jewish year 1843 as between March 21, 1843, and March 21, 1844, uncritical onlookers, knowing that the calendar year 1843 had ended, had already begun to "shout victory" over the Millerites.

---

[1] *Signs of the Times,* Jan. 31. 1844, p 195

Miller wished to strengthen their faith that Christ would come before the twenty-first of March, then less than three months away. He reasoned that the faith of some would now be weakening because the Jewish year was so nearly ended. He called to his aid the command of the ancient Bible prophet that though the vision "tarry, wait for it." Habakkuk 2:3. He summarized "some of the reasons why I believe that Jesus will come this Jewish year," and said to the believers, "Let us hold fast our faith without wrath or doubting, and let us be careful that the enemy get no advantage over us."

Probably with the prophet's words in his mind that the vision might "tarry" he declared, "If time continues until the end of this Jewish year, we shall be assailed by the enemy in every place where he can have any prospect of hurling in a dart."

Miller well realized the spiritual danger present in such a situation. He knew they would be tempted to throw away their hope. "This," said he, "would be a fatal stab in our Saviour's side."

But he had a further fear. He wished to warn the believers against the danger of self-righteousness, lest the devil "persuade us that we are holy; and that anything we may think or do, is not sin." Miller believed that those who thus thought themselves holy were walking on "enchanted ground." He considered this false idea of self-righteousness as a travesty on the doctrine of "true gospel holiness." It would be hard to see how a leader of a religious movement could have written with keener insight into the dangers attendant upon fervent religious interest, or how such a leader could have given more earnest or more definite warning against such dangers. In his warning statement he came to this climax:

"I call heaven and yourselves to witness, my brethren, that I have never taught anything to make you throw away any part of God's Word. I have never pretended to preach anything but the Bible. I have used no sophistry. My preaching has not been with words of man's wisdom. I have not countenanced fanaticism in any form. I use no dreams or visions except those in the Word of God. I have not advised anyone to separate from the churches to which they may have belonged, unless their brethren cast them out, or deny them religious privileges. I have taught you no precept of man; nor the creed of any sect. I have never designed to make a new sect. . . . I have wronged no man; neither have I sought for your honors or gold. I have preached about 4,500 lectures in about twelve years, to at least 500,000 different people. I have broken my constitution and lost my health; and for what? That if possible I might be the means of saving some. . . . "I hope, my brethren, you will continue faithful unto the end." [2] *

The first issues of the Millerite papers in 1844 were filled with letters from ministers, lecturers, and other believers in the advent. But midwinter presented many handicaps to the holding of general meetings, particularly the kind that the Millerites were accustomed to hold. In the rural areas the winter months were largely devoted to smaller or less pretentious gatherings. In the large cities along the Atlantic seaboard important conferences and other public meetings were held.

The first of these was in Boston, beginning January 28. This conference is important as an indicator of the increasing interest of the public in the subject of the advent.

Miller delivered a series of lectures in the tabernacle for a week, beginning on Sunday the twenty-eighth. On that day not only were all the seats filled but all the aisles. Men and women, young and old, stood for hours to hear what Miller had to say. "Had the tabernacle been twice its size, it would probably have been densely filled, as multitudes were obliged to go away, unable to obtain admittance." [3]

---

[2] *Ibid.*, p. 196.
[3] *The Midnight Cry*, Feb. 22, 1844, p. 242.

* There is preserved a manuscript by Miller entitled "A New Year's Address to Those Who Believe in the Second Advent of Jesus Christ," which is evidently the first draft of the message finally sent to the *Signs of the Times* for publication. This first draft contains many phrases and some sentences identical with those in the printed address, but the opening paragraph employs a somewhat different and more colorful figure of speech:

"Brethren, The Roman [year] 1843 is past [the Jewish sacred year would end in the spring of 1844] and our hopes are not realized. Shall we give up the ship? No, no, methinks I hear responding from everyone on board. But why not? the land lubber says our reckoning has run out. And you see that yonder ships on our lee are now feasting and drinking, rejoicing at the failure of our log book. Yes, yes, says the pilot. They have kept no reckoning and they desire no port; therefore, are they scoffing. They do not see the signs of land which are passing our noble ship on every wave. They heed not the land breeze which makes our sails fill, and gives hope to the sailor's breast that he will soon be anchored in the broad bay of the new heavens and the new earth. We do not yet believe our reckoning has run out. It takes all of 457 and 1843 to make 2300, and must of course run as far into '44 as it began in the year 457 before Christ."

Early in February a second advent convention was held in New York City. Here again the attendance was beyond all expectation. Miller, in company with other important leaders, was present for a brief time. From there the scene changed quickly to Philadelphia, as one after another of the principal cities on the coast became the place of a Millerite conference. Again the place of meeting was "filled to overflowing," the attendance being variously "estimated at from four to five thousand." [4]

The closing days of February found Miller, Himes, and others in the capital city of Washington. There were lectures morning, afternoon, and evening. Millerism was the topic of interest even in the city that was the center of discussion for so many subjects. Himes seemed particularly encouraged over the hearing that was given them, for he wrote:

"Men of the world who heard us, told us that Mr. Miller had been misrepresented, and that whatever his opponents might say about him, it would be difficult for them to disprove the doctrine by the Bible. We have advocates of our views, in the circles of the high and low. And although we never visited a place where we saw so *few Bibles,* yet every Bible there is, seems to be in good demand. The Bible has been read more generally within a few weeks, than for years before." [5]

He told of a Senator who asked a reporter whether the Millerites were in town. The reporter said they were. "I thought so," replied the Senator, "for I never heard so much singing and praying in Washington before."

It seems that there was a watchman stationed at the navy yard who was a good Millerite. He whimsically remarked to Himes: "You have made me a great deal of trouble. . . . Why, before you came, I found it difficult to introduce the subject of the advent to the soldiers and officers of the Navy, but now they are all upon me: I have as much as I can do to hear and answer questions." [6]

---

[4] *Ibid.,* p. 241.
[5] *The Advent Herald,* March 20, 1844, p. 52.
[6] *Ibid.*

While the meeting was in progress, Miller wrote that Brother Himes was "scattering his papers and his tracts" among the people, "by thousands, and a more hungry class of anxious inquirers I never saw. They throng us constantly for papers, books or tracts, for information on this important subject." He tells of requests coming in from the near-by areas, and from "old Virginia." He feels a thrill of new hope and confidence as he relates briefly how multitudes have listened in Boston, New York, Philadelphia, "and now in the capital of our country, the prospect is fair, yes, very fair; we shall triumph beyond our expectation.... When the last trying moment has come, and our enemies supposed that the advent cause would slumber in the tomb of bygone days; behold from hill and dale, from village and hamlet, from city and country, from kingdoms and states, from continents and isles, a redoubled shout is heard, ON! ON!! To victory." [7]

Everywhere the interest exceeded the expectation. The meetings in Washington had been planned for a Baptist church, but this quickly had to be abandoned for Apollo Hall. Millerism was anything but dead, despite the fact that the sands of the fateful year were almost run out. Miller was writing this report on Washington only three weeks before March 21, but there is nothing in his letter to indicate that he intended to conclude his activities on March 21 if the Lord did not come. On the contrary he declared in the letter: "If Christ comes, as we expect, we will sing the song of victory soon; if not, we will watch, and pray, and preach until He comes, for soon our time, and all prophetic days, will have been filled."

This attitude of mind was shared by others in the movement. It may be explained by the text Miller himself had used in January in that letter he wrote to the second advent believers, in which he quotes the Bible prophet concerning "the vision," that might "tarry." Perhaps in the mysterious plans of God there would be a little delay in the fulfillment of the promise in

---

[7] *Ibid.*, March 6, 1844, p. 39.

order to test their faith. So they reasoned. Then, too, Miller had always declared that his forecast had in it one possible element of uncertainty, the errors in chronology that might have crept into the reckoning of events through the centuries. There was still another closely related reason for not drawing the line hard and fast at March 21. There was more than one way of reckoning the Jewish year, the Millerites decided as they examined the subject more fully. They increasingly inclined to the position that the reckoning of Jewish time kept by the Karaite Jews was the true Biblical reckoning. This would mean that the Jewish year 1843 would not end until one lunar month later than they had first reckoned.[8]

An editorial in *The Midnight Cry,* in February, declared: "If we are mistaken in the time, we feel the fullest confidence that the event we have anticipated is the next great event in the world's history." [9] This probably describes the attitude of mind of Millerite spokesmen in the opening months of 1844.[10]

The Millerite papers at this time were filled with accounts of ministers and laymen either being expelled from their churches or withdrawing voluntarily. One minister * wrote an extended report of his trial for heresy before the presiding elder in the Portland district of the Maine Conference of the Methodist Episcopal Church. The charge against him was "disseminating doctrines contrary to our articles of religion, as explained by our standard authors." This charge was brought against him in harmony with a series of resolutions that had been passed some time before by the Maine Conference. These resolutions discussed Millerism very specifically and described the teachings of the movement as "contrary to the standards of our church," and "as among the erroneous and strange doctrines which we are pledged to banish and drive away."

---

[8] See *The Midnight Cry,* March 28, 1844, p. 289; also issue of April 4, 1844, p. 297.
[9] *The Midnight Cry,* Feb. 15, 1844, p. 237.
[10] *Ibid.,* April 18, 1844, p. 317.

* This Methodist minister was L. S. Stockman. Ellen Harmon, later Mrs. Ellen G. White, refers to him in certain of her writings. She accepted Millerism as a girl and went to Stockman for spiritual counsel. (See Ellen G. White, *Early Writings,* pp. 12, 17.)

The resolutions granted that high motives might control those who preached such views, but declared "that those who persist in disseminating these peculiarities, either in public or in private, and especially those who have left their appropriate work for this purpose, [should] be admonished by the chair, and all be hereby required to refrain entirely from disseminating them in future." [11]

About the same time a short news item appeared in *The Midnight Cry,* stating that "Brother A. M. Osgood has resigned his charge as pastor of the Methodist E. Church in Salem, N. H., and, in company with Brother Eastman, has gone to the great West to labor in the vicinity of Rochester." [12]

The next week's issue contained an item about a Cumberland Presbyterian minister, J. P. Weethee, president of a college in Beverly, Ohio, as being "a firm Adventist." The report states that while he was occupied during the weekdays in his school, he had "during the evenings . . . and the vacations, . . . been faithfully and zealously engaged in sounding the midnight cry." [13]

The next issue reports that Elon Galusha, pastor of the Baptist church in Lockport, New York, "tendered his resignation last Sabbath, and is now free to preach the whole truth, without being desired to conform his preaching to the taste of a Laodicean church." [14]

In the same issue another minister wrote to state: "I am now disengaged and ready to sound the alarm wherever the Lord may open the door." This minister wrote from Sandy Hill, only a few miles from Miller's home.

As might be expected, the belief that the Protestant churches were a part of Babylon, which had begun to take hold of Millerite thinking in 1843, was now gaining general acceptance. Had not the churches been increasingly hostile to the doctrine of the literal

---

[11] See report by L. S. Stockman in *The Advent Herald,* Feb. 14, 1844, p. 13; see also issue of Feb. 21, 1844, pp. 17, 18; *Signs of the Times,* Sept. 13, 1843, p. 32; *Maine Inquirer* (Bath), July 26, 1843.
[12] *The Midnight Cry,* Jan. 25, 1844, p. 215.
[13] *Ibid.,* Feb. 1, 1844, p. 224.
[14] *Ibid.,* Feb. 8, 1844, p. 229.

advent of Christ? Had they not ridiculed those who preached it? Had they not made it increasingly difficult for them to bear testimony to their faith? Had they not even on occasion disfellowshiped them? There was only one answer to all these questions. And the answer had become so emphatic that it finally began to reflect itself in actions taken at second advent conferences. For example, the conference held in New York City on February 7, 1844, recommended to those believers who were "denied the privilege of the open advocacy of the doctrine of the Lord's speedy coming, to withdraw themselves from all sectarian organizations, since they cannot remain in such fellowship but at the expense of piety, peace and usefulness." [15]

The first issue of *The Midnight Cry* in February, 1844, contains a long article on Babylon. In an introductory editorial the author is quoted as saying:

"I consider it of *primary* consequence, nay, that it should take *precedence,* at this stage of the advent cause. I ask your attention to the fact, that John [the revelator] heard, as distinctly, 'a voice from heaven, saying, COME OUT OF HER, MY PEOPLE,' as he did that '*the hour of His judgment is come.*' And you may depend that this cry must be as *distinctly,* and as *fully* made as the other." [16]

The editor, who only a few months before had dissented from the views of another writer on this subject, was now ready to introduce the present article with the commendatory note:

"We have not had the time . . . to give *all* its parts that thorough scrutiny which might enable us to say, *there is no error here,* but we are *sure,* so much of it is true and Scriptural, that we are happy, with great earnestness, to say to our readers, *do* read it, *immediately,* and lay not the subject aside till, with humble, prayerful searching, you have *decided* as to *your* duty; and then fearlessly *do* your duty, for, 'Behold the JUDGE standeth before the door.'" [17]

As they increasingly withdrew from the churches the problem of securing meeting places became acute. It is of the genius of

---
[15] *The Advent Herald,* Feb. 21, 1844, p. 21.
[16] *The Midnight Cry,* Feb. 1, 1844, p. 218.
[17] *Ibid.*

the Christian religion that believers meet together in religious services to hear the preaching of the Word. The Millerites were certainly no exception. In various places where a substantial company of second advent believers were located, inexpensive structures, often called tabernacles, began to be reared.

The speed and fervor with which they constructed such tabernacles is illustrated by the experience of the Millerites in Toronto, Canada. An Adventist lecturer found that a large hall in the city, the only one they could secure, was quite too small to hold the crowd who thronged the meetings. He told them he would have to go on to other towns to preach, if they could not find a place that could hold the congregation. That seemed impossible, because "every hall in the city, and every church" was closed against them. A decision was speedily made to "erect a plain, simple, but convenient house for our meetings." How quickly was the plan consummated? Here is the answer in the words of the lecturer himself:

"In two hours from the time that the proposition was started in a prayer meeting, where our friends had met for worship, the whole amount was subscribed. One brother gave the land, another the nails, another a quantity of lumber, and more than a score of brethren offered to work on the building; besides money enough being subscribed to pay all other expenses. Our house will be a temporary affair, expecting soon, as we do, to exchange it for that which has foundations, whose builder is God. It will be about thirty feet, by ninety, and will be finished in six or eight days. The excitement through the city, is immense: and it is hourly on the increase." [18]

That was the tempo of the movement in the early months of 1844. The Millerites showed their faith by their works.

Though the Millerite ministers and lecturers were now quite generally preaching that the believers should come out of Babylon, Miller did not give this teaching his endorsement. He was loath to depart from the position he had taken at the very beginning, that his mission was to revive the true Bible teaching of the second advent of our Lord, without disturbing existing church organizations, or creating a new one. In a personal letter to

---

[18] *The Midnight Cry*, Feb. 22, 1844, p. 245.

"Brother Galusha" in the spring of '44 he discussed various questions that were troubling him, and declared:

"But one thing more that has been a trouble on my mind. Do give me light. You are well aware that many of our advent brethren are giving another cry, *'Come out of her My people.'* I must tell you where my fear lies. 1st, I fear the enemy has a hand in this, to divert our attention from the true issue, the midnight cry, *'Behold the Bridegroom cometh.'* Again 2d, I fear we do err in our application of 'her.' " [19]

Miller was not sure that the "her" included Protestantism However, this teaching regarding "Babylon" must have been making some impression on his mind, for in a letter to Himes he wrote:

"I am not certain but that God will confound all of our sectarian churches, and bring out His people from among them. Yet it is plain God did command His people to associate themselves in churches, and bid them to walk in His precepts, and obey His ordinances. Now what must we do? To disobey God, I dare not. And to walk with and have a good fellowship with those who by their traditions, make void the law of God, I must not. To fellowship those who say and act as if they spoke the truth, that Christ will never come again to earth, . . . in me it would be wicked." [20]

Miller was in a dilemma. He thought "it would be wicked" "to fellowship" those who denied the Bible truth on the advent. But he feared that any move toward a clear-cut withdrawal might make him responsible for organizing into a new body all "who call themselves Adventists." He was not blind to the fact that many who liked to call themselves such were "living in error by neglecting the plain commands of God in His Word." There was nothing to prevent anyone, anywhere, from declaring that he was a believer in the advent as Miller taught it, but that did not mean that his beliefs on other vital doctrines conformed to the Scriptures.

If Miller had really been the self-seeking adventurer that his enemies so often charged, he probably would have been the first to sound the cry "Come out," in the hope of establishing a new

---

[19] Manuscript letter, April 5, 1844.
[20] *The Advent Herald,* May 1, 1844, p. 97.

organization of his own choosing, controlled and disciplined by him. It is a revealing fact regarding Miller's character and name, that he held back to the very end from joining in what otherwise soon became a unanimous chorus, "Come out."

But vigorous and prominent as were the discussions in the churches regarding Millerism, such discussions were not confined to them. In the city of Washington, D. C., in early April, was held the National Institute Convention, a gathering of the learned. The session on the evening of Thursday, April 4, was devoted to an address by Dr. E. Nott, president of Union College, Schenectady, New York, on the "Origin, Duration, and End of the World." The newspaper reporters wrote briefly:

"From the great excitement which had been produced by the visionary speculations and abortive prophecies of Miller on the immediate destruction of the world by fire, the subject selected by Doctor Nott was one calculated to produce great interest in his hearers. . . . He then spoke of the duration of the earth, alluded to Miller's predictions; quoted passages from the Bible in opposition to Miller's interpretation. . . . He said that the Scripture declared that the heaven and earth were to wax old, etc.; but that though great changes had taken place, nothing yet indicated that it had grown old. . . . He agreed that it would at last, however, be brought to an end; the Bible declares that the world will have an end, and nature confirms the truth of this declaration in language not less impressive and awful. How long, he asked, would those internal fires, volcanoes, etc., which have been so alarming and dreadful, but which were in fact safety valves, be kept open? Should they be closed up, and the crust of the earth rent open, destruction would follow." [21]

The learned doctor did not believe in Miller's view of how the world was to come to an end, but apparently he saw another way which might bring it to a close, some possible condition that would repress volcanoes and the like, so that they would rend the crust of the earth and bring destruction. Probably the savants who listened to him were duly impressed. The reporter did not indicate that anyone took exception to his view of how the last holocaust might come. Doubtless it seemed more scien-

---

[21] *Daily National Intelligencer* (Washington, D. C.), April 5, 1844.

THE FIRST DISAPPOINTMENT 169

tific to them to have fires come up from below than to descend from above.

While the learned were expressing their dissent from Miller in measured, dignified tones, others were taking a more earthy and active course of opposition. A Millerite minister, S. C. Chandler, wrote to Miller from West Troy, New York, telling of mob action against his meeting. While they were holding their service in a district schoolhouse a mob appeared and demanded that they leave immediately. Remonstrances were in vain. The Millerites decided to retire to the home of one of the brethren. Out they marched from the schoolhouse in a body, singing, "Religion makes us happy," and "I am fighting for a kingdom." Chandler added: "We are building a tabernacle and expect to have it done by the 7th of May next, if time continues." [22] They did not intend to be dependent on unbelievers for a place of meeting.

"If time continues." The phrase well describes the feelings of these people as they came to what appeared to be the end of all their prophetic reckoning. There was no sudden disappointment or disillusionment, because, as already explained, they thought the vision might "tarry" or that they might have made a small error in computing the chronology.

Immediately after March 21 Miller wrote to Himes:

"I am now seated at my old desk in my east room. Having obtained help of God until the present time, I am still looking for the Dear Saviour, the Son of God from heaven, and for the fulfillment of the promise made to our fathers, and confirmed unto us by them that heard Him, that He would come again and would receive us to Himself.... The time, as I have calculated it, is now filled up; and I expect every moment to see the Saviour descend from heaven. I have now nothing to look for but this glorious hope." [23]

That was the message he had for all his followers, for this letter, like most of those he addressed to Himes, was written for publication in the Millerite papers.

---

[22] Manuscript letter, April 18, 1844.
[23] Letter, March 25, 1844, in *The Advent Herald,* April 10, 1844, p. 77.

In the personal letter he wrote to Brother Galusha on April 5, and from which we have made one quotation in this chapter, he declared, regarding his faith in the advent:

"My faith is strong, unwavering, and I hope true. I now am looking every day and hour for Christ to come. My time is full. The end of days is come, and at the end the vision shall speak and will not lie. I now have fixed my mind to watch and look and pray until my Saviour comes. It is a glorious hope. I soon shall be like Him, whom twenty-eight years ago I loved. . . . I thought before this time I should be with Him, yet I am here a pilgrim and a stranger, waiting for a change from mortal to immortal."

His reference to "twenty-eight years ago" takes our minds back to the year 1816 when he was converted. He went on to say that he was sure now that scoffers would scoff and say, "Where is the promise of His coming?" "But," he observed calmly, "I must let them scoff. God will take care of me, His truth, and scoffers too. Why then should I complain? If God should give a few days, or even months more as probation time, for some to find salvation and others to fill up the measure of their cup, . . . it is my Saviour's will and I rejoice that He will do things right."

Early in April there appeared almost simultaneously in the two leading Millerite papers a statement entitled "Future Operations." The editor declared that it had been his solemn conviction for three years past that the "advent . . . would have taken place before the present time." He affirmed his faith that it could not be far away, and that "it is not safe, therefore, for us to defer in our minds the event for an hour, but to live in constant expectation, and readiness to meet our Judge." Because of this he felt that any plans laid should be "in conformity with these views of the shortness and uncertainty of time." There was no idea that they should cease their labors, which had produced such an influence upon "all classes." He realized that this influence would be "perverted, or lost, unless it be followed up by continued effort, while probation shall last." The very fact that "the mass of the church and ministry" are seeking so militantly to "neutralize the vital influence of the 'midnight cry,' furnishes the strongest reasons for united and persevering effort." The conclusion was that "lecturing, conferences, tent, and camp meetings, and the distribution of publications" should continue.[24]

The announcements of camp meetings and conferences that appear in succeeding issues of their papers carry qualifying phrases like these: "Providence permitting," or "If time continue." [25]

On May 2, six weeks after the fateful March 21, Miller felt that the time had come to make a frank statement that there was an error in his preaching. He addressed a communication "to second advent believers," in which he said:

"Were I to live my life over again, with the same evidence that I then had, to be honest with God and man I should have to do as I have done. Although opposers said it would not come, they produced no weighty arguments. It was evidently guesswork with them; and I then thought, and do now, that their denial was based more on an unwillingness for the Lord to come than on any arguments leading to such a conclusion.

"I *confess my error,* and acknowledge *my disappointment;* yet I still believe that the day of the Lord is near, even at the door; and I exhort you, my brethren, to be watchful, and not let that day come upon you unawares." [26]

He warned the believers "not to be drawn away from the truth," and not to "neglect the Scriptures." "Let us," he said, "be careful not to be drawn away from the manner and object of Christ's coming; for the next attack of the adversary will be to induce unbelief respecting these." [27]

In the last week in May, 1844, a large advent conference was held in the tabernacle in Boston, at which Miller, Himes, and others of the leaders were present. In one of the meetings of this conference Miller arose and "frankly" confessed "his mistake in the definite time at which he supposed the prophetic periods would run out."

Another speaker at the conference called attention to the

---

[24] *The Advent Herald,* April 10, 1844, p. 80; *The Midnight Cry,* April 11, 1844, p. 305.
[25] See *The Advent Herald,* May 22, 1844, p. 128.
[26] Sylvester Bliss, *Memoirs of William Miller,* p. 256.
[27] *Ibid.*

different occasions when it looked as if the movement "must come to nothing." But "some unforeseen circumstance" always arose "to give the work greater power and stability than ever." This led Whiting, a prominent Millerite leader, to remark "that if every Adventist connected with the cause should abandon it tomorrow, God would raise up new instruments to sustain and carry it forward." This revealed how strong was their faith in what they described as "a favoring providence." [28]

From the council went out an address "to the disciples of Christ, who are waiting for His second appearing." The introductory paragraph of the address remarks on the handicap of not having a close-knit organization, "which has left us to a great extent in a scattered condition, and deprives us of the benefit of mutual counsel."

The address reaffirmed their "position" in the matter of doctrine, set forth a program for "future operations," "affectionately" admonished the believers "to beware of every thing which would exclude" the doctrine of the advent "from the first place in your hearts, or deny it the first claim upon your efforts," and warned them against taking any course that would lead to fanaticism.[29]

Millerism was not dead, nor even dormant. The Millerites were disappointed, but not disillusioned. Nor is this to be explained simply by the fact that there was some elasticity in their reckoning, which could reduce the shock of disappointment. Millerism was something larger than a point of time, as was evidenced by the fact that there had been strong men in the movement from the very beginning who did not accept the time aspect of the preaching. True, they were baffled for a little while, as they sought to adjust their hopes and their preaching to this springtime disappointment. Miller was as perplexed as others. A reporter gives this firsthand account of a meeting in New York at which Miller spoke:

---

[28] *The Advent Herald,* June 5, 1844, p. 140.
[29] See also *The Midnight Cry,* June 13, 1844, pp. 377, 378.

The first page of a manuscript by Miller in which he exhorts the advent believers to hold to their faith despite the fact that the predicted year of the advent, 1843, is now almost gone. He says the "Roman 1843 is past." In other words, December 31, 1843, had passed. Miller believed the prophetic year 1843 should be reckoned from March 21, 1843, to March 21, 1844. This manuscript appears to be the first draft of the New Year's message that was printed in the Millerite publications. (See page 160, footnote.)

Prominent leaders in the Millerite movement. The pictures of Miller, Himes, and Fitch, show them about the time the movement was active. The pictures of Litch and Bates were made many years afterward.

THE FIRST DISAPPOINTMENT

"He tried to define his present position, but appeared not himself to know what it was. One moment he would confess that he was mistaken, and the next say that he could discover no possible mistake, and go over his old calculations. . . . One moment he would say that henceforth he could set no time, and the next he would say in words which I copied as they fell from his lips, 'I don't believe that we can possibly even imagine that it can be off a year,' and again, 'I believe it is as near, perhaps, as the spring is to the summer, or the summer to the harvest.' . . . Then he would refer to his promise to confess himself wrong, if his prediction did not come true, and would say, 'Well, what must I confess? I'm willing to confess that Christ did not come in 1843—but I can't see where I'm wrong.' " [30]

However, the movement was not to be in a state of uncertainty for long. A few Millerite ministers were already re-examining the chronology and beginning to offer a revised and specific date for the advent. But before we tell the story of high hope and deep disappointment in the months ahead, let us turn aside to look at the group of ministers and lecturers who, with Miller, were responsible for the vitality and the expansion of the movement.

---

[30] *Christian Watchman,* quoted in *Vermont Chronicle* (Windsor), June 26, 1844.

CHAPTER 12

The Millerite Leaders—Courageous Individualists

WHAT kind of men were the officers of the steadily growing army of the Millerites that was drawing its recruits from every walk of life and every religious persuasion? Unfortunately it is not possible to give a complete or an altogether clear answer to this question. Few of the leaders of the movement left for posterity any sketch of their lives. However, there are sufficient authentic records of these men to enable us to draw a composite picture. With the exception of a half dozen very prominent preachers, it would be difficult to classify in relative order of importance the large company of men who preached in the movement. Here are the bold outlines of the picture.

In the forefront is Himes. The reader already visualizes him as a man of action, a born promoter, a good businessman, and an ardent religionist. He was born on May 19, 1805, in Rhode Island, and became a member of the Christian Church in 1823. He early revealed a bent toward the ministry, displaying abilities as an exhorter. Four years after his conversion he turned wholly to the work of the ministry. He was soon appointed an evangelist for the Massachusetts Christian Conference. Not long after this he became pastor of the First Christian Church of Boston, which pastorate he held for seven years. Then in 1837 he organized the Second Christian Church, and the next year built a chapel in Chardon Street. In this Chardon Street Chapel he was serving as pastor when he met Miller in 1839.*

---

* The Boston City Directory first lists Himes' name in 1831, and from then on continuously until the year 1862. During this period of time his address changed thirteen times; six of these changes were in the first ten years.

Chardon Street Chapel quickly became known as a rallying point for reform movements, for Himes was also a born reformer. He had an interest in great causes. We shall see in a later chapter that describes the kind of world in which Millerism developed, that the 1830's and 1840's were a period of ferment and reform. Common among the reforms was that of abolitionism, a movement to abolish slavery. This movement sprang from the passionate heart of William Lloyd Garrison and developed under the most adverse conditions and bitter opposition. Garrison found in Himes a good friend, and in Chardon Street Chapel a place for meetings.

Closely related to abolitionism, in fact, the very underlying philosophy of it, was the doctrine of nonresistance, or what we would probably describe today as pacifism. Garrison believed that physical force should never be exercised by one person against another to enforce his will on that other person. When the Non-Resistance Society was formed, some of its first meetings were held in Chardon Street Chapel on May 29, 30, 1839. Himes was one of three men who signed the circular letter of invitation to the first annual meeting of the Non-Resistance Society, which was called to meet in Chardon Street Chapel, September 25, 1839. The arches of that chapel rang to the sound of William Lloyd Garrison's voice as he read his annual report. In the spring of 1842 Garrison's antislavery weekly, *The Liberator,* contained this news item concerning its antislavery convention:

"Chardon Street Chapel.—The meetings of the New England Convention will be holden in this chapel—a building which is destined to be honorably famous in the history of Boston, and for which we entertain more respect and affection than we do for any other in the city." [1]

If nothing else were known about Himes than his connection with the abolitionists, we could safely draw the conclusion that we were dealing with a courageous individual. It took courage to be an abolitionist in the early days of the movement. In 1835 Garrison was dragged through the streets of Boston by a howling

---
[1] *The Liberator,* May 20, 1842.

mob and with a halter around his neck. Nor was the mob constituted of hoodlums, but rather of influential Bostonians, who at that time seemed to hate abolitionism as much as did the Southern slaveholders. Despite the danger of violence, Himes opened the doors of the Chardon Street Chapel to Garrison and his abolition movement. And it must be assumed that he shared in some degree the opposition and opprobrium that confronted Garrison.*

The very fact that the subject of slavery was an explosive one in the first days of the abolition movement, so that men actually risked their lives as well as their reputation in being affiliated with it, means that we have here one sure rule for measuring the courage of men. Men might have courage without being abolitionists, but they could not be abolitionists without having courage. Himes was an abolitionist. We may properly conclude then that with him right was more important than reputation, and that a despised cause had only the greater claim upon his support, provided he believed it was the cause of truth.

Himes allowed his active interest in abolitionism to subside as he became swallowed up in the all-absorbing task of promoting a movement which expected, shortly, to meet the Lord face to face. But that does not in any way minimize the significance of his abolitionist connections in the preceding years. From the brief references to abolition and other political reforms of the day that are found in Millerite literature, we conclude that Miller and his associates believed more and more that they were set for the one task of making men ready for the day of God, and that by thus making men ready to meet God they would deal the strongest blow to all the forces of evil.

---

* It is important that the reader understand these few facts concerning abolitionism, because only in this way is it possible to measure the moral courage of various of the men who became active in the Millerite movement. Little has been written on the antislavery connections of the Millerite ministers. When Sylvester Bliss wrote his biography of Miller in 1853, he made no reference to Miller's hostile attitude toward abolitionists in the 1830's nor to what we shall discover in a later chapter was Miller's final friendly attitude toward the slaves. The Millerite papers say little on the matter. We believe the explanation of the silence in their journals is that they wished to hold the movement to its one chief objective—bringing men back to the Bible teachings on the second advent. Any discussion of political or social questions of the day could serve only to bring discord and friction in a movement drawn from all churches and from all classes of society.

THE MILLERITE LEADERS

Of those who later became leading Millerite ministers, Henry Jones was probably the first to take a serious interest in Miller's views of prophecy. In an earlier chapter we quoted from the first letter he wrote to Miller, in 1832. Jones at that time was an "agent for the circulation of temperance newspapers." Temperance was one of the reforms beginning to receive serious attention, and which met with bitter opposition on all sides, including opposition from many of the clergy. Jones was a Congregational minister. His was the inquiring type of mind. When he heard of Miller's teachings, through conversation with another minister and reading some articles by Miller, he declared that he had "been led to read over and over the whole book of Revelation, together with such parts of the saying of the prophets, of Christ and His apostles, as have seemed to have the most direct bearing upon the subject, and to pray over them, to be enlightened on the question, and especially, to be kept from imbibing dangerous or delusive notions concerning those important things." [2]

In another letter to Miller, written early the next year, he threw further light upon his reform activities:

"Notwithstanding my studious disposition, my temperance agency seems to call so loud for labor by night and day among strangers and from town to town and house to house that it is almost impossible to find time to attend closely to this study as I would. And besides, other new branches of reform are loading upon my shoulders, which make my burden heavy, in regard to study and labor. I am taking considerable hold of temperance in regard to *food* and *dress* and am endeavoring to preach it *practically* as well as in theory, for the theory has been tried long enough, to no effect, for want of practice." [3]

Then follows this sentence, revealing that in the very earliest days of the abolition movement Jones turned his attention and interest toward it:

"My mind has recently become enlightened and awakened on the subject of abolition, or antislavery." He went on to say

---
[2] Manuscript letter, Dec. 27, 1832.
[3] Manuscript letter, Feb. 21, 1833.

that he was definitely allying himself with the abolitionist movement. Jones was aware that in joining with the abolition cause he was inviting danger. In the very closing lines of his letter he remarked: "If I mistake not, the call for abolition now to be made, will wake up a tremendous opposition of Satan's kingdom."

A few months later he again wrote to Miller of his "work of public moral reform in regard to temperance, antislavery, etc.," and declared that there was more opposition stirred up by his antislavery work than by his temperance work. He grieved over the fact that there were so many, of whom better things might have been expected, "who are using all their efforts against abolition." [4]

In a letter to Miller in the fall of that year Jones told of his further study of the prophecies and declared:

"Though as yet but a little learned on this subject, I have been so interested that I have not, on all occasions, refrained from attempt at teaching others more ignorant than myself—have in a few cases lectured upon it before small and unlearned congregations, so far as it has been clear in my own mind. I have also spent a day in writing a dissertation upon it, or rather a comment upon the 24th of Matthew and the 20th of Revelation, with particular reference to Christ's second coming at the commencement of the thousand years." [5]

There was something about the study of prophecy, particularly as it is related to the cardinal theme of Christ's second coming, that led men to feel they must begin telling it to others, sharing with them what they had found.

Further on in this letter Jones expressed the fervent hope that erelong his travels would take him near Low Hampton, so that he could turn aside for a week to study prophecies more fully under Miller's tutelage.

Jones already knew something of humiliation and self-denial in connection with his reform work, for he told of being debarred from churches because of his abolitionist views. But he realized that if he accepted Miller's view on prophecy, he

---

[4] Manuscript letter, May 13, 1833.
[5] Manuscript letter, Sept. 1, 1833.

must reach new depths of self-denial and humiliation in order to promote those views effectively. He discussed this point in his letter, and added:

> "Notwithstanding all this, it was suggested to me about ten days ago, as I was walking with my wallet shouldered, all alone, from Princeton to Trenton, that the time might not be remote when God would make it known, as a duty, to change the object of my travels, so as to give my time, writing and preaching, almost exclusively, as I pass from place to place, to the subject of Christ's second coming."

In view of the position that Millerite preachers in 1843 began to take, that the Protestant churches are a part of "Babylon," a letter of Jones to Miller in the spring of 1834 takes on special interest. He was anticipating by several years this particular belief. He inquired in his letter:

> "In the 18th chapter [of Revelation] the saints are commanded to come out of Babylon. Will you tell me, brother, does Babylon here mean the papal church, the united wickedness of the wicked, or the present visible church of various names? When I look at the slavery, intemperance, wars, Sabbathbreaking, lewdness, gambling, extravagance, pride, covetousness, persecution of saints, etc., etc., now fellowshiped by the church, I inquire, does this Babylon mean particularly *our* churches?" [6]

In the fall of 1834 he told Miller that he had "committed to memory" the whole of "the book of Revelation." He added immediately that he had repeated and studied this book many times over in his "travels from place to place." Besides this, he said: "I have been several times through with all the old prophets without committing to memory. . . . I have taken down brief shorthand notes of the substance and apparent interpretation of all the prophets" as their writings seemed in any way to be related to the prophecies in certain chapters of the book of Revelation.[7]

Of Jones' interest, studies, and activities in the next few years we know little. We do know that he wrote two books on the

---
[6] Manuscript letter, May 19, 1834.
[7] Manuscript letter, Nov. 14, 1834.

study of prophecy and the study of the Scriptures. In 1840 we find his name with that of Miller, Himes, and others, signed to the call that was made through the *Signs of the Times* for the holding of the first general conference in October of that year. He served as one of the secretaries of the conference, and was prominent in the movement from that time onward.

Joseph Bates was another of those who signed his name to the call for that first conference. He must have had prominent standing in the movement, for his name appears in connection with various sessions of the general conference, either as a vice-chairman or secretary or committee member. At the important conference held in Boston in the spring of 1842 he was chairman. Years afterward he wrote the story of his life. We can touch on it only briefly here.

Bates was born into a good Congregational family in 1792 and spent his childhood in New Bedford, Massachusetts. He early took to the sea, was impressed by the British, and became a prisoner of war during the War of 1812. Later he rose to the rank of captain and sailed the seven seas for many years. But he was no ordinary captain. He saw what rum did to sailors, and decided that so far as he was concerned he would never again drink ardent spirits, not even wine. Not long afterward he decided to give up smoking. Yet none of these moves were made because of religious conviction, but simply from a desire to live more healthfully.

Before he sailed on one of his journeys, his wife placed a New Testament in his trunk. This was the beginning of his real religious life, though he was to pass through a struggle before he became a Christian.

After his conversion on the high seas he took occasion, on a trip home, to be baptized. After the baptismal service, he wrote, "While we were changing our clothes, I solicited Elder M., who baptized me, to assist me in raising a temperance society."[8] Bates had seen the evils of drink and had decided against it himself.

---

[8] Joseph Bates, *Autobiography*, p. 205.

Now that he had become a member of the church, why should he not immediately engage to fight against the evil? That was the way Bates reasoned. Here again we see the directness and the vigor of the men who became Millerite leaders.

Though this minister failed to respond, Bates took steps immediately to organize in his town of Fairhaven the Fairhaven Temperance Society, one of the very first temperance societies formed in America.

He was a man of strong convictions, who felt that he ought to put his beliefs into action. Before he sailed again he gathered all the officers and men together on the quarter deck and read them the rules that were to govern their trip. These were probably the most astounding set of rules that any company of sailors had ever heard read to them. There was to be no swearing. There was to be no mending of clothes on Sunday. And perhaps most incredible of all, in a day when sailors considered a daily portion of rum an inalienable right, there was to be no liquor on board.[9]

He related that around the year 1832 antislavery societies began to be organized, and that "as the work progressed, antislavery advocates were maltreated and mobbed in many places where they attempted to organize and hold meetings."[10] After he had looked into this matter for a time he wrote that he "began to feel the importance of taking a decided stand on the side of the oppressed." Then follows this revealing statement on the price that a man pays for pioneering a new reform:

"My labor in the cause of temperance had caused a pretty thorough sifting of my friends, and I felt that I had no more that I wished to part with; but duty was clear that I could not be a consistent Christian if I stood on the side of the oppressor, for God was not there. Neither could I claim His promises if I stood on neutral ground. My only alternative was to plead for the slave, and thus I decided."[11]

A little later he, with about forty others, citizens of

---
[9] *Ibid.*, pp. 209-211.
[10] *Ibid.*, p. 235.
[11] *Ibid.*, p. 236.

Fairhaven, organized a "Fairhaven Antislavery Society, auxiliary to the New England Antislavery Society." [12]

In the early days of abolitionism, ministers in some sections of the North, to say nothing of the South, could not speak in favor of abolition without running the risk of being "driven from their parishes." They ran that risk for even admitting "antislavery lectures" or "reading notices" of such services.[13]

In the year 1839 Bates made his first contact with Millerism. He listened to a Millerite lecturer, then secured a copy of Miller's book of lectures. He accepted the teachings of Miller on the prophecies and, as already stated, joined with others in 1840 to issue a call for a conference of believers in the advent.

The way was made particularly easy for him to take an active part in the movement, because, said he:

"I had known Elder Himes from his youth, and for many years had been intimately acquainted and associated with him in the reforms of the day, and often cheered, strengthened and edified under his preaching." [14]

As Bates became increasingly interested in promoting the doctrine of the second advent, he inevitably gave less time to the meetings and the activities of the reform organizations of which he was a member. The change of interest he explained thus, in the reply he made to fellow members of reform organizations:

"My reply was, that in embracing the doctrine of the second coming of the Saviour, I found enough to engage my whole time in getting ready for such an event, and aiding others to do the same, and that all who embraced this doctrine would and must necessarily be advocates of temperance and the abolition of slavery; and those who opposed the doctrine of the second advent could not be very effective laborers in moral reform." [15]

He went on to say that in seeking to make men "every way right" for the coming of Christ he was "working at the fountainhead" of reform. In other words, he was no less a believer in abolition and temperance, but he was now approaching

---

[12] *Ibid.*
[13] See *William Lloyd Garrison, The Story of His Life Told by His Children*, Vol. II, p. 422, footnote.
[14] Joseph Bates, *Autobiography*, p. 250.
[15] *Ibid.*, p. 262.

the problem of reform from the religious rather than the political or social standpoint.

When he with a number of other advent believers had to wait in the Salem railway station for a few hours on their way home from a camp meeting, they filled the time of waiting for their delayed train by "singing advent hymns." This was something new to the people of Salem, who "came out in crowds, and seemed to listen with breathless attention." At least there was enough attention and interest so that Silas Hawley, a preacher who at that time had just accepted Millerism, was invited to preach on the subject the next Sunday. He had an estimated audience of seven thousand.[16]

Bates soon became an active Millerite minister. He sold his home, most of his real estate, paid up his debts and sought to find some way "to go down south into the slaveholding States with the message." He knew that previously two Millerite ministers, one at least of whom was well known for his earlier abolitionist activity, had been ordered out of a town in Virginia, and he said:

"I was told that if I went south the slaveholders would kill me for being an abolitionist. I saw there was some danger, but imperative duty and a desire to benefit them and unburden my own soul, overbalanced all such obstacles." [17]

He went down to Annapolis, then across the Chesapeake Bay to Kent Island, where he began holding meetings. Near the close of his series of lectures someone told him and his fellow lecturer that "there was a company about two miles off at a rum store" preparing to attack them. Then, as if that was not sufficiently disquieting, up rose a man in the meeting to denounce what Bates had been preaching. His denunciations soon become so violent that he "began to talk about riding us on a rail." To which Bates calmly replied:

"We are all ready for that, sir. If you will put a saddle on it, we would

---
[16] *Ibid.*, pp. 268, 269.
[17] *Ibid.*, p. 277.

rather ride than walk. . . . You must not think that we have come six hundred miles through the ice and snow, at our own expense, to give you the midnight cry, without first sitting down and counting the cost. And now, if the Lord has no more for us to do, we had as lief lie at the bottom of the Chesapeake Bay as anywhere else until the Lord comes. But if He has any more work for us to do, you can't touch us!" [18]

These were calm, courageous words for a man to speak a hundred years ago in a slaveholding State.*

At another place in his tour of Maryland, Bates was accosted thus by a leading citizen: "Mr. Bates, I understand that you are an abolitionist, and have come here to get away our slaves." Replied Bates:

"Yes, Judge, I am an abolitionist, and have come to get your slaves, and *you too!* As to getting your slaves *from* you, we have no such intention; for if you should give us all you have (and I was informed he owned quite a number), we should not know what to do with them. We teach that Christ is coming, and we want you all saved." [19]

The story must have spread abroad over the whole area where Bates and his fellow lecturer were preaching, that two very strange men were in that area. Bates relates that as they were walking on foot toward a village a man in great haste overtook them, inquiring if they were the two Millerites who were going to lecture there. Hardly waiting for an answer, he continued, "I have traveled 13 miles this morning to see you," and stood gazing at them. "How do we look?" inquired Bates. To which the man could only reply in honesty, though apparently in great amazement: "You look like other men." [20]

If people had such queer ideas about the actual physical appearance of a Millerite preacher, though they had absolutely no foundation for such ideas, is it hard to see how they could

---

[18] *Ibid.*, p. 279.
[19] *Ibid.*, p. 281.
[20] *Ibid.*, p. 283.

* The newspaper version of this story, as related at the time, is to the effect that Bates replied, "If you place a saddle upon the rail, I should greatly prefer it to walking on these muddy streets." To which the editor added this appropriate comment: "The wreck of matter and the crush of worlds is but a small consideration to one who can take things so cooly as this."—*Newark Daily Advertiser, March 2, 1844.*

have equally groundless ideas as to what the Millerites believed and did?*

When the tour through Maryland ended, Bates and his companions went north by boat. But did they idle away their time? No, they hung up their chart, sang an advent hymn, and when the passengers gathered around and began to inquire, they were informed that if they wished to sit down they could hear a lecture on the subject. The lecture was interrupted later by a heavy gale that blew up. When the passengers were finally transferred at the port to a train north, the lecture was continued. That was the spirit of the Millerite movement.

Still another very prominent Millerite leader was Charles Fitch. Our knowledge of him, though limited, is sufficient to reveal something of the character of the man. We know that he was a student at Brown University in 1826. That is the address on a rather well-written, original poem of his. The first significant light on the man is found in a pamphlet he wrote entitled *Slaveholding Weighed in the Balance of Truth and Its Comparative Guilt.* This was about 1837. The argument in the pamphlet is cogent and the language forceful. The author is listed on the title page as "pastor of the First Free Congregational Church, Boston."

In an earlier chapter we quoted from the letter Fitch wrote to Miller in 1838, in which he told of having secured a copy of Miller's lectures, having read them with intense interest and a growing conviction. In that letter he told of a meeting of the ministerial association in Boston, at which he was to speak, and that he planned to discuss some of Miller's views.

We have to wait three years for the sequel to this letter. In 1841 he wrote a letter to Josiah Litch, who was then actively beginning to promote Millerism.† It seems that Litch had been carrying on missionary work with Fitch, for the letter opens with this reminder:

---
* We throw out this question in passing. In later chapters we shall discuss at length the series of charges made against the Millerites.
† This letter, printed in the form of a seventy-two page pamphlet, bears the date November, 1841.

"You will, doubtless, remember that when you called at my house some months ago, you requested me to examine the Bible doctrine respecting the second coming of Christ, and write you the result of my investigation." [21]

Then recalling the time when he had first made contact with Miller in 1838, he declared:

"It is now somewhat more than three years and a half, since the lectures of William Miller on this subject were put in my hands. . . . I devoured it with a more intense interest than any other book I had ever read, and continued to feel the same interest in it until I had read it from beginning to end for the sixth time." [22]

He goes on to say that he then preached two sermons in his church in Boston, "to lay before them the theory of Christ's second coming at hand, . . . telling them I express no opinion of my own." [23]

He referred to the discussion that took place after he had spoken at the Ministerial Association meeting in 1838. It seems that the ministers responded by saying that Miller's ideas were simply "moonshine." [24] Fitch then related that his courage failed him. When a member of the Ministerial Association asked him a little later as to what he thought of Miller's book, he replied: "I was much overwhelmed with it at first, but now I don't think anything of it." He added immediately, "The truth is, that the fear of man brought me into a snare." [25]

Fitch was not the first, nor the last, minister who in his private study had been deeply impressed with the views of Miller, but who was afraid to stand against ridicule. It was not until near the end of 1841 that Fitch fully and actively associated himself with the Millerite movement. From that time onward he was one of the most aggressive and successful leaders. He spent a large part of his time in Ohio, where he was permanently located. He must have had some standing and ability, for he was given the opportunity of delivering a series of lectures at Oberlin

---
[21] Charles Fitch, *Letter to Reverend J. Litch on the Second Coming of Christ*, p. 6.
[22] *Ibid.*
[23] *Ibid.*, p. 7.
[24] *Ibid.*, p. 6.
[25] *Ibid.*, pp. 8, 9.

College in Ohio, in 1842, on the subject of the second advent, and was invited to deliver a second series in 1843. True, the professors of the college quite generally took issue with him. That was what might be expected. The point is, that his being invited to come one year and then come the next, to a rather prominent educational center, speaks rather well for the character and qualifications of Fitch.

Fitch was the deeply spiritual, pious type. This is clearly revealed in a series of letters written to his wife during the early 1840's. These letters are a rare blending of expressions of love for his wife and for his Lord.

In a letter he wrote to "My dear Brother and Sister Palmer," from Boston, in the summer of 1842 (July 26), he refers to his experience in first coming under conviction concerning the second advent. Being of the very devout type he had had a great burden to preach on the doctrine of holiness, but had found no opportunity to go on a speaking tour through the churches to unburden his heart and to call men everywhere to a higher level of spiritual living. While grieving over this, said he:

"Brother Litch, whom I had never seen, called and said, 'Brother, you need the doctrine of the second advent to put with the doctrine of holiness.' He knew that I had looked at the subject before I left Boston; which was a good while before I saw dear Brother and Sister Palmer. I had indeed looked at it and been overwhelmed with the evidence in proof of it, but laid it wholly aside." [26]

He was referring to his experience in 1838. He added that when Litch brought the second advent to his serious attention—

"I went to the Lord; I read my Bible and all the works that I could obtain. I possessed myself of all the evidences in the case that I could; and then with fasting and prayer I laid them and myself . . . before the Lord, desiring only that the blessed Spirit might guide me into all truth."

But now "came a severe struggle." He had once sacrificed many friends, he explained, because of his fervent belief in holier levels of living; now if he began to preach the second advent, he

---

[26] Manuscript letter, July 26, 1842

could expect only a further alienation of friends. But he did not consider the price too great to pay:

> "So soon as I was ready to come out on the second advent, the door before me was thrown wide open, and I have been wholly unable for the last eight months to meet one half the calls which I have received. Wherever I have been God has been with me. Since the first of December last I have preached as often as every day and about sixty times besides. I have been in all the New England States. Congregations have been large in all places."

A minister who heard of Millerism almost at the same time as Charles Fitch was Josiah Litch. No summary of Millerite leaders would be complete without mention of him. He was one of the very first ministers in New England to preach on the subject of the advent in the setting of Miller's views. Litch was a member of the New England Methodist Episcopal Conference. A copy of Miller's lectures was placed in his hand in 1838. He was sure that there could be little merit in its distinctive views, and, as he wrote the story himself in the third person singular, he recounted:

> "He could scarcely make up his mind to give the book a perusal. No doubt came into his mind but what he could entirely overthrow the whole system in five minutes. . . . However, to gratify a friend, and from a curiosity to know what arguments could be adduced in support of so novel a doctrine, the book was read." [27]

However, the arguments in the book must have been very persuasive, for he continued:

> "Before concluding the book, I became fully satisfied that the arguments were so clear, so simple, and withal so Scriptural, that it was impossible to disprove the position which Mr. Miller had endeavored to establish." [28]

Immediately he was confronted with the questions: "If this doctrine is true, ought you not, as a minister of the gospel, to understand and proclaim it?" "But what if it does not come true—where will my reputation be?" He finally decided:

---

[27] *The Advent Shield and Review*, May, 1844, p. 54.
[28] *Ibid.*, p. 55.

"If it is true that the Lord is coming so soon, the world should know it: if it is not true, it should be discussed, and the error exposed. I believe the Bible teaches the doctrine; and while I believe thus, it is my duty to make it known to the extent of my power. It is a Scriptural subject, and one full of interest; and the discussion of it cannot do harm. These prophecies and periods are in the Bible, and mean something:—if they do not mean this, what do they mean? Thus I reasoned, until the Lord, in a night dream, . . . made me willing to bear reproach for Christ, when I resolved, at any cost, to present the truth on this subject." [29]

He soon began to write and to publish "a series of letters, embodying a synopsis of Mr. Miller's views." This made a forty-eight-page pamphlet, which was printed in 1838. He stated that at this time he knew of no other minister in New England who had advocated these views of the advent except Fitch, who had that year preached two sermons on the subject. Then, said Litch, Fitch fell away from his belief for a time; "thus I was still alone as an advocate of the doctrine." Litch soon brought out a more extensive work, a volume of 204 pages, entitled *The Probability of the Second Coming of Christ About 1843*. This was published about June, 1838. The preface to that book well described the feelings of many Millerite preachers:

"The writer has, in the course of his research on this subject, seen so much which has been literally fulfilled as predicted, that although all he has written on this subject, should prove to have been founded in ignorance, he cannot doubt but that the prophecies have a meaning, and that they were written by direction and influence of the unerring Spirit of the Holy One, and will, in due time, be fulfilled. But at the same time, he must be permitted to express his firm conviction, that these calculations are founded in truth, and will stand the ordeal they must very soon pass—the unerring test of time." [30]

In June, 1841, Litch attended the Methodist Conference at Providence, Rhode Island. He was questioned by the presiding bishop as to his relation to the Millerite doctrine. Litch sought to explain what he really believed on the subject, to which the bishop replied. "Do you think that is Methodism?" Litch

---
[29] *Ibid.*
[30] *Ibid.*, p. 56.

responded, "I do. At least it is not contrary to the articles of religion of the Methodist Episcopal Church." After extended discussion "the conference came to the conclusion that I held nothing contrary to Methodism, although I went in some points beyond it. They then at my own request granted me a location and thus left me at liberty to devote my whole time to the dissemination of this important subject, and if it is heresy, they have taken a measure of the responsibility for it." [31] On second thought, however, said Litch:

"I came to the conclusion to dissolve my connection with the itinerant ministry of the M. E. Church, with whom I had labored in sweetest fellowship for eight years of my life. . . . Nothing but a solemn conviction of duty to God and my fellow men, to throw my entire influence into the enterprise in which *we* are engaged, could have induced me to take the step." [32]

It was at this time that Litch became an agent for the Millerite publications and an associate with Himes on the editorial staff of *Signs of the Times*.

---

[31] *Signs of the Times*, Sept. 1, 1841, p. 85.
[32] *Ibid.*, pp. 85, 86.

CHAPTER 13

Other Millerite Spokesmen

IN ADDITION TO THE SMALL GROUP of men who might be described as the initial leaders of the movement, who were really outstanding, there were a number of other ministers and lecturers who were more or less prominent. Among these was George Storrs. Though he did not join the movement until the fall of 1842, his name appears more or less frequently in the Millerite papers from that time onward. He was a Methodist preacher, having joined "the Methodist traveling connection in 1825." He continued in this line of labor until 1836, when he became a "local preacher, but traveled more extensively than ever." And what was one of the principal themes of his preaching and lecturing? We give the answer in the words of his daughter, Hattie W. Storrs:

"For three years he spent most of his time lecturing and preaching on the subject of slavery, in a time which tried men's souls; as nearly the whole Methodist E. Church was hostile to an agitation of that subject. That hostility manifested itself specially through the bishops, who endeavored by every possible means to suppress the discussion of the subject. That opposition convinced Mr. Storrs that *individual* responsibility was the true ground to occupy, and he could not submit to leave his responsibility in the hands of bishops, nor any body of men, however good they might be. . . . He withdrew from said church entirely, in 1840, after a connection with it of sixteen years." [1]

Once again we have the picture of the courageous individualist, the kind of man who thought the cause of right much more important than his own reputation.

---

[1] "Memoir," *Bible Examiner*, March, 1880, p. 399.

Little further need be said regarding Storrs. He had some ability in writing as well as in speaking. Early in 1843 he published, on his own responsibility, *Bible Examiner.* His idea was to bring out an issue occasionally, as need might require. But with more or less regularity it was published until the time of his death, in 1880.

Storrs had one distinctive view of theology which sometimes prevented him from having the closest fellowship with other Millerite ministers. He did not believe in an ever-burning hell. He considered such a doctrine a blot on the character of God. He believed that all who do not accept Christ will be finally annihilated, and that only those who accept Christ receive immortality and an endless life beyond the resurrection.*

The prominent Millerite paper, *The Midnight Cry,* had as its editor Nathaniel Southard. Previous to his connection with *The Midnight Cry* he had been the editor of a weekly paper called *Youth's Cabinet,* and for a time he had served as acting editor of the *Emancipator,* an antislavery paper. For years before he became interested in Millerism he was concerned in the promotion "of temperance, antislavery, and education." [2]

There were others whose names appeared in the Millerite papers quite frequently but of whom scarcely anything can be said because of the scantiness of the record. There was Henry Dana Ward, chairman of the first General Conference of Christians Expecting the Advent of the Lord Jesus Christ, held

---

[2] See Isaac C. Wellcome, *History of the Second Advent Message,* p. 272.

* Storrs held this belief before he became a Millerite and sought to continue his promotion of it after he came into the movement. He was given space in the Millerite papers for an extended presentation of his view, which speaks well for the charity of spirit of his associates, almost all of whom disagreed with him. The rejoinders to his view, so far as the Millerite leaders expressed themselves in print, were very temperate, even though decided. The perplexity which some of them felt because of the promotion of what they thought were heretical views, is revealed in a letter from I. E. Jones to Miller, which opens thus:

"I had the pleasure of seeing Brother Litch and Brother Whiting last week, and the last, again this week, and they think as do our Boston brethren, Himes, Bliss and Hale, that something ought to be done to separate our influence from Brother Storrs' view of the end of the wicked; for, as it now is, he virtually wields from our silence, the whole, or almost the whole advent influence." Jones felt that the matter had "been let alone quite too long." He informed Miller that "two sheets are to be issued week after next, one at Boston, the other at Philadelphia, giving our views, independent of advent papers. A kind and conciliatory course will be taken, and may God direct and bless."—*Manuscript letter, I. E. Jones to Miller, dated "New York, April 6, 1844."*

in Boston in 1840. He was a graduate of Harvard, and became an Episcopal minister in 1844. He believed in the doctrine of the nearness of the advent, but not in the setting of any specific time. He evidently became less and less prominent in the movement as it drew toward a climax. We infer that by the absence of his name from reports in the Millerite papers toward the close.

N. N. Whiting, a Baptist minister, who in 1845 became editor of *The Midnight Cry* under its new name, the *Morning Watch,* is quite frequently mentioned in the publications of the movement. He must have been a man of exceptional learning for he had made a new translation of the New Testament, under the auspices of the Baptist denomination.[3]

Brief reference has already been made in an earlier chapter to Joseph Marsh, as an editor of the *Christian Palladium,* an organ of the Christian Church. He held what might be considered an important position in that religious body. He served as an editor from the time of the founding of the journal until he resigned twelve years later to cast in his lot with the Millerite movement. On November 23, 1842, he wrote this brief note to the *Signs of the Times,* that reveals the resoluteness of his decision and his realization that it might mean trouble for him:

"I am fully convinced as to the time, and mean to proclaim it fearlessly from the pulpit and the press. My course is fixed—let the consequences follow. I fear not the result. God will defend His cause." [4]

From the *Palladium* office he wrote Miller in the summer of 1843:

"The *Palladium* is now in other hands. I have the privilege of writing only one third of the editorial. Nearly every other communication on the coming of Christ is shut out of the paper. Oh! Can it be possible that professed *'Christians'* should be so unwilling to hear of the return of *Him* whose *name* they bear?" [5]

---
[3] See *Signs of the Times,* March 15, 1843, p. 9.
[4] *Signs of the Times,* Dec. 21, 1842, p. 105.
[5] Manuscript letter, Aug. 17, 1843.

Two months after this he completely severed his connection with the *Christian Palladium* and with the activities of the Christian Church.[6]

His daughter, writing about forty-five years later, reveals a little of the opposition that confronted her father. He had been a respected citizen in Union Mills, New York, where the *Christian Palladium* was published. He was not only an editor on this journal but also "pastor of the only congregation in the place" and postmaster. His daughter was about seven years old at the time he accepted Millerism. Though in looking back over the years she viewed the movement as a delusion, she wrote sympathetically of her father and his relationship to it:

"My first remembrance of the 'tidings' is hearing the doctrine ridiculed. Everybody was laughing at my father's believing what he did, calling him a Millerite, and asking to see our ascension robes. I can remember a consciousness that we had become *peculiar*—a thrust-out feeling which was very painful, a conviction that my father was unjustly and wickedly treated, and that by those he had believed to be his friends. . . . The excitement in the little settlement was something to be remembered. In the hail of ridicule and persecution my father's faith intensified, of course. He could bear ridicule better than the pleading of near friends. We children heard it all, lived it all—what the committee said, what the congregation said, why So-and-so would not hear him preach his farewell sermon, and who had been converted to his new gospel, with all the worldly gossip about the struggle for the post office and the editorship. Our going away from X——— to live in a great city, the little while longer that time should last, was a merciful diversion for us who saw a martyr's halo around our father's head."[7]

Of their moving from their old home, and of the missionary fervor of the converts, Marsh's daughter wrote:

"February, 1844, saw us moving away from X———, some of my father's old parishioners, converts to Millerism, carrying us and our goods in their big sleighs as far as Utica—a long journey, the weather bitter cold, the roads blocked with snow. It was a 'shovel brigade,' and to cheer our hearts, father and the brethren would sing of 'the coming' when they could.

---

[6] See *The Midnight Cry,* Nov. 16, 1843, pp. 108, 109.
[7] Jane Marsh Parker, "A Little Millerite," *Century Magazine,* December, 1886, pp. 311, 314.

They left leaflets at many of the houses we passed—warnings and expositions of prophecy—and father preached at the inns where we stopped at night." [8]

When they reached their new abode and the landlord inquired how long they would want the house they were renting, her father replied calmly, "Until the Lord comes." The daughter continued:

" 'If time lasts' was the condition of every anticipation and promise. Father brought little furniture for the new home, only what was needed for the free hospitality of a 'pilgrims' hotel.' The walls were covered with charts illustrating apocalyptic and prophetical visions." [9]

It was not only ministers and adults in general who needed great moral courage to ally themselves with Millerism; their children needed it also, as Marsh's daughter wrote:

"There were notable saints among those Millerite children. 'Millerite! Millerite! When are you going up?' was shouted at us from the marketplace. We were, in a sense, isolated—not considered safe comrades for children whose parents were on the rock of respectable orthodoxy." [10]

The daughter made this brief comment on the leaders of the movement:

"The leaders in Millerism were not illiterate men, but Bible students, who, as a rule, had filled pulpits of comparative eminence before 'going into Millerism.' " [11]

In the next chapter we shall hear something of a Millerite minister, Samuel S. Snow. At a meeting on the evening of December 31, 1843, at the tabernacle in Boston, he related briefly the story of his life. Until his thirty-fifth year he was "a settled unbeliever in the Bible." In fact, for a time he was the most militant type of infidel, serving as an agent for the *Boston Investigator,* an avowedly infidel paper.* In 1839 a peddler sold to his brother a book written by Miller, and thus

---

[8] *Ibid.,* p. 314.
[9] *Ibid.*
[10] *Ibid.*
[11] *Ibid.,* p. 315.

* This literary weekly, during the early 1840's, boldly announced in the subtitle on the front page its advocacy of infidelity. From 1842 to 1844 the following subtitle was carried; "Devoted to the Protection and Development of Infidel Principles,"

there came under his eye a discussion of the Bible entirely different from anything he had ever read before. Said he, "I saw the perfect harmony between Daniel and the Revelation, and the history which is a perfect fulfillment of these revelations." The reading of this book resulted in his conversion, and in the fall of 1840 he united with a Congregational church. At the Millerite camp meeting at East Kingston, New Hampshire, in 1842, he fully dedicated himself to the work of promoting the movement. Unquestionably Millerism drew its ministers from a variety of sources.[12]

In attendance at another Millerite camp meeting in 1842 was a young man, James White. He had previously attended second advent meetings, but at this camp meeting he was fully persuaded that he must go out to preach. He would not be described as one of the Millerite leaders, but rather one of that large company of lecturers and ministers who went from place to place to promote the doctrine of the "advent near." * He had been the teacher of a country school. His experiences, which he wrote out in detail some years later, provide an excellent illustration of the fervor and zeal that prompted young men without ministerial training to mount the lecture platform in behalf of Millerism. James White was only twenty-one years old when he attended that camp meeting in Exeter, Maine.

What could a penniless young country schoolteacher do to advance the movement?

"I had neither horse, saddle, bridle, nor money, yet felt that I must go. I had used my past winter's earnings in necessary clothing, in attending second advent meetings, and in the purchase of books and the chart. But my father offered me the use of a horse for the winter, and Elder Polley gave me a saddle with both pads torn off, and several pieces of an old bridle. I gladly accepted these, and cheerfully placed the saddle on a beech log and nailed on the pads, fastened the pieces of the bridle together with malleable nails, folded my chart, with a few pamphlets on the subject of the advent,

---

[12] See *The Midnight Cry*, March 7, 1844, p. 260.

* The activities of James White are of more than ordinary interest and significance, because he later became one of the leaders in a religious body that grew out of Millerism, the Seventh-day Adventist denomination.

over my breast, snugly buttoned up in my coat, and left my father's house on horseback." [13]

He had only a few prepared lectures when he started out, but he found that as he spoke in each place he could begin to divide his subjects. The result was that he constantly added to the total of his lectures. He early discovered that the preaching of the prophecies brought to the hearers a deep conviction of heart. When he had completed a series of seven lectures in one place, "sixty arose for prayers." He did not know what to do. How could he carry on into the days ahead with a revival series of sermons? "My little pond of thought, in the course of seven lectures, had run out." [14] He called on his brother, who was a minister, to come to the town. The result was that many were baptized and a large church was organized.

The only way of travel was by horseback. And in midwinter in Maine that is a heroic way, especially when one is "thinly clad" and must travel "more than a hundred miles." [15]

He tells of a mob that surrounded the meetinghouse in one place where he was preaching, and hurled snowballs through the windows. He kept on preaching, changing from a lecture to an exhortation to men to repent. The mob finally quieted down. A revival followed. "I closed with benediction, took my chart and Bible, and made my way out through the subdued crowd." [16]

At another place even the "school children committed to memory all my texts, and almost everywhere you might hear them repeating" the prophetic statement in Daniel 8:14. [17]

Millerite ministers gave little thought to their own comfort. They were made of sterner stuff than that. As the sun was setting, White completed a series of lectures in a certain town. There was no time to rest. He was scheduled to speak that night at a place sixteen miles away:

---

[13] James White, *Life Incidents*, p. 73.
[14] *Ibid.*, p. 74.
[15] *Ibid.*, p. 75.
[16] *Ibid.*, p. 79.
[17] *Ibid.*, p. 85.

"My clothes were wet with sweat. I needed rest. But there was my next appointment. The people would be together in about an hour, and I had sixteen miles to go. So I hastily said farewell to the friends with whom and for whom I had labored, mounted my horse and galloped away toward Lisbon Plains, in a stinging cold February evening. I was chilled, but there was no time to call and warm. My damp clothing nearly froze to me, but I galloped on." [18]

He recorded that when he got up to speak his chattering teeth cut off some of his words, but that he soon warmed up and felt great freedom in speaking. In early April, 1843, White was riding his horse over drifts of snow higher than the fencetops. Then:

"Rain came on, and the firmly trodden drifts became soft, so that my horse with my weight upon him would frequently sink to his body in the snow. I rode all day with my feet out of the stirrups, and as he would plunge into the snow, I would instantly slide off and relieve him of my weight, that he might better struggle out, or if he could not do this alone, assist him by lifting where most needed." [19]

He must have given real evidence of a call to the ministry, because when he returned to his home town in 1843 he "received ordination to the work of the ministry from the hands of ministers of the Christian denomination" of which he was a member.[20]

During part of the summer of '43 he "labored in the hay-field to earn clothing for the winter." [21]

When he returned to one place where he had lectured formerly, a minister who doubtless wished to make sport of his preaching on the second advent of Christ, exclaimed, "Why, Mr. White, are you yet in the land of the living?"

His prompt reply was, "No, sir, I am in the land of the dying, but at the coming of the Lord I expect to go to the land of the living." [22]

---

[18] *Ibid.*, p. 92.
[19] *Ibid.*, p. 97.
[20] *Ibid.*, p. 104.
[21] *Ibid.*
[22] *Ibid.*, p. 108.

That was typical of the Millerite viewpoint. They were not morbid men. They were radiantly happy. They were sure that the future was going to provide them with release from "the land of the dying." Nothing would be farther from the truth than to picture the Millerite preachers as sad-eyed, mournful, melancholy, and filled with foreboding of impending doom. They were the very opposite. They were noted for their singing of advent hymns. They looked constantly for a better country. They were strangely akin to the Christians described in the New Testament, who looked forward to the second advent as providing the happy ending to an unhappy world.

White well set forth in one terse sentence the conviction that drove him forward: "God forbid that I should fold my arms in lazy-lock while sinners are sinking to eternal night." [23]

Another Millerite lecturer, writing of the hardships of his travels, reported this in a letter to the *Signs of the Times:*

"I have traveled in the forty days, two hundred and seventy-five miles, had my beast fall twice, while on horseback, in sloughs; and once in the midst of Kennebec River while fording, where the current was considerably rapid, and up to the stirrups. As I was cast into the river, the horse fell upon me; but I escaped unhurt, with the exception of a lame ankle, on which I was unable to bear my weight for some days. But none of these things moved me. I could hobble with the assistance of a staff into the desk, happy in having the privilege still of arousing a slumbering church to a sense of the immediate 'appearing of the great God, and our Saviour Jesus Christ.' " [24]

In the city of Haverhill, Massachusetts, lived the influential Hale family, engaged in the milling business. Ezekiel Hale, Jr., it will be recalled, was the chairman of the committee that selected the site of the first Millerite camp meeting, about ten miles north of Haverhill, at East Kingston, New Hampshire. Hale was one of that number of Millerite promoters who would not be described as a minister nor yet perhaps even as a lecturer. He was rather a businessman, who, having accepted the Millerite

---

[23] Letter, March 4, 1843, in *Signs of the Times,* March 22, 1843, p. 21.
[24] Letter from Joel Spaulding, Nov. 24, 1842, in *Signs of the Times,* Dec. 14, 1842, p. 103.

beliefs, turned his energies and resources in such ways as he could to the advancement of the movement. The planning of that camp meeting was an illustration of his activities. He also published certain literature.

Although he hardly occupied a prominent position in the movement, there is more known about his life than about that of almost any other of the group who assisted Miller. This is because of a suit in equity that he instituted in 1845, to recover certain properties from his own son. He had deeded these to his son in anticipation of the end of the world. But there was involved in the transaction the element of fraud and deception, the father charged. Sworn testimony was taken from seventy-nine persons in connection with the suit. Somewhere in the testimony of almost all the deponents is found a statement regarding the temperament, character, and activities of Ezekiel Hale, Jr. Though the testimony is sworn, it is unconsciously colored by the fact that the one testifying is either speaking for the defendant or for the plaintiff.*

He was a keen businessman, building upon the thrift and industry of his father. He entered the War of 1812 as a private and later became a captain. When the first temperance society was organized in Haverhill in 1828, Hale was not only a member but an officer. Some religious differences arose in the Congregational church of which he was a member, and he with several others withdrew and built a new church. He did not believe that there should be delay in holding services again. By resourcefulness and driving energy he saw that the new building was sufficiently constructed within fifteen days to permit of services being held within it.

In 1839 Miller held a series of lectures in Haverhill, then again early in 1840. Hale attended and became a Millerite. Soon thereafter, according to the testimony of some whose affidavits are found in the legal record, Hale became less and less interested in his milling business, and more and more

---

* These 79 depositions are found in a printed report of the case that fills 591 pages.

absorbed in Millerism. Some testified that he was not so cheerful as before; others testified the opposite. It would be easy to see how there could be differing viewpoints on this. He was away from home frequently, attending Millerite meetings, and was constantly reasoning and arguing in behalf of the second advent. One of those testifying said of him: "He always reasoned well, as the people who believed the Second Advent did." [25]

Some thought that he had now become credulous, whereas formerly he was very incredulous. Anyone who did not believe in Millerism would inevitably conclude that a Millerite was credulous, especially if he gave any attention to dreams, as some said he did. However, a hundred years ago there were many besides Millerites who gave significance to dreams.

Hale gave very liberally to the advent cause. Particular mention is made in the testimony of a hundred dollars that he gave toward paying for the great tent that was voted at the East Kingston camp meeting. He is credited, in the deposition of George O. Harmon, of Haverhill, as having "originated" the idea of having the great tent constructed.[26]

He is also credited with printing a chart, and a copy of it appears in the legal record.

In 1842 Charles Fitch was located in Haverhill as pastor of the Winter Street Church. Hale usually attended that church.

Mr. Harmon, in his deposition, stated that he himself was a Millerite and an abolitionist. As to Hale, he said:

"I think he was favorable to the non-resistant views soon after they were advocated by Mr. Garrison. I do not think that he ever fully embraced them or joined a non-resistant society. He has for a considerable time been a friend of Sylvester Graham, and has embraced his views as to diet. He entertained these as early as 1840, and still continues to entertain them." [27]

Another deponent testified that Hale "was a great antislavery man, and used to take much pains to circulate tracts on that subject; sent me many; he was always a zealous man in

---
[25] Suit in equity, *Ezekiel Hale, Jr., vs. E. J. M. Hale*, p. 79.
[26] *Ibid.*, p. 206.
[27] *Ibid.*, p. 212.

anything he undertook. . . . He was much interested in the temperance cause at one time, also." [28]

A cousin of Hale's included this statement in his deposition:

"His [Hale's] appearance seemed to be that of an insane man, in regard to the business of this world. His Millerism gave a peculiar coloring to his appearance and conversation." [29]

However, a printer in Haverhill testified that Hale "appeared to me to have as much capacity for doing business as men in general. . . . There was no want of sharpness or shrewdness in his bargains with me, though he generally trusted to me." [30] Perhaps the cousin had thought Hale a bit out of his head because he had no concern for material possessions for himself, as repeated testimony in the suit reveals. The printer told of having printed, for Hale, some notices for a Graham lecture, and a temperance lecture, and a work on Millerism.

The deposition of the wife of the plaintiff's brother stated that she had "daily intercourse" with the family, and made this comment on Hale:

"I don't recollect of anything particularly different from his previous conduct of the ordinary transactions of life. His mind was very much occupied on the subject of Millerism, but he attended to little affairs for the comfort and convenience of his family, as much as at any time; and I remember his making the remark that we should attend to our everyday matters, just as particularly as if we did not anticipate the immediate coming of the Lord, or words to that effect." [31]

His sister-in-law, however, was testifying for the defendant, who wished to prove that his father was in every way normal in his actions and speech and thus competent to transfer his property. Perhaps we might come nearer to the truth by drawing a line midway between the testimony of those who said that he was just as much engaged in business as before, and those who said that he gave it over completely. We might draw the

---

[28] *Ibid.*, p. 584.
[29] *Ibid.*, pp. 285, 286.
[30] *Ibid.*, p. 502.
[31] *Ibid.*, p. 561.

same middle line between those who testified that he quite forgot about the interests of his family, and those who testified that he was as solicitous as ever regarding them. It is hardly possible to believe that a man could become swallowed up in a great movement like Millerism without its affecting in some degree his interest in his ordinary pursuits, and his interest in his family. Even our Lord declared that the family must be secondary to service for Him.

This sketch of Hale is important, because it provides us with the only instance where we have a description of a Millerite in terms of sworn legal testimony, and by people who were testifying while their memories were still fresh. The wild stories about Millerites that filled the newspapers at that time, and have increasingly filled the air for a hundred years since are not sworn statements, nor is there any opportunity of resurrecting their originators and making them swear to their statements. If this were possible, how disastrous it would be to many a "good" story. But with Ezekiel Hale, Jr., we have both sides of the story, the testimony for defendant and plaintiff. And those who testified could be described, as a grandnephew of Ezekiel Hale well described them, as a "Who's Who" of Haverhill.*

A pioneer in the temperance movement, a sympathizer with Garrison, and a supporter of the diet reforms of Graham—Hale fits the picture that is now firmly fixed in our minds of the typical Millerite promoter. There was contempt for convention, a willingness to support new causes and to explore new fields of thought and reform. Such men might not be easy to live with, but we live much easier today because this type of men lived before us. We do not argue from this fact of the courageous individualism of the Millerite leaders that there was worth in the Miller-

---

* The "Bill of Complaint" by Ezekiel Hale, Jr., in the opening pages of the legal report on the case, carries the names of none others than Daniel Webster and Rufus Choate. Notable legal counsel indeed! According to a grandnephew, Henry Hale Gilman, who wrote a story of the incident long years afterward, there were six hundred copies of the legal report printed. He adds that the Hale family were so embarrassed by the public airing of this controversy between father and son that they bought up and destroyed all except two copies. In 1943 one of these copies came into the possession of the Haverhill Public Library. (See Henry Hale Gilman, *The Mill and the Millerite*, p. 13.)

ite movement. That must be established on other grounds and with other evidence. We present the picture of the character and courage of these men simply to show that the Millerite spokesmen were drawn from the ranks of that rare class in society who are best known for their independent thinking, their moral courage, and the contribution which they, through their reforms, have made to the world. Millerism does not suffer by an examination of the quality of the men most responsible for its progress.

There were two main classes of Millerite spokesmen—ministers and lecturers. Under the title of ministers came those who had a bona fide ministerial background. Under the title of lecturers came those who were drawn from the farm, the workbench, the office, to speak in public in behalf of the advent near.

In the spring of 1844 Litch declared that those who were preaching in behalf of Millerism were drawn from the following churches:

"Protestant Episcopal, Methodist Episcopal, Methodist Protestant, Primitive Methodist, Wesleyan Methodist, Close Communion Baptist, and Open Communion Baptist, Calvinistic and Arminian Baptists, Presbyterians, Old and New School Congregationalists, Old and New School Lutheran, Dutch Reformed, etc., etc." [32]

A year later Miller, in looking at the movement in retrospect, estimated that "about two hundred ministers" embraced his views and proclaimed them, and that "about 500 public lecturers" were engaged in speaking. As to the number of advent congregations and believers, he declared: "In nearly a thousand places advent congregations have been raised up, numbering, as near as I can estimate, some fifty thousand believers." [33]

Neither Miller nor his associates made extravagant claims as to the number of adherents.* That was left for others to do.

---

[32] *The Advent Shield and Review*, May, 1844, p. 90.
[33] William Miller, *Apology and Defence*, p. 22.

* We believe that the estimate of fifty thousand is a very conservative one. If only the membership of well-defined "advent congregations" is reckoned, as is apparently the case in this statement by Miller, then fifty thousand may be a relatively correct total. In the very nature of the case a loose-knit movement, which stirred the whole country, must have had many adherents who did not belong to any particular advent congregation. Then, too, there was the "mixed multitude" who were more or less impressed by the preaching, and who

The public press of the time occasionally quoted very large figures, and the figures have not shrunk in the retelling, but men and women paid too great a price in ridicule to take up easily with Millerism. In view of that price, we marvel, not that the membership failed to go much higher, but that it went as high as it did. Particularly impressive is the fact that two hundred ministers risked all their future ministerial standing to give their support to the movement. It must have made a tremendous appeal to their hearts and minds.

How great was the price that both laymen and ministers paid will be revealed more fully in the following chapters.

---

displayed at least a surface loyalty to it. How great the true total of Millerites was, will ever remain an insoluble statistical problem. We believe we are warranted in assuming that it was definitely more than fifty thousand.

CHAPTER 14

"Behold, the Bridegroom Cometh"

WE PICK UP THE THREAD OF our story again in the spring of 1844. The year of the end of the world had ended, but Millerism had not. The predictions of the Millerites had failed, but so also had the predictions of their enemies, who had confidently forecast that when 1843 came to a close the Millerites would become infidels, burn their Bibles, and do numerous other ungodly things, because of their disappointment. But the Millerites did none of these. Though some who had been only lukewarm in the movement fell away from it, many maintained both their faith and their fervor. They were ready to attribute the disappointment to some minor error in calculating chronology.

The public press, both secular and religious, had much to say in the late spring and early summer of 1844 about the Millerites' renouncing their faith. As with most of the stories that had appeared in the press in the preceding years, these also were quite groundless. Perhaps the wish was father to the thought. *The Advent Herald* devotes a column to such stories.[1]

In fact, it was right in the springtime, when disappointment appeared certain, that the Millerites began to adopt a distinctive name. It seemed that they were to be in this world for a little while yet—they knew not how long—and they most certainly expected to continue as a well-defined movement until the great day. Hence, why not adopt a name that would properly describe them? They had been known up to this time only as Millerites. The editor of *The Advent Herald* explained that they had "no

---

[1] *The Advent Herald,* July 17, 1844, p. 187.

particular objection to being called 'Millerites,' the current name applied to us by those who are in the habit of using nicknames, in speaking of their neighbors; but there are many of our number who do not believe with Mr. Miller in several important particulars.* It is also his special wish that we should not be distinguished by that appellation." [2] The most exact title or name they could assume, the editor concluded, would be Adventists. The name "marks the real ground of difference between us and the great body of our opponents." He explained this statement thus:

> "We are fully aware that they [the opponents] have endeavored to keep the question of time before the public as the obnoxious and heretical point, (and we fully believe the time to be as distinctly revealed as any other part of the subject. On that account we have defended it, and thus it has become so prominent,) still that is not, nor has it ever been, the only, or the main question in dispute. In fact, there is a greater difference between us and our opposers on the *nature of the events* predicted, than upon the interpretation of the prophetic periods, or their termination." [3]

The very fact that Millerism was more than a point of time, as this quotation from *The Advent Herald* reiterates, explains in part why the Millerite movement did not automatically disintegrate and disappear with the disappointment on the time element of the preaching in the spring of 1844.

Then, too, as we have already mentioned, the Millerites felt that the disappointment could probably be explained on the ground that there was some minor error in chronology, for chronology has always been a field of debate for historians.

Even before this uncertainty began to trouble the Millerites, a new date was already being suggested. Samuel S. Snow, in *The Midnight Cry,* as early as February, 1844, put forth the view that the great time prophecy of 2300 prophetic days (Dan. 8:13,

---

[2] *Ibid.*, March 20, 1844, p. 53.
[3] *Ibid.*

* As stated in an earlier chapter, we use the term "Millerite," after the passage of a hundred years, not as a nickname, but simply as the most obvious, and the only all-comprehensive term, to describe the movement that developed under the special leadership of William Miller.

14), which is at the heart of all Millerite reckoning, would not end until the autumn of 1844. We need not here go into the details of his reasoning, though it should be said that his arguments were not intended to alter in any way the basic premises of Millerite belief, but only to make more exact the calculations.[4]

Snow's letter in *The Midnight Cry* was prefaced with an editorial note which expressed serious doubt as to the correctness of his reasoning. That was the position generally taken by the Millerite leaders for some time, but the leaven of Snow's idea was working, and after the spring disappointment it naturally received more serious attention, though still actively opposed by many of the prominent spokesmen.

Thus matters stood at the opening of the summer of 1844. For two years, now, the summer had proved the golden time for evangelistic activity and promotion, the ideal time for camp meetings. The Millerites saw no reason why they should not go forth again to proclaim to all men the soon coming of Christ.

Miller and Himes set out on a tour west, which was to take them as far as Ohio. About the middle of July, and just before starting on this trip, Himes described what he felt was the general attitude of believers in relation to the advent:

"I have never witnessed a stronger, or more active faith. Indeed, the faith and confidence of the brethren in the prophetic word was never stronger. I find few, if any who ever believed on Bible *evidence,* that are at all shaken in the faith; while others are embracing our views."[5]

Of the interest in the city of Philadelphia, for example, Himes wrote after a brief visit there the middle of July:

"The trying crisis is past, and the cause is on the rise in this city. The calls for lectures in the vicinity, were never more pressing than now. The minister in charge of the Ebenezer station, Kensington, (Protestant Methodist,) has just come out on the doctrine in full. He has been *driven out,* and many have followed him. They have set up a meeting, and there is a considerable interest to hear on the subject."[6]

---
[4] See letter from S. S. Snow, Feb. 16, 1844, in *The Midnight Cry,* Feb. 22, 1844, pp. 243, 244.
[5] *The Advent Herald,* July 17, 1844, p. 188.
[6] *Ibid.,* July 24, 1844, p. 200.

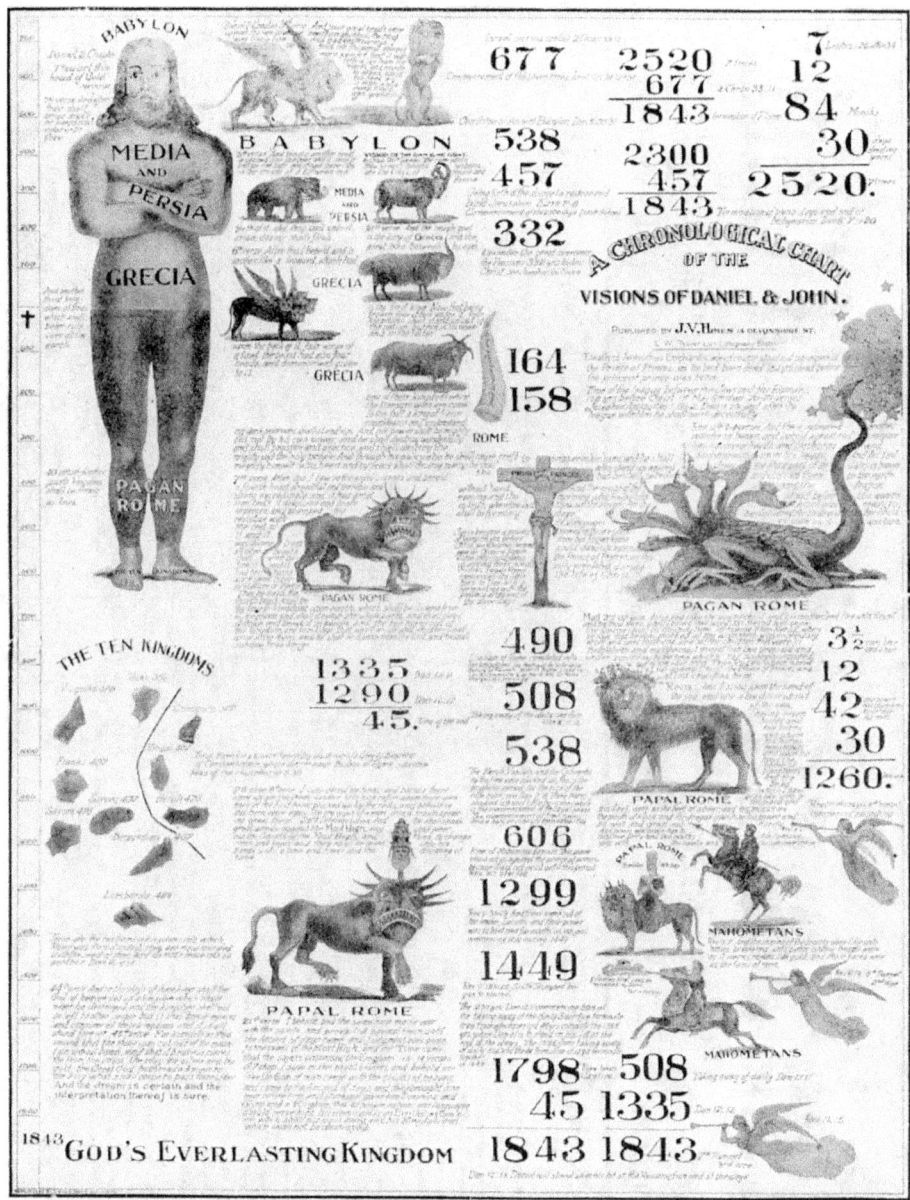

The 1843 prophetic chart. This was the chart originally designed by Charles Fitch and Apollos Hale, of which 300 copies were ordered printed by action of the Millerite general conference held in Boston in May, 1842. This chart, prominently displayed at Millerite meetings everywhere, was one of the most distinguishing marks of the movement. After the failure of their advent expectations in 1843 the Millerites had to revise their chart.

The Second Advent of Christ.

Vol. 3.　　　　C. FITCH, Editor.　　　　CLEVELAND, WEDNESDAY, JULY 26, 1843.　　　　T. H. SMEAD, Publisher.　　　　No. 2.

[Please Read and Circulate.]

"COME OUT OF HER, MY PEOPLE,"
A SERMON, BY C. FITCH.

Rev. 18th chapter, 1 verse.

"And after these things I saw another angel come down from heaven, having great power, and the earth was lightened with his glory. And he cried mightily with a strong voice, saying, Babylon the great is fallen, is fallen, and is become the habitation of devils, and the hold of every foul spirit, and a cage of every unclean and hateful bird. For all nations have drunk of the wine of the wrath of her fornication, and the kings of the earth have committed fornication with her, and the merchants of the earth are waxed rich through the abundance of her delicacies.

And I heard another voice from heaven saying, Come out of her my people, that ye be not partakers of her sins, and that ye receive not of her plagues. For her sins have reached unto heaven, and God hath remembered her iniquities."

21st verse. "And a mighty angel took up a stone like a great millstone, and cast it into the sea, saying, Thus with violence shall that great city Babylon be thrown down, and shall be found no more at all."

Rev. 14: 6. "And I saw another angel fly in the midst of Heaven, having the everlasting gospel to preach unto them that dwell on the earth, and to every nation, and kingdom and tongue and people; saying with a loud voice, Fear God and give glory to Him,

every spirit that confesseth that Jesus Christ is come in the flesh, is of God: and every spirit that cometh not that Jesus Christ is come in the flesh, is not of God: AND THIS IS THAT SPIRIT OF ANTICHRIST whereof ye have heard that it should come, and even now already is it in the world." 2 John, verse 7, "For many deceivers are entered into the world, who confess not that Jesus Christ is come in the flesh. This is a deceiver AND AN ANTICHRIST."

It must be admitted that a spirit which is of God, while it confesses that Jesus Christ is come in the flesh, will readily assent and conform to all the objects for which He came. To confess with the lips that Jesus Christ is come in the flesh, and yet to be opposed in heart and life to the objects for which he came, is certainly to be Antichrist. The spirit therefore which is of God, while it confesses that Jesus Christ is come in the flesh, will cordially embrace, and heartily enter into all the objects for which he was thus manifested. All else must be Antichrist. What then was the end for which Jesus Christ was manifested in the flesh? Luke 24: 45, "Then opened he their understandings that they might understand the scriptures, and said unto them, Thus it is written, and thus it behoved Christ to suffer and to rise from the dead the third day; and that repentance and remission of sins should be preached in His name among all nations, beginning at Jerusalem." This was one object of Christ's coming in the flesh; and when Peter, 2d Peter 3d chap., speaks of the new earth wherein dwelleth righteousness, rebuked Him for foretelling

his ascension, personal, so surely his coming must be. As he has taught, in the 19th of Luke, he is now gone into a far country to receive to himself a kingdom and to return; and "he shall so come again in like manner as ye have seen him go into heaven." In the 9th Ps. we read, "Once have I sworn by my Holiness that I will not lie unto David; his seed shall endure forever, and his throne as the sun before me. It shall be established forever as the moon, and as a faithful witness in heaven."

Then Jesus Christ has come in the flesh to sit on David's throne. he is to sit upon it personally and forever. For at the sounding of the seventh trumpet, "THERE SHALL be heard great voices in heaven saying, "THE KINGDOMS OF THIS WORLD are become the kingdoms of our Lord and of his Christ, and he shall reign forever and ever." "He shall have dominion also from sea to sea, and from the river to the ends of the earth." Ps. 72: 8. He said then at the bar of Pilate, "My kingdom is not of this world;" and for the reason that the earth which now is, is kept in store, reserved unto fire against the day of judgment and perdition of ungodly men; and as Christ's kingdom can have no end, God has promised a new earth wherein dwelleth righteousness, and has said, "As the new heavens and the new earth which I will make shall remain before me, so shall your seed and your name remain. See 65th and 66th chap. of Isaiah and 2d Peter 3d chap. In the new earth wherein dwelleth righteousness, the saints will sit upon

the church of God, have always, when they could, looked for support to the secular power, instead of trusting God to maintain them. Hence God accuses them of committing fornication with the kings of the earth: and the Romish church is called the great whore that did corrupt the nations; drawing them from the worship and service of the true God, to support her in her nameless and horrid abominations. But,

2d. Is the Catholic church only, opposed to the personal reign of Christ? What shall we say of Protestant Christendom in this respect? Among all the sects into which the Protestant church is divided, where is one that is not decidedly hostile to the Bible truth that Christ has been raised up to sit personally on David's throne? Indeed where has such a notion originated, as that Christ is to have only a spiritual reign? There is nothing in the Bible that furnishes the least shadow of a foundation for such an idea. Peter has however given us a clue to the origin of the very thing. 2 Peter 3: 3, "For the time will come when they will not endure sound doctrine, but after their own lusts shall they heap to themselves teachers, having itching ears, and they shall turn away their ears from the truth, and shall be turned to fables." This is at present true of all sects in Protestant Christendom. The sound, scriptural doctrine of the personal reign of Christ on David's throne cannot now be endured, and hence the teachers which the various

---

The sermon, "Come Out of Her, My People," by Charles Fitch, marked the real beginning of the Millerite exodus from the churches. (See pages 148, 149.)

From Troy, New York, Himes wrote a week later to describe a camp meeting held near that city, at which "it was estimated that 4,000 were present on the Sabbath." Then he added: "We had invitations to lecture in many places, which we could not supply." [7]

On the twenty-fourth of July, Himes wrote from Rochester that he was lecturing to large audiences. He was so impressed with the opportunities that this trip was revealing that he declared:

"We want one thousand faithful men, 'full of faith and the Holy Spirit,' to enter the field east, west, north, and south, to 'give meat in due season,' —the warning voice. Who will forsake all for Christ and go?" [8]

This hardly looks like Millerism disintegrating, or the interest dying out.

On July 31 Miller wrote from Buffalo to correct the interpretation that had been given to his words in the springtime when he admitted he had made an error in calculation. He wanted all men to know that he had not cast away his confidence in God or His Word. "I am now waiting every hour for what I then looked for," he declared. He continued to insist that the only basis on which he would change his thinking would be the basis of better Scriptural interpretation or understanding, and not on the basis of ridicule. Said he:

"Our opposers ought to see that nothing will draw us from our present faith, but a better construction of Scripture. Let them give us this, *and we yield*. But misrepresentation, burlesque and ridicule, will never make a real Adventist give up his hope." [9]

From Cleveland, Himes wrote early in August of his plan to go to England in October, "if time be prolonged," for the purpose of quickening the interest already present there. Literature had been sent out. Various ministers in other lands had taken up the cry, "Behold, the Bridegroom cometh." But Himes thought that

---
[7] *Ibid.*, Aug. 7, 1844, p. 4.
[8] *Ibid.*
[9] *Ibid.*, Aug. 14, 1844, p. 14.

now he and others with him from America should go forth to strengthen the endeavors abroad. Said he:

"If time be continued a few months, we shall send the *glad tidings* out in a number of different languages, among Protestant and Catholic nations. . . .

"A press shall be established at London, and lecturers will go out in every direction, and we trust the Word of the Lord will have a free course and be glorified. What we shall accomplish we cannot tell. But we wish to do our duty." [10]

Thus even as Himes and Miller moved westward expanding the work, they envisioned a still greater work overseas. Yet all the while they admitted that the day of the Lord might come very soon and very suddenly. They sought to accomplish that difficult but important spiritual feat of being in instant readiness for the coming of the Lord and yet of planning great and expansive activity for His cause.

Later in August, Himes could report that in Cleveland the meeting place could not begin to hold the congregation. An awning had to be placed in the rear of the house for those who could not be seated within, and the speaker stood in the door "so that most could see and also hear." There had come down to this meeting advent believers from Michigan and Wisconsin "and many other parts of the West, desiring *help*. Faithful men, 'apt to teach,' are called for, in all parts of this Western field." [11]

About a hundred of the advent believers in Akron chartered a boat and came up the canal to the meeting. Miller and Himes returned with them in the boat, the time of the return trip being "spent in singing, prayer, and a lecture by Brother Miller." In the city of Akron the believers had erected a tabernacle for their meetings.

In Cincinnati an equally great interest was evident. On the first evening Miller lectured "to about 4,000 people, who listened to him with almost breathless attention." [12] In that city also the

---
[10] *Ibid.*, Aug. 21, 1844, p. 20.
[11] *Ibid.*, Sept. 4, 1844, p. 36.
[12] *Ibid.*

believers had erected a building of their own, "with brick walls, 80 ft. square." [13]

The fervent devotion of those who attended these gatherings is strikingly illustrated by this incident: At the close of a service when testimonies were being given by the believers, one man mentioned some facts about the extent of the literature distribution by his brother in Boston. He explained that the funds for such large literature distribution had been made possible "chiefly by ladies' gold rings and other freewill offerings." Believers in the Rochester, New York, area, where this incident was being related, were not to be outdone in liberality by those in Boston. He had hardly finished his testimony when one of the Millerite ministers placed a ring in his hand, then one after another of the sisters dropped "rings, breastpins, strings of gold beads, ear rings, etc., etc.—now and then a brother with a watch key." [14]

The issues of the Millerite papers during these months admitted to their columns a number of articles that called for Adventists to come out of the churches. Finally Himes himself endorsed this belief in the summer of 1844. Writing from Ohio on the subject of "Separation From the Churches," he reviewed the policy the Millerites had followed through the years of not attempting "to convert men to a sect, or party in religion." He told of ministers who had invited Millerites to speak in their churches, but who *"had not* sincerely embraced the doctrine." These ministers saw that they must go with the doctrine, and preach and maintain it, or in the *crisis* which was right upon them they would have difficulty with the *decided and determined believers.* They therefore decided against the doctrine, and determined, some by one policy and some by another, to suppress the subject." [15] He recounted the ridicule that had been heaped upon the believers, which finally caused many of them to arise "in the majesty of their strength" to shake "off the yoke," and raise the cry, *"Come out of her, My people."*

---

[13] *The Midnight Cry,* June 20, 1844, p. 388.
[14] *The Midnight Cry,* Aug. 1, 1844, p. 22.
[15] Letter, Aug. 29, 1844, in *The Midnight Cry,* Sept. 12, 1844, p. 80.

He quoted the scripture concerning Paul, that when he found that "divers were hardened, and believed not, but spake evil of that way before the multitude, he departed from them, and separated *the disciples.*" Acts 19:9. He believed that there was a parallel to this in the experience of the Millerites, that the churches that continued to speak evil of the truth on the second coming of the Lord, which was also central in Paul's preaching, could be "none other than the daughters of the mystic Babylon." Without dogmatizing on just what constituted Babylon, Himes wished to make this clear:

"We are agreed in the *instant* and final separation from all who oppose the doctrine of the coming and kingdom of God at hand. We believe it to be a case of life and death. It is death to remain connected with those bodies that speak lightly of, or oppose the coming of the Lord. It is life to come out from all human tradition, and stand upon the Word of God, and look daily for the appearing of the Lord. We therefore now say to all who are in any way entangled in the yoke of bondage, 'Come out from among them, and be ye *separate,* saith the Lord.' " [16]

This letter from Himes virtually brought to an end any difference of viewpoint among Millerite leaders regarding the right and the necessity of separating from the churches. While Miller really never accepted this view, he evidently did not openly go on record against it at this time. The die had been cast. By the summer of 1844 Millerism stood sharp and clear on the religious horizon as a well-defined and more or less separate movement, with ministers, second advent associations, and meeting houses.

Though the two dominant leaders, Miller and Himes, were in the West, accompanied for a part of the time by another prominent leader, Litch, all the Millerite activity and fervor that summer was not concentrated out there. Far from it. There are notices of numerous camp meetings to be held in the New England States, always, of course, with some such proviso in the announcement as "providence permitting," or "if time lingers." And all

---

[16] *Ibid.*

the while Snow with his convincing evidence for the ending of the 2300-day time prophecy in the fall of that year was writing and preaching on this theme. In fact, he had not been studying it long before he finally set October 22, 1844, as the date for the termination of the prophetic period.*

Perhaps not so much from the preaching and writing of Snow, as from a deep conviction that the end of all things could not be far away, some of the believers in northern New Hampshire, even before summer began, failed to plow their fields because the Lord would surely come "before another winter." This conviction grew among others in that area so that even if they had planted their fields they felt it would be inconsistent with their faith to take in their crops. We read:

"Some, on going into their fields to cut their grass, found themselves entirely unable to proceed, and, conforming to their sense of duty, left their crops standing in the field, to show their faith by their works, and thus to condemn the world. This rapidly extended through the north of New England." [17]

Such conviction naturally prepared men to give a sympathetic ear to the proclamation that the day of the Lord would come on October 22. By midsummer a new stimulus had been given to Millerism in New England. Backsliders were reclaimed, and new ardor controlled those Adventists who accepted Snow's reckoning, as they went out to proclaim the cry, "Behold, the Bridegroom cometh, go ye out to meet Him." Indeed, Snow declared that only now was the true midnight cry being given.†

On the twelfth of August a five-day camp meeting opened in Exeter, New Hampshire, only a few miles away from East

---

[17] *The Advent Herald,* Oct. 30, 1844, p. 93.

* This date was equivalent, in the Karaite Jews' reckoning, to the "tenth day of the seventh month" of the Jewish sacred calendar, which brought the ancient symbolic services of the Jews to a grand climax in a Day of Atonement.

† His reasoning briefly was this: Disappointment had come in the spring of 1844, and now in the language of Christ's parable, the ten virgins were sleeping while the "bridegroom tarried." But the parable declared that at midnight the cry was raised, "Behold, the Bridegroom cometh." Now in prophecy a twenty-four-hour day symbolizes a year; hence a night symbolizes a half year. Midnight would be midway of that six-month period, when the true cry should be sounded. Snow stressed the fact that in the midst of that six-month period, the cry, that is, the announcement of the exact time of the advent, really began to go forth.

Kingston, where the first Adventist camp meeting in the United States had been held just two years earlier. It was at this Exeter meeting, according to the united testimony of all the Millerite writers, that this new belief concerning the specific date, October 22, finally took full hold of the Adventists in New England, changing their indefinite, though very real conviction of the nearness of the Lord's coming, into a belief so specific as to send them forth with a crusading zeal to warn men in the little while that remained.[18]

The services at this Exeter encampment were dragging perceptibly. Joseph Bates was in the speaker's stand, seeking to quicken the hearts of the hearers, and to enlighten their minds. But he was making little progress. In the rather informal style of those open-air meetings a middle-aged, quiet-spoken woman arose and addressed him thus:

"It is too late to spend our time upon these truths, with which we are familiar, and which have been blessed to us in the past, and have served their purpose and their time."

The preacher sat down. Every eye was fixed on this woman as she continued:

"It is too late, brethren, to spend precious time as we have since this camp meeting commenced. Time is short. The Lord has servants here who have meat in due season for His household. Let them speak, and let the people hear them. 'Behold, the Bridegroom cometh, go ye out to meet Him.' " [19]

Snow had come on the campground. He had hardly dismounted from his panting horse before the word spread around that here was a man who had a message.* That is what the middle-aged sister meant when she interrupted Bates' discourse. When Snow had presented his views, the whole spirit of the camp

---

[18] *Ibid.*
[19] James White, *Life Incidents*, pp. 159, 160.

* J. N. Loughborough stated that Joseph Bates was speaking that morning when Snow came on the grounds. According to Loughborough's account, Snow sat down beside an elder and his wife and whispered to them what his new light was. Whereupon the sister arose and addressed Bates. (See *Advent Review and Sabbath Herald*, Aug. 18, 1921, p. 5.)

meeting was changed. A tentful of fanatics from Watertown, Massachusetts, who had inflicted themselves on the camp, and whose influence was growing because of the idle curiosity of many who gathered about them, now became silent. They seemed smitten dumb by the awesome message. The campers had something more important to give ear to. They must make ready for the coming of the Lord in a little more than two months. Writing of this camp meeting only three years afterward, when the memory of it was still vivid, Bates told of setting out for the meeting with the thought constantly coming to his mind: "You are going to have new light here, something that will give a new impetus to this work." Then he added:

"There was light given and received there, sure enough; and when that meeting closed, the granite hills of New Hampshire rang with the mighty cry, 'Behold, the Bridegroom cometh, go ye' out to meet Him!' As the stages and railroad cars rolled away through the different States, cities, and villages of New England, the rumbling of the cry was still distinctly heard. Behold the Bridegroom cometh! Christ is coming on the tenth day of the seventh month! Time is short! Get ready! Get ready!! . . . Who does not still remember how this message flew as it were upon the wings of the wind—men and women moving on all the cardinal points of the compass, going with all the speed of locomotives, in steamboats and rail cars, freighted with bundles of books and papers, wherever they went distributing them almost as profusely as the flying leaves of autumn." [20]

There had been set in motion here in New Hampshire a movement within the movement—for the Millerite leaders were very slow to accept the argument for a definite time—a movement which was soon to give a new tempo to the thinking and the activity of the advent believers over the whole country, and to bring Millerism to a dramatic and speedy climax.

Immediately after the Exeter camp meeting *The Advent Herald* gave a brief report of the meeting, mentioning almost casually that "Brother Snow remarked with great energy on the *time* [October 22, 1844], and displayed much research in his presentation of the evidence which, in his view, points to the tenth

---

[20] Joseph Bates, *Second Advent Way Marks and High Heaps*, pp. 30, 31.

day of the seventh month of the Jewish sacred year, as the day of the Lord's advent." [21]

However, in writing in retrospect a "history of the late movement" the editor described the Exeter camp meeting and declared that the message which came out from it "rapidly spread through all the advent bands in the land." Then he added immediately:

"At first the definite time was generally opposed; but there seemed to be an irresistible power attending its proclamation, which prostrated all before it. It swept over the land with the velocity of a tornado, and it reached hearts in different and distant places almost simultaneously, and in a manner which can be accounted for only on the supposition that God was [in] it. . . .

"The lecturers among the Adventists were the last to embrace the views of the time, and the more prominent ones came into it last of all. It seemed not to be the work of men, but to be brought about in spite of men. The several advent papers came into the view only at a late hour; and this paper [*The Advent Herald*] was the last to raise its voice in the spread of the cry. For a long time we were determined to take no part in the movement, either in opposition, or in the advocacy of it. . . . It was not until within about two weeks of the commencement of the seventh month [about the first of October], that we were particularly impressed with the progress of the movement, when we had such a view of it, that to oppose it, or even to remain silent longer, seemed to us to be opposing the work of the Holy Spirit; and in entering upon the work with all our souls, we could but exclaim, 'What were we, that we should resist God?' It seemed to us to have been so independent of human agency, that we could but regard it as a fulfillment of the 'midnight cry.' " [22]

Thus the stage was set for the grand climax of Millerism.

---

[21] *The Advent Herald,* Aug. 21, 1844, p. 20.
[22] *Ibid.,* Oct. 30, 1844, p. 93.

CHAPTER 15

Hastening on to the Climax

EVENTS crowded one upon another in the brief period from mid-August to October 22. It is on the happenings of this period of about ten weeks that the critics of Millerism from that day to this have relied so heavily in their endeavor to picture the movement as simply a wildly fanatical one, led on by firebrands. But were even these last two months so delirious as rumor would have it?

One of the first glimpses we have of a large Millerite gathering after the Exeter meeting is that given to us by John Greenleaf Whittier, who visited the camp meeting held at Derry, New Hampshire, about the middle of September, 1844. Did he picture the camp as a place of wild fanaticism? A sensitive spirit like Whittier's would be easily offended. In fact, his report of the meeting includes a critical comment on some of the hymns, because of the literal and, to him, gross way of describing the abode of the saints and their exultation over the destruction of the sinners.

If Whittier's sensitive ear was sufficiently "shocked" to cause him to comment on the language of these hymns—many of which were like hymns sung in the staid denominations—he surely would not have failed to mention fanaticism if it had been present. But this is the way he described the Millerites in attendance:

"Here were sober, intelligent men, gentle and pious women, who, verily believing the end to be close at hand, had left their counting-rooms, and workshops, and household cares to publish the great tidings, and to startle, if possible, a careless and unbelieving generation into preparation for the day of the Lord and for that blessed millennium,—the restored paradise,— when, renovated and renewed by its fire-purgation, the earth shall become as of old the garden of the Lord, and the saints alone shall inherit it. . . .

"As might be expected, the effect of this belief in the speedy destruction of the world and the personal coming of the Messiah, acting upon a class of uncultivated, and, in some cases, gross minds, is not always in keeping with the enlightened Christian's ideal of the better day." [1]

He followed this statement immediately with the comment on the advent hymns to which we have just referred, as though indicating that this illustrated his remark about the effect of adventism not always being "in keeping with the enlightened Christian's ideal of the better day." But he said that not only were there "in some cases, gross minds," as would be true in any general gathering, but also were there "indeed occasionally to be found among the believers men of refined and exalted spiritualism [spirit] who in their lives and conversation remind one of Tennyson's Christian knight errant in his yearning towards the hope set before him." [2]

We doubt whether Whittier would have described any camp meeting held by any denomination in those days in more kindly language than this. Yet this meeting was dominated by the belief that the Lord would come on October 22.*

During the summer the great tent was pitched in various places in Ohio, then in Indiana, and finally in Louisville, Kentucky, where a series of lectures was begun on September 25. This

---

[1] John Greenleaf Whittier, *Prose Works*, Vol. 1, p. 423.
[2] *Ibid.*

* Whittier followed this eyewitness description of the Derry camp meeting with the recital of a bit of hearsay: "One of the most ludicrous examples of the sensual phase of Millerism, the incongruous blending of the sublime with the ridiculous, was mentioned to me not long since. A fashionable young woman in the western part of this State became an enthusiastic believer in the doctrine. On the day which had been designated as the closing one of time she packed all her fine dresses and toilet valuables in a large trunk, with long straps attached to it, and, seating herself upon it, buckled the straps over her shoulders, patiently awaiting the crisis, shrewdly calculating that, as she must herself go upwards, her goods and chattels would of necessity follow."—*John Greenleaf Whittier, Writings, Vol. 5, Prose Works, Vol. 1, p. 424.*

Had Whittier talked with this young woman? No. Did he even say that the person who told him the story had talked with the young woman? No. Here is an illustration of the numerous rumors and stories that were afloat about the Millerites. Most of the stories were patently made out of whole cloth; a few have threads of truth in them. In later chapters we shall give extended consideration to charges of fanaticism and shall weigh the value of the numerous stories that were current. We should add, however, that we have not found other than in Whittier's work, this story of the young woman and the strapped trunk. Most "good" stories had a rather general circulation.

was less than a month before the anticipated end of the world.

On October 1 the *Louisville Morning Courier* wrote a story about the big tent. Said the newspaper reporter:

"We gratified ourselves last night with a visit to the big tent. . . . If the most perfect decorum, the faithful reading and exposition of the prophetic writings, the sincerity and faithfulness of the speakers, and the absence of everything like selfishness and folly, are objects of any attraction to the people of Louisville, we recommend a visit to this tent. . . . These men are the bearers of no common message—they deserve a hearing of the proper kind, and we earnestly hope they will get it." [3]

Here is what a New York paper tells of that Louisville tent meeting, giving the *Louisville Courier* as its source: "The high, the low, the rich, the poor, the aristocrat, the democrat, preachers, saints, and sinners" were in attendance at the great tent.

"After the sermon had been preached—and it was a very reasonable, sensible sermon, which no one could object to—came a scene which beggars description. The mourners or converts, of whom there were a very large number, threw themselves in the dust and dirt around the pulpit, and for nearly an hour, men and women were praying, singing, shouting, groaning, and weeping bitterly." [4]

Two points stand out in this news story—the actions of the preachers and the actions of the hearers. The Millerite movement was responsible for the former but not necessarily for the latter. The preaching is described as above reproach, but the actions of the listeners as rather in contrast. The reporter says that the mourners prostrated themselves on the dirt floor. That was the only floor there was. How fervently they may have prayed or sung, shouted or wept, might easily be reported very differently by different eyewitnesses. Even if we grant—and probably we should—that the mourners gave very bold and

---

[3] *Louisville Morning Courier,* Oct. 1, 1844, quoted in *The Midnight Cry,* Oct. 12, 1844, p. 127. We are dependent in this instance, as in several others, on a Millerite paper for this newspaper quotation. No file of the *Louisville Morning Courier* of October 1, 1844, is extant. But the Millerites would have been running a great and unnecessary risk, in their constant controversy with their adversaries, to print a garbled report from a newspaper. Someone would have quickly made capital of this and exposed them. There is no record anywhere of anyone's attempting to do that. Evidently the Millerites were careful when they quoted.

[4] *Evening Post for the Country* (New York), Oct. 22, 1844.

audible expression to their contrition for sin, even to the extent of creating a brief babel, it would be nothing more than was common and even customary in connection with camp meetings and revivals in those days. But, we repeat, the kind of sermon here described—"reasonable," "sensible," "which no one could object to"—sounds much more restrained than the fervent evangelistic preaching of the typical camp meetings of the time. Indeed, would the "high," the "rich," the "aristocrat," and the "preachers," have been attending these Millerite meetings unless they were conducted within the bounds of what was considered propriety in religious services?

Speaking of the impression created in the minds of men regarding the religious principles and convictions of the Millerites, even in advance of the last solemn weeks of October, this incident is illustrative: The editor of a religious paper in Boston rebuked a man for an outburst of profanity. The man turned upon him inquiring, "Well, you are a follower of *Miller,* ain't you?" This led the editor to muse:

"What, thought I, are the 'followers of Miller' the only ones in Boston from whom the profane have expected any reproof? Have the great mass of professing Christians here been conformed to the world, and not rebukers of iniquity? Alas! it is too true. Now, whatever blame may be attached to the 'followers of Miller,' and with what degree of justice or injustice, it is just to them that it should be remembered that they have firmly rebuked both the religious and the irreligious profanity, which the great mass of professed Christians have winked at. 'Honor to whom honor is due.' " [5]

Early in October mobs, which had been intermittently troublesome to Millerite meetings, became a grave menace to them in some of the leading cities. In Boston, on Saturday evening, the twelfth of October, while the sexton was sweeping the tabernacle and preparing it for the services of the next day, a mob broke into the building. They were dispersed by the police. On Sunday, the next day, after the Millerites were in the tabernacle for their service a great crowd gathered on the streets in front.

---

[5] *Genius of Christianity,* quoted in *The Midnight Cry,* July 4, 1844, p. 404.

To avoid further disturbance, the Millerites decided to hold no meeting in their tabernacle Sunday night. But early Sunday evening the mob was again milling in the street around the building.⁶

The situation was such that the Millerites decided they would have to abandon holding meetings in the tabernacle. Himes then drafted a statement of the matter for publication in the Boston newspapers, addressed "to the public" and entitled "Disturbances at the Tabernacle." *

Himes devoted the opening paragraph of his statement to the reasons why the Adventists were now looking to October 22 as the date of the Lord's coming, and declared that their having announced this date "has produced an unexpected sensation." Because of this hope of the Lord's coming, which was then only ten days away, he said:

"We were desirous to meet once more, to mingle our prayers and to encourage one another in the last work of preparation; and for this purpose we had met at our well known place of worship in this city. We gave no special notice of our meeting; we made no appeal to the public; and it was characterized by no exercises which were calculated to excite either the mirth or vengeance of any portion of the community.

"We were serious, we were bowed in penitence and prayer before God, or heartily affected by the mutual confessions of tried and dear friends. We had no ill feeling to indulge towards any man; we felt that we were done with the world, and had forgiven them the many injuries they had inflicted upon us; but stale and silly slanders in reference to us were revived; the restless spirits of the community have been aroused; we could not meet in peace, and our meetings, in consequence, have been suspended. And we now make these remarks to disabuse the public, and with the hope that some who would not otherwise give their attention to the calls of the present time, may lay them to heart.

"To the city authorities, who faithfully tendered their services, we are grateful, though we could not promote the objects of the meeting, when such protection was needed.

---

⁶ See *The Advent Herald,* Oct. 30, 1844, p. 93.

* This statement was dated October 14, 1844, and appeared in the *Boston Daily Mail* the next day, and in the Boston *Daily Evening Transcript* on the sixteenth. This statement was also quoted in papers of other cities. For example, it was printed in the *Portland Daily American,* (Maine), October 18. It was also published in the Millerite papers.

"We forgive our enemies. They have not injured us. And oh, that they could see how much they have injured themselves." [7]

This is the major part of Himes' statement to the public. To the very last, he was following the policy of seeking to keep the record clear. In the midst of mob excitement, when "stale and silly slanders" were befogging the air, he wished the unprejudiced mind to have an opportunity to hear the other side of the question.

Himes had a record as clear as that of Miller, in the matter of militantly discountenancing anything fanatical. Yet if one were to believe simply what the newspapers in various cities reported about the disturbances at the tabernacle in Boston, one might easily conclude that the Millerites themselves were responsible for all their troubles, that they had generated so much excitement in their meetings they found it necessary to close them.

Regarding the manner in which the mob action in Boston was colored and turned as it was copied from one paper to another, take this illustration. A Baltimore newspaper, on October 17, stated that at the Millerite meeting in Boston last Saturday night the constabulary stopped the "noisy proceedings." And borrowing its ideas from the *Boston Times,* it continued:

"This, says the *Boston Times,* is well advised—for the strange doings there were very much in the nature of a breach of the peace, and from all accounts some of the nightly performances might well come under the demonstration of nuisances." [8]

A Portland, Maine, newspaper, on October 15, observed editorially:

"In Boston, the scenes in reference to this delusion [of Millerism] are equally painful and wicked. The *Post* informs us that the excitement at the Miller tabernacle, produced by the second advent believers, rose to so high a pitch on Saturday that the principal authors of it became alarmed and announced that there would be no more public lectures there at present and advised their deluded followers to repair to their homes." [9]

---

[7] *The Midnight Cry,* Oct. 19, 1844, p. 136.
[8] *Sun* (Baltimore), Oct. 17, 1844.
[9] *Daily Eastern Argus* (Portland, Maine), Oct. 15, 1844.

Now the only excitement "produced by the second advent believers" on Saturday the twelfth was that caused by the sexton industriously wielding his broom, preparing the empty building for the services of the morrow.

Very appropriately did the editor of the *Portland Daily Advertiser,* shortly after the climax of Millerism, remark:

"We have never before written a paragraph on this subject, and during the whole period of the agitation, but very few statements concerning it of any kind have been allowed a place in our paper. It has appeared to us that much of the newspaper gossip about it has been exceedingly idle, and not a little that is very mischievous. So far as related to the actual believers in the immediate advent, the remarks have been mostly of a ridiculous character, and have done good to the enthusiasts themselves." [10]

While this newspaper deplored the mistaken teachings of the Millerites, it preferred no charges of fanaticism against them. Evidently the editor had a very low estimate of his fellow editors of the daily press, at least so far as their handling of the Millerite movement was concerned. This editorial found in the *Portland Daily Advertiser* is typical of several revealing statements written by certain editors who were outraged by the groundless attacks on the Millerites.

In Philadelphia the Millerites had similar difficulties with mob interference, so that the police would not permit them to hold meetings at night. In a Philadelphia newspaper on Monday, October 14, appeared a notice by the Millerites informing the public that the services at the second advent chapel on Julianna Street "were closed last evening by order of the sheriff, in consequence of a large gathering of persons on the outside of the chapel. There will be no further evening services. Providence permitting, the chapel will be open daily at 9 A. M. and 2 P. M." [11]

A New Hampshire paper discusses the Millerites and riots in Philadelphia, stating that the sheriff of the city and county of

---

[10] *Portland Daily Advertiser* (Maine), Oct. 26, 1844.
[11] *Philadelphia Public Ledger,* Oct. 14, 1844, quoted in *The Midnight Cry,* Oct. 19, 1844, p. 132.

Philadelphia with his officers had gone "to the different places of meeting of the Millerites, and caused them to desist from any further lectures, as great crowds of persons were attracted by their proceedings, and many were disposed to riot." This was too much even for a newspaper in New Hampshire, where the papers certainly had not been sympathetic to Millerism, for it adds immediately: "This is Philadelphian police, and miserable indeed. It is like telling a householder—'you must not presume to have glass windows in your house, because many unruly boys are disposed to break them.' " [12]

The action of the sheriff provoked a vigorous protest from a citizen of Philadelphia, who signed himself "an anti-Millerite." Addressing the editors of the *Public Ledger,* he said:

"As fully convinced of the fallacy of the Millerite doctrine as yourselves, and having therefore no personal grievances to complain of in the closing of their place of worship in the evening by order of the sheriff, I would respectfully inquire by what authority this was done. A resident of Philadelphia all my lifetime, I have frequently noticed that whenever a party or a congregation of people, holding opinions opposite to those popular with the great mass, are disturbed in their meetings by rude boys or lawless men, the disturbed are invariably ordered to cease from meeting, and the disturbers, having gained their object, exult in having put down 'fanatical notions.' In regard to the Julianna Street Church, I believe it is admitted, that however much mistaken, the congregation had a full right to hold meetings. Why then, instead of protecting them in the exercise of that right, and dispersing or arresting their disturbers, were they ordered to close in the evening for fear of being still further disturbed?... No journal has ventured to express its opinion—not even your own; of which, judging from its whole course, permit me frankly to say, better things were expected by An Anti-Millerite." [13]

The pages of this chapter could be filled with newspaper accounts of mob attacks on the Millerites, particularly in the closing weeks of the movement. Every endeavor seemed to be made by lawless elements to bring confusion and distraction to the meetings. Sometimes windows were broken, sometimes bon-

---

[12] *Portsmouth Journal* (N. H.), Oct. 19, 1844.
[13] *Philadelphia Public Ledger,* Oct. 21, 1844.

fires were lighted outside. In one instance Roman candles were fired near by to create a weird light and to bring panic and confusion to the audience within.[14]

It would seem that there was much more excitement and irrational action outside the Millerite meeting places than in them. Of course the actions of a mob are never described as fanatical. That term is reserved for religious people who happen at the moment to be the object of general condemnation.

Now, with such rowdy proceedings going on around Millerite buildings, sometimes even to the extent of causing panic within or the breaking up of the meeting entirely, is it reasonable to believe that a very accurate report was brought to the newspapers of what actually was taking place in the Millerite meetings?

It should be remembered that the newspapers of those days were very different from our present ones. They had no wire service, no great news-gathering or news-distributing agencies, no photographers to take a visual record, and apparently very few reporters, for it is a common thing to have news items in those papers prefaced with "It is reported," "We are informed," "It is said," and not too infrequently, "It is rumored." Take for example this brief item on the Millerites that appeared in a Philadelphia paper about a week before the great day of climax: The news item makes a terse reference to the Millerite meetings and ends thus: "We have not attended any of their assemblies, but those who have been present at their meetings, assure us that the scene is appalling."[15]

What more need be said? Here is a respectable newspaper telling us that "the scene is appalling" at Millerite meetings. Why should we doubt the story? The editor assures us that he has been assured by those "who have been present" as to the facts in the case.

---

[14] See, for example, *Herald* (New York), Oct. 12, 1844; *New York Spectator*, Oct. 16, 1844; *Philadelphia Public Ledger*, Oct. 15, 1844; *Newark Daily Advertiser*, Oct. 19, 1844; *Daily National Intelligencer* (Washington, D. C.), Oct. 21, 1844; *Philadelphia Public Ledger*, Oct. 21, 1844.
[15] *United States Gazette* (Philadelphia), Oct. 16, 1844.

However, another Philadelphia newspaper, the day before the anticipated end of the world, carried this item:

"We took occasion to go to a Millerite chapel in this city, to witness the proceedings of the fanatical persons who attended them, and were surprised at the apparent intelligence and actual respectability of the members. Discourses were pronounced in smooth terms, full of argument, such as it was, in favor of conflagration." [16]

This newspaper reporter was "surprised" at what he saw and heard. Apparently he had been taking at face value the rumors that were abroad, and too, he may have been "assured" by the same persons who assured the other newspaper of how "appalling" the Millerite meetings were.*

A third Philadelphia newspaper, writing in the same week, had this to say about the Millerites:

"Very many persons believe that the deplorable delusion of Millerism is confined to persons in the humbler walks of life, to the ignorant and utterly uninstructed. This is a great mistake. There are to be found among the followers of Miller persons from almost every rank of society; from the educated professional man to the unlettered day laborer; and of women attached to the doctrines of the pretended prophet might be selected many whose presence would grace a fashionable drawing room, and numbers who as wives and mothers are exemplary in every particular of womanly duty. In the public meetings of the sect held in this city addresses and prayers are made which in all points of rhetoric and requisites of correct declamation would not discredit many admired and popular pulpits. To hear these is to be convinced of the sincerity of the speakers and their auditory, and moved to the keenest pity by the manifestations of contrition and horror felt by the individuals of the assembly." [17]

The Millerites could hardly have asked for a more flattering description than this. They might possibly have taken a little exception to the closing statement that "horror" was felt by the individuals of the assembly, but perhaps not. There were always enough strangers and unconverted who had been brought to the

---

[16] *Philadelphia Public Ledger,* Oct. 21, 1844.
[17] *North American* (Philadelphia), Oct. 16, 1844.

* This reporter's testimony is even more important in view of the fact that he was most certainly opposed to Millerism as a blight and a curse. He goes on in his news story to state that the evil effects of Millerism include even "idiocy." Today we blame that malady on the poor victims' ancestors!

meetings, and who saw only judgment and destruction ahead, rather than deliverance out of this evil world. The best testimony available is that the Millerites themselves were filled with joyful anticipation. But we need not quibble on this one point. The reporter's story speaks for itself, as to the kind of people present and the kind of preaching delivered. Such people and such preaching do not produce wildly fanatical results.

A Boston newspaper, commenting on the Millerites the day following the fateful twenty-second of October, spoke of them as "intelligent, respectable, pious people." [18]

A Baltimore newspaper on October 15 described a Millerite baptism, at which it was estimated that about ten thousand persons attended as spectators. Now here was an excellent opportunity for the Millerites in the very week before their anticipated ascension to display fanaticism. The setting was ideal. Here were ten thousand people to watch them. Anyone who has ever attended an open-air baptismal service knows that there are almost certainly moments when those who are disposed to laugh will find occasion for doing so. For example, someone may stumble going into the water or coming out. Here is the comment of the newspaper:

"Good order prevailed, though an occasional peal of laughter at something of a ludicrous character in the proceeding, made manifest the prevailing emotions in the minds of the multitude at the novel spectacle." [19]

Incredible! "Good order prevailed"! Yet the service was conducted by allegedly fanatical Millerites at whose services the most "appalling" incidents were rumored to be taking place.

---

[18] *Boston Daily Mail,* Oct. 23, 1844.
[19] *Sun* (Baltimore), Oct. 15, 1844.

CHAPTER 16

The Great Day of Hope

FROM MOB SCENES AND MASS MEETINGS in great cities we turn our eyes now to the quiet spot called Low Hampton. Miller had completed his summer's trip west, and was once more at home resting from the arduous labors that had told so heavily on his meager physical resources. He was acquainted with the evidence and argument on which a rapidly increasing number of the believers were relying for their hope that Christ would come on October 22. But he had not accepted this view. He was loath to do so. He always had held that no man could know the day or the hour of the Lord's coming. He had never felt free to be more specific than to foretell it in terms of the year. In a letter written September 30 he said:

"I am once more at home, worn down with the fatigue of my journey, my strength so exhausted and my bodily infirmities so great, that I am about concluding I shall never be able again to labor in the vineyard as heretofore." [1]

Miller had been the one man who had stood out to the last against the idea of any general withdrawal from the churches. Perhaps because of his constant traveling he had not come so intimately in contact with the kind of spiritual and social problem that confronted the Adventist believers as they sought to continue fellowship in their own local churches that were often actively and openly hostile to them. Now Miller himself was to feel the force of this opposition, for in this same letter he declared:

"I found on my arrival here that my brethren had relinquished the meetinghouse to a small minority of our church, who separated from us

---

[1] Sylvester Bliss, *Memoirs of William Miller*, p. 268.

last spring, because the second coming of Christ was there preached—though they claim to be looking for Him. Rather than contend with them, our brethren have peaceably relinquished the chapel to them, and will build, if time continues." [2]

In the week that followed the writing of this letter Miller must have given very serious study to the claims made for October 22, the tenth day of the seventh month, according to the Karaite reckoning of the Jewish sacred calendar. The "seventh-month movement," as this late development in Millerism was known, was now finally to gain the support of Miller. On October 6, scarcely more than two weeks before the anticipated great day, he wrote Himes a letter which began thus:

"I see a glory in the seventh month which I never saw before. Although the Lord had shown me the typical bearing of the seventh month, one year and a half ago, yet I did not realize the force of the types.* Now, blessed be the name of the Lord, I see a beauty, a harmony, and an agreement in the Scriptures, for which I have long prayed, but did not see until today. Thank the Lord. . . . I am almost home, Glory! Glory!! Glory!!!" [3]

Almost at the same time the other prominent leaders were placing themselves on record as believing that the Lord would come on October 22. Southard, the editor of *The Midnight Cry*, declared in the first issue of October:

---

[2] *Ibid.*, pp. 268, 269.
[3] *The Midnight Cry,* Oct. 12, 1844, p. 121.

* Miller is referring to a letter he wrote Himes on May 3, 1843, which was published in *The Midnight Cry,* June 1, 1843. In this letter he declared: "If you will examine, you will find all the ceremonies of the typical law that were observed in the first month, or vernal equinox, had their fulfillment in Christ's first advent and sufferings; but all the feasts and ceremonies in the seventh month or autumnal equinox, can only have their fulfillment at his second advent." Miller set forth a series of reasons for the position he took, such as: "The atonement was made on the tenth day seventh month, and this is certainly typical of the atonement Christ is now making for us. . . . When the high priest came out of the holy of holies, after making the atonement, he blessed the people. . . . So will our great High Priest. Heb. 9:28. This was on the seventh month tenth day."
The editor made a brief, favorable comment on Miller's letter, and there the matter rested until Snow, early in 1844, drew on it in building his argument for the ending of the 2300-day prophecy on the typical day of atonement, October 22, 1844.
In the seventh-month movement the thinking of the Millerites was turned to the sanctuary above, which was not the case up to that time. In the weeks and months just preceding October 22, there were frequent references to Christ's activity as High Priest above, and to His completing His priestly work on October 22, when He would come out to bless His waiting people. The reader is referred to a closing chapter where the transition in thinking— from the idea that Christ left the most holy on the twenty-second, to the view that He entered the most holy on that day—is presented in connection with a description of the rise of Seventh-day Adventists.

"The weight of evidence that the Lord will come on the tenth day of the seventh month is so strong that I heartily yield to its force, and I intend, by the help of the Lord, to act as if there was no possibility of mistake:— to act as if I *knew* that in less than one month the opening heavens would reveal my Saviour." [4]

In the first issue of *The Advent Herald* in October, Himes announced that his "mission to Europe," which he had intended to carry out in October, had been canceled. He explained that "the recent remarkable movement among the advent brethren on the *time,* and the great work which God is doing for His people, certainly gives a new indication of the near approach of the glorious Bridegroom." [5]

However, Himes was not yet fully convinced of the soundness of the evidence when that October 2 issue of *The Advent Herald* went to press. He stated that he was printing the articles of Brother Snow and others, that the readers might have all the evidence before them, and asked them to examine the whole question "seriously and prayerfully." But he added:

"While there is much evidence clustering around that day, sufficient to induce all who love the Lord's appearing, to hope He will then come, yet if the evidence may fail of making it a demonstration, why should any who are *waiting* for His appearing, feel to oppose the idea that the Lord may then come?" [6]

In the issue of October 9 he finally came out firmly as a believer in the "seventh-month movement" and set forth at length his reason. Said he in conclusion: "We are shut up to this faith, and shall, by the grace of God, look for the event, and act accordingly." [7] This statement was signed also by Sylvester Bliss, who was associated with Himes in editorial work on *The Advent Herald.**

---

[4] *Ibid.,* Oct. 3, 1844, p. 100.
[5] *The Advent Herald,* Oct. 2, 1844, p. 68.
[6] *Ibid.,* p. 72.
[7] *Ibid.,* Oct. 9, 1844, p. 80.

* On October 10, 1844, a Mrs. E. C. Clemons, writing to Miller, told of the activities at the Boston Advent Tabernacle, declaring: "Brother Himes came out last Sabbath [October 6] (on his return from N. Y.), & expressed his belief that the Lord would come on the tenth of the seventh month." Himes wrote a penciled note to Miller at the close of the Clemons letter,

About this same time Charles Fitch, another of the very prominent leaders, accepted the belief in October 22 as the day of the advent. He was lying ill in Buffalo, and someone read to him the articles in behalf of the seventh-month view.[8] But he did not live to suffer disappointment with the others. He baptized a company of believers in a river in the chill autumn weather, became ill, and died October 14.

Josiah Litch wrote from Philadelphia on October 12, to say, "My difficulties have all vanished," and I live "in joyful expectation of seeing the King of kings within ten days." [9]

The most active endeavors were made by the Millerites during these closing weeks to broadcast what they believed was the truth concerning the exact time of Christ's advent. Extra issues of *The Midnight Cry* and *The Advent Herald* were published. The editor of *The Midnight Cry* stated that in order to provide the literature needed they were keeping "four steam presses almost constantly in motion." [10]

Did the Millerite leaders quite lose their heads as they contemplated the awesome event that was almost upon them, and counsel the advent believers to do foolish and fanatical things in preparation for heaven? Let the record speak for itself. Take this editorial in *The Midnight Cry*, entitled "Take Heed to Yourselves." Said the editor:

"My dear brethren and sisters, we are in a solemn hour, when temptations will beset us, on every side. . . . We are in great danger of letting our business and labors in warning others so occupy our hearts and minds, that we shall forget ourselves. . . .

"Redeem time for secret prayer at any sacrifice, and maintain the

---

stating his firm faith in October 22. The note is dated "Oct. 10, 1844." On the very day, October 6, when Himes was avowing his faith in the October 22 date at the Boston Tabernacle, Miller was writing his letter of acceptance of that date for the advent. Mrs. Clemons opened her letter to Miller by saying, "I was deeply interested in hearing yours of the 6th inst. read at the tabernacle last evening."

Because this Clemons letter is one of the few original sources we have from which to draw our picture of Millerite meetings immediately preceding the great day, the full text of the letter is given in Appendix B.

[8] See *The Midnight Cry*, Oct. 12, 1844, p. 124.
[9] *Ibid.*, p. 125.
[10] *Ibid.*, p. 126.

spirit of prayer in all your labors. Beware of being drawn away from your duty to yourself, by exciting labors for others. Satan may tell you, and tell you truly, that you have not done your duty to your friends and neighbors, and your own family in times past. But the duty of yesterday you can never do, and your first duty today is, to see that all is right between yourself and God. Till that is settled, you may labor in vain for others. Don't run away from your first duty today, because you neglected your first and second duties yesterday. . . .

"When you go into company, or go into the world, guard against the first approach to levity, but maintain a settled joy in God. . . .

"Study the Bible much especially those parts which are most heart searching. Live out your faith, and your lives will preach." [11]

Place alongside this the concluding paragraph of an extended editorial on Christ's coming in the next day's issue of *The Midnight Cry,* for it was issued daily for three days:

"How important it is, that we should meditate on His coming; that it should be the subject of our nightly prayer, the burden of our morning thoughts, and the theme of our noonday conversation. It should occupy our sleeping, and our waking hours. How solemn the thought that the LORD COMETH! Those words should be in our hearts continually, and we should teach them diligently to our children; we should talk of them when we sit in the house, and when we walk by the way; when we lie down, and when we rise up,—and when we are about our daily occupation." [12]

Frankly, all this sounds like a very intense application to spiritual things and a very penetrating scrutiny of the heart. If the Millerite leaders had counseled any less than this, they would have been charged with hypocrisy by their ministerial opponents. But there is nothing in this counsel that incites to foolish or fanatical acts, or gives any license to them. Rather the contrary. There is nothing that savors of self-righteousness or smug spiritual complacency, those false paths down which religious fanatics so frequently walk. So far from being smugly satisfied with himself, we find that Himes addressed a communication "to our readers" in which he declared:

---
[11] *Ibid.,* Oct. 10, 1844, p. 108.
[12] *Ibid.,* Oct. 11, 1844, p. 116.

"We feel sensible of our many imperfections. Whilst we have contended for what we believe to be truth, we can see that pride of opinion and self, have arisen. . . .

"We ask forgiveness of God and all men, for every thing which may have been inconsistent with His honor and glory; and we desire to lay ourselves upon His altar. Here we lay our friends and worldly interests, and trust alone in the merits of Christ's atoning blood, through the efficacious and sanctifying influence of God's Holy Spirit, for pardon and forgiveness and acceptance at the Father's mercy seat. May the blessing of God rest upon all of us; and that we may all meet in God's everlasting kingdom, is the prayer of your unworthy servant." [13]

Immediately below this statement which Himes signed is a note from the editor, Southard: "I heartily join in the prayer and confession expressed by Brother H."

The Midnight Cry of October 19, the last number issued before the anticipated advent, offered this interesting suggestion on the relation of diet to temperate living in anticipation of Christ's coming:

"Let us imitate Daniel, who would not defile himself with the king's meat. Let us abstain from every article of food which was unclean to the Jews, for the Lord had a reason for all His laws. Eating swine's flesh is mentioned as something abominable, in each of the last two chapters of Isaiah, the only chapters in the Old Testament which directly introduce us to the new heavens and the new earth. When Adam was in Paradise God gave him the best of food, and it consisted wholly of that which grew from the earth. We can lay down no rule for others, but hope our readers will all keep the body under, as Paul did, lest having preached the gospel to others, he himself should be a castaway. . . . Let us live every day on that food which is simplest, plainest, least exciting, and most easily prepared, and be very temperate." [14]

Millerite leaders must have been a little in advance of their day on the basic idea that one's diet has a very direct relationship to one's health and one's state of mind. They were not seeking to dogmatize, for the subject was one on which they could not hope to feel too confident. But who will say that there was not a measure of good dietetic and religious counsel in the appeal?

---
[13] *Ibid.*, p. 120.
[14] *Ibid.*, Oct. 19, 1844, p. 132.

"Let us live every day on that food which is simplest, plainest, least exciting, and most easily prepared."

The printed page was an important factor to the very last. All were urged to send in their orders immediately for literature, telling whether they wished it delivered by mail or express. These supplies were offered to them free.

The Millerites had no precedent to guide them as they approached October 22. Just how should men act and speak, and just how should they counsel others who with them are expecting to meet their Lord face to face at a certain date in the very near future? What does the record reveal? We do not mean the record in the newspapers that were largely hostile, and unblushingly printed rumors and gossip. Nor do we refer to the word-of-mouth stories that have come down through the century and have grown with each generation. There is only one place where the official and authentic record of the actions and pronouncements of the Millerites can be found, and that is in their publications. That is why we have quoted them at length.

A striking fact presents itself to the one who reads the issues of these papers for October—the relatively calm and measured way in which they approached the great day. A person reading these papers who had not previously heard gossip or rumor about the Millerites would find scarcely anything there to suggest to his mind that the Millerites were other than circumspect, godly men and women, who anticipated with solemnity and yet with joy the appearing of their Lord. Nor should this seem at all unreasonable. If a Christian may prepare to enter the valley of the shadow of death with a serene, happy spirit, why should it not be possible for him to anticipate being lifted to the heights of eternal day with at least equal serenity and happiness?

We do not say that the preparation of all Millerites for this anticipated event was above question or that there was no evidence of unwarranted hope or action that passed the proper bounds of faith. There *were* some exceptions, but the point is, they were exceptions. These instances will be examined fully in a later chapter. But no movement should be measured by its exceptions. The true measure of Millerism in these closing weeks of its history is the same that should be used for rightly evaluating it in the preceding year, namely, its own official publications, and the words and actions of its acknowledged spokesmen.

In this same final issue of *The Midnight Cry* is an editorial, entitled, in the language of Paul, "Finally, Brethren, Farewell." The editorial opens with the text of Scripture: "Be perfect, be of good comfort, be of one mind, live in peace; and the God of love and peace shall be with you." Then follows immediately this editorial: "You are exposed to two opposite temptations. 1st to despair of yourself, or, 2d, to presume on your safety." The editorial is devoted to a discussion of these two temptations, and ends thus: "Trust as implicitly as if you expected all from God, and, in His strength, labor as earnestly as if you expected all from yourself." [15]

What we have here quoted hardly makes exciting reading, but it is the official record. The kind of counsel that these Millerites gave sounds strangely like many things we read in the Holy Scriptures. Even the suggestion on diet reminds one of the words of Paul: "Whether therefore ye eat, or drink, or whatsoever ye do, do all to the glory of God." 1 Corinthians 10:31.

Two questions that troubled the minds of the Millerites these last few weeks before the expected end of all things, were whether they should give up their usual occupation and whether they should dispose of what they possessed. In former chapters we have repeatedly called attention to the counsel that was given, the resolutions passed in sessions of their general conference, as to being diligent in business as well as fervent in spirit, serving the Lord. Millerite leaders had been quite emphatic through the years in counseling all, except the few who might be clearly called to be preachers, to stay by the workbench or the farm, earning an honorable living, while, of course, at the same time devoting proper time to missionary activity.

---

[15] *Ibid.*

This counsel had never been revoked, though as the summer of 1844 came on, there were some in northern New England, as already mentioned, who were so certain the Lord would come before the next winter, that they had not planted their crops. But this action and attitude was very far from general. The great majority of Millerites were still engaged in the various lawful occupations.

However, the day of the Lord was now right upon them. Should they, or should they not, withdraw completely from the world with all its interests and activities and spend the little remaining time in making ready for the advent? The question was a practical one. It was also a very perplexing one. An editorial in the final issue of *The Midnight Cry,* under the Scripture title, "Occupy Till I Come," warns the believers:

"These words of the Lord have been pressed into the service of Mammon, and they are now in the mouths of thousands to justify them for being wholly absorbed in the affairs of the world. . . .

"Think for eternity! thousands may be lulled to sleep by hearing your actions say: 'This world is worth my whole energies. The world to come is a vain shadow.' O, reverse this practical sermon, *instantly!* Break loose from the world as much as possible. If indispensable duty calls you into the world for a moment, go as a man would run to do a piece of work in the rain. Run and hasten through it, and let it be known that you leave it with alacrity for something better. Let your actions preach in the clearest tones: 'The Lord is coming'—'The time is short'—'This world passeth away'—'Prepare to meet thy God.' " [16]

This editorial reveals the dilemma that confronted the Millerites in what they thought were the last few days of their stay on earth. To go forward nonchalantly to all their routine labors and employment until the last day might rightly have laid them open to that worst charge that can ever be brought against a religious person—the charge of hypocrisy. Loud would their enemies have shouted that the whole movement was a hoax as they had always charged, that the Millerites never really believed what they said they did.

---

[16] *Ibid.,* p. 133.

However, to take the opposite position and encourage the advent believers to cease all their ordinary activities, to liquidate any possessions they had and turn in the proceeds to a common fund, could only result in having an embarrassing charge hurled against them, the charge of being fanatics.

The editorial here quoted reveals the endeavor of the Millerite leaders to steer between these two extremes. Perhaps someone with the wisdom of Solomon might have steered more successfully. But the Millerite leaders were not Solomons; rather they were men of the same limitations as we. We think they gave rather rational counsel in the light of their belief, and kept fairly away from either extreme.

It was not that they feared particularly the charge of fanaticism. They had been accustomed to that charge. What they did fear was providing their enemies with any just ground for bringing the charge. They did not feel that it was necessarily foolish or fanatical, much less sinful, for a believer to neglect worldly business or even to give of his possessions to the poor in these closing days before the anticipated advent. Across the page from the editorial we have just quoted is one entitled "Charge of Fanaticism," which reads in part:

"The papers abound in paragraphs, detailing the dreadful effects of Millerism. The amount of them is, that we are neglecting worldly business, and those who have this world's goods give freely to the poor.

"Materials for such paragraphs were abundant in the times of Christ and His apostles. Matthew left a good business that he might follow one who had not even a place to lodge. Peter left the labor which was his living, and so did James and John, and left their father also, to follow the same leader. Many rich men sold their property, and in one place property worth 50,000 pieces of silver was burned up, under the influence of what the world called a *delusion*." [17]

Farther down in the same column is a paragraph that provides a concrete illustration of the endeavor that was made to walk a middle path between two extremes in this matter:

---

[17] *Ibid.*, p. 132.

"We cannot all wholly abstain from labor, but we can imitate the example of a brother in this city, who is a wood-sawyer. He said he found that by living temperately, he could sustain his body by laboring half a day, and then he could seek for food for his soul, the other half." [18]

There were two reasons why the believers in the advent would wish to have more free time from their ordinary occupation as the great day drew near. First, they might feel that they needed these extra hours for meditation and spiritual preparation for the great day. There are numbers of precedents in the history of the Christian church for such a procedure as this. Even today retreats are conducted for the purpose of taking busy men away from all their activities for a time to meditate on spiritual things. The second reason why the Millerites might wish to be free from their ordinary labors was that they might engage wholly in a last endeavor to proclaim what they believed was the truth concerning the second advent. Could a man do other than turn his first time and thought to warning neighbors and friends if he sincerely believed the end of all things was at hand? To do otherwise would lay him open to the charge of spiritual exclusiveness, of viewing religion as a very selfish possession which he need not share with anyone else. A short news item in *The Midnight Cry* informs us:

"Many are leaving all, to go out and warn the brethren and the world. In Philadelphia, thirteen volunteered at one meeting (after hearing Brother Storrs,) to go out and sound the alarm. . . . In both cities [New York and Philadelphia], stores are being closed, and they preach in tones the world understands, though they may not heed it." [19]

It seems that some who were in business closed their stores not only to leave themselves footloose for evangelistic activity, but also to provide a witness to all men that the day of the Lord was near. A typical illustration of a Millerite's closing his store as a witness, was related in a Philadelphia newspaper on October 11. The paper informs us that in the window of a store in that city appeared the following sign:

---
[18] *Ibid.*
[19] *Ibid.*, Oct. 3, 1844, p. 104.

THE GREAT DAY OF HOPE

"This shop is closed in honor of the King of kings, who will appear about the 20th of October. Get ready, friends, to crown Him Lord of all." [20]

There were several reasons why the believers in a number of instances sold their possessions in part or in whole. First, they wished to have more money with which to support the cause. It took money to support four presses running constantly, pouring out literature on Millerism. Second, they wished to have all their dealings with their fellow men honorably concluded before the advent, including full payment of all their debts. Third, with that fervent love for others, which true religion certainly ought to generate in the hearts of men, Millerites who owed no debts themselves sought to help others pay their debts. Some Millerites, stimulated by the realization that soon earthly gold would be worthless, and warmed in their hearts with a love for their fellow men, wished to make gifts to the poor, both within and without the faith.

The editor of *The Midnight Cry* ran this notice above his signature: "If any human being has a just pecuniary claim against me, he is requested to inform me instantly." [21]

A New York newspaper tells of the owner of a dry-goods store who offered his wares at special prices, and for this reason: "My only object in offering my goods for sale, is that I may meet all obligations to my fellow men as far as possible, before that day arrives. All persons indebted, will oblige by settling the same immediately—and all to whom I am indebted will please send their accounts for settlement." [22] *

A Philadelphia newspaper reported that one believer brought to a Millerite meeting a bill of $22, expressing fear that he could not pay it before the end came, and that the money to pay the bill was quickly subscribed by others.[23]

---

[20] *Philadelphia Public Ledger,* Oct. 11, 1844.
[21] *The Midnight Cry,* Oct. 3, 1844, p. 104.
[22] *New York Spectator,* Oct. 19, 1844.
[23] See *Spirit of the Times* (Philadelphia), Oct. 15, 1844.

* The store owner's name is given as Richard Plumer, and the date of his notice as October 16. Another paper, doubtless referring to the same incident, gives the location of this store as Newburyport, Massachusetts. (See *Evening Post for the Country* [New York], Oct. 18, 1844.)

Another newspaper tells of an officer in the New York custom house who resigned his position because he had accepted Millerism, and who wove into his letter of resignation this word of appeal to his superior: "And may the Lord by His spirit convince you of the truth and prepare you to meet Him with yours in the hope of a better inheritance." The letter was dated September 4, 1844.[24]

Newspapers also carry certain stories about Millerites throwing their money on the streets and tradesmen their wares on the sidewalks. These alleged acts will be considered in a later chapter that deals with the examination of evidence on fanaticism.

There are numbers of news items in the papers regarding the payment of debts and the restoring of stolen property, because men's consciences were quickened by the preaching that the day of the Lord was near at hand. For example, the secretary of the United States Treasury received $5 conscience money from a man who identified himself as being now a believer in Millerism.[25] A man sent $120 to a New York insurance company with this note: "The Lord is at hand. This was unlawfully taken from you, and I ask forgiveness, for the Lord has forgiven me much." [26]

Large crimes and small crimes were confessed. Shortly before the great day came, a "conscience-struck Millerite," as the newspaper described him, returned a shawl and a spoon to someone with an explanatory note to the effect that his conscience had been quickened through Millerism.[27]

In an earlier chapter we described the "caricature prints" that began to appear in 1843, that strange array of broadsides and other printed material with ludicrous cartoons of Millerites and their preaching. October, 1844, saw these scurrilous sheets reaching new heights, or rather new depths, of ridicule and sacrilege. Few of these broadsides have been preserved, but

---
[24] *Sun* (Baltimore), Oct. 22, 1844.
[25] See *Boston Post,* Oct. 25, 1844.
[26] *Neal's Saturday Gazette* (Philadelphia), Oct. 19, 1844.
[27] See *Boston Daily Bee,* Oct. 22, 1844.

there lies before us as we write one such masterpiece of the press, about three feet long and two feet wide. It bears a flaming title, "End of the World." And immediately underneath it in a little smaller type, "October 22, 1844!!" Then on a third line in still smaller type: "Behold the Bridegroom Cometh!! Go ye out to meet Him!!!" The upper half of the broadside is almost wholly filled with a large picture of the second coming of Christ in judgment. The person reading the columns of text matter on the lower half of the broadside would have to come nearly to the close before finding anything other than material quoted from the Millerite papers; but the last column contains a short article entitled "Strange Doings at the Tabernacle," which ridicules Millerites and their services at the Boston tabernacle.* One might be pardoned for doubting that such broadsides were actually printed, and with so evident an intent to deceive, were it not that some of these broadsides are still preserved for our amazed inspection.

An obviously scurrilous broadside, of which copies are still preserved, is entitled in very large type "Grand Ascension of the Miller Tabernacle!" In smaller type underneath is the subtitle "Miller in His Glory, Saints and Sinners in One Great Conglomeration!" The upper half of this broadside, which is also about three feet long and two feet wide, consists of a cartoon

---

* This broadside bears no date, but it could not have been published earlier than October 12, because it carries an article from *The Advent Herald* of that date, and it must have been published before October 19, because *The Midnight Cry,* in its issue of that date, carries this item on the last page:

"*N. B. The public are informed that none of our sheets are offered for sale.* As many have been imposed upon by a sheet sold by the newsboys, entitled, 'THE END OF THE WORLD!' supposing it to be from the Advent office, we hereby inform all who wish to read our views in detail that they may obtain the sheet containing them *gratuitously* at 14 Devonshire Street, Boston."

This particular broadside has an interesting connection with one that was printed anonymously in the spring of 1843. The 1843 broadside, copies of which are still preserved, carries the same title, "END OF THE WORLD," in large, bold type. And the same striking picture of the second advent of Christ is used, with the same caption. But in this case all the material, and also all the prophetic pictures, excepting the second coming scene, are taken from the Millerite publications. The material had simply been pirated by a conscienceless printer and brought out in spectacular broadside style to increase its sales possibilities. The Millerite papers at the time exposed the deception and expressed their emphatic disapproval of any attempt to picture so sublime an event as the second advent. The Millerites were evidently quite conservative in their handling of the theme of the second advent, if they would not even approve of a picturization of it. They described any such artistic attempts as "presumptuous in the extreme." (See *Signs of the Times,* May 10, 1843, p. 76.)

showing the Boston Tabernacle lifted from its foundations, and soaring in the clouds, with various of the Millerites holding to it precariously, and with a basket swinging from the sky, apparently filled with provisions. The lower part of the picture shows a seething mass of people on the Boston streets looking upward at the strange sight. On the rostrum of the tabernacle, which is pictured as still standing on the street, is a caricature of Himes, with money bags about him, and with the names of the Millerite papers inscribed on the side of the rostrum. Himes is shown as reaching upward, but as unable to ascend because behind him crouches the devil, in all his cloven-hoofed grandeur, holding on to Himes' coattails, and declaring, "Joshua V., you must stay with me." This simply pictured the charge that had been hurled at Himes for years, that he was a conscienceless adventurer who had made great money out of publishing the Millerite literature.

The lower half of this broadside contains columns of doggerel verse in ridicule of Millerism, and also columns of prose that consisted of a rehash of all the foolish stories and charges that had been made against Millerism. At the bottom of the broadside is a line of display type:

"Here endeth the end of the world, and the grand tableaux of October 22d, 1844." *

We may well marvel, not that some Millerite acted irrationally, as a few of them did, but that the great body of them maintained their poise at all under the barrage of broadsides and other scurrilous material that poured from the press.†

The Advent Herald was a weekly paper published each Wednesday. On the front page of the issue that came out six days before the expected end—for the twenty-second was a Tuesday—Himes published a statement in which he said:

---

* This broadside, like the other we have just described, bears neither a date nor the name of a printer, but it was evidently brought out just before October 22, if not on that day. It was printed not earlier than six days before, because the story of an alleged "eyewitness" to the strange activities of the Millerites bears date of October 16.

† There was one clear-cut incident of a not very prudent move made by a group of about two hundred Millerites who went out from Philadelphia the day before the expected end, believing they should leave the cities even as Lot fled Sodom before its destruction. This incident will be discussed at some length in a chapter devoted to fanaticism.

"As the date of the present number of the *Herald* is our last day of publication before the tenth day of the seventh month, we shall make no provision for issuing a paper for the week following. . . . We feel called upon to suspend our labors and await the result." [28]

The last words were being said by the Millerites. And for that matter their opponents also were bringing on their last arguments, for occasionally they did change from ridicule to serious argument. The *Philadelphia Public Ledger,* on the fifteenth day of October, ran a rather lengthy editorial discussing Millerism and seeking to prove that it was impossible for the world to break into fire. The editor declared there was no chance from spontaneous combustion, or volcanoes, or colliding stars, and inquired solemnly, "From what other source can the destruction proceed?" The main substance of the argument was reprinted in the issue of October 21.

At last came the great day. Where did it find the Millerites? In their churches, one would naturally answer, in view of the fact that they were deeply religious and in numbers of main cities had been holding daily meetings for the preceding week or more. Newspapers are tantalizingly brief in their reports on the Millerites on that day. But from such specific information as they did give, we conclude that our supposition is right, that the Millerites were at their meetinghouses, in those cities where they had a place of worship. For example, a New York newspaper reported:

"The last evening being the one before the great 'going out' of the Millerites, there was some anxiety in the public mind as to what and how they were preparing for this, to the Millerites, great event, and it was generally expected that something more than ordinary display would be made at the different places of worship. The attendance thereat was pretty great." [29]

The reporter then went on to say that some of the Millerite meeting places in New York City were already closed by the police on account of mobs. He remarked that in front of some

---
[28] *The Advent Herald,* Oct. 16, 1844, p. 81.
[29] *Herald* (New York), Oct. 23, 1844.

of these closed meeting places curious persons gathered to discuss the matter of the Millerites' anticipated ascension that day. He added in comment:

"It was pretty generally understood that these poor deluded individuals had formed themselves into small parties at their several houses, to comfort and bear each other company in their anticipated trip; where private prayer meetings were held, in consequence of the authorities interfering in closing their meeting houses to prevent disturbance." [30]

In New York City, then, it seems that the Millerites on that great day were present in their meeting places if they were still left open by the police, or else were gathered in small companies for religious services in their homes. The reporter does not even suggest that anything fanatical happened in connection with their services.

Of the Millerites in Baltimore, the leading newspaper in that city said shortly after the great day:

"The Millerites . . . kept it up all night before last, and yesterday they went to bed—their public haunts are silent as the grave." [31]

"Public haunts" was evidently the newspaper's slurring name for the meeting places of the Millerites. And at these meeting places they had been on that great day. A Cleveland newspaper gives a similar report concerning the Millerites in that city:

"Our second advent friends watched for the coming at the tabernacle most of last night. Their meetings have been kept up today." [32]

We have been able to find only one instance where a reporter actually attended a Millerite meeting on the twenty-second and wrote a firsthand report. This was in the city of Cincinnati, which was a strong Millerite center. They owned their large tabernacle. In the absence of any good reason for thinking otherwise we may rightly conclude that the Cincinnati meeting was typical of Millerite meetings held on that day. The report is written by a correspondent of the *Cincinnati Chronicle*. It seems that he

---
[30] *Ibid.*
[31] *Sun* (Baltimore), Oct. 25, 1844.
[32] *Cleveland Herald*, Oct. 22, 1844.

knew of no other plans that the Millerites had in Cincinnati than to hold services in their tabernacle, as they awaited the solemn moment of Christ's return. Said the reporter:

"As the consummation of all terrestrial things was expected to have taken place last evening, and being desirous of seeing the effect of such belief upon its votaries at their last earthly meeting, I took the liberty . . . of being present. The assemblage, indoors and out, probably numbered 1,500 persons. If rightly informed about the capacity of the house, about 1,200 were inside. . . . There was less excitement than I expected, and a great deal more cheerfulness manifested in the countenances of the believers than could have been supposed at the hour of so serious a crisis. . . .

"Considering the crowd, the meeting was very orderly. Two or three attempts were made by a set of rowdies outdoor to raise a breeze by noise and clamor, but the assertion of the preacher, that a strong police was present, calmed the multitude, and he was enabled to proceed with what he at the close said was, in his opinion, his last warning to a sinful world. . . . Before nine o'clock the benediction was pronounced, and the people advised to go quietly home and await the awful coming, which not unlikely might transpire at the hour of midnight, while most of us were wrapped in sleep. Notwithstanding all this, daylight, yea, a most splendid day of sunshine, is again upon us." [33] *

A few years later another writer tells of having gone to the Cincinnati tabernacle about nine o'clock on the morning of that eventful day. His words convey the impression that a great many of the Millerites had stayed at the tabernacle in religious service throughout the night, for he declared: "On our arrival there we found the house still about two-thirds full." He described briefly the singing and informal exhortation, but made no charge that anything fanatical or startling happened. He said the people decided they should go home in the afternoon. It is hard to

---

[33] *Cincinnati Chronicle,* quoted in *United States Saturday Post,* Nov. 9, 1844.

* In Cincinnati at this time there was published monthly by Charles Cist, the *Cincinnati Miscellany,* which gave a current history of the city. Under the title "Millerism—The Finale Here" there is found in the November, 1844, issue a description of Millerite activities in the days leading up to October 22, which tells of the meetings held at the tabernacle on Monday and Tuesday, October 21 and 22, and of the crowds that gathered around. This detailed article does not even imply that the services were other than proper. He makes this general comment near the close: "In most popular delusions, the leaders are crafty, designing and dishonest men, and the mass, honest dupes. I have watched this movement in every stage of its progress, and believe that all concerned, 'Priest and people alike' were sincere in their convictions."—*Pages 42, 43.*

believe that he would cover over fanatical proceedings with the mantle of vague phrases, for he was a preacher and frankly stated that he thought Millerism a rank delusion. It seems there was nothing sensational to report.[34]

What individual Millerites here or there may have done on that great day we cannot say. But so far as the record is specific with regard to the main companies of Millerites, they attended religious services or were in little companies in their homes. The very brevity of the record argues strongly that those services must have been sufficiently decorous and regular to be lacking in news value. And when we examine the one newspaper story that gives a reporter's firsthand account of a Millerite meeting, we are doubly persuaded that these advent services on the twenty-second of October were orderly and proper.

No words of ours can describe the heights of spiritual exaltation and hope on which the Millerites moved as they entered that great day. They truly believed they would meet Him, whom not having seen, they loved; that they would gaze into the face of the One who had been the object of all their prayers and adoration. They were confident that with others "loved long since, and lost awhile," they would be gathered into a blest abode where sorrow, sickness, and death are no more. From that high level of hope and happiness they were suddenly to be dashed to the depths of dark disappointment.

---

[34] See Maxwell Pierson Gaddis, *Footprints of an Itinerant,* pp. 362-364.

THE TRUE MIDNIGHT CRY.

BEHOLD, THE BRIDEGROOM COMETH; GO YE OUT TO MEET HIM.

Vol. I.   Edited by S. S. Snow, and published by E. Hale. Jr.; Haverhill, Ms. Aug. 22, 1844.   No. I.

Our blessed Lord and Master has promised that he will come again and receive his people to himself; that where he is, they may be also. The place where he and they are to dwell forever, is the New Jerusalem, that holy city, which God hath prepared for them, and which is to come down from God out of heaven, and that New Earth, wherein dwelleth righteousness.

Concerning the *time* of that coming, he says, in Mark xiii. 32, "But of that day and hour knoweth no man, no, not the angels which are in heaven, neither the Son, but the Father." It is thought by many, that this passage proves that men are never to know the time. But if it prove this, it likewise proves that the Son of God himself is never to know the time: for the passage declares precisely the same concerning him, that it does concerning angels and men. But can any person believe that our glorious Lord, to whom all power in heaven and earth is given, is, and will remain ignorant of the time until the very moment that he comes to judge the world? If not, then certainly this text can never prove that men may not be made to understand the time. An old English version of the passage reads, "But that day and hour no man maketh known neither the angels which are in heaven, neither the Son, but the Father." This is the correct reading according to several of the ablest critics of the age. The word *know* is used here in the same sense as it is by Paul in 1 Cor. ii. 2. Paul well understood many other things besides Christ and him crucified, but he determined to *make known* nothing else among them. So in the passage first quoted, it is declared that none but God the Father maketh known the day and hour, that is, the *definite time* of the second coming of his Son. And this necessarily implies that God makes the time known. The Old Testament contains the testimony of the Father concerning his Son, and concerning the *time* of both his first and second comings. Therefore the time is to be understood. See Dan. xii. 10, "Many shall be purified, and made white, and tried; but the wicked shall do wickedly; and none of the wicked shall understand; but the wise shall understand." Rom. xv. 4, "For whatsoever things were written aforetime were written for our learning, that we through patience and comfort of the Scriptures might have hope." It is by the teaching of his word, as we are led therein by the Holy Spirit, that we are to understand the time of the coming of our GLORIOUS KING. As further proof of this, see Dan. ix. 25, "Know therefore and understand, that from the going forth of the commandment, to restore and build Jerusalem, unto the Messiah, the Prince, shall be seven weeks, and threescore and two weeks." Mark i. 14, 15, "Now after that John was put in prison, Jesus came into Galilee, preaching the gospel of the Kingdom of God, and saying the *time* is fulfilled." Luke xix. 43, 44, "For the day shall come upon thee that thine enemies shall cast a trench about thee, and compass thee round and keep thee in on every side, and shall lay thee even with the ground, and thy children within thee, and they shall not leave in thee one stone upon another; because thou knewest not the time of thy visitation." 1 Pet. i. 9–11, "Searching what, or what manner of time the spirit of Christ, which was in them, did signify, when it testified beforehand the sufferings of Christ, and the glory that should follow." Isa. xl. 1–5; Acts xvii. 30, 31, "He hath appointed a day in the which he will judge the world in righteousness." Ecc. iii. 17, "God shall judge the righteous and the wicked; for there is a time there for every purpose and for every work." Ecc. viii. 5–7, "Whoso keepeth the commandment shall feel no evil thing; and a wise man's heart discerneth both time and judgment." Jer. viii. 6–9, "I hearkened and heard, but they spake not aright; no man repented him of his wickedness, saying, what have I done? every one turned to his course as the horse rusheth into the battle. Yea, the stork in the heaven knoweth her appointed times; and the turtle, and crane, and the swallow, observe the time of their coming; but my people know not the judgment of the Lord. How do ye say, we are wise, and the law of the Lord is with us? Lo certainly in vain made he it; the pen of the scribes is in vain. The wise men are ashamed, they are dismayed and taken; lo, they have rejected the word of the Lord; and what wisdom is in them? Hosea ix. 7–9, "The days of visitation are come, the days of recompense are come; Israel shall know it." The prophet is a fool, the spiritual man is mad." Rom. xiii. 11–14, "And that knowing the time, that now it is high time to awake out of sleep."

THE SIX THOUSAND YEARS. The period of time allotted for this world, in its present state, is 6000 years, at the termination of which commences the great millennial Sabbath, spoken of in Rev. xx, and which will be ushered in by the personal appearing of Christ and the first Resurrection; see Isa. xlvi. 9, 10; Gen. ii. 1–3; Heb. iv. 4–9; Isa. xi. 10; 2 Pet. iii. 8. According to Usher's chronology, which is commonly received, the Christian Era commenced in the year of the world 4004, but Usher has lost in the time of the judges 153 years. From the division of the Land of Canaan to the beginning of Samuel's administration, he gives but 295 years; whereas Paul, in Acts xiii. 20, gives us "about the space of 450." From the book of Judges we obtain 430 years, and Josephus gives us 18 more for the elders and anarchy, before any judge ruled; this added to 430 make 448 which

The first page of a four-page paper published to present the arguments for the October 22, 1844, date for the advent. Note the reasoning employed to escape the Bible declaration that no one knows the day of Christ's coming.

Boston 10th Oct. 1844.

Dear Brother Miller,

I was deeply interested in hearing yours of the 6th inst, read at the Tabernacle last evening by brother Himes, & gladly write you in compliance with his request.

The Midnight Cry is searching our souls through & through. We feel to humble ourselves in the dust & magnify the Lord.

He that is mighty hath done great things & holy is his name. We had never been brought into this faith had we not known the voice of God. He has said My sheep hear my voice & they follow me. There was something sweet, soul-subduing & heavenly in the sound of this cry when I first heard it at the Exeter Camp Meeting. Yet I was kept back by "wise & prudent" considerations from embracing the present truth until about a week since when I came to this place.

Such a breaking down of soul I never saw — no power but the Sword of the Spirit can slay in this manner.

First part of a letter from Mrs. E. C. Clemons to Miller. This letter is historically important because it provides one of the few descriptions written by Millerites of the real temper of the movement shortly before the great day.

Dear Bro. Miller:

The above is written at my request. I know you will excuse me for not writing you at length — The time is short. I am resigned up to the Judgment. I never felt it so before. God is now testing us — Do we believe what we have preached — We have got to answer it — on the answer, yea or nay, depends our Salvation.

Love to all the Brethren. My faith is given in the Herald. God bless you — And may we meet soon in the Kingdom.

J. V. Himes

Oct. 10. 1844.

A short penciled note from Himes to Miller that was written at the bottom of Mrs. Clemons' letter. (See Appendix B.)

The upper part of the first pages of the first issues of the *Signs of the Times* and *The Midnight Cry*, the two leading Millerite papers. In these is to be found the most authentic and most detailed record of the activities of the movement.

A portion of the first page of a two-page extra of the *New-York Tribune* on Millerism. The text matter is by Dowling, a militant and widely quoted opponent of Miller's.

CHAPTER 17

The Great Disappointment

THE MILLERITES WHO GATHERED in their churches that twenty-second day of October were no longer believers in the "advent near," they were believers in the advent here. With unwavering faith and full confidence, they had expected their Lord's return on that day. But as the sun sank in the west, their hopes sank with it. From the heights of happiness and hope they fell to the depths of the deepest disappointment.

On October 24 Josiah Litch, who was in Philadelphia, wrote to Miller these sorrowful words: "It is a cloudy and dark day here—the sheep are scattered—and the Lord has not come yet." [1]

Even if the weather actually was cloudy, and the day literally dark in Philadelphia, we cannot escape the feeling that Litch was speaking of a figurative darkness that enveloped them.

Joseph Bates truly observed that "the effect of this disappointment can be realized only by those who experienced it." [2]

Another of the Millerites, telling of that experience, described how high were their expectations, how they looked for their "coming Lord until the clock tolled twelve at midnight." Then their "disappointment became a certainty." But let Hiram Edson tell in his own words of the sorrow that took hold upon him:

"Our fondest hopes and expectations were blasted, and such a spirit of weeping came over us as I never experienced before. It seemed that the loss of all earthly friends could have been no comparison. We wept, and

---

[1] Manuscript letter, Oct. 24, 1844.
[2] Joseph Bates, *Autobiography*, p. 300.

wept, till the day dawn. I mused in my own heart, saying, My advent experience has been the richest and brightest of all my Christian experience. If this had proved a failure, what was the rest of my Christian experience worth? Has the Bible proved a failure? Is there no God, no heaven, no golden home city, no paradise? Is all this but a cunningly devised fable? Is there no reality to our fondest hope and expectation of these things? And thus we had something to grieve and weep over, if all our fond hopes were lost. And as I said, we wept till the day dawn." [3]

The shock, the sorrow, and the darkness were so great that at least for the moment even the most devout found themselves tormented with disquieting thoughts.

The keenness of that disappointment was so great that another Millerite, writing long afterward of the event, could describe it in the most vivid language. Here are his words:

"That day came and passed, and the darkness of another night closed in upon the world. But with that darkness came a pang of disappointment to the advent believers that can find a parallel only in the sorrow of the disciples after the crucifixion of their Lord. The passing of the time was a bitter disappointment. True believers had given up all for Christ, and had shared His presence as never before. The love of Jesus filled every soul; and with inexpressible desire they prayed, 'Come, Lord Jesus, and come quickly;' but He did not come. And now, to turn again to the cares, perplexities, and dangers of life, in full view of jeering and reviling unbelievers who scoffed as never before, was a terrible trial of faith and patience. When Elder Himes visited Waterbury, Vt., a short time after the passing of the time, and stated that the brethren should prepare for another cold winter, my feelings were almost uncontrollable. I left the place of meeting and wept like a child." [4]

Luther Boutelle, a Millerite lecturer, tells of the disappointment and embarrassment that confronted them:

"The 22d of October passed, making unspeakably sad the faithful and longing ones; but causing the unbelieving and wicked to rejoice. All was still. No *Advent Herald;* no meetings as formerly. Everyone felt lonely, with hardly a desire to speak to anyone. Still in the cold world! No deliverance—the Lord [had] not come! No words can express the feelings

---

[3] Hiram Edson, Fragment of manuscript on his life and experience, pp. 8, 9.
[4] Washington Morse, "Remembrance of Former Days," *The Advent Review and Sabbath Herald,* May 7, 1901, p. 291.

THE GREAT DISAPPOINTMENT

of disappointment of a true Adventist then. Those only who experienced it can enter into the subject as it was. It was a humiliating thing, and we all felt it alike. . . .

"Not quite content with being housed, after such stirring times, I went to Boston. Found *The Advent Herald* office closed, and all still. I next went to New Bedford. Found the brethren in a confused state. Had a few meetings; comforted those who came as best I could, telling them to hold fast, for I believed there would be a good come out of this matter. . . . Some fanaticism was seen, but the many were sober watchers for the Lord." [5]

He was told "of a company that had come together to stay until the Lord came." He decided to visit them and cheer them in their disappointment:

"I found about 70 believers in a large house, living there and having meetings daily. They had put all their money in a milk pan, and when they paid for anything they took the money from the pan. All was common stock. We held a meeting with them and advised them as best we could to keep the faith and separate, and see to their individual interests, and those of their families, which advice they kindly took, and very soon separated, each going to his or her calling." [6]

Here again is evidence in support of the conclusion that the Millerites were gathered in religious services on that day, services held in private homes when regular meetinghouses were not available.* The description of their common funds sounds strangely like the story in the Bible of the common fund which the early Christians had, by which the needs of all were supplied.[7]

To suffer so keen a disappointment was exquisite pain in itself, but to that were added the jeers and ridicule of scoffers. The Millerites knew they were in an alien, hostile world. They

---

[5] Luther Boutelle, *Life and Religious Experience*, pp. 67, 68.
[6] *Ibid.*, pp. 68, 69.
[7] See Acts 4:34, 35.

* Another Millerite, writing from Boston a year afterward, gave this account of his experience on Tuesday, October 22: "I waited all Tuesday and dear Jesus did not come;—I waited all the forenoon of Wednesday, and was well in body as I ever was, but after 12 o'clock I began to feel faint, and before dark I needed someone to help me up to my chamber, as my natural strength was leaving me very fast, and I lay prostrate for 2 days without any pain—sick with disappointment—then all my strength returned suddenly. Blessed be God."—*Letter from H. Emmons, Oct. 10, 1845,* in *The Day-Star, Oct. 25, 1845, p. 6.*

This writer did his waiting, not out in a graveyard, or some other strange place, but in a downstairs room of his home! This supports the previous testimony presented regarding the location of the Millerites on the twenty-second.

shrank from mingling with others. They knew not how to answer the taunting question, "Why didn't you go up?" though one of them silenced an inquirer by asking sternly in return, "And if I *had* gone up, where would you have gone?" Miller himself, in a personal letter a few weeks afterward, told a fellow believer of what happened at Low Hampton in connection with the great day. He spoke of it as "a solemn time" when "even the wicked scoffers stood mute." But, said he:

"It passed. And the next day it seemed as though all the demons from the bottomless pit were let loose upon us. The same ones and many more who were crying for mercy two days before, were now mixed with the rabble and mocking, scoffing, and threatening in a most blasphemous manner." [8]

This letter of Miller's reveals that there were not simply two classes at that time—the sincere Millerites, and the open scoffers. There was a third class—a group who had come to the Millerite services, not because they loved the Lord's appearing, but rather because they feared it. They hoped that in some way they might ward off the judgments of God by coming into the circle of the Millerites at the last moment and mingling their fear-inspired prayers with the exultant songs of the true believers. This has always been true in the history of religion since the days of the mixed multitude that came out with the Israelites from the land of Egypt. But the sudden revelation of this fact to the startled eyes and ears of true Millerites would only add to their overwhelming sorrow. Of these counterfeit Adventists, Miller declared in this letter that none now "come near our meeting."

From N. N. Whiting came a letter to Miller just two days after the disappointment, describing the troubles that confronted the advent believers on Long Island when the day of the advent had passed. Said Whiting:

"The excitement against us here already begins to die away. We were in some danger from the mob last Sabbath [October 20], at Franklin Hall

---

[8] Manuscript letter to I. O. Orr, M. D., Dec. 13, 1844.

[New York City]. The mayor, however, offered to put down the mob with strong hand if a meeting should be held in the evening. Our brethren concluded to close the house." [9]

Whiting was not sure on the twenty-fourth that mob violence of some form or other might not trouble them. He revealed this in an unusual way. While the salutation at the beginning of his letter read, "Dear Brother W. Miller," the letter was addressed to "Mr. George Miller," his son. His reason for thus addressing the letter he explained in a postscript: "I have directed this to George Miller, lest it should be intercepted or opened."

The mobs and the excitement soon quieted down. But this still left one problem troubling the leaders. They must take some step to care for those advent believers who had impoverished themselves by selling their possessions. In the first issue of *The Midnight Cry* published after the disappointment there appeared a signed editorial by Himes entitled "Provision for the Destitute." In it he said:

"As many of our brethren and sisters have disposed of their substance, and given alms, agreeable to Luke 12:33, in the confident expectation of the speedy coming of the Lord, I wish to have immediate provision made for the comforts and wants of all such persons, and families, by the advent brethren. We must not permit them to be dependent upon the world, or that portion of the professed church, who scoff at our hope. We hope no application will be made to such for aid in this work of charity. . . .

"Let committees of faithful and judicious men, be raised in every city and town, to whom contributions may be given for the poor saints. . . .

"Some among us still have this world's goods, and can render present aid to the destitute. I doubt not all will do their duty." [10]

Himes, it appears, believed there were sufficient resources within the circle of the movement to care for all who might be destitute. We conclude, therefore, that the Millerites followed no general policy of selling possessions. While farmers in many instances did not harvest their crops, there seems to have been no selling of the farms. Most of the believers, however, gave

---

[9] Manuscript letter, Oct. 24, 1844.
[10] *The Midnight Cry*, Oct. 31, 1844, p. 140.

up all their worldly occupations for the last few days, and some for the last few weeks, before the expected end of the world. The testimony on this is clear.[11]

This abstaining from labor at the very last in order to attend meetings or to engage in missionary work seems largely to have been a spontaneous action, without any clear instruction from the principal leaders. However, there was at least one among the Millerite ministers who must have advised the believers to leave all worldly activity as the end drew near. We find that George Storrs made this confession a few days after the disappointment:

"I confess that I have been led into error, and thereby have led others astray, in advising advent believers to leave business entirely and attend meetings only; though I have usually qualified that advice by excepting business *absolutely* necessary for *present necessity.*"[12]

But the postscript to this letter of confession Storrs sent to *The Midnight Cry* shows he still had some good counsel to offer. He suggested that the believers visit the office of *The Midnight Cry* only when they have "business necessary to be attended to there" and that the visit should "be as short as possible." And why? Because "spending our time there in *speculation* on the Scriptures, or *disputation* on any subject, I fear, will *disqualify* rather than *prepare* us for an admission into the kingdom of God."[13]

That was good counsel under the circumstances. The believers were bewildered for the moment. There had been no time for calm study and re-examination of the evidence. Nothing could be gained by indulging in idle speculation or dispute.

However, the problem of providing aid for the needy had a sinister side to it in the minds of unfriendly critics of the movement. For years Himes and others had been accused of profiting by the promotion of the movement. In view of the fact that numbers of the believers had turned their possessions into

---

[11] See Sylvester Bliss, *Memoirs of William Miller*, p. 276.
[12] *The Midnight Cry*, Oct. 31, 1844, p. 144.
[13] *Ibid.*

cash, and that no small part of this money was used to purchase literature or in some other way to advance the movement, new insinuations and open charges were made that the Millerite leaders, particularly Himes, had personally profited.

One New York newspaper actually charged that Himes took everything the poor had and left them destitute.[14] A Boston paper insinuated that Himes had short-changed people, and that public indignation against him was high.[15] A week later this paper quoted a Philadelphia paper which accused the Millerite leaders of being knaves who had been "filling their pockets."[16] A Providence paper carried this item: "It is reported that Brother Himes, the treasurer of the Millerites, is missing. It is supposed that he has ascended, and that he has carried the money with him."[17] A New Hampshire paper wrote, "Himes, one of the high priests of Miller, it is said decamped a short time since, with a fund, no one knows how large, collected from the advent believers, but has been arrested and taken to Boston."[18] About ten days later another newspaper had improved on the story to the extent of reporting that several Millerite leaders had been arrested for fraudulently inducing their followers to part with their money, and named Himes particularly.[19]

Apparently the only foundation in fact for these stories about Himes and others being arrested after October 22, is the case of I. R. Gates of Baltimore. He was arrested not *after* the disappointment but *before*. The charge was *not* that of swindling people out of money but that of disturbing the peace. And he was not put in jail but immediately discharged, unconditionally. In a letter to *The Midnight Cry,* Gates told his version of the newspaper story about a Millerite preacher arrested in Baltimore. He stated, "I was brought before Caesar

---
[14] *New York Spectator,* Nov. 2, 1844.
[15] *American Traveller* (Boston), Nov. 2, 1844.
[16] *Ibid.,* Nov. 9, 1844.
[17] *Providence Daily Journal* (R. I.), Oct. 24, 1844.
[18] *New Hampshire Statesman* (Concord), Oct. 25, 1844.
[19] *Caledonian* (St. Johnsbury, Vt.), Nov. 4, 1844.

on a charge of disturbing the peace of society, but was immediately discharged." Some newspapers had reported that he was released by the court on his own recognizance until after the great day of the advent. And a Millerite paper, trusting the press to this extent, copied the statement. But Gates declared emphatically, "There was no such condition whatever."

He explained that the "ground of this prosecution" was that he held meetings, and that the Millerites would "occasionally shout and praise God above a whisper, which made some of the people very angry, and they took that plan to vent their spite at me." The judge, by releasing him unconditionally, gave evidence he must have thought that spite, or some reason equally groundless, actuated Gates' accusers. Gates made very clear that he felt his accusers were inconsistent in their charge, for he remarked in the very next sentence that he had heard "last night from twelve o'clock until break of day," very "enthusiastic shoutings" over Mr. Polk, in connection with the Presidential election. Yet everyone seemed to think that such exuberance of spirit was wholly proper.

Gates also took occasion to refer to the furor that had been raised about the Adventists' having sold their possessions to give alms to the poor. With fine irony he declared:

"The world affects to have great sympathy for us, for fear we will become poor; but I ask what is the reason that they don't have any sympathy for those of our cities who have been made poor and wretched through other causes, such as politics, gambling, drunkenness and idleness? Nothing is said about them in the papers. They might starve and freeze to death in many cases, and the editors of those corrupt papers would be the last to seek them out and appeal to the sympathy of the world in their behalf, without being paid for it. Does any ask, what is the principle by which they are governed in this case towards us? I answer, precisely that of Judas, and others, who found fault with Mary, to our blessed Lord, for the expensive box of ointment she poured upon His head. It was not that they cared for the poor, they aimed their thrust at Him. So in this case their death blow is aimed at Christ's second coming." [20]

---

[20] Letter, Nov. 7, 1844, in *The Midnight Cry*, Nov. 14, 1844, p. 159.

THE GREAT DISAPPOINTMENT

Gates' response was typical of the Millerite attitude in relation to all attacks upon them. They firmly believed in the oft-proved military maxim that attack is the best defense. We need not endorse their strategy of militant rejoinder in order to agree that the Millerites were quite able to defend themselves. They were certainly not a group of bewildered ignoramuses who simply shouted hallelujahs when not struck dumb by a withering attack from opponents. On that point the record is too clear to admit of debate.

On viewing the array of wild charges in the press, particularly with regard to his alleged arrest, Himes wished at the outset to make a blanket denial. Through *The Advent Herald* he delivered his soul in the robust editorial style current in that day:

"It is no time for us to defend ourself now, against the thousand rumors that are rife in the community. We have been a close observer of all the movements and doings in the enemy's camp, but as yet we have not seen a *single truth*. Lies! Lies!! Lies!!!" [21]

A little further on in the same issue he referred specifically to stories that he had been arrested, and added this comment: "We have not seen the *officer* nor his *warrant*. If there is one we should be very happy to see it." [22]

Himes must have reconsidered shortly his position that "it is no time for us to defend ourself now," because we find him a few days later drafting a detailed answer to a series of charges against him and the movement. This refutation of charges was prepared originally for *The Advent Herald*. But on second thought Himes decided to try to have it published in a newspaper. In this he was successful. It appeared in full on the front page of the *Boston Post*. The statement was prefaced with a brief letter from Himes to the editor, dated October 31, which said in part:

"The following article was prepared originally for *The Advent Herald*, but as you have generously offered to give it a place in the *Post*, I thankfully

---
[21] *The Advent Herald*, Oct. 30, 1844, p. 94.
[22] *Ibid.*, p. 96.

avail myself of the opportunity. The insertion of it in your columns will truly make the *amende honorable*. Permit me to say that I hope the religious and secular press who have given circulation to the slanderous reports relative to my character will be as prompt and honorable in doing me the same justice." [23]

He quoted in the opening paragraph of his article what the *Boston Post* itself, along with other newspapers, had printed of slander, gossip, and rumor regarding him. Said he:

"I have been represented as dishonest, speculating out of the fears of the community, a disturber of the peace, as duping the unsuspecting, and obtaining money under false pretenses,—soliciting it for public purposes, and appropriating it to private uses. I have been reported as having absconded, not only to England, but also both to Canada and Texas; and also as being liable to arrest under warrants already issued; as having been arrested and confined in Leverett Street jail, and as having committed suicide." [24]

He called on all "registers of deeds" to "report any real estate on record at their respective offices," for if people had really deeded property to Himes there must be a record of it. As to his transfers of money—for one of the rumors was that Himes took a large sum of money out of the bank shortly before October 22 to buy English securities—he said: "My deposits have been made at the Merchants' Bank, and if I have had money deposited there in a larger amount, or drawn it out in sums otherwise than the regular transaction of my business would naturally render necessary, the officers of that bank are requested to make it public." He declared that books showing his publishing and other business transactions would be "open to the inspection of all proper or interested persons."

His lengthy statement bristles with names of people and of places, of dates and detailed discussion of transactions with various people, in answer to specific charges. It is not the kind of reply that a guilty man makes to charges. Such a man who felt he must say something in the public press in defense of himself would not, if he were even half as shrewd as Himes was

---

[23] *Boston Post*, Nov. 2, 1844.
[24] *Ibid.*

credited with being, do other than bluster and make a few vague general denials.

After answering a series of specific, libelous charges against himself, he then turned to an examination of certain general charges against the movement.

The very fact that the editor of a prominent Boston newspaper published this lengthy statement by Himes on the front page rather suggests that he must have thought Himes made out a pretty good case. That was on Saturday. Newspapers in different cities made reference to the *Post* statement by Himes. While they could hardly be expected to say much in favor of it, which would be equivalent to indicting themselves as having been publishers of slanderous stories, they do not make any attempt to refute his answer. Remarkable indeed! Himes, with his very specific and detailed rejoinder had given them a golden opportunity. Some of them even admitted, grudgingly, as did one newspaper in Philadelphia, that Himes had met the charges against him and the movement with "tolerable success."[25] *

The reader may ask why we take time at this late date to go into the details of long-dead charges. We reply: First, to give a true history, that the reader may really know how dark and how difficult were the times the Millerites passed through. Second, because the charges, though long, are not dead. They have lengthened with the years but have refused to die.† It is really impossible to see the Millerites in true focus until the fog of false charges has been blown away. There is a very special reason for discussing this statement by Himes. It deals largely with the kind of charges that are most easily capable of clear proof or

---

[25] *Pennsylvanian* (Philadelphia) Nov. 8, 1844.

* Another paper, the *Boston Daily Mail*, went so far as to say in its comments on Himes' defense in the *Post:* "It is but justice to say that he most effectively disarms his enemies and nails their slanders to the counter."—*Daily Mail, Nov. 4, 1844.* In the same issue it published Himes' statement in somewhat condensed form. The *Boston Bee* also reported Himes' statement from the *Boston Post.* (See *Boston Daily Bee,* Nov. 4, 1844.)

† About the year 1850 several persons who had been more or less associated with Himes preferred charges against him, some of them in the same category as these. See Appendix C for an examination of these later charges.

disproof. Did people deed their property to Himes? Let the recorders of deeds speak up, he declared. Did he take unusual sums of money out of the bank? The bank officials are openly invited by him to tell what they wished about his affairs.

Now if each of the charges that had been made with such positiveness and plausibility as regards financial dealings proves false, then perhaps other charges not so easily subject to proof might also be considered groundless, or at least highly questionable. The same public press which was bringing one set of charges was bringing all the other charges.*

There *are* other charges against Millerism besides the allegedly shady financial dealings of the leaders. These will be considered in succeeding chapters. When we are examining them we shall make further reference to this statement by Himes. But we have here given enough of the discussion in the *Boston Post* to illustrate how the Millerites' sorrows of disappointment were sharpened by a renewed outburst of libelous charges against their leaders. Almost at the same time that Himes was preparing for the *Post* his defense of the movement in general and himself in particular, Miller was writing a personal letter in defense of his course to a "Brother Baxter." The letter opens in this unusual fashion: "I received an anonymous letter a few days since of your handwriting, and I presume was dictated by a very wicked heart." In those days there were no typewriters to aid an anonymous letter writer in hiding his identity. From Miller's reply we conclude that Baxter had raked up all the silly slanders of the past regarding Miller, despite the fact that he had been rather well acquainted with him and should have known better. Said Miller:

"You came into our meeting a few nights since and pretended you wanted light. Your conduct since shows you wanted no such thing. Your object was to find fault, and you have improved it to the entire satisfaction

---

* The courts, which through the centuries have sought to establish judicial procedures that will ensure a fair trial, have established certain rules regarding the credibility of witnesses. If a witness is discovered to be giving false testimony on even one point, opposing counsel is permitted to appeal to the jury to disregard any and all testimony by that witness. The presumption is that if he will lie on one matter he will lie on others.

of your master and his children. Then, you have loved and reported lies, and some of them you have been the father of. You have reported that my object in preaching was to make money. You knew better; for you have been with me time and again, and you know of no place where I received enough to pay my expenses. You have made and reported a lie, about the 'stone wall,' and many things more equally as untrue." [26]

The story, circulated years before, that Miller had just built a new stone wall around his farm, and therefore did not believe the Lord was coming soon, had often been disproved, but lived on. Continuing the letter:

"You say you should be ashamed to lift up your head, if you had been mistaken as I have. I suppose you would, because you have forsaken the way and looked back."

It was hard enough to meet the opposition of those who had always been enemies, but it was doubly painful to meet the charges of one who had to some degree at least formerly associated himself with the movement. But that was part of the pain of the disappointment. Miller ended his letter thus:

"Your criminal charge against me, 'that I have caused more suicide and insanity within six years than had been for sixty years before'—if you will be an honest man, and own your own handwriting, I will give you a chance to prove it. I am satisfied you dare not give me the opportunity. A deceitful man is always dishonest. I remain as ever opposed to deceit of any kind."

It is one thing to read of the charges that were made against a man who lived a hundred years ago. It is quite another thing to picture yourself in that man's place, subjected to a steady barrage of the most outrageous charges which, if only one tenth true, would make you a fit subject, if not for the asylum, then for the penitentiary.

But the very same week that Baxter's scurrilous letter was being brought to Miller by the postal service, another letter, by personal messenger, was on its way to him. This letter has no bearing on the story of the aftermath of the great disappointment. It belongs, rather, with the story of the

---

[26] Manuscript letter, Nov. 5, 1844.

abolitionist sentiments of Miller's associates. But the chronology of the letter places it here, and we turn aside to examine it. The letter sets forth Miller in a vastly different light than does the one from Baxter. It is written from South Granville, a town south of Low Hampton, in the same county. Here is its very unusual message:

"Dear Brother Miller:
"The bearer is a fugitive from the iron hand of slavery and, as appears from letters in his possession and his own statements, of some considerable consequence to his claimant. His master, with United States officers, is in hot pursuit of him. Not being acquainted with anyone in your section that would be more ready to feed the hungry and direct a stranger fleeing to a city of refuge than yourself, I have directed him to you.
"I think it is best for him to keep on through Vermont as far as Vergennes or Burlington, at least, before he strikes the Lake. You will probably be able to refer him to some abolitionist on his way north. Should you think any other course more safe, you will advise him.
"Yours for the slave,
"(Signed) Philander Barbour.
"If anything important transpires, let me know it." [27]

Miller may not have had any standing with Baxter, or the multitudes who thought like him, but he had very great standing with Philander Barbour—and the slave fleeing to freedom. This letter reveals that Miller had come to espouse the much-maligned abolitionist movement, which in itself reveals qualities of moral courage. It would be interesting to speculate on how he was brought to support the abolition movement. He could hardly escape doing so without being in opposition to some of his closest and most trusted associates. However, no man would take hold of abolitionism in those days who did not put conviction ahead of reputation. Miller could qualify in that respect.

---

[27] Manuscript letter, Nov. 8, 1844.

CHAPTER 18

Confident in Defeat

LESS THAN ONE MONTH AFTER the disappointment a lengthy statement was published in the two leading Millerite papers.¹ This was entitled "Address to the Public." The subtitle revealed its purpose: "Our Confession—Defense of Our Course —Opposition." There was first a frank confession that they had been "twice disappointed." This referred to the disappointment in connection with the prophetic year 1843, and also to the disappointment of October 22, 1844. "Those who do not believe with us," continued the address, "honestly suppose that such disappointments cannot be reconciled with an adherence to our faith." The purpose of most of the address that followed was to show how a person could still be a consistent, sensible Adventist after these disappointments. Commenting on the conclusion the public immediately reached, that "we must relinquish all our hopes, and abandon all our expectations," the address declared:

"We, however, do not thus feel. As great a paradox as it may be to our opponents, yet we can discern in it the leadings of God's providence; and when we are reviled and censured by those to whom the world look as the Gamaliels of our age, we feel that they are only speaking evil of the things they understand not." ²

The Millerites believed that in the mysterious plans of God this preaching of an exact date when men must meet God, served the purpose of a test to discover those who really loved the Lord

---
¹ See *The Advent Herald*, Nov. 13, 1844, pp. 108-112; *The Midnight Cry*, Nov. 21, 1844, pp. 161-166.
² *The Midnight Cry*, Nov. 21, 1844, pp. 162, 163.

and His appearing. They reasoned that God overruled to make this disappointing experience serve a divine purpose. Orthodox Christian theology holds the view that many happenings in our lives, while not attributable to any plan of God's for us, are often overruled by Him to His glory. The Millerites used the illustration of Jonah preaching to Nineveh. Said they:

"We as much believe that we have done the will of God in thus sounding the alarm, as we believe that Jonah did when he entered into Nineveh a day's journey, and cried, saying, 'Yet forty days and Nineveh shall be overthrown.' Nineveh was not then overthrown; nor has the Lord yet wrought deliverance in the earth, or the inhabitants of the earth fallen. Was Jonah a false prophet when he preached the *time* of Nineveh's destruction? No; he had only preached the preaching that God had bid him. . . . We thus have an instance on record where God has justified the preaching of *time,* although the event did not occur as predicted. And the men of Nineveh will rise up in the judgment against this generation and condemn it, for they repented at the preaching of Jonah; but this generation have not repented." [3]

They cited also the singular experience of Abraham when, in harmony with the command of God, he laid his son upon the altar of Mount Moriah to offer him up as a burnt offering:

"Had Abraham stopped to inquire if he might not after all be mistaken, he would have sinned; but, believing God, and accounting that He was able to raise him even from the dead, he laid his only son on an altar and stretched forth the knife in his hand to slay him. God thus having tested him and proved his faith, spared him the offering; 'for' said God, 'now I know that thou fearest God, seeing thou hast not withholden thy son, thine only son from Me.' . . . Even so do we believe that God permitted the preaching of this last time for the same purpose respecting His children now, to test their faith." [4]

As to their present position, the address declared:

"We now find ourselves occupying a time, beyond which we can extend none of the prophetic periods, according to our chronology and date of their commencement. . . . We admit that it is proved that we do not yet know the definite time; but we have seen no evidence yet to disprove that it is at the

---

[3] *Ibid.,* p. 163.
[4] *Ibid.*

very door, that it cannot be long delayed, and that the events are those for which we look." ⁵

This led them naturally to conclude:

"We are, therefore, now occupying a period of time in which we are to take heed to ourselves, lest at any time our hearts be overcharged with surfeiting and drunkenness, and cares of this life, and so that day come upon us unawares. Our position, therefore, is one of continual and confident expectation. . . . It will be our purpose the 'little while' we may continue here, to present the doctrine of the advent in all its purity." ⁶ *

In the concluding section of their address they dealt with the opposition that had confronted them all along the way:

"Believing as we do that we are living in the very *crisis* of this world's history, we have endeavored to be faithful, in presenting to the world the evidence of our belief. In doing this we have not trespassed on the rights of any, or conducted ourselves differently than our enemies acknowledged they would do if they believed with us. Yet to our astonishment, men of all classes and parties have united in opposing us—not with arguments, but the most malicious falsehoods that a depraved heart could suggest. Why is this? we inquire. It has been replied that we encourage idleness, and induce men to leave their business, to waste their property, and to leave their families unprovided for. This is not true. While some have thus taught, we have protested against it. . . . We have, however, advised those who wished to be relieved from the cares of this world for a few days before they expected the Lord, to lay by for a time, and prepare for and await the result. But if this was a crime in us, it is also a crime in those who accuse us." ⁷

In support of this countercharge they quoted the appeal that a Whig newspaper in Massachusetts made to the members of the party a few days before the national election took place. The fight was between Clay and Polk, and a vigorous fight it was:†

---

⁵ *Ibid.*
⁶ *Ibid.*, p. 164.
⁷ *Ibid.*, p. 166.

* Then followed a discussion of the relationship of their basic views on prophecy and the advent, to the views held on this subject by others. We defer consideration of this to a closing chapter.

† The Millerites, in their address, gave only a portion of this newspaper statement. We quote it in full as it appeared in the newspaper.

"*Whig* READER! Have you, through all the contest done anything to secure the election of Clay and Frelinghuysen to the presidency and vice-presidency? If not, spend the little remaining time in hard work among the doubting, the luke-warm, and the open enemy. Forget business —forget everything but your country till the election is over, and then you will read the result with a clear conscience." [8]

The Millerite address made this comment:

"We know that in advocating the present election, more time and money have been expended, a thousand times over, than have been expended in circulating the evidences of the coming of the King of kings. In the opinion of the world, this is, however, all right and proper; but if we act in accordance with our faith, in view of our eternal well-being, we are, by those who do the same things, condemned and censured as inconsistent." [9]

Then followed immediately a statement regarding the disposition of Millerite property in the fervent days before October 22. This is probably the most authoritative Millerite pronouncement on this moot point:

"We have advised none to waste their property, but we have taught that we were only stewards of *God,* and that if any have this world's goods, having the love of God in them, and seeing their brother have need, they will not shut up their bowels of compassion; and also, that if any man can do more good in the advancement of the cause of God than in their regular occupation, they will do so. But we have examples for thus doing in the days of the apostles. Matthew left a good business that he might follow One who had not even a place to lodge. Peter left the labor which was his living; and so did James and John, and left their father also, to follow the same leader." [10]

In conclusion they asked a question:

"The various falsehoods which have been industriously circulated against us, we have refuted, and in vain challenged the world for their proof. And again we ask, why is it? Why should the preaching of the immediate coming of the Lord awaken such opposition from such different quarters? The gambler, the libertine, the drunkard, and the profane all unite in opposition to this doctrine; and strange as it may seem, the professed church of Christ has united with them in opposing it. How could this be, unless the church

---

[8] *Evening Mercantile Journal* (Boston), Nov. 6, 1844.
[9] *The Midnight Cry,* Nov. 21, 1844, p. 166.
[10] *Ibid.*

had lost her love for the Saviour's return?—Unless, as Professor Gaussen, of Geneva, says, 'These are times of lax theology and infidelity'?" [11]

The same issue of *The Midnight Cry* that contained this address to the public, carried an editorial that sought to steer the believers in a middle course between two extremes, now that they must carry on in the world a time before the Lord should come. Their attention was called to the evil of pursuing "earthly gain" and grasping for money. "But in seeking to avoid that fatal snare" they were to be careful not to go about idly and listlessly. "The body and mind were made for action, and if they are not active in doing good, they will be led into sinful action,—or sinful *inaction*." Yet the brethren who had "laid aside their worldly business" were warned to "great watchfulness when returning to it, lest they are led insensibly into a worldly spirit, in forming plans for the future."

As to the study of prophecy the attention of the believers was called to the fact that the Christian churches had been "almost entirely disregarding prophetic times, and giving very little heed to the prophetic time." This was an evil to be avoided. But, said the editorial, "In avoiding that extreme, we have been in danger of fixing upon exact times with too great positiveness; and of finding signs where God has not given them." Yet again, in avoiding in the future the danger of looking "with such deep interest to a particular day, we are in danger of relaxing our watchfulness, and saying, in our hearts, 'My Lord delayeth His coming.'" Finally, believers were reminded once more that the churches generally had discounted the value of all prophetic study. But in seeking to avoid this evil extreme and to obey the inspired command to "take heed to the sure word of prophecy," they faced another danger. This, the editorial reminded them again, was the "danger of applying Scriptures to events in our own times, to which they cannot apply except by a warping and straining, which would make them mere playthings." The editorial ended with this word of counsel given by the apostle

---

[11] *Ibid.*

Paul: " 'Let your moderation be known unto all men. The Lord is at hand.' " [12]

If this formula for religious living and study had been followed by all the Millerites, how stable and aggressive the advent movement might have become! But the days of the movement as one well-defined religious group were almost numbered. There was to be a period of transition before the spiritual forces released and the doctrinal views set forth by Millerites finally crystallized themselves into stable and enduring religious bodies. But we must not run ahead of our story.

About this time Miller wrote a letter to Himes. Miller's faith never wavered; his faith in God and the Bible were quite unshaken by disappointment. Said he:

"Although I have been twice disappointed, I am not yet cast down or discouraged. God has been with me in spirit, and has comforted me. I have now much more evidence that I do believe in God's Word; and although surrounded with enemies and scoffers, yet my mind is perfectly calm, and my hope in the coming of Christ is as strong as ever. I have done only what after years of sober consideration I felt to be my solemn duty to do. If I have erred, it has been on the side of charity, the love of my fellow men, and my conviction of duty to God. . . . I had not a distant thought of disturbing our churches, ministers, or religious editors, or departing from the best Biblical commentaries or rules which had been recommended for the study of the Scriptures." [13]

He recalled the evil names that were hurled at the advent believers, of how their motives were impugned, but he added:

"Many of our brethren caught a measure of this spirit, and began to defend themselves in like manner, against the attacks of the several sects. The name of 'Babylon,' and I am sorry to say it, was applied to *all* of our churches without any discrimination, although in *too many* instances it was not unjustly applied. We were thus placed at the time we expected our deliverance; and if Christ had come and found us in this condition, who would have been ready, purified and made white? But the time passed, and the Adventists were humbled; and thus we see that our God was wise

---

[12] *Ibid.*, p. 167.
[13] Letter, Nov. 10, 1844, in *The Midnight Cry*, Dec. 5, 1844, p. 179.

and good, in the tarrying of the vision, to humble, purify and prepare us for an admittance into His blessed kingdom." [14]

Here is a searching self-criticism of the movement he loved that is truly remarkable. We feel at times, in reading some of his letters of the period following the disappointment, that he almost overdid the matter of self-condemnation.

He encouraged Himes to continue publishing *The Advent Herald* and *The Midnight Cry*, "so that amid the moral darkness which has shrouded the people on the prophecies, we may have light in all our dwellings."

He was sure that the end could not be far away, and addressing himself to the whole fellowship of the faith, he continued:

"*Brethren*, hold fast; let no man take your crown. I have fixed my mind upon another time, and here I mean to stand until God gives me more light. —And that is *Today*, TODAY, and TODAY, until He comes, and I see HIM for whom my soul yearns." [15]

Thus wrote Miller from his home in Low Hampton as he sought to establish the hearts of the believers. The position he took of looking for Christ "today, today, and today, until He comes," is reiterated by him in later correspondence. In a letter to Doctor Orr, from which we have already quoted, he used almost exactly the same language, and followed with this declaration:

"I have reckoned all the time I can. I must now wait and watch until He is graciously pleased to answer the ten thousand prayers that daily and nightly ascend His holy hill, 'Come, Lord Jesus, come quickly.' " [16]

Though Miller thus refused to set further time, because he believed all the great time prophecies were fulfilled, he could not quite escape the conviction that his reckoning of prophecy was surely correct, and therefore he might firmly believe in the coming of the Lord before that Jewish year ended. He had not come

---
[14] *Ibid.*, p. 180.
[15] *Ibid.*
[16] Manuscript letter, Dec. 13, 1844.

to his conclusion in haste. He had spent long years in his study. He did not want to discard the results of that long study. In another letter to Himes he declared:

"I feel as confident as ever, that God will justify us in fixing the year. And I believe as firmly, that this Jewish year will not terminate before this wicked and corrupted earth's history will all be told. The amount of scoffing and mocking at the present time, is beyond any calculation. We can hardly pass a man, professor or nonprofessor, but what he scoffingly inquires, 'You have not gone up,' or 'God cannot burn the world,' etc., ridiculing the Bible itself, and blaspheming the Word and power of God." [17]

How very human was Miller. One moment he realized that the strict logic of events demanded that he forgo for the future all predictions and look only day by day for the Lord's coming. The next moment he thought again over all the long years of his confident belief and unburdened his mind in such words as we have just quoted. There is really no great conflict between the two thoughts. He had no new prophetic period to fix upon. At the same time he believed that perhaps a small error in the reckoning of chronology might still explain the Lord's delay in coming.

The Millerite papers of this time contain a number of letters from Adventist ministers expressing full confidence and faith in the movement. For example, Litch wrote:

"But while I say, the same confidence which we felt in the coming of the Lord in 1843, is not warranted in respect to any given time in the future, I do not mean to say that our ground of confidence in His immediate coming, is any less than then; but on the contrary, it increases day by day." [18]

Some of the Millerite ministers did not accept the view that the Lord would come on October 22. Thus the disappointment on that day did not shake their faith in the belief in the near coming of the Lord. For example, there was G. F. Cox, a Millerite minister in Maine, who addressed a letter to Miller, Litch, and Himes, in which he said:

---
[17] Letter, Nov. 18, 1844, in *The Advent Herald,* Dec. 11, 1844, p. 142.
[18] Letter, Nov. 14, 1844, in *The Midnight Cry,* Dec. 12, 1844, p. 187.

"Had we adopted the two ideas, 'ye know not when the time is,—and, when ye see these things come to pass, KNOW YE that He is NEAR, even at the doors,' and brought all our arguments to bear upon these two points, we should probably have come at the truth." [19]

He assured them, however, that he never "felt greater confidence in the great principles of interpretation" that had distinguished the Millerite movement.

Then, thinking of the fact that advent congregations had been quite severed from the different denominations, he offered a prayer of hope "that provision will be made, if not done already, that in all the advent congregations, the sacraments— baptism and the Lord's supper, be duly administered—as well as Bible discipline—as those *who cannot* abide in the churches without suppressing their faith, may have a place to flee to." [20]

Thus step by step the Millerites were thinking their way through to the creation of a distinct church organization, separate from other religious bodies.

Lest they might by any chance mistake his true feeling in the matter, Cox declared in his closing paragraph: "The object of this is to say, I am an Adventist still. My heart is in the great work." Though, of course, he had been critical of setting the definite date, October 22, for the advent, he freely admitted: "I doubt not but in the movements of Providence, it may have been permitted for wise purposes that specific time should have been so successfully preached."

Whiting was another of the Millerite ministers who did not accept the argument for October 22. We have already quoted from his letter to Miller regarding the opposition of mobs in connection with the great day. This letter opens thus:

"It has pleased God, who knows how to humble man that He alone may be exalted, to allow almost all our brethren to make another mistake as to the time of His coming. . . . I have always believed that 'the day and hour'

---

[19] Letter, Nov. 7, 1844, in *The Advent Herald,* Nov. 27, 1844, p. 126.
[20] *Ibid.,* p. 127.

of the Saviour's coming were among the secret things which belong to God alone." [21]

Though he was critical of the acts of some in connection with the seventh-month movement, he believed the Millerite movement itself was valid. He inquired, "The question now is, What shall be done?" He followed immediately with these words of faith: "I believe that the principles formerly taught by the Adventists are true. They have lost none of their weight in consequence of this very general mistake."

So far as the record reveals there was apparently only one of the Millerite ministers, who, having had a part in preaching the October 22 advent date, failed to see in that preaching any action of an overruling Providence. George Storrs, who was more or less prominent in the movement, declared that "human influence, which I call *mesmerism*," explained why he had actually preached a definite date. He confessed that it would not have been wrong for him "or anyone else, to preach the strong probability of the Lord's coming at that time." He thought they should have "contented" themselves respecting such a position, but, said he, "some influence drove some of us beyond the just bounds of discretion. For one, I am sorry for it, and I am willing all should know it. I am now looking *daily* for the coming of our Lord, and striving by grace, to be always ready for it." [22] *

Early in December, Miller wrote to Himes and Bliss. His constant, day-by-day anticipation of the advent is revealed in the opening sentence:

"I cannot sit down to write, without the reflection that this letter may never reach its destination.—Yet I believe in occupying until Christ shall

---

[21] Manuscript letter, Oct. 24, 1844.
[22] Letter, Nov. 8, 1844, in *The Midnight Cry,* Nov. 14, 1844, p. 157.

* It seems that some wrongly understood him in his use of the word "mesmerism." He wrote again, therefore, to explain just what he meant by the word: "It is the influence which one body, or *person,* has over another, to act upon them to produce certain results. In other words, it is a mere *human* influence. In itself, it is not evil." It is evident that Storrs was not using this term in any precise technical sense, or as a synonym for hypnotism. In reading the several paragraphs he wrote in explanation of the use of the word, it becomes evident he simply meant to say that his mind had been strongly influenced by the minds of others, and that this explained why he joined his energy with them to preach what now proved to be a mistake. (See *Morning Watch,* Feb. 20, 1845, pp. 59, 60.)

come. . . . I have never enjoyed more calmness of mind, nor more resignation to the holy will of God, and patience of spirit, than I have within a few weeks past." [23]

He is confident that Providence overruled in the preaching of the definite time, October 22:

"It is to me almost a demonstration, that God's hand is seen in this thing. Many thousands, to all human appearance, have been made to study the Scriptures by the preaching of the time; and by that means, through faith and the sprinkling of the blood of Christ, have been reconciled to God." [24]

He feels that they had been blessed and others likewise, by this preaching, just as Nineveh had been blessed by the preaching of Jonah. But he immediately adds this acute comment on the ways of God toward man:

"If this should be the real state of the case, and we should go on and set other times in the future, we might possibly be found frustrating, or trying to, at least, the purposes of God, and receive no blessing." He does not want anyone to conclude that simply because the preaching of a set time had been providentially used of God that once, therefore they should set particular dates in the future in order to receive a further blessing.

In concluding this letter he comes again to what is not an infrequent theme in his letters, self-analysis of the frailties and mistakes of himself and his associates in the movement. He declares that there had been "pride, fanaticism, and sectarianism." He believed that pride, that ancient vice of the human heart, revealed itself in various ways, often in a failure to give God the glory for success in silencing opponents of the advent. His comments on fanaticism we shall discuss later.* The charge of sectarianism brought him back again to the question of whether Adventists had rightly used the word

---

[23] Letter, Dec. 3, 1844, in *The Advent Herald,* Dec. 18, 1844, p. 147.
[24] *Ibid.*

* Because the critics of Millerism have capitalized on his statement regarding fanaticism, we wish to give it more extended consideration than is warranted in this connection. See Appendix D.

"Babylon" when they applied it indiscriminately to all religious bodies. In a previous letter he had frankly admitted that he believed it applied in many instances.

No one can say that Miller was blind to the human frailties of the movement which he himself was so largely responsible for raising up. To the last he retained his keen powers of self-analysis and was as free to point out the mistakes of the men in the movement as he was to point out the mistakes of those who were opponents. We fear that Miller could hardly qualify as a fanatic. Fanatics do not have such powers of analysis. They and theirs are always right, above question, in fact, almost perfect. Miller could be sure of his faith in God, sure of the essential soundness of the basic premises on which rested the beliefs that created the movement, and yet could coolly analyze his own mistakes and those of the men most closely and sympathetically associated with him.

The last important event of 1844 was the holding of an advent conference at Low Hampton on December 28 and 29. Here for two days gathered Millerite leaders to strengthen one another's faith and to clarify their own thinking. The conference asked Miller to prepare an "Address to Advent Believers," which address constituted the report of the principal committee. This address recounted the hopes of the Adventists, took note of slanderous charges, encouraged the believers to hold fast, and offered an explanation for the disappointment. The explanation was that all their reckonings were subject to the fallible element of human chronology and that therefore there *might* be an error of a few years in the computation of the key time-prophecy of 2300 years. On this point the address declared:

"The discrepancy, we believe, is in the human part of the chronology, and as there are four or five years in dispute among our best chronological writers, which cannot be satisfactorily settled, we feel that we have a good right to this disputed period; and candid and reasonable men will all allow this to be right. Therefore we must patiently wait the time in dispute, before we can honestly confess we are wrong in time." [25]

---

[25] *The Advent Herald*, Jan. 15, 1845, p. 183.

This feeling that there might be four or five years yet for the prophecy to run—though they had formerly found themselves quite unanimous in placing the beginning of the prophetic period in 457 B. C.—provided the buffer to soften the blow of disappointment.*

The year 1844, so crowded with activity, had come to its close. Himes frankly stated the financial difficulties that confronted the cause and that very particularly confronted him, in seeking to continue the Millerite publications, and appealed for sustaining aid.[26] In the last issue of *The Midnight Cry* for December he explained that the seventh volume of that paper was ending, and that it had been suggested that in the future the name be changed to the *Morning Watch*. Said he, "If our pilgrimage is prolonged we expect to commence a new volume." [27]

---

[26] See *The Midnight Cry*, Dec. 12, 1844, p. 189.
[27] *Ibid.*, Dec. 26, 1844, p. 205.

* One is tempted to conclude that here is a case of the wish being father to the thought. It was a pardonable wish, to be sure, but one that had little, if any, historical support. In the days preceding October 22, 1844, the leaders in the movement did not present the matter in terms of a sliding scale. They had rightly become sure of the date 457 B. C., as the time for the beginning of the 70-week and thus of the 2300-day prophecy. But when disappointment came on October 22, it never seemd to occur to them to question their interpretation of the meaning of the sanctuary cleansing. They questioned the date instead. They interpreted the phrase in the prophecy, "Then shall the sanctuary be cleansed" (Dan. 8:14), as involving the advent of Christ and the purging of the earth by fire. Christ had not come; hence the 2300-day prophecy had not ended! Therefore they must advance the date of the fulfillment of the prophecy. Ultimately, of course, all who thus interpreted the prophecy were forced to declare that they did not know when the prophecy was supposed to end. To take this position, they had to renounce the view that Miller took at the outset, and without which there is no hope of discovering the bounds of the 2300-day prophecy, namely, that the seventy-week prophecy, whose starting point can be known, constitutes the first part of the 2300-day prophecy. For a further discussion of this matter, particularly as regards a different interpretation to the phrase, "then shall the sanctuary be cleansed," see the comment in Chapter 29.

CHAPTER 19

The Movement Called Millerism Draws to Its Close

FOR YEARS THE RIVER OF MILLERISM had flowed on in ever-increasing volume. It was no meandering stream, listlessly spreading over flat country for lack of sharply defined banks. There was a sense of urgency, of hastening toward a destination, that gave velocity and a sharply defined course to the river. Though there were eddies and swirls and cross currents and even marshy spots along the banks, these were mere incidentals. The main course and character of the stream were evident to all.

Now the river of Millerism expected to be swallowed up in the ocean of eternity on October 22—Millerite charts marked out no land beyond that point. Instead, the erstwhile fast-moving stream poured out over an arid, uncharted waste. The scorching sun of disappointment beat down, and the burning winds of ridicule swept in from every side. The river suddenly lost its velocity. There was no momentum to cut a clearly marked channel in this new, parched land. Sun and wind quickly began to play havoc with this directionless body of water, now spread thinly over a wide area. While a central stream of what had once been an impressive river, was more or less well defined, there were many lesser streams, which often ended in miniature dead seas, where stagnation and evaporation soon did their work. Indeed, no small part of the once large river, when evaporated under the scorching sun of disappointment, was finally returned to the sources from whence it came, the other rivers in the religious world.

To turn to literal language, the Millerite movement was

not constituted to meet the conditions that confronted it after 1844. Miller had consistently held before the movement the ideal of an interchurch awakening on the doctrine of the soon coming of Christ. The various advent conferences repeatedly declared that Millerism did not seek to create another denomination nor disturb the church relationship of anyone. And even the cry to come out of the churches, which was finally sounded, did not have as its purpose creating a new church, but simply lifting men out of a hostile atmosphere in anticipation of the immediate advent of Christ. Why should the leaders build a close-knit organization! They expected the perfect order and organization of heaven to shape their affairs in a very little while.

It is therefore no occasion for surprise, nor any indictment of Millerism, that the movement so markedly subsided after 1844. The history of religion is replete with illustrations of an awakening on some phase of spiritual truth, followed, generally, by a return to something less than wakefulness on the part of Christendom. Generally, the flaming evangel who has warmed and wakened hearts for the little while has earned for himself the commendation of a few and the condemnation of a multitude. Occasionally he may have had the spiritual astuteness to set up an organization to preserve and promote the spiritual convictions that he believed so important. In that event there is maintained in the Christian world a continuing light and an awakening note on some particular truth that might otherwise have been ignored or forgotten.

But in the very nature of the case Miller was debarred by the logic of his own belief from planning anything beyond 1844. Nor could he have great reason to sense the need of the stabilizing value of an organized church body. To borrow another simple illustration:

A bicycle, even though the most unstable of conveyances, easily keeps its course as long as it is in motion. Indeed, the more rapid the motion, the easier it is to maintain the course. But let the forward motion cease, or only markedly decrease, and the rider finds himself more likely to suffer disaster, or at least to wander off the road, than to keep on the path he had set for himself. And the likelihood of disaster is not decreased by the presence of more than one rider!

Thus with Millerism. As long as it was truly a movement, it tended to hold all steadily to a course. But when the sudden halt came in October, 1844, the inevitable happened. There was disaster for some, as they fell by the way, and a turning into bypaths for others. There were even collisions at times. The very fact that a new movement always draws in some who are inherently unstable and others whose chief quality is their ability to stand alone, or travel alone, only increased the spiritual traffic problem that confronted Millerism as 1845 opened.

This picture of human nature in relation to a spiritual crisis may be discouraging, but it is not new. The history of church councils is none too edifying, no matter what period of the church is considered. There have been occasions when bishops offered violence to brother bishops—even in some of the early centuries of the Christian Era. Piety has frequently yielded to prejudice, and saintly men have too often acted in unsaintly fashion. There is fiery, fervent Luther refusing even to shake hands with Zwingli after their debate on the Lord's supper.* And there are the fierce controversies between the disciples of Calvin, notably Presbyterians, who hold to predestination, and the disciples of Arminius, Methodists for example, who hold to the doctrine of the free will of man. The controversies that have raged in that area of theology probably found their most militant and colorful expression in the blazing declaration of one Arminian minister to his Calvinistic brother minister, "Your God is my devil." When the Westminster divines in England hotly debated theology as they sought to formulate a creed, Cromwell appealed to them, "I beseech you by the bowels of Christ, bethink you that ye might be mistaken."

---

* This is one of the classic examples of the frailty of even the best of men when under the tension of religious debate. See Samuel Simpson, *Life of Ulrich Zwingli*, pp. 164-210; Jean Grob, *Life of Ulric Zwingli*, pp. 147-154.

Thus the record might be embarrassingly enlarged. And what does it all prove? Not that the great spiritual problems that provoked the controversies were not worthy of solemn study, but simply that those who were studying the problems were a strange mixture of heaven and earth, with the earthy part too often predominating. They dealt with the treasure of spiritual truth, but they had this treasure in earthen vessels, as the Holy Word reminds us. Ever since apostolic days, when Paul rebuked Peter to his face, and engaged in hot debate with Barnabas, church leaders have too often revealed how earthen is the vessel. And the more sincerely and devoutly men believe that they have the truth of God, the greater is their temptation to denounce all who oppose them—should not error be rebuked!

And why have we made this digression from the story of Millerism to tell of the frailties of churchmen in past ages? Simply that the reader might see in proper perspective the picture we are now to present. It is a picture of strong-minded men seeking each in his own way to find an explanation for a staggering disappointment, and displaying too often a lack of charity toward the explanation offered by others. One Millerite leader in Boston, writing to Miller early in 1845, opened his letter thus:

"I will just inform you that I am still in the land of the living; and though tried am not destroyed; though disappointed, am endeavoring to be patient; though in the midst of 'confusion worse confounded,' am striving to keep my head cool and my heart warm. But oh, how difficult, in this stormy latitude of time, amidst the flatteries, frowns and sophistry of the church, our friends and the world, together with one's inward temptations, to maintain a perfect equilibrium of mind! I do not wonder that the Saviour closed all His discourses on the end of time with the injunction to especially watch and pray. He foresaw that the circumstances of this time would abundantly demand it.

"Our brethren this way are catching at every conceivable hypothesis to reconcile the movement of the tenth [day of the seventh month, that is, October 22]. . . .

"But supremely ridiculous, painful and dangerous, as is this state of things among ourselves, it is not as much so as the ranks of our opponents present. Who can think of the endless diversity of opinion among them on the prophecies and atonement, free will, baptism, conversion, and every

Bible truth; and not say in view of his temptations to leave this [advent] cause: 'To whom shall we go?' . . .

"Oh, I sigh for home. Home; sweet, sweet home. But, patience, my soul." [1]

In a letter to Himes, Miller told of his sorrow of heart over the discord that quickly developed in the ranks of the advent believers:

"I must confess I am pained at heart to see the battle we are now in. . . . After having silenced our common enemy, . . . that we should now turn our weapons against each other! Every paper which has come into my hands recently is full of fight, and that, too, against our friends." [2]

Remembering that Himes was still the chief publisher and editor, Miller had a suggestion:

"The dear editors can do much in stopping this seeming controversy, . . . which can never in this world be settled to the satisfaction of all parties. You are the organs through whom we communicate our thoughts one to another. Our tried situation actually calls for an interchange of thought and opinion; the lambs want milk. Many of us, and in this case, I know I ought to say *we,* may write some foolish things of which by and by we may be ashamed. Very well, you suppress it; that is your duty, and when by and by comes, and we see our folly, which we most assuredly shall in nine cases out of ten if we have eyes, we shall then love our editors better and better. Let nothing personal go into your papers in a hurry. Let no piece written with a spirit to find fault with any brother find a corner there. . . .

"Unless we are harmless and wise, there are breakers ahead which will be to much damage and loss. And more depends on you as pilots of our gallant ship now, than any time since we launched our little all on board."

However, Miller was not overwhelmed by the fact of controversy. We are again led to remark on his keen insight into human nature and his knowledge of church history. He knew that in past ages, when church authority was strong, controversy could sometimes be suppressed and a false appearance of calm be made to prevail. He neither possessed nor desired such authority. Commenting further, he said:

---

[1] Manuscript letter from I. E. Jones, Feb. 14, 1845.
[2] Manuscript letter, undated, probably written, as internal evidence indicates, early in 1845.

"It would be remarkable if there were no discordant views among us, for there is no sect or church under the whole heaven, where men enjoy religious freedom or liberty, but there will be various opinions. And our great men, leaders, and religious demagogues have long since discovered [this], and therefore come creeds, bishops and popes. We must then, either let our brethren have the freedom of thought, opinion and speech, or we must resort to creeds and formulas, bishops and popes. . . . I see no other alternative. While we are in this state of things we have to let the light of God's Word shine in the darkness, or we must establish a light of our own, which will only make darkness more visible and eventually drown men in perdition. God have mercy on us, and send Jesus Christ who is our light to restore all things.

"Do, I beseech of you my brother, let all speak that use proper and affectionate language, and especially those who pretend to have Bible for what they believe. Have we not blamed the sects and churches for shutting their eyes, ears, doors, pulpits and presses against this light? And shall we become as one of them? No. God forbid. . . . We had better suffer the abuse of liberty, than to strengthen the bands of tyranny."

Thus did Miller feel and thus did he analyze the situation as he endeavored to find light for the movement in the darkness of the disappointment. The stature of the man did not decrease in defeat.

Miller's faith was as bright as ever, even though he stood in the shadows. He did not doubt the Bible, even though he could not see where his mistakes might be. A helpful side light is thrown on the man at this very time by a letter he wrote early in 1845 to the *Boston Investigator,* avowed organ of infidelity. The editor had invited letters from those who claimed they had been converted from doubt to faith and from infidelity to Christianity. In his letter Miller told the story of his youthful infection with deism, and of how he later found the Bible to be true and the one source of joy and hope to him. Addressing himself, then, directly to the editor, he added:

"And now, Sir, let me tell you, Millerism is to believe, try to understand, love, and proclaim to others, the good news contained in the Bible. This is all I have ever done to call down the slander of the several sects which I have received. I can say, honestly, I have never designed to proclaim or publish any sentiment, word, or doctrine, but such as I found clearly taught in that blessed Inspired Volume. Let God be my judge, I know I believe it. And I pray God that you, my dear sir, may become a Millerite too." [3]

It took a measure of calm confidence for Miller, in his hour of disappointment, to write thus to the keen-minded, critical editor of an infidel weekly. The editor evidently sensed both the news value and the sincerity of the letter, for he published it on the front page, and appended a note which read in part: "We have not the least doubt of Mr. Miller's entire sincerity in his views of the Bible." On the editorial page appeared this further comment on his letter:

"The mere fact of his sending us a friendly letter, is presumptive proof at least, of kind feelings; it shows a good intention, and this of itself, is worth something—nay, it is worth to us a great deal, not only because it is unexpected, but because it is evidence of improvement. We thank Mr. Miller that he has exhibited this good intention; and thank him, also, for the example he has set, that a man may be a Christian and yet be a gentleman—a doctrine that but very few Christians exemplify in their practice, since but very few of them know how to treat an infidel with even common civility, to say nothing of kindness." [4]

We repeat, the stature of Miller did not decrease in the hour of defeat and dark disappointment.

Because confusion was resulting inevitably from differing views, a number of Millerite leaders decided to issue a call for a "Mutual Conference of Adventists" to be held at Albany, New York, beginning April 29, 1845. This conference, rather well attended, drew up a brief statement of belief, which was unanimously adopted, and passed certain resolutions. Among these was a resolution which, in different language, had been voted in conferences of earlier years, denouncing fanaticism in rather specific fashion. There was also an appeal to the believers "to continue in obedience to the great commission to preach the gospel to every creature."

The "Address to the Brethren Scattered Abroad," which was sent out from the conference, opened thus:

---
[3] Letter, Jan. 27, 1845, in *Boston Investigator*, Feb. 12, 1845.
[4] *Boston Investigator*, Feb. 12, 1845.

MILLERISM DRAWS TO ITS CLOSE

"The present state of our faith and hope, with the severe trials which many of us experience, call for much brotherly love, forbearance, patience, and prayer. No cause, be it ever so holy, can exist in this present world, without its attendant evils. Therefore, it becomes necessary for all who are connected with this cause, to exercise great charity; for charity covers a multitude of sins.

"The cause we advocate calls upon all men to read the Word of God, and to reason, judge, compare, and digest for themselves. This is certainly right, and is the privilege of all rational members of the community. Yet this very liberty may become a stumbling-block to many, and, without charity, be the means of scattering, dividing, and causing contention among brethren. . . .

"We are commanded to be sober and hope to the end, for that grace which is to be brought unto us at the revelation of Jesus Christ. Our disappointment as to the time should have no effect upon our hope. We know that Christ has not yet been revealed, and the object of our hope is yet in the future. Therefore, if we believe in God's Word, as we profess, we ought to be thankful for the trial of our faith." [5]

These main points of the conference proceedings enable us to see that despite the disappointment and the ensuing divisions, that had developed since October, 1844, the Millerites showed remarkably good judgment and set forth judicious principles as rules to guide the believers in the second advent. There were objections, of course, to the actions taken. There were good men who looked askance at any attempt to set forth a statement of belief, lest the movement become like the various sects in formulating a creed that would rigidly bind the membership. There were also fears among others that such a conference might be the first step toward organizing a clearly defined denomination, and that this would be returning to Babylon. So real was this fear with some that they protested even the use of the name "Adventist" as particularly descriptive of the movement. How extensive the opposition was, there is no way of knowing. We do know that Joseph Marsh, who edited *The Voice of Truth* at Rochester, New York, and who had been a rather prominent

---

[5] *The Advent Herald*, May 14, 1845, p. 108.

Millerite minister in that State, voiced such protests and fears as these in his paper.[6]

To all these objectors Miller made an eloquent and cogent reply through *The Advent Herald*. He declared that the conference had no thought of formulating a creed or creating any specific organization, though he insisted that any group of men ought to be permitted to state what they believed and to recommend "the adoption of such principles of association and order," as will best conduce to true church order. As to the name "Adventist" he inquired:

"Was the term Adventist in use ten years ago? No,—it is not in the dictionary; it is a newly coined word. . . . The coiners of the word are entitled to it, and those who associate with them. But let it be distinctly understood, that at the Albany conference, the question did not arise whether we should adopt that name. It was already upon us; and the only question that arose respecting it, was whether when speaking of some fanatics who call themselves Adventists, the word should be permitted to remain in that connection." [7]

This Albany conference in the spring of 1845 marks the final endeavor to hold the movement together as a united body encompassing all who had had a part in Millerism, and even that conference did not include all the leaders. It was inevitable that the movement should come on hard and dangerous times. The illustration of the river reveals that. The very endeavor that had been made prior to October, 1844, to keep the movement from becoming a separate sect, now arose to plague such men as Miller and Himes, who clearly saw that some kind of church order and discipline would be needed for the future.

The source material on this period is less complete than the careful writer would like. Critics have been very willing to dismiss the matter with a general statement that the whole movement simply disintegrated into fanaticism, or disappeared in the

---

[6] See *The Voice of Truth and Glad Tidings*, May 21, 1845, pp. 61, 62.
[7] *The Advent Herald*, June 4, 1845, p. 130. See also Miller's manuscript letter to Himes, May 20, 1845, in which he declared that certain ones who protested the actions of the Albany conference were "disorganizers."

arid sands of doubt and bewilderment. There is just enough truth in such generalizations to make them sound plausible. But the complete picture is very much different, as the reader may judge from the summary of the actions of the Albany conference and from the facts set forth in a closing chapter. There *were* those who disappeared in doubts. And there were some fanatics. They were nothing new, but they were less handicapped in their actions. They were rivulets that ran out on all sides from the main stream, and ended as stagnant pools, with no onrushing current to cleanse them. And it takes only a few stagnant pools to create a dank and evil odor over a large area.

The stabilizing influence of the Albany conference served to hold a substantial majority of the Adventists together for years—that, plus the personal presence and influence of such men as Miller and Himes, who continued to travel and preach and publish.*— In August, 1845, Miller published his *Apology and Defence*, in which he recounted his life's experiences as they related to religion. The document constitutes a pamphlet of thirty-six pages. It is written in simple, straightforward style. Almost all the facts he there set forth have already been woven into this narrative. As to his orthodoxy, he declared:

"In all the essential doctrines of the Bible, as they have been held by the pious of the church in all ages, [which] were given to the saints, and for which we are commanded earnestly to contend, I have never seen any reason to change my faith." [8]

He declared himself in opposition to "any of the new theories" that developed immediately after October 22, in an endeavor to explain the disappointment. Inasmuch as Christ did not come on that date he unhesitatingly affirmed that it was not "a fulfillment of prophecy in any sense." [9]

He also wished to make clear that the doctrine that the wicked will finally be annihilated, and that the dead lie uncon-

---

[8] William Miller, *Apology and Defence*, p. 27.
[9] On this point see also Miller's manuscript letter to J. B. Cook, Sept. 16, 1845.

* See Chapter 20 for a more specific statement on this matter of the divisions into which the Adventist movement separated after 1844.

scious in their graves until the resurrection, was not an integral part of the Millerite movement. He considered it necessary to make this statement because some who were more or less prominent in the movement, such as Storrs and Fitch, until his untimely death preached these views.

He referred to the description in Revelation 14:6, 7, of the angel proclaiming the hour of God's judgment as having come, and observed, "This proclamation must of course continue until Christ shall actually come to judge the quick and dead at His appearing and kingdom." [10] Miller believed that the message he and his associates had been preaching fulfilled this prophetic description.

In conclusion, he declared that he had given "a plain and simple statement of the manner" of his arriving "at the views" he had preached, and added:

"That I have been mistaken in the time, I freely confess; and I have no desire to defend my course any further than I have been actuated by pure motives, and it has resulted to God's glory. My mistakes and errors God, I trust, will forgive. I cannot, however, reproach myself for having preached definite time; for as I believe that whatsoever was written aforetime was written for our learning, the prophetic periods are as much a subject of investigation, as any other portion of the Word. . . .

"But while I frankly acknowledge my disappointment in the exact time, I wish to enquire whether my teachings have been thereby materially affected. My view of exact time depended entirely upon the accuracy of chronology: of this I had no absolute demonstration. . . . Other chronologers had assigned later dates for the events from which I reckoned; and if they are correct, we are only brought into a circle of a few years, during which we may rationally look for the Lord's appearing. As the prophetic periods, counting from the dates from which I have reckoned, have not brought us to the end; and as I cannot tell the exact time that chronology may vary from my calculations, I can only live in continual expectation of the event. I am persuaded that I cannot be far out of the way, and I believe that God will still justify my preaching to the world.

"With respect to other features of my views, I can see no reason to change my belief. We are living under the last form of the divided fourth kingdom, which brings us to the end. The prophecies which were to be

---

[10] William Miller, *Apology and Defence*, pp. 30, 31.

fulfilled previous to the end, have been so far fulfilled that I find nothing in them to delay the Lord's coming. The signs of the times thicken on every hand; and the prophetic periods I think must certainly have brought us into the neighborhood of the event.

"There is not a point in my belief in which I am not sustained by some one of the numerous writers who have opposed my views." [11]

In support of this last statement he cited various theological lights of his own day, and of course there were many theologians of past days whom he might have quoted. Then followed "a word of exhortation" to all Christians to examine what he had said, an appeal to "unconverted friends," and fatherly counsel to the advent believers. To the last group he wrote:

"Avoid everything that shall cause offences. Let your lives be models of goodness and propriety. . . . Let your conversation be in heaven, from whence you look for the blessed hope. Avoid unnecessary controversy, and questions that gender strifes. Be not many masters; all are not competent to advise and direct. God will raise up those to whom He will commit the direction of His cause." [12]

That closing sentence should be read in the light of Miller's oft-repeated declarations that he felt his days would soon be numbered. He had been in very poor health for several years. He was to live four years more. So far as his strength permitted, those years were filled with traveling and preaching for the cause he loved. Early in 1848 his health began to decline, and with it his eyesight. An unfinished letter written in the spring of 1849, in a large, shaky hand, bears mute testimony that the hour of his dissolution was drawing near. But his indomitable faith burned bright. Perhaps the letter was to his boon companion in labor, Himes; we know not. The salutation is simply "Dear Brother." The letter opens thus:

"I cannot refrain from writing a word or two, although I cannot see. All is well. The Bridegroom [Christ] is coming; no mistake. . . . The King must come. Lift up your head, be of good cheer, be not faithless but believing. We shall soon see Him for whom we have looked and waited." [13]

---
[11] *Ibid.,* pp. 33, 34.
[12] *Ibid.,* p. 36.
[13] Unfinished manuscript letter, April 10, 1849

He followed this with certain revisions of his views that led him to believe that though Christ did not come in 1844, He would come very shortly. His hope and confident belief to the last were that some minor error in chronology, particularly as touching the key prophecy of 2300 days, with its interlocking prophecy of seventy weeks, explained the disappointment. He died in the very literal expectation of the immediate coming of Christ.

Death came to him on December 20, 1849, in the sixty-eighth year of his life. At his bedside stood the man who in Chardon Street Chapel, in December, 1839, had made a solemn compact with him to promote and publish his views to all America and beyond. It was fitting that Himes should be there at Low Hampton to say a last word to the old warrior who first served his country in the War of 1812 and later his God in a far more arduous war. Miller lies buried in a little graveyard about half a mile from his old home. At the top of the tombstone are the appropriate words of Holy Writ: "At the time appointed the end shall be." Below his name are carved the equally fitting words of Inspiration: "But go thou thy way till the end be: for thou shalt rest, and stand in thy lot at the end of the days."

Commenting on his death, the editor of a prominent literary journal remarked in part:

"We heard 'Father Miller' preach on this great subject [of the second advent] to an immense audience one night in Philadelphia. His evident sincerity, earnestness and simplicity attracted to him our greatest respect. We think the success which marked his labors, . . . arose from his bringing prominently forward a neglected truth. And it is to be feared that his confident and ill-founded predictions as to *the time,* will throw temporary discredit upon the great burden of many prophecies—the second coming of Christ." [14]

This editor's explanation of the secret of Miller's success is echoed years later by the author of an impressive volume on great events of American history:

"Perhaps the simple secret of Mr. Miller's wonderful success, was his

---

[14] *Littel's Living Age,* Jan. 19, 1850, p. 138.

bringing prominently forward a somewhat neglected but vividly important truth." [15]

It would be hard to find a more simple or more satisfactory explanation of Miller's appeal to the hearts of his hearers.

Thus ends the narrative of William Miller and the Millerites. For reasons already given we have not turned aside along the way to consider in detail any of the major charges that were brought against the Millerites. Yet no final judgment can be passed on the movement until those charges have been examined. We believe that the documented record in the preceding chapters will lead most readers to discount the charges in advance. In order to study these charges in their proper setting we should look beyond the circle of the movement itself out into the world in which the movement lived. In what kind of world did Millerism flourish?

---

[15] R. M. Devens, *The Great Events of Our Past Century*, p. 310.

CHAPTER 20

The Kind of World in Which Millerism Flourished

THE FAMILY ALBUM IS PROBABLY the best proof that people of a former generation cannot fairly be judged in terms of what we today consider sober and sensible. The picture of grandpa and grandma is generally good only for a laugh. We forget that fashions change, and that grandfather doubtless thought the painting of his grandfather in wig and knee breeches queer. We also forget that our children will look back and offer the same comment on us.

Now there are fashions in thought and in deportment, as well as in dress. People think and act and speak differently in relation to various situations in different generations. Yet these differing reactions to a situation may no more be the true measure of people than the clothes they happen to wear in their generation. We must place ourselves back at the time when those people lived if we would rightly measure their actions and words.

What kind of world did the Millerites live in? Certainly it was not the kind we live in today. The highly colored stories that are current regarding the activities and fervency of the Millerites might appear at first blush as sure proof that they were feverishly infected with fanaticism. But perhaps it was the style of that day to be more fervent, more vocal, more vigorous. And if so, then the activities of the Millerites immediately take on a different complexion.

In the fall of 1840 as Millerism was slowly emerging as a well-defined movement, a great national campaign was being waged. Van Buren was running for re-election as President.

Opposing him was Harrison, with his running mate, Tyler. The electorate were not content to sit calmly in their homes and read the speeches of Presidential aspirants. They took their politics straight and in very large doses. Harrison, whose name became synonymous with "Tippecanoe," which recalled his military prowess as a general, was carried forward in his campaign on the lilting lines of a song that began "Tippecanoe and Tyler too." The song went on through an endless number of stanzas. The party headquarters for Harrison in various places were constructed of log cabins to dramatize Harrison's humble beginning. Speaking of these log cabins one historian declared:

"Here were held mass meetings to which from many miles around came farmers with their families to spend days and nights in singing songs and shouting 'Tippecanoe and Tyler too.' It became impossible to count them and surveyors were employed to measure the throngs by the acre. . . . It was like a religious revival. . . . Whole towns and counties turned their population into a line of march often five miles long and sometimes stretching from one State into another." [1]

Even if we discount sharply this amazing picture of political fervor on the part of the populace, we still have a remarkably uninhibited America in the year 1840. It was simply the custom of that age for people to give very fervent and vocal expression to their feelings and beliefs.

In the fall of 1844, when Polk and Clay were the opposing candidates for the Presidency, one newspaper wrote:

"One of the characteristic features of the present campaign, and we believe a new element in political contests, is the getting up of torchlight processions and meetings. The two parties in New York have been vying with each other in these splendid parades and displays. Voters on either side, counted by thousands and tens of thousands, intoxicated with *patriotic ardor,* assemble in the night time—arrange themselves at the sound of soul-inspiring music, with hundreds of banners waving over them, and guided by the brilliant glare of ten thousand torches, march through the illuminated streets of the great city, amidst the gaze and shouts of a hundred thousand spectators. We can scarcely imagine a more picturesque and animating scene.

---

[1] F. A. Ogg, Builders of the Republic, pp. 268, 269.

But like a thousand other scenes, its enchanting power is felt most at a distance. Its *scenic* effect is far better than its *moral* effect." ²

In connection with this same campaign a newspaper advocating the election of Clay, feverishly appealed to Whig party members, as quoted in a previous chapter, to "spend the little remaining time [before election] in hard work among the doubting, the lukewarm, and the open enemy. Forget business—forget everything but your country till the election is over, and then you will read the result with a clear conscience." ³

We have no way of knowing how clear the Whig conscience was, or how faithfully they carried out the appeal to forget business and everything else in behalf of the election, but we do know that they were mistaken in their hopes, and sadly disappointed when Clay was not elected President.*

In the realm of social and moral reforms the same fervent forces were at work in the 1830's and 1840's. We are likely to think of our forebears of a century ago as staid and even stuffy, bound hand and foot by the conventions of all the past generations. But this is not a true picture. There were great stirrings in the souls of many Americans a hundred years ago. Various social and moral reforms were in their formative stages. The public were anything but passive or apathetic in their relationship to these new ideas. Indeed, a public that could shout itself hoarse on "Tippecanoe and Tyler too" and could warm its soul to a fever heat by the flickering tapers in a torchlight parade, could hardly be expected to view new moral or social reforms in a passive manner. On the contrary, the very spirit of pioneering and daring that brought the original settlers to America, and which was soon to push the frontiers far west to the gold coast of

---

² *Vermont Phoenix* (Brattleboro), Nov. 15, 1844.
³ *Evening Mercantile Journal* (Boston), Nov. 6, 1844.

* How militant and uninhibited were some political campaigners in the 1840's is indicated by this item from a Cincinnati paper, quoting the *Richland Bugle:* "The *Richland Bugle* gives the following passage from a speech of David Tod [candidate for governor of Ohio] at Lima: 'My opponent, Bartley, is an imbecile old man—he is a farmer, and cannot make a speech. His friends did haul him to Cleveland and propped him up on the stand, while he spoke about a minute and a half and frizzled out. Do you want a man of such a stamp to rule over you?' "—*Cincinnati Daily Gazette, Oct. 7, 1844.*

California, might rightly be expected to reveal itself in pioneering ideas in the social realm. In an essay entitled "New Englander Reformers," Ralph Waldo Emerson said in 1844:

"Whoever has had opportunity of acquaintance with society in New England during the last twenty-five years, with those middle and with those leading sections that may constitute any just representation of the character and aim of the community, will have been struck with the great activity of thought and experimenting. His attention must be commanded by the signs that the church, or religious party, is falling from the church nominal, and is appearing in temperance and nonresistance societies; in movements of abolitionists and of socialists; and in very significant assemblies called Sabbath and Bible conventions; composed of ultraists, of seekers, of all the soul of the soldiery of dissent, and meeting to call in question the authority of the Sabbath, of the priesthood, and of the church." [4]

Lest the reader might think to dismiss such unusual stirrings in supposedly staid New England as the activities merely of a lunatic fringe of society, it should be added immediately that some of the most eminent names of New England were included among the "reformers" of whom Emerson was writing.

For example, there were those who thought to reform the social structure by advocating a communal form of living. That is, they advocated that people live as one great household and have all things in common; that they share alike in the labor and in the fruits of the labor, which would be put in a common fund. In 1841 one such community, known as Brook Farm, was set up a few miles from Boston. This particular social venture, which was only one of several of that kind, lasted for at least six or seven years. A quarterly literary journal, *The Dial,* was a principal organ for the promotion of the social and philosophical ideas and ideals of those who belonged to the community. And who were numbered among those making so novel an experiment? The secretary of the group was none other than Charles Dana, who later became famous as one of the editors of the *New York Tribune.* Another was Bronson Alcott, who was perhaps famous because of what his daughter Louisa May wrote. Na-

---

[4] *The Complete Writings of Ralph Waldo Emerson,* p. 313.

thaniel Hawthorne was also among the group. Concerning this venture, Emerson wrote: "In and around Brook Farm, whether as members, boarders or visitors, were many remarkable persons, for character, intellect or accomplishments." [5]

It would be hard to visualize a similar social venture today on the part of prominent literary and intellectual persons. In fact, we would consider the idea rather fantastic. But not so a hundred years ago. Then people tried out new things, and leading citizens were often in the forefront of such experiments.

Attempts at social reform were made in the field of temperance. The name of John B. Gough, a reformed drunkard, is found frequently in the newspapers of the 1840's. Gough stirred mighty mass meetings with his fervent speaking, and rallied strong support for the temperance movement. Large temperance conventions were held in various cities. In 1844 a mammoth temperance convention was held in Boston. The railways gave half-fare rates to those attending. It was a colorful parade that moved along the streets of supposedly staid Boston. In the procession was a whole boatload of whalers who had come in from the seven seas. It seemed that the railways conveyed free to Boston, the boats, harpoons, and other gear that the whalers used in the parade. One newspaper remarked: "The appearance of the gallant sons of the ocean on such an occasion must have an imposing effect." [6]

Another newspaper, writing the day after the parade, stated that the usually busy streets of Boston were filled with thousands of people who had come to the temperance convention.[7]

In an earlier chapter reference has already been made to the abolitionist movement that began to develop under William Lloyd Garrison in the early 1830's and to the great mob of so-called respectable Boston citizens who manhandled Garrison as he sought to flee from them through the winding streets of that

---
[5] "Life and Letters in New England," *The Complete Writings of Ralph Waldo Emerson*, p. 1055.
[6] *Lowell Courier* (Mass.), May 18, 1844.
[7] See *Lowell Advertiser* (Mass.), May 31, 1844.

city on a day in 1835. Men not only had strong beliefs in those days; they also had strong disbeliefs.

It is easier to understand how men took such militant stands on one side or another of a new movement when we remember that in the 1840's the duel, as a means of settling differences, had not yet been wholly abandoned. One newspaper, in October, 1844, remarks regarding dueling:

> "The *duellum,* or war of two, is with other forms of war, losing ground in the public estimation. The time is not distant, when to show that a man is not a scoundrel, some other proof will be required than a willingness to be shot at, with chance of shooting somebody else." [8]

This newspaper was certain the day was "not distant" when this robust form of self-expression would be outlawed, but that day had not yet arrived. This is a point to remember in creating a picture of America in the 1840's.

In a different class from social reforms, but significant as showing the ferment of new ideas, were certain medical and dietetic views that aroused great interest and hot debate. There was Sylvester Graham, who gave his name to Graham bread. He held certain dietetic ideas, particularly as to the advantages of a vegetarian diet and the superiority of whole grains over refined milled products. Today we would think of a man with new dietetic views, for example, as evoking, at the worst, some critical comment through the press. But a hundred years ago the people expressed their opposition rather militantly even in matters of diet. Not only were the butchers opposed to him, but also the bakers. He argued that better bread could be made at home.

When he was lecturing in Boston in 1837 the bakers made such a hostile demonstration that the owner of the hall feared for the safety of his property and refused to let Graham continue his lectures. The friends of Graham's views were no less militant. They found another place for the lecturer, provided themselves with a quantity of slaked lime, which they shoveled out

---

[8] *Evening Mirror* (New York), quoted in *Daily Morning Post* (Pittsburgh), Oct. 30, 1844.

from second-story windows on the hostile mob with immediate and immensely satisfying results. This caustic medicine for mobs provides picturesque proof that Americans a hundred years ago did not relate themselves passively to new ideas.

Even in the field of religion, where propriety and gravity may most reasonably be expected, there was often audible fervor, not infrequently physical manifestations, and sometimes even fanaticism, on the part of the worshipers. Camp meetings probably provide the best illustration. Such meetings were first held in America in 1799, under the joint auspices of Presbyterians and Methodists. The first few years camp meetings were rather confined to the area of Kentucky and Tennessee, frontier States at the opening of the nineteenth century. The Magee brothers, one a Presbyterian and the other a Methodist, are generally credited with starting camp meetings. John Magee, one of the brothers, thus describes his fervent action at a Presbyterian meetinghouse on the eve of the camp meeting era:

"The power of God was strong upon me; I turned again, and, losing sight of the fear of man, I went through the house shouting and exhorting with all possible ecstasy and energy, and the floor was soon covered with the slain. . . . This was the beginning of that glorious revival of religion in this country which was so great a blessing to thousands." [9]

Bishop Asbury, a prominent and pious Methodist leader, commenting on what he saw at a camp meeting in 1800, declared:

"The ministers of God, Methodists and Presbyterians, united their labors and mingled with the childlike simplicity of primitive times. Fires blazing here and there dispelled the darkness, and the shouts of the redeemed captives and the cries of precious souls struggling into life broke the silence of midnight." [10]

The authoritative history of Methodism, in which the foregoing quotations are found, remarks concerning physical manifestations, or what might be called fanatical acts:

---

[9] John Fletcher Hurst, *The History of Methodism*, Vol. 5, p. 526.
[10] *Ibid.*, p. 524.

"Strange physical phenomena were observed at many of these revival meetings. The 'falling exercise' was by far the most common; indeed a preacher scarcely considered his labors owned of God unless 'the slain' fell about him." [11]

Another historian of Methodism adds this further description of those early camp meetings:

"Sometimes as many as twenty thousand were present. Presbyterian and Methodist ministers united in the work. The assemblage divided into groups, which were addressed by as many speakers. So many were struck to the ground at one meeting that, to prevent their being trodden underfoot by the multitude, they were laid out in order on two squares of the central meeting house." [12]

From this vigorous beginning at the turn of the century, camp meetings spread from the Kentucky-Tennessee area north and east, to become a fixed part of the religious life of many in America for generations to come. Despite the fact that Presbyterians lost interest in such meetings because of the great excitement often created, Methodists and others fostered and promoted camp meetings as a well-defined form of religious activity.

In the autobiographies of various ministers is found a picture of the religious life and enthusiasm of at least a certain portion of the public who lived contemporaneously with the Millerites. For example, a Methodist minister, Gaddis, who labored during the first half of the nineteenth century in the State of Ohio, gives us a real insight into the life of Methodism in the second quarter of the nineteenth century. He throws this side light on a revival service and the vigor of the penitents as they pleaded for mercy: "The cries of the 'stricken ones' still at the altar were borne far off by the night winds." [13]

There were held in those days what were known as "protracted meetings." As the name implies, these were meetings which were carried on for days and sometimes for weeks. People would come day by day and also evening by evening to the meet-

---
[11] *Ibid.*, p. 532.
[12] James M. Buckley, *A History of Methodists in the United States*, p. 298.
[13] Maxwell Pierson Gaddis, *Footprints of an Itinerant*, p. 74.

ings, with a view to reviving their spiritual experience or gaining conversion. This type of meeting was introduced by the Methodists. Speaking of one such meeting that had been in progress for a time, and was making successful gains, Gaddis said:

"The next day the battle waxed much hotter, and farmers laid aside their work and brought their families with them to the house of God. During the balance of that week we held meeting twice every day, and for three days we ate our dinners at the church, because we could not find time to go home between the morning service and the exercises at three o'clock, P. M." [14]

Of a night service which closed his ministry in a certain place, he wrote:

"It was near the hour of twelve o'clock before all the congregation had left the house. Some were so filled with the Spirit that they praised God aloud in the streets as they returned to their homes." [15]

He told of listening in 1837 to a powerful address by a spokesman for the American Bible Society: "My feelings were so excited that I gave away nearly all the money I had." [16]

Lest the reader think that this picture of spiritual exuberance was true only of the more western areas, like Ohio, where Gaddis itinerated, we quote the following description of the closing service of a Methodist camp meeting on Martha's Vineyard, off the coast of Massachusetts, in the year 1842:

"On Monday evening the public services closed with the usual parting ceremony, and at eight o'clock we retired to our tents to besiege the enemy in his lurking places. The battle waxed warmer and warmer till after ten o'clock, when the enemy gave way and the shout of triumph rang through all our lines. Some now retired to rest, but many remained upon the field to celebrate a glorious victory.

"At half past two o'clock on Tuesday morning the encampment was aroused by a procession of singers, who after marching several times around the circle, engaged in a prayer meeting which continued till broad daylight.

---

[14] *Ibid.*, p. 176.
[15] *Ibid.*, p. 187.
[16] *Ibid.*, p. 188.

Several of the companies moved to the shore singing the songs of Zion." [17] *

In his *Encyclopedia of Methodism*, Matthew Simpson, a Methodist bishop, wrote this in 1878, regarding camp meetings:

"These meetings have been disapproved of by many because of the great excitement which sometimes attends them, and because of extravagances, in which a few persons have sometimes indulged. . . . While there undoubtedly have been instances of persons attending these meetings for improper purposes, and there may have been scenes of disorder, especially in the outskirts, yet the history of these meetings shows that wonderful reformations have been accomplished by their agencies." [18]

The reader is warranted in assuming that those who disapproved of camp meetings were not so restrained in their description of "extravagances" and "scenes of disorder."

It should also be noted that the bishop did not state that such extravagances and disorders as did break out were confined to the fringes of the then civilized America. The facts are that a hundred years ago, when religion was taken more seriously by the masses of the people, when men really believed there was a heaven to win and a hell to shun, there was inevitably some excitement and at least occasionally extravagances and disorders in great public meetings, whether those meetings were held in a tent or in a building. Indeed, in a day when people became mightily stirred over a political campaign, or over a social reform, should

---

[17] Reverend H. Vincent, *A History of the Wesleyan Grove, Martha's Vineyard, Camp Meeting*, pp. 65, 66.
[18] Matthew Simpson, *Encyclopedia of Methodism*, p. 162, art. "Camp Meetings."

* In the year 1854 a book was written by a minister on the subject of camp meetings, which was chiefly a defense of such meetings against various charges and objections. The book was printed in Boston. This minister, a Methodist, answered, for example, the objection that camp meetings lead to disorder. He replied in part:

"What strikes many persons as disorder in a religious exercise is, when rightly viewed, no more than a proper and Scriptural instance of religious zeal."—*Reverend B. W. Gorham, Camp Meeting Manual, p. 53.*

We need not turn aside to discuss how valid his answer was. We are interested here only in giving a brief sketch of the tempo of various religious services at the time that Millerism flourished. It is, of course, reasonable to presume that what a critic might describe as "disorder" in a religious exercise, could easily be described by a sympathetic onlooker as simply "religious zeal."

Another objection answered by this same writer reveals that in the middle of the nineteenth century there were physical manifestations in connection with camp meetings, for he considered the objection: "But I have known persons lose their strength at camp meetings." He did not deny this charge that people were prostrated at times at camp meetings under the preaching. He simply replied by citing instances in the Scriptures, where holy men of old were prostrated, completely losing their strength when they received great revelations and light from God.

we expect to see them remaining absolutely calm and passive under the fervent preaching of a minister who was setting before them the question of their eternal destiny?

Fervency in camp meetings and other religious services was not the only way in which people militantly expressed their religious beliefs and convictions a century ago. There were strong tensions between Protestantism and Catholicism. In 1837 the Native American party was founded. Beginning as a movement opposed to unlimited immigration, it quickly became openly anti-Catholic. In May of 1844 the city of Philadelphia was the scene of rioting between Catholic and anti-Catholic elements. In July rioting was renewed. Several persons were killed and many injured, and some Catholic churches were burned.

Incredible as it may seem, the following news item appeared in a Massachusetts newspaper in 1844:

"Doctor O. A. Brownson was baptized into the Catholic faith last Sabbath. We cannot too sincerely congratulate the Protestants on the fact, for if the doctor should render his new friends the same sort of service that he has his old friends, Catholicism will soon be at an end." [19]

Nor were vigorous utterances in the field of religion confined to disputes between Protestants and Catholics. In the city of New York in the year 1844 were published two prominent Protestant religious weeklies, the *New York Evangelist* and the *New York Observer*. It seems that the *Evangelist* had written an article on which the *Observer* made some rather critical remarks. This led the *Evangelist* to state editorially:

"To our painful surprise our contemporary has seized on the article with singular avidity, and by detaching some unguarded expressions from their obvious connection has *labored* with malignant perversion of our meaning, to fasten on us the expression of sentiments which we utterly disclaim and abhor. . . . A more unparalleled and wicked perversion we can scarcely call to mind." [20]

To which the *Observer* replied in similar vein two days later:

---

[19] *Concord Freeman* (Mass.), Oct. 25, 1844.
[20] *New York Evangelist*, Jan. 11, 1844.

"The religious press, instead of being a blessing to the church, will become its severest curse, the vehicle of poison and death, if such doctrines are promulgated and then excused on the ground of carelessness or haste." [21]

Another revealing side light on our forebears is the way they related themselves to "tall" stories. Generally speaking the public a century ago were not unwilling to accept a rather incredible story. A newspaper editor in 1843 related that there called upon him a minister who stated that his wife had vomited up a half-grown frog, and that evidently she must have swallowed it in tadpole form some weeks ago when she was drinking in the dark. The news story went on to relate that the frog jumped around a little, and then rolled over and died. The editor assured his readers that he would not have believed the story had not a minister told him.*

In a Boston paper in 1844 appeared an article entitled "An Elk Suckled by a Woman." The story related that a traveler in the territory of Missouri came to the home of some hardy pioneers, and found there a "four-legged child." According to the story the woman had suckled the elk "until it had grown to the size and perfection of the perfect animal described in history, which all know is large and beautiful." Then the newspaper added immediately: "We give this as a curious and interesting fact." [22] The story was widely quoted in the newspapers, some printing it as fact, and others expressing a doubt or uncertainty as to its genuineness.

Occasionally the newspapers brightened up their columns of routine news by inserting whimsical items written in the same style as the news and distinguishable from bona fide news items only by their incredibility. For example, there was the item that appeared in numbers of papers, entitled "Forty Thousand Tame Frogs." In grave, matter-of-fact language the reader is in-

---

[21] *New York Observer*, Jan. 13, 1844.
[22] *Boston Daily Bee*, Oct. 24, 1844.

* The most remarkable part of this whole story is that the newspaper in which we found it, credited the news item to the *Boston Transcript*, a newspaper which at that time and for long afterward was always to be found in the best homes in that cultural center of America. (See *Massachusetts Spy* [Worcester], Sept. 13, 1843.)

formed that a trip was made by Mr. Wise, United States Minister to Brazil, to the Peake of Teneriffe. On this trip Lieutenant J. B. Dale described, "among other notable things" which were seen, a huge cistern in the garden of the American Consul, whence, at twilight, issued the voices of forty thousand frogs, cultivated with care for their musical talent.[23]

This frog story was surely intended to be understood by the newspaper readers simply as a whimsy and as a delightful "tall" story. But we wonder whether a public, seriously asked to believe that a tadpole could change to a frog in a woman's stomach, could be safely counted on to view these Brazilian frogs only as a figment of the editor's imagination.

There was another characteristic of those times, the tendency to judge a man by some minor external feature. For example, a Boston newspaper, describing the defendant in a case of seduction, wrote:

"He is very dark, scowls frightfully and wears a goatee, itself *prima facie* evidence of animal propensities and small wit." [24]

The reader may feel that in this chapter we have wandered far afield from the subject of Millerism. We think not. This brief picture of the world in which Millerism flourished will aid us in evaluating the Millerite movement and the charges brought against it. We can now see that the fervent preaching of the Millerites and the exuberance of spirit that sometimes revealed itself at their meetings was quite in line with the temper of the times. By the same token we may be permitted to discount in advance a large part of the militant attacks upon Millerism, both in the secular and in the religious press. That was merely the style of the day. No one seemed to have many scruples about expressing himself vigorously and sometimes in conscienceless fashion against those who held contrary views, particularly in religion.

---
[23] *Boston Post,* Oct. 9, 1844.
[24] *Boston Daily Mail,* Oct. 24, 1844.

WORLD IN WHICH MILLERISM FLOURISHED

And when it is remembered that the Millerite leaders were oftentimes also abolitionists, it is doubly easy to see why they would be the objects of much blind hatred and groundless stories. For abolitionists, in the early days of their work, were often hated as heartily in the North as they were in the South. In this connection it should be mentioned that when the Millerites began to declare that the Protestant churches were a part of Babylon, they sometimes offered as part of their proof the fact that many churches endorsed slavery and many more condoned it.

The simple fact that the Millerites lived in an age of militancy is sufficient, we repeat, to explain most of the charges made against them. When we add to this the fact that they frequently coupled Millerism and abolitionism, indicting the churches because of their attitude toward slavery, we have almost a sufficient explanation of why they were the objects of ribaldry and defamatory stories.

And in the light of the fact that the newspapers straight-facedly told their readers such stories as that of the frog in the woman's stomach, and that of the elk nurtured on human milk, we can only expect that the press would themselves believe, and pass on to their readers to believe, equally fantastic stories about the Millerites. To say the least, we should be very much on our guard and view with a critical eye the "good" stories about the Millerites that were printed in the public press or given circulation by word of mouth. Such stories ranged all the way from the obvious joke to the patently grave charge that was intended to be taken at full value.

Here is a sample of the stories that passed for high humor. An editor saw a dog trotting by his window. The dog had its tail curled up in the form of a figure 3, and of course was running on its four legs, thus giving the number 43. The beast looked to be about eighteen years old. Thus, said the editor, he reached the conclusion that this canine signified 1843. All this, of course, was intended to be a most uproarious joke on the Millerite predictions concerning 1843. The yarn was typical of the brand of humor in which many editors engaged. This particular story was widely printed. Many other stories of similar nature appeared in the papers. The only conclusion one is able to reach from reading such jokes is that the enemies of Millerism must have been rather hard put to find really bona fide stories to print about the movement. Evidently the Millerites did not do enough nonsensical and wildly fanatical things to make really colorful reading. Hence a primitive form of humor had to be invoked to make them appear ridiculous.[25]

However, the papers sometimes printed as a serious charge what we today would consider as whimsical. For example, in the spring of 1843 a Massachusetts newspaper stated that a woman in Andover, New Hampshire, according to Doctor Tibbets, was delivered in March "of a nondescript child, with two heads and a double set of hands and feet, and nine toes on one foot. She had been excited at a Miller meeting, and looking at the disgusting animals on the Miller diagrams." [26]

And now to a consideration of the major charges against the Millerites.

---

[25] See, for example, *Portland Bulletin* (Maine), May 23, 1843; *Daily Evening Transcript* (Boston), May 25, 1843.
[26] *Haverhill Gazette* (Mass.), April 15, 1843.

CHAPTER 21

Did the Millerites Indulge in Fanatical Practices?

THE MILLERITES HAVE PROBABLY been charged with more colorful varieties of fanaticism than almost any other religious movement in modern history. They have been indicted as guilty of conducting wild, hysterically emotional meetings, accompanied by the most incredible physical manifestations; of clothing themselves in ghostly white ascension robes to wander over hill and vale and through graveyards; of filling the asylums with deluded creatures made mad by their preaching; of promoting fantastic, new beliefs.

In brief, these are the charges—grave ones, indeed! They have been told and retold until almost everyone is *sure* they are true. They have actually been woven into history books and reference works. But what are the facts?

The reader has already noted that many of the newspaper stories about the Millerites were introduced unblushingly with the words, "It is said," "It is reported," and even "It is rumored" —inadmissable as testimony in court. And we have taken occasion, because it was so interlocked with the narrative, to examine one of the charges, namely, that the Millerite leaders were unscrupulous men in financial matters. The examination of that charge revealed that it had only rumor for foundation.

But the main charges still remain to be considered. In introducing our examination of these we wish to stress an obviously sound principle that a whole movement must not be judged by the actions of a few; most certainly not if those actions are condemned by the movement. This applies particularly to a loose-knit movement, as any new religious movement is almost sure to be. Unless this principle is followed, no organization—religious, social, or political—could hope to escape condemnation. And the condemnation would come no matter how close-knit the organization. The favorite sport of skeptics is to point to individual hypocrites in the church and declare that all Christianity is a fraud. And of course it is a fact that there was a cursing Peter and a traitorous Judas in the earliest Christian church. Dictator nations have made capital of lawless incidents in connection with our elections to prove that democracy is a failure.

Rivers have not only a main channel, in which flows the great body of water, they have also marshy spots along the banks, a backwater or stagnant lagoon here and there, perhaps even a crosscurrent occasionally. But English literature would provide us no glorious descriptions of rivers if the poets had fixed their eyes on the marshy spots along the bank—Bobby Burns' "Sweet Afton" would have been neither "sweet" nor "murmuring." True, the marsh and the stagnant lagoon are related to the river, but no one in his right senses ever thinks of describing a river in terms of them. Nor would anyone think of charting the course of a stream by focusing his eye on the eddies or swirls.

Now, a religious movement, or any other movement for that matter, has something in common with a river. Millerism, for example, began small, like a tiny rivulet. Enlarged by the constant inflowing of members from all sides, this religious stream became a river, rolling onward in ever-increasing volume. Along the edges a marshy spot was to be found here and there, an eddy or a swirl, or even a crosscurrent occasionally.

Certainly there were abnormal, fanatical incidents to be found along the courses of Millerism. The people who constituted it were human beings, gathered out of all classes. On the law of averages there could hardly fail to be found at least a few who were erratic mentally or spiritually, or both. Someone long ago observed that every movement, whether religious, political, or social, has its "lunatic fringe." Unfortunately a new move-

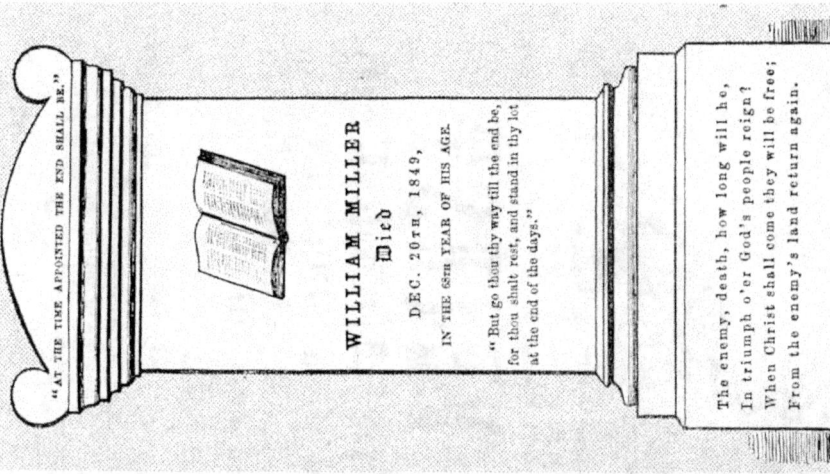

To Dr. I. O. Orr, December 13, 1844, Miller describes events connected with October 22 ("The next day" of the opening phrase) at Low Hampton. (See pages 250, 267.)

Above Miller's grave stands this tombstone, with its appropriate quotations.

THE

MILLERITE HUMBUG;

OR THE

Raising of the Wind!!

A Comedy

IN FIVE ACTS,

AS PERFORMED WITH UNBOUNDED APPLAUSE IN BOSTON AND OTHER PARTS OF THE UNION!

COMPILED AND ARRANGED

BY ASMODEUS IN AMERICA,

OR THE DEVIL ON TWO STICKS.

BOSTON:
PRINTED FOR THE PUBLISHER.
1845.

Title page of a play satirizing Millerism. The play was based on the October, 1844, Millerite hopes.

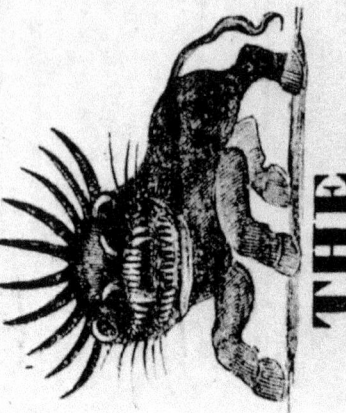

THE

HIGH PRIEST

Of Millerism Unmasked,

Or, a brief account of a Millerite Camp Meeting, held in East Kingston, N. H., from June 28th to July 5th, 1842.

One Joshua Himes of Boston,
Great things hath done of late,
While holding a Camp meeting,
In the old Granite State.

He strated as Chief Marshal,
Before a host of tools ;
And showed the world how partial
Are all self-righteous fools.

But when all others they can gag :
They will be *Simon Pure*.

God gave his servant victory,
And error fled the field ;
The sons of hell were hurl'd from heav'n,
And priestcraft had to yield.

A portion of a broadside devoted in part to an attack on the Millerites in general and Joshua V. Himes in particular. This doggerel attack runs on for many verses. Versifying seemed to be a popular style in the 1840's for lampooning one's foes.

ment, because of its loose-knit structure and absence of well-defined central control, cannot easily prove to a critical world that its "lunatic fringe" is really on the fringe and is not of the warp and woof of the movement.

The malady called fanaticism has plagued Christendom from the earliest times. The apostle Paul had to deal with it in some of the churches he raised up. He even had to plead with one church to have all things "done decently and in order." 1 Corinthians 14:40. The early church fathers have left a record of numerous fanatical outbreaks in the church. Luther, the leader of the Protestant Reformation, was gravely embarrassed for a time by a fanatical group that he had to denounce. The great religious movement under the preaching of John Wesley was also troubled from time to time with fanatical individuals or groups. This fact is not questioned even by those church historians who write sympathetically of Wesley's great work.

Because the Wesleyan religious awakening was near enough in time to warrant comparison with Millerism, let us look at the record as it deals with fanaticism. Wrote one historian, who was obviously not biased against Methodism:

"The purest gold is sometimes mixed with dross; and so it was with Methodism. Some of the Foundery Society fanatically talked of feeling the blood of Christ running upon their arms, their breasts, their hearts, and down their throats. Wesley met them, and denounced their folly as the empty dreams of heated imaginations. Good John Brown, of Tanfield Leigh, two or three days after his conversion, came riding through Newcastle, hallooing and shouting, and driving all the people before him; telling them that God had revealed to him that he should be a king, and should tread all his enemies beneath his feet. Wesley arrested him, and sent him home immediately, advising him to cry day and night to God, lest the devil should gain an advantage over him. These were rare exceptions, and were promptly checked." [1]

This same historian tells also of a George Bell who was converted and pretended to be sanctified, and who wrote Wesley "in a letter tinged with a frenzy."

---

[1] L. Tyerman, *The Life and Times of the Rev. John Wesley,* Vol. 1, p. 395.

"Bell soon developed into a full blown enthusiast. . . . He began to hold meetings of his own, declaring, that God . . . was to be found nowhere but in the assemblies of himself and his London friends. . . . His admirers fancied themselves more holy than our first parents. . . . They professed to have the gift of healing." [2]

Quite apart from these fanatical acts, there were many unusual manifestations in connection with Wesley's revival meetings. Critical onlookers generally called such manifestations fanatical.

Wesley records that while he was holding a meeting "a well-dressed, middle-aged woman suddenly cried out as in the agonies of death." This continued for a time, and she was finally converted.[3]

On another occasion Wesley had hardly started preaching when he was interrupted by the cries and groans of a man under conviction.

"Another person dropped down, close to the one who was a strong asserter of the contrary doctrine. . . . A little boy near him was seized in the same manner. A young man who stood up behind fixed eyes on him, and sunk down himself as one dead; but soon began to roar out and beat himself against the ground, so that six men could scarcely hold him. His name was Thomas Maxfield [footnote says he became a lay helper to Wesley]. Except John Haydon, I never saw one so torn of the Evil One. Meanwhile many others began to cry out to the 'Saviour of all,' that He would come and help them, insomuch that all the house (and indeed all the street for some space) was in an uproar. But we continued in prayer, and before ten the greater part found rest to their souls." [4]

Wesley warned of the dangers of fanaticism and rebuked fanatics. The text of these warnings shows how similar is the pattern of fanaticism in every century, and how every religious awakening has been plagued by it. There are those who have false ideas of holiness, and of living above sin; those who feel that their impressions or dreams should guide them, no matter how strange the impressions; those who believe they have the

---

[2] *Ibid.*, Vol. 2, p. 434.
[3] See *The Journal of the Rev. John Wesley*, Vol. 2, pp. 131, 132.
[4] *Ibid.*, pp. 203, 204.

gifts of healing and divination of spirits, or perhaps the gift of tongues. Such false thinking and claims confronted Wesley and he went on record against them. Despite this, the whole Wesleyan movement was described by staid Anglican bishops as simply a display of fanaticism, with John Wesley himself the chief fanatic.[5]

The dictionary has embalmed for our sober inspection today a definition formerly given to the word "fanatic" in England, where all who practiced religions not conforming to the Church of England were considered outside the pale of respectability. Says the New Standard Dictionary, "Fanatic. . . . An English nonconformist: used opprobriously."

Though the dictionary informs us that this usage of the word is now obsolete, the term is still employed by many to cover any unusual acts or views of anyone who may differ from the majority in religion. Fanatic is the smear word, par excellence, in the religious arena. We should keep this fact in mind in any consideration of charges of fanaticism.

Certainly there were fanatical acts in connection with Millerism. If Millerism could have arisen and carried on its work wholly free of the virus of fanaticism, it would have constituted one of the seven wonders of the religious world. The virulent germ of fanatical thought and action seems ever to be present in the spiritual bloodstream of some types of religionists and needs only the stimulus of a religious awakening in the community, to bring on its dread fever in such individuals.

Yes, Millerism was troubled with fanatics. How do we discover this? Must we turn to the writings of enemies in order to learn the facts? No, when fanaticism broke out here and there in the movement, it was generally discussed frankly, even baldly, in the Millerite papers. The Millerite doctors proceeded on the belief that the best way to treat a focus of fanatical infection was to expose it to the blazing light of their scorn.

---

[5] See *The Letters of John Wesley,* Vol. 4, pp. 338-384, for Wesley's reply to Doctor Warburton, Bishop of Gloucester, who had charged him with being a fanatic.

In the spring of 1843 one of the Millerite lecturers, Calvin French, embraced the heretical view that Christians can become so holy as to be above sin. This distortion of the true doctrine of Christian perfection caused men to feel that inasmuch as they were above sin, anything they desired to do must be a reflection of the promptings of the Spirit of God and altogether right to do. The evil possibilities in such reasoning are evident.

And what did the Millerites do when French took up with such false teachings? They publicly denounced him and his course in their own papers, and were "glad to be able thus early to expose" him. The committee's report said that they could no longer have "confidence in Mr. French, as a man of purity and integrity."[6] A movement that will frankly admit and expose a major mistake on the part of one of its lecturers is entitled to be heard and believed when it denies various charges against the movement, charges which even if true could rarely be as grave as this which it freely admits.

It was in the year 1843 that the virus of fanaticism first began in a troublesome way to affect the Millerite movement. In the spring of '43, in Joshua V. Himes' own Chardon Street Chapel in Boston, occurred an incident that throws further light on this question of fanaticism and how Millerite leaders dealt with it. Because Himes had to be away from his church increasingly in the promotion of the movement, an assistant pastor, John Starkweather, had been engaged. He was a graduate of Andover Theological Seminary and a minister in good standing in the "Orthodox Congregational denomination." A man of strong personality, "he taught that conversion, however full and thorough, did not fit one for God's favor without a second work; and that this second work was usually indicated by some bodily sensation." The natural result was that there were strong physical manifestations soon taking place in the Chardon Street Chapel. Some members were impressed that this might be of God; others were not sure, but feared that by opposing such

---

[6] *Signs of the Times*, April 19, 1843, p. 56.

DID MILLERITES INDULGE IN FANATICISM? 309

manifestations they might be sinning against the Holy Ghost.

When Himes returned from one of his extended journeys, he sensed that all was not well. But when he sought to show that the tendency of the manifestations was in the wrong direction, Starkweather and some of his zealous adherents declared that Himes would drive away the Holy Ghost. Some cried out, "You are throwing on cold water." "Throwing on cold water!" replied Himes with vigor; "I would throw on the Atlantic Ocean before I would be identified with such abominations as these, or suffer them in this place unrebuked."[7] Here was the true spirit of Millerism expressing itself.*

In an earlier chapter we discussed the Millerite camp meetings of 1843 and stated that there was one marked exception to the otherwise orderly series of meetings that summer—a trio of camp meetings held in Connecticut.

At these three meetings were certain groups who engaged in fanatical acts. There were those who thought they had acquired the gift of discerning of spirits, and could tell who were saved or who were lost simply by touching them on the forehead. One woman felt impressed that she could walk on the water even as Peter did, and only with difficulty could be restrained from testing her faith in the near-by Connecticut River. The virus of this fanaticism affected one after another of three camp meetings held at the following places in Connecticut: Plainfield, Stepney (near Bridgeport), and Windsor. The fanatical

---

[7] See Sylvester Bliss, *Memoirs of William Miller*, pp. 231-233.

* Though thus rebuked, Starkweather continued to associate himself with the movement to a greater or lesser degree. Even an occasional article by him is found in the Millerite papers. Perhaps this was not wholly consistent on the part of the Millerite leaders. However, it should be remembered that Starkweather was not guilty of any immorality. The "abominations" of which Himes spoke, consisted only in silly manifestations that outraged Himes' sense of religious decorum. To have dealt too hardly with a man who was guilty of what many in those days would have viewed only as excess enthusiasm, would have placed the Millerite leaders in the light of harsh and rigorous men who permitted no variation from their views of propriety. However, an article from his pen that was published in *The Midnight Cry*, October 12, 1844, was prefaced by an editorial note that indicates that the Millerite editor wished Starkweather's remarks to be taken with spiritual caution. Early in 1846 the following note appeared in *The Advent Herald*: "J. STARKWEATHER.—We have frequent complaints from brethren in relation to this individual. His course is one of disaster and mischief wherever he goes. We cannot help our brethren in this matter. Unless they take their stand against such extravagant and fanatical pretenders, they may always expect discord, and every evil work among them."—*March 25, 1846, p. 56.*

element at these camp meetings was restrained only after the severest rebukes.

The daily press, which too generally had been forced to content itself with unfounded, irrelevant rumors in defamation of Millerism, found in these Connecticut meetings a choice morsel. The story was soon printed in papers over the land and lost nothing in the retelling.[8]

There seems to be no clear evidence that the infection of fanaticism was present in any definite way in 1843 beyond these Connecticut camp meetings. Certainly if it had been, the press would have made special mention of it.* What is even more important, the Millerite papers themselves would doubtless have discussed it. We may conclude this from the fact that both the *Signs of the Times* and *The Midnight Cry* contained vigorous discussions and denunciations of the fanatical outbreaks that occurred in connection with the Connecticut meetings. Josiah Litch, one of the most prominent of the Millerite leaders, was in attendance at the Stepney camp meeting. Immediately afterward he wrote a letter to *The Midnight Cry* in which he excoriated the fanatics and analyzed the false reasoning that produces such fanaticism. Said he:

"I find in the papers of this morning an account of the second advent camp meeting near Bridgeport, Connecticut. The picture is, to be sure, a dark one, but no more so than the truth will warrant. All the scenes

---

[8] See, for example, *Philadelphia Public Ledger,* Sept. 11, 1843; *Newark Daily Advertiser* (N. J.), Sept. 14, 1843; *Pittsfield Sun* (Mass.), Sept. 28, 1843.

* Because the term "fanaticism" has often been used in a very loose way, we should state that we are here using it to describe acts, attitudes, and beliefs which, when compared with Bible standards, or with the acts and beliefs of the great majority of Christians, are found to be outside the pale. Unquestionably, a person who thinks that by touching another person on the forehead he can tell whether that person is saved—which was the case at the Connecticut camp meetings—is guilty of fanaticism, by the definition here given. But a person who is simply exuberant and somewhat uninhibited in his expressions of religious joy would not necessarily be viewed as fanatical by our definition. Religious history and Sacred Writ provide enough illustrations of holy men who were thus vocal and vigorous in their religious deportment to make us hesitate to indict as fanatical, with all the odium that attaches to that term, a person who is guilty of nothing more than fervent actions and expressions. In the preceding chapter we have given a number of illustrations of the vigorous way in which many people related themselves, not only to religion, but to politics and social reform in the early nineteenth century. Therefore, when we speak of instances of fanaticism by Millerites, we are primarily concerned with acts and beliefs that conform to the definition in this note. It is true that Miller himself seems to have used the word "fanaticism" in a loose and general sense in a criticism of the movement late in 1844. For a discussion of his criticism, see Appendix D.

described there are true, without exaggeration. A more disgraceful scene, under the garb of piety I have rarely witnessed." [9]

Not even the most captious critic of Millerism could say that Litch was attempting to smooth over an unfortunate incident. In his righteous indignation Litch really outdid the newspapers. But this was not the first time he had been confronted with fanatical scenes. Previous to his active connection with Millerism in 1841, he had been a Methodist Episcopal minister for a number of years, and had had occasion to attend various kinds of religious gatherings. He continued:

"For the last ten years I have come in contact nearly every year, more or less, with the same spirit, and have marked its developments, its beginning and its result; and am now prepared to say that it is *evil, and only evil, and that continually.* I have uniformly opposed it, wherever it has made its appearance. . . . The origin of it, is, the idea that the individuals thus exercised are entirely under the influence of the Spirit of God, are His children, and that He will not deceive them and lead them astray; hence every impulse which comes upon them is yielded to as coming from God, and following it there is no length of fanaticism to which they will not go. . . .

"I wish to enter my most solemn protest against the whole concern of *fanaticism* as I witnessed it at the *Stepney camp meeting*. I wish to have no part nor lot in such a concern. And if second advent meetings must be the scenes of such disgraceful proceedings as I there witnessed, I protest against more being held." [10]

There is no hedging here; Litch's soul was outraged. He was jealous for the good name of the movement. Fervently he prayed in almost the closing line of his letter, "May the Lord save us from all such fanaticism in the few days which yet remain, until He comes." [11]

Perhaps if fanaticism had not broken out in spots we might never have had a record of the feeling and attitude of the Millerite leaders toward such religious excesses. A letter like this by Litch leaves us in no doubt.

---

[9] Letter, Sept. 11, 1843, in *The Midnight Cry,* Sept. 14, 1843, p. 29.
[10] *Ibid.*
[11] *Ibid.,* p. 30.

But Litch was not the only one to express himself in writing on these Connecticut camp meeting incidents. Over in Ohio, Himes read this militant protest and added the following postscript to a letter he was ready to send to the *Signs of the Times:* "I have just received *The Midnight Cry* containing Brother Litch's 'Protest.' *I heartily join in it.*" [12]

At the Windsor, Connecticut, camp meeting, L. C. Collins, another Millerite minister, was present. Immediately afterward he wrote for the *Signs of the Times* a forthright rebuke to the fanaticism that arose at the meeting, and set forth some of the factors that led to fanaticism. These Millerite spokesmen had a clear understanding of the causes, both spiritual and physical, that are involved in fanaticism. They were neither surprised nor nonplused by it, nor need anyone be who has read the history of religion and noted the more or less standard pattern that fanaticism has assumed as it has broken out here and there through all the centuries. Wrote Collins:

"Many good things might be said of this meeting. . . . But with unmingled grief I have to state that we found a spirit developing itself among us, which we are *perfectly satisfied is not of God,* but directly opposed to the letter and spirit of His Word. It is no *new* thing, it has been trying to graft itself upon the meek, and gentle, and unassuming, and rational, and consistent religion of the Bible in every age since the days of Christ." [13]

Fearing lest his detailed description and denunciation might convey to the reader the mistaken idea that these fanatical outbursts on the part of a few, presented a true picture of the whole camp meeting, he said in a concluding paragraph:

"This was only a noxious worm that had commenced gnawing the leaves upon the outer branches, but which if permitted to propagate would destroy the tree. But God has shaken it off, and enabled us to crush it underfoot." [14]

He mentioned the names of other lecturers who were in

---

[12] Letter, Sept. 21, 1843, in *Signs of the Times,* Oct. 4, 1843, p. 56.
[13] Letter, Sept. 22, 1843, in *Signs of the Times,* Sept. 27, 1843, p. 45.
[14] *Ibid.,* p. 46.

attendance with him and who wished to be on record with him in protest against the fanaticism.

A sequel to Collins' letter against the fanatics at the Windsor camp meeting is a resolution passed by the second advent believers in Worcester on September 25, just five days after the Windsor meeting closed. It seems that at this Windsor meeting "the Worcester tent," that is, the tent in which the believers from Worcester had lived, "had the reputation of being the seat of the peculiar exercises" that had been the cause of the fanatical trouble at the meeting. Did the occupants of the Worcester tent truly represent the second advent believers in that city? Evidently the Millerites in Worcester wanted it clearly known that this was not so. At a special meeting called on the twenty-fifth, a formal series of resolutions was passed. These resolutions deplored what had happened as the result of "the fanatical spirit and movement of some brethren connected with the Worcester tent at the Windsor camp meeting." The resolution protested "against all such sentiments and proceedings, whether seen at that meeting or any other," and went on to describe the fanatical spirit as being "of the devil." The secretary of the meeting added this:

"I would just say that I regard the above as a correct expression of the feeling of Adventists here. . . . Several of the friends, who partially drunk into the strange spirit, have seen their error, and regret the whole affair. With only two or three exceptions, we are all right on this subject." [15]

The one most pained by such displays was Miller. Said he:

"My heart was deeply pained during my tour east, to see in some few of my former friends, a proneness to the wild and foolish extremes of some vain delusions, such as working miracles, discerning of spirits, vague and loose views on sanctification." [16]

While the Millerite leaders deplored any display of fanaticism, they saw no reason why they should therefore be placed on the defensive in relation to other religious bodies.

---
[15] *Signs of the Times*, Oct. 11, 1843, p. 64.
[16] Letter, Oct. 12, 1843, in *Signs of the Times*, Nov. 8, 1843, p. 97.

What the editor of the *Signs of the Times* had to say in comment on a critical statement that had appeared in a religious journal, applies, in principle, to the whole question of fanatical acts:

"The *Hartford Christian Secretary*, has a long article on the fanaticism attending the Bridgeport camp meeting. We would ask Brother Burr, if it would not be an act of justice to state in connection with it, that such doings are entirely discountenanced by us and by the Adventists generally?

"The article states that 'Millerism is the *hotbed* in which the *exotic* is nurtured and grown.' Then was the Reformation the *hotbed* in which the fanaticism of that day was nurtured; so was *Christianity* the *hotbed* in which the excesses grew, against which the apostles warned the primitive church; and so is religion ever the hotbed in which all fanaticism germinates. A hotbed that will not produce some weeds will not produce any good fruit. The tares and wheat will grow *together* till the harvest; and where the Spirit of the Lord is, the devil will be with his counterfeits. Brother B. knows very well that this argument would be as good against the Baptist, and every other evangelical denomination, as against those of the Adventists. Their operations in spite of the most judicious efforts, and to the pain of the servants of God in these branches of the church, have been accompanied by these extravagances; and the absence of the exotic may at the present time be as much a call for sorrow as for pride and censoriousness. The devil may be too well pleased with their condition to tempt them with fanaticism. He has but little choice whether men are *frozen* or *burnt up*, if anything he prefers the frost where nothing can grow, but in the torrid zone there is sure to be something valuable amid the luxuriant herbage." [17]

Up to the close of 1843, apart from the incidents at the Connecticut camp meetings, almost the only charge* brought against the Millerites in the matter of fanaticism was the accusation that their meetings were scenes of undue excitement, contrary to the spirit of good religion, and that people were even

---

[17] *Signs of the Times*, Sept. 27, 1843, pp. 44, 45.

* We realize that a generalization like this is always open to challenge by anyone who may discover that in a particular city certain Millerites were said to have done thus and so. We admit that we can never say with absolute certainty that we have considered every charge that is entitled to be heard, for rumor and hearsay are so interwoven with facts as to bewilder, at times, even the most careful investigator. This book would be larger than an unabridged dictionary if we gave serious consideration to all the stories that are prefaced with "It is said," or "It is rumored," or even to stories that begin plausibly by stating that this is what a friend of mine told me of what he saw. All such testimony and evidence are worthless in court. We see no good reason why they should be considered of more value here.

As a sample of the material that confronts a researcher in this field—and it is much more plausible than most newspaper items—take the following:

made insane by such excitement. The insanity charge was generally very specific, occasionally mentioning names of alleged victims. We shall examine the charge in detail in later chapters. The accusation that they held exciting meetings was almost invariably in vague language.

Now the charge of undue excitement at religious services, particularly revivals, is an old one and was invented by skeptics long before Miller was born. Doubtless the charge has been well founded at times. As shown in the preceding chapter, the revivals in connection with the camp meetings of various bodies in the early decades of the nineteenth century in America were exceedingly fervent affairs, to say the least. We think that Miller and his associates would have offered some criticism of them. Yet the great religious bodies that conducted those camp meetings seem not to have it held against them today.

However, in these early decades the religious press felt it necessary at times to justify the excitement that was present at many revivals. In 1840, for example, *Zion's Banner* reprinted approvingly a long article from the *Christian Watchman* on "Revivals and Excitement." The article defends both, seeking to show that there was much excitement in connection with the preaching of Christ and the apostles, and concludes thus:

"Excitement has always attended the rapid spread of religion and always will. And why should not a subject of such awful moment produce excitement? Men may be excited in politics without reproach. The political press often speaks with praise on the 'enthusiasm' in favor of this or that candidate. . . . We hope therefore that the vain talk about excitement will deter no one from bold, active, constant effort to bring sinners to

---

The editor of a Portland, Maine, paper wrote a critical editorial on Millerism. He described a meeting where "ten or twelve persons" were rolling around on the floor and screaming, and declared that one of them, the next day, explained that they "had been receiving sanctification." (See *Portland Bulletin,* Jan. 17, 1843.) Even if this report were taken at face value it would prove only that a group of people of the Holy Roller type—there have been such people in every age—had woven into their thinking the Miller teachings on the advent. The report would not prove Millerism, as such, a fanatical movement, and for the simple reason that every bona fide spokesman for Millerism denounced all such bodily exercises. But was this editor actually testifying as an eye witness? No. He said that "a gentleman of our acquaintance" was the source of his information. Furthermore, that this "gentleman" had received part of his information from "several individuals" who "stood around" watching these exercises. Finally, that a further source of the editor's information was some unnamed person who "interrogated" one of the worshipers the next day! Impressive testimony indeed!

Christ. Let the use of all Scriptural means be resorted to without fear, to convert sinners, and if excitement be the consequence, it is not our fault." [18]

Then why should the Millerites need to defend themselves against the charge of excitement? Their meetings could be very fervent and tense, with strong cryings and tears, and still be in line with the usual revival services of those times. But the evidence already presented, including the testimony of newspaper reporters who visited Millerite meetings, shows that those meetings were generally decorous, and the preaching dignified, even in the last climactic days before October 22, 1844.

In the year 1844, until October, there were apparently few well-defined fanatical incidents on which the newspapers could build a story. However, one camp meeting, at least, was disturbed by a group of fanatics that summer. The Millerites stated this themselves in their own papers. The most definite instance recorded was in connection with the notable Exeter, New Hampshire, camp meeting, from which dates the real beginning of the seventh-month movement, that set October 22 as the time of the advent. The report of that camp meeting in *The Advent Herald* contains the following brief statement regarding the disturbance that developed:

"This refreshing season was somewhat disturbed and greatly annoyed by a company who came on the ground with a tent, having no sympathy with the object for which the meeting was called, and in whose exercises and extravagances the meeting had no sympathy. It is altogether too late to palm off, as the fruits of God's Holy Spirit, the works of the flesh, which are in all things directly the opposite." [19]

Writing some years later concerning this camp meeting, James White, one of the younger Millerite ministers, stated that the "company" in this disturbing tent were from Watertown, Massachusetts. He himself was in the tent that housed a company from Portland, Maine. He told of how the Portland tent had been "pitched close to this tent from Watertown, before the condition of those who occupied it was generally known," and

---
[18] *Zion's Banner*, May 6, 1840.
[19] *The Advent Herald*, Aug. 21, 1844, p. 20.

DID MILLERITES INDULGE IN FANATICISM? 317

that when it became impossible to quiet those in the fanatical tent, the "Portland brethren moved their tent to a distant part of the ground." Fanaticism, though a disease of the mind and of the spirit, seems to have something in common with certain diseases of the body. It is contagious. White stated that the very act of the Portland brethren in moving their tent away caused the Watertown people to raise the "cry of persecution" and led some unthinking onlookers to join with them in the cry. White then related how a minister "who had the especial charge of the meeting" took a vigorous stand against the fanaticism:[20]

"He stated, in the most solemn manner, that he had no objections to shouts of praise to God, over victories won in His name. But when persons had shouted 'Glory to God' nine hundred and ninety-nine times, with no evidence of one victory gained, and had blistered their hands in striking them together with violence, he thought it was time for them to stop. But if they would not change their course, it was time for all who wished to be consistent Christians to withdraw their sympathy from them, and show their disapproval of their course by keeping entirely away from them. These remarks helped the people generally, but not those who were wild with fanaticism." [21]

It was when Snow addressed the camp, as mentioned in an earlier chapter, leading them to believe that they must be ready to meet God in October, that the fanatics were suddenly quieted, and none gave them more heed.

There is a background to this Watertown-tent incident. About a month before the Exeter camp meeting *The Advent Herald* published a "statement and protest of advent believers in Watertown, Mass." This is a rather extended statement by a group whose names are signed at the close, regarding the troubles they had had with some who had come into their midst advocating and practicing strange views. The Millerites in Watertown wanted all men to know that "we can have no sympathy with their opinions, their spirit or practices." The published protest declares:

---
[20] See James White, *Life Incidents*, pp. 157, 158.
[21] *Ibid.*, pp. 158, 159.

"We have, therefore, resolved to separate ourselves from all who walk thus disorderly and unscripturally, and so contrary to the views of all intelligent and consistent Adventists. . . . We can hold no fellowship with them in these things." [22]

They had no way of driving out the fanatics, so the advent believers themselves left. That reveals how strongly they felt about separating from these disturbers. It is hard to see how better proof could be offered of the resolute course taken by Millerites against fanaticism.

In the light of this the reader may wonder how the disturbers with their strangely fanatical views were permitted on the campground. The answer is that in the camp meetings of those times, whether Millerite or otherwise, the general practice was to allow all who called themselves Christians to pitch their tents and join in the services. These fanatics coming from Watertown looked the same as other people, and their fanaticism did not become evident until after they were located. To deal with them then by attempting physically to eject them from the ground might be to employ a remedy that would be worse than the disease.*

Among the few specific newspaper references to fanaticism at Millerite camp meetings in 1844, there is a news story on the meeting in Wallingford, Connecticut, in October, where some of the people thought they possessed the gift of healing and the gift of tongues.[23]

Fanaticism, like some other maladies, seems to be resident in certain areas. In other words, a fanatically disposed group may

---

[22] "Statement and Protest," Watertown, July 7, 1844, in *The Advent Herald*, July 17, 1844, p. 189.
[23] See *Albany Evening Journal* (N. Y.), Oct. 25, 1844, quoting *Herald* (New Haven, Conn.), Oct. 17, 1844; *Litchfield Enquirer* (Conn.), Oct. 24, 1844.

* If these few facts about the nature of oldtime camp meetings are kept in mind, the reader will have little difficulty separating in his mind the fanatical occupants of a particular tent from the general activities and deportment of the remainder of the encampment. In view of the lure that a large encampment with its stirring preaching would have for spiritually unstable persons, the marvel is not that fanaticism broke out occasionally at such meetings, but that it did not break out more often. Unless great care had been exercised, all the Millerite encampments might easily have become infected with a fanatical fever. That they did not is excellent proof that the Millerite doctors were constantly on their guard against it.

be found in a particular community, and whenever a public meeting or revival is conducted in that area, there are always reports of fanaticism. The simple reason is that these fanatical persons generally made it a point to attend, and to display their fanaticism. It is in the setting of this fact that we find particular significance in the statement made by a Millerite minister in reporting a Connecticut camp meeting in the summer of 1844:

"Of the *'Fanaticism'* which is said to exist among the brethren in that region, I can only say, that I witnessed nothing that I had not seen twenty-five years ago, among our Methodist brethren at their camp meetings." [24]

In view of the very limited references in the press to allegedly fanatical acts at the Millerite camp meetings that final summer of 1844, we may reasonably conclude that Millerism did not suddenly deteriorate into a series of fanatical orgies in the last great camp meeting season.

In the summer of 1844 the public press referred to a Miss Ann Matthewson who was mentioned in the Millerite papers. It seems that this young woman had been very ill for some time, that her life had been despaired of, that in some way she was almost miraculously sustained, and that she had been uttering certain warnings that sounded strangely like those of the Millerites. The casual reader might easily conclude that Miss Matthewson was a Millerite and that her strange acts were to be explained as a manifestation of Millerite fanaticism.

The facts were that she had no connection with the Millerites. The editor of *The Advent Herald* so stated.[25] Naturally, many Millerites were impressed by her ominous words and her apparently inexplicable hold on life. Several articles appeared in their papers in favorable comment on the phenomenon. But this much should be said in their defense—and we believe it is sufficient—they were evidently no more impressed than were multitudes of others. The record reveals that there were hosts of people of all religious persuasions who came to see this

---
[24] *The Midnight Cry,* Sept. 5, 1844, p. 71.
[25] *The Advent Herald,* July 10, 1844, pp. 180, 181.

singular young woman. The Millerites were neither more nor less credulous than others who lived at that time. If Miss Matthewson was a fraud, or a fanatic, she was not chargeable to Millerism, for neither she nor her parents were Millerites.

Late in 1844 the newspapers commented on an article that appeared in *The Midnight Cry,* reporting certain "cases of bodily cure by the power of faith." [26] The article is not long. It deals briefly with five cases. The Millerite editor confessed that he accepted as true this report of miraculous healings that had been sent in to him. Now any orthodox believer in the Scriptures agrees that the Bible offers a formula for the healing of the sick by prayer, provided always, the request is according to the will of God.[27] Medical science has belatedly been testifying to the remarkable interlocking of body, mind, and spirit.

However, to accept at face value the account of all these five cases gives evidence of what we today would certainly describe as credulity. But if credulity is a sure proof of fanaticism, then a very great host of pious people in all past generations stand equally condemned. It might also be remarked that the credulity here revealed is no greater than that which was displayed by the public generally in the 1840's.*

---

[26] *The Midnight Cry,* Oct. 12, 1844, p. 125.
[27] See James 5:14, 15.

* For example, the newspaper editor's write-up of what a minister told him about the tadpole that changed to a frog in a woman's stomach. See Chapter 20.

CHAPTER 22

Was Fanaticism Rampant in October, 1844?

AS TO THE CHARGE THAT THE MILLERITES were fanatical, there remain for our examination only the stories told regarding their activities in October, 1844, when they were making final plans for the great day of Christ's advent. According to newspaper stories and tradition a very large percentage of the alleged irrational acts of the Millerites occurred on October 22 and the days immediately preceding.

The reader already has in mind the main facts about the Millerites during this period, as set forth in their official publications. These reveal, above all else, that the leaders did not lose their heads in those last climactic days and begin to incite the advent believers to wild excesses; rather, the very opposite. Then how shall we judge the colorful stories that have come down to us of Millerites going out into the fields and graveyards, and up on mountaintops and housetops, of children dying by cold and exposure from being thus out in the open in the chill October weather?

The Millerite publications themselves, remaining frank to the very last in their exposure of any fanaticism, not only stated that there were some fanatical acts, but described certain of them. The great majority of the specific and lurid newspaper reports on Millerite excesses in connection with October 22, focus on certain happenings in Philadelphia. That is the first and most important fact to keep in mind. While the newspapers in other principal cities like Washington, New York, Boston, Portland, Rochester, Cleveland, and Cincinnati, published general remarks about allegedly foolish Millerites in their cities on October 22, almost invariably their reports are irritatingly vague and consist almost wholly of what they themselves generally admit are hearsay and rumor. Even in Boston, as we discovered in an earlier chapter in our discussion of the mob disturbances at the tabernacle, the reports in the city papers deal only in generalities and rumor, the unreliability of which we have already shown. But they almost all quote from the Philadelphia papers regarding fanaticism there.

First, what did the newspapers of Philadelphia say about the Millerites in their city? Here is the heart of the story as it appeared in the *Philadelphia Public Ledger* on October 22:

"Several large parties of persons believing in the Millerite doctrine, left the city yesterday morning, with the design of encamping outside the city, and awaiting the great change of temporal affairs, as predicted by their leaders and expected by them." [1]

On Thursday, October 24, the same paper stated that these Millerites left their campground on the Darby Road and removed their tent on Tuesday, some of them returning home according to report while others sought some spot "more safe from annoyance and threat than the ground they left." [2]

Around this central news item various newspapers in Philadelphia placed other details. One paper stated that "there were about two hundred persons in the encampment, men and women." [3]

On October 22, another of the Philadelphia newspapers, in telling of the Millerites who had left for the encampment the day before, reported that one of them threw away money in the streets, and that "one little girl showed us $3.50 she had gathered." [4]

On October 23 the same paper carried a note about the Millerites returning from their encampment "looking the picture of wretchedness." [5]

---

[1] *Philadelphia Public Ledger,* Oct. 22, 1844.
[2] *Ibid.,* Oct. 24, 1844.
[3] *Pennsylvania Inquirer* (Philadelphia), Oct. 22, 1844.
[4] *Spirit of the Times* (Philadelphia), Oct. 22, 1844.
[5] *Ibid.,* Oct. 23, 1844.

On October 24 this paper carried the following rumor item:

"It was rumored yesterday that four of the converts to the Miller humbug who went to the encampment, near Darby are dead from the effects of overexcitement and exposure. We understand that one of the female believers gave birth to a child in one of the tents." [6]

Another Philadelphia paper told of the pitching of the first tent on the Darby Road, Monday noon, of the little children of the Millerites being "exposed to the peltings of the pitiless storm," because "on Monday commenced a cold storm, and Monday night was most bitter and inclement." This newspaper gave as its opinion that on account of the inclement weather and related factors it was "next to impossible" that all should "escape death." The paper remarked that "it is currently reported" that some of the leaders had decamped with large sums.[7]

In 1844 Philadelphia had at least ten newspapers.* Seven of these were published daily, and three weekly; hence the encampment received a wide and varied reporting.

Here is a sensational story, to say the least—Millerites pouring out of the great city of Philadelphia, southwest, down Darby Road, men, women, and little children, throwing away their money as they journeyed on Monday morning, October 21, poorly housed in two large tents over the night in cold weather, and then the trek back to the city on Tuesday for most of them.

This story appeared in every corner of the land. What more proof did the public need that Millerism was a wildly fanatical movement? Here was a clear demonstration. The ordinary newspaper reader would naturally conclude that these people went out on instruction from the Millerite leaders and that this encampment, of course, was simply typical of what must have been similar open-air activities everywhere else on the part of these very foolish people on October 22.

Now what are the real facts in the case? How much of the

---
[6] *Ibid.*, Oct. 24, 1844.
[7] *United States Saturday Post* (Philadelphia), Oct. 26, 1844.
* This was the total number for which we could find a file.

story is true and how much false? What did the reporters actually see and hear, and what did they record of rumor and hearsay? Shortly before October 22 a Dr. C. R. Gorgas claimed to have a special revelation for the Millerites in relation to the great day. Who this Doctor Gorgas was, we know not. We do know that he was *not* a Millerite leader. Apparently his name is not even found in any of the Millerite literature until October, 1844. He declared that according to a revelation given him the righteous were to flee out of the cities just before the day of destruction, the same as Lot fled from Sodom. The report on this man and his activity up to October 22 we have drawn from a statement by Lewis C. Gunn, one of the more or less prominent Millerites of Philadelphia.*

Gunn said that Gorgas believed it had been "revealed to him that the advent would take place at three o'clock, on the morning of the 22d." †

Copies of the broadside containing this warning "were sent to Baltimore and to this city," that is, Philadelphia, and "the brethren in both places immediately opposed it." [8] Gorgas is described as a man of magnetic personality, the kind of person who very easily and powerfully influences others.

Of the relation of the Millerite leaders to the Gorgas fanaticism, Gunn testified:

"Joshua V. Himes, the chief publisher of advent papers, came to this city and strongly opposed Doctor Gorgas, as also Josiah Litch, well known as one of the first and most prominent among the Advent preachers. ‡

---

[8] *The Midnight Cry,* Nov. 7, 1844, p. 147.

* This statement was first published in one of the Philadelphia papers, and then in *The Midnight Cry.* Inasmuch as no newspaper challenged anything he said, despite the critical stories they had published on the encampment, we may properly attach great weight to the statement that he made on the matter.

† This statement is corroborated by the evidence in a broadside that bears Gorgas' name and carries a prominent display line that reads: "At 3 O'Clock in the Morning, 22d of October, HE will Come, Child Believe it. At the 9th Hour of the night, Jewish Time." —*Broadside, "In Honor of the King of Kings."*

‡ This statement finds corroboration in a letter, from which we have already quoted, that Josiah Litch wrote to Miller from Philadelphia on October 24: "Dr. Gorgas, with the help of C. S. M[inor], in spite of all I could do, led off about one hundred and fifty to flee from the city [Philadelphia] on Monday morning."

Perhaps Gunn did not know it, but he might also have given Whiting's name in support of his declaration that Gorgas' views were opposed by Millerite leaders. In his

Brother Himes also went to New York, and arrested the republication there of the doctor's chart." [9] *

Gorgas' few converts in Philadelphia were "distributing his charts very freely," related Gunn, "and the public therefore received the impression that these charts set forth the expectation of second advent believers generally, who on the contrary rejected *in toto* the pretended inspiration." The result was:

"The influence he [Gorgas] had exerted over a few, and then their influence over others, led to the encampment—a most unhappy step—over which none can grieve more bitterly than the advent preachers and advent believers generally. It was the result of a few following a mere man, instead of the Inspired Word of the living God." [10]

Gunn stated that "only from one to two hundred, out of nearly three thousand believers" in the city of Philadelphia, "were deluded by this." † Then he added: "The arrangements

---

letter of October 24 to Miller, and from which we quoted in another connection, Whiting referred to the view set forth in the area where he lived, that the Millerites should "flee into the open country as Lot did." This was specifically Gorgas' view. Whiting also referred to some fanatical ideas being "preached especially by a Mrs. Higgins." So far from giving his endorsement, Whiting describes these views and ideas, and the results they produced on those who gave ear to them, as "a tempest of real fanaticism." See Appendix E for a more extended discussion of Whiting's statement.

[9] *Ibid.*
[10] *Ibid.*

* This refers to the attempt made to have this Gorgas chart, or broadside, printed and sent out to all the subscribers of *The Midnight Cry*. Southard, the editor, told of his relationship to the matter, and what he described as "an humble confession to God and our readers in relation to a little sheet [Gorgas chart] which was issued from this office on Friday evening, Oct. 18th, headed *Midnight Cry* Extra." He stated that the sheet was brought to him by Storrs. Because Storrs had some standing, and because time was late, the chart "was given to the printer without being examined by any person connected with *The Midnight Cry*." Southard explained this unusual move by saying, "We did not feel like opposing its circulation." He stated that he "inconsiderately" placed the line "*Midnight Cry* Extra" at the top of the chart so that it might be mailed to the subscribers like any other issue. This, said he, was his own act, and with a view to saving the subscribers money, "and not by Brother Storrs' request. He would have preferred to have it go out, as it came from its author, that the responsibility might rest on him alone." Southard then remarked, "We did not feel that we expressed an opinion on the authenticity of the sheet by placing that heading at the top. This was our great mistake. Several hundred were mailed Friday evening. The next day we reflected more on the subject and felt that we had acted hastily. . . . The press was stopped, and the sheets burned on Saturday."—*The Midnight Cry, Oct. 31, 1844, p. 144.*

Some of these "several hundred" that were mailed out, fell into newspaper editors' hands, with the unhappy publicity that that involved, and of course without Southard's explanation, as here given, to place the Extra in its proper light in relation to the Millerite movement. (See, for example, *New York Express*, Oct. 21, 1844; *Newburyport Daily Herald*, Mass., Oct. 21, 1844.)

† Gunn's statement as to the number of persons who went to the encampment agrees with Litch's letter, with the report in the Philadelphia *Inquirer*, of October 22, and with the estimate of George Grigg from whom we shall quote in the next paragraph. There is

for the encampment were made so hastily that those opposed had no opportunity to consider and try to counteract it." [11]

The Midnight Cry soon after the disappointment published a letter from George Grigg, who confessed that he with one other "took the lead in the matter" of the encampment. He not only confessed that he had been deceived, but gave an extended account of the encampment. He did not have to make a confession, much less write one for publication. The letter was written in response to a request from the editor of *The Midnight Cry* for any comment he might wish to make on the stories of the encampment that were in the newspapers. When a man willingly confesses that he has been duped and deceived—in other words, has made a fool of himself—there is hardly anything more embarrassing he could confess. Hence, if he does not paint the rest of the picture regarding the encampment incident as luridly as did the newspapers, we may reasonably presume that those other details were probably not as lurid as reported. We shall let Grigg speak for himself:

"Sister [C. S.] Minor and myself took the lead in the matter. I should think the whole number that went out, including children, to be about one hundred and fifty. We encamped in the field of one of our brethren, on the Darby Road, about four miles from Market Street Bridge. We had two large tents, and being quite near the house of our brother, and also within a short distance of several country stores, we obtained all the necessaries we wanted.* The next morning (Tuesday) my faith in the

---

no reason to believe that either Litch or Gunn or Grigg minimized the number. Why should they hesitate to speak frankly on this point, when they spoke so definitely on other points? Litch is on record, from his account of the Connecticut camp meetings, for denouncing fanaticism forthrightly, and without any minimizing. Nor did Litch or Gunn or Grigg refer to any other than the one encampment, the one prompted by the Gorgas vision, which went out on Darby Road. There is no good reason to believe that they would have hesitated to mention it if there had been more than one encampment. We feel warranted in concluding, therefore, that the rumors printed in the various Philadelphia papers about companies going to various places were only rumors. We think one paper stated the matter truthfully, when, in referring to the "place where the Millerites had gone to hold meetings," it remarked, "The reports were various and could not be relied upon."
—*Pennsylvanian, Philadelphia, Oct. 22, 1844.*

[11] *Ibid.*

* Reference to a map of Philadelphia for the year 1847 shows that the Darby Road was one of the principal thoroughfares leading southwest out of Philadelphia, and that along that road were a number of houses. In other words, the encampment was not out in some wild, isolated spot far from any place where provisions might be secured. (See "Map of the Circuit of Ten Miles Around the City of Philadelphia," by J. C. Sidney, C. E.)

pretended vision of Dr. C. R. Gorgas entirely failed, and at ten minutes after three [Gorgas had claimed that Christ would come at three o'clock Tuesday morning] I laid myself on the floor in the house, and slept soundly till five." [12]

On awakening he counseled with others and virtually all agreed to return home.

"Some few persons took boarding at a farmhouse near by. Some twelve or sixteen went farther on. The remainder returned to the city with their families." [13]

What light does Grigg throw on the newspaper rumors about sickness and death at the encampment, and about a Millerite preacher decamping with money? Here are his own words in the very next paragraph:

"I now wish to say, so far as my knowledge extends, and I think my opportunity for knowing is as good as that of any person in or out of the city of Philadelphia, that there was *no death or sickness* among any who went out with us on the occasion, and I think there can be no ground for the reports that are in circulation, of the brethren and sisters throwing money into the streets, and along the road.

"The rumor that a professed brother had absconded with $1900, I presume must have referred to myself. For the last eighteen months, I have acted as treasurer of the Philadelphia S[econd] A[dventist] Association, and have kept an account of all the receipts and disbursements up to October 11, 1844, and reported weekly to the general committee. For ten days, during the intense excitement, when many persons were handing to me various sums of money to be given to brethren standing in need, the great number of applicants at the close of each service made it impossible for me to keep any regular account of the money received or given out. I have been asked what amount of money I received during those ten days. My reply has been, According to my best judgment, not more than fifteen hundred dollars, nor less than twelve. Many of the sisters were anxious to have me dispose of their property and household goods, but I declined so doing in every instance. Had I been so disposed, I could have had a large amount of money. . . . In every instance I appropriated the various sums according to the wishes of the donors and my best judgment. After

---

[12] *The Midnight Cry*, Oct. 31, 1844, p. 141.
[13] *Ibid*.

making the distribution at the camp [to enable the campers to return, or to buy food], I found I had but $3.50 left." [14]

In the very closing lines of his letter he again confessed to his mistake: "I am fully persuaded that I should have not gone out of the city had I not . . . been under a mesmeric influence." [15]

Let us examine this letter. The writer of it was the "treasurer" of the Philadelphia Second Adventist Association. Presumably he would have more money in his possession than anyone else. Well might he "presume" that the newspapers "referred" to him when they printed the rumor about a Millerite's having decamped with $1,900. But here is the treasurer himself writing a letter for publication, and informing everyone of his whereabouts. Right at this point let it be repeated that newspapers were quite careful readers of *The Midnight Cry,* for they made frequent reference to it. Grigg well knew when he wrote out his statement for publication, that he would run the risk that any man does when he puts statements in print—of having those statements challenged. This was no private confession Grigg made into the ear of the editor.

From the evidence before us, we must conclude that the reports that those at the encampment suffered hunger were groundless. These people did not leave Philadelphia until sometime Monday morning, and most of them returned Tuesday morning. They would certainly have planned provisions enough for the remainder of Monday, for, according to Gorgas, they did not expect the Lord to come until 3 A.M. Tuesday.

And what of the story that the accommodations were so limited that the children were pushed out into the open field in the pelting, cold rain? There were "two large tents" and near by was the house of a Millerite brother. It would seem that these accommodations would certainly be large enough to house 150 to 200 people in an emergency. Furthermore, how cold was it? On Monday, at 9 in the morning the temperature was 46°, at noon

---

[14] *Ibid.,* pp. 141, 142.
[15] *Ibid.,* p. 142.

54°, and at 3 P.M., 52°. At nine o'clock Tuesday morning, it was 55° and at noon 56°.[16] *

In addition to the general stories of the encampment that appeared in the numerous Philadelphia newspapers, there was one daily paper that carried a story about a "body of Millerites encamped on Monday in the vicinity of Phoenixville," a few miles west of Philadelphia. They were said to have been there through Tuesday, the twenty-second. The report stated that Wednesday morning "two little children were found in the encampment, perfectly cold, stiff, and dead." [17] †

This frozen-babes story has caused many a shiver of horror and indignation on the part of countless people from 1844 onward to our own time. Was the story true? The Millerites denied that anyone died, as Grigg's statement reveals. Himes described the story as "false" in his lengthy statement on the front page of the *Boston Post,* November 2, 1844. If the babes

---

[16] See *United States Saturday Post* (Philadelphia), Nov. 2, 1844.
[17] *Pennsylvania Inquirer,* Oct. 24, 1844.

* There are no temperature records available for the night. But the record shows a slow but steady rise in temperature for the week ending October 26.
  When writing of the Millerites the newspapers eloquently described an October rain as "cold" and as a "pitiless storm," which from the emphasis on the word "cold," might be presumed to have blown in from the arctic. The very idea of these Philadelphia Millerites going out into the country to dwell in some tents for a day or two seemed to the newspapers as about the surest proof of fanaticism, if not mild insanity. Unquestionably there *was* fanaticism involved—fanaticism in the *reason* that prompted them to go out, that is, Gorgas' alleged vision. For the newspapers, this point was lost. They expressed a general condemnation of the very idea of the Millerites' leaving the city to abide in tents.
  But the idea of going out into the country for a special convention, either political or religious, was really nothing strange in those days, as suggested by evidence presented in an earlier chapter. For example, only three weeks before the Millerite incident in Philadelphia, a great political rally by the Whig party was held in open country on the boundary line between Ohio and Indiana. Reported one Cincinnati newspaper: "The tents extended for a distance of nearly a mile in length by half a mile in breadth. . . . Many came from a distance of 100 miles. . . . Early on Saturday morning, a cold rain set in, which lasted for 24 hours. . . . Nothing however could dampen the ardor of the Whigs." —*The Daily Atlas, Oct. 1, 1844.* Here is a tent encampment; here is a cold rain; here is unbounded ardor. But we were unable to find any criticism of the gathering—at least not in Whig newspapers—and no suggestion that anyone had suffered or died from the fearful experience of being caught in a cold rain at an encampment. And to think that all the ardor was wasted! The Whigs were disappointed; they did not elect their candidate for President!

† Though Philadelphia had seven dailies at this time, we found this story in only one paper other than the *Inquirer.* A Philadelphia weekly carried it later, but this was presumably a rewrite job. With all one possible exception, all the out-of-town newspapers we examined, that quoted the story of the Phoenixville babes, gave the *Inquirer* as the source. That a story of sudden death should be missing from most of the papers in a city is in itself almost sufficient to warrant the conclusion that the story has no foundation in fact. The *Inquirer* gave as its authority, "we learn."

had really died, how easy it would have been for someone to point to two tombstones, or at least to a death certificate or some physical evidence or document in connection with the tragedy. The fact that the Philadelphia papers, generally, did not carry the story, is further presumptive evidence against its being true. In fact, the failure of most of these papers even to mention a Phoenixville encampment, lends strong support to the testimony of the Millerites that there was only the Darby Road encampment. The further fact that the temperature, as we have already noted, was far above the freezing point, is still further evidence against the story. Finally, the record of "interments" of the Philadelphia health office fails to provide support for the story.* Evidently we have here simply one more illustration of the groundless rumors that circulated regarding the Millerites. Our only apology to the reader for examining so seriously this story is that it has been accepted seriously by the public for a hundred years. †

Let us sum up the case: The Philadelphia encampment consisted of not more than two hundred Millerites out of the very conservatively estimated fifty thousand Millerites in the country. Only one Millerite minister of any prominence became a party to it, namely, Storrs, by his desire to have the Gorgas chart come under the eyes of all the believers for serious study, though Storrs himself did not join in the encampment. The rest of the Millerite leaders did not condone the movement; they militantly condemned it. ‡

---

* The records of "interments," as given out by the health office of Philadelphia, separate deaths of "children" from those of "adults," and state the "diseases" responsible for the deaths. The report for the week ending October 26 lists interments of forty-six children, but none of the forty-six are recorded as having died from freezing or from exposure to the cold. (See *United States Saturday Post*, Philadelphia, Nov. 2, 1844.) There are no coroner's reports on file for 1844. However, some Philadelphia newspapers published rather routinely the news items about coroner's reports. But these news items do not include one regarding two babes who died from the cold.

† The story is embalmed in the impressive *History of the People of the United States*, by John B. McMaster, Vol. 7, p. 141. The babes were brought out for popular inspection more recently in *The American Mercury*, November, 1942, article by R. C. Toomey, "Gabriel, Blow That Horn," which was reprinted in *The Reader's Digest*, January, 1943.

‡ However, they did not wish to condemn any of the believers who went out of the city to the encampment, and so stated, for the faith and sincerity of this little group were real, even though they were deluded. Thus *The Midnight Cry* could say regarding the incident, "We

Despite the colorful stories in the press and the evident folly of their going out to the encampment under Gorgas' guiding, there is no good evidence that they engaged in any fanatical act in connection with the journey, or while there, or that they suffered from lack of food, or that anyone died.

But we repeat, the critics of the Millerite movement have never taken time to secure the real facts regarding this encampment. Hence the story of it has gathered glamor and momentum as it has come down through the years. For example, a large three-volume history of Philadelphia, published in 1884, just forty years after the incident, contains a rather lurid story of this encampment. This history states that "the crowd at Darby were gathered within two tents, but so great was it that the children for two days were obliged to run about the fields exposed to the peltings of a pitiless storm." [18] However, "the crowd" were there only *one* day. The "storm" gathered tremendous momentum through the forty years. Listen to the description of what struck the poor Millerites while they were in the encampment:

"While here a furious hurricane strengthened the faith of the Millerites and struck awful terror to the souls of the timid. It swept over the city, destroying shipping and demolishing houses." [19]

Of course the first question that any rational person would ask is this: How did those two frail tents hold up in a hurricane that knocked down ships and houses? Yet we are calmly assured that the children ran around in the rain for two days because there was no room in the tents. Strange that the children were not blown away! No Philadelphia paper mentions a hurricane on the twenty-first or the twenty-second of October, when the Millerites were at the camp. Singular, indeed! Hurricanes are always front-page news. But the press *does* say that early Saturday morning, October 19—two days before the Mill-

---

have full confidence that it will all be overruled for the glory of God and the good of His waiting children."—*The Midnight Cry, Nov. 7, 1844, p. 150*. There is a difference between condemning the deceiver and his deception, and condemning the deceived. See Appendix E for Himes' comment on the Gorgas incident a few months later.

[18] Thomas Scharf and Thompson Westcott, *History of Philadelphia*, Vol. 2, p. 1448.
[19] *Ibid.*

erites left Philadelphia—a freak "hurricane" played havoc in the city.* But that is not all. The historians' statement of the effect of the hurricane upon Millerite morale is strangely like a sentence in the *Philadelphia Public Ledger* the day before the expected end. The paper remarked that in the preceding century in England, according to Walpole's Letters, a similar day was forecast:

"The day set apart for destruction was signalized by a tremendous thunderstorm, which struck terror into the souls of the faithful. If on the 22d or 23d of this month there should be a storm, . . . it will add to the delusion." [20]

Apparently a "hurricane" early on October 19, plus a "tremendous" thunderstorm in England the preceding century, "which struck terror into the souls of the faithful," were combined to make a "furious hurricane" on the twenty-first or twenty-second which "struck awful terror to the souls of the timid." Thus breezy history is written!

The 1884 historians picture the campers as exhausted from hunger. They did not go out to the camp until sometime Monday morning, and most of them returned early Tuesday morning. Yet in a relatively few hours the poor people "were almost exhausted for want of food." [21] A lack of "adequate provisions" according to the none-too-conservative press of 1844, becomes an absence of food, to the point of near exhaustion, in a sober history book of 1884.

Thus only forty years after the event, two sedate historians provide us with a synthetic hurricane and synthetic starvation to enlarge the legend of the Millerites. Telling of the return of the Millerites to Philadelphia, these writers declared:

"When the woebegone company arrived in the city, the first intelligence

---

[20] *Philadelphia Public Ledger*, Oct. 21, 1844.
[21] Thomas Scharf and Thompson Westcott, *History of Philadelphia*, Vol. 2, p. 1448.

* Here is what one Philadelphia paper wrote on Monday, October 21, regarding this hurricane: "On Saturday morning, between three and four o'clock Philadelphia was visited by a perfect hurricane of wind, accompanied by a deluging rain. . . . The storm, while it lasted, was the most frightful one which has occurred for a great length of time."—*Spirit of the Times, Oct. 21, 1844.*

from their former associates was that one of their preachers had decamped out West with several thousand dollars." [22]

It was bad enough in 1844 for the newspapers to print the rumor that a Philadelphia Millerite preacher had fled with some money, but it is adding insult to injury to picture this rumor as having such basis in fact that the source of the report is the "former associates" of these people at the encampment, that is, the regular body of Millerites in Philadelphia. They denied that there was any truth in the story. That denial was published in a leading newspaper in Philadelphia, as well as in a Millerite paper. We confess that it makes much more exciting reading to tell the story the way this three-volume 1884 history tells it, than the way the facts demand. Beyond that, nothing can be said in favor of such writing.*

This Philadelphia encampment is unquestionably the source of no small number of the stories that have been told regarding the Millerites from that day to this, particularly stories that describe the Millerites as leaving their homes everywhere on October 22 and going out into the fields and into graveyards and onto mountaintops, to await the Lord's coming. Speaking of going into the country, it should be kept in mind that even if it were true that many Millerites went afield, there would be nothing necessarily fanatical in this. The great saints and sages

---

[22] *Ibid.*, p. 1449.

* We have given this extended comment on the statements made by these Philadelphia historians, not simply because their history is a standard work, but because it illustrates the kind of distortion frequently found in historical sketches of Millerism. However, in justice to historians it ought to be said that during the last half of the nineteenth century there was at least one serious and very reputable work that presented a restrained statement on the fanatical aspects of the Millerite movement in general, and this encampment in particular. Here is what the historian wrote:

"That irregularities of one kind and another attended a religious movement so widespread, intense and enthusiastic, as this, is not to be wondered at; but it is doubtless true that the majority of the incidents thus circulated were the easy inventions of opponents. The most notable incident was that which occurred in Philadelphia. In opposition to the earnest expostulations of Mr. Litch and other judicious and influential persons, a company of about one hundred and fifty, responding to the pretended 'vision' of one Gorgas, on the 21st of October went out on the Darby Street Road, about four miles from Market Street bridge, and encamped in a field under two large tents, provided with all needed comforts. The next morning, their faith in the vision having failed, all but about a dozen returned to the city; a few days later, the others returned. This act met the emphatic disapproval of Mr. Miller, and of the Adventists generally."—R. M. Devens, *The Great Events of Our Past Century*, pp. 312, 313.

of all ages frequently withdrew from their fellows to commune with their God on hilltop and in valley.

In view of this it may seem quite pointless, in this chapter devoted to an examination of fanatical acts, to discuss the question of whether the Millerites went out in great companies to mountaintops, fields, or even graveyards. Nor would we take time to discuss it here, were it not that the stories of a general exodus of the Millerites out into the open country provide a most plausible setting for the ascension-robe stories we shall consider in a later chapter. It is not very dramatic to picture Millerites quietly sitting at home in flowing robes. How much more colorful to picture them streaming out of the cities in great nightly processions, enveloped in wraithlike, ghostly garments. How greatly it heightens the story to have these weirdly clad Millerites seated upon the heights to the amazement of a goggle-eyed world below. Or as a variant to the story, how thrilling and chilling to be able to relate having seen, yes, actually seen, "by the struggling moonbeam's misty light," whole graveyards filled with these phantomlike creatures awaiting the resurrection morning.

In a preceding chapter we showed that such clear testimony as there is regarding the Millerites on October 22 almost invariably describes them as in their churches, or if their churches had been closed by mobs, then in little companies in their own homes. But, someone will ask, do not the newspapers also tell of great companies of Millerites streaming out of various cities into the open country or into graveyards in October, 1844? Except for the Philadelphia encampment, the answer is No.*

The papers everywhere published a lurid story of that encampment. Why did they fail on all the rest? Why did New England papers, for example, depend on a Pennsylvania story of an encampment when, if tradition be true, they had far better stories close at hand?

---

* See Appendix E for further comment on this point. Also see Chapter 25, which refers to a number of newspaper stories and rumors about Millerites who allegedly went to graveyards and mountaintops in early 1843.

Turning to another charge against the Millerites, we find the newspapers in October and November carrying a few news items about attempts being made to have guardians appointed over the property and persons of certain Millerites. In the words of one newspaper, the charge was that they "have been neglecting their business and suffering their property to go to waste, to run after the Miller phantom." [23]

This newspaper story is discussing the case of a group of Millerites in Meredith, New Hampshire. This seems to be the incident most frequently referred to. The story has grown until today the number of Millerites of Meredith who needed guardianship is very great. But the original newspaper report says only "eight or ten individuals." [24] And were the newspapers in the habit of minimizing any charge against the Millerites?

There are also several stories, copied and recopied by the newspapers, about Millerites in business who either burned up their stock or threw it in the street, and who opened the door and invited people to come in and help themselves. There are not many such stories, but they are sensational in their very nature, and thus were widely quoted in the press. Probably the most frequently quoted was that of a Millerite shoemaker in New York, identified only as being located on Division Street, who was said to have given away his shoes until his son stopped him and had him committed to an asylum.*

Under the heading "Reports and Rumors," *The Midnight Cry* discusses this story, stating that not only was the shoe dealer supposed to have been taken to the asylum but "some said they had conversed with those who had seen him there." Here is a paragraph from *The Midnight Cry* statement:

---

[23] *Portland Bulletin* (Maine), Nov. 30, 1844.
[24] *Ibid.*

* Apparently the origin of this story is a report on Millerite activities written by a Mrs. Child, New York correspondent of the *Boston Daily Courier*, and published in that paper on October 17, 1844. The item was widely quoted. See, for example, *Evening Post for the Country*, New York, Oct. 18, 1844; *Newark Daily Advertiser*, Oct. 19, 1844; *Daily National Intelligencer*, Washington, D. C., Oct. 21, 1844; *Philadelphia Public Ledger*, Oct. 21, 1844; and *National Aegis*, Worcester, Mass., Oct. 23, 1844.

"Brother Abraham Riker, a well-known shoe dealer, in Division Street, who was for many years a class leader in the M. E. Church, closed his store and spent considerable time in distributing papers, attending meetings, and warning others. It was soon reported that he was scattering his goods in the street, and crowds of people assembled around his doors at night, and the report soon went abroad that he had killed himself, and a minister in a neighboring town in New Jersey repeated it in the pulpit. The coroner actually called at his house to hold an inquest, but he found him in health and in his right mind. He declared that he was too anxious to behold his coming Saviour, to commit suicide." [25]

Is it not obviously profitless to attempt to run down all such stories? We are willing to grant that some of them may have been true, probably were, at least in part, for the Millerites were drawn from all classes, and most certainly included in their number some erratic, even unbalanced persons. But to admit all this is merely to admit what any organization has to admit, particularly a newly formed one. The Millerite leaders frankly declared that there was some fanaticism, and they spoke of it rather specifically so that we need be in no doubt. We hardly believe a reasonable-minded reader will ask us to accomplish the impossible feat of running down and disproving every bit of "newspaper gossip," [26] as the editor of the Portland *Advertiser* described most of the anti-Millerite stories, before drawing the conclusion that the Millerites as a body were sane, sensible people, even in the climactic days of October, 1844.

---

[25] *The Midnight Cry*, Oct. 31, 1844, p. 141.
[26] *Portland Daily Advertiser* (Maine), Oct. 26, 1844.

CHAPTER 23

Did Millerism Cause Insanity, Suicide, and Murder?

ONE OF THE MOST COMMON CHARGES made against the Millerites was that they were filling the asylums with people made insane by their preaching. However, it was not uncommon in those days for critics of religion to bring such a charge against religious groups. In an earlier chapter we quoted from the autobiography by Gaddis, a Methodist minister who labored in the State of Ohio in the first half of the nineteenth century. Writing of his mother's conversion at a Methodist meeting, and the dismay she brought to her own staid church by shouting aloud for joy at public services, he said, "Mother was now considered, by all of them, partially deranged, and, if not restored, would soon be a fit subject for the insane asylum." [1]

Some years later another Methodist minister, writing on the subject of revivals, defended them against certain charges. One of the charges he examined was this: "It is objected that revivals sometimes lead to *insanity* and *suicide*." [2]

One cannot read very far in any newspaper in 1843 or 1844 without finding some indictment of Millerism in the matter of insanity. For example, a Portland (Maine) newspaper in the spring of 1843 speaks of Millerism as "filling our insane hospitals." [3] About the same time a Baltimore paper informed its readers that "fifteen Miller lunatics are now confined in the asylum at Brattleboro, Vermont." [4] A Boston paper, in the

---
[1] Maxwell Pierson Gaddis, *Footprints of an Itinerant*, p. 57.
[2] James Porter, *Revivals of Religion*, p. 201.
[3] *Portland Bulletin* (Maine), March 30, 1843.
[4] *Sun* (Baltimore), May 4, 1843.

spring of 1844, speaks of Miller and "the mischief he has done the past year in filling our lunatic asylums." [5] A Vermont newspaper, late in 1844, tells of many made "raving crazy" by Millerism. [6]

These are typical. Sometimes not only insanity, but suicide and murder were laid at the door of Millerism. This, of course, was all very plausible, for in some forms of insanity suicide or murder might result. One newspaper, telling of a certain woman's being sent to an asylum, declared:

"It appeared that she had been listening to the ranting of Himes, Miller, and Co., and had become perfectly demented. So much for the machinations of these spiritual wolves." [7]

Sometimes the newspapers became specific by mentioning the names of people who, they declared, had been sent to asylums, suffering from Millerism-produced insanity. It is the mention of specific names that gives us our first opportunity to check on the truth of these newspaper stories.

The Millerites themselves certainly did not remain silent under the accusations. For example, in the spring of 1843 there appeared an article in *The Midnight Cry,* entitled "Insanity." The opening paragraph reads thus:

"Once more we must say a word on this touchstone, revealing the nature of the opposition to us.

"A few days ago, a preacher in this city [New York] professed to have received information, direct from the asylum at Blackwell's Island, that eleven insane persons were there as the 'fruits of Millerism.' Some of our brethren, after visiting the prisoners on the island, were invited to go up to the asylum. They there inquired respecting the truth of the report. The superintendent instantly replied that the number should be *four* instead of *eleven.* Having thus cut off the *increase* which the story had gained in rolling down four miles into the city, he mentioned the names of the four." [8]

Then follows a column of discussion listing by name the four persons, giving something of their history, and quoting certain

---
[5] *Daily Evening Transcript* (Boston), March 28, 1844.
[6] *Vermont Watchman and State Journal* (Montpelier), Nov. 15, 1844.
[7] *Sun* (Baltimore), Oct. 25, 1844.
[8] *The Midnight Cry,* April 20, 1843, p. 21.

letters and testimony that the Millerites had secured to prove that the four asylum inmates were not victims of Millerism.

We earlier mentioned that immediately after the great disappointment in October, 1844, Himes prepared a defense of himself and of the movement that was published on the front page of the *Boston Post*. One of the charges he answered was that regarding insanity and suicide. He was as specific on this point as on others we have already considered. We quote part of his rejoinder:

"A Brother Williamson, in Medford, has been reported as having committed suicide, and left his family destitute:—He informs us that ten ship carpenters board at his house, who would not, if the family were very destitute. Brother Riker, of New York City, on whose body the coroner went *twice* to sit, is still very happy in looking for the Lord. [Riker was the shoemaker on Division Street, whom rumor reported as having thrown all his shoes out in the street when he anticipated the Lord's coming.] Brother Wyatt, of Dover, who has been reported to have poisoned himself to death, is also still well. Every other case of suicide and death that we have been able to trace—not excepting the two children which froze to death one night near Philadelphia—are equally false." [9]

Himes may be pardoned for the ironical vein in which he wrote. How easy it would have been for an accuser to make short shrift of Himes' defense if the charge under consideration had been true. It is not difficult to tell whether a person is dead or alive, especially if that person's name and his place of abode are commonly known. But there is no record anywhere of anyone's pointing to a tombstone to refute Himes' defense.

However, we are not left to Millerite denials in examining the charge of insanity. The records of the asylums of New England that were in existence in the 1840's are still preserved. Through the kindness of the medical superintendents of those institutions, we have had opportunity to examine the original records, the case histories of those admitted. We chose for our study the years 1842, 1843, and 1844. Beyond question these are the years when Millerism was the subject of general discussion

---

[9] *Boston Post*, Nov. 2, 1844.

throughout New England. The area selected was Maine, New Hampshire, Vermont, and Massachusetts, where Millerism was most active. On the findings from these original case history records, and statements found in the published annual reports of the medical superintendents of the 1840's, we shall build this and the following chapter.*

Before going into a detailed examination of what these old case histories and annual reports reveal, let us test some of the newspaper stories about specific individuals made insane by Millerism, against the case history record of those individuals in the asylums. †

In view of the fact that the charge of insanity was sometimes coupled with the charge of murder, we shall take as our first exhibit the case of a Mr. B., who lived in the town of Sumner, Maine. In April, 1841, he murdered his wife and two of his children. According to the newspapers, "he had been subject to fits of insanity, and it is said that, in a fit of religious frenzy he committed this horrid deed, '*to save his family from eternal ruin, at the approaching end of the world.*' This, we presume, is another fruit of the Miller humbug." [10]

Note first the admission that "he had been subject to fits of insanity." This admission ought to be sufficient to dismiss the case immediately. The very fact that the papers insisted, nevertheless, in seeking to charge Millerism with his foul deeds, proves most clearly that they must have been hard pressed to find some plausible ground for indicting this new religion. Why charge against even the most irrational religion the actions of a man whose past history is one of insanity?

---

[10] *Republican Herald* (Providence, R. I.), citing the *Portland Daily Advertiser* (Maine), as quoted in *Signs of the Times*, June 1, 1841, p. 40.

* In making reference to case history records only initials may be used. This will explain why, in the case of certain persons mentioned in our quotations from newspapers, only the initials are given. In referring to institutions for the insane we shall use the term "asylum," because that was the term used both by the institutions themselves in those days, and by newspapers.

† In several instances where newspapers named a certain person as being sent to a particular asylum, an examination of the records of that asylum failed to show the admission of such a person. This is nothing more than we would expect in view of the fact that many of the newspaper stories were admittedly rumor and hearsay. On the other hand, it is possible in a number of instances to compare the newspaper story with a case history record.

DID MILLERISM CAUSE INSANITY, SUICIDE, MURDER? 341

Even if it were true that Mr. B. committed this murder "to save his family from eternal ruin, at the approaching end of the world," how does that necessarily prove that Millerism was responsible? Do the statements of insane persons as to the motive for their crimes provide us with the dependable information needed to explain their deeds?

But was the newspaper sure that Mr. B. even offered as the reason for his deed that "he wished to save his family from eternal ruin, at the approaching end of the world"? No. The statement is introduced with the elusive and irresponsible phrase, "It is said." And in the next sentence is the equally unimpressive phrase, "we presume." The Millerite paper *Signs of the Times* commented thus on the newspaper editor's story:

"Don't you know certain, Mr. Editor? Dare you only *presume* that this 'horrible tragedy,' was the 'fruit of the Miller humbug.' This sagacious editor ought to have *known,* that no murders, or any dreadful evils *could* take place without Mr. Miller's aid." [11]

This Mr. B. was not hanged for his crime, but was placed in the local jail. This is *prima facie* proof that the court must have been sure that he was really an insane person. A hundred years ago it was very difficult to escape the noose on the flimsy plea of temporary insanity, no matter what caused it. On June 26, 1844, he was transferred from the jail to the State asylum in Augusta that had been opened a few months before. April 15, 1854, he was discharged as fully recovered. But on May 26, 1862, he was readmitted. After four years he was again discharged, August 5, 1866, as recovered. Commenting on his case history, the medical superintendent of Augusta State Hospital in 1944, said:

"The religious ideas expressed do not appear to have been more prominent than those we find in many depressed cases of the present day and his psychosis could hardly be attributed to attendance at any religious meeting. It seems quite evident from the symptomatology as detailed in the old history that this was a case of manic-depressive insanity." [12]

---

[11] *Signs of the Times,* June 1, 1841, p. 40.
[12] Personal letter to the author from F. C. Tyson, M. D., Jan. 11, 1944.

This case has been discussed at length because it provides us one of the few instances where a newspaper charge of Millerism-provoked murder can be checked by the records. Almost invariably the stories of such cases have no sequel in the asylum records later. Did heartless courts hang men who had really been deprived of their reason by Millerism and who were thus legally not responsible for their deeds? Or were the courts unable to discover in the evidence submitted anything to support the newspaper stories that the murderers were made insane by Millerism or any other ism?

Newark, New Jersey, is the scene of the next crime we shall examine. This is a case of suicide and murder. Early in 1843 there appeared in a Newark newspaper a story about a Mrs. Jonathan S. Leverich, who poisoned herself and her two small children, causing the death of all three. The reason for her administering the arsenic is thus stated by the paper:

"She yielded at last to a fear apprehension that she could not recover her own health and that her little ones must suffer in the world if she should be taken from them. It is said further that her mind had been troubled some time on the subject of Millerism, though we do not learn that she said much on that subject during her last moments. It is believed however by her friends that it had much influence on her mind, and had its effect in producing the fatal consequences here recorded." [13]

The story occupied about six inches of space in the Newark paper, which was describing a tragedy that had happened locally. But two days later an Albany, New York, paper, quoting a New York City paper, the *Plebeian,* as its authority, wrote this brief news item on the case:

"Yesterday morning the wife of Mr. Jonathan Leveridge [the name was variously spelled as the story was copied from paper to paper], a respectable mechanic residing in Newark, N. J., having become a maniac owing to the Miller excitement, administered a dose of arsenic first to her two youngest children, . . . then took a quantity herself, which caused the death of the children about twelve, and the unfortunate female about 6

---

[13] *Newark Daily Advertiser* (N. J.), Feb. 25, 1843.

o'clock. She had been attending the Miller meetings, and no other cause can be attributed for the rash act." [14]

Up in Maine a newspaper told very briefly of this suicide and double murder, remarking, "Mrs. Leverich had been unwell for some days, and exhibited symptoms of insanity, having been troubled for some time by the preaching of the Millerites." [15]

Far west in Chicago a newspaper had a paragraph on the tragedy, with this comment on the cause: "It is supposed under the influence of Millerism." [16]

This group of quotations hardly needs comment. The original story gave as a statement of fact a reason for the crime that had nothing to do with Millerism, and then added as a rumor, "It is said further that her mind had been troubled some time on the subject of Millerism." Even this rumor or surmise seemed to lack weight, by the admission that immediately followed. But the out-of-town papers quickly changed rumors to facts. They were sure she had been actually "attending" Millerite meetings, that she was "under the influence of Millerism" and that "no other cause can be attributed for the rash act."

If these newspaper stories were worthy of serious rebuttal, we would ask: If Mrs. Leverich had really become enough acquainted with Millerite teachings to believe them and to order her life in the light of those teachings, why would she have been dominated by a fear of the fate of her children in this world, seeing the Millerites believed the world was to end that year?

The sequel to this newspaper reporting of the Leverich case is found in two items: one that appeared in the Millerite weekly, *The Midnight Cry*, and the other in the *New York Daily Tribune*. *The Midnight Cry* declared:

"We have taken the pains to make particular inquiry touching this singular tragedy, and find that '*Millerism*' had no more to do with it, than

---
[14] *Albany Evening Journal* (New York), Feb. 27, 1843.
[15] *Maine Inquirer* (Bath, Maine), March 8, 1843.
[16] *Chicago Express*, March 8, 1843.

it had with the late lunar phenomenon; and we are authorized by Mr. *Jacob Wheeler* who works in the same establishment with the unfortunate husband of the deceased, and got his information from the husband, to say, that *Millerism* had nothing to do with the matter." [17]

The *New York Daily Tribune,* about a month after this tragedy, published an editorial entitled "Millerism and Insanity." The editorial cites two cases specifically. We quote the comment on what is quite evidently the Leverich case, as the press at that particular time carried no other similar story:

> "So in the case of the woman who poisoned her children and attempted to commit suicide some weeks since—*her* insanity was attributed to Millerism, but entirely without reason. Doubtless the like has been the case in many other instances." [18]

So much for Millerism-induced suicide and murder. But what of less lurid cases of insanity where sudden and violent death does not play a part? The press had hardly finished telling the story of Mrs. Leverich when they published the story of another woman, a Mrs. L. of Massachusetts, who "was made a raving maniac by the preaching of Millerism." [19] This unfortunate person appears as case No. 1588 in the Worcester, Massachusetts, asylum. The cause of her insanity is given as "religious excitement," a phrase very commonly used by asylums for many years. There is no mention of Millerism in the case history. The record is brief. She was in the asylum eleven days, dying of "brain fever." To a modern psychiatrist this would appear to be a case of death due to some condition that had little or no relation to religious excitement.

A New York paper on March 11, 1843, quoted the Augusta, Maine, *Gospel Banner* as authority for the statement that four persons were brought to the hospital in Augusta the preceding week from one town to the east, "who were made insane by the Miller delusion." [20] This would be the week ending February

---

[17] *The Midnight Cry,* March 3, 1843, p. 25.
[18] *New York Daily Tribune,* March 24, 1843.
[19] *Maine Inquirer* (Bath, Maine), March 22, 1843.
[20] *New York Daily Tribune,* March 11, 1843.

25.* In that week four cases were admitted, Nos. 228 to 231. Were they all from one town? No, they were from four different towns. What does the asylum record say concerning each of them? For Case No. 228, Millerism was given as the cause. But the record states that this person had had several previous attacks of insanity. Here was a clear case of periodical insanity. Case No. 229 makes no mention of Millerism, but states that this person "has been insane eighteen years." Case No. 230 makes no mention of religion. The case history of No. 231 states that he recently attended "two lectures," just before he became insane, but there is no indication that these lectures had any relationship to Millerism. Furthermore the record states that his grandfather, father, and mother had been insane. The poor man had no chance, lectures or no lectures, Millerism or no Millerism!

That is what we discover when we examine the records of the Augusta Asylum for the week ending February 25, 1843. Yet the *Gospel Banner's* story about four persons from one town in one week made mad by Millerism, was published to all New York through one of its leading newspapers, and was similarly published in other newspapers throughout the land. †

A little later a Maine newspaper told its readers that it learned from the *Gospel Banner* that a man "from Buckfield" was carried to the asylum last week, and that the cause was Millerism.[21] This is Case No. 243 in the Maine asylum. The man was admitted April 24, 1843. The case history states that he had attended protracted meetings six weeks previously. Who conducted the meetings is not disclosed. Protracted meetings were commonly held by various religious bodies. But the record

---

[21] *Maine Inquirer* (Bath, Maine), May 3, 1843.

* The *Gospel Banner* was a weekly paper. The latest issue which the *Tribune* could have received previous to the publication of this story in New York on the eleventh, would be the *Gospel Banner* of Saturday, the fourth of March. The editor of this paper, writing a news item during the week ending March 4, would be discussing the week ending February 25.

† If by chance the *Tribune* was referring to the *Gospel Banner* of February 25, instead of March 4, the asylum records provide no better support. In fact the Augusta records will be searched in vain for long weeks preceding February 25, for any seven-day period when four persons were brought in from "one town" who were made insane by any one cause, religious or otherwise.

does say that he had "had an attack of insanity twelve years ago, caused at that time by religious excitement." That would be in 1831. No one in Maine had ever heard of Millerism at that time.

A Portland newspaper in the summer of 1844 contained this news item, reported by "an eyewitness":

> "L——, of Gilmanton Village, who, as has been supposed, had his reason shaken at the Gilmanton camp meeting of 1843, and for a time afterward showed symptoms of insanity, has had his mental faculties at this camp meeting completely dethroned, and is now a raving maniac of the worst kind, and is within the walls of the insane hospital at Concord." [22]

Now here is an eyewitness's story of a poor Mr. L. who first had his reason shaken at the Millerite camp meeting in 1843, and who suffered final mental collapse at the Millerite camp meeting in 1844. This man appears as Case No. 190 in the New Hampshire asylum at Concord. He was admitted July 8, 1844. The case history states: "Second advent excitement was the cause." But the record also states: "Insane by spells for two years, violent since Friday last. . . . Had fever two years ago at Baltimore. . . . Has not been well since fever." The newspaper story would lead the reader to believe that Mr. L.'s reason was first shaken at the Millerite camp meeting in 1843, though the "eyewitness" protects himself by the phrase "as has been supposed." But the asylum record reveals the insanity began in 1842, and at Baltimore, Maryland, rather than at Gilmanton Village, New Hampshire. Furthermore, that a "fever" marked the beginning of the trouble instead of a camp meeting. What the case history means by speaking of the "second advent excitement" as the "cause" is that it was the cause of his latest outbreak.

In October, 1844, various newspapers in New England gave circulation to a strange story of insanity and suicide charged to Millerism, plus the intriguing angle of mistaken identity. A Boston newspaper tells of a Gilman Gale, of Landaff, who "in a

---

[22] *Portland Bulletin* (Maine), July 23, 1844.

paroxysm of mental derangement, from religious fanaticism produced by attending meetings of the Millerites," wandered off and has not been heard from since.[23] Other newspapers in New England related the same story about this Mr. Gale.

At the same time various newspapers were telling the story of a Moses Clark of Landaff, who had committed suicide because he "fell into the miserable delusion of Millerism, and reason was ousted from her throne." [24]

This story spread as far as the Gilman Gale story. Was it really true that two men living in one little town, Landaff, had been struck mad by Millerism at the same time? The mystery is cleared up by an item in a Portsmouth, New Hampshire, newspaper on November 9, quoting from another newspaper:

"The Haverhill, New Hampshire, *Republican* states that Moses Clark, Esq., the second advent man who has been so extensively killed by the newspapers, is alive and well; it was Mr. Gale who was drowned accidentally while in a state of religious insanity." [25]

How did the confusion of names come about? We venture this guess: Moses Clark was well known in Landaff. He held a public office. His religious beliefs as a Millerite were also well known. And if anyone heard that one of the townspeople of Landaff had become insane from Millerism, it would be natural to conclude that the Millerite, Clark, was the man. The story was inaccurate not only as regards names but as regards the charge of suicide. Mr. Gale was "drowned accidentally." *

In instances where suicide climaxed the case before the person could be taken to an asylum, there is no way of checking on the individual's history. The press very generally carried the dramatic story of a young man by the name of Kulp who jumped

---

[23] *Boston Daily Bee,* Oct. 16, 1844.
[24] *Sun* (Baltimore), Oct. 28, 1844.
[25] *Portsmouth Journal* (N. H.), Nov. 9, 1844.

* There is a humorous sequel to the story. Though the case of mistaken identity was cleared up by the newspaper item on November 9, the *Kennebec Journal,* in Augusta, Maine, was belatedly telling its readers on November 15 of the tragic suicide of poor Mr. Clark, the second advent man.

into the Niagara River because he had been made insane by
Millerism. Obviously he carried his story with him. We cannot
check his record. In the cases already discussed it is evident that
Millerism was not the true cause of insanity. But there are
several cases mentioned in the press, which, when checked with
the asylum records, are apparently chargeable to Millerism.
That is, the record fails to show that the person had been
previously insane, had insane relatives, or could otherwise be
clearly eliminated as a Millerism case.

Should we therefore conclude that Millerism must be held
accountable for certain cases of insanity? The answer to this
question must be found in an examination of the annual reports
of the medical superintendents of the asylums, coupled with a
more comprehensive study of all the data to be secured from a
wide reading of case histories for the period 1842-1844.

CHAPTER 24

Old Asylum Records Offer Further Testimony

HERE ARE SOME OF THE FACTS that have come to light when the annual asylum reports are examined:

First, many insane persons, who today would most certainly be committed to institutions, were at large. There were three principal reasons for this: Asylums were still relatively new institutions in the early 1840's. For example, the State asylum at Concord, New Hampshire, was not opened until October, 1842. There was naturally a hesitancy on the part of families to commit some member to an institution. Then there was the expense. The general policy of the asylums was to charge a certain amount per week, which, while not great, was a heavy drain on poor families. Finally, there was sometimes a shortage of rooms in the asylums, even when people were willing and financially able to send a member of the family. The asylum reports often speak of building on a new wing to an institution, and of its being filled almost immediately upon completion.

All this means that to a degree probably unknown today in any part of the United States, insane persons were at large in the community, or confined at home, or in penal institutions. It is a well-established fact that many clearly defined mental cases have lucid intervals, or reveal their insanity only when discussing certain subjects. There was nothing to prevent such persons from overhearing or joining in the conversation of other members of the family, or perhaps even attending a religious service. There must inevitably have been numbers of instances where mentally unbalanced persons drew into their disordered thinking the prophetic phrases that described the momentous Millerite doctrine. In some forms of insanity, at least, the mind tends to take on the color and view of the latest and most stimulating ideas and happenings of the world about it.

The second important fact that these asylum reports of the 1840's reveal, is that there was little scientific knowledge at that time concerning the care of the insane or the causes of insanity. This is no reflection on the medical staffs of those institutions, in contrast to medical men generally at that time. Scientific knowledge in all fields was very limited. The medical profession relied on powerful purgatives as the main standby in their practice. They were still truly doctors of physic. One doctor who declared that calomel was the Samson of the *materia medica* was reminded by a waggish critic that like Samson it had slain its thousands. Bleeding a patient was still an approved procedure in treating diseases, both of the body and the mind. The old faded-ink records of the asylums tell of instances where unusually large amounts of blood were drawn off, followed by the notation that the patient was very quiet for a considerable time afterward!

These facts naturally raise the question, Can we be sure that the causes of insanity as assigned in the case histories are always accurate? This leads us to the third and rather startling revelation that the records provide—the strange array of "causes" assigned. Here are some of the causes given for certain cases admitted to the Worcester, Massachusetts, asylum from 1842 to 1844: "Family trouble," "disappointed ambition," "asthma," "animal magnetism," "fear of poverty," "excitement," "inventions," "overexertion," "domestic affliction," "rheumatism," "eruption," "hard study," "hard labor," "exposure to cold," "going into the water." *

This brings us to the fourth fact revealed by the records. The cause assigned for the insanity of a person admitted to an

---

* Such a list of causes, with interesting variations, and with the addition of other and more plausible causes, could be duplicated in the records of most of the other asylums. For example, the Maryland Hospital Annual Report for 1844 includes the following as causes of insanity: "Loss of friends," "disappointed ambition," "mortified pride," "political excitement."

asylum was not the result of a diagnosis made by the medical staff of the institution, but strange as it seems to us today, the cause assigned was that which was given by friends and relatives at the time of admitting the patient. For example, the table of causes of insanity given in the first report published by the New Hampshire asylum, carries this heading: "Supposed causes of insanity, as assigned by their friends." [1] In the next year's report of this same institution the superintendent stated:

"The 'supposed cause,' put down in this table [referring to a table of "supposed causes of insanity"], is the one assigned by those who bring patients to the asylum; and it is the one that seems to the friends most prominent in producing the disease." [2]

The reports of the Worcester, Massachusetts, asylum contain this statement:

"There are usually several circumstances, all of which conspire to bring on that state of brain and nervous system that results in mental derangement. The one that seems most prominent to the friends is the one here recorded." [3]

These are typical admissions by the medical superintendents. This brings us to the fifth fact disclosed by the records; namely, that the medical superintendents were generally skeptical as to the validity of the causes assigned, and especially when "religious excitement" was given as the cause. Said the superintendent of the Maine asylum, in his 1842 report:

"Pains are taken to ascertain the causes of the disease, and the results are duly recorded. These I have not presented in tabular form, as is commonly done in reports of this kind, because I have doubted whether the information we are in the habit of receiving, is sufficiently exact and trustworthy to be made the basis of any very useful general conclusions. . . . It is often a matter of accident, whether the accounts we derive from friends are uniform and consistent, or vague and contradictory. If we happen to meet only those friends who entertain the same views, the existence of any diversity of opinion on the subject may never be made known to us. Those

---

[1] *Report of the Board of Visitors, of the Trustees, and of the Superintendent of the New Hampshire Asylum for the Insane, for the Year Ending May 31, 1843*, p. 14.
[2] *Ibid.*, for Year Ending May 31, 1844, p. 19.
[3] *Annual Report of the Trustees of the State Lunatic Hospital at Worcester, for Year Ending Nov. 30, 1846*, pp. 49, 50.

who bring the patient, may agree, for instance, in the statement that he showed no signs of insanity till he began to attend religious meetings, where he became unduly excited and soon deranged. Months afterward, perhaps, we meet with an intimate friend of the patient, who is confident that long before the religious meetings, he observed something strange in his demeanor that suggested to him a strong suspicion of his insanity, and which he attributed to a certain loss of property, or domestic affliction. Of the 54 cases to which we have assigned a particular cause, I should not be surprised to find, could we have their history complete and unquestionable, that in a large portion, we have been mistaken. Those upon whom we have been obliged to depend for our information, are often ill qualified to give it, either from an imperfect acquaintance with the patient, or from an inability to observe such a peculiar order of facts as the early manifestations of a disordered mind. Any prominent circumstances or event in which the patient is concerned, happening near the commencement of his illness, is very often set down as its cause, where the relation was merely accidental, or perhaps an effect rather than a cause." [4]

The medical superintendent of the New Hampshire asylum stated in his 1846 report:

"The influence of religion in deranging the operations of the mind, is too often introduced by those who reason from untenable positions upon this important subject. Cases, in which the delusions of the insane are connected with the subject, are frequent; but is it not probable that the deranged ideas had a prior existence in the brain, caused by inappreciable causes?" [5]

In his report in the year 1848 the medical superintendent of this New Hampshire institution declared:

"It is no unusual thing, for those made insane from causes particularly depressing in their nature, to exhibit the highest exhilaration in their insane manifestations, and *vice versa*. Devotional exercises may totally engross the attention of the lunatic, and religion may have had nothing to do in the production of the insanity. The emperors, knights errant and queens to be found in every lunatic hospital, are as frequently from classes of society where no hopes of political preferment could be supposed to exist. This fact essentially detracts from the value of the causes of insanity, as given by

---

[4] *Annual Report of the Directors of the Maine Insane Hospital (Augusta), for the Year Ending Dec. 31, 1842*, p. 15.
[5] *Report of the Board of Visitors, of the Trustees, and of the Superintendent of the New Hampshire Asylum for the Insane, for the Year Ending May 31, 1846*, p. 19.

those who commit friends to the asylum, and so marked is the disposition to seize upon some accidental bias, which the insane mind exhibits in its waywardness, and signify as a cause what is merely the exhibition of an effect, that, with many who have written upon the subject, I confess, that all the data thus obtained, either at this or any other asylum, are to be received with extreme caution, if not viewed as nearly valueless." [6]

The medical superintendent of the Worcester asylum declared regarding the causes of insanity:

"It is difficult, and often impossible to ascertain the true and relative bearing of the various circumstances around us, upon our own minds, but it is much more difficult to ascertain the precise objects that suggest each successive link in the chain of thought that is passing through the mind of another." [7]

The medical superintendent of McLean Asylum, a part of Massachusetts General Hospital, said in his 1841 report:

"As to the *causes* of disease and its duration before admission, I must give my testimony that receiving patients principally from the better educated and most intelligent classes of society, and from the proximity of the residence of most of their friends to the asylum being in such constant communication, as enables us to ascertain and verify antecedent facts to the highest practicable extent, there is not one case in ten where a satisfactory or adequate single cause can be decided upon as certain, and I suspect that in a majority of cases, the first impressions of the probable causes of disease, as derived from friends will be changed on more mature examination." [8]

For this reason reports of the McLean Asylum give no tables of "causes."

The medical superintendent of the Boston Lunatic Hospital stated in his 1844 report: "No point in the history of our patients is more difficult to ascertain than the causes of their insanity." [9]

The same conviction as to the unreliability of assigned causes was also held by medical superintendents of institutions beyond

---

[6] *Ibid., for Year Ending May 31, 1848,* pp. 18, 19.
[7] *Annual Report of the Trustees of the State Lunatic Hospital at Worcester, for Year Ending Nov. 30, 1846,* pp. 49, 50.
[8] *Annual Report of the Board of Trustees of the Massachusetts General Hospital, for the year 1841,* p. 13.
[9] *Report of the Superintendent of the Boston Lunatic Hospital and Physician of the Public Institutions at South Boston, for the Year Ending June 30, 1844,* p. 17.

New England. For example, here is a statement in the annual report of the Pennsylvania Hospital for the Insane in 1841:

"The friends of patients constantly mistake *effect* for *cause,* and without care the physician may be deceived in a similar manner. As an example, we have on several occasions been assured that the disease was to be attributed to religious excitement, when a careful inquiry proved conclusively that the death of a near relative, or the loss of property, or the disappointment of long-cherished hopes, has really been the *cause,* and the Religious Excitement only an *effect,* made striking by the public manner in which it had been manifested." [10]

The medical superintendent of the State asylum at Columbus, Ohio, in his 1842 report, discussed the difficulty of making sure as to the true causes of insanity, and added:

"These remarks apply with peculiar force to those denominated religious causes, which, it will be seen, occupy a leading position in our table. . . . As the result of some attention to this matter, we feel satisfied that the true remote cause of insanity very frequently lies behind the religious influences which appear so conspicuous that, at most, religion can only be accused as the occasional exciting cause of a disease whose foundation is completely established in the system. . . . In not a few instances, so far is the disease of the mind from a religious origin, that it is clearly and properly chargeable to the indulgence of vicious habits. It is certainly a fact that a maniac may imbibe a religious as well as any other extravagant delusion, and yet his derangement may be occasioned by the very reverse of anything like a religious cause." [11]

Despite all these vigorous criticisms of assigned causes, there are found in the annual reports some statements that *seem* to support the charge that religious revivals in general, and Millerism in particular, were the cause of insanity in certain cases.

The New Hampshire asylum report in 1844 contained this statement:

"Religious perplexity and excitement will, whenever our divine aspirations are directed by bigoted and zealous men, be ranked high among

---

[10] *Report of the Pennsylvania Hospital for the Insane (Philadelphia), for Year Ending Dec. 31, 1841,* p. 40.
[11] *Annual Report of the Directors and Superintendents of the Ohio Lunatic Hospital, for Year Ending Nov. 15, 1842,* p. 52.

the causes of this malady. Three cases of 'Millerism' and one of 'Swedenborgianism,' have come to us this year." [12]

The Worcester asylum report for 1843 asserts:

"The number of cases of insanity from religious causes has increased the past year in most of the institutions in this country. In this hospital, 28 cases of 220 are supposed to have arisen from this cause, 15 of which were attributed to the Miller excitement, and much larger proportions are ascribed to the same cause in some of the New England institutions. It is rare that a popular religious error has produced so much excitement in the community and rendered so many insane. This is not surprising as the subject is momentous, the time fixed for the final consummation of all things so near at hand, and the truth of all sustained by unerring mathematics." [13]

In his 1842 report the medical superintendent of the Maine asylum observed:

"Of the 87 cases admitted during the past year, 13 were attributed, with as much certainty as can ever be obtained on this subject, to *religious excitement;* not to mention a few in which this cause contributed its share with others in developing the disease. In all but one of the above 13, the disease commenced within the present year. This is an unusually large proportion, and is referable, no doubt, to the extraordinary variety and vehemence of the religious movements that have characterized the past year. There has not only been a remarkable awakening of enthusiasm among the older and more regular sects, but Mormonism, Millerism, and other eccentric manifestations of the religious sentiment, by powerfully addressing the credulity and marvelousness of men, have agitated the public mind to an astonishing and alarming extent.

"When such moral epidemics, if I may be allowed the expression, sweep over the face of society, it is to be expected that many a mind already affected with a strong predisposition to insanity, should be overthrown by their resistless force. Even under ordinary circumstances, religious excitement will always be a prolific cause of insanity, wherever, as in New England, religion is a subject of great popular interest and regard." [14]

These are the most prominent statements in the New England annual reports of the 1840's that seem to contradict the emphatic

---

[12] *Report of the Board of Visitors, of the Trustees, and of the Superintendent of the New Hampshire Asylum for the Insane, for the Year Ending May 31, 1844,* pp. 19, 20.
[13] *Annual Report of the Trustees of the State Lunatic Hospital at Worcester, for the Year Ending Nov. 30, 1843,* p. 52.
[14] *Annual Report of the Directors of the Maine Insane Hospital (Augusta), for the Year Ending Dec. 31, 1842,* pp. 18, 19.

declarations in these same reports as to the unreliability of the causes assigned by friends and relatives. How shall we harmonize this apparent contradiction? Fortunately this is not very difficult to do. We say fortunately, because not only Millerism but all religions seem to stand indicted by these last-quoted statements. Only a fraction of the cases supposedly due to religious excitement are charged to Millerism. The Maine asylum superintendent spoke of the "remarkable awakening of enthusiasm among the older and more regular sects."

But a further reading of his report reveals that he had in mind two different kinds of causes: "constitutional" and "exciting." By "constitutional" cause he meant "the predisposition to the disease founded on some organic peculiarity not well understood." By "exciting" cause he meant "the occasional, exciting influence, that fully develops the disease to which the constitution is already disposed." He deplored the fact that these two causes were confused in various asylum reports, and added:

"When I speak of the causes of insanity, I refer exclusively to the exciting causes—those which give rise to the disease in a constitution in which the predisposition to it already exists." [15]

It is in the light of this explanation that we are to understand his statement about thirteen cases which he charges to religious excitement. He did not charge religion, whether of the "regular sects" or the "eccentric" ones, as being anything more than the "exciting" cause which gave "rise to the disease in a constitution in which the predisposition to it already exists."

This distinction between constitutional and exciting causes is not always made in asylum reports. The confusing of the two would obviously lead to unsound conclusions. The superintendent of the Maine asylum expressed distress over such confusing of causes. In our reading of the Worcester asylum reports of the 1840's we did not find any definite statement that would suggest

---

[15] *Ibid.*, p. 15.

a distinction between these two kinds of causes. This may have a bearing on the statement in the 1843 report from that asylum, from which we quoted, that tells of twenty-eight cases that were "supposed" to have resulted from religious causes, "15 of which were attributed to the Miller excitement." The words "supposed" and "attributed" are the weak links in this indictment. The friends and relatives "supposed" and "attributed," and the asylum very solemnly recorded those suppositions.

The medical superintendent of the New Hampshire asylum in the 1840's was very skeptical of the validity of the assigned causes, particularly where religion was involved. This is evident from the quotations given. This same skepticism, plus a clear distinction between constitutional and exciting causes, is set forth by a later medical superintendent in the 1852 report. But this same report also contains a withering indictment of Millerism as a cause of insanity. In fact, this is unquestionably the worst indictment of Millerism to be found in any asylum report. Because it is the worst, and because it seems to us that the context in which the charge is found provides almost a complete refutation, we quote at some length:

"It would be the easiest thing imaginable to give the causes commonly alleged by those who commit patients to our care; but it by no means follows that the causes given at that time are reliable. . . .

"Hard study, hard work, grief at the loss of friends, and causes generally which reflect no blemish on the character of the individual, would naturally be given, before those ranked in the category of vicious excesses. And, even the narration of those remote circumstances is sometimes withheld, which, if frankly given, throw great light upon cases. The existence of hereditary predisposition, of natural eccentricity of character, of mental deficiency, etc., is often studiously concealed, from a regard for that kind of charity which is extended to the unfortunate. A correct result under this head is also obscured by a fallacy like the following:

"A person, previously of no strongly developed moral principles, becomes unaccountably fond of his Bible; attends the most exciting religious meetings within his reach; is affected with an extreme concern for his future welfare, and finally falls into a religious frenzy, with the constant declaration upon his lips that he 'has committed the unpardonable sin.' Instead of ascribing the insanity, in this instance, to religious excitement, as is usually the case, it is far safer to consider his religious proclivity, as, of itself, the bias of a lapsing mind; the cause of whose disturbance lay far back of any religious inclinations. So untrustworthy are the usually given causes of insanity, and so frequently, as in the above instance, are effects mistaken for causes, that approximations even, are not obtainable. Moreover, all who give a philosophical attention to the subject are brought to a belief, that, in a majority of cases, what are called *exciting* causes are worth little, in comparison with those far anterior constitutional disturbances—sometimes acquired but more frequently inherited—which keep multitudes in all walks of life hanging over an abyss into which they are precipitated upon the slightest excitement. . . . [Then follow several paragraphs discussing other factors popularly thought to play a part in insanity.]

"On the whole, the declaration may safely be made, that, of those admitted to this institution, two thirds will show, if the case be thoroughly investigated, some inherited predisposition to mental disease. In a great majority of this number, the exciting cause is either not discernible; or, when given by friends, found to be altogether a fanciful one; or, else, although it be a plausible one, it is too trifling to have disturbed the equipoise of reason in any well-balanced mind. Of the remaining third of cases, febrile affections, where the brain has suffered; the puerperal state; protracted anxiety or grief, and physical excesses, comprise the larger number; leaving a small margin for those unusual cases which are more frequently displayed on the page of fiction than in the sober domain of fact.

"Current popular delusions usually leave the most enduring traces of their passage on the records of lunatic hospitals. The first page of entries on the folio records of the asylum, commencing with the 29th of Oct., 1842, and terminating Feb. 25th, 1843, is a page of instructive history, that has no precedent or analogy. History records many instances of the insanity that has suddenly affected multitudes, but all have failed to leave so sad a history written as this volume will preserve of the 'Miller Delusion,' which was just reaching its acme as the doors of this institution were opportunely thrown open to receive its infatuated victims. It will be observed—perhaps with a smile—that 'Spiritual Rappings,' as the current instance in point, has furnished us its small quota. To the credit of our race be it spoken, however, that the multitude, thus 'borne about by every wind of doctrine,' is really not so great as at first sight appears. A certain small number in the community, by assuming, in the succession of a very few years, such a variety of strange and fantastic garbs of doctrine, may bear the appearance of a multitude; causing us to forget, in the facility with which a new disguise is put on, that the passing masquerade is really composed of but few individuals. The victims of the *isms* of the day are either of the class already enumerated, in whom but a breath is necessary to submerge frail reason, or else of grade with him

" 'Who never had a dozen thoughts
In all his life, and never changed their course.' " [16]

The context clearly shows that at worst Millerism is indicted only as the exciting cause and that it ushered into the asylum only those "in whom but a breath" was sufficient to unbalance them, or on the other hand, those who never had any minds. But how did this medical superintendent in 1852 know that a group, even of these two types, were ushered into the asylum a decade before as a result of Millerism? He explained that the proof is found on the "first page of entries on the folio records of the asylum." In other words, he simply looked at the first page of the admissions ledger, which notes the cause assigned when the patient was admitted, but gives no case history data. And who assigned the cause in each case? The friends or relatives or others who brought in the patient. And how dependable did this superintendent believe that such a diagnosis was? In his own words: "So untrustworthy are the usually given causes of insanity, and so frequently, as in the above instance [where religious excitement is wrongly given as the cause], are effects mistaken for causes, that approximations even, are not attainable." What would he have found regarding the so-called religious excitement cases listed on that first page of the admissions ledger, if he had taken time to examine the detailed case histories? Let us see.

In Appendix F is an analysis of every one of the so-called religious excitement cases from the opening of the asylum on October 29, 1842, down to February 25, 1843, the period under discussion by the superintendent in his 1852 report. During this time fifteen cases were admitted in which religious excitement or sometimes specifically Millerism was given as the cause. In every instance where Millerism is mentioned in the case history, that fact is noted.

---

[16] *Report of the Board of Visitors, of the Trustees, and of the Superintendent of the New Hampshire Asylum for the Insane, for the Year Ending May 31, 1852*, pp. 13-17.

The facts that come to light from the analysis of the fifteen cases give virtually no support to the charge against Millerism. The New Hampshire asylum medical superintendent apparently did what even the most learned do at times; he made a sweeping, general statement without carefully consulting his sources.

Turn, now, to the records of the State asylum at Augusta, Maine. We quoted the medical superintendent as declaring in his report for the year 1842: "Of the 87 cases admitted during the past year, 13 were attributed, with as much certainty as can ever be obtained on this subject, to *religious excitement;* not to mention a few in which this cause contributed its share with others in developing the disease." The superintendent charged all this up to a "remarkable awakening of enthusiasm among the older and regular sects" as well as to "Mormonism, Millerism, and other eccentric manifestations of the religious sentiment." He explained, of course, that he was referring only to the "exciting causes."

An examination of the original case history records shows nineteen cases in the year 1842 in which religion is mentioned either as the cause or as a factor in the insanity. In thirteen of the nineteen cases hereditary insanity or periodical insanity stand revealed. Only four of the nineteen case histories mention Millerism either directly or by inference, and in three of the four cases the factor of hereditary or periodical insanity is mentioned. Space limits do not permit discussion of each of these nineteen cases, nor do we believe it is necessary, in view of the facts just stated. The picture that these nineteen cases present is strangely similar to that of the fifteen cases in the New Hampshire asylum.

But what of the cases in the large asylum at Worcester, Massachusetts? We quoted a very critical statement by the medical superintendent in his report for the year ending November 30, 1843: "In this hospital, 28 cases of 220 are supposed to have arisen from this cause [religious excitement], 15 of which were attributed to the Miller excitement."

And what does an examination of the case histories of these twenty-eight people reveal? First and most important, that seventeen of the twenty-eight cases carry the notation "hereditary —periodical," meaning that one or the other or both factors are present in these seventeen cases.* This leaves a total of eleven cases which, at least so far as the records go, fail to reveal that some other member of the family had been insane, or that the patient himself had had previous attacks of insanity. Of these eleven remaining cases, only four mention Millerism. Of the four, one was readmitted at a later date, which properly marks that case as periodical. Of the three cases remaining, one carried the significant statement in the case history: "Mind is very susceptible."

These findings for the year 1843 in the Worcester asylum are more or less similar to what we find for the years 1842 and 1844, the three years for which case histories were examined.

Besides the large State institution at Worcester, there were two other asylums in Massachusetts in the 1840's. We have already quoted from one of the annual reports of the medical superintendent of the McLean Asylum in Massachusetts, in which he discounted all causes of insanity assigned by friends and relatives when patients were brought to the asylum. His annual reports for the 1840's contain no tables of causes, nor any statement that is in any way an indictment of religion or Millerism. The case histories of this asylum were not examined. There was also the Boston Lunatic Hospital. This was a relatively small institution. In the annual reports of this hospital for the three-year period 1842-44, a total of only eight cases of "religious anxiety" are recorded, three of these cases being allegedly due to "Millerism." In the medical superintendent's annual report in the year 1845 is found this statement:

"It is to be noticed, that the causes in all cases are *supposed,* or are such as are *assigned* by the friends of the patients. With all the art and skill a

---

* One of these religious excitement cases, No. 1677, admitted in June, made a visit home on October 30 and was readmitted as case No. 1768 on November 9. Hence there were not twenty-eight but only twenty-seven persons admitted to the Worcester asylum in 1843 whose case histories carry the notation "Religious Excitement." And, as already stated, seventeen of these carry the telltale comment, "hereditary—periodical."

physician may possess, he can never, perhaps, pronounce with confidence and certainty what may have been the originating movement towards insanity in the madman's brain." [17]

The case histories of the Boston Lunatic Hospital were not examined.

The asylum serving all Vermont in the 1840's was located at Brattleboro. The annual reports of this asylum for the 1842-44 period contain no reference to any causes of insanity, nor do these annual reports refer directly or indirectly to Millerism or religious excitement. The case histories themselves were examined for this period. They present a picture very similar to that of the group of New Hampshire cases which we have set forth in some detail in Appendix F.

A table in Appendix G summarizes certain of our findings from an examination of the original case histories in the asylums of Maine, New Hampshire, Vermont, and the one principal Massachusetts State institution at Worcester. Reference to this table will show that during the three-year period 1842-44—which is the limited period when Millerism was widely preached by a group of ministers—there was a total of 1,516 admissions to these asylums. Of this grand total, 199 are marked as cases of religious excitement, of which 101 cases reveal the telltale information in their history of either hereditary or periodical insanity. Of the remaining ninety-eight religious excitement cases, thirty-nine mention Millerism. In other words, after eliminating from our consideration all cases where insanity is in the family or where the patient himself has recurring attacks, there are left for consideration only thirty-nine cases of so-called Millerism-induced insanity in the four institutions that served the major part of the New England area where Millerism was most active.

Now it is evident from the group of New Hampshire cases that are presented in some detail in Appendix F, that a case

---

[17] *Report of the Superintendent of the Boston Lunatic Hospital and Physician of the Public Institutions at South Boston, for Year Ending June 30, 1845,* pp. 18, 19.

need not be in the hereditary-periodical group in order to be eliminated from serious consideration. Even the insignificant total of thirty-nine cases begins to melt rapidly under case history scrutiny. Thus virtually disappears the charge that Millerism filled the asylums.

But someone may ask: Is it not true that the grand total of admissions to these institutions during this three-year period showed a marked rise above the average before and after, thus indicating a mentally disturbing factor of some kind at work in these States? The answer is No. The increase in admissions to the various asylums in the United States during the 1840's presents no uniform pattern. An asylum may go along for several years with minor fluctuations in admissions and then suddenly rise to a definitely higher level. Virtually without exception the explanation is found in the fact that a further addition has been made to the asylum, thus making possible the admission of a certain predetermined total of patients beyond the former capacity of the institution. In a few instances the opening of an asylum in a State withdrew from an asylum in an adjoining State a certain total of patients. Sometimes a change in the rate charged for weekly care affected the total of admissions. These were the principal factors affecting asylum populations in the 1840's.

There is another interesting point that comes to light when the figures of the different asylums are compared, and that is the percentage of the cases that are attributed to religious excitement. Even if all the asylums presented a uniform picture of an exceptionally high percentage charged to religious excitement in the 1842-44 period, it would not necessarily prove anything, as the facts already set forth establish. But the absence of such uniformity is in itself one more argument against the validity of the charge that Millerism filled the asylums. The superintendent of the Worcester institution made a special point out of the high percentage of cases charged to religious excitement in the year 1843 in that asylum. Thirteen per cent of the cases admitted were charged to religious excitement that year. This is the highest percentage for any year from the opening of the asylum in 1833 to the year 1852.[18] But if this truly reflected the disturbing of men's minds by Millerism, we would certainly expect the percentage to be as high, if not higher, in 1844, because the whole Millerite movement rose to its climax in October, 1844. But the percentage charged to religious excitement for 1844 is 9 per cent, which is the same as for the year 1842. What is much more interesting, this 9 per cent is the same as for the years 1838 and 1833.

Turning far west to the Ohio State asylum, we find that in the year 1840 the percentage of cases supposed to be caused by "religious anxiety," a variant phrase for "religious excitement," was 14.75 per cent, dropping to 14 per cent in 1841, then rising to 15.25 per cent in 1842, dropping sharply to 9.25 per cent in 1843, and to 7.50 per cent in 1844.[19]

Now, Millerism was scarcely known, much less preached in a definite way, in Ohio in 1840 and 1841; it really began to be preached, although in a very limited manner, in 1842. From then on Millerite activity increased rapidly until it came to its climax near the close of 1844, yet the percentages here work in the reverse order.

If we totaled all the cases of religious excitement in New England asylums in the years 1842 to 1844, we would find that the average percentage relation to total admissions was certainly under 10 per cent.* Now in 1869, or twenty-five years after Millerism had come to its climax in 1844, the percentage of the cases admitted to all the asylums in the United States because of "religious excitement" was almost 10, or 9.91 per cent to be exact.[20]

In other words, the 1869 percentage for religious excite-

---

[18] See *Annual Report of the Trustees of the State Lunatic Hospital at Worcester, for the Year Ending Nov. 30, 1851*, p. 58.
[19] See *Annual Report of the Directors and Superintendents of the Ohio Lunatic Hospital, for the Year Ending Nov. 15, 1851*, p. 81.
[20] See *Insanity and Insane Asylums*, Report of E. T. Wilkins, M. D., Commissioner in Lunacy for the State of California, Dec. 2, 1871, p. 233.

* It is true that the table in Appendix G shows a higher percentage than this for the group of asylums studied. But as we there explain, that table includes a number of cases that would not ordinarily be classed in an asylum report as "religious excitement" cases.

ment cases in all asylums was higher than for the Worcester asylum in the climax year of Millerism, for the Worcester asylum in 1844 showed only 9 per cent religious excitement cases. Yet the medical superintendent in his annual report for 1844 said, "The number of cases from religious causes, continues to be large. The last year has been as prolific of excitement on the subject as any of the past years. Millerism has had as many victims as in any former years." [21]

From this and similar data that might be presented, it would seem that the period 1842-44 was not so distinctive a one for the New England asylums in relation to religion as many have been led to believe.

Speaking of figures working in the opposite direction from what would be expected if Millerism had really produced an avalanche of insanity, note again the 1852 report of the New Hampshire asylum. In that report the medical superintendent stated that the "Miller delusion . . . was just reaching its acme as the doors of this institution were opportunely thrown open to receive its infatuated victims" in October, 1842. But Millerism was not reaching its climax in October, 1842. The climax was reached in October, 1844. In New England and elsewhere there was far more widespread preaching of Millerism in 1843 than there had been in 1842, and certainly more preaching of it in 1844 than in 1843. Furthermore, in the summer and fall of 1844 the whole Millerite movement took on a tone of intensity and fervor unknown before, because in that summer a specific day was set for the end of the world. In the light of this we wish to call attention to the fact that an examination of the case histories of the various New England asylums fails to show an increase in the number of religious excitement cases that even mention Millerism in the year 1844. On the contrary, there is a drop as compared with 1843. Here are the figures for Maine, New Hampshire, Vermont:

---

[21] *Annual Report of the Trustees of the State Lunatic Hospital at Worcester, for the Year Ending Nov. 30, 1844*, p. 52.

TOTAL NUMBER OF RELIGIOUS EXCITEMENT CASES ADMITTED 1842-1844 TO THE ASYLUMS OF THREE STATES, THAT MENTION MILLERISM

(By Calendar Years)

1842	Maine	New Hampshire	Vermont	Grand Totals by Years
1st q.	0	(Opened	0	
2d q.	3	Oct. 29/42)	1	
3d q.	0		0	
4th q.	1	8	0	
	4	8	1	13
1843				
1st q.	3	6	4	
2d q.	1	3	5	
3d q.	0	1	3	
4th q.	1	6	2	
	5	16	14	35
1844				
1st q.	1	0	0	
2d q.	1	1	0	
3d q.	0	2	1	
4th q.	0	1	4	
	2	4	5	11
Grand totals by States	11	28	20	

The above figures, which include all cases that mention Millerism in the case histories, reveal in the fullest degree possible the relationship of Millerism to insanity with no deductions of cases where hereditary or periodical insanity is present. See the table in Appendix G for a more detailed analysis.

Why this marked and rather general decline in totals of cases that even mention Millerism? This is really a question to be answered by those who have made the charge that Millerism filled the asylums. However, we venture this explanation: By the year 1843 Millerism had finally spread out over the whole country to such an extent that everyone was discussing it. Despite the fact that the preaching was much more intense in 1844, and many more were preaching, the subject was no longer a new topic of interest. Now the minds of those who are unbalanced or on the border line have a way of taking on the color of the changing scenes in the world about them. Their thoughts and their conversations reflect the latest exciting event that they hear discussed.

Whether this explanation is valid or not, the fact remains that instead of the "Millerism" cases increasing in the asylums, when the climactic year arrived, the cases actually declined, and that very sharply. All this supports emphatically the conclusion, which was already evident from all the facts before us, that Millerism was not really the cause of anyone's insanity.

At substantially this conclusion the *New York Tribune* arrived in 1843. In an editorial entitled "Millerism and Insanity," from which we have already quoted, the editor discussed two cases of insanity that had been charged to Millerism, admitted that the charges were unfounded, and then added:

"Doubtless the like has been the case in many other instances. Those who know anything of insanity are aware that it very commonly takes its hue from the most exciting topic of the hour, so that hundreds of persons have been reported as victims of *'religious* mania,' when in fact their insanity was caused by functional disorders.... Of those who are currently reported as rendered insane by 'revivals' or 'Millerism', a great portion would be found, on due inquiry, to have been constitutionally disposed to insanity, and often to have inherited that malady. In other cases, physical derangement consequent on personal excesses, such as intemperance, gluttony, and other forms of sensuality, was the true cause.—We cannot exclude from our columns accounts of remarkable casualties, but our readers will know how to make due allowance for the causes to which they are often mistakenly attributed." [22]

The only sense in which Millerism could possibly be said to be related to cases of insanity might be instances where, to borrow the language of the 1852 New Hampshire annual report, "but a breath is necessary to submerge frail reason." We agree with the Methodist writer who, in answering the charge "that revivals

---

[22] *New York Daily Tribune,* March 24, 1843.

sometimes lead to insanity and suicide," replied, "It is well known that minds of a certain kind cannot endure excitement from any source." [23]

We have never heard of a politician's being indicted for the murder of a man who died of a weak heart under the excitement of a political meeting. Then why indict preachers because of the mental collapse of some people whose minds are too weak to stand the so-called excitement of a fervent religious service?

The answer is that physicians trained in the modern science of psychiatry quite generally exonerate preachers and religion of any responsibility in such cases. The medical superintendent of the Augusta State Hospital (Maine), in speaking of the effects of religious movements on certain kinds of minds, declared:

"The personality conflicts find expression in these religious movements. But the religious movements are not the cause of the disturbances. In my opinion, there is no such thing as religious insanity. . . . I feel, and I think it is the consensus of opinion of modern psychiatrists, that these religious trends are used by the individual to sublimate his internal difficulties; that their concern over religion is the result, rather than the cause of their difficulties." [24]

The assistant superintendent of the New Hampshire State Hospital observed regarding the cause assigned for insanity in the asylums a hundred years ago:

"In general it is my opinion that all cases that were formerly diagnosed as 'religious mania,' or similar expressions, could, if seen at the present time, be fitted into one of the modern psychiatric classifications. The majority of these cases, I believe, would be diagnosed psychoneurosis, hysterical type. Schizophrenia would follow as a close second, and some would be diagnosed manic-depressive psychosis, manic phase. There would be a few who would have other diagnoses. For example, delusions of a religious nature sometimes accompany general paresis and other organic brain diseases. We now regard a delusion of this type not as a disease entity, but as a symptom. In order to determine what disease this is a symptom of, it is necessary to consider the whole picture of the patient from psychiatric, medical, and laboratory standpoints.

---

[23] James Porter, *Revivals of Religion*, p. 201.
[24] F. C. Tyson, M. D., in a personal letter to the author, Oct. 15, 1943

"I doubt if preoccupation with religion alone ever caused a psychosis. It was merely a symptom of underlying changes, which we can now classify more accurately, although our classification is still far from perfect. On the other hand, I think religious excitement did frequently precipitate psychotic or psychoneurotic manifestations in people who were already predisposed to a psychiatric breakdown. This is probably even more true in the psychoneuroses than in the psychoses. As you have found in your researches on this subject, many of these people who had an illness for which religion was blamed, are people who had previous or subsequent breakdowns to which other causes were assigned." [25]

All of which leads to the inevitable conclusion that the charge that Millerite preaching filled the asylums owes its origin either to religious prejudice, psychiatric ignorance, or the native ability of some people to invent a sensational story—or perhaps to a combination of all three.

---

[25] W. C. Brinegar, M. D., in a personal letter to the author, Oct. 29, 1943.

NOTE

The discussion on Millerism and insanity, consisting of the two preceding chapters and appendices F and G, has been read and approved by the following:

Dr. Willard C. Brinegar, assistant superintendent, New Hampshire State Hospital, Concord, New Hampshire. (In 1840's, New Hampshire Asylum for the Insane.)

Dr. George A. Elliott, superintendent, Brattleboro Retreat, Brattleboro, Vermont. (In 1840's, Vermont Asylum for the Insane.)

Dr. George T. Harding, medical superintendent, Harding Sanitarium, Worthington, Ohio.

Dr. Alfred B. Olsen, consulting psychiatrist, Hinsdale Sanitarium and Hospital, Hinsdale, Illinois.

Dr. Harold Shryock, assistant professor of anatomy (neurology), College of Medical Evangelists, Loma Linda, California.

Dr. Forrest C. Tyson, superintendent, Augusta State Hospital, Augusta, Maine. (In 1840's, Maine Insane Hospital.)

The foregoing group of doctors confined their reading to the section of the manuscript devoted to insanity in relation to Millerism, and have expressed their scientific and medical opinion only on that question. The author is deeply indebted to them for their great kindness in examining this part of his work.

CHAPTER 25

Did the Millerites Wear Ascension Robes?

NO STORY OF THE MILLERITES is more widely known nor more firmly believed than that of their wearing ascension robes on the momentous day when they expected Christ to come to this world. Just what these ascension robes were supposed to look like no one has ever said with any great definiteness. A researcher receives only the vague impression that they must have looked like old-fashioned, oversized nightgowns. The most specific thing said regarding them is that they were white and generally that they were of muslin.

Now, if the Millerites wore such robes, they would stand convicted of something far more grave than simply displaying silly ideas in dress. They would be guilty of holding silly ideas on religion. A person could fall into no more foolish error than to think that by robing himself in some special white garment he was thus fitted for entrance into heaven. Were the religious ideas of the Millerites this gross?

The reader will recall that while the great day of the expected advent was October 22, 1844, there had earlier been a whole year, beginning with March 21, 1843, which could be described as the year of the end of the world. In other words, the Millerites first thought that sometime during that twelve-month period the Lord would come, though there was no general agreement among the believers as to any particular date within that year. We therefore look for the ascension robe story to begin to have currency as the year of the end of the world drew near. And this is the case.

We do not know the date when the story was first published, nor is this knowledge necessary to our investigation of the charge.

We do know that in the very opening weeks of 1843 various newspapers were carrying news items about Millerites and ascension robes. For example, a leading Philadelphia newspaper quoted the *Bay State Democrat* of Boston as its authority for the following news item:

"It is now well known, that in this city [Boston], many of the believers in the doctrine that the world will come to an end this year, are having ascension robes made, with which to mount up to the regions of bliss." [1]

In January also a Maine newspaper declared, quoting the *Boston Daily Bee:*

"We learn from unquestionable authority (says the *Bee,*) that the most sanguine of the Millerites in Groton, Massachusetts, are busily engaged in making their 'ascension robes'!" [2]

A Boston newspaper, also in January, quoted from the *Journal of Commerce,* New York, a story that Miller had found an error of a thousand years in his reckoning, which would put off the advent into the dim future, and added this comment by the New York paper: "The 'ascension robes' with which many of the Millerites on Long Island have provided themselves, are not likely to be wanted." [3]

A Portsmouth, New Hampshire, paper in February of 1843 quoted the Nashua (New Hampshire) *Telegraph* as stating:

"We have seen going the rounds of the newspapers, statements that many of the Millerites have provided themselves with white robes in which to ascend to meet their Lord, but have regarded them only as the invention of the enemy. We are assured, however, that not a few of them in town, have actually provided themselves with long white robes for the expected occasion." [4]

In February also appeared an item in a Philadelphia paper, which was quoted from the *New York Express,* regarding a group of Millerites who were said to have fixed on a certain day, then

---

[1] *Philadelphia Public Ledger,* Jan. 16, 1843.
[2] *Maine Inquirer* (Bath), Jan. 18, 1843.
[3] *Daily Evening Transcript,* Boston, Jan. 23, 1843.
[4] *Portsmouth Journal* (N. H.), Feb. 11, 1843.

past, for the end of the world, and that "it is even said that some had prepared *white robes* in which to be translated from earth!" [5]

These are typical of the newspaper stories on Millerite ascension robes in the opening months of 1843. No writer said that he saw anyone in an ascension robe, much less a group of people. In fact, the charge is only that the Millerites were making robes, or had provided themselves with robes. And what is the authority for the stories? "It is now well known" is the guaranty for one story. And what better guaranty would anyone ask for a good story! "We learn from unquestionable authority" also leaves nothing to be desired, even though the writer forgot to tell us who his "authority" was. "We have seen going the rounds of the newspapers," is rather roundabout proof, which the newspaper honestly confessed was not sufficient, so it added, "We are assured." "It is even said," is the foundation for another story on Millerite robes.

Now the only trouble with such authorities as these is that we have had our confidence in them shaken completely by our examination of other charges against the Millerites. We had every rightful reason to hope that when we came to investigate the ascension robe story, which is now certified by its inclusion in ponderous encyclopedias, we would find original sources that would provide us with unquestionable authority for that story.

The form in which the ascension robe story is generally heard today is that the Millerite leaders instructed their followers to wear such robes. Therefore, it is with some interest that we examine the pages of the Millerite papers in the opening months of 1843, to see what they had to say on this subject. Do they confirm the newspaper stories? Or do they deny them? Or are they simply silent on the matter? They certainly ought to have known better than anyone else whether the stories were true, and whether they, as Millerite leaders, really believed in having their followers wear robes. The reader will recall that the Millerite papers carried a "Liar's Department" in which they

---

[5] *Philadelphia Public Ledger,* Feb. 18, 1843.

placed newspaper stories that they considered were made out of "whole cloth," and which were so patently a fabrication that they scarcely called for comment. Indeed, Millerite editors oftentimes made no comment on newspaper items that they reprinted in this rather sulphurous department. Early in 1843 a Millerite paper printed in its Liar's Department the item from the New York *Journal of Commerce,* about Miller's finding an error of a thousand years in his reckoning, with the result that the Millerites on Long Island would have no need of the ascension robes they had prepared.[6] Other than to list the names of a number of papers, some secular, some religious, that had printed this story, the Millerite editor offered no comment. The title of the department was considered comment enough.

Thus the issue was drawn almost two years before that great day of October 22, 1844, when, according to the current version of the story, all the Millerites went forth, under the instructions of their leaders, garbed in ascension robes. Did those leaders later change their position and endorse what they at first denounced as a lie? The answer to this question will be provided as the story unfolds.

Two weeks after its initial attack on the story, the same Millerite paper printed a letter written by Joshua V. Himes, in New York. In this letter Himes referred to the *Journal of Commerce* story of a thousand-year error in Millerite reckoning, and the Long Island Millerites' no longer needing their ascension robes, and said:

> "I called upon the editor (Mr. D. Hale) today, who assured us that it was published in the evening edition of his paper *without the knowledge or consent of the editors,* and that it was written by one of the clerks of the office, as a *hoax!"* [7]

We know, of course, that Miller never announced a thousand-year error in his reckoning. This point was fully discussed in an earlier chapter. But on this alleged error is built one of the

---

[6] *Signs of the Times,* Feb. 1, 1843, p. 157.
[7] Letter, Jan. 20, 1843, in *Signs of the Times,* Feb. 15, 1843, p. 173.

earliest versions of the robe story—a rather unstable foundation, to say the least, for a story that has grown tall, very "tall," through a hundred years. Indeed, this very foundation is unreal, for the whole story is admitted to be a hoax, if we may believe Himes' very explicit letter in which he mentions the newspaper editor by name.*

Early in March of 1843 *The Midnight Cry,* in its department entitled "Scoffers and Liars," discussed certain comments that had been made on Millerism in the *New York Observer,* by its editor, the Reverend Samuel I. Prime. The *Observer* was a leading religious weekly and, in common with the religious press of that day, was very ready to swing its sword lustily against any newcomer in that field. We quote several paragraphs, that the reader may see how a "good" story grows, how it changes its geographical location each time it is told, and what the Millerites themselves had to say in comment on such a recital, which in this instance is a story of ascension robes. Says the Millerite paper in its usual vigorous style:

"We cut the following from the *Observer* of last week, where it stood without comment:

"'The *Millerites* at Providence had decided that the great end of things was to come about last Wednesday, and preparations were made to meet it. Over one hundred passed the night in the burying ground, on the west side, some of whom, if report speaks true, were dressed in their ascension robes. They went there to witness the resurrection of their friends, with whom they expected to rise into the clouds!'

"This story about the ascension robes is a pure invention, and was manufactured somewhere in Massachusetts, where the scene was first laid. David Hale of the *Journal of Commerce* next suffered the story to travel the rounds, *credited to him,* with the scene on Long Island. Here, Mr. Prime, or some handler of the scissors, employed by Sidney E. Morse & Co., passes it along, as occurring at Rhode Island. Next, to cap the climax of lying, and obtain the first premium from the infernal court, we have a

---

* We need hardly remind the reader of what has been stressed in earlier chapters; namely, that the Millerite papers were very carefully read by newspaper editors, and that the Millerites seemed to be quite sure of their ground when they took issue with the public press. At least, we have yet to find an instance where a newspaper seriously challenged the truth of a rejoinder made by the Millerites in their journals. The presumption, therefore, is strongly in favor of the truth of Himes' statement in his letter from which we have quoted.

version, of which *N. P. Willis* is said to be the author. We cut it from the Springfield, Mass., *Gazette:*

" 'The New York correspondent of the *National Intelligencer* states that "several believers in Miller's theory were nearly frozen to death last Wednesday, on the heights of Hoboken, sitting in the snow in their ascension robes," in momentary expectation of the second advent. These ascension robes have created a great demand for drab Mackintosh cloth, and other draperies suitable for the liveries of the saints; and should the *finale* fail to come in 1844, the Chatham Street brokers will make a great "operation" in the cast-off heavenly apparel.' " [8]

The Millerite editor's comments on this robes story have at least this much in their favor. They cannot be misunderstood. He described the story as "a pure invention" and as going on from one falsehood to another until the retailers of the story finally "cap the climax of lying."

Now, in the light of this, and before we go further in our investigation, it is pertinent to raise two or three questions: If the Millerites in different places like Providence, Long Island, Massachusetts, and Hoboken, were simultaneously proceeding to array themselves in ascension robes, as the press declared, would it not reasonably follow that they had received instruction from some central headquarters? We think the answer is Yes. Ascension robes are such an unusual kind of attire that it is unreasonable to believe that groups of people in different places would all suddenly decide to wear such freakish apparel. What headquarters office would that be? The editorial office of one of the leading Millerite papers. That was the only kind of headquarters office the Millerites had. Furthermore, in what manner would the leaders be expected to send out their counsel? Through the pages of their publications, naturally. But when we turn to their publications we find them denouncing the ascension robe story as "a pure invention."

An interesting side light on the early controversy between the Millerites and the public press regarding ascension robes was a comment that appeared in the *Boston Investigator*. This was

---

[8] *The Midnight Cry,* March 10, 1843, p. 45.

an ably edited weekly, devoted to the promotion of infidel principles, as it boldly declared. No religious leader or movement was exempt from its critical analysis and comment. But it must be said to the credit of the *Investigator* that it displayed a certain element of fair play, that was strikingly absent from most of the press, particularly the dogmatic and often intolerant religious publications of that time. Though the *Investigator* had no love for the Millerites, it was outraged by the way the religious press attacked this new movement. When the ascension robe story was started, the *Investigator* noted what the Millerite papers said in reply, and remarked:

"The story of the 'ascension robes' turns out to be what we thought it was, when we first heard of it—a hoax invented by Christians to bring contempt upon those who believe in the second advent. Any way to put the Millerites down, appears to be the motto of their Christian opposers, and they act upon it most faithfully." [9]

This forthright statement made in the middle of March, 1843, is all the more significant in view of the fact that the *Investigator,* only six weeks earlier, had apparently given some credence to the robes story by making an incidental reference to such robes in a paragraph about Millerites.[10] Critical of all religion though it was, the *Investigator,* on reading the Millerite denials, was willing to go on record as believing those denials. Nor did it take any stretch of charity or any special faith in the Millerites to believe their denials. Should they not know better than anyone else what they had been doing or wearing? And if the leaders had really counseled their followers to wear such strange garments, those leaders were not the kind of men to turn around immediately and disown their own counsel. This much has to be said for the Millerites: They were not ashamed of what they taught. Evidently they did not teach their followers to wear ascension robes. That is the only conclusion to reach.

But we are not through with the ascension robe story. In

---
[9] *Boston Investigator,* March 15, 1843.
[10] See *Boston Investigator,* Feb. 1, 1843.

fact, we have only begun. In March of 1843 the public press changed from its vague stories and rumors about Millerites' preparing their robes, or groups of them allegedly sitting at midnight on hilltops or in graveyards, and gave circulation to a story about a specifically named individual. Here is the story as it appeared in a Maine paper, quoting a Massachusetts paper:

"The *Haverhill Gazette* relates what follows:—In Pelham, New Hampshire, Mr. Shortridge, formally enrobed himself in a long white dress, and climbed into a tree, to be prepared to ascend, believing that the second advent was to take place on that day—in attempting to *rise* he fell to the ground and broke his neck." [11]

The story is given in a little more detail in the *New York Observer,* under the head "Distressing Effects of Millerism":

"We find in the New Hampshire papers an account of the death of Mr. Shortridge, aged fifty-five. He was formerly a merchant of respectable standing in Portsmouth, but, by misfortune in business, had been several years reduced in his pecuniary affairs, and suffered much from an almost incessant mental derangement. At the day of his death he was imagining the time of the second advent was to take place. He had made a garb for the occasion, and with this he was waiting; until, becoming impatient, he climbed to the top of a high tree. There, *mantled in his long white ascension robe,* he made one aspiring effort, but was precipitated to the ground, and instantly died from a broken neck." [12]

Now even if this story were true, why should Millerism be held accountable for the deeds of a man who "suffered much from an almost incessant mental derangement"? The story does not even suggest that his insanity was produced by Millerism. Rather we are permitted to believe that it was the result of misfortune in business. Yet the death of Mr. Shortridge is described as one of the "distressing effects of Millerism."

But is this story true? Did this man really jump from a tree and die from a broken neck in the spring of 1843? Not long after this news item was published there began to appear retractions of it. The *New York Daily Tribune* thought its

---
[11] *Portland Bulletin* (Maine), March 14, 1843.
[12] *New York Observer,* quoted in *The Midnight Cry,* March 24, 1843, p. 80.

retraction worthy of an editorial note, in which it discussed not only this case but another case under the general title "Millerism and Insanity." In the preceding chapter we quoted from the last half of the editorial. We quote now from the first part, which deals with the sad case of Mr. Shortridge:

"We lately published a statement that a Mr. Shortridge, of New Hampshire, had run mad with Millerism, and attempted to ascend to heaven from an apple tree, but found the attraction of gravitation too strong for his celestial aspirations, and came to the ground with such momentum as to cause his death. We have just seen two letters of late date from different sources in Portsmouth, N. H., stating that letters have been received there from this same Mr. Shortridge, making no mention of his 'ground and lofty tumbling' or death circumstances so remarkable that they could hardly have escaped his notice had they actually occurred. We have heard from another source that this same Mr. S. was crazy ten years ago." [13]

We agree with the *Tribune* editor that Mr. Shortridge himself was probably the best authority on the subject of his alleged death. And if he was insane "ten years ago," his insanity began when Millerism was scarcely known in New Hampshire.

The *New York Observer* also printed a retraction in which is found this statement:

"He has been insane for years, but the report of his death has been contradicted in the Portsmouth *Journal,* and has since been proven false by a letter from the man himself." [14]

Apparently Mr. Shortridge had lucid intervals and took direct action against the papers that had published the story of his death. He wrote to them to deny it and presumably to demand a retraction. The very fact that this man wrote letters to the papers probably explains why we have a retraction of a really "good" Millerite story, something rare in the press.*

---

[13] *New York Daily Tribune,* March 24, 1843.
[14] *New York Observer,* April 1, 1843.
* The records of the New Hampshire Asylum for the Insane provide the complete refutation of the stories of the death of Mr. Shortridge in the spring of 1843. John H. Shortridge of Portsmouth, New Hampshire, was admitted to the asylum on October 21, 1843, as case No. 121. The exciting cause is given as "pecuniary embarrassment." He was 55 years of age and a "merchant." He remained in the asylum until his death on June 2, 1845. The case history is very brief and gives no information as to the length of time he was insane before admission. There is no reference to Millerism even by implication.

With Mr. Shortridge out of the tree and with his neck intact —or did he even climb a tree or wear a robe?—we go forward in our search for ascension robes. There are other mentions of robes in the newspapers during the spring of 1843. The vague character of these stories is indicated by the following from a Philadelphia paper:

"It seems that, a few nights ago, a number of the proselytes of Millerism, anxious to see the 'final finish,' dressed themselves in their ascension robes, and ascended one of the church steeples in Utica, New York." [15]

Did a reporter see these people? On what authority does the story rest? The answer is, "It seems that."

A Massachusetts paper quoted from another paper a circuitous story told to the writer "by a gentleman late from the headquarters of Millerism in Albany," that, among other things, "the saints are to be ready with their ascension robes, and are to be taken up into the comet, out of harm's way, till all is over." [16]

Do the Millerite papers contain any such information or instruction? The answer is No. On the contrary, Millerite papers discussed the comet that was then bright in the skies in a very matter-of-fact fashion, certainly not as a dwelling place for the Millerites.

A Maine newspaper quoted from another newspaper to the effect that many of the most fervent Millerite "converts, not content with making ascension robes for themselves, are preparing garments for the Saviour when He makes His appearance on earth." [17]

This tale is too obviously silly to be worthy of serious comment. Even the Millerite papers did not deign to comment on it.

This Maine newspaper on the same day carried the following item: "The Millerite encampment at Salem will be reopened

---

[15] *Philadelphia Public Ledger,* March 23, 1843.
[16] *Salem Register* (Massachusetts), April 3, 1843.
[17] *Maine Inquirer* (Bath) April 5, 1843.

on the first of April.—Great preparations are being made in the way of ascension robes." [18]

Did any newspaper in 1843, describing the activities of the Millerites at their camp meeting, tell of actually having seen anyone in an ascension robe at those public services? No.

A Massachusetts paper, early in April, remarked on the fact that the Miller tabernacle was progressing very slowly toward completion, and added:

"The 23d of April is close at hand; what is to be done by those who have been deeming it necessary to their salvation, to be assembled, in their 'ascension robes,' within the walls of the tabernacle on that awful day, I know not." [19]

In the same fictitious class is the story from a news weekly quoting "a writer in the *Providence Journal*" stating that on April 23 "several Millerites in that city walked the streets and fields all day arrayed in their ascension robes, dripping from top to bottom, looking for the Saviour to come in the pouring clouds." [20]

Now, were any of the Millerites looking for the Lord to come on April 23, 1843? No. The reader will recall that this date owes its origin to a newspaper story, which the Millerites in their publications exposed and refuted well in advance of the date. Yet so quickly did the story spread, and so firmly did it become fixed in men's minds, that when the day arrived some papers contained accounts of Millerites expecting their Lord on that day, and for good measure an occasional rumored item dressed them up in ascension robes. Now, the Millerites had to risk every kind of ridicule to follow the instruction of their leaders. How unreasonable, then, to believe they would proceed to bring upon themselves unnecessary reproach by going out to meet their Lord on an ascension date denounced by the Millerite leaders as false, and attired in garments described by those same leaders as a malicious caricature of Millerism.

---

[18] *Ibid.*
[19] *Hingham Patriot* (Massachusetts), April 8, 1843.
[20] *Niles National Register*, May 6, 1843.

These ascension robe stories in the public press, of which the foregoing are most representative, are found not infrequently in the newspapers and the religious press in the first few months of 1843. In other words, a crop of such stories sprang up at the beginning of the year of the end of the world. That, of course, was the very time for such stories to spring up. But as suddenly as the stories appeared, they disappeared, or virtually so, for after the spring of 1843 we find scarcely a reference to ascension robes in the public press until the fall of 1844. Why these stories so suddenly disappeared we know not. Perhaps they collapsed of their own absurdity.

But before these fantastic stories had died out of the newspapers the yarn took on new life in a pictorial form. We mentioned in an earlier chapter the "caricature prints" which were brought out in the spring of 1843 and then again in the fall of 1844. From the descriptions in the Millerite papers, and from the few prints that have been preserved, these caricature prints were simply one expression of the robust 1840's, when men freely lampooned their enemies, political, social, or religious, by publishing large sheets devoted in part or in whole to a cartoon. Himes, writing to Charles Fitch in the spring of 1843, said in part:

"Another class of men have arisen up of late, who seem to have been encouraged by the opposition of the *religious* press, [and] are publishing the most obscene and blasphemous caricature prints, which are enough to shock the sensibilities of a fiend. So we see, as the time draws nearer, the opposition is more vile and fiendish. It is very remarkable, that they have fixed upon the same things used by our more decent opponents, such as 'ascension robes,' etc., etc., in order to bring not only us, but the Bible, and all its most sacred truths into contempt." [21]

If the public had begun to doubt the newspaper stories concerning ascension robes, they were now given visual proof that the Millerites wore such garments. The cartoonists set out to draw pictures of them. If one picture is worth a thousand

---

[21] *Signs of the Times*, April 19, 1843, p. 53.

words, then these numerous caricature prints ought to have fastened quite firmly on a multitude of minds the general impression, at least, that Millerites wore robes—an impression that memory long years afterward could easily transform into a sure conviction that the Millerites *did* wear ascension robes.

In April, 1843, the editor of *The Midnight Cry* quoted a varied array of stories in the press concerning ascension-robe preparations by the Millerites, including the report that "$5,000 worth of silk" had been ordered by the Millerites in one town to be used for ascension robes, and then added this comment: "We trust our readers will pardon our seeming insult to their understandings in publishing these weak inventions of those who love lies." [22]

By the middle of 1843, as already stated, the ascension robe story had quite run its course, and the press turned to other rumors about Millerism. In its first issue in 1844 *The Midnight Cry* devoted a column to "Errors Corrected" and summed up certain of the principal false stories concerning Millerism that had had currency up to that time. One subhead in this column is entitled "The Fiction About Ascension Robes." The paragraph that follows refers to some of the forms in which the story had appeared in print, and concludes thus:

"From such weak falsehoods multitudes have formed their opinions respecting a subject of momentous interest. Large rewards have been offered for the sight of an ascension robe, but none have been produced, for none existed." [23]

Two weeks later this same Millerite paper published a letter from a Sarah T. Bolton, of Indianapolis, who describes a Brother Stevens that had come to their city to preach:

"It had been represented to us, through the public prints, that the second advent believers were a set of deluded fanatics, better fitting a lunatic asylum, than society. It was reported that they have prepared ascension robes, in which to meet the Saviour, and that the howlings of the

---

[22] *The Midnight Cry*, April 7, 1843, p. 106.
[23] *Ibid.*, Jan. 4, 1844, p. 189.

deluded creatures might be heard for miles. After having heard all this, imagine my astonishment if you can, when I saw how Brother Stevens conducted his lectures. There was no attempt to create excitement through the feelings or imagination of the people." [24]

In March, 1844, Himes wrote a letter to *The Midnight Cry*, telling of Miller's lectures in Baltimore, and of the opposition they met in the form of a printed sermon that was widely circulated. The author of it was evidently engaged in promoting many of the discredited stories about Millerism. Himes remarked: "His taunts about 'ascension robes!' etc., show that he is very ignorant or wicked. Any man of common sense ought to know better." [25]

In the spring of 1844 Josiah Litch wrote a long article on "The Rise and Progress of Adventism," which was published in a Millerite quarterly. This quarterly presented seriously and at length the doctrines of Millerism with a view to catching the eye and the mind of studious persons. In his article Litch discussed, among other things, the prophetic year 1843, throughout which year different groups of Millerites looked with varying degrees of interest to certain dates as the possible exact time of the advent. Said Litch concerning these particular periods of time within that year:

"Those periods came and passed with no unusual occurrence. As soon as they had gone by, a flood of scoffing, reviling and persecution burst forth, not from the infidel world, so much, but from the professed friends of the Saviour; the most idle and foolish stories of ascension robes, and going out into the graveyards to watch, going to the tops of houses, etc., etc.; these were repeated again and again, both from pulpit and press, until the public were, many of them at least, almost persuaded to believe them true." [26]

Now if it were common knowledge that the Millerites had actually gone into graveyards and sat on housetops in ascension robes, could Litch hope to convict the minds of serious students by denying so obvious a fact—denying it indeed at the very time

---

[24] *Ibid.*, Jan. 18, 1844, p. 207.
[25] *Ibid.*, March 21, 1844, p. 273.
[26] "The Rise and Progress of Adventism," *The Advent Shield and Review*, May, 1844, p. 74.

when men would have an immediate and present knowledge of it?

The Advent Herald, in midsummer of 1844, spoke of an opponent who had "given circulation to the silly story of 'ascension robes,'" and declared that the only reason why he would tell so "silly" a story was that his former attempts to refute Millerism, by writing a serious book against it, had proved quite ineffective.[27]

These and other quotations that might be given from Millerite papers carry us down to the fall of 1844. The testimony of the Millerite publications is consistent from the first in its denunciation of the ascension robe story as a silly fabrication, intended only to bring discredit upon Millerism. We come now to the closing, climactic weeks of the Millerite movement. Events were moving rapidly toward the great day, October 22, when, according to the faith of a rapidly increasing number of Millerites, they expected the end of all things earthly to take place. The reader will recall that in those last few weeks the public press printed a great many items about the Millerites, some good, some bad, some silly, some serious. Scarcely anything of significance concerning the activities of the Millerites was overlooked by the newspapers. We would therefore expect the press to revive the story of ascension robes.

In the month of October, 1844, are found a few newspaper references to ascension robes. They are as vague as the stories that came out in the spring of 1843—or even more vague if that were possible. For example, a New York newspaper on October 16, tells of a Millerite church in that city surrounded by a mob which burned blue lights and fireworks, and caused a stampede and panic. Then follows this sentence: "We are informed that the followers of Miller were, on that occasion, assembled in their *ascension dresses,* waiting for 'the end of all things.'"[28]

With blue lights, fireworks, a stampede and a panic, in the

---
[27] See *The Advent Herald,* July 24, 1844, p. 197.
[28] *New York Spectator,* Oct. 16, 1844.

night, it might be a little difficult even for a reporter on the ground to say with certainty how the worshipers in a church were dressed. But the newspaper is not writing this story in terms of a reporter's account, a rather rare thing in those days. No, the editor simply stated, "We are informed."

On the nineteenth of October a newspaper in Philadelphia carried a story of an attempt that was made to break up a Millerite meeting in that city:

> "Just at midnight on the 15th inst., when the final catastrophe was expected, a strange scene arose from the sudden and obstreperous blowing of horns, by a gang of mischievous lads, the persons inside rushing forth in their 'ascension robes' to be preserved from the general destruction." [29]

Again we may ask whether, in the midst of tumult, panic, and darkness, any true account of the dress of the Millerites was given.*

Another reference to ascension robes just prior to October 22 is an item in a Philadelphia weekly newspaper. On the editorial page in a column entitled "Our Weekly Gossip" is an extended discussion of Millerism, in the rather vague language of rumor. Near the close is found this paragraph:

> "The most singular feature of the whole matter, is the preparation of 'ascension robes,' of white cloth, by the believers, in which they actually sit clothed to await the coming! But we spare the reading of further remarks upon a subject on which sufficient is said elsewhere, in this day's paper." [30]

The "elsewhere" referred to is an editorial on the same page, entitled "Millerism," which is devoted almost wholly to a narration of various predictions concerning the end of the world that have been made during past centuries. The opening paragraph includes this:

---

[29] *Neal's Saturday Gazette* (Philadelphia), Oct. 19, 1844.
[30] *United States Saturday Post* (Philadelphia), Oct. 19, 1844.

* But there is something more serious the matter with this story. It was written in advance of October 22 and deals with a meeting on the fifteenth, which is alleged to be the last great night. Was this newspaper anxious to "scoop" its competitors and tell just how the Millerites dressed and acted on the last great day when that great day was still a week away? But the record is clear in the Millerite papers, and was very generally understood by the press, that the end was not expected until the twenty-second.

25

"We hear of women arrayed in 'ascension robes,' deserting the care of their households, and sitting down in upper rooms, some even in unfinished garrets, to be as near to heaven as possible, and there awaiting the 'second advent.' " [31]

Beyond this the paper gives no details concerning the alleged ascension robes. Now, on what were these two statements based? The first appeared under the title "Our Weekly Gossip." The second is introduced with the phrase, "We hear of." But this second statement, which admittedly had nothing more than hearsay to support it, was very widely republished by the press in other cities.

Thus the public was prepared to expect that on October 22 the thousands of Millerites would provide the country with a spectacular procession of white-robed creatures who would wend their eerie way to places even higher than garrets, yes, even to mountaintops, there to let their white robes flutter in the breezes. Surely a most reasonable expectation! Why would the Millerite women have dress rehearsals for days ahead and then not come out in their dresses on the great day for which those dresses had been made! That would hardly be in the feminine tradition!

This public expectation of a white-robed procession of Millerites on the great day was heightened in the public mind by a news item that received amazing circulation in the press of the country. A Mrs. Child, the New York correspondent for the *Boston Courier,* wrote a story for her paper concerning the Millerites in New York City. She mentioned among other items having seen in a dry-goods store window in the Bowery a sign reading, "Muslin for Ascension Robes." Her comment on the sign was, "I know not whether this was done for waggery, or from that spirit of trade, which is ever willing to turn a penny on war, pestilence or conflagration." [32]

This item was copied over the length and breadth of the land, but often without Mrs. Child's comment as to the

---
[31] *Ibid.*
[32] *Boston Daily Courier,* Oct. 17, 1844.

possibility that the placard was only a bit of "waggery." In such instances the readers were simply to conclude that here was a sober statement that muslin was being offered for sale for ascension robes in a Bowery store.[33]

In an earlier chapter we described a broadside printed a few days before October 22, which devoted half its space to a cartoon showing the Boston Tabernacle ascending and the Millerites on the roof, or hanging onto the windows. The cartoonist pictured the women dressed in long, flowing robes.

We also mentioned another large broadside, which was intended to appear as actually a Millerite production—but which was exposed and denounced by them in their publications. This pictured the advent in awesome fashion and printed below certain excerpts from Millerite literature. There is only one item that reveals the hostile spirit that prompted the printing of the broadside. This item is entitled "Strange Doings at the Tabernacle," and is found in the last column. This is supposed to be a description of the way the Millerites looked and acted as they awaited the end, and holds them up to ridicule and scorn. The second paragraph opens thus: "The flowing robes and pantaletts, the round-a-bout jackets and corduroys were all prepared in due season." Even the writer of this broadside, who had all the latitude that anonymity gives, did not picture the Millerites as *wearing* the "flowing robes," though he went into details about the people and their actions, and though he allegedly described a last meeting of these people who "intended to take their departure for a celestial home at 4 o'clock, P.M." He simply said that the "robes" had been "prepared in due season." He certainly missed an excellent chance to describe the Millerites in these strange garments. That really would have made sensational reading. Did he feel that the known facts about the Millerites in Boston would not permit of his going this far in his

---

[33] See, for example, *Philadelphia Public Ledger*, Oct. 21, 1844; *Albany Evening Journal*, Oct. 21, 1844; *Daily National Intelligencer* (Washington, D. C.), Oct. 21, 1844; *National Aegis* (Worcester, Mass.), Oct. 23, 1844.

caricature without hopelessly exposing the whole fraudulent broadside?

Now to sum up the material on ascension robes that we have unearthed for the period just preceding October 22, 1844. There was the placard in the Bowery dry-goods store window offering "Muslin for Ascension Robes." There were the hearsay and "Weekly Gossip" column stories in the Philadelphia paper about Millerites preparing and donning robes to sit down in garrets. There was the story of the Millerites in a New York and in a Philadelphia church who allegedly rushed out in the darkness in a panic in their robes. And there were two anonymous broadsides, one picturing the Millerites ascending in robes, the other declaring that they had "prepared" robes. These items, some of them reproduced widely in the public press, are what we found for the weeks immediately preceding October 22. Perhaps there were others we missed. That is really immaterial, for the real test of the truth of the robes charge is to be found in what actually occurred on October 22. If the Millerites had indeed prepared robes, then the great day would disclose that fact. There should be no lack of witnesses to establish the truth or the falsity of the story. Indeed, there should be ten thousand, yes, many times ten thousand, eyewitnesses to testify to the facts. A company of white-robed people on a mountaintop ought easily to be seen by multitudes, and were there not many such companies? There should be no difficulty in finding the record in the newspapers, for all the principal cities and many towns had excellent newspaper coverage, and the files of no small number of these papers are preserved for our scrutiny today. There would not be the slightest tendency on the part of the newspapers to suppress such a story, for the press had a consistent record of going out of its way for years to print any and every kind of item on Millerism, even to publishing banal jokes about them. October 22 should have proved a field day for the reporters, a sort of high day, provided, of course, all the Millerites were out in the fields, or high on the hills, as the now current legend says they were.

However, the reader must surely already have his grave doubts as to how great a field day the reporters had, because in a preceding chapter newspaper testimony was presented which showed as conclusively as available sources can ever hope to show, that the Millerites on that great day were quite generally either in churches or in little companies in private homes, praying and waiting for the advent of the Lord.

Then, too, if the Millerites over the whole country actually did array themselves in ascension robes on that great day, it would most certainly indicate that some unified counsel and instruction had gone out from Millerite headquarters. The point will bear repeating here that it passes credulity to believe that people living in widely separated places would all spontaneously come out at one time in one kind of new garb, the like of which had never before been seen. But if Millerite headquarters did give such instruction for October 22, then the leaders reversed themselves completely on the position they had taken unitedly in their publications, of denouncing the idea of robes from the time the ascension robe story first started. Their publications contain no instructions on dress for October 22.

With these facts in mind the reader will have less difficulty in adjusting his mind to the report we are now to make as to what the newspapers said regarding the Millerites and ascension robes on October 22. We found not one news item that described any gathering of Millerites in ascension robes anywhere, or even alleged that someone was reported to have seen some Millerite somewhere, in some strange garment, on October 22.* Be it said to the credit of the newspapers, which were generally none too creditable in their news reporting in the 1840's, that they did not give space on October 22, or on the

---

* We did not accomplish the herculean task of reading every newspaper published in the United States in October, 1844, of which a file is now preserved. But the ninety-one newspapers we did examine, cover very fully the whole geographical area where Millerism was active. During this period of time the newspapers continued their former practices of reprinting items from other papers regarding Millerites. Thus long before we had examined all of these papers, we had read virtually all the news items that any of the papers wrote on the subject. This fact of reprinting suggests also that on the law of averages if we overlooked a Millerite item in one paper we would find it in our examination of some other paper.

days following, to the printing of fanciful rumors, hearsay, and gossip, concerning Millerites allegedly wearing ascension robes. The silence of the newspapers is the loudest testimony that can be heard in proof that the Millerites did not wear ascension robes on the great day. To think otherwise is to entertain the impossible idea that the newspapers would fail to feature the most spectacular and climactic act in the whole of Millerite history, which the wearing of ascension robes certainly would have been, and particularly if those robes had been fluttering from mountaintops or draped over the edges of gravestones.

Perhaps both the press and the public were so nonplused by the generally quiet and undramatic actions of the Millerites on that day—for sitting in church or in one's own home is hopelessly undramatic—that they could not immediately think up a good story on robes. Furthermore, such a tale would have seemed too implausible, when compared with the known facts as to how the Millerites generally deported themselves on that day. In view of the fact that ascension robe stories were in circulation just before October 22, it is doubly remarkable that not even a rumor regarding Millerites' wearing ascension robes on that day seems to have made its way into the columns of the newspapers on October 22 or the days immediately following.

We did find, however, in our reading of the newspapers, one reference to Millerites and ascension robes in connection with the great day, but the reporter does not say that the Millerites were wearing the robes. This story is unique, in that it is the only eyewitness story we have found from the pen of any reporter, actually describing what happened at a great Millerite meeting on October 22. The account is by a correspondent of the *Cincinnati Chronicle,* who attended the service held at the large Millerite tabernacle in that city on October 22. We have already quoted from this, in part, in a previous chapter. Here is what he wrote regarding robes:

"As the consummation of all terrestrial things was expected to have taken place last evening, and being desirous of seeing the effect of such belief upon its votaries at their last earthly meeting, I took the liberty, without putting on any *material* ascension robe, as did a vast multitude of others, of being present. The assemblage, indoors and out, probably numbered fifteen hundred persons. If rightly informed about the capacity of the house, about twelve hundred were inside. I observed no ascension robes on, and conclude that the rumor of a wagon load having been taken there yesterday, was only a slander. There was less excitement than I expected, and a great deal more cheerfulness manifest in the countenances of the believers than could have been supposed at the hour of so serious a crisis." [34]

There is no reason to believe that this great Millerite gathering in Cincinnati was other than typical of Millerite gatherings everywhere. Cincinnati was one of the main centers of Millerism in the west, and the Millerites in that city had received much of the personal ministry and labor of Millerite leaders. Thus the thinking and the actions of that large company may rightly be viewed as reflecting Millerism generally. The twelve hundred people in that tabernacle made up a number sufficiently large to include all varieties of temperament, idiosyncrasies, and shades of opinion. In other words, here was a cross-section of Millerism. Said the newspaper writer: "I observed no ascension robes on." It is evident from the context that he had expected to see the Millerites thus clothed. He mentioned the "rumor" of a wagon load of ascension robes having been taken to the tabernacle the preceding day, and concluded that this could have been "only a slander." *

And what happened to all the muslin for ascension robes allegedly offered for sale by that Bowery dry-goods store, whose single window card received probably the best publicity in the nation's press that any dry-goods store had ever received?

---

[34] *Cincinnati Chronicle,* quoted in *United States Saturday Post* (Philadelphia), Nov. 9, 1844.

* There is no file of the *Cincinnati Chronicle* to be found in any library today. We quote the correspondent's story as reproduced at length in the *United States Saturday Post,* of Philadelphia. We mention this fact because it was this newspaper that gave birth, on October 19, to the two ascension robe rumors most widely reprinted in the press on the eve of the great day. When all the shouting and the tumult had died away, the only ascension robe news story that this Philadelphia paper could actually publish was this Cincinnati reporter's eyewitness account of his not having seen ascension robes on anyone.

For some strange reason this reporter's story of the Cincinnati Millerite meeting had no large circulation. We found it reprinted only in the Philadelphia paper. But then, there was nothing sensational in the report, to make it a story worth reprinting—simply a description of a quiet assembly of worshipers listening to a sermon.

Apparently the reporter who first wrote up this story was correct in her surmise that it might have been "done for waggery."

As to the story of the Millerites in the two churches, one in New York and the other in Philadelphia, who allegedly rushed out in the darkness a week ahead of time in ascension robes, we can only conclude that this must be placed in a class with the ascension robe stories that appeared in the press in the early months of 1843. Even if the Millerites in Philadelphia, for example, were really wearing robes a week early, we would expect them to be none the less spectacularly clothed when the great day finally came. But the files of ten different Philadelphia newspapers fail to provide support for the idea that any of the Millerites in that city wore robes on October 22.

This silence of the Philadelphia papers is even more remarkable when it is remembered that Philadelphia was the scene of the one well-defined fanatical move on the part of any definite group of Millerites. We refer to the Doctor Gorgas incident mentioned in an earlier chapter. Here was a group of a hundred and fifty to two hundred Millerites who drove out of the city the day before to an encampment along the Darby Road. But even this little fanatical element, which acted contrary to the best counsel of leading Millerites by going on that trek, did not wear robes. They left on a Monday morning. Everyone could see them. The newspapers of Philadelphia all gave the story. But, we repeat, there was no reference to ascension robes in any of the stories.

The virtually complete absence of robe stories in the religious press in the days immediately following October 22 is still more remarkable. The religious press had been even more free to give currency to defamatory stories than the secular press. It is a sorry fact that the record of religious disputation through the centuries has frequently been written in blood and brimstone. In a rather extensive reading of religious publications of the time we found only one that contained a story about Millerites wearing robes on the great day. This was a report that appeared in a leading weekly. The story was dated

"Philadelphia, October 26, 1844," being a report of the Philadelphia correspondent of that paper.

This story purports to describe the activity of the Millerites as a body, in connection with their preparation for October 22, but proves to be simply a description of the Gorgas incident, which drew off only a small fraction of the Philadelphia Millerites. This major blunder in reporting suggests in itself that the correspondent did not make very close contact with the Millerites or with the facts involved. He almost borrowed the language of some of the newspapers which a few days earlier had told of the Philadelphia encampment and of the children, "forced outside into the cold and rain." Then follows the statement found in *no* newspaper report: "Some of them [at the encampment] had prepared ascension robes, and stood ready for their departure. But three o'clock came, and brought nothing but cold and rain." [35]

Now we could ask: Did this correspondent of the *New York Evangelist* see something that the reporters for ten Philadelphia newspapers failed to see? Or did he just add this ascension robe sentence to give a little color and variation to his story? Of course, we might also ask, did this correspondent actually hire a horse and buggy to drive four miles out along the country road in "the cold and rain" on Monday afternoon to *see* the Millerites who had "prepared ascension robes, and stood ready for their departure"? If he had really gone out and done a bona fide reporting job, he would have quickly discovered that he was dealing, not with the Millerite movement of Philadelphia, but with an insignificant fraction who could not conceivably be viewed as representing the movement. In that event honesty would have required him to write quite a different story about the Millerites of Philadelphia. But if he did not go out, how could he really know the manner in which those Millerites "stood ready for their departure"? We would apologize to the reader for such a detailed scrutiny of evidence, were it not for the fact that today

---

[35] *New York Evangelist,* Oct. 31, 1844.

the ascension robe legend is so firmly embedded in men's minds that almost heroic steps are needed to destroy it.

In a religious paper in November, 1844, a brief item regarding the Millerites included this sentence:

"Repentance, faith, and holiness constitute the best ascension robes, although they are not so easily put on as the white garments which many ignorant people were led to believe formed a sufficient preparation to meet the Lord at His coming." [36]

This belongs in the category of vague statements; it does not deal with any specific incident, place, or time. In fact, it says nothing specific except this, that people "were led to believe" that ascension robes "formed a sufficient preparation to meet the Lord at His coming." Certainly, the only ones who would lead people thus to believe would be the Millerite preachers. When we turn to their writings, we find them denouncing ascension robes. Need we pursue further such groundless, irresponsible statements?

We turn, now, from an examination of the secular and the religious press to that of the Millerite papers to see what they themselves might have to say concerning ascension robes in the days immediately following October 22. There are good reasons why we should expect them to make at least *some* reference to robes, even though their most prominent opponents, the newspapers, had given them no provocation. Undoubtedly the word-of-mouth rumors that were abroad regarding robes must have come to their ears. Then, too, the cartoon broadsides showing Millerites in ascension robes could not have failed to stir up discussion in the market place and to cause the public to believe there might be some truth to the story. Then, there were burlesques on the Millerites in connection with the great day that gave further plausibility to the idea that the Millerites were dressed in white robes. Here is an account in a Millerite paper of what happened in Connecticut:

"In one place, the prophecies in Revelation were mimicked in a daringly blasphemous manner. A large procession paraded the streets in the night.

---

[36] *The Presbyterian,* Nov. 16, 1844.

One went before on a red horse, dressed in a grotesque manner, with a speaking trumpet proclaiming, 'Behold He cometh.' He was followed by one on a white horse, in a white robe, to represent Christ, and a large number on white horses rode behind him, dressed in white, with various instruments, making all manner of discordant sounds. Their proceedings were so outrageous that the civil authorities interfered to stop them." [37]

There are a few references to ascension robes in the Millerite papers in the weeks immediately following October 22. But none of these references discuss any newspaper item on the subject. Did the Millerites suddenly lose their militant fighting ability and change from their long-established practice of exposing false newspaper stories in their journals? We cannot thus conclude, because a reading of the Millerite papers in 1845 and onward shows the leaders as militant as ever, and actively challenging any false newspaper story. Therefore, the only conclusion to reach is that the newspapers carried no robe stories in connection with October 22 for the Millerites to refute. That squares with what we found, or rather failed to find, from a survey of the newspapers. The reader will recall the reference made in an earlier chapter to Himes' defense of the movement in general and himself in particular, that was published on the front page of the *Boston Post,* on November 2, 1844. We have already quoted from this in connection with an examination of the charge that Millerite leaders were making money out of the movement, and also in connection with the charge that Millerism was responsible for insanity and suicide. A paragraph devoted to refuting this last charge closes with this sentence: "Every other case of suicide and death that we have been able to trace ... [is] equally false,—and also every story about ascension robes, etc." [38]

In our earlier discussion of this Himes defense, we called attention to the fact that though many newspapers referred to his defense, we found none that attempted to refute it, and some even admitted that he had made out a very excellent case. Now Himes would have lacked the very shrewdness with which

---
[37] *The Midnight Cry,* Nov. 14, 1844, p. 157.
[38] *Boston Post,* Nov. 2, 1844.

his enemies credited him, if he had made this sweeping front-page denial of all ascension robe stories, without being very sure of what he was saying. Nor is it reasonable to believe that the daily press, which so widely referred to his defense, would have permitted this ascension robe denial to go unchallenged if they had knowledge of any bona fide cases of ascension robes' being worn by Millerites. Himes also published this defense in the two leading Millerite papers, so that it received a maximum of circulation.[39]

The Advent Herald of November 20 contains an article on the front page that examines a long array of false stories, and makes a passing allusion to the "slander about 'ascension robes.'"[40]

In *The Advent Herald* of December 4 is an editorial entitled "Credulous," which discusses the "readiness with which the press will believe and publish anything which happens to be put in circulation." We quote:

"No matter how absurd or ridiculous it may be, if it only reflects on the character of others, it is at once reported as true. Nor are the religious papers free from this; for they seem to be the most easily gulled of any.

"We have been led to these remarks from the perusal of a pretended 'Curse of the Pope,' which we found in the *N. E. Puritan, N. H. Baptist Register,* and other grave and dignified prints. It was copied in them from the *Olive Branch,* and is said to be a papal bull against one William Hogan."[41]

After quoting a portion of the curse the Millerite editor concluded:

"But, will it be believed, the entire pretended curse is word for word from the 'Life of Tristram Shandy,' a fictitious work written many years since by the celebrated Rev. Lawrence Sterne, and purports to be a malediction which one Doctor Slop pronounced against one Obadiah for accidentally furiously riding against the doctor at an angle in the road, and thus upsetting both him and his horse.

---

[39] *The Advent Herald,* Nov. 6, 1844, p. 101; *The Midnight Cry,* Nov. 7, 1844, p. 150.
[40] *The Advent Herald,* Nov. 20, 1844, p. 113.
[41] *Ibid.,* Dec. 4, 1844, p. 136.

DID MILLERITES WEAR ASCENSION ROBES? 397

"If such papers are so easily hoaxed in reference to a matter so apparent as this, we need not wonder that the press should everywhere so readily receive, believe, and publish so many silly stories respecting the freezing of advent babies, *ascension robes,* etc., etc. The credulity of the age is one of the striking characteristics of this day. Men will believe anything but the Word of God: this is too much for them to believe; and although they are thus easily gulled themselves, yet they are ready to decry as credulous 'Millerite' any who dare believe those scriptures which speak of the signs of Christ's immediate appearing, and His reign on earth." [42]

After reading this who will say that the Millerite leaders had lost any of their keenness in debate or any of their skill at finding a weak place in the armor of their accusers. This last quotation may be viewed as a general rejoinder to all the "silly stories," of which the ascension robe story was one, that appeared, particularly in the religious press, throughout the history of the movement.

On December 28 and 29, 1844, an advent conference, was held at Low Hampton, Miller's home. During that conference an "Address to Advent Believers," "prepared by Brother Miller, at the request of the brethren, was presented by a committee, and unanimously adopted by the conference." In this formal address Miller declared that the Adventists could not have fellowship with those who made light of Bible doctrines, and added:

"We cannot sit under preaching where the Bible is discarded from the pulpit, except as a textbook, and the plainest passages are mysticized and explained away, . . . and the promise of being caught up in the air ridiculed by the oft-repeated slang of ascension robes. These things we cannot fellowship, we will not hear them repeated." [43]

To understand this quotation we need to know how the word "slang" was often used in the early nineteenth century. At that time it was employed as a synonym for "abuse," "humbug," or "nonsense." [44] Miller, therefore, was speaking of the ascension robe story as a humbug or nonsense or abuse, a caricature of

---
[42] *Ibid.*
[43] *Ibid.,* Jan. 15, 1845, p. 183.
[44] See *A New English Dictionary on Historical Principles,* generally known as the Oxford Dictionary, under the word "slang."

the spiritual teaching that at the second advent the righteous are caught up in the clouds to meet the Lord in the air. This formal denunciation of the ascension robe story was part of the address that was unanimously voted by the advent leaders meeting at Low Hampton from different parts of the country. It would go counter to everything we know of William Miller and his associates, and of the whole Millerite movement, to believe that they would thus formally denounce the ascension robe story, sending out the denunciation to the advent believers everywhere, as a part of their "Address to Advent Believers," if the Millerites had actually worn ascension robes on October 22. It should also be remembered that this conference included Millerite spokesmen from different geographical areas who could rightly be expected to know how the believers had deported themselves in different places. The Millerites did not fear to do something unusual if they thought it right. Nor did they hesitate to admit blunders or even fanaticism in their midst. These facts give added significance to this sweeping denial of the robe story.

We might properly conclude the matter at this point. The testimony of the original sources is clear and unmistakable, and the verdict must be that the Millerites did not wear ascension robes. But the story has made such a unique place for itself in the folklore of America and is so firmly embedded even in reputable reference works that we wish to trace in the following chapters some of the principal references to this story through the century that spans the years between the Millerites and us.

CHAPTER 26

Tracing the Robe Story Through the Years

IN AN EARLIER CHAPTER we described one of the prominent Millerites, Ezekiel Hale, Jr., and the suit he instituted in 1845 to recover his property from his son, to whom he had willed it in anticipation of the Lord's coming. We stated that the legal tome dealing with the suit described quite minutely all the changing moods and attitudes and any unusual acts of this Millerite. If it could be proved that a sound businessman had become so erratic and unbalanced as to be quite abnormal, that would be an excellent argument against the validity of his legal transaction in deeding his property to his son. Now Hale was a leader of the Millerite group in Haverhill, Massachusetts. If, on October 22, he had clothed himself in a kind of glorified, oversized white nightgown—which is the nearest we can come to describing this elusive apparel—and had walked through the streets of Haverhill and up to a hilltop in his billowing robes, what further evidence of irresponsibility would the courts have needed! Why would the lawyers spend time securing depositions as they did, to attempt to show that Hale was not quite as thoughtful of his family as in former time—a state into which too many men, legally sound in mind, fall as their married life lengthens—if it were possible to prove that Hale did so fantastic a thing as to wear an ascension robe on October 22? But does this lengthy legal report of the case mention any such colorful incident as this? It does not. Yet the nearly fourscore persons making the depositions were those who best knew Hale, and who lived in that immediate vicinity. They were testifying within five years of the time the Millerites expected the Lord to come, and were mentioning even the most trivial details of his life.

Now, why do we mention this case, since it throws no new light on the question, and the absence of any mention of robes is simply what we would expect in view of the evidence we have examined thus far in the chapter? The reason is this: Long years after 1844, and long after Ezekiel Hale, Jr., had been gathered to his fathers, a grandnephew, Henry Hale Gilman, made an address to a gathering in Haverhill, in which he reminisced on the legal controversy between Ezekiel Hale, Jr., and his son in the 1840's. In that address he mentioned casually that on the great day of expectation Ezekiel Hale, Jr., in his white robe, headed a similarly robed company of Millerites down the streets of Haverhill and up to an eminence on a near-by hill. Gilman gave as the authority for this story his mother, who was a young girl at the time.*

Is Gilman's knowledge of the long ago, as passed on to him through his mother, to be accepted at face value, even though it runs counter to the best evidence available in the original sources? If so, then we ought to accept *in toto* the ascension robe story regarding all the Millerites. Gilman is only one of a host of people in the twentieth century who declare, on the strength of a story told them by someone of a former generation, that either the Millerites in general or some Millerite in particular wore an ascension robe. That is why we have the generally believed story of ascension robes today. We submit that the silence of the legal record of the suit in equity on this matter of robes speaks far more loudly than the voice of the grandnephew of Ezekiel Hale testifying long years after the event. The same is true of the silence of the Haverhill newspapers of October, 1844, and of all the newspapers for that matter.

The question at issue here is the worth of testimony that is being offered. According to one of the most firmly established rules for the admissibility of evidence that has governed courts

---

* Unfortunately, the typewritten copy of Gilman's address bears no date, but internal evidence places it clearly in the twentieth century, and very probably within the last twenty years. In other words, he was giving a reminiscence on an event three quarters of a century in the past. (See Henry Hale Gilman, *The Mill and the Millerites*, p. 11.)

The upper halves of two anonymous, anti-Millerite broadsides circulated in October, 1844. Note the ascension robes in the cartoon. (See pages 241, 387.)

A correspondent of the Cincinnati Chronicle gives the following account of the last night, in that city:

"As the consummation of all terrestrial things was expected to have taken place last evening, and being desirous of seeing the effect of such belief upon its votaries at their last earthly meeting, I took the liberty, without putting on any *material* ascension robe, as did a vast multitude of others, of being present. The assemblage, indoors and out, probably numbered fifteen hundred persons. If rightly informed about the capacity of the house, about twelve hundred were inside. I observed no ascension robes on, and conclude that the rumor of a wagon load having been taken there yesterday, was only a slander. There was less excitement than I expected, and a great deal more cheerfulness manifest in the countenances of the believers than could have been supposed at the hour of so serious a crisis; why, I cannot, of course, undertake to say; perhaps it was owing to the firmness of their faith, but I could not help but think and feel (the states of those around us are often perceptible from their sphere, a sort of spiritual atmosphere, so to speak, that surrounds them,) that they were experiencing an inward joy from the hope and expectation that they were to be permitted to stay with us sinners a little longer.

"Considering the crowd, the meeting was very orderly. Two or three attempts were made by a set of rowdies out door to raise a breeze by noise and clamor, but the assertion of the preacher, that a strong police was present, calmed the multitude, and he was enabled to proceed with what he at the close said was, in his opinion, his last warning to a sinful world. He finished by shaking his coat tails in token of clearing his skirts of the blood of those he had thus warned to prepare for the great event, by him, hourly expected. Before nine o'clock the benediction was pronounced, and the people advised to go quietly home, and await the awful coming, which not unlikely might transpire at the hour of midnight, while most of us were wrapped in sleep. Notwithstanding all this, daylight, yea, a most splendid day of sunshine, is again upon us

A newspaper reporter's story of the Millerite meeting, October 22, 1844, in Cincinnati. (See pages 244, 390.)

MILLERISM AND INSANITY.—We lately published a statement that a Mr. Shortridge, of New Hampshire, had run mad with Millerism, and attempted to ascend to Heaven from an apple-tree, but found the attraction of gravitation too strong for his celestial aspirations, and came to the ground with such momentum as to cause his death. We have just seen two letters of late date from different sources in Portsmouth, N. H., stating that letters had been received there from this same Mr. Shortridge, making no mention of his 'ground and lofty tumbling' or death-circumstances so remarkable that they could hardly have escaped his notice had they actually occurred. We have heard from another source that this same Mr. S. was crazy ten years ago. So in the case of the woman who poisoned her children and attempted to commit suicide some weeks since—*her* insanity was attributed to Millerism, but entirely without reason. Doubtless the like has been the case in many other instances. Those who know any thing of Insanity are aware that it very commonly takes its hue from the most exciting topic of the hour, so that hundreds of persons have been reported as victims of '*religious* mania,' when in fact their insanity was caused by functional disorders, often having its seat in the digestive organs and only by sympathy affecting the brain. Of those who are currently reported as rendered insane by 'Revivals' or "Millerism,' a great portion would be found, on due inquiry, to have been constitutionally disposed to insanity, and often to have inherited that malady. In other cases, physical derangement consequent on personal excesses, such as intemperance, gluttony, and other forms of sensuality, was the true cause.—We cannot exclude from our columns accounts of remarkable casualties, but our readers will know how to make due allowance for the causes to which they are often mistakenly attributed.

An editorial from the *New York Daily Tribune*, March 24, 1843. The Shortridge case here discussed is the basis of the stories of tree-climbing, robed Millerites. The suicide and murder incident is unquestionably that of Mrs. Jonathan Leverich, whose dark deed was alleged by some to be due to Millerism-induced insanity. (See pages 378, 342-344.)

A Bro. Williamson, in Medford, has been reported as having committed suicide, and left his family destitute :—He informs us that ten ship carpenters board at his house, who would not, if the family were very destitute. Bro. Riker, of New York city, on whose body the Coroner went *twice* to sit, is still very happy in looking for the Lord. Bro. Wyatt, of Dover, who has been reported to have poisoned himself to death, is also still well. Every other case of suicide and death that we have been able to trace—not excepting the two children which froze to death one night near Philadelphia,—are equally false,—and also every story about ascension robes, etc.

A small section of the article by Joshua V. Himes in defense of the Millerite movement that appeared on the front page of the *Boston Post* November 2, 1844. Note the unqualified, sweeping denial of all stories "about ascension robes." (See pages 255-258, 339, 395, 396.)

through the long years, a man's testimony is admissible only if he is testifying of those things which he personally knows. Gilman did not claim to have seen Ezekiel Hale going down the street in an ascension robe. Obviously he could not, for he had not yet been born. He was simply testifying to what someone else was said to have seen, and that makes a world of difference. All experience teaches us, as it long ago taught the courts, that there is a vast difference between the kind of testimony a man can offer regarding what he saw himself and that which he says someone else saw. Because that difference is so great and so frequently makes all the difference between valid and worthless testimony, the courts simply do not accept secondhand testimony. Their refusal to accept it, and our refusal likewise, does not necessarily imply that the person offering the testimony is knowingly distorting the truth or seeking to foist an untruth upon the world, but simply that secondhand testimony, like anything else secondhand, is likely to be contaminated. And the germs of distortion, inaccuracy, and untruth that contaminate the testimony, are, like most other dangerous germs, not easily detected. Certainly no one in search of truth should have any difficulty in deciding which to accept—secondhand testimony or firsthand evidence such as is set forth in the preceding chapter.

But what if someone long years after the Millerite movement should declare that he personally had a memory of the Millerites wearing robes? Should his testimony therefore be immediately accepted, and all the contrary evidence we have been considering be thrown out? Might not memory play tricks with a man after the passage of many years, and as he grows into old age? The courts take account of the fact that a long passage of time has a bearing on the credibility of testimony. Here is what a legal authority says on this point:

"The fact that a long period of time has elapsed between the occurrences as to which a witness testifies and the giving of his testimony is proper to be considered as bearing on credibility." [1]

---

[1] *Corpus Juris*, Vol. 70, p. 769.

The reasonableness of this principle is evident. Let us say that you had in court a suit to quiet title on a piece of property, and had produced all the documents of fifty years ago that described the transfer now being considered by the court. Would you think that the judge or the jury ought to discount all that written evidence simply because some person full of years and memories testified that his memory of the matter went contrary to the documents before the courts? No, you say, the documentary evidence should stand, and the personal memories of the long ago should be discounted. How doubly unreasonable is the idea of accepting a man's testimony against the written documents, when he is testifying not out of his personal memory but simply out of his memory of what others had told him they had seen or heard or read!

For these and other equally valid reasons we give little or no weight to all the stories of later years, drawn from the memories —we almost said imagination—of people, regarding ascension robes. But for the sheer delight of tracing the history of a "good" story we shall continue our journey through the nineteenth century.

After the end of the Millerite movement the ascension robe story first began to be incorporated definitely in American literature in the field of fiction. What better soil in which to nurture this story that is to grow large enough, finally, to find a place in the minds of virtually all men! The first reference we have found to the robe story in fiction is in Longfellow's "Kavanagh," written in 1849. His references are few and casual, merely embodying the rumor that had been afloat since 1843. Fiction writers do not need to offer proof for their statements. As the years passed by, other novels wove in the story in the same casual fashion. The robe story was not the first nor will it be the last historical error that novels have fixed in the minds of men.

In 1853 Sylvester Bliss, who had been a prominent Millerite, wrote his *Memoirs of William Miller*. In that biography, written and circulated at a time when the memories of all his readers regarding events of 1844 would be still very good, Bliss declared:

"All reports respecting the preparation of ascension robes, etc., and which are still by many believed, were demonstrated over and over again to be false and scandalous. In the investigation of the truth of such, no labor and expense were spared; and it became morally certain that *no instance of the kind anywhere occurred.*" [2]

In the general church paper of the Seventh-day Adventists—a movement that began in late 1844—whose first leaders were men that had preached in the Millerite movement, are found repeated references to ascension robes. This church paper, founded in 1850, contains in some of its earliest issues denials of the ascension robe story.[3]

In that church paper in 1868 was published an article by James White, who had been a preacher in the Millerite movement and was then one of the most prominent in the Seventh-day Adventist denomination. He told of how he and his fellow ministers had been confronted with the robe story on every side. Being a man of action he had finally decided to take a more vigorous step than simply denying the charge. He therefore ended his article thus:

"FIFTY DOLLARS REWARD is offered to any person who will present unquestionable proofs of the truthfulness of these statements that believers in the second advent of Christ, on the day of expectation, did put on ascension robes. Those who can produce such proofs, are requested to forward them immediately to the writer, at Greenville, Montcalm Co., Mich. and receive $50.00 by the return of the mail." [4]

To James White in 1868, fifty dollars was probably worth as much as several hundred dollars would be to us today. But he was willing to publish his offer for all men to read. True, his church paper did not have a large circulation in 1868, but it did have religious critics who read its pages. Here was a wonderful opportunity to make a little easy money.

---

[2] Sylvester Bliss, *Memoirs of William Miller*, p. 276.
[3] See *Advent Review and Sabbath Herald*, Aug. 19, 1851, p. 11, and May 27, 1852, p. 16
[4] *Advent Review and Sabbath Herald*, April 14, 1868, p. 281.

Did anyone accept the offer to provide proof? The answer is best given in the words of a writer in the same journal thirteen years later. In an article entitled "William Miller and the Ascension-Robe Scandal," W. H. Littlejohn quoted from James White's 1868 article the paragraph that set forth the fifty-dollar offer, and added this comment:

> "Up to the present time, but one man has ever endeavored to make out a case entitling him to the reward. The facts proved that his inordinate inquisitiveness had made him the victim of a practical joke, and that the ascension robes in question were nothing more, and nothing less, than certain night-dresses, similar in material and make-up to those found in every lady's wardrobe." [5]

In this same church paper there appeared, early in 1870, an extended editorial on ascension robes, in which all the arguments against the truthfulness of the story are cogently set forth. The closing paragraph refers to specific instances where rewards of a hundred dollars were offered in an endeavor to track down ascension robe stories in certain areas, but all to no effect.[6]

In June of that year there was a further discussion of ascension robes in this same church paper and another offer of a hundred-dollar reward by another person in another area who was seeking to run down an ascension robe story. There was also an exchange of letters from persons whose names had been offered in support of the ascension robe story by a minister of another denomination. The upshot of the whole exchange of letters was that the woman whose name had been submitted as a witness in behalf of the story wrote that she had been misunderstood and that she had no knowledge of ascension robes' ever having been worn by any Adventists.

This is typical of the discussions of ascension robes that appear in the Seventh-day Adventist church paper through the years. Every opportunity was given for critics to present valid evidence. No pains were spared by Seventh-day Adventist

---

[5] *Ibid.*, Oct. 11, 1881, p. 227.
[6] *Ibid.*, Feb. 15, 1870, p. 67.

writers and speakers in running down clues. But even with the aid of rewards, no robe ever materialized.

It was in the same year, 1870, that a very illuminating discussion of ascension robes took place in the *Independent*. This was one of the most important and most widely circulated journals at that time.* In an issue in February, 1870, is found a statement by a book reviewer about persons having "prepared their ascension robes."[7] The statement was merely incidental in a book review of a work on the coming of Christ. But two weeks later a Mr. J. T. Dixon, of Rocky Brook, Rhode Island, wrote to the editor, taking issue with the statement, and inquiring:

"Will you be so kind as to announce in the *Independent* that the sum of $100.00 will be paid if proof positive can be produced that an ascension robe was ever donned by any of the Second Adventists at any time. I, like others, have been misled by that slander."[8]

To which the editor appended this comment:

"Mr. Dixon will observe that the writer of the [book] notice in the *Independent* did not say that ascension robes had been donned; but only that they had been prepared, ready to be donned. But we suspect that even this cannot be proved. The writer probably erred in assuming the truth of idle stories set afloat in a time of excitement to satirize Second Adventists."[9]

Here was an offer being made through the columns of a most reputable, widely circulated journal. Surely there ought to have been a thousand persons ready to respond by the next mail. The first response appeared in the issue of March 17. The evidence that the letter writer presented was in the form of an affidavit from a neighbor, a Mr. C. C. Bellows. In his affidavit Mr. Bellows simply offered indirect testimony that robes had been worn—he had seen women sewing on white gowns but had not seen anyone gowned. †

---

[7] *Independent* (New York), February 3, 1870.
[8] *Ibid.*, Feb. 17, 1870.
[9] *Ibid.*

* The American Newspaper Rate-Book of 1870 lists the *Independent* as having a "circulation about 68,000." An advertisement of the *Independent* in that Rate-Book says in part, "The widest circulation of any weekly religious newspaper in the world."

† The affidavit by Mr. Bellows reads thus: "On the 23d October, 1844, while boarding

But were there not hundreds, yes, thousands, who wrote to the *Independent,* telling of actually *seeing* a Millerite in an ascension robe? That was what Mr. Dixon was specifically asking for, even as others have asked all through the years. A search of the pages of the *Independent* for the issues of thirteen weeks failed to produce another response! The editor himself, who doubtless had as clear a memory of events in 1844 as any of his subscribers, did not attempt to win the $100. He described the rumors of robes' being worn by Millerites as "idle stories." It is too bad that those who today so confidently write in encyclopedias that robes were worn, did not live back in 1870. They could have had an opportunity to make a little easy money.*

In 1884 the ascension robe story had successfully made the journey from the realm of rumor to the field of fact, at least so far as a history of Philadelphia is concerned. In that year there was published the rather impressive three-volume work entitled *History of Philadelphia,* to which we referred in Chapter 22. We quoted in part what it said regarding the Philadelphia encampment of the Millerites on the Darby Road. We have already called attention to some of its evident historical inaccuracies. After speaking of the little group who went out to the

---

in Providence, R. I., I saw two ladies, fellow boarders—the name of one I well remember—who firmly believed they were to ascend to heaven that night, and appeared very anxious that I, with four or five other boarders, should go with them to the general meeting of the Millerites and place of ascension. I had frequently seen these ladies sewing on fine white goods for several days. They said to me they were for ascension robes. They were made longer than ordinary dresses of that day. My engagements did not permit me to accompany them to the meeting; but those who went, one of them my own brother, since dead, told me there were over thirty in the company of about two hundred that were ready *with their ascension robes* on, and that the excitement was very great."

Mr. Dixon replied in the issue of March 24 that he considered the evidence unsatisfactory. The editor added the note, "Mr. Dixon fortifies his position by an argument for which we cannot find room."

We venture that Mr. Dixon's reasons for rejecting the Bellows statement would include the following: Bellows was not present at the meeting and hence did not offer firsthand testimony. Few men are competent to describe accurately women's clothes, particularly when they are in process of being made. Again, Mr. Bellows was describing the conversation of members of a boarding house group. After twenty-five years could he really be sure whether one of these two ladies made the remark about ascension robes, or whether one of "the four or five other boarders" jokingly made it?

At this late date the only check that can be made on this Bellows affidavit, if indeed it is entitled to any checking, is the silence of the Providence, Rhode Island, newspapers regarding robed Millerites on the great October day in 1844.

* See Appendix H for a discussion of the affidavit of a Jacob Wheeler who declared that he had seen two people in ascension robes.

encampment, and of the poor children running around in the cold rain, the historians add immediately: "The parents clad in thin white 'ascension robes,' were almost exhausted for want of food." [10]

And where did these authors find the ascension robes with which to clothe these unfortunate people? Certainly they did not find them in the files of the newspapers of that day. And to think that these authors, forty years later, should have been able to see what ten newspapers failed to see, or what even the imaginative eye of rumor was unable to provide for the public press on October 22, 1844. These historians inform us that not only were robes worn, but also they were "thin." The weight of the cloth is needed to give weight to their statement that the weather was cold, with its implication that the Millerites were suffering from it. We have already shown that these authors created a synthetic hurricane and synthetic starvation in describing the Millerites at the encampment. We must now credit them with creating synthetic ascension robes.

In 1886 the *Century Magazine* carried an article by Jane Marsh Parker, the daughter of Joseph Marsh, a Millerite preacher. During 1844 he was located in Rochester, New York, and there published the Millerite paper, *The Voice of Truth*. His daughter was about eight years old in October, 1844. She later became something of a literary woman, writing at least one novel and a number of articles. Though naturally sympathetic toward her father, she never considered herself a Millerite.* Wrote Mrs. Parker:

"Now, if the Millerites had ascension robes, how is it I never saw one? I well remember hearing them talked about. My ascension robe was

---

[10] Thomas Scharf and Thompson Westcott, *History of Philadelphia*, Vol. 2, p. 1448.

* This *Century Magazine* article was written forty-two years after the Millerite movement; hence the author of it is subject to all the frailties of memory that are likely to develop in anyone after so long a period of time. But her writing has this advantage: It is the personal reminiscence of a child who actually lived in a Millerite home. We quote her statement on ascension robes, not as proof against the reality of robes—for we are proceeding on the principle that that point was fully established by the firsthand source material in the year 1844 itself—but simply to provide the reader with a running story of the discussion that has been carried on through the years.

something I was quite used to hearing inquired after. Father Miller took great pains to find one, but never succeeded. But the world is never going to give up its belief that the Millerites had long white garments in which they clothed themselves preparatory for 'going up.' The ascension robe has a place in history in spite of every effort to prove it a myth." [11]

In 1887 there appeared in the March and April issues of a widely circulated woman's magazine a piece of fiction entitled "The Last Day." This was a story of a widow and a bachelor, both of them supposed to be Millerites. Romance and ascension robes are rather prominent in the story. In the April installment the artist actually pictured two of a Millerite group in long, flowing ascension robes. The artist, of course, was simply seeking to illustrate the story, and the story did not trouble to provide any proof for the ascension robes. That is one of the advantages of writing fiction. You are not expected to be methodically accurate. The story is written in dialect. At one point in the story two characters are discussing the strange phenomenon whereby an unfounded rumor finally is accepted as truth. They are not discussing the subject of ascension robes, but what one of these characters says to the other one concerning the strange phenomenon in connection with rumor, is worth quoting here:

"Curius, hain't it? How folks will get to tellin' things and tellin' 'em, and finelly tell 'em so much, that they will get to believin' of 'em themselves." [12]

"Curius, hain't it?" No more appropriate comment could be made on the ascension robe myth!

In 1891 Jane Marsh Parker wrote another article on Millerism, in which she again made reference to ascension robes. We share with the reader this delicious line: "The ascension robe which my father was charged with having proved to be his long night-shirt, and which had been seen on our clothes-line." [13]

---

[11] Jane Marsh Parker, "A Little Millerite," *Century Magazine*, December, 1886, p. 316.
[12] Josiah Allen's Wife, "The Last Day," *Ladies' Home Journal and Practical Housekeeper*, March, 1887, p. 1.
[13] Jane Marsh Parker, "A Spiritual Cyclone: The Millerite Delusion," *Magazine of Christian Literature* (September), 1891, p. 325.

In the September, 1894, issue of *Harper's Magazine* appeared a short story entitled "A New England Prophet," which wove ascension robes into the narrative of the doings of a group of Millerites. This prompted a response from Jane Marsh Parker in the form of an article in *The Outlook,* entitled "Did the Millerites Have Ascension Robes?"[14] The article presents nothing essentially new, but is significant for the reason that it prompted a number of letters to the editor. *The Outlook* was a very prominent weekly, whose editor at that time was Lyman Abbott. What do these letters to the editor reveal? Did a number of people write to state that they had seen Millerites in ascension robes? True, 1894 was fifty years after the Millerite movement had really ended, but then the older generation ought to be able to provide a good many letters reviving memories of the long ago.

The Outlook of October 27, 1894, contained a letter from a man who declared he had seen Millerites in robes at a large gathering, and that to be thus dressed "was the instruction given by the leaders." Indeed! He evidently had never read a Millerite publication. And who was this man? We do not know. He signed himself simply "1844." The editor invited him to identify himself, but he did not respond. The editor said he wished "to substantiate the evidence one way or the other." Perhaps that is what caused the writer to remain anonymous!

The issue of November 3, 1894, contains letters from three persons, but they provide no satisfactory evidence. The first of the three said he had not seen any robes, but that his wife had seen robes owned by a Millerite family. The second said that his father was a Millerite and "did not prepare ascension robes." But this letter writer said that he believed such robes were worn, because the "matter was common talk and generally accepted as a fact." The third was "An Old Millerite," who ridiculed the idea of robes.

---

[14] See Mary E. Wilkins, "A New England Prophet," *Harper's Magazine,* September, 1894, p. 601; Jane Marsh Parker, "Did the Millerites Have Ascension Robes?" *The Outlook,* Oct. 13, 1894, p. 582.

In the issue of November 24, 1894, appeared two more letters, which closed the discussion in *The Outlook*. One of these two was a long letter from Joshua V. Himes, who at that time was rector of St. Andrew's Episcopal Church, Elk Point, South Dakota, as he indicated at the close of his letter. The letter is dated October 29, 1894. He told of a long and intimate acquaintance with the whole Millerite movement, and on the strength of that he declared:

"I *know* the whole story of ascension robes to be a concoction of the enemies of the Adventists, begotten of religious prejudices, and that there is not a scintilla of truth in it. No wonder the writer in *The Outlook* of October 27 [anonymous Mr. "1844"] did not give his name and address. The statement that 'to be prepared, dressed in their ascension robes, was the instruction given by their leaders to the rank and file of the Millerites,' is almost too silly to be noticed." [15]

Himes admitted that "there were some excesses, such as always attend great religious upheavals, but they were not committed by the 'instruction of their leaders,' and the putting on of ascension robes was not one of these excesses." [16] He then went on immediately to state:

"When these stories first started, and while I was publishing in the interests of the adventist cause, I kept a standing offer, in the paper of which I was editor, of a large reward for one well authenticated case where an ascension robe was worn by those looking for the Lord's return. No such proof has ever been forthcoming. It was always rumor, and nothing more. ... I have refuted the story hundreds of times, in both the *'Advent Herald'* in Boston, Mass., and in the *'Midnight Cry'* in New York, which had a circulation of tens of thousands of copies; and no accusers ever made an attempt to defend themselves, although I held my columns open to them to do so. And now, at the age of ninety years, with a full personal experience of those times, before God, who is my judge, and before whose tribunal I must soon appear, I declare again that the ascension-robe story is a tissue of falsehoods from beginning to end, and I am glad of the opportunity to deny it once more before I die.

"The preparation urged upon the 'rank and file' of those looking for the coming of the Lord was a preparation of heart and life by a confession of

---

[15] *The Outlook*, Nov. 24, 1894, p. 875.
[16] *Ibid.*

Christ, a forsaking of their sins and living a godly life; and the only robes they were exhorted to put on were the robes of righteousness, obtained by faith in Jesus Christ—garments made white in the blood of the Lamb. Nothing of an outward appearance was ever thought of or mentioned." [17]

This forthright testimony of Himes, who had intimate knowledge of all that happened in the Millerite movement, is not wholly accurate. No matter how intimately a man may be related to events and incidents, he is still subject to the frailties of memory. Fifty years had passed by; Himes was a very old man, and his memory played a trick on him when he declared that he kept a standing offer in the paper of which he was an editor of a large reward for one well-authenticated case of an ascension robe having been worn by a Millerite. No "standing offer" is found in the 1843-44 files of the two great Millerite papers, one published in Boston and the other in New York, under the immediate direction of Himes. However, it is easy to see how he made this error in his statement. The numerous quotations we have given from the Millerite papers in refutation of ascension robes, show how militantly the story was challenged. In one of the quotations is found this reference to a reward: "Large rewards have been offered for the sight of an ascension robe, but none have been produced, for none existed." [18]

It is evident, therefore, that rewards actually were offered in some form or other, for the sight of an ascension robe. Hence Himes was not very far from the truth. It is probable that the offers were made from the platform.

When he declared that he had "refuted the story hundreds of times" in the Millerite papers, he was indulging in a little hyperbole, which is perhaps pardonable. In the two principal Millerite papers, in the years 1843 and 1844, and into the first months of 1845, we have found twenty-nine references to ascension robes, all of them exposures of the story.* If any

---

[17] *Ibid.*
[18] *The Midnight Cry,* Jan. 4, 1844, p. 189.

* Probably in some other of the Millerite papers circulated in different parts of the country he may have had something to say on the matter, though we have not gone through these with a fine-tooth comb. See Appendix I for the list of these references.

reader edited a journal today and through its pages refuted a story twenty-six times, he would be very likely to think he had done it hundreds of times. No, Himes is not accurate to the last detail in his statement. Nor are we presenting his letter here as though it settled the issue. That issue, we repeat, is settled, not by the memory of friend or foe, a half century afterward, but by the records and the evidence at the time the robes were alleged to have been worn.

Immediately below the Himes' letter in *The Outlook* is another one on the same subject, which reads as follows:

"I can answer for ascension robes on the Millerites in Troy, N. Y., but cannot tell the date. They were gathered in an assembly room on the west side of Fourth Street, just below what was then Albany Street, but now Broadway. I was a child, and, with other children (I think we were coming from school), went up the steps softly and carefully, as though we were approaching a horror or something uncanny; arriving at the door we peeked in, taking one good look, and then scampered away as fast as our feet could carry us, scared at having seen the saints in their white robes." [19]

This letter scarcely calls for comment. We hardly believe the reader would be willing to have his case settled in court by the testimony of a scared child as to what he saw in one peep through a door, especially if he was recalling that one peepful a half century afterward.

At the head of the column in *The Outlook* containing this Himes' letter and the short one below it that we have just quoted, is found this introductory paragraph by "the editors":

"We are glad to be able to print the following letter from 'Father Himes,' who is undoubtedly the best living authority on the question which has interested so many of our readers. We have also received several other letters from correspondents to the effect that they had heard of ascension robes, or knew of the general belief in them, but no one has, we believe, asserted that he actually laid eyes on an ascension robe, with the exception of the writer of the short letter added to that of Mr. Himes." [20]

---

[19] *The Outlook*, Nov. 24, 1894, p. 875.
[20] *Ibid.*

In other words, the wide circle of subscribers of this influential weekly failed to include anyone who wrote a letter stating that he actually "laid eyes on an ascension robe," excepting the small boy who made one scared peep through a door and announced that he had "seen the saints in their white robes." Now the editor, Lyman Abbott, was himself about nine years old in October, 1844, and ought to have been able to testify personally if robes had been worn at that time by the Millerites. But he had no such testimony to offer.

This, in brief, is the record of the ascension robe story through the nineteenth century. The farther we move from 1844 the more people we find ready to write a letter to an editor stating that they believed the Millerites wore robes. But no writer produces evidence in support of his belief, at least not the kind of evidence that will stand a moment's investigation. Even rewards fail to bring forth the desired proof. However, we must not be discouraged in our search. Time works many wonders, not the least of which is to transform rumors into reliable facts. Ascension robes really come into their own in the twentieth century, as we shall discover in the next chapter.

CHAPTER 27

The Ascension Robe Story in Twentieth Century Dress

IN ENCYCLOPEDIAS, HISTORIES, and other works of the present day are found statements regarding the Millerites. In some instances these statements are quite accurate throughout, including an exposure of the ascension robe hoax.* In other instances old rumors and stories, including those on robes, have been solemnly introduced. This makes the reference works much more readable! For example, a biographical cyclopedia thus describes an alleged incident in Millerite history shortly before October 22, 1844: "Muslin for ascension robes was freely given away, tradesmen closed their shops, and all repaired to the fields." [1]

In 1844 the newspapers had a story that muslin for robes was for sale in a Bowery dry-goods store. Some papers even admitted the "for sale" sign might have been "waggery." But in the twentieth century we are gravely informed that the muslin was "freely given away." By whom? Not the store! And certainly not the Millerite headquarters! This present-day work sweeps all the Millerites into the fields, even though the best testimony

---

[1] *National Cyclopaedia of American Biography*, Vol. 6, p. 373, art. "Miller, William." (Volume 6 was printed in 1910.)

* For example, the *Cyclopaedia of American Biography* says, "They [the Millerites] did not array themselves in ascension robes."—*Volume IV*, art. "Miller, William." This cyclopedia is the new enlarged edition of *Appleton's Cyclopaedia of American Biography*, and was printed in 1915, by Press Association Compilers, Inc., New York. The original Appleton's, printed in 1888, makes the same statement regarding ascension robes.
  The *Dictionary of American Biography* declares: "Miller's followers were accused of donning ascension robes and assembling in graveyards and on high places to await their Saviour. These charges, according to the best evidence, are not based on facts, although tradition to this day readily affirms them."—*Volume XII*, art. "Miller, William." This dictionary was published by Charles Scribner's Sons, New York. in 1933.

of the sources is that they were in religious services, generally, on the great day. To speak of them as all in the the fields makes airy reading, but it sacrifices accuracy to oxygen in an attempt to provide an expansive setting for the wearing of the flowing muslin robes.

Then there is the strange case of the appearance of ascension robes in none other than the *Encyclopaedia Britannica*. The ninth edition was the first to contain a biographical sketch of Miller. This was a brief, restrained, and rather accurate statement.* The eleventh edition, printed in 1910-1911, contains a new and longer biographical sketch of Miller, with this sentence standing in the middle of the sketch: "Many of them [the Millerites] left their business, and in white muslin robes, on housetops and hills, awaited the epiphany." [2] The robe story was in circulation when the ninth edition was published. Why did it not find inclusion until the eleventh was written? Time accomplishes many miracles, not the least of them being to give increasing plausibility to "good" stories.

A much-quoted United States history devotes eight pages to Millerism. The authorities cited for most of the statements are various newspapers of 1843 and 1844. This is another way of saying that the author provides his readers with a very colorful account of the Millerites.

His description of the movement includes certain references to ascension robes. The reader will immediately recognize this one: "At Portsmouth [New Hampshire] a Millerite was in such haste to see the coming of the Lord, that clad in his ascension robes, he climbed a tree, attempted to fly into heaven, fell to earth and broke his neck." [3]

This is our old friend, Mr. Shortridge, who did not fall and break his neck, but who had been insane ten years, and whose

---

[2] *Encyclopaedia Britannica* (11th ed.), Vol. 18, p. 465, art. "Miller, William."
[3] John B. McMaster, *A History of the People of the United States*, Vol. 7, p. 137. (Volume 7 was published in 1910.)

* The ninth edition was published over a period of years, from 1875 to 1889. The tenth edition is simply an expansion of the ninth.

actions, whatever they may have been, were no more related to Millerism than ours are. Yet all this is incorporated in a serious history of the United States. Perhaps the author was in haste. If he had read a little further he would have found in a number of the papers a frank admission that the story was groundless.

This history further informs us that the Millerites were "anxiously awaiting the coming of Christ on the 23d of April, 1843," [4] and that "on the appointed day great crowds abandoned their houses, left the cities and towns and, in their ascension robes, betook themselves to the fields in the full expectation that the Saviour would come with His angels to receive them and set the world afire." [5] The reader will recall that this April 23, 1843, date was a fictitious one published by the newspapers and that the Millerites denounced the fiction well in advance of April 23. Therefore they could hardly be expected to be anticipating the Lord's coming on that day, much less dressing for the event. Yet this history of the United States not only falls into the error of certain newspapers in the spring of 1843 by declaring that the Millerites were expecting the Lord's coming on April 23, but goes most of the newspapers one better by actually taking "great crowds" of the Millerites out into the fields on that day in ascension robes.

In 1924 there was published a book, *Days of Delusion,* devoted to a description of the Millerite movement. It is a very readable volume, the only one of its kind, for no one else in our modern day has set out to write a book devoted exclusively to the Millerite movement. In preparing this volume the author, Clara Endicott Sears, drew very largely on the reminiscences of friends, acquaintances, and others. We are indebted to her for crystallizing in a group of about two hundred sixty letters the current form of the Millerism legend, particularly as it relates to ascension robes.* These letters were written to her in the years

---
[4] *Ibid.,* p. 136.
[5] *Ibid.,* p. 138.

* These letters are on file in the office of the Society for the Preservation of New England Antiquities in Boston. We have read them through, and before us now as we write is a summarization of each letter.

On the morning after the great disappointment Hiram Edson finds a new explanation for key phrase, "the cleansing of the sanctuary." (See pages 457-460.)

Top: Oldest Seventh-day Adventist church still in use, Washington, New Hampshire. Middle, left to right: Hiram Edson, who first set forth the new view on the cleansing of the sanctuary. William Farnsworth, first Seventh-day Adventist in Washington, New Hampshire. Frederick Wheeler, first Seventh-day Adventist ordained minister. Below: James White and his wife, Ellen G. White, prominent pioneers in Seventh-day Adventist denomination.

between 1920 and 1923, as the result of the following notice she inserted in various New England newspapers:

"Has any reader of this paper any recollection of having heard parents or grandparents tell of the great religious excitement in 1843, the year that William Miller predicted the end of the world?

"Any anecdotes of that period, or any information however trivial will be gratefully received by

Clara Endicott Sears
[Address, etc., etc.]" [6]

In the notices sent to some of the newspapers particular reference was made to the matter of ascension robes, though that was probably unnecessary, when asking people to tell what they had heard about the Millerite movement.

We are quite unable to draw from these letters the general conclusion that is drawn by the author of *Days of Delusion*. She finds in them strong support for the idea that the Millerites were a fanatical group in general, and in one specific way revealed that fanaticism markedly by wearing ascension robes in trees, on housetops, and otherwise. We see in these letters a rather lurid story that has been growing for a hundred years and which runs contrary to the undebatable facts that stand revealed in the records of 1844.

In the first place, these letters were written nearly eighty years after the event, which is another way of saying that virtually all these letters give only secondhand testimony. They relate what parents or grandparents, friends or acquaintances, one or two generations removed, had told the writers of the letters. Not infrequently the letter writers merely recite some vague rumor they had heard in some past day, without giving any particular authority for it. By the rules of evidence that were long ago set down by the courts to protect the lives and reputations of men—rules whose protection every one of us today would demand if our reputations were at stake in court—virtually all these letters would be thrown out immediately. This rule, which

---

[6] Clara Endicott Sears, *Days of Delusion*, Preface, p. v.

we have already discussed, that testimony must be firsthand, is not a bit of legal red tape invented to complicate judicial procedure. It reflects the distilled wisdom of the ages.

Probably the next most distinguishing mark of these letters is a certain quality of vagueness. This was probably inevitable in the very nature of the case. But it is a very grave indictment of evidence to say that it is vague. After reading all the letters, one reaches the conclusion that the writers of them—that is, some of them—might be sure that there had been robes, but rarely does anyone ever claim to have actually seen one. In fact, it is rather difficult to determine from the letters whether anyone really did think he saw robes, though for the sake of argument the point might be conceded that a few did think so. In that event they would be people well along in their eighties who were seeking to recall what had happened when they were very small children. Most people have difficulty in remembering with certainty what happened ten years ago. But here are writers attempting to remember events after nearly eighty years, and trying to keep actual historical events separate from rumor and gossip that were alive at the time they are endeavoring to recall. Such firsthand testimony is patently worth no more than most secondhand testimony. The courts have ruled that the testimony of a person relating events of his early childhood may be properly challenged as to credibility unless his testimony possesses a certain consistency not demanded of testimony offered on current happenings.[7]

Within the very group of letters themselves is found one of the best proofs, we believe, of their undependability as historical source material. Take, for illustration, three different versions of the activities of Doctor S., a Millerite, in connection with the great day. One woman wrote in her letter that Doctor S. joined with other white-robed Millerites, and went up on a hill to meet the Lord. Apparently she was drawing her story from something her father had told her, for she added that her father

---

[7] See *Corpus Juris*, Vol. 70, p. 766.

"stanchly" vouched for it. But a few days later she sent in a second letter enclosing one from two aged sisters, whose memories ran back to 1844. They took issue with the story that this woman had sent in about Doctor S., declaring that it was "apocryphal." Then they proceeded to give an entirely different story. This second story does not have Doctor S. in a robe. A third letter, from another person, stated that Doctor S. sat in his front hall three days and nights with his wife, waiting for the Lord to come. It is an understatement to say that these three accounts differ widely, and that all three can hardly be true. The implication in the third letter is plain that the wife of Doctor S. joined with him in waiting. But the first letter declared that while Doctor S. was out on the hill with the other white-robed Millerites, Mrs. S. was at home sleeping the sleep of a good Congregationalist. Any one of these letters taken by itself might seem plausible, at least as plausible as any reminiscences of long ago can be; but when the three letters are put together we discover that the memories of people differ widely, and in a contradictory fashion.

But there is a further interesting point about this Doctor S. story. The first of the three letters we have cited declares that when Doctor S. came home early the next morning from his mountaintop experience he knocked at the front door, shouting, "This is Doctor Smith, let me in." To which the wife is said to have replied, "No, that can't be; he has gone up." Now, this is a good story and, told only once about only one man, would not only be a good story but also a plausible one. However, another correspondent—not the writer of one of the above three letters—told of a certain Millerite woman who sat up on a housetop. When she went home and knocked on the door, her husband refused her entrance, saying that his wife had gone to heaven hours ago, and then "he shut down the window and the wife never did get in." This letter writer gave her grandmother as the source of her story. Still another letter writer related a Millerite story that he heard one time by listening to a trio of old cronies. According to the letter, one of these cronies had a Millerite wife who was said to have "made a beautiful white shroud for the ascension," and in the middle of the night she rang the door bell, but her husband called out that his wife had gone to heaven.

Now, did all these nonbelieving spouses simultaneously think up such a sparkling bit of repartee when suddenly roused from their sleep on the night following the great day? *

If these different letter writers and others were not relating actual incidents, but only a "good" story, where did that story originate? We would not venture a dogmatic answer, but we offer at least a very plausible one. In the large broadside entitled "Grand Ascension of the Miller Tabernacle," with its picture of the ascending tabernacle and the robed Millerites, which was circulated just before the great day, is found a story of Joanna Southcote, who had lived in England, and who had certain ideas with regard to the coming of the Messiah. According to the story on this broadside, one of Joanna Southcote's proselytes, the wife of a hard-working man, went out one night to meet an angel who was to take her to some blissful abode. Becoming disillusioned she returned very early in the morning and knocked at the door of her home, with the result that this hard-laboring, simple peasant husband in Manchester, England, engaged in brilliant repartee with his shivering wife, who was standing outside in the snow. And that repartee sounds strangely like what is given in these various letters in the Sears collection!

If these letter writers thus reveal that their reminiscences on one alleged, sensational Millerite incident can be traced back through an anonymous caricature print, how can we be sure that other reminiscences do not have an equally worthless foundation? Certainly, whoever read the Joanna Southcote story on that broadside could not fail to have had impressed on his mind, also, the large cartoon picture that filled the upper half of the broadside showing Millerites draped over the sides of the ascending Boston tabernacle, in long, flowing white robes.

---

* We mentioned this story to the grandson of William Miller, Willis Bartholomew, who lives in Fair Haven, Vermont. He smiled and replied that this story was told about his grandfather in Low Hampton.

Then there is the trio of hell-fire stories. A letter writer says a Millerite on a hilltop went to sleep; some prankish boys threw hay in a circle round him and then lighted it, with the result that he awakened and exclaimed, "In the middle of hell, just as I expected." A second letter writer related the story of a Millerite who sat down by a tree to rest as he journeyed home from meeting, fell asleep, was wakened by straw fires set by prankish boys, and made a remark about hell strangely like that of the other fire-encircled man. A third letter writer tells of a Millerite farmer and his wife who lay down to sleep in the loft of their barn in order to be very near to heaven. The farmer's pipe started the hay ablaze, and they awakened to make the very same observation on hell.

We agree that this story has everything that a "good" story ought to have—warmth, color, and action. But it is related at least once too many times to justify considering it as anything more than a "good" *story*. Yet it is told as gravely as the incidents related by any of the approximately 260 letter writers.

Two writers of letters told of Millerites' building platforms from which they hoped to ascend, dressed in white. One of the two writers remarked that "this was a common thing at the time." Indeed, think of specially built platforms here and there throughout New England, one of them described as a tower thirty feet high, as the other letter writer stated, on which these strangely dressed Millerites were perched on the great day. Were all the newspaper reporters on October 22 blind or dead? We have had to wait till more modern times for the story to grow "tall" enough to place the Millerites on high platforms!

Several letters told of Millerites being congregated in a city park in Philadelphia in their robes, on the anticipated ascension day, one writer declaring that this was "an absolute fact," and that he had often heard his father speak on the subject of the Millerites. He added that many townspeople and some police were present. But why did everyone keep it so secret from the press? We examined ten Philadelphia newspapers and none of them carried the story.

Standing out prominently in this whole collection of letters, many of which were scribbled in pencil and in poor handwriting, is a well composed, typewritten letter on a business letterhead. It reads impressively. The writer declared that his father was about thirty-two years of age in 1844, and nearly became a Millerite. His father had told him that on one occasion Miller exhibited on the lecture platform "the ascension robe he had caused to be made to wear," and that the robe was made of "black silk." Furthermore, that Miller "pretended that the Almighty had prescribed the form of it." Now if we had no knowledge of the historical facts in the case, especially of the consistent position taken by the Millerite leaders in denunciation of the ascension robe story, we might be impressed by this letter. But if the story set forth in *this* letter, which has more of a ring of authenticity to it than almost any other letter in the whole group, must certainly be discarded as a worthless rumor, then what must be said of all the remaining letters?

Another letter writer tells that he learned from a friend who had heard of a group in Concord, New Hampshire, who bought white wings for every member, and then went to the top of a hill to wait. Why not wings as well as white robes? One is as sensible as the other, and certainly the addition of wings would be very helpful to the Millerites in reaching the tops of mountains, or houses, or even the tops of high platforms. The only trouble with this added touch to the story is that the wings fall off somewhere along the years as we go back to 1844. They seem to be a rather modern addition, unless we think of Mr. Shortridge in the apple tree as having them in embryonic form.*

---

* Perhaps we should modify this statement. We found no story, or even rumor, in the newspapers of 1843 or 1844 to the effect that Millerites had prepared wings to ascend. But we have found a curious item in an almanac of 1844 that might possibly be the source of the wings story—other stories that have come down to our day regarding the Millerites have as grotesque an origin. The almanac prints the story of a colored child in Boston who had come into possession of a pair of fairy's wings when the Tremont Theater stage properties were being moved. He gathered other urchins around him and harangued them thus: "I say boys, I'se a Millerite. . . . Wish I had one ob dem 'ere 'cension robes. . . . Whoora fur brodder Himes and parson Miller!"—*The Great Western Almanac for 1844, p. 12.* Here is a combining of wings and robes into what is at least a "good" story. Probably almanacs were as widely read as any printed matter in the 1840's. If people could draw from broadside caricatures for "good" Millerite stories, why might they not draw from almanacs also?

A woman wrote that she remembered being told that a certain sea captain accepted Millerism and sailed his boat to the Holy Land, reaching there about six months later. In a second letter she added that Miller went along with the party that sailed from New York, but did not return with them.

But Miller was never outside America, at least not during the years he was preaching. His diaries make that clear.

Still another letter writer told of having heard that the Millerites erected a machine near Bunker Hill Monument, to take them up. What an excitement would have been created in Boston if the Millerites had constructed a mechanical contraption to take people to heaven! How the news would have spread as day after day anvils resounded to the Millerite hammers. But once again the newspapers apparently missed a good story. We found no records of this marvelous product of Millerite inventiveness in any of the daily papers.

Several letters tell of having heard of a Millerite who climbed a tree in flowing white robes. The writers of one or two of the letters recalled having heard that it was an apple tree. Some of the letters also tell of a Millerite jumping out of a tree, and in one version of the story as given in these letters, a Millerite broke his arm.

Now this sounds strangely like the story of our old friend, Mr. Shortridge, of Portsmouth, New Hampshire, whose alleged apple-tree-climbing in an ascension robe, followed by a disastrous jump that supposedly broke his neck, we have already discussed. In our reading of the papers in the 1840's we found no other alleged tree-climbing by an ascension-robed person, though we did find the Shortridge story rather widely published. Of course, as has already been stated, the Shortridge story proved to be unfounded. At least when the public press afterward admitted there was no truth to the story that he had jumped to the ground with fatal effects, there was no attempt to maintain that *any* part of the story was true.

The singular resemblances that these present-day stories bear to the Shortridge story of long ago prompt us to remark that in many of the 260 odd letters are found certain phrases and vaguely mentioned incidents that sound strangely like the fanciful stories and charges that were brought against the Millerites in the 1840's. We hardly believe that the reader will wish any further analysis of this collection of letters in order to reach the conclusion that they provide little more than unreliable rumors, or at best historical incidents hopelessly distorted by aged memories. Even the most plausible letters in the collection are open to this indictment, as we have already seen. Indeed, the letter quoted by the author of *Days of Delusion* as apparently Exhibit A, and which she declares is "certainly sufficiently definite" proof that ascension robes were worn, is a letter that would not be admitted as evidence in any court. Here it is:

"I have heard my mother tell that when she was a girl she remembers that her mother made a white robe, put her house in order, put lamps in the windows and sat up all night waiting for the end of the world to come." [8]

This letter was written August 21, 1921, or seventy-seven years after the time of the alleged incident. Was the writer telling of something she saw? No, she was not even alive at the time. Instead, she was giving us the benefit of what her memory recalled of what in turn her mother's memory recalled, of the time when "she was a girl" and "her mother made a white robe." Such testimony is interesting but worthless. Numbers of the letters we have cited from this collection have as good authority for their stories as this letter; or perhaps even better. And fortunately, as we have discovered, some of those letters contain statements that are capable of being checked, and when thus checked, they failed to square with the facts of history.

In the case of the Exhibit A letter, where the woman's grandmother was said to have made a white robe, how interesting it would have been if we could have questioned the mother, or better still, the grandmother. We would have liked to ask the mother one question: Did *your* mother make a "white *robe*" or

---

[8] Quoted by Clara Endicott Sears in *Days of Delusion*, pp. 259, 260, footnote.

simply a white *dress?* This is no technical point. White was the color very frequently used by women in the 1840's for their best dresses, the Sunday-go-to-meeting kind of dresses. The pages of Godey's *Lady's Book,* the fashion authority of a century ago, show white to have been a dominant color for ladies' dresses in the 1840's. One of the letters in the Sears collection mentions that it was the custom back there to wear white on church occasions. That is why we say we would like to have asked the question: Are you *sure* your mother made a white *robe,* or was it simply a white *dress?*

The making of a white dress would have signified nothing more than that this woman wished to be dressed as appropriately on this holy day when she expected to meet her Lord in person as she would have liked to be dressed had she expected to meet Him in spirit in a church service. We have already discovered from the documentary evidence of the times that most of the Millerites either were in church services on the great day or else met together in private homes for a religious service or prayer meeting. Why should they be less appropriately dressed on such a solemn religious day than they would have been had they gone to a regular church service on a Sunday?

Is it difficult to see how a dress could change into a "robe," especially when seventy-seven years are allowed for the change, and the dress must be passed on from the memory of one person to that of another? *

Thus ends our search over hill and valley, across broad fields, through eerie graveyards, and even into the privacy of the homes

---

* Perhaps a word should be added regarding the testimony of a centenarian that is cited by the author of *Days of Delusion.* This person is quoted as testifying that she made an ascension robe for "Aaron Mason's daughter." But this testimony gives a delightfully new turn to the story: "Aaron Mason's daughter had to be satisfied with white cotton cloth that had a little black sprig pattern scattered over it, because all the plain white cloth available there had been sold to others for robes."—*Clara Endicott Sears, Days of Delusion, p. 191.*

Think of it, dry-goods stores bare of "plain white cloth." What a host of robed Millerites there must have been in that area. We are ashamed to trouble the reader with further obvious comments. We would merely be repeating the comments we have been forced to make on other modern so-called proofs that the Millerites were robed. We do not even suggest we would like to have cross-examined this centenarian on the witness stand. That would make us appear cruel and captious.

For further comments on the book *Days of Delusion,* see Appendix I. For a discussion of the question, How did the ascension robe story start? see Appendix J.

of the Millerites themselves, in search of that nondescript garment said to have been white—or was it black?—and to have been made of muslin—or was it linen, or silk?—and picturesquely called an ascension robe. But how could we hope to find one now, when diligent inquiry for a century has failed to produce a robe, even though the lure of a reward has at times been offered? Everyone today is sure that robes were worn. Hundreds of people can write letters tantalizing us, but no one ever seems to have produced anything that had the semblance of a white robe, unless it be the white nightgown of a Millerite leader that was seen harmlessly sunning itself on the clothesline of a Millerite home. Something like this, of which everyone is certain, and yet has ever eluded capture, is worthy of the attention of a Sherlock Holmes or some other master of fiction. In fact, it belongs in fiction. It *is* fiction!

CHAPTER 28

Did the Millerites Set Forth Strange, New Beliefs?

ALMOST EVERYONE WHO HAS HEARD of the Millerites is as sure that they taught fanciful doctrines as that they wore fanciful clothes. But what are the facts? Did they really set forth strange, new beliefs?

We shall concern ourselves only with their *distinctive views*, because it must be remembered that Millerism began as an interchurch movement. Ministers from various denominations became Millerite preachers. And laymen from all the various churches were finally numbered as a part of the movement. But neither ministers nor laymen were asked to surrender their denominational beliefs except where those beliefs differed with the literal Scriptural teaching on the second advent. On the contrary the Millerite movement went on record repeatedly as declaring that it did not desire to interfere with the church connections of those who joined the movement. True, toward the close there was a call to come out of the churches, because of the way they treated the Millerites, but this had little to do with the basic doctrines of the churches.

The reader will recall that when Miller first began to study the Bible, he drafted a statement of his Christian beliefs and that these beliefs were very orthodox. They could have been accepted quite generally, except for his statement that he believed the second coming of Christ would take place "on or before 1843." Miller and his close associates were unquestionably orthodox Baptists, Methodists, Congregationalists, and so on, so far as the basic tenets of the Christian faith are concerned. They set forth no strange, new ideas on God and salvation. Most of them retained their ministerial connections with their own denominations until near the climax of the movement.

Nevertheless there was something very distinctive about their preaching. This made Millerism a definite movement and brought down upon the Millerites the opposition and ridicule of many secular and religious leaders. But what was the distinctive belief that could justify the charge that they were preaching strange, new beliefs? The edifice called Millerism was built on the foundation idea that there will be an end to the world. The edifice itself was constructed of the belief that the end of the world will be sudden, precipitated by the supernatural second coming of Christ in the clouds of heaven, to bring destruction to the wicked and salvation to the righteous. The furnishings were constructed of the idea that the time of the end of the world can be known, and indeed has been revealed in prophecy. These furnishings were so appealing to many minds and seemed to be so flawlessly constructed that many thousands of sincere people soon made Millerism their spiritual home.

Was this Millerite edifice a freak when measured by the standards of Christian doctrinal architecture? In our endeavor to find an answer let us begin with the foundation. Did Miller build on a strange, new idea when he reared his structure on the belief that there will be an end to the world? The Bible has much to say about the end of the world. Christ and the holy prophets and apostles often spoke of this great event. There is probably no teaching more definitely set forth in the Bible than that there will be an end to this world as we know it today, an end to this age. The doctrine of the end of the world is one that has been held through all the history of the Christian church. Poets have woven the idea into verse, as did Tennyson when he wrote:

> "One God, one law, one element,
> And one far-off divine event,
> To which the whole creation moves." [1]

---

[1] *In Memoriam, The Poetic and Dramatic Works of Alfred Lord Tennyson* (Cambridge ed.), p. 198.

The poet Whittier, in his prose description of a Millerite camp meeting, discussed this basic idea "of a radical change in our planet," which was the foundation of Millerite preaching:

"In every age since the Christian Era, from the caves, and forests, and secluded 'upper chambers' of the times of the first missionaries of the cross, from the Gothic temples of the Middle Ages, from the bleak mountain gorges of the Alps, where the hunted heretics put up their expostulation, 'How long, O Lord, how long?' down to the present time, and from this Derry campground, have been uttered the prophecy and the prayer for its fulfillment....

"And, after all, is the idea itself a vain one? Shall tomorrow be as today? shall the antagonism of good and evil continue as heretofore forever? Is there no hope that this world-wide prophecy of the human soul, uttered in all climes, in all times, shall yet be fulfilled? Who shall say it may not be true? Nay, is not its truth proved by its universality? The hope of all earnest souls *must* be realized.... That hope and that faith which constitute, as it were, the world's life, and without which it would be dark and dead, cannot be in vain." [2]

Unquestionably, the edifice of Millerism rested on a very ancient foundation, the belief that there is to be an end to the world. But what of the structure itself? What of the idea that the end of the world will be suddenly precipitated by the supernatural second coming of Christ in flaming fire, to bring death to the wicked and salvation to the righteous? Is this a new, unorthodox idea? No, the Bible very clearly teaches it.

A New Testament writer informs us that this doctrine of the coming of the Lord in judgment was prophesied by one of the first of the godly men of the human race. Describing the wicked and the judgments that were to come upon them, the apostolic writer, Jude, declares:

"And Enoch also, the seventh from Adam, prophesied of these, saying, Behold, the Lord cometh with ten thousands of His saints, to execute judgment upon all." [3]

David, the sweet singer of Israel, whose songs have quickened the spiritual thinking of multitudes through the millenniums, prophesied thus of the coming of the Lord:

---

[2] John Greenleaf Whittier, *Prose Works,* Vol. I, pp. 421, 422.
[3] Jude 14, 15.

"Our God shall come, and shall not keep silence: a fire shall devour before Him, and it shall be very tempestuous round about Him." [4]

The same thought is expressed by the apostle Paul. Writing to the Christians who were troubled with persecution, he declared:

"And to you who are troubled rest with us, when the Lord Jesus shall be revealed from heaven with His mighty angels, in flaming fire taking vengeance on them that know not God, and that obey not the gospel of our Lord Jesus Christ: who shall be punished with everlasting destruction from the presence of the Lord, and from the glory of His power; when He shall come to be glorified in His saints, and to be admired in all them that believe." [5]

This scripture is very explicit in picturing both the righteous and the wicked as living in the world until the day of the advent. In other words, the Bible teaches that when the Lord returns it will be to the kind of world we know, where good and evil exist side by side. Christ, in one of His parables, makes this doubly clear. He describes the "kingdom of heaven" as like "unto a man which sowed good seed in his field: but while men slept, his enemy came and sowed tares among the wheat, and went his way." The man's servants asked if they should not pull up the tares. But the man replied: "Let both grow together until the harvest: and in the time of harvest I will say to the reapers, Gather ye together first the tares, and bind them in bundles to burn them: but gather the wheat into my barn."

The meaning of the parable is also given: "The field is the world; the good seed are the children of the kingdom; but the tares are the children of the wicked one; the enemy that sowed them is the devil; the harvest is the end of the world; and the reapers are the angels." [6] It would be difficult to find a more explicit statement of the doctrine that the world will continue to be populated by both the righteous and the wicked until "the end of the world," when God will mete out final rewards to all.

---

[4] Psalms 50:3.
[5] 2 Thessalonians 1:7-10.
[6] Matthew 13:24-30, 38, 39.

DID MILLERITES SET FORTH STRANGE BELIEFS? 431

The Bible also contains many warnings to the faithful regarding the suddenness and the unexpectedness of the advent of the Lord. Take for example these words of Christ to His followers:

"Take heed to yourselves, lest at any time your hearts be overcharged with surfeiting, and drunkenness, and cares of this life, and so that day come upon you unawares. For as a snare shall it come on all them that dwell on the face of the whole earth." [7]

Many other texts might be quoted to show how Scriptural, and thus how ancient and orthodox, is the belief that the end of the world, or more precisely, the end of this sinful age, is to be brought about by the sudden, supernatural appearing of Christ in glory to destroy the wicked and to redeem the righteous.

This idea of the return of our Lord as the climax to earthly history, when separation is made between righteous and wicked, is woven into the creeds of Christendom from the very earliest centuries. One of the first of these is the so-called Apostles' Creed, in which is found the statement that Christ "ascended into the heavens; sitteth on the right hand of God the Father; from thence He shall come to judge the quick and the dead." [8]

The Nicene Creed, another of the very oldest and most widely accepted creeds, employs almost this same language.

The Athanasian Creed, still another of the confessions of faith of the early centuries, affirms this concerning Christ:

"He ascended into heaven, He sitteth on the right hand of the Father God Almighty. From whence He shall come to judge the quick and the dead. At whose coming all men shall rise again with their bodies; and shall give account for their own works. And they that have done good shall go into life everlasting: and they that have done evil, into everlasting fire." [9]

In the Reformation times, and afterward, when various creeds and confessions of faith were formulated, this same doctrine concerning Christ's coming is found. Take for example

---
[7] Luke 21:34, 35.
[8] Philip Schaff, *The Creeds of Christendom*, Vol. 2, p. 50.
[9] *Ibid.*, pp. 69, 70.

the Augsburg Confession, which is described as "the fundamental and generally received symbol of the Lutheran Church." [10]

"In the consummation of the world, Christ shall appear to judge, and shall raise up all the dead, and shall give unto the godly and elect eternal life and everlasting joys; but ungodly men and the devils shall He condemn unto endless torments." [11]

The Thirty-nine Articles of the Church of England simply echo the words of the ancient creed in declaring that Christ "ascended into heaven, and there sitteth, until He returns to judge all men at the last day." [12]

The Irish Articles of Religion, formally adopted by the Irish Episcopal Church in 1615, declare in Paragraph 103:

"At the end of this world the Lord Jesus shall come in the clouds with the glory of His Father; at which time, by the almighty power of God, the living shall be changed and the dead shall be raised; and all shall appear both in body and soul before His judgment seat, to receive according to that which they have done in their bodies, whether good or evil." [13]

The Westminster Confession of Faith was adopted in 1647, and is perhaps the most important of all Protestant creeds. It appropriately devotes its closing chapter to the events of the last day and the judgment, when "the righteous go into everlasting life" and the wicked are "punished with everlasting destruction from the presence of the Lord." The concluding paragraph of the chapter, and thus of the Westminster Confession itself, declares concerning the suddenness of Christ's coming and of the danger of being found in the ranks of evildoers:

"As Christ would have us certainly to be persuaded that there shall be a day of judgment, both to deter all men from sin, and for the greater consolation of the godly in their adversity: so will He have that day unknown to men, that they may shake off all carnal security, and be always watchful, because they know not at what hour the Lord will come; and may be ever prepared to say, Come, Lord Jesus, come quickly. Amen." [14]

---

[10] *Ibid.*, Vol. 1, p. 234.
[11] *Ibid.*, Vol. 3, pp. 17, 18.
[12] *Ibid.*, p. 489.
[13] *Ibid.*, p. 544.
[14] *Ibid.*, pp. 672, 673.

DID MILLERITES SET FORTH STRANGE BELIEFS? 433

Certain creeds formulated down even in the nineteenth century set forth the same belief. Take, for example, the Baptist New Hampshire Confession drawn up about the year 1833, and according to Schaff, "widely accepted by Baptists, especially in the Northern and Western States." [15] The closing section contains this statement:

"We believe that the end of the world is approaching; that at the last day Christ will descend from heaven, and raise the dead from the graves to final retribution; that a solemn separation will then take place; that the wicked will be adjudged to endless punishment, and the righteous to endless joy; and that this judgment will fix forever the final state of men in heaven or hell, on principles of righteousness." [16]

Much more might be quoted from confessions and creeds and statements of belief. But the foregoing are surely more than sufficient to show how Scriptural, ancient, and widely accepted in Christendom is the belief that the end of this world will be brought about by the second coming of Christ, who descends with summary judgment for the righteous and the wicked, both of which classes, we are given to understand, will be living in the world at the time of the end.

According to the blueprint of these ancient beliefs concerning the advent, Miller and his associates built the edifice of Millerism. And it is with regard to the house itself before we even come to the furnishings—the time element—that a controversy developed between the Millerites and their religious opponents.* Indeed, they were often more involved in controversy over *what* was to take place than *when* it would take place. This is made clear in an editorial in *The Advent Herald* in the spring of 1844. Himes was discussing the reasons why the Millerites should adopt

---

[15] *Ibid.*, p. 742.
[16] *Ibid.*, p. 748.

* In earlier chapters we called attention to the fact that at the very beginning of the year of the end of the world a Millerite paper made clear that Millerism was more than "a mere point of time." (See *The Midnight Cry,* June 15, 1843, p. 112.) Some of the most prominent Millerites were not even believers in a "point of time"; for example, Henry Dana Ward and Henry Jones, chairman and secretary, respectively, of the first advent conference in 1840, and N. N. Whiting, who became editor of the *Morning Watch.* In various advent conferences it was explicitly stated that a person need not believe in a definite date for the advent in order to be in good standing in the conference.

the name Adventist, which signifies a belief in the "personal advent (or coming) of our Lord Jesus Christ." He said that this name is "proper, because it marks the real ground of difference between us and the great body of our opponents," and added:

"We are fully aware that they [the opponents] have endeavored to keep the question of time before the public as the obnoxious and heretical point, (and we fully believe the time to be as distinctly revealed as any other part of the subject. On that account we have defended it, and thus it has become so prominent,) still that is not, nor has it ever been, the only, or the main question in dispute. In fact, there is a greater difference between us and our opposers on the *nature of the events* predicted, than upon the interpretation of the prophetic periods, or their termination; for some of them believe these periods terminate about this time, only they are looking for different events from those which the Adventists expect; and those who give the periods a different termination, while they differ more widely upon the events predicted, are more positive in asserting their termination, though entirely without proof, than Mr. Miller has ever been." [17]

No truer statement was ever made by a Millerite leader. As Millerism took shape in a definite movement it was more than "a mere point of time"; it was an endeavor to restore a true belief as to the nature of impending events.

Viewed negatively, Millerism was an attack on the belief that had then become popular, and is now quite generally held, that the world will gradually become more holy by the spread of Christianity, until finally the forces of righteousness will well-nigh, if not wholly, control the earth. Specifically, the millennium of the Apocalypse, when the righteous reign with Christ, is interpreted as finding fulfillment in a thousand-year period of holiness on this earth as the result of the final victory of Christianity over wickedness. This filling of the earth with righteousness through the working of the Spirit of Christ, was in Miller's day, and is now, quite generally viewed as the coming of Christ—a spiritual coming.

There are variants of the doctrine, but it is not necessary to discuss them here. The essence of this view of the future of our

---

[17] *The Advent Herald,* March 20, 1844, p. 53.

world is that the whole world—or virtually so—will be converted, that the change from a wicked world to a righteous one will be gradual, and that the advent of Christ is the coming of His Spirit in mighty power to this earth to win the battle for righteousness in men's hearts. The doctrine of the world's conversion, which is the very heart of this view of earth's final destiny, generally has coupled with it the doctrine of the conversion of the Jews and their return to Palestine.

The Millerites declared that the doctrine of a spiritual coming took the reality and personality out of the second advent. Cogently they argued that the idea of the world's conversion is really the idea of universal salvation, a view that has been condemned by virtually all Christian spokesmen through the centuries. In brief, the Millerites argued that the popular view concerning the end of all things, which had gained increasing acceptance for a century, hopelessly blurred the true and ancient teachings regarding the second advent, the end of the world, and the salvation of men.*

When ideas akin to this were aired at the time of the Protestant Reformation, they received no endorsement and no place in the creeds or confessions. On the contrary, such ideas were sometimes vigorously and specifically condemned. Take, for example, the statement found in the Augsburg Confession, under Article XVII, which treats "of Christ's return to judg-

---

* The idea that the world will gradually grow better and become an ideal place for man, seems to be a revival in transcendental form, of an old Jewish tradition that the present material world, with Jerusalem at its head, will finally blossom as the rose, and be the abode of righteousness. This idea, dressed in Christian garb, and in variant forms, found only a limited support in Protestant thinking until the opening of the eighteenth century. At that time the idea of a world transformed to holiness by the gradual operation of spiritual forces began to gain a dignified status in theological circles, and on allegedly Scriptural grounds, very particularly a new interpretation of the millennium of the Apocalypse. At the same time the idea received a special impetus from the philosophical view then gaining favor, that man is capable, of himself and in this present world, of attaining to increasing perfection if given fortunate surroundings and opportunities. It is easy to see how this philosophical idea of progress unto perfection provides a natural setting for the theological idea of world betterment and conversion. And because the idea of progress panders to the vanity of the human heart, it is therefore not hard to accept.

Out of a combination of these ideas—Jewish tradition, the philosophical idea of progress, and a new interpretation of certain scriptures—was constructed a doctrine of the world's finale that was widely accepted by Miller's time. This view is even more widely held today.

For a discussion of the history and significance of the idea that man is inherently capable of progress, see J. B. Bury, *The Idea of Progress*.

ment." This article speaks of certain things that the churches condemned:

> "They condemn others also, who now scatter Jewish opinions, that, before the resurrection of the dead, the godly shall occupy the kingdom of the world, the wicked being everywhere suppressed." [18]

All the Reformation creeds, as we have already seen, set forth the doctrine either explicitly or implicitly, that Christ's coming to this earth will be a coming in judgment to a world in which both the righteous and the wicked are living.

The Millerites viewed themselves as reformers, seeking to turn men back to the Bible teaching regarding the second coming of Christ and the end of the world. Whatever else we may think of the Millerites, we can hardly question their claim that in challenging the views that had gained currency in their day, they were standing on a venerable platform. Their house of second advent hope and belief was both stable and ancient. Apostles, martyrs, and Reformers had found comfort and protection within its walls.

But what of the furnishings of this spiritual abode? This brings us to the third distinctive point in their preaching, the *time* of the second advent. Was the fabric of the upholstery spun wholly out of the imagination of Miller, or were the strands drawn from the prophetic scriptures and simply woven into a wrong pattern? Unquestionably, the pattern Miller wove was alluring to the minds and hearts of those who longed to see their Lord, but fell apart when subjected to the test of time. There is another question, also, that may properly be raised: What kind of time element, if any, did Miller's opponents give to the views *they* presented of a world of holiness that is to evolve out of the present evil world, without the supernatural intervention of Christ's coming? Both these questions need to be considered if we are to see Millerism in its true historical perspective.

Generations before Miller sat down to explore the prophe-

---

[18] Philip Schaff, *The Creeds of Christendom*, Vol. 3, p. 18.

DID MILLERITES SET FORTH STRANGE BELIEFS? 437

cies, pious and scholarly theologians of various religious bodies had been studying the prophetic portions of the Bible. Such study was carried on even by eminent men who were not theologians; for example, by Sir Isaac Newton, one of the most brilliant scholars of all time, who wrote a work on prophecy in the early part of the eighteenth century. These men rather generally believed that the major prophecies were rapidly coming to their end, and that beyond them lay only one great prophetic event to be fulfilled, the climactic event of the second advent of Christ in glory.

Now, in what way did Miller differ from all these learned men who studied and wrote on prophecy in the years before him? Obviously, the difference is not found, as some critics have declared, in the position Miller took that the prophecies can be understood. It is not correct to picture him as seeking to understand mysteries that the devout up to his day had reverently left alone. Nor is the real difference to be found in the major conclusions Miller reached as to most of the prophecies of Daniel and the Revelation, nor in the principles of interpretation he employed in his study. This is all the more remarkable when it is remembered—and Miller's critics have always sought to make capital of it—that Miller did not go to a theological school, but sat down with his Bible and concordance, to study the Scriptures.* The very fact that he did this, and yet reached the same conclusion that scholarly theologians of the past had reached on so many of the major prophecies of the Bible, argues something more

---

* In Chapter 10 we quoted the statement by the Millerite editor, Southard, regarding the sources from which Miller drew in formulating his basic views on prophecy. Speaking of the Bible and concordance in Miller's study, Southard wrote: "These two books were almost the only ones he looked at while preparing his lectures. . . . He never had a commentary in his house, and did not remember reading any work upon the prophecies, except Newton and Faber, about thirty years ago."—*The Midnight Cry, Oct. 26, 1843, p. 88.*

We do know that Miller read history very widely. That is evident from his writings. Southard makes a distinction between theological and other works, leaving us to infer that Miller did read widely in other fields. However, all the evidence leads to the conclusion that while Miller was not guided by, or may not even have read, any prophetic works, except the two mentioned, at the time he formulated his prophetic views, he must have done some reading of such works later on. Else how could he have declared that his prophetic views were not original with him, but harmonized very largely with the views held by students of prophecy in past generations? However, there is no real conflict here, for there is a basic difference between studying prophetic works in connection with formulating one's views, and scanning or even reading carefully such works later on, in order to compare views.

For a summary of the Millerite interpretation of major prophecies, see Appendix K.

than the saneness of Miller's study. It argues that the prophecies of the Bible are not incapable of being understood, as some believe.

When drawn into controversy, Miller referred to theologians of generations past in support of virtually all the positions he took regarding prophecy. In fact, he could even call on certain eminent men of his own time in support of some of his most basic views. In order that the reader may see the full force of this fact, it should be explained that one of the most primary points to be settled in interpreting Bible prophecy is the value or meaning to be given to the word "day." This is because the prophecies mention a number of periods of time, such as 1260 days, 2300 days, 42 months, 1290 days. Now obviously if the prophets gave a symbolic value to the word "day," and it was meant to stand for a much longer period than a literal day, then the various periods of time mentioned by the prophets immediately become of the greatest significance. They become long measuring sticks marking off the plans of God for our world down through the Christian Era.

Miller's preaching on prophecy rested squarely on the primary position that a day in prophetic language stands for a year. In other words, when the prophet spoke of 1260 days he intended us to understand 1260 years. In the language of the theologians, this is known as the year-day principle in the interpretation of prophecy.

Now was this a new, strange idea? No! An examination of classic works on Bible prophecy through the centuries reveals that this year-day principle has the most eminent support. In fact, some theologians who wrote against Miller in his own day were very ready to admit this. The evidence on this point is unequivocal.

In the year 1842 Professor Moses Stuart, of Andover Theological Seminary, wrote a book on prophecy. As the preface implies, it was written because of the Millerite preaching. Though he himself did not accept the year-day principle, he freely made this admission:

"It is a singular fact, that the great mass of interpreters in the English and American world have, for many years, been wont to understand the *days* designated in Daniel and in the Apocalypse [the Revelation] as representatives or symbols of *years*. I have found it difficult to trace the origin of this general, I might say almost universal, custom." [19]

In the spring of 1844 the Millerites published a pamphlet consisting of an exchange of letters between Miller and the Rev. George Bush, professor of Hebrew and Oriental literature, New York City University. Miller described Bush as his most "gentlemanly opponent." In his letter Bush set forth his reasons for rejecting Miller's views on the advent. Before giving the reasons that he believed have caused "multitudes" to reject Miller's views, Bush confessed that the "multitudes in their most decided rejection of the cardinal tenets" of Miller's belief, may have been affected by "prejudice." But he added:

"I think I may confidently affirm that this prejudice is not founded,—

"1. Upon your high estimate and diligent investigation of the Prophetic Scriptures. We are commanded to give heed to the 'sure word of prophecy, as to a lamp that shineth in a dark place,' and the devout study of this part of the divine oracles is to be regarded rather as a matter of commendation than of censure.

"2. Neither is it to be objected, as I conceive, to yourself or your friends, that you have devoted much time and attention to the study of the *chronology* of prophecy, and have labored much to determine the commencing and closing dates of its great periods. If these periods are actually given by the Holy Ghost in the prophetic books, it was doubtless with the design that they *should* be studied, and probably, in the end, fully understood; and no man is to be charged with presumptuous folly who reverently makes the attempt to do this. On this point, I have myself no charges to bring against you. Nay, I am even ready to go so far as to say, that I do not conceive your errors on the subject of chronology to be at all of a serious nature, or in fact to be *very* wide of the truth. In taking a *day* as the prophetical term for a *year,* I believe you are sustained by the soundest exegesis, as well as fortified by the high names of Mede, Sir I. Newton, Bishop Newton, Kirby, Scott, Keith, and a host of others who have long since come to *substantially* your conclusions on this head. They all agree that the leading periods mentioned by Daniel and John, do actually expire *about this age of the world,* and it

---

[19] Moses Stuart, *Hints on the Interpretation of Prophecy,* p. 74.

would be a strange logic that would convict you of heresy for holding in effect the same views which stand forth so prominent in the notices of these eminent divines. Your error, as I apprehend, lies in another direction than your *chronology;* not, however, that I am prepared to admit all the details of your calculations, but, in general, your results in this field of inquiry do not strike me so far out of the way as to affect any of the great interests of truth or duty." [20]

Another learned divine who wrote on Bible prophecy about this time was Irah Chase, D. D., professor of ecclesiastical history in the Newton Theological Institution. In the preface to his work he referred obviously to Millerism, and declared:

"We need not wonder that the minds of many have, within a few years, been greatly agitated by an expectation of the speedy fulfillment of certain predictions in the book of Daniel. The way for this was prepared by some of our standard English writers on the prophecies, men of former ages, venerated for their piety and their erudition." [21]

Chase went on to state that these learned and venerated writers on the prophecies were, according to his views, not wholly accurate in the "principles of interpretation" that they employed. But he continued:

"Instead, now, of being offended, or of looking scornfully at those who have only carried out and applied according to their best understanding, the principles taught by bishops and learned commentators, let each one for himself; first of all, see to it that he be prepared to meet, without dismay whatever may occur, and to stand before his final judge; and then, let him, as his situation and circumstances may permit, endeavor, with fervent prayer, and diligent study, and holy living, to ascertain what God has revealed, and what He has enjoined.

"There was much of candor and of good sense in the reply which Mr. Miller once made to an individual who had asked what would convince him that his explanation was wrong: 'Give a better one.' " [22]

A book reviewer in one of the leading monthlies of the day wrote in somewhat similar vein in his review of a Millerite book:

---

[20] Second Advent Library, No. XLIV, *Reasons for Rejecting Mr. Miller's Views on the Advent,* by Rev. George Bush, *With Mr. Miller's Reply,* pp. 6, 7; see also *The Advent Herald,* March 6, 1844, p. 38.
[21] Irah Chase, *Remarks on the Book of Daniel,* p. v.
[22] *Ibid.,* pp. v, vi.

"It may not be out of place to say, that we think Mr. Miller is very unfairly dealt by in many respects, and that many of his views are far easier mocked than answered. Some of them we think are entirely unsound, and many more crude and ill digested. It is also worthy of remembrance that he is in no respect the originator of the system which passes under his name; but that every leading feature of it, if we understand it even tolerably, has been over and over advanced by men, some of whom are of the very highest note." [23]

These are remarkable admissions, to say the least. They are largely from prominent theologians of the time, who had no love for Miller, but who were willing to admit that he was supported by learned men of the past generations in many of his conclusions on prophecy, and particularly in his use of the year-day principle.

In view of these admissions the question immediately arises: In what respect then *did* Miller run counter to the great interpreters of the past, and to what extent did such contemporaries as we have here quoted take issue with him? To answer that question we must look a little more closely at the specific views that Miller held regarding prophecy. He believed that certain great periods of time mentioned in prophecy expired either in the closing years of the eighteenth century or about the year 1843, and that when this latter group ended, the next and immediate event would be the second advent of Christ. One of these prophetic periods, the longest of all, was the heart of his whole prophetic teaching. All his other arguments from prophecy or Scriptural analogy were in a definite sense secondary to, or in corroboration of, this major line of prophecy. And what is it? We find the answer in one of the very earliest statements of his views that Miller presented. We refer to a manuscript of 1831. The opening lines of that manuscript read thus:

"The first proof we have, as it respects Christ's second coming as to time, is in Daniel 8:14, 'Unto 2300 days; then shall the sanctuary be cleansed.' By days we are to understand years, sanctuary we understand the church, cleansed we may reasonably suppose means that complete

---

[23] Review of pamphlet by J. Litch, *Judaism Overthrown*, in *Spirit of the XIX Century*, March, 1843, p. 190.

redemption from sin, both soul and body, after the resurrection when Christ comes the second time, 'without sin unto salvation.' " [24]

Miller immediately added, after having given what he considered to be the meaning of "days," "sanctuary," and "cleansed," that "the greatest difficulty is to know when Daniel's vision begins." The immediate context of the eighth chapter of Daniel does not give any clue to the beginning of the prophecy. And, of course, we cannot tell when it ends unless we can tell when it begins.

Without going into a detailed discussion of prophecy, which would take us beyond the range of this book, it may be said briefly that Miller took the position that the date of the beginning of the 2300-day prophecy is explained in the ninth chapter of Daniel. The prophet closes the eighth chapter with these words: "I was astonished at the vision, but none understood it." In the ninth chapter he declares that the angel Gabriel, whom he "had seen in the vision at the beginning," appeared to him again, and said, "O Daniel, I am now come forth to give thee skill and understanding. . . . Therefore, understand the matter, and consider the vision."

Immediately upon commanding Daniel to "consider the vision," the angel Gabriel declares, "Seventy weeks are determined upon thy people, . . . to make reconciliation for iniquity, and to bring in everlasting righteousness, and to seal up the vision and prophecy, and to anoint the most holy."

Miller learned from his study that the word "determined" may properly be translated "cut off." Believing that the angel's statements were an explanation of the prophecy of 2300 days, he concluded that these "seventy weeks," or 490 days, of prophetic time were "cut off" from the 2300-day period, that is, from the first part of the period.* Now, the angel Gabriel told Daniel

---

[24] Manuscript dated Feb. 15, 1831, *A Few Evidences of the Time of the Second Coming of Christ, to Elder Andrus by William Miller.*

* The "seventy weeks" could not be understood as being cut off from the end of the 2300-day period, because all the events of the seventy prophetic weeks were to carry on down only to the time of Christ, whereas the 2300 days, or years, must carry far beyond that date.

DID MILLERITES SET FORTH STRANGE BELIEFS? 443

that he should begin to measure the "seventy weeks" "from the going forth of the commandment to restore and to build Jerusalem." Miller believed that this "commandment" went forth about the year 457 B. C.

Thus he had a starting point for the longer prophecy of 2300 days, or years, and by simple addition was able to reach the conclusion that that prophecy would end "about the year 1843." The reader will recall that neither Miller nor his associates were altogether certain at the outset as to the exact point of time of the going forth of the commandment to restore and to build Jerusalem, and hence were not altogether certain about the time that the prophecy would end. The time of the advent was first forecast as due "about the year 1843," but the date was later revised to read exactly, "October 22, 1844."

Miller's opponents clearly understood that this 2300-day prophecy, as tied in with the prophecy of the seventy weeks, was the heart of Miller's prophetic teachings, so far as setting a date for the second advent was concerned. Take the statement, for example, by John Dowling, who wrote one of the most widely circulated books against Miller:

"Every reader of Mr. Miller's book, has doubtless noticed the stress which he lays upon his interpretation and comparison of the vision of the seventy weeks, and of the two thousand, three hundred days. This is the key to all his other dates; from the strange supposition, that these are two prophetic periods which begin at one and the same *date,* he fixes upon the year 1843 as the end of the world. Having obtained this date, nothing is easier than to fix the time of his other prophetic periods, by simple subtraction or addition.*

"This is the foundation of the whole system; and Mr. M. himself seems so to regard it." [25]

In the light of this statement of Miller's central teaching on prophecy, which brought him to his 1843 conclusion, we return

---

[25] John Dowling, *An Exposition of the Prophecies, Supposed by William Miller to Predict the Second Coming of Christ, in 1843,* p. 40.

* For a summary of Miller's secondary arguments for the advent of Christ in 1843, see Appendix L.

to the question, What did his theological opponents have to say on these particular teachings? Or to state the question in more pertinent form: How strange or new were these particular views as compared with the prophetic beliefs of learned interpreters of the past?

We have already discovered that Miller followed a principle long employed by eminent theologians in understanding a prophetic day to mean a year, and that those who opposed him admitted this frankly. Indeed, some of them employed the same principle themselves.* But what of the position Miller took that the 2300-day prophecy was interlocked with the seventy-week prophecy, and that therefore this long prophecy, central to his views on the time of the advent, began about 457 B. C.? There were theologians of good standing before the days of Miller who thus tied these two prophecies together. Silas Hawley, in his dedicatory sermon at the Boston Tabernacle, canvassed very fully the question of the relation of Miller's prophetic views to those held by eminent theologians through the centuries, and set forth specific proof in support of his proposition that "in all that is essential in our view, we have with us the highest and most respected authorities of the whole church." In that sermon he

---

* However, certain of these opponents, while accepting the year-day principle, did not believe that this principle applied in the particular instance of the prophecy of the 2300 days. In brief, their argument generally was that the original word translated "day" in this particular prophecy was a different word from that used in other great time prophecies of the Bible, therefore literal time is intended. Hence the prophecy was viewed as dealing only with a brief incident in the history of the ancient Jews. This was the position taken by Dowling, for example. However, Dowling admits that Miller has excellent support for employing the year-day principle in this particular prophecy of the 2300 days. "Mr. Miller contends that we are to understand in this place 2300 years, a day for a year. In this I cannot agree with him, though many of the modern commentators think that years and not days are intended."—John Dowling, *An Exposition of the Prophecies, Supposed by William Miller to Predict the Second Coming of Christ, in 1843,* p. 71.

Dowling certainly would not have admitted this if the evidence from the writings of other theologians had not demanded it, for he was a bitter opponent of Miller. When Dowling said that "many of the modern commentators think that years and not days are intended" in this 2300-day prophecy, he probably meant commentators who had written within the last generation or two.

This in itself would be sufficient to protect Miller against the charge of setting forth a unique interpretation on this particular point at least. However, we can go far back behind the days of Miller and Dowling and find commentators holding that the year-day principle in prophecy applies in this 2300-day prophecy, the same as in others. It is interesting to note that Sir Isaac Newton, writing a hundred years before the time of Miller, quoted the words of Daniel, " 'Unto two thousand and three hundred days; then shall the sanctuary be cleansed,' " and added immediately, "Daniel's days are years." (See Sir Isaac Newton, *Observations Upon the Prophecies,* p. 122.)

credited Professor George Bush,* "and others of our day" with tying the 2300-day and seventy-week prophecies together, having them both begin, therefore, at the same point of time.[26]

There were other learned theologians, who though they apparently did not tie the two prophecies together, nevertheless believed that the long 2300-day prophecy was about to end. Take, for example, Irah Chase, from whom we quoted earlier as declaring that the present "expectation of the speedy fulfillment of certain predictions in the book of Daniel" is built on the interpretation of prophecy that has been given by "men of former ages, venerated for their piety and their erudition." He illustrated this admission thus:

"Doctor Scott, in his notes on Daniel 8:13, 14, after quoting, with approbation, the remarks of Lowth and Newton, adds, 'no doubt the end of the two thousand and three hundred days, or years, is not very distant.' "[27]

The writers he mentioned—Scott, Lowth, and Newton (probably Bishop Newton of the Church of England)—were all theologians, "venerated for their piety and their erudition." Hence we conclude there was nothing new or strange in Miller's belief that prophetic days mean years, including the 2300-day prophecy, or in his belief that this prophecy was about to end. As for tying together the 2300-day and 70-week prophecy, he could find support for that also. Regarding his belief that the great prophecies were ending, learned commentators of the past, as Bush admitted, "all agree that the leading periods mentioned by Daniel and John, do actually expire *about this age of the world.*" Therefore, what *was* new and strange about Miller's preaching? His opponent Dowling declared:

"The two chief peculiarities by which Mr. Miller's book [of lectures which set forth his prophetic ideas] is distinguished, are,

---

[26] See *The Midnight Cry,* July 20, 1843, pp. 170, 171.
[27] Irah Chase, *Remarks on the Book of Daniel,* p. v.

* We do not have the particular work by George Bush from which Hawley draws his statement. But we may repeat here what has been said before, that Millerite preachers were generally quite careful in quoting their sources, so as not to give their adversaries an opportunity to charge them either with deceit or inaccuracy. It will be evident from a quotation we shall soon give from Professor Bush that he most certainly must have believed that the 2300-day prophecy began about the year 457 B. C.

"1. That the coming of Christ spoken of in the following and kindred passages in the Old and New Testament, is not to follow, but to precede the *millennium,* or latter-day glory. [Then follows a long passage of Scripture describing the second coming of the Lord in glory.] . . .

"2. That the solemn event described in the above passages [of Scripture] is at hand, even at the door, and that 'about the year 1843,' as expressed in the title page of Mr. M.'s book, we are to expect 'the second coming of Christ.'

"In both of these articles Mr. M. has adopted a belief entirely different from that which is held by the great body of evangelical Christians." [28]

Miller preached that Christ was to come suddenly with final judgment for all, while the wicked world is going on in its usual round, and that the millennium begins *after* the wicked have been destroyed by the brightness of the Lord's coming, and the righteous have received their reward. Dowling declared that this was "a belief entirely different from that which is held by the great body of evangelical Christians." There lay the primary point of controversy.

It is perhaps true that Miller's belief was "entirely different" from that held by many in his day. But as we have already discovered, this was due to the fact that for something like one hundred years before Miller and his opponents argued the case, there had been a gradual change in the view held by theologians concerning the nature of the second advent and the events connected with it. Not Miller but his opponents were the holders of new, strange doctrine, teachings that had been denounced in classic Protestant creeds as heresy.

No wonder the Millerites declared that their preaching dealt with more than "a mere point of time." Dowling admitted as much in his statement on what he considered the first of the "two chief peculiarities" of Miller's views. Himes was stating an obvious truth when he declared:

"There is a greater difference between us and our opposers on the *nature of the events* predicted, than upon the interpretation of the prophetic

---

[28] John Dowling, *An Exposition of the Prophecies, Supposed by William Miller to Predict the Second Coming of Christ, in 1843,* pp. 29, 30.

DID MILLERITES SET FORTH STRANGE BELIEFS? 447

periods, or their termination; for some of them believe these periods terminate about this time, only they are looking for different events from those which the Adventists expect." [29]

Now if many prophetic commentators of the past, as well as prominent theologians of Miller's own day, believed that the major time prophecies of the Bible were drawing to an end, what did they believe was to follow the ending of these prophecies? The theologians of former days, to whom Bush and Chase referred, rather generally held that the second advent of Christ was the next great event, though they did not hold that it was to follow immediately at the close of the time prophecies. Miller differed from the eminent divines of the past in placing the supernatural second appearing of Christ at the immediate conclusion of one of these time prophecies, that of the 2300 days.

And what did the theologians of Miller's day believe? We know they did not believe Christ was to come in judgment "about the year 1843." Indeed, as we have already seen, they took issue with the basic idea that the present sinful world is suddenly to be brought to the bar of divine justice by the second appearing of Christ. Yet some of his most prominent opponents believed the major prophecies were ending in their day. But what did they believe was to *take place* when the prophecies ended? We shall let Bush answer the question. He is the man who wrote in his letter to Miller, "Your error, as I apprehend, lies in another direction than your chronology." Then where did Miller's "error" lie? Bush explained:

"While I have no question that well-informed students of prophecy will admit that your calculation of *Times,* with the above exception [one of the "details" of Miller's "calculation" that Bush considered invalid], is not materially erroneous, they will still, I believe, maintain that you have entirely mistaken *the nature of the events* which are to occur when those periods have expired. This is the head and front of your expository offending. You have *assumed* that the close of the 2300 days of Daniel, for instance, is also the close of the period of human probation—that it is the epoch of the visible and personal second coming of Christ—of the resurrection of the righteous

---

[29] *The Advent Herald,* March 20, 1844, p. 53.

dead—and of the dissolution of the present mundane [earthly] system. All this I affirm to be gratuitously and groundlessly asserted. Admitting, as I readily do, that we have arrived at a momentous era of the world, and that the expiration of these periods is to introduce, by *gradual steps,* a new order of things, intellectual, political and moral, I still peremptorily deny that the Scriptures, soundly interpreted, warrant the expectation of any such sudden and miraculous disruption of the existing order of things, as yourself, and those usually termed Adventists, are in the habit of teaching.

"The great event before the world is not its *physical conflagration*,* but its *moral regeneration;* and for once I am happy to think that, by your own limitation, the question is so soon to be put to the test of indisputable fact." [30]

Professor Bush did not believe that Christ would come in 1843 to bring a fiery judgment to evildoers. But he based this disbelief, not on a difference of view as to the time of the ending of certain Bible prophecies, but on a difference of view regarding what was to take place when the prophecies ended. He could agree with Miller that great events were impending, but he could not agree on the events. He believed that the "moral regeneration" of the world was due to begin. In other words, Bush believed that 1843 would mark the beginning of an earthly millennium, with righteousness gaining domination of the world "by gradual steps."

Dowling differed with Miller on this same fundamental point. Said he:

"What Mr. Miller regards as introductory to the coming of Christ upon His 'great white throne,' I regard as introductory to the millennium [an earthly millennium such as Bush believed in]. I wish, therefore, to be distinctly understood, that whenever in the following pages, I attempt to

---

[30] Second Advent Library, No. XLIV, *Reasons for Rejecting Mr. Miller's Views on the Advent,* by Rev. George Bush, *With Mr. Miller's Reply,* p. 11; see also *The Advent Herald,* March 13, 1844, p. 41.

* From a statement made in an earlier paragraph of his letter to Miller, it is evident that Bush used the phrase "physical conflagration" to mean the annihilation of the physical world. He imputed this belief to the Millerites because he thought they interpreted the Scriptural phrase, the "end of the world," as meaning the physical world. But this was not Millerite belief generally. They knew, as all students of Greek know, that "world" is here translated from a Greek word meaning "age." In other words, the Millerites anticipated "the end of the age," "about the year 1843," the age of God's mercy, the age of sinful men. (See *The Advent Herald,* March 6, 1844, p. 39.) However, there was one pamphlet by a Millerite that sought to prove that the physical world as well as sinners would be destroyed. (See bibliography under Gunn, L. C.)

DID MILLERITES SET FORTH STRANGE BELIEFS? 449

correct the time of the fulfillment of prophetic periods which he applies to the former-named event, I apply the dates, so corrected, to the latter." [31]

He described the millennium as the time "when true religion shall prevail in all the world, and the church of Christ shall be raised to a state of prosperity, far greater than has ever yet been enjoyed." [32] Then he proceeded to discuss the point of "the most probable *time of the commencement* of this glorious era." [33] Because of his uncertainty as to when certain time prophecies would end, Dowling thought that "this glorious era" might begin in 1866, or 1987, or A. D. 2015, and declared:

"My own opinion is in favor of the last, viz.: A. D. 2015, because I think it rests upon the most solid foundation; though I think it more consistent with my own views of the uncertainty of unfulfilled prophecy, to say that it will probably commence *about the year 2000,* than positively to fix upon any particular year." [34]

Interesting indeed! Miller's opponents flayed him for predicting, on the strength of his understanding of Bible prophecy, that a great event would take place at a certain time, namely, "about the year 1843." But his opponent, Bush, calmly announced a similarly stupendous, though not so immediately spectacular, event, as due at the very same time. Dowling agreed with Bush on the nature of the event, and was specific regarding the date, except that he set his date later. Miller was denounced because he said that "about the year 1843" Christ would come. But Dowling, using a strangely similar phrase, predicted that "about the year 2000" would occur an event no less far-reaching in its influence on the world, even though different in nature.

Bush and Dowling were not setting forth isolated, personal ideas, but on the contrary were presenting opinions held by a number of theologians of their time. In fact, they implied in all

---

[31] John Dowling, *An Exposition of the Prophecies, Supposed by William Miller to Predict the Second Coming of Christ, in 1843,* pp. 31, 32.
[32] *Ibid.,* p. 172.
[33] *Ibid.,* p. 186.
[34] *Ibid.,* p. 191.

their arguments that they expressed the consensus of religious thinking, while Miller held "a belief entirely different from that which is held by the great body of evangelical Christians."

Again we remark, how true Himes was when he said that it was "the nature of the events predicted" that most definitely distinguished Miller from his opponents. Well did Josiah Litch, another ardent Millerite spokesman, declare in an "Address to the Clergy," which was an appeal to the ministry to give Millerism a hearing:

"Finally the question resolves itself into this. Is the millennium of the Scripture to be in a *temporal* [earthly], or an *eternal* state? [In other words, is the world gradually to improve, as Bush, Dowling, and others affirm, or is it suddenly to be cleansed of all evil by the flaming appearance of Christ in judgment?] If the former, then the [Millerite] theory advocated in these pages must fall. But if the latter, then the objection as to the time vanishes. For the warmest opponents of this [Millerite] theory admit the prophetic period, by which we arrive at the time, to begin and end at the same time contended for in these sheets. They believe the termination of the 2300 days of Daniel 8:14 will introduce a *temporal millennium,* and the literal restoration of the Jews; but here [in this Millerite publication] it is contended that no such events as these are to be looked for; but that the event is *the establishment of a glorious and everlasting kingdom of God on earth, at the resurrection of the just.* There can, therefore, be no more absurdity in saying that the glorious kingdom of God will be established at a given time, than there is in saying that the [prophetic] period will terminate at that time, but in another event. For the Scripture must decide what the event is." [35]

We may therefore sum up the matter thus: If Miller in his charts, which showed the time prophecies all ending in his day, had indicated that at the close of these prophecies the "moral regeneration" of the world would begin, his opponents would have found little fault with him. Of course, they might have challenged some "details" of his "calculations"—they disagreed among themselves on details. But that would have been minor.

Miller's opponents kept reminding him that time would soon put his views to the test. Obviously that was so. They even

---

[35] *Signs of the Times,* Jan. 1, 1842, p. 151.

DID MILLERITES SET FORTH STRANGE BELIEFS? 451

inquired in advance as to what he intended to do or to say when time proved him wrong. We know what he and his associates said; we have already quoted their admissions of error. The question that clamors for attention is what his opponents had to say when their equally specific and dogmatic predictions failed to come true. Of course Dowling was saved from embarrassment because he forecast the beginning of the "moral regeneration" "about the year 2000." But not so with Bush, and all others who either agreed with him specifically on 1843, or on some relatively early date. We wait, still, for their answer. Evidently church people generally felt so relieved when Miller's predictions did not come true that it never occurred to them then or afterward to inquire of their ministers why the "moral regeneration" of the world had not definitely begun. And anyway, Bush had so cautiously worded his forecast that its failure to come true was not immediately evident. He declared that "by *gradual steps,* a new order of things" was to be introduced.

When the year 1843 ended, bringing its first disappointment to the Millerites, the following item appeared in one of their papers:

"Not long since, Doctor Brownlee, preaching in Newark, New Jersey, collected together his proofs and labored to show from the signs of the present times, together with the prophetic periods, that in the year 1843 a great *moral change,* the greatest the world ever experienced, would take place.*

"Professor Bush has also, for some time, been telling the people substantially the same thing. Both have acknowledged the 'Millerites' to be

---

* The reader will recall that in Chapter 8 we gave excerpts from the daily reports of the New York *Herald* reporter who wrote up the story of the Millerite camp meeting at Newark, New Jersey, in November, 1842. Included in his reports was a lengthy summary of a sermon preached by Doctor Brownlee. This learned doctor felt it necessary to preach a sermon in Newark against Millerism. The reporter presents the sermon at great length and credits Brownlee with teaching that "in 1843 or 1844 we may see the first dawn of light preparing for the millennium, in the restoration of all the Jews to the Holy Land." Then Brownlee is reported to have described other events that precede "the commencement of the millennium," and to have concluded that "by 2016, all but the millennium will be accomplished."—*New York Herald, Nov. 11, 1842.* This view is very similar to what we have quoted from Dowling, who thought the temporal millennium would begin "about the year 2000." The fact that the reporter did rather accurate work in writing up Miller's sermons, warrants us in concluding that he probably reported Brownlee correctly also.

right as regarded the time; at the same time contending that they were wrong as to the nature of the expected event.

"Well, 1843 has passed, and where is the anticipated great moral change? And who thinks of treating the great Doctor Brownlee or the great Professor Bush with mocking and ridicule? But those who have been, and still are, looking for the blessed hope of the Lord's speedy appearing, because the vision tarries beyond the time when many of them were expecting the coming of their glorious King, are compelled to hear from the scoffers of these last days, from the chair of the theological professor down to the dregs of the dram shop, the taunting remark, 'Well, you have not gone up yet.'" [36]

After their great disappointment on October 22, 1844, the Millerites touched the real crux of the matter in their "Address to the Public." After summing up the evidence that showed they were "sustained" in their "views of prophecy by the standard commentators," and after stating that even their theological opponents believed a great event was impending, they came to this conclusion:

"That we are on the eve of some mighty and wonderful event, all are ready to admit. . . . What is the nature of these events? is the great question at issue." [37]

In the light of all this it can hardly be said that Miller's views were very strange or fanciful. He was distinctive and different in one respect only: he declared that the *advent* was to take place immediately at the close of the 2300-day prophecy. Both he and his opponents were mistaken in what was to take place about that time, with Miller certainly no more mistaken than they. Indeed, the scales tip in favor of Miller. He had the creeds of the earliest centuries, and the principal Protestant creeds of later centuries, to justify him in watching for the advent of Christ in judgment. He also had the strong testimony of an impressive line of prophetic commentators to warrant him in believing that the event was not far away. His opponents not only forecast the wrong event for 1843 or thereabouts; they

---

[36] *The Midnight Cry*, May 9, 1844, p. 344.
[37] *Ibid.*, Nov. 21, 1844, p. 164.

actually forecast an event that the writers of the ancient creeds, and also of the classic Protestant creeds, quite evidently never believed would occur, and which one of the historic creeds placed in the category of "Jewish opinions."

We might perhaps bring our study of Millerism to a close at this point, and let Miller and his opponents, who have all gone to their graves, rest in peace. Certainly it would be most unkind to rouse his opponents from their dusty beds lest they be shocked by the startling fact that their predicted "moral regeneration," which ought to have made a hundred years headway, has been sadly interrupted by two world wars, unparalleled in history. They would be even more startled to discover that the potentialities of destruction are now so great that even statesmen speak of the possibility of the end of civilization and the suicide of the human race.

But there is one more question that should be answered, in order to bring this study to a proper close: Did Millerism die with William Miller? Or stated in another way: Did the prophetic awakening produced by that loosely knit but fervent movement cease with the great disappointment? Did the key prophecy of the 2300 days, which not only Miller but certain of his opponents believed terminated about 1844, become meaningless to the Millerites in the years that followed, or did this prophecy take on new significance?

CHAPTER 29

Did the Advent Faith Miller Kindled, Die With Him?

MILLER HAD EXPECTED TO SEE Christ come in his day. To the last he had buoyed up his hope by declaring that possible errors in chronology permitted him to expect the advent within a few years after 1844. We can only surmise as to what interpretation he would have given to the 2300-day prophecy, the keystone of his prophetic arch, had he lived many years. But we do know that he unwaveringly believed to the last that the cleansing of the "sanctuary" at the close of the 2300 days involved divine acts that could take place only at Christ's coming. Hence, to all who continued to accept his interpretation, he left a heritage of speculation as to the year, if not the day, of Christ's coming. Why should not they seek to fix with certainty the chronology of the 2300-day prophecy? Even eminent opponents had admitted that the prophecy was due to end in their very day. The practical result was, of course, a constant setting of dates by various persons, though there was no unanimity, and no dramatic days of expectation. This continued actively for about a decade after 1844.

One of the last important instances of time setting as it affected any definite segment of the Adventists—as they now called themselves—was in 1853. The promoters of this date believed that the Lord would come in the autumn of 1853 or the spring of 1854. This view was not acceptable to those Adventists who had abandoned any attempt to extend the 2300-day prophecy further, and who controlled *The Advent Herald*. Hence, the promoters of the new time began the publication of a separate paper to rally those who accepted this new date. When time proved them wrong they had already moved so definitely away from other Adventists who were still held in loose bonds of fellowship by the actions of the Albany conference, that they decided to form a separate body. One of the prime reasons for this decision was that they had incorporated in their beliefs the doctrine that man is by nature mortal and that the dead lie unconscious in their graves until the resurrection. This newly created group organized the Advent Christian Association at Worcester, Massachusetts, November 6, 1861, and are known as the Advent Christian Church.

This church constitutes today the principal segment of what might be described in simplest terms as First-day Adventists, coming down from the Millerite movement, in contrast to Seventh-day Adventists, of whom we shall speak shortly. The Advent Christian Church holds much in common with other Protestant bodies, its most distinguishing marks being the emphasis on the advent doctrine and the tenet which treats of the nature of man. A more circumspect body of Christians it would be hard to find. Regarding the doctrine of the advent they declare: "Bible prophecy indicates the approximate time of Christ's return, and the great duty of the hour is the proclamation of this soon-coming redemption." [1] *

In a personal letter to the author the executive secretary of the Advent Christian General Conference of America, the Rev. C. H. Hewitt, speaks more specifically as to their views on prophecy:

"In reply to your two questions concerning prophecy,† it is true (1) that

---
[1] United States Department of Commerce, Bureau of the Census, *Religious Bodies, 1936*, Vol. 2, Part 1, p. 16.

* The Bureau of the Census follows the practice of securing from each religious body an authoritative statement regarding the history and beliefs of the body. Hence the statement here quoted rightly describes the view of the Advent Christian Church on the point discussed. The same may be said of the statements quoted from the census report regarding Seventh-day Adventists later in this chapter.

† The two queries in our letter, regarding the doctrine of the advent, were: (1) "Are there certain particular great time prophecies which your denomination sets forth as proof of this article of your faith, and if so, which ones are they?" (2) "Particularly, I would like to know what interpretation your church gives to the prophecy of Daniel 8:13, 14."

we point to the great trunk line prophecies in Daniel 2 and 7, the culminating fulfillment of Matthew 24, and the apparent historic realization of most of the symbols of Revelation, as well as other prophecies, in support of our belief that the near return of Christ is indicated; and (2) that we realize that Miller's interpretation of Daniel 8:13, 14 [the 2300-day prophecy] was proved incorrect by the passing of the time; also, that his interpretation was probably based upon a wrong premise and should be abandoned. It is doubtful, however, if there is any unanimity among us with respect to an alternative interpretation. I think we feel that the key to a correct understanding will sometime be discovered, but it would not be correct to represent that as a group we are vitally concerned with this particular item of prophecy today." [2]

In the same letter are given statistics for 1942-43, which show a total membership in the United States and Canada of 30,115, and overseas of "approximately 2,700 members," or a grand total of approximately 32,815 members.*

Retracing our steps, we come again to 1844 to sketch the rise of another Adventist body, Seventh-day Adventists. We quote from a statement prepared by this denomination and published in 1926:

"The movement which resulted in the formation of the Seventh-day Adventist denomination originated in a discussion as to the correct interpretation of the passage in Daniel viii, 13, 14, 'Then shall the sanctuary be cleansed,' which Mr. Miller and other Adventist leaders had interpreted as referring to the cleansing of the earth at the coming of Christ, which they looked for in 1844. With the passing of that period, there arose renewed investigation, and some were convinced that while there had been no mistake in regard to the time, there had been an error in interpreting the character of the event." [3]

In a later prepared statement, which sketches, first, the general advent awakening in many lands in the early nineteenth century, is found this further information regarding the origin of Seventh-day Adventists:

---

[2] Personal letter to the author, May 24, 1944.
[3] United States Department of Commerce, Bureau of the Census, *Religious Bodies, 1926*, Vol. 2, p. 24.

* The limits of this book do not permit of our discussing other and much smaller First-day Adventist churches, none of which have as many as 5,000 members. The reader is referred to the 1936 Federal Census of Religious Bodies.

"In the United States and Canada came a parallel [advent] movement. ... It was from among the Adventists engaged in this movement in America that there arose a small group in 1844, in Washington, N. H., who began to observe the seventh-day Sabbath, as they found it enjoined in the fourth commandment of the Decalogue. Thus came the first Seventh-day Adventists, though the name was not formally adopted until later years.

"Prominent among those who pioneered the work were Joseph Bates, James White, his wife, Mrs. Ellen G. White, Hiram Edson, Frederick Wheeler, and S. W. Rhodes." [4] [*]

These two quotations give us the heart of the matter regarding the genesis of the distinctive religious body known as Seventh-day Adventists.

Seventh-day Adventists, as a distinct religious body, most correctly could be described as beginning at the moment that a new interpretation was given to the prophecy of the 2300 days. That new interpretation was born the morning after the great disappointment. A Millerite, Hiram Edson, living in the State of New York, watched for the Lord to come on October 22. His sorrow, and that of others in his group, was so keen when night fell that they "wept till the day dawn" of October 23, as we have already quoted in the chapter on the disappointment. We wish now to quote again from his story in his own handwriting. After stating that they wept till morning, he declared:

"A second glance over past experience, and the lessons learned, and how when brought into strait places where light and help was needed by seeking the Lord He had answered by a voice and other ways, I began to feel there might be light and help for us in our present distress. I said to some of my brethren, 'Let us go to the barn.' We entered the granary, shut the doors about us and bowed before the Lord. We prayed earnestly, for we felt our necessity. We continued in earnest prayer until the witness

---

[4] *Ibid.*, 1936, Vol. 2, Part 1, p. 27.

[*] The reader will recognize the first two names as those of Millerite preachers, Bates having held key positions in various of the advent conferences of the early 1840's. Ellen G. White was a young woman who with her parents had been disfellowshiped from a Methodist church in Portland, Maine, for "long absence from our Church and ordinances and supporting an anti-Methodist doctrine and congregation, viz.: Millerism, etc."—*Records of Stewards and Leaders of Chestnut Street M. E. Church of Portland, Maine, from February to September, 1843, regarding the case of Robert Harmon, Eunice Harmon, Sarah B. Harmon, and Ellen Harmon.* (Ellen Harmon became Mrs. James White in 1846.) Edson, Wheeler, and Rhodes were Millerites also.

of the Spirit was given that our prayer was accepted, and that light should be given—our disappointment be explained, and made clear and satisfactory.

"After breakfast I said to one of my brethren, 'Let us go and see, and encourage some of our brethren.' We started, and while passing through a large field I was stopped about midway of the field. Heaven seemed open to my view, and I saw distinctly and clearly that instead of our High Priest coming out of the Most Holy of the heavenly sanctuary to come to this earth on the tenth day of the seventh month, at the end of the 2300 days, He for the first time entered on that day the second apartment of that sanctuary; and that He had a work to perform in the most holy before coming to this earth. That He came to the marriage at that time [as mentioned in the parable of the Ten Virgins]; in other words, to the Ancient of days to receive a kingdom, dominion, and glory; and we must wait for His return *from the wedding*. . . .

"While I was thus standing in the midst of the field, my comrade passed on almost beyond speaking distance before missing me. He inquired why I was stopping so long. I replied, 'The Lord was answering our morning prayer, by giving light with regard to our disappointment.' " [5]

The prophecy under discussion declares that at the end of the 2300 days, "then shall the sanctuary be cleansed." Hiram Edson believed that the Lord illuminated his mind, not to see a new and later date, or a revised chronology, but a different *event* as the explanation of the prophetic statement regarding the cleansing of the sanctuary. He concluded that the prophet Daniel was speaking of a work that was to be accomplished in the sanctuary in heaven, beginning at the close of the 2300 days. His views and those of his associates with whom he discussed the matter might be summed up thus:

The most simple and most literal interpretation to give to the word "sanctuary," is the place where the sacrificial work was carried on by the priests in the daily ministration of ancient Israel, or the true original of this place, that is in heaven above. The earthly sanctuary was made according to the pattern of the divine; the earthly sacrifices were but symbolic of the divine sacrifice of Christ, and the work of the High Priest in heaven, even Christ. In the earthly sanctuary the sacrificial service was

---

[5] Fragment of manuscript on his life and experiences, by Hiram Edson.

carried on throughout the year in the first of the two apartments of the sanctuary, known as the holy place. Only on the closing day of the yearly cycle of symbolic services did the high priest go into the second apartment, the most holy place. His service on that day was to cleanse the sanctuary of the uncleanness of the people, that is, from their sins, which had been brought to it during the year's ministration. This was a great day in ancient Israel, and is still a solemn day to all Jews, who consider it a day of judgment. It is known as *Yom Kippur*.

The conclusion they drew from these facts was this: If the earthly service was truly a shadow of the heavenly, then we should look for a concluding work in heaven by Christ, our High Priest, that would correspond to the concluding service of cleansing the earthly sanctuary. There can be no doubt that Daniel is speaking of the true sanctuary in heaven when he uses the word "sanctuary" in his prophecy of the 2300 days, for the earthly type would have long been ended before the prophecy was due to be fulfilled. Therefore, the prophetic event forecast in the phrase, "then shall the sanctuary be cleansed," is the entering of Christ into the most holy place in the heavenly sanctuary, there to complete His mediatorial work before coming to this earth "the second time without sin unto salvation." [6]

Edson talked over the matter with two other Millerites, O. R. L. Crosier and F. B. Hahn, with whom, he explained, "I was closely associated." Edson and Hahn were associated with Crosier in the publication of a paper called *The Day Dawn*. They decided to publish their views, and *"The Day Dawn* was sent out bearing the light on the sanctuary subject. It fell into the hands of Elders James White and Joseph Bates, who readily endorsed the view." [7] * Edson and his associates published their paper in

---

[6] See Leviticus 16; Hebrews 5 to 10.
[7] Edson manuscript.

* There is no file of *The Day Dawn* known to exist today. However, a very full statement of the view of Edson and his associates on the cleansing of the sanctuary was published in an Extra of *The Day-Star,* February 7, 1846, over the name of O. R. L. Crosier. (*The Day-Star* was a Millerite paper published in Cincinnati, Ohio.) The article fills seven and a half pages of small type and carries the rather vague and inexact title "The Law of Moses," a phrase borrowed from Malachi 4:4, which is quoted in introduction. The article

Canandaigua, New York, whereas White and Bates were in New England. That explains Edson's next statement: "This number of *The Day Dawn* opened a communication between us and these Eastern brethren." The result was: "We appointed a conference of the scattered brethren to be held at my house, and invited these our Eastern brethren to meet with us. Brother W[hite] made the effort to come; but his way was hedged up. Father Bates came on. His light was the seventh-day Sabbath." [8]

Here in a few bold strokes from the pen of a pioneer of the Seventh-day Adventists, we have the story of the beginnings of this religious body, at least so far as the key doctrine of the cleansing of the heavenly sanctuary is concerned. This branch of the river of Millerism that poured out over arid, uncharted land on October 23, 1844, began very small.* Doubtless the stream of Seventh-day Adventism would have attracted many more advent rivulets into its channel in those earliest days had it not been for the doctrine of the seventh-day Sabbath. This seemed a very great obstacle in the eyes of many. Even though the genius of the whole Millerite movement had been to study the Bible with a view to reviving and promoting long-neglected truths, the economic and social handicaps of keeping the seventh day of the week seemed too great for most Adventists. There were some, of course, who were drawn in by the force of the simple fact that the Ten Commandments specifically declare that

---

is followed by a brief note "To the Brethren and Sisters Scattered Abroad," appealing for funds to pay the cost of publication. The note is signed by Hiram Edson and F. B. Hahn. The view of the cleansing of the sanctuary set forth in this *Day-Star* article by Crosier was unqualifiedly endorsed by Ellen G. White. (See her endorsement in *A Word to the "Little Flock,"* p. 12.)

[8] *Ibid.*

* For about seven years this stream sought to increase its volume almost exclusively by drawing in those who were a part of the Millerite movement in 1844. This was due to the fact that at the very first there was held a too-restricted view of the ministry of Christ in the most holy place, coupled with the belief that the day of grace for the rejecters of the advent message had passed. In 1852 James White declared that "from the time of the great disappointment in 1844, to 1846, a number of advent brethren in different States embraced the Sabbath."—*The Advent Review and Sabbath Herald*, May 6, 1852, p. 5. But at the time of his writing in 1852 he could add: "This work is not confined to those only who have had an experience in the past advent movement. A large portion of those who are sharing the blessings attending the present truth were not connected with the advent cause in 1844."— *Ibid.*, pp. 4, 5.

"the seventh day is the Sabbath," [9] and that nowhere in the Bible is there to be found an annulment of this commandment or the giving of a new command to keep the first day of the week.

There were others of the Adventist groups who were especially attracted into the channel of this slowly enlarging stream, because the interpretation given to the 2300-day prophecy enabled them to believe that there had been truly a significance to the awakening of the world on prophecy at this very time, that indeed something of vast import in the plans of God for man had taken place in 1844. But the number of Adventists thus attracted did not greatly swell the stream.

This fact, coupled with an expanding vision and conviction on the part of those who headed the now developing Seventh-day Adventist movement, that it had a message for *all* men, set the pattern very shortly for a nation-wide and then a world-wide crusade of evangelism. But though these early leaders turned their eyes to the future, they did not turn their backs on the movement from which they had sprung. On the contrary, they found in their connection with it the primary proof that they were carrying on to completion a work divinely foretold in prophecy. This was because they believed that God's special message for men in the last days of earth's history is symbolically set forth by the messages of three angels,[10] that the first two of these messages began to be preached in a most definite way during the Millerite movement, and that the third was to follow immediately. Seventh-day Adventists from the days of the pioneers of the movement, have believed that they were the bearers of this threefold message to the world.* In 1868 James White wrote a book, the title page of which reads thus: *Life Incidents, in Connection With the Great Advent Movement, as Illustrated*

---

[9] See Exodus 20:8-11.
[10] See Revelation 14:6-11.

* This does not mean that Seventh-day Adventists confine their beliefs or their preaching to the distinctive, and as they believe, timely truths represented by this threefold message. They hold much in common with the classic creeds of Christendom. For a statement of all the major beliefs of Seventh-day Adventists see *Year Book of the Seventh-day Adventist Denomination, for 1944,* pages 4-6.

by the Three Angels of Revelation XIV. In this work he declared:

"The truth and work of God in this [advent] movement, commencing with the labors of William Miller, and reaching to the close of probation, is illustrated by these three angels [of Revelation 14:6-11]. The first was a time message, and related to the Judgment. The second described the condition of corrupted Christianity. The third is a solemn warning relative to what men may not do, and what they must do, in order to be saved at the coming of Christ. These angels illustrate the three great divisions of the genuine movement. . . .

"Seventh-day Adventists hold fast the great advent movement, hence have use for the messages. . . . They cannot spare these links in the golden chain of truth, that connect the past with the present and future, and show a beautiful harmony in the great whole. . . .

"I repeat it. The three messages symbolize the three parts of the genuine movement." [11]

Ellen G. White offers a similar testimony regarding the connection between Seventh-day Adventists and the Millerite movement:

"Miller and his associates fulfilled prophecy, and gave a message which Inspiration had foretold should be given to the world, but which they could not have given had they fully understood the prophecies pointing out their disappointment, and presenting another message to be preached to all nations before the Lord should come. The first and second angels' messages [of Revelation 14:6-8] were given at the right time, and accomplished the work which God designed to accomplish by them." [12]

"The passing of the time in 1844 was followed by a period of great trial to those who still held the advent faith. Their only relief, so far as ascertaining their true position was concerned, was the light which directed their minds to the sanctuary above. . . . They had a clearer understanding of the first and second angels' messages, and were prepared to receive and give to the world the solemn warning of the third angel of Revelation 14." [13]

Seventh-day Adventists believe that the third angel's message, when viewed in positive terms, is a call to men to honor the true Sabbath of God, the "seventh day" Sabbath of the Decalogue,

---

[11] James White, *Life Incidents*, pp. 306, 307.
[12] Ellen G. White, *The Great Controversy*, p. 405.
[13] *Ibid.*, pp. 431, 432.

that is, the day commonly known as Saturday.¹⁴ The preaching of the seventh-day Sabbath in the prophetic setting of the third angel of Revelation 14, soon became a distinctive part of this newly developing religious movement.

There have been a singular strength and an evangelizing fervor inherent in Seventh-day Adventism from the first, because of its conviction that it is to carry forward to completion a divinely foretold prophetic work that had been started under the preaching of Miller. There is found in the membership a sense of destiny and divine commission.

Seventh-day Adventists were at first largely confined to the New England States. In 1855 the headquarters was moved to Battle Creek, Michigan. In 1860,* the name "Seventh-day Adventist" was officially adopted. In May, 1863, a formal denominational organization was created. In 1903 the headquarters was moved to Washington, D. C.

The growth of the Seventh-day Adventist movement through the years would probably not be described as spectacular, and for three definite reasons. First, the doctrine of the seventh-day Sabbath has ever proved an obstacle too great for the majority of people to surmount. This, coupled with a code of living that bans liquor, tobacco, the theater, the dance, and kindred amusements, has prevented all but the most ardent believers in the teachings of the movement from becoming members. It is one thing to believe the truth of certain teachings, it is quite another thing to order one's life according to those teachings, especially if that means a complete reordering of the life. Yet no one is counted as a member unless his life is thus ordered.

Second, anything of a sensational or fanatical character has been discountenanced and condemned. From the very first, the leaders have viewed holy living as having no connection with sensationalism in conduct. †

---

¹⁴ See Exodus 20:8-11.

* At a conference held in Battle Creek, September 20 to October 1.

† The writings of Ellen G. White carry repeated denunciation of everything bordering on fanatical actions. This is particularly true in her writings in the early years, when the

Third, the Seventh-day Adventist body has always held that the exact time of the advent cannot be discovered from a study of prophecy. This has inevitably kept the movement from rising to any climaxes of dramatic appeal to the multitudes, which climaxes might have resulted in at least temporarily large expansions of the membership.

These three reasons which help to explain why the growth has not been spectacular, also suggest that the growth has probably been solid. It might even be reasonably presumed that a membership consisting of men and women who hold their beliefs, despite the economic and social handicaps involved, may really be far more significant as a spiritual force in the world than mere statistics of membership would suggest. The membership in the United States and Canada, as of December 31, 1943, was 201,111. The overseas membership at that date, and as nearly as war conditions permitted the gathering of statistics, was 343,599. This gives a grand total of at least 544,710 members. The grand total Sabbath school membership stood at 654,370 at the end of 1943.

But this does not really provide an accurate picture of the vigor of the movement. Its activities and commitments over the world give us a sharper picture. World figures at the close of 1943 show 61 publishing houses and branches, with a total sale of denominational literature of $7,682,683.94. There is a world total of 173 hospitals, sanitariums, clinics, and dispensaries. The church school system consists of 3,304 schools, counting grammar schools, intermediate schools, and colleges, with a total enrollment in 1943 of 128,529 students. Mission stations are found in every continent and in every island group in the world. Seventh-day Adventist literature is published in 200 languages and dialects, and is preached in more than 800.

---

movement might have easily attracted to itself an unstable element. Such an element can swell the membership figures, but there is only weakness in such numbers. This is not to say that no fanatics have arisen at any time. That could not be said of even the most perfect church organization in the history of Christendom. But it is a simple statement of fact that the movement has ever given fanaticism a chill reception. The emphasis has ever been on practical godliness.

DID THE ADVENT FAITH DIE WITH MILLER? 465

The willingness of a man to back up his beliefs with his cash is generally considered, even by skeptics, as a good test of the vitality of his religion. Seventh-day Adventists give 10 per cent, a tithe, of their income, before spending any of that income on themselves. They believe that this 10 per cent belongs to God, and quote Scripture in support of the belief. In addition, they give freewill offerings to support home and foreign missions and their private school system. In 1943 their per capita payment of tithes and offerings in the United States and Canada, for all purposes, was $101.04, or a total for the 201,111 members of $20,322,228.32. The 1943 appropriation for overseas mission work for the year 1944 was $5,616,166.89.*

The explanation for this is to be found in the strong confidence of Seventh-day Adventists in the belief that they are the inheritors of a sacred trust, that to them has been given the task of calling on all men to make ready for the second advent of Christ and for a better world which God has prepared for those who love Him. As already stated, Seventh-day Adventists do not set a time for Christ to come. They take very literally His declaration, "Of that day and hour knoweth no man, no, not the angels of heaven, but My Father only." [15] But they do believe, on the strength of Christ's equally clear-cut statement, that when certain prophecies are fulfilled, and certain signs which He described, take place, we may know that His coming "is near, even at the doors." [16]

Christ illustrated this statement by declaring that when we see the buds breaking forth in the springtime we know that summer is nigh, even though those buds provide no exact measure of the nearness of the summer. He also called on His followers to be in constant anticipation of His coming. In response to the inquiry of His disciples, "What shall be the sign of Thy coming,

---

[15] Matthew 24:36.
[16] Matthew 24:33.

*Needless to say, these figures, when viewed on a per capita basis, stand in a class apart, in the comparative tables of contributions or mission appropriations that are prepared by interchurch organizations.

and of the end of the world?" He gave an extended forecast of events. In that forecast He refers to the writings of "Daniel the prophet" and adds: "Whoso readeth, let him understand." [17] The last book of the Bible, called the Revelation, and written by Christ's beloved disciple, John, opens with these words:

"The Revelation of Jesus Christ, which God gave unto Him, to show unto His servants things which must shortly come to pass; and He sent and signified it by His angel unto His servant John.... Blessed is he that readeth, and they that hear the words of this prophecy, and keep those things which are written therein: for the time is at hand." [18]

This book of Revelation, like that of the book of Daniel in the Old Testament, is filled with prophetic statements concerning events that are to take place, ending with the climax of the second advent of Christ. Seventh-day Adventists declare that the man who believes in the inspiration of the Bible can come to only one conclusion after studying such texts as those just quoted. That conclusion is this: While finite man cannot know the exact time of Christ's advent, he can know when it is near, even at the doors, and that he is to gain this knowledge by a study of the prophecies in the Book of God.

Seventh-day Adventists stress the fact that this is precisely the conclusion that pious men through the centuries have reached. The Millerites made no claim to being the first to search the Bible prophecies in an endeavor to learn something of God's plan for the future of our world. On the contrary, those who took part in the advent awakening a hundred years ago declared emphatically that they were proclaiming the ancient doctrine of the second advent in the setting of the fulfilling prophecies, and that their understanding of these prophecies accorded with the conclusions of the most devout and learned theologians of previous generations.

The subject of Bible prophecy has occupied the studious hours, not only of pious men, but of very wise, scholarly Christians as well. Contrary to a shallow, skeptical view,

---
[17] See Matthew 24.
[18] Revelation 1:1-3.

scholarship and the love of the Scriptures have often gone hand in hand, and included in that has been a profound interest in the inspired prophecies of Scripture. The searching of these prophecies is not the peculiar pastime of fanatics or crackpots. Although the learned who have made prophecy their special study have differed on many points, the number of their points of agreement is most encouraging to all who believe that the Bible is inspired and that the more it is studied the better it can be understood.

Everyone is acquainted with the name of Sir Isaac Newton, doubtless one of the most brilliant men who ever lived, the scientist who formulated the law of gravitation and certain of the laws of motion. But few people know that Sir Isaac spent his energy, not simply in delving into the things of the natural world, but also into those of the spiritual. He was a great student of Bible prophecy and wrote a book entitled *Observations Upon the Prophecies of Daniel, and the Apocalypse of St. John.* He took the position that God designs that men shall understand the various prophecies when the time of their fulfillment is at hand. He did not believe that God intended that the prophecies should be used by any interpreter far in advance to foretell events that could not otherwise be known, as though God intended to make a prophet of him. This led him to conclude:

"But if the last age, the age of opening these things, be now approaching, as by the great successes of late interpreters it seems to be, we have more encouragement than ever to look into these things. If the general preaching of the gospel be approaching, it is to us and our posterity that those words mainly belong: 'In the time of the end the wise shall understand, but none of the wicked shall understand. Blessed is he that readeth, and they that hear the words of this prophecy, and keep those things which are written therein.' ...

"There is already so much of the prophecy fulfilled, that as many as will take pains in this study, may see sufficient instances of God's providence: but then the signal revolutions predicted by all the holy prophets, will at once both turn men's eyes upon considering the predictions, and plainly interpret them. Till then we must content ourselves with interpreting what hath been already fulfilled.

"Amongst the interpreters of the last age there is scarce one of note who hath not made some discovery worth knowing; and thence I seem to gather that God is about opening these mysteries. The success of others put me upon considering it; and if I have done anything which may be useful to following writers, I have my design." [19]

In the same connection Sir Isaac draws this parallel between Christ's first and second advents:

"As the few and obscure prophecies concerning Christ's first coming were for setting up the Christian religion, which all nations have since corrupted; so the many and clear prophecies concerning the things to be done at Christ's second coming, are not only for predicting but also for effecting a recovery and re-establishment of the long lost truth, and setting up a kingdom wherein dwells righteousness." [20]

Said Sir Isaac: "I seem to gather that God is about opening these mysteries." This was written about one hundred years before Miller began to preach. Seventh-day Adventists agree heartily with Newton that the prophecies concerning Christ's second coming are intended to play an important part in "effecting a recovery and re-establishment of the long lost truth, and setting up a kingdom wherein dwells righteousness."

There have been only two views of the future of our world that have had any standing in Christendom; one is that man by his own inherent powers, or through some measure of imparted wisdom and goodness, will finally drive out wickedness from the earth and remake this evil world; the other view is that God will suddenly bring an end to this evil age and supernaturally set up a new earth wherein dwells righteousness. The former belief is probably at its worst discount today.* With a world prostrated the second time in a generation by international carnage, even the most ardent believers in man's inherent potentialities for goodness have been forced to confess that there may be truth in the old-fashioned doctrine of man's sinfulness. Nor is there any reason to believe that the most perfect peace plan for Europe

---

[19] Sir Isaac Newton, *Observations Upon the Prophecies*, pp. 251-253.
[20] *Ibid.*, p. 252.
* See Appendix M.

or the world can remove from man that evil thing called sin, that deep-seated force that breaks out in envy, jealousy, avarice, hatred, murder, and a thousand kindred ways. Hence if we are to look for a better world through human endeavor, we are committed to a doctrine of pessimism.

The latter view, that God's day of grace for those who are determined to do evil, is to come to an end, and that then Christ will return, is a view that has the support of the prophets and apostles, and the creeds of the great religious bodies through the long centuries. To that genuinely optimistic view Seventh-day Adventists are committed. For its promotion they spend their energies and resources. They promote it in the setting of Bible prophecies, which, by the confession of many commentators, have been fulfilled in the last century or so of the Christian Era. And they believe with these prophetic commentators that the next great event is the coming of Christ. Seventh-day Adventists view themselves as in the spiritual succession of those who have ever looked to God and not to man for the solution of the tragedy of an evil world. Nor do they feel they must long wait for the solution, for they believe that Christ's coming is "near, even at the doors."

CHAPTER 30

The Case for the Defense Summed Up

THE MOST IMPRESSIVE CHARGES against Millerism have been considered in the preceding chapters. We do not say we have examined every charge or story or rumor that has gained currency during the century. That would be impossible. But we do feel safe in saying that all the major charges that seemed to have any semblance of truth have been examined. We believe that the evidence submitted, which has been drawn from original sources, leads to the following conclusions:

1. That the advent awakening in America, known as Millerism, was paralleled by a similar, spontaneous awakening of interest in other parts of the world.

2. That Miller was a sensible, respectable man of good standing in his community, who went forth to preach his views out of a sincere conviction that he had a message for his fellow man, and that because of his respectable standing his testimony in defense of himself and the movement may properly be given great weight.

3. That Miller's principal ministerial associates, who constituted the core of the movement, were likewise men of blameless character who proceeded in good faith in the undertaking called Millerism, and therefore their testimony in defense of the movement may properly be given great weight.

4. That the movement consisted of a cross section of America, including even some of the cultured in its circle, and that the great body of these Millerites were normal in their religious life and circumspect in their deportment.

5. That while there were occasional fanatical acts by

THE CASE FOR THE DEFENSE SUMMED UP 471

individuals, or by small groups who accepted Millerism, such acts should not rightly be charged against the movement, because:

a. No movement, religious or otherwise, should in fairness be judged by exceptional cases, particularly if the movement is too new or loose-knit to possess the power to control the individual who uses its name while acting contrary to its principles.

b. The Millerite leaders consistently were on record, in both a general and a specific way, against all fanaticism.*

6. That in view of the fact that the Millerites forthrightly discussed and denounced certain fanatical acts within the movement, their equally forthright denials of numerous charges, which would generally have been no more embarrassing to admit, ought to be given great weight.

7. That the various charges against the Millerites have been built largely on rumor and hearsay, which no court of law would accept as evidence.

8. That Millerite preaching did not fill the asylums or cause men and women to do insane, violent acts, such as committing suicide or murder.

9. That with the exception of the incidents noted, the Millerites did not engage in fanatical acts, either in fields or on housetop or mountaintops, in connection with the day of expectation, October 22, 1844; that, on the contrary, the best evidence requires us to believe that the majority, at least, were gathered for prayer, in churches or homes, happy but calm in anticipation of the advent.

10. That the Millerites did not wear ascension robes.

11. That instead of producing fanatical excesses, the preaching of Millerism produced genuine revivals of religious life, as illustrated by the quickening of men's consciences to make restitution for thefts and other crimes.

12. That Millerism was not a new religious sect with a strange array of new doctrines, but was, instead, an interchurch

---

* Such credulity as some of them displayed in regard to a phenomenon like Sister Matthewson, merely reflected the credulity of the majority of people in those days.

movement that sought to revive and to stress one great doctrine: the ancient Christian teaching as to the personal coming of Christ to bring judgment to the wicked and redemption to the righteous.

13. That Millerism was much more than a mere point of time.

14. That some of their most prominent theological opponents were as definitely predicting, in terms of Bible prophecy, an end to the present evil world—by the gradual ushering in of a better one—and were as definitely mistaken, as were the Millerites. (At least we think these opponents, if raised from their graves to survey the ruins of the world after World War II, would not have the hardihood to contend that their predictions had been fulfilled. In fact, we think they might be rather willing to return to their graves.)

15. That these theological opponents frankly admitted that the Millerites had the best of scholarly support for their basic principles of prophetic interpretation; and an examination of learned prophetic works of former days reveals that the Millerite teachings regarding the major prophecies also had the most eminent support.

16. That in view of this admission, the fact that the Millerites made one major mistake—their interpretation of the sanctuary cleansing in Daniel 8:13, 14—is in itself no valid reason for discounting *in toto* this second advent movement, or for describing the Millerites as fanatical and irrational. No one has ever heard their equally mistaken opponents thus described.

17. That scholarly theologians for a century or two preceding Miller had been coming to an increasing understanding of Bible prophecies and to the conclusion that the great day of God was drawing on apace.

18. That Sir Isaac Newton had been so strongly impressed by the success attending the endeavors to understand prophecy that he saw in this very fact of the unsealing of prophecy an evidence that the time of the fulfillment of the last events of earth's history must not be very far away.

19. That in view of the fact that the Millerites employed

the same prophetic principles and reached the same conclusions on the major prophecies as the great majority of these earlier students of prophecy, Millerism should be viewed as really an expansion and popularization of prophetic study that formerly had largely been confined to cloisters and seminary classrooms.

20. That thus viewed, Millerism takes its place in the unfolding plan of the great God who has promised increasing light on the prophecies, with increasing wisdom to understand them in the last days. (The error in Millerite interpretation need not be blurred over in order to view the movement in this way. There is ever the human as well as the divine element present in the best of religious movements. Even Christ's disciples suffered a great disappointment at the crucifixion because they had not rightly interpreted one of the key statements of the prophets concerning Christ, that He must suffer humiliation and death before He could be glorified.)

These conclusions, we believe, logically flow from the evidence set forth in the preceding chapters. With the fogs of rumor and religious prejudice thus removed, Millerism stands out, not as a flawless movement, either in doctrine or in deportment—there never has been such—but as a movement that does not suffer by comparison with other religious awakenings that have taken place through the centuries.

The very genius of the movement may be described as the active endeavor of a company of Christians to understand more fully the will and ways of God toward man, in anticipation of meeting Him face to face. And that endeavor to understand was in terms of an ardent study of the Bible, emphasizing the historic Protestant principle of employing the literal meaning wherever possible, in contrast to the growing practice of spiritualizing away the clear-cut declarations of Holy Writ. As Miller himself well expressed it in his letter to an infidel editor: "Millerism is to believe, try to understand, love, and proclaim to others, the good news contained in the Bible." [1] Millerism

---

[1] Letter from Miller, Jan. 27, 1845, in *Boston Investigator*, Feb. 12, 1845.

was a focusing on the climactic "good news" of the Bible, that Christ will come "the second time without sin unto salvation." [2] In other words, Millerism was the revival and bringing into prominence of the ancient belief and hope in the supernatural second advent of Christ, the hope which lighted the path of patriarchs, prophets, and apostles, and gave fortitude to the martyrs. We believe that the growth and success of Millerism is best explained by a secular editor whose obituary notice on Miller we have already quoted. This editor recalled having heard Miller preach on the second advent and observed:

"His evident sincerity, earnestness and simplicity attracted to him our greatest respect. We think the success which marked his labors . . . arose from his bringing prominently forward a neglected truth." [3]

Eminent theologians, both in the Old World and in the New, who specialized in the field of prophecy had been declaring for generations that the principal Bible prophecies were ending and that no other great event but the second advent lay ahead. Was it not time for some movement to arise to turn the minds and hearts of men to this central truth of the second advent of Christ in the setting of Bible prophecy?

---

[2] Hebrews 9:28.
[3] *Littel's Living Age,* Jan. 19, 1850, p. 138.

ACKNOWLEDGMENTS

The saying is both old and inspired, that no man liveth unto himself. Certainly no author who wishes to do thorough work can hope to live to himself. He is beholden to a wide circle of helpful friends. And those friends may run the whole gamut from a learned archivist in a great institution to an obscure individual in a humble cottage. Sometimes it is the latter who supplies, with a faded letter, a link in the chain that might otherwise ever be missing. It is always a pleasure to make acknowledgments. It is also a perplexity. An author wishes to name specifically those whose aid has been of major significance, but he cannot extend the list indefinitely, lest it get out of bounds. Hence the perplexity in deciding where to draw the line. The following have given assistance of very real and substantial value in the preparation of this work:

In the field of research: William Sumner Appleton, corresponding secretary, The Society for the Preservation of New England Antiquities, Boston, Massachusetts; Elbert Benton and Margaret Dempster, director and librarian respectively of the Western Reserve Historical Society, Cleveland, Ohio; Clarence S. Brigham and Clifford K. Shipton, director and librarian respectively of the American Antiquarian Society, Worcester, Massachusetts; Everett N. Dick, professor of history and political science, Union College, Lincoln, Nebraska; LeRoy E. Froom, curator of the Advent Source Collection, Washington, D. C.; Orrin Roe Jenks, president emeritus, Aurora College, and curator of the Adventual Collection, Aurora, Illinois; Lucy W. Markley, librarian, Union Theological Seminary, New York City; Earle Williams Newton, director of the Vermont Historical Society, Montpelier, Vermont; Arthur W. Spalding, director of social education, Madison College, Tennessee;

Arthur L. White, secretary of the Ellen G. White Publications, Washington, D. C.

As readers of the manuscript of this book (including some mentioned in the preceding paragraph): G. T. Anderson, H. M. Blunden, C. L. Bond, A. S. Maxwell, D. E. Rebok, M. L. Rice, D. E. Robinson, F. M. Wilcox.

As readers of the section of the manuscript that deals with Millerism and insanity: See special note of acknowledgment on page 369, at the close of Chapter 24.

As readers of portions of the manuscript that deal with points of law and evidence: Philip M. M. Phelps, attorney at law, Fair Haven, Vermont; Millward C. Taft, attorney at law, Washington, D. C.

As a reader of the manuscript in order to prepare an artistic layout and illustrations for the book: T. K. Martin.

In addition to the foregoing whose assistance can be classified into well-defined divisions, there are a number who gave very real aid in various ways. We mention the following: Mrs. Ella L. Adams, Grace E. Amadon, Alonzo L. Baker, Edward L. Bartholomew, Willis J. Bartholomew, Mary Elizabeth Brown, Donald K. Campbell, R. E. Crawford, Mary Jane Dybdahl, Charles O. Farnham, J. R. Ferren, C. H. Hewitt, B. P. Hoffman, Hazel E. Malick, Edith G. McClellan, Mrs. J. Lewis Neal, Walter M. Ost, Stanley H. Perry, Clara Endicott Sears, Clifton L. Taylor, H. E. Thompson, Charles E. Weniger.

And then there is that group who by the traditions of the publishing business ever remain the unsung heroes of the literary world—the book editor, the copy editors, and the proofreaders. They are the silent branch of the service. They convoy the author safely across the turbulent seas of solecisms, split infinitives, and dangling participles, to the port of publication. Some authors might make the journey without them. This one could not.

APPENDICES

Appendix A

MILLER FAMILY GENEALOGY

According to the best sources available the genealogy of William Miller may be traced from the seventeenth century onward as follows:

Thomas Miller: born, Springfield, Massachusetts. Killed by Indians in King Philip's War, 1675.

Ensign John Miller: born, Springfield, Massachusetts, April 23, 1657; died in 1735.

Captain Joseph Miller: born, Springfield, Massachusetts, March 12, 1700; died April 25, 1760.

William Miller: born, Springfield, Massachusetts, March 29, 1730.

Captain William Miller: born, Pittsfield, Massachusetts, December 14, 1757; moved to Low Hampton, New York, April, 1786; died December 23, 1812.

Captain William Miller: born, Pittsfield, Massachusetts, February 15, 1782; moved to Low Hampton, New York, April, 1786; died December 20, 1849. Leader of the Millerite movement.

Miller's father was a soldier in the Revolutionary War and later became a captain of the State militia of New York.

Miller had ten children. The youngest child, Lucy Ann, born March 1, 1825, married Warren Bartholomew. Two of their children are living at the time of this writing (September 26, 1944): a son, Willis J. (born June 27, 1868); and a daughter, Ella L. Adams (born March 12, 1871). These are the only surviving grandchildren of William Miller.

The sources from which this genealogy has been constructed are:

The genealogical pages in a Miller family Bible in the possession of a great-grandson, Philip M. M. Phelps, Fair Haven, Vermont.

The genealogical pages in a Miller family Bible in the possession of a great-grandson, Edward L. Bartholomew (nephew of Willis J.), Marblehead, Massachusetts.

C. S. Williams, *Descendants of Captain Joseph Miller of Springfield, Massachusetts, 1698-1908.*

The Miller Family Magazine, edited by William Montgomery Clemens, New York City, Vol. I, No. 3, July, 1916.

Sylvester Bliss, *Memoirs of William Miller,* pp. 1-7.

As is true of the genealogical records of many families, there are discrepancies in the Miller genealogy as given by different writers. However, these discrepancies are small, having to do with minor variations in dates of birth of one or two ancestors, etc. Where there is a discrepancy, the figures given are in harmony with the weight of evidence.

Appendix B

THE CLEMONS LETTER ON MILLERITE ACTIVITIES IN OCTOBER, 1844

[The following manuscript letter provides one of the best descriptions of the tempo of Millerism in the days just before the expected advent. Spelling, punctuation, capitalization, unedited.]

Boston 10th Oct. 1844.

Dear Brother Miller,

I was deeply interested in hearing yours of the 6th inst.* read at the Tabernacle last evening by Brother Himes, & gladly write you in compliance with his request.

The Midnight Cry is searching our souls through & through. We feel to humble ourselves in the dust & magnify the Lord.

He that is mighty hath done great things: & holy is his name. We had never been brought into this faith had we not known the voice of God. He has said My sheep hear my voice & they follow me. There was something sweet, soul-subduing & heavenly in the sound of this Cry when I first heard it at the Exeter Campmeeting. Yet I was kept back by "wise & prudent" considerations from embracing the present truth until about a week since when I came to this place.

Such a breaking down of soul I never saw—no power but the sword of the Spirit can slay in this manner. Tuesday evening Brother Jones† lectured in the Tabernacle on this Cry which he had got into his soul with all its blessedness. He is clear & strong in the faith & his words have mighty power

---

* This is the letter in which Miller declared, "I see a glory in the seventh month," and expressed his belief that the Lord would come October 22.

† This is very likely I. E. Jones, who was in Boston about this time, as a letter of his to Miller a little later reveals. Henry Jones, early in October, was recovering from an illness in Vergennes, Vermont.

—this is the case with all who receive it from the Lord. Brother Himes came out last Sabbath (on his return from N. Y.) & expressed his belief that the Lord would come on the tenth of the seventh month. A great sensation was produced. Many had been hoping that he would not embrace the trying truth & that they in consequence would have an excuse to shelter them in the day of the Lord. These souls Brother Himes very emphatically shook off from his skirts. He then gave a summary of the work of arousing the world to judgment. First there was the proclamation that the Lord was coming. Then came the defence of this truth—the settling the controversies of Zion—& lastly the preparation for the Saviour's coming which is our present work. The Tabernacle is crowded, every night & doubtless will be by day now that the Conference has commenced. At six o'clock this morning there was a prayer meeting at that place. Br. Himes is in a sea of business. Two power presses running constantly day & night can scarcely supply the demand for the last [Advent] Herald. Multitudes are pouring in from the country to attend the Conference—comparatively few lecturers come however, they are going on the wings of steam to sound the glorious Cry. Brother Brown arrived last evening from Nantucket stopping at New Bedford on his way. He give an interesting account of the state of things at those places. As in other places the cry arose all at once & thrilled through the souls of all. Brother Brown thinks he cannot stop here scarcely at all—but has concluded to relieve Brother Himes by remaining today & assisting at the Tabernacle. We would gladly have you with us, but the Lord's will be done—as you say we shall meet in a few days. The Spirit of the Lord moved upon my dear father to accompany me to this place. He attended the meetings at the Tabernacle for several days & is quite broken down before the truth—he says it is God's work & if he could have the broken & contrite heart of an Adventist he would be willing to be called by that name! Praise the Lord!

Last evening (Wed.) Brother Himes addressed the immense congregation at the T. His subject was in Dan. 9th showing that it was *time* that caused the prophet to set his face unto the Lord God to seek by prayer & supplication, with fasting & sackcloth & ashes. Before closing he read your very welcome letter & we all felt to praise the Lord. We knew you would embrace the faith for we read when the cry was made, "all those virgins arose & trimmed their lamps."

Brother Bliss has left for Hartford to sound the alarm. His wife & family have arrived in this place. Sister B is penitent & believing & designs going forward in baptism. Brother Litch arrived yesterday. Sister Hedge at whose house I am stopping, has dismissed her boarders, & thrown open her doors to the Advent people. Her movement is speaking loudly The Lord is Coming!

Glory be to God! dear brother we shall soon meet in the kingdom—
Till then a short farewell!

In the glorious hope of seeing Jesus on the tenth of the seventh month,

Your sister,

[Signed] E. C. Clemons.

[Immediately below Mrs. Clemons' letter is the following penciled note from Himes to Miller.]

Dear Br. Miller:

The above is written at my request. I know you will excuse me for not writting you at length—The time is short. I am reigned up to the Judgment. I never felt it so before. God is now *testing us*. Do we believe what we have preached—We have got to answer it—on the *answer, yea,* or *nay,* depends our Salvation.

Love to all the Brethren. My faith is given in the [Advent] Herald. God bless you. And may we *meet* Soon in the Kingdom.

Oct. 10, 1844. [Signed] J. V. Himes.

Appendix C

THE SO-CALLED TRIAL OF JOSHUA V. HIMES

While Millerism was flourishing in the early 1840's, open enemies charged Himes with profiting personally by his connection with the publishing business of the movement, and of being generally unscrupulous. These charges he met vigorously and forthrightly with detailed rejoinders, as the reader has noted in the quotations from him in this book. A faint echo of these charges is found in a now rare pamphlet of 135 pages entitled *The Trial of Elder J. V. Himes Before the Chardon Street Church Together With a Vindication of the Course Taken by Prof. J. P. Weethee and Elder George Needham Relative to the Late Difficulties. Published by Order of the Church.*

This pamphlet was printed in 1850. It describes what is alleged to be the trial of Himes before the Chardon Street Church on seven charges. Most of these charges have to do with personalities and situations on which it would be very difficult for anyone to reach a satisfactory decision. The accusers also charged that Himes held certain properties, like *The Advent Herald,* as personal, while drawing funds for the support of them on the ground that he was simply the agent of the advent movement. Even these charges as framed by his accusers provide very little reason to believe that Himes *personally* profited by his various transactions.

The answer to these charges is found in another equally rare pamphlet published in 1851 entitled *Defence of Elder Joshua V. Himes: Being a History of the Fanaticism, Puerilities and Secret Workings of Those Who, Under the Garb of Friendship, Have Proved the Most Deadly Enemies of the Advent Cause.* (Published by Order of the Chardon Street Church.)

This 1851 pamphlet fills 268 pages. The 1850 pamphlet states specifically that Himes was tried "before the Chardon Street Church." The 1851 defense pamphlet not only declares it is "published by order of the Chardon-Street Church," but prints on the reverse side of the title page the text of the "Action of the Chardon-Street Church" authorizing the preparation and publication of the pamphlet, and gives the names of the persons appointed as a committee to prepare the defense. Included are the names of two well-known Millerite leaders, Sylvester Bliss and Apollos Hale.

The defense pamphlet gives a detailed history of the activities of a dissident faction, culminating in the withdrawal from the church in the summer of 1850, of a portion of the church, under the leadership of J. P. Weethee. Himes was in very poor health and Weethee had for a time been serving as pastor of the church. When this faction withdrew they boldly presumed to call themselves still the Chardon Street Church. This explains why both pamphlets declare on the title page that they are published by order of the church. There was no "trial" of Himes in the usually accepted sense of the word. Evidently he was tried in absentia, his accusers serving as prosecutors, jury, and judge. Certainly the 1850 pamphlet of the "trial" gives no defense testimony and consists wholly of accusations and elaborations on the accusations. It is conservative to say that the 1851 pamphlet, in defense, presents a rather convincing case.

Appendix D

MILLER'S ACCUSATION OF FANATICISM

In Chapter 18 Miller was quoted as declaring that the movement had been guilty of fanaticism. Much has been made of this by critics. We do not think Miller's statement, when viewed in the setting of a series of facts, provides any basis for the conclusion that the movement was distinguished by fanaticism. He is writing of "the causes which required God's chastising hand upon us." In his opinion these were "pride, fanaticism, and sectarianism." Pride was displayed, he feared, in not giving God the glory for victories won; and sectarianism in blanketing all other religious bodies under the indictment "Babylon," for Miller had been the one leading Millerite who declined to the very end to endorse any divisive element in the preaching of the advent. Of fanaticism he said:

"I know our enemies accused of this before we were guilty; but this did not excuse us for running into it. A thousand expressions were used, without thought or reflection, and I thought sometimes very irreverently, such as 'Bless God,' etc. I was afraid it was done in very many cases to the appearance of outward piety, rather than as the hidden manna of the heart. Sometimes our meetings were distinguished by noise and confusion, and, forgive me brethren, if I express myself too strongly, it appeared to me more like Babel, than a solemn assembly of penitents bowing in humble reverence before a holy God. I have often obtained more evidence of inward piety from a *kindling eye,* a *wet cheek,* and a *choked utterance,* than from all the *noise* in Christendom." [1]

The first fact to have in mind in evaluating this statement is that Miller was ultraconservative in his ideas about propriety. That is evident from the whole story of his life. He stated in one of his letters, from which we quoted, that he used no "anxious seats," so dramatically employed by many revivalists in those times to bring penitents to a decision. He said that he preferred simply using the naked sword of the Spirit and applying the strong arguments from the Word. There is further proof of his exceptional conservatism in his aversion to the use of various "expressions" so commonly employed in many religious services in his day, like "Bless God." We are certain Miller would have found occasion to write several long letters against "fanaticism" if he had participated in the usual camp meetings of the day that had no connection with Millerism.

The next fact to remember is that throughout the whole camp meeting season in 1844 he had been far west, as Ohio and western New York were then described. With the exception of a meeting or two on the Eastern seaboard en route home in the fall, he had been out of touch with the whole body of Adventists in the main centers of the East. This, his diary reveals. Now we have already presented evidence to show that all camp meetings in the early nineteenth century were rather fervent affairs, and especially was this true out west. It is easy to imagine that the multitudes who came to the meetings of Miller, Himes, and others on that western tour in 1844 were not too restrained. They doubtless acted as they had been accustomed to act at their camp meetings and great revivals. And let it not be forgotten that whereas the meetings were Millerite meetings, in that they were sponsored by them, many thousands of those who attended were not Millerites. Hosts of people came out of curiosity to hear what this new doctrine was.

The third fact to remember is that when Miller returned to Low Hampton, wondering, perhaps, how affairs stood with all the believers in the

---

[1] *The Advent Herald,* Dec. 18, 1844, p. 147.

East, there came to him the letters from Litch and Whiting, which we have quoted. Those letters, particularly Litch's, described the fanatical view of Gorgas, about fleeing from the cities. And Whiting's letter added a brief statement about the fanatical enthusiasm of Mrs. Higgins, a woman who had done some preaching and was now infecting others with her unwarranted confidence in strange signs and wonders. Perhaps Whiting's letter was unduly critical. He had never accepted the "seventh-month movement," but he was a leader among the Millerites, and his words, along with those of Litch, would naturally have very great weight with Miller. Furthermore, the very fact that Miller had not been traveling in the summer of 1844 in New England, and had visited only a few places on the eastern seaboard, where most of the Millerite interest was found, made him depend almost wholly on letters in forming his judgments.

Now an examination of the Miller correspondence of this period immediately after the disappointment reveals that it contains few letters from leaders, persons on whose general opinion he would be likely to rely. The Litch and Whiting letters therefore stand out prominently. Yet they were describing very circumscribed incidents, as we have discovered.

The last fact to remember is that almost immediately afterward there appeared in *The Advent Herald* a letter from Elon Galusha, a rather prominent Millerite, which took definite exception to Miller's statement about fanaticism. Miller had written his letter on December 3, and it was published in *The Advent Herald* on December 18. Galusha wrote on December 25, as follows:

"I fear Brother Miller's frank and unguarded expressions in his last letter published in the *Herald*, will furnish an unrighteous weapon in the hands of the enemies of the cause. His admissions as to the fault of Adventists are true in their application to the *few*, but not to the many. Our opponents will seize upon them with avidity and use them as though they were intended for general application—as they did Brother Storrs' confession. In admitting, (as we should honestly do) the faults of Adventists, we must *discriminate*—else we shall prove our own slanderers. The host of *honest, discreet,* and *consistent* Adventists, must not be charged (either by admissions or implications) with the faults of the few. Our dear unsuspecting brother, uses the pronoun *we,* when he ought to use the *third person they.* While we patiently bear the buffetings of the wicked, and the unsparing denunciations of Christian editors and ministers, for our integrity—and while we meekly submit to chastening for our *real* faults—let us be careful not inadvertently to furnish deadly weapons for the use of our antagonists." [2]

Miller's comment on this criticism by Galusha is found in a letter he

---

[2] *Ibid.*, Jan. 8, 1845, p. 173.

wrote on January 15, 1845, to Joseph Marsh. Marsh printed the letter in his paper, *The Voice of Truth*. Wrote Miller:

"I see in the *Herald* of January 8th my good brethren Galusha and Mansfield have administered a good, hearty rebuke to me, for giving our enemies, priests and editors, a chance to slander us, by my unguarded remarks, in which, after all is summed up, the fault lies in using the little word *we* instead of *they*. In justification, permit me to say, brethren, that when I write to or speak of those whom my soul loves, it is to me more natural and more congenial to my heart to use the word we; therefore, if I have erred, it is an error of the heart, and shows me wrong in this case certainly. . . . To me, the word *we* has so much Christian fellowship and love in it, so little dogmatism and selfishness in it, that I cannot help but love, admire and esteem it for its simplicity and honesty." [3]

In the light of this series of facts Miller's statement is placed in proper focus and accepted, without weakening in any way the evidence submitted as to the decorous manner in which the Millerite movement in general was conducted even during the climactic days of October, 1844.

Appendix E

HIMES' COMMENT ON GORGAS INCIDENT

In Chapter 22 the Philadelphia encampment, led by Doctor Gorgas, is discussed. There, evidence from two Philadelphia Millerites was presented to show that Gorgas deceived not more than two hundred Philadelphia Adventists into going out to a camp about four miles from the city, and that despite the fact that they followed the extravagant notions of Gorgas in thus going out, there was no evidence that any fanatical acts were indulged in at the encampment. In that chapter we reached the conclusion that outside of the Philadelphia encampment there is no dependable evidence that any well-defined group of Millerites went afield, either through the urgings of a visionary like Gorgas or simply through a natural desire to be far from a sinful city on the great day.

This conclusion may seem to run counter to a statement made by Himes about six months after the incident. Referring briefly to the Gorgas affair, he wrote: "In some places, many embraced his view, and carried it out, in all its extravagance." [1] Does this statement require us to revise all our conclusions in Chapter 22? We think not, and for the following reasons:

1. Immediately after the Gorgas incident *The Midnight Cry* published the detailed account of the affair as it applied to Philadelphia. It seems

---

[3] *The Voice of Truth*, Feb. 5, 1845, p. 5.
[1] *The Morning Watch*, April 3, 1845, p. 112.

unreasonable to think that if there had been similar encampments in other cities, no word of them would have been printed in the Millerite papers. The very reason that prompted the write-up of the Philadelphia encampment, explained *The Midnight Cry* editor, was his desire to know the facts regarding the stories that had appeared in the public press concerning that encampment. Would he not have had an equal desire to know the truth of stories in the papers about encampments in other cities—if such encampments had been written up in the public press?

2. That brings us, logically, to the inquiry: If the Philadelphia papers wrote up the story of the encampment near their city, would not the papers of other cities have likewise printed the startling news of a similar encampment near their cities—if there had been such encampments? These papers copied the story of the Philadelphia encampment, which proves they considered such an incident news. We did find one item in a Philadelphia paper, quoting the Harrisburg, Pennsylvania, *Intelligencer,* to the effect that some Millerites at Middletown went out Monday afternoon, October 21, to an island in the Susquehanna River, "there to engage in prayer, etc., and to wait the coming of the Messiah." [2] This is one of the rare references to Millerites' going away from their homes. Accepting this news item at face value—which is probably not warranted—we do not find in it anything to suggest fanatical extravagance in connection with their going to this island. In fact, we are told that they went there for prayer. It is, of course, possible that this going out of the Middletown group reflects the activities of Gorgas, for it was within easy radius of Philadelphia, and his charts were sent out through the mails. If Gorgas did figure in this in any way, apparently the Middletown Millerites were sufficiently circumspect to avoid a write-up in the papers regarding their activities while away from home. It was at this time that the newspapers were so eager to publish stories on Millerite activities that they actually printed, for example, a banal news item to the effect that a young woman was baptized by the Millerites and became "excited" on coming up out of the water. The item is very brief and no details are given. Yet this pointless little squib was copied from one newspaper to another. We repeat: the silence of the newspapers regarding any encampments like that at Philadelphia becomes the loudest proof that there were none.

3. With one exception the letters to Miller immediately after October 22 fail to mention any preaching of Gorgas' views except at Philadelphia. The one exception is a letter from N. N. Whiting. He wrote from Williamsburgh, Long Island, immediately after the October disappointment, a long letter describing his feelings and views. Included are

---

[2] *Pennsylvania Inquirer,* Oct. 28, 1844.

several sentences that speak of fanaticism. He introduces his remarks about fanaticism by saying that where he lived the spirit of brotherly love, which was said to dominate the movement elsewhere, was not present. The reason was that those who believed in the October 22 date were unwilling to allow those who did not accept the date to speak in their meetings—Whiting was one who did not accept the date. "We were completely proscribed," he wrote. "The very things which they had censured in the conduct of the churches, they now practiced themselves, and this while they told us that in a few hours they expected to be with Christ. In this region we had a tempest of real fanaticism. Our poor brethren were deluded into a belief of 'signs and lying wonders'—gift of tongues and modern prophecies. These things were preached especially by a Mrs. Higgins. They were urged to quit their employment, and they did so in great numbers. I heard one of our well-known lecturers teach his hearers that they must abandon the cities and large villages and flee into the open country as Lot did, or they would lose their lives and probably their souls. But I cannot tell you the half of what I saw and heard, nor is it necessary." [3]

This is clearly an illustration of what the Millerite papers meant when they said that there were instances of fanaticism. This sounds like the standard pattern of fanaticism as it has revealed itself all through the centuries. However, Whiting does not imply that it was very widespread. In fact, he suggests, rather, that it centered in the preaching of "a Mrs. Higgins." It would also be proper to observe that Whiting, who did not believe in the setting of a date, and was very critical of the seventh-month movement, would not be likely to understate the case; being human, he might even have overstated it a little.

However, we are not here concerned with the general question of fanaticism, but with the specific Gorgas incident. We venture the guess that Whiting is referring to Storrs as the lecturer who taught that they should flee from the cities as did Lot. Storrs, as we have learned, was the one Millerite of any prominence—though certainly not a leader of primary rank—who gave credence to Gorgas' views. We know that Storrs did come to New York to secure publication of the Gorgas chart. Hence, the area where Whiting lived could have been one of the "places" to which Himes referred, in speaking of the range of Gorgas' influence. Storrs was also the one Millerite spokesman who is on record as encouraging the believers, finally, to quit their regular work. However, while Whiting states that a number of the people responded to the appeal to leave their employment, he says nothing of any response to the warning to flee the cities. Perhaps the people did respond. If so, they evidently departed in such an unob-

---

[3] Manuscript letter, Oct. 24, 1844.

trusive fashion and so free of any strange acts, as to escape publicity in the public press.

4. References to Millerism in historical works, years afterward, mention only the Philadelphia encampment, when they become specific about Millerite activities of this character.

5. Himes himself mentions only Philadelphia in the one long paragraph he devotes to "the movement of Dr. Gorgas." Perhaps this specific reference to Philadelphia should be explained by the context that discusses Mrs. Minor's relation to the incident, seeing that she went out from that city. Himes states that he thinks she "owes the advent cause, if not the church, and world, a confession, of the sore evils of that movement, in which she took so conspicuous a part, against the remonstrances of Brother Litch, and others, and by which the advent cause in Philadelphia, received its heaviest blow." However, inasmuch as he sets out to discuss "the movement of Dr. Gorgas," it does seem a little strange that he should have become specific only regarding Philadelphia and the "blow" that the advent cause received there.

Himes' statement about Gorgas, that "in some places, many embraced his view, and carried it out, in all its extravagance," should probably be viewed as an illustration of that loose and rather sweeping language into which even the most careful writers fall at times in making generalizations. Himes, like other leaders, was no man to minimize in his description of any evil work. It is possible, of course, in the confused state that existed immediately after the disappointment, that Himes may have given some credence to newspaper stories about a number of Millerite companies radiating out from different places in the Philadelphia area. Of course, there need not be many "places," in order to warrant the use of "some." We know there were Philadelphia, Williamsburgh, and possibly Middletown. As to the "many" who "embraced" the Gorgas view, we do know, according to the united testimony appearing in *The Midnight Cry,* and from Litch's letter to Miller, that the number leaving Philadelphia was not more than two hundred. And Philadelphia is the only city that produced enough excitement in the matter of an encampment to catch the eye of the newspapers. The number leaving that city must have been the chief item of news, for there is no dependable evidence that the campers did anything very spectacular in connection with the encampment.

Himes' statement that certain Millerites "carried . . . out" Gorgas' view, "in all its extravagance," does not necessarily mean that they did anything more than leave the city. There is nothing in the sources, or in the charges of enemies, to warrant the conclusion that Gorgas' views called for anything more than that. But that in itself was an extravagant view, being an irrational analogy to Lot's experience, coupled with an alleged revelation. We think Himes so intended his words to be understood. To read into his use of the word "extravagance" the idea of sensational acts would place him in conflict with the emphatic declarations in his own *Midnight Cry,* at the very time of the Gorgas incident, that sensational acts were absent.

In the light of the foregoing, we see no good reason for revising our conclusions in Chapter 22 relative to the Millerites and encampments.

Appendix F

CERTAIN CASES IN THE NEW HAMPSHIRE STATE ASYLUM

Following is a summary of the case histories of all the cases admitted to the New Hampshire State asylum from the opening date, October 29, 1842, to February 25, 1843, in which religious excitement is said to have been the cause of the insanity. These cases are the ones referred to by the asylum superintendent in his 1852 report. See the discussion of this in Chapter 24, "Old Asylum Records Offer Further Testimony."

Case No. 1. Admitted Oct. 29, 1842. "Of nervous and bilious temperament." "His aunt and a sister have been insane." "Protracted second advent meeting was held in the vicinity and he attended. He took part in the meetings. Said he could do his own preaching and was Jesus Christ Himself. He soon became noisy and at times violent."

Case No. 4. Admitted Nov. 18, 1842. "Large preponderance of the nervous in his temperament, but moderate . . . in his movements and conversation. Some 14 years ago was for a short time insane and very violently so, soon after he was admitted to the church. He has a large family, some children by each wife, lived pleasantly with the first. The second has not assisted him much, as he says, to get along, she having many years been deranged, which made his home at times very trying to him. . . . For some time has been reading the second advent books lent to him by a neighborly woman who manifested great interest in snatching his soul from the great conflagration that is to be next spring. He labored hard and probably took cold, for he afterward said that he worked some nights most all night. Was sleepless and lost his appetite for two or three weeks. Soon he became violent." Discharged Dec. 17, 1842, as recovered.

Case No. 8. Admitted Dec. 1, 1842. "His grandfather was at the time he 'experienced religion' insane about three months. Has been a hard-working farmer and is one of the selectmen. Married. For several months he spent much of his time in attending meetings and examining the Bible to prove the second advent doctrines." After recovering from his insanity he stated he had looked into Millerism for three months and he "supposed he became insane from attending to one subject for so long a time to the exclusion of all others." Discharged April 1, 1843, but readmitted to the asylum Oct. 20, 1853, as case No. 1117.

Case No. 9. Admitted Dec. 2, 1842. "Insane one week. Caused as friends supposed by religious excitement as it came on during a religious excitement which was engaged in. Two years ago was at McLean [asylum] nine months, brought on then by taking cold." The case history makes no reference directly or indirectly to Millerism. Discharged April 1, 1843, as recovered. Readmitted Sept. 27, 1843, as Case No. 116.

Case No. 14. Admitted Dec. 10, 1842. "Mild and affectionate with a very susceptible nervous system. She came within the range of the all-absorbing and mind-desolating influence of the second advent preaching. Soon her ardent feelings became enlisted and her whole soul engaged in preparing for that great day of Christ's second coming. . . . The great joy produced by these delightful anticipations soon wrought up her feelings to such a state of commotion that her intellect was unable to withstand the shock. Whenever she was in the company of others she was excited. For six weeks this state of things continued. When the catamenial turn [menstruation] came she thought if she was baptized it would be safe with her and she would be ready then to meet the Saviour and to go up with the true believers. She went into the water and was baptized. This about the 5th of December. December 10 she took cold, entire suppression [of the menses] took place and raving madness supervened." Discharged July 1, 1843. "She left with her husband as well as ever, he said."

Case No. 15. Admitted Dec. 10, 1842. "Has two aunts and a grandfather insane. She has been insane six weeks. For some time she has been studying the Bible in search of arguments to support the Miller doctrine and became a full believer in its truth. The friends suppose the second advent doctrines caused her insanity." But the record adds that she had been "into a meetinghouse but twice to hear preaching. She is a good Christian. Her temperament is highly nervous." Discharged March 8, 1843, as "fast convalescing."

Case No. 16. Admitted Dec. 11, 1842. "She was insane 12 years ago three months and has had four slight attacks since, but soon got over them. Caused by the 'Miller doctrines' and trouble with a family in her house whom she endeavored to get out of it but they refused to go and as she said 'threatened her life.'" Discharged April 19, 1843, as recovered, but readmitted Dec. 21, 1843, as Case No. 136. Then long afterward in May, 1870, readmitted as Case No. 2803.

Case No. 17. Admitted Dec. 12, 1842. "Hereditary, has for three years turns of being unwell, has been insane three months, was admitted to the church about six weeks ago. Caused by second advent doctrines. Father was insane before marriage." Discharged some time later as "not improved."

Case No. 18. Admitted Dec. 16, 1842. "Insane 14 years and the last 10 bad. Six years ago went to McLean [asylum] three months. . . . This was brought upon him by the religious excitement." Discharged June 21, 1843.

Case No. 20. Admitted Dec. 24, 1842. "Exciting cause—Millerism. . . . For some time has had wild spells. Insane seven weeks and has been chained five weeks. 'The Miller excitement' has had something to do in hastening on his insanity." Discharged June 15, 1843, as recovered, but readmitted in 1854, as Case No. 1231. Once more readmitted in 1856 as Case No. 1399.

Case No. 33. Admitted January 24, 1843. "Respectable man, not hereditary. About four months ago became converted as himself and friends supposed under the Methodist preaching in the neighborhood, but did not join himself to the church. About one month after the Miller meetings began he attended constantly for about four weeks and then he became insane. . . . He is a small person of nervous and phlegmatic temperament. Said at first to have been excited but now is dull almost to catalepsy." He died in the asylum ten years later.

Case No. 34. Admitted Jan. 29, 1843. "For a year has been reading the Bible and Clarke's Commentaries. He has often talked about the Miller doctrine, said it was not true and that he could convince anyone that it was not. Some of his neighbors have talked with him upon the subject but he has not for more than a year read anything upon the subject of the second advent nor has ever heard a lecture upon it. And yet his friends and the doctor say that his insanity was caused by the Miller doctrines. One week before he came to the asylum he attended an evening meeting and during this he got up and said a few words. He stopped and went home suddenly. His friends thought it strange in him but he was not much wild until Tuesday. . . . He talks about religion and Millerism." Discharged April 26, 1843, as recovered.

Case No. 35. Admitted Jan. 31, 1843. Causes assigned, "religion, hereditary." "She united with Presbyterian church in London and moved to Rumney where her friends were Free-Will Baptists. They would not let her unite with their church, said she was not worthy for she had not been baptized. She became perplexed on the subject and the same time her husband was sick (practically insane). She became insane, violent, destroying clothing. Now she falls in with the Miller doctrine. . . . A grandmother was insane." Discharged May 20, 1843, as relieved.

APPENDICES 491

Case No. 38. Admitted Feb. 10, 1843. "Three weeks insane. Caused by religious excitement. . . . He says he is a Universalist, and last spring he began to be serious, turned his thoughts to religious subjects and has believed himself ever since a better man. Thinks he has knowingly done no bad thing since, was badly injured by something about the cart, falling onto his bowels which he says made him what they call crazy." Discharged March 21, 1843, as relieved.

Case No. 39. Admitted Feb. 11, 1843. "Caused by religious excitement. Studying the Bible when in ill-health." "He is nonresistant and inclined to Millerism." Discharged May 13, 1843, as relieved.

These fifteen cases represent the total of cases in which religion is set down as the possible cause, that were admitted to the New Hampshire asylum between the opening date, the twenty-ninth of October, 1842, and February 25, 1843, the period of time mentioned by the medical superintendent in his 1852 report. Let us analyze these cases. Cases 9, 18, and 38 do not mention Millerism, either directly or indirectly. That leaves twelve cases for scrutiny. Cases 1, 4, 8, 15, 16, 17, 20, and 35 show the factor of either hereditary or periodical insanity. That is, either some other member of the family has been, or is, insane, or else the patient himself suffers from recurring attacks of insanity. Certainly such cases are sufficiently explained without bringing Millerism into the picture. This leaves only four cases for consideration, as follows:

Case No. 14.—She had "a very susceptible nervous system." As a result of accepting the advent teachings "she was excited" whenever "she was in the company of others." We would like to have a report on whether this woman with the "very susceptible nervous system" had formerly displayed calmness when in the company of others. She went into the water and was baptized about the fifth of December, during a menstrual period. Then follows this statement: "December 10 she took cold, entire suppression [of the menses] took place and raving madness supervened." Baptisms frequently took place in rivers or lakes in the 1840's. It is therefore quite possible that this woman was thus baptized, which means that she was immersed in bitterly cold water. Now the "raving madness" did not develop as soon as "she came within the range of the all-absorbing and mind-desolating influence of the second advent preaching," not even after she had been within range of it for six weeks. But less than a week after her baptism, and on the very day she took cold, with suppression of the menses, "raving madness supervened." Further comment seems unnecessary. However, it might be remarked, in passing, that in writing the phrase, "mind-desolating influence of the second advent preaching," the asylum physician seems not to be dispassionately chronicling facts for the record, but rather indulging in the reprehensible business of name-calling that disgraced so much of religious discussion a century ago. It is at least possible that some case histories may have been colored by the prejudices of the times.

Case No. 33.—This man came from the town of East Kingston, New Hampshire, located a few miles above Haverhill, Massachusetts. In a Haverhill newspaper there was published a story about this man's being taken to the asylum as a victim of Millerism. In reply to this the Millerite minister in Haverhill, Henry Plummer, addressed a letter to the editor of the newspaper in which he said: "We have heard much of the insanity effected by what is called Millerism, but I believe it has not been proved in any instance, that preaching that doctrine has caused insanity. When cases so reported have been examined, they have invariably proved false, as the following certificates go to prove, in the case of Mr. B——, so glaringly set forth in your paper of April 29th. By publishing the following communication you will do an act of justice to those you deem fanatic, and your humble servant will be obliged." Then follow two letters addressed "To Whom It May Concern," one by Stephen Morrill and the other by Jonathan W. Tappan, both dated East Kingston, May 13, 1843. Both men state that they are not believers in Millerism, and that they are ready to repeat under oath the statements they are about to make. The substance of their letters is that they have been acquainted with Mr. B—— for a considerable time, that his health has long been poor, that he was not known to have attended Millerite meetings, though he did attend some Methodist meetings, that there was no reason in the world to believe that Millerism had anything to do with his insanity.[1]

Case No. 34.—One is tempted to become whimsical in commenting on this case. Here was a man who had never even heard a lecture on Millerism, nor had even read anything on the subject of the second advent for a year preceding his insanity, and in fact had never even inclined toward Millerism; "yet his friends and the doctor say that his insanity was caused by the Miller doctrines." Presumably "the doctor" would be his family physician that brought him to the asylum. Probably the only comment needed on the case is this: If the Miller doctrines were really so mind shattering that a man's reason could be unseated without his attending a lecture, without his sympathizing with it, and without his reading anything on the subject for a long time, then why did not all New England go insane?

Case No. 39.—The data on this case, as touching the question of religion, are too brief or too ambiguous to permit any definite conclusion. There is nothing to indicate that this man had been reading Miller's works, or attending Millerite lectures, but simply that he was "inclined to Millerism."

---

[1] See *Haverhill Gazette* (Mass.), May 20, 1843.

Appendix G

HEREDITARY AND PERIODICAL INSANITY IN RELATION TO SO-CALLED RELIGION-INDUCED INSANITY

A study was made of the factor of hereditary and periodical insanity in so-called religion-induced insanity, particularly Millerism-induced cases. The findings are summarized in the table accompanying this appendix. The survey covered certain New England asylums for the calendar years 1842-44. The procedure was as follows:

Where the case histories reveal that some close relative, or relatives, of the patient have been, or are, insane, we have made the notation "hereditary." Where the patient himself had had previous attacks of insanity or was readmitted to an asylum subsequent to 1844, we have made the notation, "periodical." In this table all cases that reveal either hereditary or periodical insanity are merged in one total under the abbreviation HP. In the asylum reports of the 1840's the term "Religious Excitement" is generally employed in the tables of "Causes of Insanity," to describe all cases supposed to have resulted from religion. That term is here employed in the abbreviated form RE.

In deciding which of the Worcester asylum cases to list as RE, we followed the notation in the ledger of admissions, which states the cause assigned for each case, but which does not otherwise discuss the nature of the case. In the examination of cases in the Maine, New Hampshire, and Vermont asylums, a more comprehensive study of the case histories themselves was made before deciding which cases should be considered as RE. The procedure was to list as RE all cases which are so designated on the title page of the case history, or—in the absence of any assigned cause on the title page or in the case history—all cases in which religion is mentioned in the history. But a case was not considered RE if title page states otherwise—even though some reference is made to religion in the case history—except when case history mentions Millerism. This ensured that every case in which any allusion is made, directly or indirectly, to Millerism would come under scrutiny. Thus the figures were weighted as heavily as possible against Millerism.

This generous method of deciding which are RE cases and, particularly, which are allegedly Millerism-induced cases, explains why the totals of such cases here given are definitely higher than those shown in certain of the annual reports of these asylums. Also the fact that all figures in this table are in terms of calendar years explains why certain of these figures do not agree with the annual reports of some of the asylums, which are on other than a calendar-year basis. In determining what figures to place in the column "RE Cases That Are Not HP but That Mention Millerism," examination was made of the case histories themselves in each instance.

In the period 1842-44 there was only one asylum in each of the following States: Maine, New Hampshire, Vermont. The records of these three institutions were examined. Thus we have a complete picture of all admissions in these three States. In Massachusetts examination was made only of the records of the asylum at Worcester, which was the principal institution of its kind in the State. In addition to the asylum at Worcester, there were McLean Asylum, a subsidiary of the Massachusetts General Hospital at Boston, and the Boston Lunatic Hospital. The medical superintendent of McLean Asylum declared in his annual reports that all so-called causes of insanity as given by friends and relatives are quite worthless, and hence no tables of "Causes" appear in the reports, nor any reference to Millerism. The annual reports of the Boston Lunatic Hospital, for the four-year period ending June 30, 1845, list a total of only twelve cases of RE, of which four are charged against "Millerism." The total admissions for McLean's and Boston Lunatic Hospital for 1842-44 were 546. The total admissions for all the other asylums in the four States of Maine, New Hampshire, Vermont, and Massachusetts in this period were 1,516, as the table shows. Hence the grand total of admissions was 2,062. The 1,516 cases analyzed in this table constitute 73 per cent of all cases admitted to asylums in these four States, from 1842 to 1844 inclusive. And it was in these States that the most intensive preaching of Millerism was carried on.

If the assumption is valid that every so-called RE case which reveals HP in the case history ought immediately to be removed from the total of cases charged against Millerism, then the grand total of all cases not thus immediately removed is only thirty-nine. Most of these thirty-nine cases, as chapters 23 and 24 and Appendix F show are clearly chargeable to some other cause than Millerism. That leaves perhaps a dozen cases concerning which it is impossible to speak with certainty, and for the simple reason that the case histories of most of these are too brief to permit of any valid conclusion as to the true cause.

In this connection the comments of Dr. George A. Elliott, superintendent of the Brattleboro Retreat (in 1840's, Vermont Asylum for the Insane), in a personal letter to the author, are most appropriate: "If the history of the cases which you have isolated for study could be more complete, it might appear even in these instances that the preaching of the Millerites was no more responsible for the mental disturbance than the spectator is for what happens at a bull fight." [1]

---

[1] Manuscript letter, May 22, 1944.

APPENDICES

	Calendar Year	Total Admissions	Cases of RE	RE Cases That Are HP	RE Cases That Are Not HP but That Mention Millerism
MAINE					
	1842	87	19	12	1
	1843	89	10	6	3
	1844	85	6	1	2
Totals		261	35	19	6
NEW HAMPSHIRE (Asylum Opened Oct. 29/42)					
	1842	22	10	8	1
	1843	115	22	9	8
	1844	101	13	9	2
Totals		238	45	26	11
VERMONT					
	1842	111	12	4	0
	1843	112	20	7	7
	1844	124	12	3	3
Totals		347	44	14	10
MASSACHUSETTS (For Worcester Asylum Only)					
	1842	205	20	13	1
	1843	222	28	18	3
	1844	243	27	11	8
Totals		670	75	42	12
Grand Totals		1,516	199	101	39

Appendix H

AN ASCENSION ROBE AFFIDAVIT

At the Vermont Historical Society office there is found with the collection of Miller material a sheet of foolscap on which is written an affidavit by a Jacob Wheeler. The affidavit reads as follows:

"I Jacob Wheeler of Castleton in the County of Rutland and State of Vermont, being duly sworn, do depose, testify and say that I shall be eighty-eight years of age next month, that I have resided in Castleton aforesaid for eighty-three years, and was a soldier in the War of 1812 for 2 years and 3 months. That I remember well the times of William Miller, or Prophet Miller so called, and knew him personally.

"I remember also that on the morning of the day set by Miller for the ascension I saw William Cook and his wife at Hydeville in this town dressed in white robes made of cambric I should think, which they called their ascension robes; afterwards they took them off, made them into a bundle and on the same day took them with them to Hampton, New York, where a great many people were convened to ascend. Further this deponent sayeth not.

"[Signed] Jacob Wheeler

"Witness
"Wm. C. Rice"

On the same sheet, immediately below the affidavit, is a statement by John Howe, "Master in Chancery" (equivalent to a notary public), to the effect that Jacob Wheeler had personally appeared before him at Castleton, Vermont, on May 25, 1878, and had made oath "that the above affidavit by him subscribed was made agreeably to the truth."

The librarian at the Historical Society office was unable to throw any light on this document. It stands as a lone page. The document is unique in that it is the only one of its kind we have been able to find. Who Jacob Wheeler was, why, or under what circumstances he swore to the affidavit, apparently will never be known. Nor is it really necessary that we know.

We sent a photostat of this affidavit to Mr. Philip M. M. Phelps, attorney at law, Fair Haven, Vermont, a few miles from Castleton, and asked for his comment. We quote the relevant part of his letter in reply:

"This affidavit would never be admitted as evidence in courts of our State. The only evidence which can be received in our courts is the testimony of witnesses, or the depositions of witnesses. The reason for this is due to the fact that an affidavit can set forth anything. The adverse party has no opportunity to cross-examine the affiant. I am sure you will find this the general rule throughout the United States, and England under the common law. . . . I certainly should give no weight whatsoever to an affidavit of this nature."[1]

Evidently there is nothing inherently awesome or weighty in an affidavit. It signifies that the person is willing to make his statements under oath, but it provides no proof that what he says is true, even though it is said in sincerity. Testifying under oath is no protection against the tricks of memory. In other words, this statement is inherently no more weighty than that of any elderly person's declaration concerning the Millerites of long ago. We have examined enough of such statements in Chapter 27 to establish that the combination of age and distance in time from the event discussed, play havoc with accuracy in remembering happenings.

Jacob Wheeler states that he is about eighty-eight. We have no way of telling how well his mind was working. The only clue to his physical state is the character of his signature. It is a shaky, wholly illegible scrawl. Everything on the foolscap sheet except Wheeler's signature is written by John Howe. And it is Howe's clear writing that enables us to decipher Wheeler's illegible signature.

Among other questions, we would have liked to ask Wheeler how near he was to "William Cook and his wife" when he "saw" them in "white robes." Surely if the Cooks bundled up their robes and went over to Hampton, to be with others "convened to ascend," they would unbundle them there and don them once more to be ready "to ascend." Now we have quoted the statement prepared by William Miller at the Low Hampton conference in December, 1844, in which he spoke of the derogatory reports of enemies regarding ascension robes. Evidently he had not heard of the Cooks, or did they keep their robes bundled up? And if so, why did Mrs. Cook spend all those hours making the robes and then fail to garb herself, even if not her husband, in the finished garment when she finally gathered with all the other Millerites "convened to ascend"?

But all such questions are profitless, because there is no answer possible at this late date. We grant that there is abundance of testimony, years after the great day, that the Millerites wore robes. The only unique point in the Wheeler testimony is his claim to having actually seen people in robes. Too bad that so rare a testimony in legal form was not prepared in such fashion as to make it admissible as testimony. Why did he not give notice as to when and where the affidavit was to be taken, so that someone might have been present to cross-interrogate, that is, ask him certain questions? His answers, under oath, might have thrown some helpful light on this intriguing, wholly one-sided document.

Since writing the chapters on ascension robes, we have found an article

---

[1] Letter to author, May 17, 1944.

that tells of certain people who said they actually saw ascension robes on Millerites. The student of this phantom subject will find this article most illuminating, or disappointing, we probably should say. The statements by these alleged eyewitnesses are printed in the church paper of the Seventh-day Adventists in October, 1885. These statements are not notarized. However, one of the persons making a statement adds as a postscript that he is willing to swear to it. They were made by people in Santa Barbara, California, in July and August of 1885. Their statements sound quite plausible, that is, until the facts printed in the remainder of the article are read. These statements concerning certain people in New England and one person in New York State, in 1843 and 1844 were investigated by persons living in the East, and the reports on their findings are published. Included is another humorous nightgown story.[2]

In regard to these 1885 statements, we are able to read the other side, and thus to check up on the claims. We do not know what Jacob Wheeler actually saw. We will have to let the reader guess.

Other than the cases above mentioned, and certain ones discussed in Chapters 26 and 27, we have found no record of anyone's having said that he *saw* a Millerite in a robe.

Appendix I

FURTHER COMMENTS ON THE BOOK *DAYS OF DELUSION*

This work by Clara Endicott Sears is the only book in modern times that is wholly devoted to the subject of Millerism; thus it is the one source of reference for many who have sought information on the Millerites. We believe the book has at least three grave weaknesses.

First, it is built very largely on reminiscences three quarters of a century after the movement thrived. How wholly unreliable are many of these reminiscences is already evident from our analysis of the letters she received from 1920 to 1923. She declares in the preface to her work that she believed "that all these [reminiscences, both the letters and the word-of-mouth stories that had come down the years] gathered together would bring before us at close range a vivid picture of one of the most peculiarly emotional and hysterical episodes in the ins and outs of our past history."[1]

Second, the book gives little evidence that contemporary sources, either secular or religious, except certain Millerite papers and a few personal

---
[2] See "Ascension Robes, A Desperate Attempt and What Came of It," *The Advent Review and Sabbath Herald*, Oct. 13, 1885, pp. 632, 633.
[1] *Days of Delusion*, p. v.

letters, were examined. The preface itself makes clear that the book presents the *current* tradition regarding the Millerite movement. Now unquestionably this makes for a very readable book, but we believe it does not make for accurate history.

Third, the book reveals that even in the investigation of the Millerite papers too limited a time was spent on them to secure a wholly accurate picture of what the Millerites really believed or did. How limited that reading was is strikingly revealed in the comment that the author makes on Joshua V. Himes' letter to *The Outlook* in 1894. Challenging "the old gentleman's memory" in regard to his claim that he had refuted the ascension robe story "hundreds of times" in the Millerite papers and had kept "a standing offer" of a reward for proof of ascension robes, Miss Sears declares:

"The author has diligently searched the files of *The Midnight Cry* and *The Advent Herald* (the latter covering the years up to 1860, of which only a few copies were missing), and has failed to find any reference whatsoever to ascension robes, or any mention of the reward the old gentleman speaks of in his letter; nor has she been able to discover the refutations which he declares he had printed in the columns of both these papers 'hundreds of times.' . . . The only reference to the very harmless act of wearing the white robes is in Elder Bliss's *Life of William Miller* which was published by Elder Himes in 1853, nine years after the great fiasco." [2]

The reader will immediately recall that in our discussion of the ascension robe charge we commented on Himes' letter and also quoted repeatedly from the Millerite papers regarding ascension robes. We did not quote every statement; there were too many. Nor would we claim to have found all of them, but we did find comments on robes, each comment being an excoriation or refutation of the story, in the following Millerite papers, the references to which are given in chronological order:

Signs of the Times, Feb. 1, 1843, p. 157.
The Midnight Cry, Feb. 3, 1843, p. 15.
Signs of the Times, Feb. 15, 1843, p. 173.
Signs of the Times, Feb. 22, 1843, p. 179.
Signs of the Times, March 8, 1843, pp. 4, 5.
The Midnight Cry, March 10, 1843, p. 45.
Signs of the Times, March 15, 1843, p. 16.
The Midnight Cry, March 17, 1843, p. 61.
The Midnight Cry, March 24, 1843, p. 80.
The Midnight Cry, April 7, 1843, p. 106.
Signs of the Times, April 12, 1843, p. 46.

---

[2] *Ibid.,* p. 259.

Signs of the Times, April 19, 1843, p. 51.
Signs of the Times, April 19, 1843, p. 53.
Signs of the Times, May 3, 1843, p. 72.
Signs of the Times, May 17, 1843, p. 88.
Signs of the Times, July 5, 1843, p. 141.
The Midnight Cry, Jan. 4, 1844, p. 189.
The Midnight Cry, Jan. 18, 1844, p. 207.
The Midnight Cry, March 21, 1844, p. 273.
The Advent Shield and Review, May, 1844, p. 74.
The Advent Herald, July 24, 1844, p. 197.
The Advent Herald, Nov. 6, 1844, p. 101.
The Midnight Cry, Nov. 7, 1844, p. 150.
The Midnight Cry, Nov. 14, 1844, p. 157.
The Advent Herald, Nov. 20, 1844, p. 113.
The Voice of Truth, Nov. 20, 1844, p. 172.
The Advent Herald, Dec. 4, 1844, p. 136.
The Advent Herald, Jan. 15, 1845, p. 183.
The Voice of Truth, Jan. 29, 1845, p. 2.

Here is a total of twenty-nine references to ascension robes during the two-year period when the movement was at its height. Most of the references, it will be noted, are to *The Midnight Cry* and *The Advent Herald,* or its predecessor. (The reader will recall that the *Signs of the Times* changed its name to *The Advent Herald* early in 1844, and the latter name is sometimes used to cover the whole period of the journal's existence.) Besides these twenty-nine references, there is the *Boston Post* story of November 2, 1844, which gives Himes' vigorous denial that robes were worn. It is, therefore, not quite accurate to say that "the only reference" by the Millerites to the robe charge was published "nine years after the great fiasco." Miss Sears' admission that she "failed to find any reference whatsoever to ascension robes" in the Millerite papers would seem to warrant the conclusion that her reading was not as extensive or perhaps as thorough as it might have been. Furthermore, in the light of this it is surely not unduly critical to suggest that possibly the author of *Days of Delusion* might also have "failed to find" other very important information contained in the publications of the Millerites—information that could have greatly changed the picture she has drawn of them. She might even have been less free in her use of such withering adjectives as "hysterical" and "fanatical" in describing them.

But how limited and cursory must have been the reading of Millerite source material by the author of *Days of Delusion* is even more strikingly revealed by the statements she makes in the sentences that immediately follow those we have quoted. Miss Sears proceeds to quote Bliss's statement in 1853 to the effect that the ascension robe story was false, and follows it with this comment:

"But Elder Luther Boutelle [a Millerite preacher], a man whose integrity has never been questioned, in writing his *Autobiography,* in which he describes the happenings of those days, quotes directly from the very page upon which this statement appears and, continuing down to the paragraph itself, stops short and totally ignores its contents; and why?—because Elder Boutelle knew perfectly well that in his own home town of Groton and in his own State of Massachusetts, especially in the rural districts, to say nothing of other localities, this perfectly innocent bit of symbolism [wearing ascension robes] was, if not universally, at least very prevalently, indulged in. Elder Boutelle, like Prophet Miller, was by nature outspoken and direct in thought and speech and free from subterfuge, and while certain of the brethren, under the sting of humiliation, denied this and denied that after the great fiasco, neither he nor his leader ever belittled the memory of their supreme disappointment by raising or refuting questions of such minor import as the one referred to." ³

Now the only deduction to draw from this statement is that Boutelle, being a man of "integrity" and "free from subterfuge," told the truth about the ascension robe story by stopping "short" in his quotation from Bliss: while Bliss, of course, must be guilty of subterfuge, indeed bald falsehood, because of the statement he made. This is a grave charge against Bliss, who was a prominent Millerite. Now what are the facts?

In Chapter X of his autobiography Boutelle quotes Bliss. The context is this: Boutelle opened this chapter with a brief description of the state of the movement as "the tenth day of the seventh month drew nigh." He declared that "with joy all the ready ones anticipated the day. Solemn, however, were the last gatherings. . . . The leading preachers of Adventism had all endorsed the tenth day of the seventh month." Then in support of these statements he referred briefly to statements from leading Millerites, concluding with a paragraph from Bliss, who pictured the last-moment preparations made for the advent. Immediately following this Boutelle said: "These quotations harmonize with what I knew to be at the time. Such a concentration of thought; such a oneness of faith was never before witnessed. . . . Meetings everywhere were being held. Confessions made, wrongs righted." ⁴

Surely it is clear that Boutelle stopped "short" on the Bliss quotation simply because it would have been irrelevant to the point he was seeking to establish, to have quoted more. We are still permitted to believe that Bliss was not guilty of distortion or falsehood!

---

³ *Ibid.,* pp. 259, 260.
⁴ Luther Boutelle, *Life and Religious Experience,* pp. 65-67.

The author of *Days of Delusion* says that Boutelle "knew perfectly well" that ascension robes were worn "very prevalently" in his own home town and in the State of Massachusetts. The reader is entitled to know that such a statement is not based on anything in Boutelle's autobiography, but on various reminiscences of people discussing Millerism three quarters of a century after 1844.

Boutelle may never have spent time "refuting" the robes story. We cannot say, for Boutelle was not a prominent Millerite in the 1844 period, and productions from his pen are rather limited. But that "his leader," William Miller, refuted the story, is a matter of record. The reader will recall our reference to the Low Hampton conference on December 28 and 29, 1844, and Miller's "Address to Advent Believers," in which he spoke of their being "ridiculed by the oft-repeated slang of ascension robes"! This address, voted by the conference, was sent out to the Millerites everywhere through *The Advent Herald*.[5]

If space limits permitted, other illustrations might be taken from *Days of Delusion* showing what we believe are clear cases of a failure to read Millerite literature as extensively or as attentively as might have been done, with a resulting distortion of Millerite history as a whole. In view of the evident inaccuracy of the ascension robe section of *Days of Delusion*—the high point of the book—we leave the reader to decide how far he should permit that book to shape his conclusions regarding the Millerites.

Appendix J

HOW DID THE ASCENSION ROBE STORY START?

There is, of course, no positive answer that can be given to the question, How did the ascension robe story start? Nor are we obliged to attempt an answer. We believe the most plausible explanation is that some listener at a Millerite meeting heard the preacher speaking of the white robes that the righteous must wear when they stand before the Lord at His coming, and began to give currency to the story that the Millerites were planning to have ascension robes made. But if such a listener had been more attentive, he would have discerned that the Millerite preacher was quoting from the figurative, symbolic language of the book of Revelation, one of the books of the Bible most quoted by the Millerites. This book speaks of the saints being arrayed in white robes, and says that the "fine linen" is the righteousness of the saints. These robes were washed and made white by the atoning blood of Christ, explained John the revelator.[1] Evidently the Millerites in

---

[5] See *The Advent Herald*, Jan. 15, 1845, p. 183.
[1] See Revelation 7:9-14; 19:8.

1844 thought that the fictional ascension robe story might have had such an origin, for a brief article on the fabulous story in one of their journals explains that the robes the Millerites expected to wear at the advent, and which indeed they hoped to be wearing daily in anticipation of the advent, are "the righteousness of the saints," and in a concluding sentence the Millerite writer exhorted, "Then let us wear the unsullied robe of righteousness." [2] This, we believe, provides probably the most plausible explanation for the first appearance of the story, when the rumor was simply that the Millerites were making ready their ascension robes.

The story that the Millerites had muslin robes apparently must be traced to the sign in the Bowery store in October, 1844, that offered "muslin for ascension robes." This story, as is stated in Chapter 25, was very widely quoted in the public press.

The robes story, of course, was given added plausibility by the large broadside circulated in October, 1844, which contained a cartoon showing Millerites in their robes, hanging onto the ascending Boston Tabernacle.

A still further plausibility was given to the story by the pranks of various rowdies. We mentioned in Chapter 25 one instance in Connecticut in which a group of rowdies were dressed in white, riding on horses. The newspapers themselves, in October, 1844, tell of many pranks played on the Millerites, such as shooting off fireworks, to disturb their meetings. In the writings of various Adventist denominations are found reminiscences of 1844 by old believers, which include accounts of pranksters who dressed up in long white robes, and actually climbed up on the roofs of Millerite buildings, while the Millerites were inside engaged in religious service. The Sears collection of letters includes one such reminiscence. (It should be mentioned, in passing, that that collection of letters contains some very stout denials of the whole ascension robe story.) However, we do not quote these reminiscences as proof, because they suffer under the same handicap as other old reminiscences. But it is at least worth remembering that there are such reminiscences.

The foregoing, we believe, provides more than a sufficient explanation for the origin of the ascension robe story. Most of the good stories that are in circulation in history books concerning famous characters have a far less plausible foundation than this. For example, there is the story that George Washington, when a little boy, cut down a cherry tree with his hatchet. The story has become a part of the folklore of America. Why should we question it? Did not George confess to his father that he did cut down the tree? This story owes its origin to Parson Weems, who wrote a life of George Washington. The hatchet story first appeared in an

---

[2] *The Voice of Truth,* Jan. 29, 1845, p. 2.

edition of his work, published in 1806. When Weems first inserted this story in the fifth edition, he "explained vaguely" (according to *Life* magazine February 19, 1940), that "it was told him 'twenty years ago by an aged lady who was a distant relative' of the Washingtons. Without further substantiation, this yarn became one of the most celebrated bits of American history."

However, the classic illustration of how fiction can change to fact, and that virtually overnight, is the celebrated story of the first bathtub in America. The story is to the effect that a man by the name of Adam Thompson, in Cincinnati, Ohio, on December 10, 1842, exhibited the first American bathtub to a group of his men friends. But the bathtub was soon to be denounced by physicians as a menace to health, with the Boston city fathers passing an ordinance prohibiting its use except on medical advice, and the legislators in Virginia imposing a $30 tax upon the installation of each bathtub, with certain other places charging extra rates for water with which to bathe in bathtubs. This, with other details giving names and places, is the form in which the story is found in many books, some of them serious reference works. Yet the story is a hoax, pure and simple.

It was invented December, 1917, by that witty, droll master of English, H. L. Mencken, for years the editor of *The American Mercury,* and a member of the staff of the Baltimore *Sun.* According to his own statement, his only motive in writing the story was to "have some harmless fun" during the tense days of World War 1. It never occurred to him that anyone would take the story seriously, because it was "packed full of absurdities." But to his utter astonishment he soon found that his story was being taken seriously in every quarter of the country and overseas. To quote his own words: "Pretty soon I began to encounter my preposterous 'facts' in the writings of other men. They began to be used by chiropractors and other such quacks as evidence of the stupidity of medical men. They began to be cited by medical men as proof of the progress of public hygiene. They got into learned journals. They were alluded to on the floor of Congress. They crossed the ocean, and were discussed solemnly in England, and on the Continent. Finally, I began to find them in standard works of reference." The story has even a more fantastic angle than this, if that is possible. The story was reprinted in the *Boston Herald,* under a four-column head, and with a two-column cartoon labeled satirically, "The American Public Will Swallow Anything." This, of course, was intended to be an exposure of the story plus a good laugh over the credulity of the American public. "And then, three weeks later, in the same editorial section, but promoted to page one, the same *Herald* reprinted my one-year-old fake—soberly and as a piece of news." It seems that even in the Baltimore *Sun,* with which Mr.

Mencken had had editorial connections through the years, the story appeared at least twice as a sober piece of news.

The preceding quotations from Mencken are found in a news column released by the Western Newspaper Union. The newspaper clipping we have is from the *Journal,* Napa, California, February 20, 1942. This clipping was enclosed in a letter H. L. Mencken wrote us in response to our inquiry concerning the facts in the case. His letter is brief and to the point: "I enclose a clipping that answers your questions. I have long since given up hope of putting that hoax down. I have exposed it myself at least three or four times, and various other persons have done the same, but it continues to flourish. Sincerely yours, [Signed] H. L. Mencken." [2]

After one hundred years no Millerite ascension robe story is half so specific as to names and places as is this bathtub story. But the bathtub story is a hoax, nevertheless.

Appendix K

MILLER'S INTERPRETATION OF MAJOR PROPHECIES

For those who are students of prophecy it will be of interest to know how the Millerites understood certain major prophecies of Daniel and the Revelation. A brief statement on this is found in the address delivered by the Millerite spokesman Silas Hawley at the dedication of the Boston Tabernacle, May 4, 1843. He set forth the Millerite interpretation of various prophecies, and affirmed that there was the most excellent authority for such interpretation. Indeed, it was consistently the position of the Millerites that they were not the inventors of new interpretations of the great prophecies, but simply that they sought to popularize and proclaim to all men the significance of the prophecies whose interpretation had already generally been agreed upon by the most learned of theologians through the past generations. Hawley declared:

"In all that is essential in our view, we have with us the highest and most respected authorities of the whole church. In fact, in almost every point raised by our opponents, we have been supported by the expositors. In the very few instances in which we have not their direct support, we have their general views and reasonings to sustain us, and the direct testimony of some of the first and most judicious of their number. This I will proceed to show." [1]

He follows with a discussion of "seven points" of prophecy on which

---

[2] Personal letter to the author, Jan. 26, 1943.
[1] *Signs of the Times,* June 7, 1843, p. 110.

"doubt or dissent" has been raised by various of Miller's opponents. He enumerates these in order:

"1. *The fourth kingdom of Daniel.* This we claim to be the Roman. . . .

"2. *The little horn of the seventh.* This we hold to be Papacy. . . .

"3. *The little horn of the eighth chapter, that became* EXCEEDING GREAT. This we believe to be *Rome.* . . .

"4. *The length of the prophetic numbers.* . . . The *days* in Daniel and John are representatives of so many *years.* . . .

"5. *The commencement of the seventy weeks.* These we believe commenced with the decree of Artaxerxes Longimanus, . . . B. C. 457. . . .

"6. *The connection between the 2300 days and the seventy weeks.* This connection we think plain. . . .

"7. *The rise of the little horn of Daniel seventh.* We believe that Papacy, symbolized by the little horn, rose by virtue of the decree of Justinian," which went into "full effect" in A. D. "538." [2]

In connection with his discussion of each point he cites eminent authorities who support the Millerite interpretation. In many instances the support is really as wide as Protestantism. He admits that the direct support for the sixth point is more limited.

Sylvester Bliss, in his *Memoirs of William Miller,* deals with this same subject of the Millerite interpretation of major prophecies. Only he extends the discussion to include virtually the whole range of Miller's teachings by adding on three more points, as follows:

"8. The nature of Christ's second advent.
"9. The return of the Jews.
"10. The epoch of the resurrection." [3]

Bliss shows that Miller was most orthodox in his views on the nature of the second advent, as measured by historic doctrinal statements on the subject. This we have considered at length in Chapter 28.

In view of his belief regarding the second advent, Miller militantly preached against the idea that the literal Jews would return to their homeland and there be converted to Christianity during the earthly millennium which some of Miller's opponents believed in. Miller placed this idea of the return of the Jews in the same category with the doctrine of the world's conversion. They were really parts of one whole. And both were tied to a doctrine of the millennium that Miller considered unscriptural. Bliss cites eminent authorities in support of Miller's position.[4]

---

[2] *Ibid.*
[3] Sylvester Bliss, *Memoirs of William Miller,* p. 185.
[4] *Ibid.,* pp. 199, 200.

The tenth point, the epoch of the resurrection, was also tied in with the doctrine of the millennium. "Miller held that the resurrection of the just will be pre-millennial, and that that of the wicked will be at the close of the millennium. This hinges on the interpretation given to Revelation 20:4-6. It is worthy of note, that during the first two centuries there was not an individual who believed in any resurrection of the dead, whose name or memory has come down to us, who denied that a literal resurrection is there taught." [5] Miller's opponents, believing as they did that the millennium would come on by "gradual steps," and without supernatural intervention, had to spiritualize away the idea of a resurrection at the beginning of the millennium. They did this by declaring, for example, that people would be converted who had been "dead in trespasses and sins." As already stated, Miller believed in a *literal* resurrection at the beginning of the millennium. And likewise, of course, he believed in a literal resurrection at the close of the millennium.

In this book, which is not a theological treatise, but rather a historical one, the preceding paragraphs must suffice to describe Miller's views regarding major prophecies and doctrines and the learned support that those views could claim. A full treatment of the subject of prophetic interpretation through the centuries, and in relation to Millerism, will be found in a forthcoming work by LeRoy Edwin Froom, entitled *The Prophetic Faith of Our Fathers,* to be published by the Review and Herald Publishing Association, Washington, D. C.

Appendix L

MILLER'S SECONDARY PROOFS FOR THE 1843 DATE

As stated in Chapter 28, Miller's main line of proof for his 1843 date (later revised to October 22, 1844) was the 2300-day prophecy, coupled with the seventy-week prophecy. In addition to this he presented what may properly be described, in the perspective of the whole history of Millerism, definitely secondary and corroborative lines of proof. In fact, we are tempted to believe there was a deal of truth to the charge of some of his opponents that after Miller had decided on 1843 as a result of his study of the 2300-day prophecy, he worked backward from that date to secure certain of the dates that he employed as the starting point of some of the secondary lines of proof. Better men than Miller have fallen into

---

[5] *Ibid.,* p. 200.

this logical fallacy called begging the question. Too often in the history of religion a man has set forth one strong line of reasoning in support of his position, only to weaken and embarrass it by secondary arguments that are fanciful. Nor has this mistake been confined to the realm of religion. The danger lurking in the path of every man who becomes devoted to one main line of study or work is that he is likely to see proofs for his views on every side—proofs which may seem fanciful even to his friends. Miller was exceedingly like other men in this respect. However, this is not intended to condone those of his secondary proofs that were farfetched—for some of them were farfetched. But the fanciful character of some of these proofs for the 1843 date does not in any way minimize the fact that his interpretation of the major prophecies of Daniel and the Revelation, as discussed in Appendix K, was similar to that of scholarly commentators of bygone days. The secondary proofs Miller offered for the 1843 date are summarized in the following paragraphs (we have, in some instances, combined several "proofs" under one head):

1. Miller understood the "seven times" of punishment upon the Jews, threatened in Leviticus 26:21, as describing a prophetic period of 2,520 years, beginning in 677 B. C., and thus ending in A. D. 1843. By the same method of reasoning, and taking the same starting date, Miller used the text in Deuteronomy 15:1, 2, regarding the "seven years," at the end of which release should come to all in bondage. The people of God were to be delivered from their bondage in 1843. Parallel to this, in his mind, was the passage in Ezekiel 39:9, 10.

2. God was six days in creating the earth and then rested the seventh day. This, Miller believed, prefigured Christ's work in laboring six figurative days in creating a new heavens and earth and finally resting on the seventh day, when the millennium begins. These figurative days, not to be confused with the "days" of prophetic periods, he declared, were a thousand years, taking 2 Peter 3:8 as his proof. In the field of Scriptural interpretation this is exhibit A of the fallacy of false analogy. Yet it is an undebatable fact that this fanciful analogy is as old as the Christian Era and dips back into Jewish thinking. It is to be found repeatedly in the writings of the early church fathers—a fact that in itself ought to have put later and more judicious theologians on their guard—and thence onward to our own days. Miller simply accepted a widespread view, hoary with age, and very naturally employed it as one of the proofs that the end of the world was near. According to his reckoning of Bible chronology, the world had lasted already about six thousand years. It is an interesting fact that Alexander Campbell, a leading founder of the church called Disciples of Christ, and a contemporary of Miller, saw in this fanciful analogy a primary reason for anticipating the soon coming of Christ, though

he set no date. He very appropriately called the religious journal he founded *The Millennial Harbinger*. Declared his biographer:

"He [Campbell] felt assured that a reformation such as he advocated, . . . could leave no room for any other religious reformation, and must of necessity be the very last effort possible to prepare the world for the coming of Christ. He did not presume to fix upon any very definite period for this event, Scripture analogies inclining him to the opinion that it would occur at the commencement of the seventh Chiliad [that is, the seventh thousand-year period], answering to the seventh day or Sabbath when God rested from the work of creation." [1]

3. The Jewish year of jubilee came every fifty years, when liberty was to be proclaimed throughout the land. Miller reasoned that seven times seven jubilees would bring a complete or perfect Sabbath. Now, viewed in prophetic values for time, this would mean 2,450 years. He began his reckoning of this period from 607 B. C., "when the Jews ceased the keeping of the Sabbaths and jubilees, at the close of Josiah's reign." Hence the period would end in 1843.

4. He took the statement in Hosea 6:1-3, "after two days will He revive us; in the third day He will raise us up, and we shall live in His sight"; gave a figurative value of a thousand years to a day; and saw in the two days a two-thousand-year period of distress for God's children beginning in 158 B. C. and ending in 1842. Thus 1843 would be "the first year in the 3d thousand years, or 3d day of the Lord." Miller was led into this fanciful reasoning because of the widely accepted fallacy resident in the creation-millennium analogy discussed under No. 2.

5. He took the statement in Daniel 12:6, 7, regarding "a time, times, and a half," which according to widely accepted prophetic views ended in 1798, and observed that the context of the prophecy dealt with events right down to the resurrection. He believed therefore that the final work of scattering "the power of the holy people" called for a certain extension of time, or sufficient to reach to 1843.

6. He took the statement in Daniel 12:11-13 regarding the 1,335 days of prophetic time, and starting in A. D. 508, "from the taking away of pagan Rome," again reached the 1843 date.

7. He took the statement of Christ in Luke 13:32, "Behold, I cast out devils, and I do cures today and tomorrow, and the third day I shall be perfected"; made the days analogous to the days in Hosea; and hence reached the same conclusion.

8. He interlocked the prophecies of the fifth and sixth trumpets in Revelation 9, ending the time of the sixth trumpet in 1840, after which the

---
[1] Robert Richardson, *Memoirs of Alexander Campbell*, Vol. 2, pp. 302, 303.

seventh trumpet, the final one, sounds. He did not make this so specific as some other lines of reasoning, but prefaced his statement with the general declaration, "The trumpets are also a revelation of time."

9. He took the statement in Revelation 11:3 regarding the two witnesses prophesying 1260 days, and terminated this period in 1798. He then tied this with the statement in verses 14 and 15 of the same chapter, which led him to conclude that the end should be expected not long after 1798.

10. He took the statement in Revelation 12:6, 14, where again the prophetic period of 1260 days is mentioned. Consistently with his other lines of evidence he ended this period in A. D. 1798, and then declared that "this also harmonizes with the *witnesses,* and the *trumpets,*" comparing Revelation 11:15 with chapter 12, verse 10.

11. He took the statement in Revelation 13:5, where the same 1260-day prophecy is presented under the phrase "forty and two months." He ended this period, of course, in 1798. Then he noted what he believed was a certain relationship between that period and the 1,335-day prophecy, which he carries down to 1843.

12. He took the statement in Revelation 13:18, which states that "the number of the beast" is 666. He understood this to mean 666 years. "This text shows the number of years that Rome would exist under the blasphemous head of paganism, after it was connected with the people of God by league, beginning B. C. 158, add 666 years, will bring us to A. D. 508, when the daily was taken away. Then add Daniel 12:12, the 1,335 to 508, makes the year 1843."

The foregoing statement, with brief quotations, is a summary of the lines of secondary proof for the 1843 date that Miller set forth in a formal way on January 1, 1843. This was included in a "Synopsis of Miller's Views," printed in *Signs of the Times,* January 25, 1843, pages 145-150. Most of these lines of proof are found woven through Miller's early writings. Some of these so-called proofs that 1843 was the climax year of prophecy are plainly fanciful. Others of the proofs were sound in their basic elements, for example, the interpretation of major prophecies, such as the 1260 days. But they were strained in the conclusions that were built upon them. Even though it could be established by certain lines of reasoning, that great prophecies ended about 1843, Miller erred in reasoning that the second advent must follow immediately. Thus his writings on prophecy mix error with truth. The truth is found in the interpretation he gave to most of the major prophecies of Daniel and the Revelation, as discussed in Appendix K. The principal errors are found in the reasoning adopted in his endeavor to create certain secondary proofs, and in the interpretation he gave to the key words "sanctuary" and "cleansed," in Daniel 8:13, 14.

Appendix M
THE IDEA OF GRADUAL WORLD IMPROVEMENT HEAVILY DISCOUNTED TODAY

By the year 1914 the great majority of intellectuals had subscribed to the idea that the world is gradually progressing upward toward a better level. Some believed that this was due to an inherent upward urge within all creation, the blind force of evolution in operation. Others, particularly those who had a definitely Christian background and who still wished to hold on to the Bible in some form, believed that this alleged upward, onward movement of humanity was due to the mysterious workings of God's divine Spirit. Such persons held that ultimately such divine action would cause this present world to evolve into a new earth, in other words, that a millennium of peace and holiness would ensue. Those who believed the very old-fashioned idea that the only solution of the tragedy of a wicked world is by the supernatural appearing of Christ to destroy the wicked and redeem the righteous, were at an increasing discount. They were viewed as calamity howlers, people who had lost faith in the possibilities of man.

Then came World War 1. That shattered sadly the pollyanna ideas of many, and produced some remarkable confessions from eminent men. For example, in 1924 none other than Winston S. Churchill wrote an article under the startling title "Shall We All Commit Suicide?" His article opens thus: "Up to the present time the means of destruction at the disposal of man have not kept pace with his ferocity." He summarizes briefly the hit-or-miss fashion in which much of the fighting of all ancient times was waged, and continues, "It was not until the dawn of the twentieth century of the Christian Era that war really began to enter into its kingdom as the potential destroyer of the human race."

He then describes how "science unfolded her treasures and her secrets to the desperate demands of men and placed in their hands agencies and apparatus almost decisive in their character." This leads him to remark:

"Such then is the peril with which mankind menaces itself. Means of destruction incalculable in their effects, wholesale and frightful in their character, and unrelated to any form of human merit; the march of science unfolding ever more appalling possibilities; and the fires of hatred burning deep in the hearts of some of the greatest people of the world, fed by the deepest sense of national wrong or national danger!"

Writing as he was, in 1924, he refers to the "blessed respite of exhaustion, offering to the nations a final chance to control their destinies and avert what may well be a general doom." He declares that "if a sense of self-preservation still exists among men, if the will to live resides not merely in individuals or nations but in humanity as a whole, the prevention of the supreme catastrophe ought to be the paramount object of all endeavor."

Gloomily he observes that "mankind has never been in this position before," and that this "is the point in human destinies to which all the glories and toils of men have at last led them." [1]

An echo of this doleful description of man's probable future fate is found in the annual report of the Rockefeller Foundation for the year 1943, prepared by its president, Raymond B. Fosdick. He declares:

"The supreme question which confronts our generation today—the question to which all other problems are merely corollaries—is whether our technology can be brought under control. Is man to be the master of the destructive energies he has created, or is he to be their victim? ... In brief, has man the wisdom and the ethical and spiritual powers to control the forces which he has himself let loose? ...

"We cannot count on geologic ages for the development of methods of social control. What we do in this generation and the next may well decide the kind of civilization, if any, which is to dominate the globe for centuries to come. We now have it within our power to tear the world to pieces whenever passion and emotion call the tune. We must hope that we have it within our power, too, although the opportunity may slip from our grasp not soon to be regained, to make this Frankenstein creature which we have built, the servant and not the master of the people.

"Nobody can be sure of the formula by which this end can be achieved. All that we know is that it will take knowledge and wisdom almost beyond what seems available at the moment." [2]

Statements like these might be multiplied manyfold. We do not recall reading anything more doleful than this in Millerite or Adventist literature anywhere. The chief difference between dire pictures such as Churchill and Fosdick draw and those drawn by the believers in the supernatural second advent of Christ, is this: The former offer no assurance of light beyond the darkness, the latter offer the light of the advent.

For the man who believes the most elementary doctrine that God lives and rules the universe, should it be thought a thing incredible that this God would finally take summary action to end the tragedy of our world? If man's intellectual, physical, and financial resources have finally been capitalized for mass suicide, for the destruction of the world as we know it, is there any rational reason that can be offered why God should longer permit this present world to continue? The idea of a sudden and supernatural end to our present world is neither incredible nor irrational, and it is eminently Scriptural.

---

[1] Winston S. Churchill, "Shall We All Commit Suicide?" *Hearst's International*, August, 1924.
[2] Raymond B. Fosdick, *The Rockefeller Foundation, A Review for 1943*, pp. 33-35.

Appendix N
"GABRIEL, BLOW THAT HORN!"

Under the title "Gabriel, Blow That Horn!" there appeared in *The American Mercury,* November, 1942, an article by Regis Canevin Toomey, describing the actions of the followers of William Miller as they anticipated the second advent of Christ in 1844. This article was reprinted in *Reader's Digest,* January, 1943. The reprint contains almost all of the original article. Because the article gives a historically distorted picture of Millerism, and because the *Reader's Digest* has so large a circulation, it seems not out of place to comment here on some of the statements made in the article. Quotations are made from the *Reader's Digest* condensation. We shall discuss ten errors of fact.

1. "This was no handful of fanatics. It was a religious movement that in one short decade boasted of a million members."

The obvious conclusion is that this was a *multitude* of fanatics. But whether "fanatics" or not, the Millerites never boasted of a million members. This error crept into the article because the author read that "million members" in McMaster's *History of the People of the United States,* but did not check original sources. McMaster gave as his authority the Millerite paper, the *Signs of the Times.* Reference to that paper reveals that it quoted at length from various religious and secular papers that had commented on the East Kingston camp meeting in the summer of 1842. One of these, the *Boston Daily Mail,* said that the Millerites claimed "not less than a million." (Quoted in *Signs of the Times,* July 13, 1842, p. 114.) But like many or most of the newspaper stories this was quite inaccurate. The Millerites never claimed more than between fifty thousand and one hundred thousand adherents.

2. The general deportment of the Millerites on the date of the expected advent of Christ is thus described: "It was a night of religious frenzy unequalled in American history." "Many indulged in wild religious dances."

The only eyewitness report by a newspaper man that we found, the one who described the large Cincinnati tabernacle meeting on October 22, stressed the decorum and quietness. There is nothing in the newspaper reports of the Millerite meetings on the great day, as the reader of this book knows, that supports any such lurid picture. However, there is an account of what might possibly be described as a wild religious dance, but it is not found in a contemporary source. Instead, it is in a book written about eighty years after the event, which depends for its "facts" on the memories of people and the word-of-mouth stories passed on from one generation to another. That book, published in 1924, by Clara Endicott Sears, and entitled *Days of Delusion,* is discussed at some length in Chapter 27, and in Appendix I. We know that the author of the article, Toomey, was conversant with her book, because he mentions it in a list of sixteen books which he kindly sent us in response to our request for the bibliography of sources from which he drew in preparing his article. Incidentally, this bibliography consists almost wholly of works written at least a generation or two after Millerism flourished. No Millerite publications of the 1840's are listed.*

3. *"Some, . . . waiting to be lifted into heaven, . . . crouched in laundry baskets and washtubs."*

This story is found in Sears' *Days of Delusion,* page 194. A woman wrote to Miss Sears, saying, "I . . . have heard my relations tell of a company of Millerites dressed in white taking baskets along to go up in." The letter writer, a woman seventy-four years of age, was writing to Miss Sears about seventy-seven years after the alleged event! And now ninety-eight years after the supposed incident, the basket story is related as though it were one of the undebatable facts of history.

4. *"One worldly young woman in Chicago packed a complete new wardrobe in a trunk, and strapped herself firmly to her treasure so that both would enter the pearly gates simultaneously."*

We do not know where the author, Toomey, found this story; we seriously doubt that he found it in a Chicago newspaper of that day, or in any other newspaper of 1844. A story that dramatic would certainly have been clipped and reprinted over the whole country within a few weeks. We did not find it in any of the ninety-one newspapers we examined, but we did find the story in John Greenleaf Whittier's *Prose Works,* Volume I, chapter, "The World's End." This chapter describes a Millerite camp meeting in September, 1844. But he places the story in "the western part of this State [Massachusetts]." Perhaps the young lady moved about with her trunk! But it was a long distance to Chicago in those days! Did Whittier say he had seen the young lady? No, he prefaces the story with the remark that it "was mentioned to me not long since." Somebody told him that somebody else in the western part of Massachusetts had done thus and so in the year 1844. By 1942 the young lady in question had drifted over to Chicago, and we are informed of her activities, not as a piece of hearsay, as Whittier confessed, when he first passed on the story, but as a solemn, undebatable incident in American history.

5. *On that last night "children scurried about, wide-eyed and frightened. . . . At one camp two were found dead next day."*

These are none other than the two sweet Millerite babes whose alleged freezing fate we discussed in Chapter 22. We found that

---
* Letter to author from R. C. Toomey, Jan. 28, 1943.

contemporary evidence gave the lie to the story—including the evidence from the health officer's record of interments, and the weather man's report of the temperature on that supposedly cold, cold night. But ninety-eight years after the gossip-generated tragedy the rumor is reported anew and as dogmatically as if it were taken from the official coroner's reports.

6. *"Great crowds left Boston, Philadelphia, New York and other thickly populated centers by the afternoon of October 22, and streamed out into the countryside clad in their thin white ascension robes."*

In view of the evidence presented in Chapter 25, we believe the reader will agree that this ghostly picture is slightly overdrawn. There is nothing in the newspapers of October 22, 1844, or the days immediately following, to warrant saying that even one Millerite was seen in an ascension robe anywhere!

7. *"A middle-aged Philadelphian, clad in a white robe, calmly stepped from his third-story window and tried to fly to heaven. In Worcester, Massachusetts, a respectable citizen donned a pair of turkey wings, climbed a towering tree and tried to fly from the topmost branch."* Etc.

In the light of the comment under No. 6, there is little need to discuss these stories, which are merely subsections of the general story about ascension robes. The reader will recall that we found in the contemporary sources only one tree-jumping story, á la robes, that the story was later retracted in the newspapers, and that the alleged jumper was admitted to have been insane for ten years. The current form of the tree-jumping story is found in the Sears work, *Days of Delusion*, and is placed in Worcester, whereas the original story placed the supposed jumper near Portsmouth, New Hampshire. But then, a man or rather a rumor, can jump quite a distance down country in ninety-eight years!

We found in the Worcester newspapers many silly stories about Millerites, but the editors apparently missed this capital story of the robe-clad tree-jumper in their town. Or had he not reached their town at that time? Yet today the tree-jumping story is given as routine history. It is remarkable what a century will do toward authenticating a story. The story of the "middle-aged Philadelphian" we have found in no newspaper of 1843 or 1844. It is probably only a variant of the jumping stories that sprang from New Hampshire.

8. *"Suicides and numerous cases of mental derangements were reported. A small asylum in Vermont held 25 Millerites whose minds had cracked under the strain of waiting."*

In 1844 there was only one asylum in Vermont. It was located at Brattleboro and was known as the Vermont Asylum for the Insane. In the newspapers in the fall of 1844 appeared this item: "Mr. Addison Davis in a letter to the editor of the Essex Co. *Washingtonian* says that 26 persons are now in the insane asylum at Brattleboro, Vt., in consequence of insanity produced by the influence of Millerism."[1] Who Mr. Davis is, we know not. He was not an official of the Brattleboro institution, so far as our reading of its annual reports reveals.

We need not here restate the facts set forth in Chapters 23 and 24, which show that the charge of insanity that was brought against Millerism disappears under detailed scrutiny of the asylum records of the 1840's. The reader will recall that the references to "causes" in the case histories reflect what the friends or relatives said, and not what the asylum doctors diagnosed! Even then, the friends and relatives, in sending patients to Brattleboro, never even thought to mention Millerism except in five cases in 1844. But now, ninety-eight years afterward, the idle gossip of a Mr. Addison Davis, in a letter to the press, regarding twenty-six cases in Brattleboro in 1844, is set forth as the most matter-of-fact piece of history.

9. "In Pennsylvania a farmer killed himself and his family because one of the older children had dared to scoff at the prophet, and in Massachusetts a Millerite cut his wife's throat for the same reason."

The story of the Pennsylvania farmer reminds us of the rather hoary catch question as to what's the matter with the story of the man who dreamed that he had died, and the shock killed him. The answer, of course, is that if he died, how do we know what he dreamed? So with the poor farmer. He is supposed to have killed himself and all his family. But then perhaps he kept a diary! We read the files of some of the leading papers of Pennsylvania, but we did not see any account of this tragedy. Perhaps we missed it. Even if it were printed, that would still leave unsolved the question of whether the poor farmer left a record of his deed. There was a story that appeared in the press in 1848 about a man in the State of Maine who killed himself and his family, and whose deed was first carelessly charged to the aftereffects of Millerism. But the papers later admitted that this charge was groundless. (For full discussion of this see *The Advent Herald,* May 27, 1848, page 136; June 17, 1848, page 156; July 15, 1848, page 188.) Perhaps rumor moved this man to Pennsylvania after ninety-eight years. It could be possible!

As to the man in Massachusetts, we do not know. We have not found this story in the papers of 1843 or 1844. We did find the story of a Mr. Nathaniel Brown of Kingston, New Hampshire, who is said to have cut his wife's throat, endangering her life. A news weekly adds:

---
[1] See, for example, *Pennsylvanian* (Philadelphia), Nov. 11, 1844.

"It is said he was partially deranged, caused by overexcitement on the Miller doctrine." [2] That sounds quite like the same story. And it is not far from New Hampshire to Massachusetts. Not nearly so far as from Massachusetts to Chicago, the distance the young lady had to go with her loaded trunk during the ninety-eight years. Now, what is the authority cited for the Nathaniel Brown Millerism-induced act? The answer is, "It is said." We have analyzed such impressive phrases as that many times in the chapters of this book and have routinely found them to be as undependable when used a century ago as when used in current speech today. But while this story, and almost every other story of suicide, murder, or attempted murder in the 1840's that was supposed to be due to Millerism, is originally prefaced with "It is said" or some similar evasive and elastic phrase, such qualifying expressions are left off in the retelling a century later.

Incidentally, if this Mr. Brown were really insane, would not the court most likely have committed him to the State asylum? But the records of the New Hampshire asylum contain no record of such a man in the 1840's. Furthermore, if there was a man in Massachusetts who was made insane by Millerism and who attempted to kill his wife, would we not most likely find a record of him in the principal State institution at Worcester? But the case histories of that institution for the years 1842, 1843, and 1844, that mention Millerism, contain no story of an unfortunate patient's having committed any such violent act. That silence in itself raises a heavy presumption against the genuineness of the whole story, though of course the man might have been taken to the McLean Asylum or to the Boston Lunatic Hospital. The superintendent of McLean's, however, was so skeptical of all alleged "causes" given by friends and relatives, that he refused to dignify such laymen's diagnoses by any formal table of causes in his annual reports.

10. *"In New York City a shoe merchant threw open the doors of his establishment and placed his stock at the disposal of the public. In Meredith, New Hampshire, the number of devout who abandoned everything became so great that the town fathers asked the courts to appoint legal guardians so that families might not be forced into poverty."*

The New York shoe merchant is undoubtedly none other than Abraham Riker, of Division Street. The groundlessness of this story we have shown in Chapter 22. The reader will recall that Mr. Riker not only was said to have given away his shoes, but also was said to have been taken to an asylum and even to have died suddenly. As to the Meredith, New Hampshire, story the contemporary sources, the

---

[2] *Niles National Register*, April 1, 1843.

newspapers, which were never known to understate in their reports on Millerism, declared that "eight or ten individuals in Meredith" were alleged to be the objects of legal action.[3] In ninety-eight years "eight or ten" become a number "so great" that they make a really worth-while story for publication. Surely the Millerites have multiplied and replenished the earth.

But why lengthen the discussion of errors in this article, which apparently is written in the tempo of sober, staid facts! There are a number more errors and, what is equally bad, half-truths. We do not believe the author purposely set out to distort history. We think he simply did what most everyone else has done: he repeated the idle stories that have gradually been incorporated in many respectable works. That is doubtless the way to write something interesting. Beyond that nothing can be said in commendation of such writing.

---

[3] *Portland Bulletin* (Maine), Nov. 30, 1844.

Bibliography

LOCATION OF PRIMARY SOURCES

For the benefit of the student of Millerite history we give here the names of libraries, etc., in which the primary Millerite sources used in this book were found. We refer to primary sources in the restricted sense of the word, the writings of the Millerites themselves, or the writings of contemporaneous authors who deal specifically with Millerism, whether as letters, pamphlets, journals, broadsides, or books. Newspapers, it is true, have a primary value. But the following list of libraries, etc., ignores the question of the location of old newspapers. They are scattered too widely over the libraries and historical society offices of all New England and elsewhere. The following list is in alphabetical order, and not necessarily in order of importance:

Advent Source Collection, Takoma Park, Washington, D. C. This collection, gathered from both Europe and America, is the largest and most complete of its kind in this field. Its value is enhanced by certain complete photostatic copies of rare European works now probably irreplacable after the destruction incident to the war. This collection is particularly rich in theological works on prophecy and the advent doctrine, not only of the Millerite period itself, but of the centuries preceding. Contains almost complete file of principal Millerite papers. Housed in the Seventh-day Adventist Theological Seminary. This collection is of greatest value to those carrying on research work in the theological areas of Millerism.

Adventual Collection, Aurora, Illinois. This is the best collection of manuscript sources on Millerism, including a group of more than 800 letters to or from Miller. Almost complete file of the principal Millerite papers, and bound volumes of certain papers that were published in the years after 1844 by various men who had had a part in the Millerite movement. Probably the most nearly complete collection of the pamphlets that constituted the Second Advent Library. Other important works on the Millerite movement are also found in this collection, which is housed at Aurora College, an institution of the Advent Christian denomination.

American Antiquarian Society, Worcester, Massachusetts. The library of this society contains a number of Millerite works, including several of the Second Advent Library series. Also some bound volumes of Millerite papers. Has a rare collection of broadsides and similar material, most of which was printed by those opposed to Millerism in the 1840's. Very extensive collection of journals of the period, a number of which contain references to Millerism. Complete file of asylum reports for the 1840's.

Boston Public Library, Boston. Contains a number of works that deal with Millerism, particularly polemical works on the doctrinal aspects of the movement.

Library of Congress, Washington, D. C. Contains a number of Millerite works and a few volumes of Millerite papers. Its map division provides the student with a true picture of every part of New England in the 1840's.

New York Public Library, New York City. This contains several works of importance. Its chief distinction is that it houses a specially indexed advent collection that is of value to the student who wishes to study the history of Seventh-day Adventists, who developed from the Millerite movement.

Phelps Collection. In the possession of Philip M. M. Phelps, of Fair Haven, Vermont, a great-grandson of Miller, are a few letters to Miller, Miller's arithmetic notebook, a few military documents, and a family Bible that contains the most complete genealogical record of the Miller family we have found.

Spalding Collection. A group of letters written by Charles Fitch to his wife, his son, and others. Also a scrapbook and a few pages of a diary by Fitch. This collection is the private property of A. W. Spalding, Madison College, Tennessee.

State Library, Concord, New Hampshire. This library contains a number of works, both by Millerites and by those who wrote against them. While it is true that almost every large library in New England contains something of value on Millerism—though oftentimes only duplicating what is found elsewhere—this library is definitely above the average.

Union Theological Seminary, New York City. The library of this seminary, which contains one of the best collections of theological works in the United States, has a number of valuable Millerite works. Also many religious papers published at that time, which discuss Millerism.

Vermont Historical Society, Montpelier, Vermont. The library of this society contains the most complete collection of manuscripts that deal with Miller's military record in the War of 1812. Miller's brief diary, with entries beginning in 1798. A copy of Miller's 64-page pamphlet, *Evidences From Scripture and History,* printed in 1833, a very rare document. A number of polemical works by contemporary theological opponents.

Western Reserve Historical Society, Cleveland, Ohio. The library of this society contains the most complete file of *The Western Midnight Cry,* and its successor, *The Day-Star.* Also a virtually complete file of *The Second Advent of Christ.*

MANUSCRIPTS

(Unless otherwise indicated, all manuscript sources listed below are in the Adventual Collection, Aurora, Illinois)

Letters

Anonymous (signed Bah!), to the "Great End of the World Man," April 22, 1843.
Barbour, Philander, to William Miller, Nov. 8, 1844.
Barry, Thomas F., to William Miller, April 11, 1840.
Brinegar, W. C., *M. D.,* to the author, Oct. 29, 1943.
Chandler, S. C., to William Miller, April 18, 1844.
Clemons, Mrs. E. C., to William Miller, Oct. 10, 1844.
Cole, Timothy, to William Miller, July 25, 1839.
Collection of letters written between 1920 and 1923 to Clara Endicott Sears. Society for the Preservation of New England Antiquities, Boston.
Elliott, George A., *M. D.,* to the author, May 22, 1944.
Fassett, Elias, to William Miller, April 10, 1813. Vermont Historical Society.
Fitch, Charles, to William Miller, March 5, 1838.
———, to "Brother and Sister [W. C.] Palmer," July 26, 1842. Spalding Collection.
Fleming, L. D., to William Miller, April 11, 1840.
Galusha, Elon, *et al.,* to William Miller, Oct. 2, 1943.
Hellweg, Capt. J. F., to the author, Feb. 21, 1944.
Hewitt, Rev. C. H., to the author, May 24, 1944.

BIBLIOGRAPHY 521

Himes, Joshua V., to William Miller, June 26, 1841; Oct. 10, 1844 (penciled note appended to letter of Mrs. E. C. Clemons of same date).
Jones, Henry, to William Miller, Dec. 27, 1832; Feb. 21, 1833; May 13, 1833; Sept. 1, 1833; May 19, 1834; Nov. 14, 1834.
Jones, I. E., to William Miller, April 6, 1844; Feb. 14, 1845.
Litch, Josiah, to William Miller, Oct. 24, 1844.
Marsh, Joseph, to William Miller, April 22, 1842; Aug. 17, 1843.
Marsh, Sarah M., to William Miller, Feb. 24, 1842.
Mencken, H. L., to the author, Jan. 26, 1943.
Miller, William, to Elisha Ashley, Oct. 3, 1824. Vermont Historical Society.
———, to Joseph Attwood (also spelled Atwood) "Dear Brother and Sisters, Emily and All," May 31, 1831.
———, to "Brother Baxter," Nov. 5, 1844.
———, to "Brother," unknown, begun April 10, 1849, unfinished.
———, to J. B. Cook, Sept. 16, 1845.
———, to [Elon] Galusha, April 5, 1844.
———, to Truman Hendryx, Aug. 9, 1831; Jan. 25, 1832; March 26, 1832; Oct. 1, 1832; Nov. 17, 1832; Feb. 8, 1833; April 10, 1833; Feb. 25, 1834; March 22, 1834; Aug. 17, 1834; Nov. 28, 1834; March 6, 1835; Aug. 27, 1835; April 2, 1836; July 21, 1836; Dec. 23, 1836; Feb. 21, 1837; July 27, 1838; May 19, 1841.
———, to Joshua V. Himes, undated [internal evidence indicates early 1845]; May 20, 1845.
———, to William S. Miller, Nov. 17, 1838; Jan. 28, 1839; March 9, 1840; Feb. 2, 1843.
———, to I. O. Orr, M. D., Dec. 13, 1844.
———, to "Friend Robins," April 27, 1814. Vermont Historical Society.
———, to John Stanley, Sept. 11, 1814.
Phelps, Philip M. M., to the author, May 17, 1944.
"R. D." to William Miller, Aug. 15, 1842.
Stebbins, H. P., to William Miller, July 23, 1842.
Stewart, Charles W., to William Miller, Feb. 21, 1842.
Toomey, R. C., to the author, Jan. 28, 1943.
Tyson, F. C:, *M. D.*, to the author, Jan. 11, 1944.
Ward, Henry Dana, to William Miller, Oct. 29, 1841.
Wescott, Isaac, to William Miller, March 12, 1835.
———, to William S. Miller, Nov. 12, 1839.
Whiting, N. N., to William Miller, Oct. 24, 1844.

WILLIAM MILLER'S PERSONAL RECORDS

Arithmetic notebook, undated. Phelps Collection.
Diary, first entry "11th day of March, 1798." Vermont Historical Society. [This is a very small notebook with brief entries that have not been made regularly. Significant as indicating early literary leanings, etc.]
Record of accounts as sheriff, 1809-11. [A small notebook containing routine entries.]
Statement of belief, Sept. 5, 1822. [Consists of twenty articles, the twentieth being unfinished.]
"Text Book," beginning Jan. 14, 1829. [Notations on sermons heard. Not to be confused with "Text Book" that follows.]
"Text Book," 2 volumes, Oct. 1, 1834, to June 9, 1839, and June 16, 1839, to June 23, 1844. [Date, place, and text of each sermon preached. Provides record of Miller's travels.]

LEGAL AND OTHER OFFICIAL DOCUMENTS

William Miller's commission as lieutenant in the Vermont militia, signed by Gov. Jonas Galusha, July 21, 1810. Vermont Historical Society.
William Miller's commission as captain in the Vermont militia, signed by Gov. Jonas Galusha, Nov. 7, 1812. Vermont Historical Society.
Roster of volunteers recruited by William Miller, Nov. 16, 1812. Phelps Collection.
William Miller's commission as justice of the peace, signed by D. Shipher, clerk of Washington County, New York, Feb. 28, 1821. Vermont Historical Society.
William Miller's license to preach, granted by the Baptist church in Hampton and White-Hall [N. Y.], Sept. 14, 1833. [Written on a small sheet of plain white paper.]
Summons signed by William Miller as justice of the peace, Feb. 13, 1834. Phelps Collection.
Records of stewards and leaders of Chestnut Street M. E. Church of Portland, Maine, from February to September, 1843, regarding the case of Robert Harmon and family. Chestnut Street M. E. Church, Portland, Maine.

Affidavit of Jacob Wheeler, notarized by John Howe, Master in Chancery, Castleton, Vt., May 25, 1878. Vermont Historical Society.

OTHER MANUSCRIPTS

Edson, Hiram. Fragment of manuscript on his life and experience. Undated. Advent Source Collection.

Gilman, Henry Hale. "The Mill and the Millerite." Undated. Haverhill, Mass., Public Library, 15 pp. [Typewritten. A brief, modern account of the suit in equity instituted in 1845 by Ezekiel Hale, Jr., against his son Ezekiel J. M. Hale, for the recovery of certain property after the great disappointment. Gilman was a grandnephew of the plaintiff.]

Miller Family. Genealogical pages in a Bible in the possession of a great-grandson, Edward L. Bartholomew.

————. Genealogical pages in a Bible in the possession of a great-grandson, Philip M. M. Phelps.

Miller, William. "The Book of Fortune." Vermont Historical Society. [A brief manuscript giving forecasts of weather if Christmas falls on Sunday, Monday, etc., also the relation of the 12 signs of the zodiac to the fortunes of mankind. No date. Handwriting indicates that it was written early in life.]

————. A commentary on the 13th, 17th, and 18th chapters of Revelation. 34 pages, dated July 12, 1844. [This is the manuscript of the Second Advent Library pamphlet *Remarks on Revelation Thirteenth, Seventeenth and Eighteenth*, q. v.]

Miller, William. Dissertation on Calumny ("Mr. Chairman and Gentlemen: Though I feel myself inadequate . . . "). Undated. Vermont Historical Society. [Internal evidence indicates that it was written during Jefferson's administration, 1801 to 1809.]

————. *Evidences From Scripture and History of the 2nd Coming of Christ About the Year A. D. 1843 and of His Personal Reign of 1000 Years*, 60 pp. [This is the manuscript of an 1833 pamphlet by this title, q. v.]

————. "A Few Evidences of the Time of the Second Coming of Christ, to Elder Andrus by William Miller," Feb. 15, 1831. 8 pp. [One of the earliest statements of any length in exposition of his views regarding 1843.]

————. "A New Year's Address to Those Who Believe in the Second Advent of Jesus Christ." [Internal evidence indicates approximately January, 1844. It is apparently the first draft of the message published in *Signs of the Times*, Jan. 31, 1844.]

————. Series of articles (the first eight) written for the *Vermont Telegraph*, Brandon, Vt. [These were printed in the *Telegraph*, beginning with the issue of May 15, 1831. They set forth Miller's theological views, particularly as touching the 1843 date. They are significant as being the very first writings of Miller that were printed.]

NEWSPAPERS

Following is a list of 91 newspapers examined and the period of time for which each was examined. This list is provided the reader because of the references in the book to the range of papers examined and our failure to find in all these papers certain news items. Newspapers were examined with particular reference to charges brought against the Millerites in October, 1844, when the end of the world was expected. However, as will be noted, a number of newspapers were examined for the two-year period 1843-44. In some instances our examination of papers has been dictated by the availability of files of papers. The fact that newspapers clipped so freely from each other makes almost certain that what the researcher misses in one he will find in another, provided of course that the item had any general news value. We would probably have examined even more fully the newspapers if we had felt they provided very dependable source material. We believe that the evidence presented in this book reveals how undependable was much that appeared in the papers. Many newspapers consisted of four pages, two of which would frequently be given over to patent medicine advertisements, a third page to a medley of literary productions and legal notices, and oftentimes only a page to definitely news matter. This page of news generally consisted of an endless series of paragraphs on different items, with no headings, not even a dividing line to mark the end of one item and the beginning of another. One of the most common forms of introduction to items was "It is reported." This was often varied by "It is said," or even "It is rumored." There were very few reporters as we know them today, and of course there were no news-gathering agencies or wire services.

Newspapers frequently varied their names. We have given the name used during the period for which the paper was examined.

BIBLIOGRAPHY

Location	Name of Paper	Frequency of Issue	Period Examined
CONNECTICUT			
Hartford	*Connecticut Courant*	Weekly	1843-44
Litchfield	*Litchfield Enquirer*	Weekly	October, 1844
Norwich	*Norwich Courier*	Weekly	1843-44
DISTRICT OF COLUMBIA			
Washington	*Daily National Intelligencer*	Daily	1844
ILLINOIS			
Chicago	*Chicago Democrat*	Daily	1844
	Chicago Express	Daily	1843
MAINE			
Augusta	*Kennebec Journal*	Weekly	1843-44
Bath	*Maine Inquirer*	Weekly	1843
Norway Village	*Norway Advertiser*	Weekly	1844
Portland	*Daily Eastern Argus*	Daily	April-Dec., 1844, 1848
	Portland Bulletin	Triweekly	1843-44
	Portland Daily Advertiser	Daily	October, 1844
	Portland Daily American	Daily	October, 1844
	Portland Transcript	Weekly	Sept.-Nov., 1844
Saco	*Maine Democrat*	Weekly	1843-44
MARYLAND			
Baltimore	*Baltimore American*	Daily	October, 1844
	Sun	Daily	1843-44
MASSACHUSETTS			
Boston	*American Traveller*	Weekly	Oct.-Dec., 1844
	Boston Daily Advertiser and Patriot	Daily	October, 1844
	Boston Daily Bee	Daily	October, 1844
	Boston Daily Courier	Daily	Oct. 15-Nov. 5, 1844
	Boston Daily Mail	Daily	Oct.-Nov., 1844
	Boston Post	Daily	Oct.-Nov., 1844
	Boston Weekly Messenger	Weekly	Oct. 16-Nov. 6, 1844
	Daily Evening Transcript	Daily	1843 and 1844
	Evening Mercantile Journal	Daily	Oct.-Nov., 1844
Concord	*Concord Freeman*	Weekly	1844
Haverhill	*Essex Banner*	Weekly	1843-44
	Haverhill Gazette	Weekly	1843-44
Hingham	*Hingham Patriot*	Weekly	1843-44
Lowell	*Lowell Advertiser*	Weekly	1844
	Lowell Courier	Triweekly	1843-44
Nantucket	*Weekly Telegraph*	Weekly	April-Sept., 1843
Newburyport	*Newburyport Daily Herald*	Daily	Oct. 21-28, 1844
Norhampton	*Hampshire Gazette*	Weekly	1843-44
Pittsfield	*Pittsfield Sun*	Weekly	1843-44
Salem	*Salem Register*	Semiweekly	1843-44
Worcester	*Massachusetts Spy*	Weekly	1843-44
	National Aegis	Weekly	1843-44
	Worcester Palladium	Weekly	October, 1844
MICHIGAN			
Detroit	*Daily Advertiser*	Daily	Sept.-Dec., 1844
NEW HAMPSHIRE			
Amherst	*Farmer's Cabinet*	Weekly	October, 1844

Location	Name of Paper	Frequency of Issue	Period Examined
Concord	New Hampshire Patriot and State Gazette	Weekly	1843-44
	New Hampshire Statesman and State Journal	Weekly	October, 1844
Exeter	Exeter News-Letter and Rockingham Advertiser	Weekly	October, 1844
Portsmouth	New Hampshire Gazette	Weekly	1843-44
	Portsmouth Journal	Weekly	1843-44

NEW JERSEY

Newark	Newark Daily Advertiser	Daily	1843-44

NEW YORK

Albany	Albany Evening Journal	Daily	Jan.-July, 1843; June-Dec., 1844
New York	Evening Mirror	Daily	October, 1844
	Evening Post for the Country	Semiweekly	October, 1844
	Herald	Daily	Nov., 1842; Oct., 1844
	New York American	Weekly	October, 1844
	New York Daily Tribune	Daily	1843-44
	New York Spectator and Semiweekly Commercial		Oct.-Nov., 1844
	Advertiser	Semiweekly	Jan.-May, 1843

OHIO

Ashtabula	Ashtabula Sentinel	Weekly	1843-44
Cincinnati	Cincinnati Daily Gazette	Daily	October, 1844
	Cincinnati Weekly Herald and Philanthropist	Weekly	1844
	Daily Cincinnati Atlas	Daily	October, 1844
Cleveland	Herald	Daily	1843-44
	Cleveland Plain Dealer	Weekly	1843-44
Columbus	Old School Republican	Weekly	1843-44
Norwalk	Experiment	Weekly	1843-44
Painesville	Telegraph	Weekly	1843-44

PENNSYLVANIA

Philadelphia	Neal's Saturday Gazette	Weekly	Oct. 12, 19, 25, 1844
	North American and Daily Advertiser	Daily	October, 1844
	Pennsylvania Inquirer and National Gazette	Daily	October, 1844
	Pennsylvanian	Daily	Oct.-Nov., 1844
	Philadelphia Gazette and Commercial Intelligencer	Daily	October, 1844
	Philadelphia Public Ledger	Daily	1843-44
	Saturday Courier	Weekly	Oct.-Nov., 1844
	Spirit of the Times	Daily	October, 1844
	United States Gazette	Daily	October, 1844
	United States Saturday Post	Weekly	Oct.-Nov., 1844
Pittsburgh	Daily Morning Post	Daily	October, 1844

RHODE ISLAND

Providence	Providence Daily Journal	Daily	Jan.-June, 1843; July-Nov., 1844

TENNESSEE

Nashville	Republican Banner	Triweekly	1844

BIBLIOGRAPHY

Location	Name of Paper	Frequency of Issue	Period Examined
VERMONT			
Bennington	*Vermont Gazette*	Weekly	Jan.-Sept., 1843; October, 1844
Brandon	*Voice of Freedom*	Weekly	Oct.-Nov., 1844
Brattleboro	*Vermont Phoenix*	Weekly	October, 1844
Burlington	*Burlington Free Press*	Weekly	1843-44
	Burlington Sentinel	Weekly	1842-July, 1844
	True Democrat	Weekly	June 7, 1843 to May 1, 1844
Danville	*North Star*	Weekly	1843-44
Montpelier	*Vermont Patriot*	Weekly	1843-44 (no ref. found)
	Vermont Watchman and State Journal	Weekly	1843-44
Rutland	*Rutland Weekly Herald*	Weekly	Oct.-Nov., 1844
St. Albans	*Vermont Republican*	Weekly	Oct.-Nov., 1844
St. Johnsbury	*Caledonian*	Weekly	1843-44
Windsor	*Vermont Chronicle*	Weekly	1842-44
VIRGINIA			
Richmond	*Richmond Enquirer*	Semiweekly	1844

Following are the references to newspapers in this work:

Albany Evening Journal (N. Y.), Feb. 27, 1843; Oct. 21, 25, 1844.
American Traveller (Boston), Nov. 2, 9, 1844.
Boston Daily Bee, Oct. 16, 22, 24, Nov. 4, 1844.
Boston Daily Courier, Oct. 17, 1844.
Boston Daily Mail, Oct. 15, 23, 24, Nov. 4, 1844.
Boston Post, Oct. 9, 25, Nov. 2, 1844.
Caledonian (St. Johnsbury, Vt.), Nov. 4, 1844.
Chicago Express, March 8, 1843.
Cincinnati Daily Gazette, Oct. 7, 1844.
Cleveland Herald, Oct. 22, 1844.
Concord Freeman (Mass.), Oct. 25, 1844.
Connecticut Courant (Hartford), Feb. 4, 25, 1843.
Daily Cincinnati Atlas, Oct. 1, 1844.
Daily Eastern Argus (Portland, Maine), Oct. 15, 1844.
Daily Evening Transcript (Boston), Jan. 23, May 25, July 10, 1843; March 28, Oct. 16, 1844.
Daily Morning Post (Pittsburgh), Oct. 30, 1844.
Daily National Intelligencer (Washington), April 5, Oct. 21, 1844.
Evening Mercantile Journal (Boston), Nov. 6, 1844.
Evening Post for the Country (New York), Oct. 18, 22, 1844.
Hampshire Gazette (Northampton, Mass.), Feb. 21, 1843.
Haverhill Gazette (Mass.), April 15, May 20, 1843.
Herald (New York), Extra, November, 1842 (reprinted from issues of Nov. 4-15); Oct. 12, Oct. 23, 1844.
Hingham Patriot (Mass.), April 8, 1843.
Journal (Napa, Calif.), Feb. 20, 1942.
Kennebec Journal (Augusta, Maine), March 10, April 28, 1843; Nov. 15, 1844.
Litchfield Enquirer (Conn.), Oct. 24, 1844.
Lowell Advertiser (Mass.), May 31, 1844.
Lowell Courier (Mass.), Feb. 23, 1843; May 18, 1844.
Maine Inquirer (Bath), Jan. 18, March 1, 8, April 5, May 3, July 26, 1843.
Massachusetts Spy (Worcester), Feb. 22, May 10, Sept. 13, 1843.
National Aegis (Worcester, Mass.), Oct. 23, 1844.
Neal's Saturday Gazette (Philadelphia), Oct. 19, 1844.
New Hampshire Statesman (Concord), Oct. 25, 1844.
New York Daily Tribune, Feb. 11, March 2 (Extra), 11, 24, 1843.

New York Express, Oct. 21, 1844.
New York Spectator, Oct. 16, 19, Nov. 2, 1844.
Newark Daily Advertiser, Feb. 25, Sept. 14, 1843; March 2, Oct. 19, 1844.
Newburyport Daily Herald (Mass.), Oct. 21, 1844.
North American (Philadelphia), Oct. 16, 1844.
Pennsylvania Inquirer (Philadelphia), Oct. 22, 24, 28, 1844.
Pennsylvanian (Philadelphia), Oct. 22, Nov. 8, 11, 1844.
Philadelphia Public Ledger, Jan. 16, Feb. 8, 18, March 23, Sept. 11, 1843; Oct. 11, 15, 21, 22, 24, 1844.
Pittsfield Sun (Mass.), Sept. 28, 1843.
Portland Bulletin (Maine), Jan. 17, March 14, 30, May 23, 1843; July 23, Nov. 30, 1844.
Portland Daily Advertiser (Maine), Oct. 26, 1844.
Portland Daily American (Maine), Oct. 18, 1844.
Portsmouth Journal (N. H.), Feb. 11, 1843; Oct. 19, Nov. 9, 1844.
Providence Daily Journal (R. I.), Feb. 10, 1843; Oct. 24, 1844.
Salem Register (Mass.), April 3, 1843.
Spirit of the Times (Philadelphia), Oct. 15, 21, 22, 23, 24, 1844.
Sun (Baltimore), May 4, 1843; Oct. 15, 17, 22, 25, 28, 1844.
United States Gazette (Philadelphia), Oct. 16, 1844.
United States Saturday Post (Philadelphia), Oct. 16, 26, Nov. 2, 9, 1844.
Vermont Chronicle (Windsor), June 26, 1844.
Vermont Phoenix (Brattleboro), Nov. 15, 1844.
Vermont Watchman and State Journal (Montpelier), Nov. 15, 1844.

PERIODICALS

Millerite and Adventist

Advent Herald, The. See Signs of the Times.

Advent Review and Sabbath Herald, Aug. 19, 1851; May 6, 27, 1852; April 14, 1868; Feb. 15, 1870; Oct. 11, 1881; Oct. 13, 1885; May 7, 1901; Aug. 18, 1921. [Started in Paris, Maine. First issue dated November, 1850. First volume called the *Second Advent Review and Sabbath Herald.* Editor, James White. From November, 1850, to March, 1851, published monthly; then semimonthly until August, 1853. Published weekly from September, 1853, onward. Printed for a time in 1851 at Saratoga Springs, N. Y., then in 1852 at Rochester, N. Y. Moved to Battle Creek, Mich., in 1855. Moved to Washington, D. C., in 1903.]

Advent Shield and Review, May, 1844. [It is difficult to know whether to list this as a book or as a periodical. It was published from May, 1844, to April, 1845, and carries a continuous numbering from page 1 to page 440. The month and year are given as part of the running title, the month sometimes changing on the same sheet, which reveals that, in certain instances at least, the issue for that month could not have been published and circulated as a separate document. The first page, in addition to the title, gives the following information: "Edited by J. V. Himes, S. Bliss, & A. Hale. Boston: Published by Joshua V. Himes, No. 14 Devonshire Street, 1844." The preface speaks of the *"contents"* of this number."—*Page 4.* But the table of contents on page 2 lists only the articles published under the running title "May, 1844," from page 1 to page 144. Following page 288 is a new title page giving the same information as the first title page, except that this second one contains the line "Vol. I" and gives the years of publication as "1844-5." However, all the pages following this second title page carry the running title "April, 1845." This publication partook definitely of the physical and editorial nature of one of our modern quarterlies. It was well edited and devoted itself quite exclusively to providing theological support for Millerism and to refuting the views of opponents. Its board of editors reveals that it was an authoritative spokesman for Millerism.]

Bible Examiner, March, 1880. [Founded by George Storrs in New York City. Published only occasionally in the early 1840's. From 1847 to 1854, published as monthly, then semimonthly until 1863. Suspended for eight years while Storrs edited a weekly paper. Revived in 1871. Final issue, March, 1880, a "Memorial Number," giving the sketch of Storrs' life. From this last issue the above data have been secured. On account of Storrs' distinctive views on the nature of man and the state of the dead, the *Bible Examiner* was almost from the first an organ of Storrs rather than an organ of the Millerite movement.]

Day-Star, The, Oct. 25, 1845; Extra, Feb. 7, 1846. [Earlier *The Western Midnight Cry,* which was founded by Himes in the fall of 1843 in Cincinnati, Ohio (see *Signs of the Times,* Oct. 4, 1843, p. 54). George Storrs was the first editor of *The Western Midnight Cry.* A little later E. Jacobs became editor. Though presumably *this periodical* was a weekly, there are many instances in which two weeks or more intervened between issues. This was probably due to shortage of funds. Name changed to *The Day-Star* with Vol. V, No. 1, Feb. 18, 1845. Himes' name does not appear on *The Day-Star.* Instead, Jacobs is both editor and publisher. This weekly rapidly moved out from the main Adventist stream after 1844. Ceased publication in 1847.]

Midnight Cry, The, Nov. 17, 23, Dec. 5, 1842; Feb. 3, March 3, 10, 17, 24, April 7, 13, 20, May 18, June 1, 22, July 6, 13, 20, Aug. 24, Sept. 7, 14, 21, Oct. 26, Nov. 2, 16, Dec. 7, 28, 1843; Jan. 4, 18, 25, Feb. 1, 8, 15, 22, March 7, 21, 28, April 4, 11, 18, May 9, June 13, 20, July 4, Aug. 1, Sept. 5, 12, Oct. 3, 10, 11, 12, 19, 31, Nov. 7, 14, 21, Dec. 5, 12, 26, 1844. *The Morning Watch,* Feb. 20, April 3, 1845. [*The Midnight Cry* was started in New York City, Nov. 17, 1842. Published daily, except Sundays, until Dec. 17, 1842. Then weekly until the end of 1844. With the first issue of 1845 the name was changed to the *Morning Watch.* Soon merged with The Advent Herald. This was one of the principal and truly official organs of the Millerite movement. It was under the direct control of Joshua V. Himes from the first.]

Morning Watch, The. See *Midnight Cry.*

Second Advent of Christ, The, July 26, 1843. [Published in Cleveland, Ohio, during most of 1843. Editor, Charles Fitch. Vol. I, No. 1, is dated Jan. 18, 1843. The standing of Fitch in the Millerite movement gave to this publication a certain significance.]

Signs of the Times, March 20, April 15, May 1, Sept. 1, 1840; April 15, June 1, July 15, Aug. 2, Sept. 1, 15, Nov. 1, 15, Dec. 1, 15, 1841; Jan. 1, 15, Feb. 15, May 4, 11, 25, June 1, 15, 22, 29, July 13, 20, 27, Aug. 3, 17, 24, Sept. 21, Oct. 12, Dec. 14, 21, 1842; Jan. 4, 18, 25, Feb. 1, 8, 15, 22, March 1, 8, 15, 22, 29, April 5, 12, 19, May. 3, 10, 17, 31, June 7, 14, July 5, 12, 19, Aug. 9, 16, Sept. 13, 27, Oct. 4, 11, Nov. 8, 15, Dec. 27, 1843; Jan. 31, 1844. *The Advent Herald,* Feb. 14, 21, March 6, 13, 20, April 10, May 1, 22, June 5, July 10, 17, 24, Aug. 7, 14, 21, Sept. 4, Oct. 2, 9, 16, 30, Nov. 6, 20, 27, Dec. 4, 11, 18, 1844; Jan. 8, 15, May 14, June 4, 1845; March 25, 1846; May 27, June 17, July 15, 1848. [*Signs of the Times* was published in Boston. Vol. 1, No. 1, bears date of March 20, 1840. (This was a reissue of a number dated Feb. 28, 1840, published by a commercial printer. See Wellcome, *History,* pp. 82, 84.) First a semimonthly, changed to a weekly with Vol. 3, No. 1, April 6, 1842. Last issue under the name *Signs of the Times,* Jan. 31, 1844. Name then changed to *The Advent Herald and Signs of the Times,* though referred to only by the first half of the title. From 1840 to 1844 the *Signs of the Times* carried varying subtitles. (This publication is not to be confused with the *Signs of the Times* founded in 1874 by the Seventh-day Adventists.) The *Signs of the Times* was one of the principal and official organs of the Millerite movement. From the beginning it was under the direct control of Joshua V. Himes. *The Advent Herald* continued publication for years after 1844 and was a chief organ of the central body of First-day Adventists.]

True Midnight Cry, The. [This is the title of a four-page paper published by E. Hale, Jr., Haverhill, Mass. Vol. I, No. 1, is dated August 22, 1844, and carries the information: "Edited by S. S. Snow." Apparently there was only one number issued. There was a reprint of this a little later in New York. This paper has particular significance because it presents in formal fashion and from the pen of the man most responsible for setting October 22, 1844, as the terminal date of the 2300-day prophecy, the arguments in behalf of that date. The paper opens with a defense of time setting in terms of a particular day for the advent, in order to offset the declaration of Christ that no man knoweth the day nor the hour of His coming.]

Voice of Elijah, The, May 30, 1843. [Published at Sherbrooke, Canada East, for some time. Editors: C. Greene, R. Hutchinson. (The only copy we have been able to find is one in the library of Aurora College, dated May 30, 1843, and bearing the further distinguishing mark "No. 2.") This publication was widely circulated in Canada and was sent abroad to British countries.]

Voice of Truth and Glad Tidings of the Kingdom at Hand, The. Nov. 20, 1844; Jan. 29, Feb. 5, May 21, 1845. [Founded by Joseph Marsh at Rochester, N. Y., Jan. 1, 1844. Published for a number of years, most of the time as a weekly.

Shortly after the great disappointment Marsh began to move away from the main Adventist group who had crystallized their thinking at the Mutual Conference in Albany, N. Y., in the spring of 1845.]

Other Millerite Periodicals. In addition to the two clearly defined weekly organs of Millerism —*Signs of the Times* and *The Midnight Cry*—and certain other Millerite papers listed in this bibliography, there were numerous publications more or less definitely tied in with the movement. Most of these enjoyed a very brief existence. In some instances a Millerite leader published a paper in connection with his series of lectures in a certain city, often for a period of thirteen weeks. In other instances a Millerite who was not a leader, but who had fervor and some money or initiative, would publish a paper for a time. With few exceptions, these papers have not been preserved. Nor have we reason to believe that if they were available they would throw much additional light on the movement. Often they confined themselves to theology, reprinting material from the *Signs of the Times* or *The Midnight Cry*. For a brief time after the great disappointment there were probably more of these short-lived papers than before. Bliss, in his *Memoirs*, states that in one week, shortly after the disappointment, Miller "received sixteen different sheets, all purporting to be advent publications, but the most of them advocating contradictory sentiments."—*Page 299*. This reflected the confusion of thought that immediately followed the disappointment.

Other Periodical Literature

(Listed by name of periodical if author and title are not available.)

Boston Investigator, Feb. 1, March 15, 1843; Feb. 12, 1845.
Brother Jonathan, Feb. 18, 1843.
Campbell, Alexander. "The Coming of the Lord—No. XXV," *Millennial Harbinger*, July, 1843, pp. 289, 296.
Churchill, Winston S. "Shall We All Commit Suicide?" *Hearst's International*, August, 1924, pp. 10, 122.
Himes, Joshua V. Letter to the editors, in "Ascension Robes Again," *Outlook*, Nov. 24, 1894, p. 875.
[Holley, Marietta.] "The Last Day," *Ladies' Home Journal and Practical Housekeeper*, March, 1887, pp. 1, 2; April, 1887, p. 4.
Independent, Feb. 3, 17, March 17, 24, 1870.
Josiah Allen's Wife. See Holley, Marietta.
Liberator, May 20, 1842.
Life, Feb. 19, 1940, p. 33.
Litch, Josiah. *Judaism Overthrown*. Reviewed in *Spirit of the XIX Century*, March, 1843, pp. 189, 190.
Littel's Living Age, Jan. 19, 1850.
Miller Family Magazine, July, 1916, pp. 33-35.
"Millerism—The Finale Here," *Cincinnati Miscellany*, November, 1844, pp. 41-43.
New York Evangelist, Jan. 11, Oct. 31, 1844.
New York Observer, April 1, 1843; Jan. 13, 1844.
Niles National Register, April 1, May 6, 1843.
Parker, Jane Marsh. "Did the Millerites Have Ascension Robes?" *Outlook*, Oct. 13, 1894, pp. 582, 583.
―――. "A Little Millerite," *Century Magazine*, December, 1886, pp. 310-317.
―――. "A Spiritual Cyclone: The Millerite Delusion," *Magazine of Christian Literature*, September, 1891, pp. 321-325.
Presbyterian, Nov. 16, 1844.
Toomey, Regis Canevin. "Gabriel, Blow That Horn!" *American Mercury*, November, 1942, pp. 600-605. Same abridged in *Reader's Digest*, January, 1943, pp. 96-98.
Wilkins, Mary E., "A New England Prophet," *Harper's Magazine*, September, 1894, pp. 601, 612.
Zion's Banner, May 6, 1840.

PAMPHLETS

[Only an arbitrary line divides between pamphlets and books. For the purposes of this bibliography we have listed as pamphlets some publications that contain as many as 100 or 200 pages, because these publications were patently tracts for the times. At least one edition of all these publications was paper bound. See note under Second Advent Library entry. To the student of Millerite history, the principal value of the following list of pamphlets—most of which are theological—is the evidence they provide of the range and vigor both of Millerite promotion and of opponents' attack.]

Address of the Building Committee, on Opening the Second Advent Tabernacle, May 4, 1843. Boston: J. V. Himes, 1843. 18 pp. [A statement of the purposes of the Millerite movement, a defense against charges, and a series of "Dangers Which Believers in the Doctrine of the Second Advent Should Avoid."]

An Appeal to the Common Sense of the People, or The Miller Delusion! ! ! ! By a citizen of Boston. Boston: I. R. Butts, 1843. 24 pp. [Anonymous. Ridicules Miller as a farmer who should not presume to teach. Charges that Millerism causes insanity and other dire disasters. Says Millerism is "like the pestiferous breath of the Simoon." —*Page 24.*]

Atkins, Robert. *A True Picture: or, A Thrilling Description of the State of the Churches Throughout Christendom. Extracted From a Discourse Recently Preached in London.* Boston: J. V. Himes, Dec. 1, 1843. 16 pp. (Second Advent Library, No. XXXIX.)

Ballou, Adin. *The True Scriptural Doctrine of the Second Advent; an Effectual Antidote to Millerism, and All Other Kindred Errors.* Milford, Mass.: Community Press, 1843. 32 pp. [Preface says, "The present is a time of great excitement and inquiry respecting the second coming of Christ. Thousands earnestly desire to understand what the Scriptures really teach on the subject." The author sets forth the singular idea that the coming of Christ and the resurrection are spiritual and began "at the end of the Mosaic age."—*Page 3.* Detailed examination of the arguments Miller set forth for the 1843 date.]

Barton, A. S. *Millerism Refuted by History, in a Series of Letters to a Friend.* Windsor, Vt.: Joseph Fairbanks, 1842. 24 pp. [In his preface the author says, "Millerism is the stalking error of the day. . . . Were Satan permitted to delude the people with an error in the garb of religion, it is believed he would adopt *Millerism.*"]

Bates, Joseph. *Second Advent Way Marks and High Heaps, or a Connected View of the Fulfillment of Prophecy by God's Peculiar People, From the Year 1840 to 1847.* New-Bedford, Mass.: Press of Benjamin Lindsey, 1847. 80 pp. [This pamphlet is largely devoted to a discussion of theological aspects of Millerism, but interwoven are historical statements regarding the movement. Of particular significance are the statements relative to events after 1844. Bates was one of the first Seventh-day Adventist leaders, and his remarks on events after 1844 throw light on the newly developing religious movement.]

Bliss [Sylvester]. *The Chronology of the Bible, Showing From the Scriptures and Undisputed Authorities That We are Near the End of Six Thousand Years From Creation.* Boston: J. V. Himes, Sept. 15, 1843. 35 pp. (Second Advent Library, No. XXXVIII.)

————. *An Exposition of the Twenty-fourth of Matthew: In Which It is Shown to Be an Historical Prophecy, Extending to the End of Time, and Literally Fulfilled.* Boston: J. V. Himes, Feb. 8, 1843. 69 pp. (Second Advent Library, No. XXVI.)

————. *Exposition of Zechariah XIV.* Boston: J. V. Himes, 1843. 12 pp. [This is probably a number in the Second Advent Library series, though it is not thus identified in the volume of pamphlets in which it is found. The pamphlet seeks to show the prophetic significance of Zechariah XIV in relation to the doctrine of the advent.]

————. *Inconsistencies of Colver's Literal Fulfilment of Daniel's Prophecy.* Boston: J. V. Himes, Feb. 1, 1843. 53 pp. (Second Advent Library, No. XXV.) [Colver published a 24-page tract giving his sermon which sought to show that literal days are signified by Daniel. Bliss seeks to refute this.]

————. *Review of Morris' "Modern Chiliasm: or the Doctrine of the Personal and Immortal Reign of Jesus Christ on the Earth, Commencing About A.D. 1843, as Advocated by William Miller, Refuted."* Boston: J. V. Himes, Oct. 15, 1842. 179 pp. (Second Advent Library, No. XVIII.) [Preface states in part, "The pamphlet under review, contains nearly all of the most prominent objections which are advanced against the doctrine of Christ's Second Advent in 1843; and also against the millenary doctrine of the primitive church." Bliss seeks to refute Morris' refutation. A polemical work.]

————. *Review of Rev. O. E. Daggett's Sermon of "Time of the End Uncertain."* In the *National Preacher of Dec., 1842.* Boston: J. V. Himes, Jan. 14, 1843. 56 pp. (Second Advent Library, No. XXVI.) [A polemic in support of the belief that the time may be known.]

Brown, F. G. *Views and Experience in Relation to Entire Consecration and the Second Advent: Addressed to the Ministers of the Portsmouth, N. H., Baptist Association.*

Boston: Joshua V. Himes, April 25, 1843. 72 pp. (Second Advent Library, No. XXXII.) [Brown is listed on the title page as "Late Pastor of the Middle Street Baptist Church, Portsmouth, N. H." He had resigned his pastorate of the Middle Street Baptist church because of his Millerite views. He describes the deeper spiritual experience he obtained at a revival service, but makes no suggestion of fanatical views regarding sanctification. He tells of listening to Fitch preach on the advent. Brown reasons that the preaching of the advent produces conversions and holy living. The material from p. 49 onward constitutes an appendix, which gives the testimony of others on this theme.]

————. *A Warning to Watchfulness.* Boston: J. V. Himes, Dec. 15, 1843. 32 pp. (Second Advent Library, No. XL.) [Brown accepted Millerism early in 1843. This pamphlet is an exhortation to constant readiness for the advent.]

Bush, Rev. George, and Miller, William. *Reasons for Rejecting Mr. Miller's Views on the Advent, by Rev. George Bush; with Mr. Miller's Reply.* Boston: Joshua V. Himes, April 15, 1844. 36 pp. (Second Advent Library, No. XLIV.) [An exchange of letters between them. There is appended a reprint of an article by Bush, who is described on the title page as "Professor of Hebrew and Oriental Literature in the New York City University," in which he strongly affirms the correctness of the year-day principle in prophetic interpretation and criticizes Prof. M. Stuart for challenging it in his "Hints on the Interpretation of Prophecy."]

Citizen of Baltimore, A. See *Return of the Jews to Their Ancient City.*

Citizen of Boston, A. See *An Appeal to the Common Sense of the People.*

Colver, Nathaniel. *The Prophecy of Daniel Literally Fulfilled.* Boston: Wm. S. Damrell, 1843. 61 pp. [Colver is listed on title page as "Pastor of First Baptist Free Church, Boston." This work is an attack upon Miller's exposition of prophecy.]

Cook, J. B. *A Solemn Appeal to Ministers and Churches, Especially to Those of the Baptist Denomination, Relative to the Speedy Coming of Christ.* Boston: Joshua V. Himes, May 25, 1843. 62 pp. (Second Advent Library, No. XXXV.) [Tells of his own experience in accepting doctrine of personal second advent, and then discusses a series of propositions relating to the nature of the events in connection with the advent.]

Cox, G. F. *Letters on the Second Coming of Christ, and the Character of His Millennial Kingdom: Together With a Reply to the Objections and Arguments of Rev. D. D. Whedon.* Boston: J. V. Himes, April 23, 1842. 132 pp. (Second Advent Library, No. XVII.) [This material was first published in a newspaper as a series of letters to the editor. The main aspects of the advent doctrine are discussed and defended against contrary views.]

Defence of Elder Joshua V. Himes: Being a History of the Fanaticism, Puerilities and Secret Workings of Those Who, Under the Garb of Friendship, Have Proved the Most Deadly Enemies of the Advent Cause. (Published by Order of the Chardon-Street Church.) Boston: No. 8 Chardon-Street, 1851. 268 pp. [See Appendix C for comments on this pamphlet.]

Dimmick, L. F. *The End of the World Not Yet. A Discourse Delivered in the North Church, Newburyport.* Newburyport, Mass.: Charles Whipple, 1842. 48 pp. [Dimmick was pastor of North Church. He sought to show by a series of propositions that the end was not yet due.]

English author, An. See *"Surely I Come Quickly." A Letter to Everybody.*

Female, A. See *Voice in New Hampshire, A; or, Reflections on Rev. J. Ward's "Brief Remarks on Miller's Lectures."*

Fitch, Charles. *"Come Out of Her, My People."* Rochester, N. Y.: J. V. Himes, 1843. 24 pp. [Reprint of sermon on the second advent of Christ, calling on the faithful to come out of their various churches.]

————. *The Glory of God in the Earth.* Boston: Joshua V. Himes, April 9, 1842. 36 pp. (Second Advent Library, No. XV.) [A sermon against the doctrine of a temporal millennium and an argument for the premillennial coming of Christ.]

————. *Letter to Rev. J. Litch, on the Second Coming of Christ, With the Sentiments of Cotton Mather on the Same Subject, Approved by Thomas Prince, Both Eminent Ministers of Boston in the Last Century.* Boston: Joshua V. Himes, 1841. 72 pp. (Second Advent Library, No. VII.) [Fitch gives a statement of his belief in Miller's teachings. Opens thus: "You will, doubtless, remember that when you called at my house some months ago, you requested me to examine the Bible doctrine respecting the second coming of Christ, and write you the result of my investigations." The preface is dated Nov., 1841. Up to this time, Fitch states, he had never seen Miller, "but his writings have greatly enlightened my mind."—*Page 63.* "It is now somewhat more than three years and a half, since the lectures of William Miller, on this subject, were put into my hands."— *Page 6.* A recital of his experience in accepting Miller's views.]

————. *Letter to the Newark Presbytery.* Newark, N. J.: Aaron Guest, 1840. 20 pp. [Sets forth Fitch's defense of his belief in entire sanctification against the charge that he was teaching "a doctrine importantly and dangerously erroneous."—*Page 20.* He adds immediately, "If you still adhere to that opinion, I must consider myself as no longer of your number, and you must do to me, and with me, as you think our Lord and Master requires." This letter gives an insight into the fervent spirit of the man. He is listed on the title page as "Pastor of the Free Presbyterian Church, Newark, N. J." Evidently he had temporarily moved from the ministry of the Congregational denomination.]

————. *Reasons for Withdrawing From the Newark Presbytery.* Newark, N. J.: Aaron Guest, 1840. 14 pp. [A companion pamphlet to Fitch's *Letter to the Newark Presbytery.* His *Reasons* is also in the form of a letter, dated April 16, 1840. He presents a series of reasons why he believes sanctification is a spiritual goal to which the Christian may rightly aspire in this present life.]

————. *Slaveholding Weighed in the Balance of Truth, and Its Comparative Guilt.* Illustrated. 2d ed. Boston: Isaac Knapp, 1837. 36 pp. [Fitch is listed on the title page as "Pastor of First Free Congregational Church, Boston." Significant as revealing the abolitionist activity of a Millerite leader. The argument is cogent and the language forceful.]

————. *Views of Sanctification.* Newark, N. J.: Aaron Guest, 1839. 24 pp. [The occasion for writing this, the preface states, was a series of nine questions, there set down, from a member of a committee chosen by the Newark Presbytery to examine Fitch's views on sanctification. The pamphlet is in the form of a letter, dated November 25, 1839. It is a general statement of Fitch's belief that holiness is obtainable in this life. The pamphlet is written in a very calm and restrained style.]

————. *A Wonderful and Horrible Thing.* Boston: J. V. Himes, April 16, 1842. 24 pp. (Second Advent Library, No. XVI.) [A discussion of the low spiritual state of the church. Title borrowed from opening text of this pamphlet. Jer. 5:29-31. Chides ministers for prophesying peace when God is about to bring judgments on the world.]

Fleming, L. D. *First Principles of the Second Advent Faith, With Scripture Proofs.* 2d ed. Boston: Joshua V. Himes, March 15, 1844. 36 pp. (Second Advent Library, No. XLIII.) [A series of thirteen propositions setting forth the Millerite belief, followed by quotations from Scripture intended to prove each proposition. The two concluding pages present "Points of Differenc Between Adventists and Their Opponents."]

————. *The Midnight Cry. A Synopsis of the Evidences of the Second Coming of Christ About A.D. 1843.* Boston: J. V. Himes, March 19, 1842. 76 pp. (Second Advent Library, No. XII.)

Fosdick, Raymond B. *The Rockefeller Foundation. A Review for 1943.* New York: The Rockefeller Foundation, 1943. 63 pp.

Galusha, Elon. *Address of Elder Elon Galusha With Reasons for Believing Christ's Second Coming at Hand.* Rochester, N. Y.: Erastus Shepard, 1844. 24 pp. [A general summary of prophetic evidences for believing the advent near.]

Gaussen, [L.]. *The German Rebuke of American Neology; a Discourse by Prof. Gaussen, of Geneva, to the Theological Students at the Opening of the Course in October Last, Entitled, Popery, An Argument for the Truth, by Its Fulfillment of Scripture Prophecies.* Boston: J. V. Himes, Sept. 2, 1844. 36 pp. (Second Advent Library, No. XLVI.) [Gaussen was a learned divine of Geneva. His address was translated and published in America by the *New York Observer,* a prominent Protestant weekly. Himes reprinted this material in a pamphlet. "Neology" was a term used to describe rationalism, which was then beginning to make inroads in American theological thinking. The Millerites viewed Gaussen's clear-cut and cogent argument that popery is the Babylon of Bible prophecy, as providing great support for their basic interpretation of the prophecies and as shutting the mouths of their contemporaries who were offering a new and rationalistic interpretation.]

Gunn, Lewis C. *The Age to Come! The Present Organization of Matter, Called Earth, to Be Destroyed by Fire at the End of This Age or Dispensation. Also, Before the Event, Christians May Know About the Time When It Shall Occur.* Revised. Boston: J. V. Himes, Feb. 15, 1844. 72 pp. (Second Advent Library, No. XLI.) [Revised and enlarged edition of his *This World to Have No Other Age.* Gunn takes the position that not only the world (the age) but also the material earth will end with the consuming fires of the second advent. He also discusses the time of the end.]

————. *This World to Have No Other Age or Dispensation.* (Trumpet of Alarm—Extra.) Philadelphia: Merrihew and Thompson, 1843. 40 pp. [Later revised and enlarged as his *The Age to Come.*]

Hale, A[pollos]. *Herald of the Bridegroom! In Which the Plagues That Await the Enemies of the King Eternal Are Considered; and the Appearing of Our Lord to Gather His Saints Is Shown to Be the Next Event Before Us, by a Scriptural Exhibition of the Order of Events From the Fall of the Papacy Down to the Establishment of the Everlasting Kingdom.* Boston: J. V. Himes, Dec. 1, 1843. 36 pp. (Second Advent Library, No. XXXIX.)

————. *Review of Dr. Pond's Letter Against the Doctrine of the Second Advent in 1843.* Boston: Joshua V. Himes, 1842. 89 pp. [Consists almost wholly of theological polemic.]

————. *The Second Advent Manual.* Boston: Joshua V. Himes, June 1, 1843. 108 pp. (Second Advent Library, No. XXXVI.) [The scope of this pamphlet is revealed in the subtitle: "The objections to calculating the prophetic times are considered; the difficulties connected with the calculation explained; and the facts and arguments on which Mr. Miller's calculations rest, are briefly stated and sustained."]

Haven, Kittredge. *The World Reprieved: Being a Critical Examination of William Miller's Theory.* Woodstock, Vt.: Haskell & Palmer, 1839. 48 pp. [In an introductory description and biographical sketch of Miller, Haven says, "We regret to say that many clergymen, who reject his peculiar views, countenance him for the purpose of preparing the way for *protracted* meetings." Charges Miller with making money out of his preaching.]

Hawley, S[ilas]. *A Declaration of Sentiments, Reported by S. Hawley to the "Christian Union Convention" Held in Syracuse, August 21, 1839.* Cazenovia: *Union Herald Office,* 1839. 16 pp. [An endeavor to show that the existence of various sects is contrary to God's order, that creeds are man made, and that there should be church union.]

————. *The Second Advent Doctrine Vindicated, a Serman Preached at the Dedication of the Tabernacle, by Rev. S. Hawley, With the Address of the Tabernacle Committee.* Boston: J. V. Himes, May 15, 1843. 107 pp. (Second Advent Library, No. XXXIV.) [The first 93 pages are devoted to his sermon which presents evidence that the main prophetic views of the Millerites harmonized with historic views. Last part of pamphlet contains committee's report.]

Hervey, N. *New Heavens and New Earth. Marriage Supper of the Lamb.* Boston: J. V. Himes, March 8, 1843. 68 pp. (Second Advent Library, No. XXX.)

————. *Prophecies of Christ's First and Second Advent. Daniel's Visions Harmonized and Explained.* Boston: J. V. Himes, March 1, 1842. 108 pp. (Second Advent Library, No. XXIX.)

————. *Witness of the Spirit in the Work of Sanctification, With a Letter From F. G. Brown.* 2d ed., enlarged. Boston: 1844. 96 pp. [A very rational presentation of the subject. Argues against necessity of miraculous happenings today in connection with outpouring of God's Spirit.]

Himes, Joshua V. *Views of the Prophecies and Prophetic Chronology, Selected From Manuscripts of William Miller With a Memoir of His Life.* Boston: Joshua V. Himes, Jan. 1, 1842. 252 pp. (Second Advent Library, No. I.) [Pages 7 to 14 are devoted to a sketch of Miller's life. Pages 15 to 19 discuss "Mr. Miller's Influence Upon the People." Pages 54 to 66 consist of "An Address to the Believers in the Second Advent Near, Scattered Abroad." These sections provide certain historical data on Miller's public life up to about 1840. The remainder of this work consists almost wholly of Miller's discussion of various prophetic and other theological questions.]

Hooper, Rev. John. *The Present Crisis: or, A Correspondence Between the Signs of the Times in Which We Live, and the Prophetic Declarations of Holy Scripture.* Boston: J. V. Himes, Feb. 19, 1842. 54 pp. With preface and notes by Joshua V. Himes. (Second Advent Library, No. VIII.)

Hopkins, John Henry. *Two Discourses on the Second Advent of the Redeemer, With Special Reference to the Year 1843.* Burlington, Vt.; G. Goodrich, 1843. 32 pp. [The author is listed as bishop of the diocese of Vermont. The preface explains that this is prepared to meet a "singularly popular delusion."]

Jacobs, E. *The Doctrine of a Thousand Years Millennium and the Return of the Jews to Palestine, Before the Second Advent of Our Saviour, Without Foundation in the Bible.* Cincinnati: Kendall and Barnard, February, 1844. 76 pp. [A presentation of the Scripture evidence against the doctrine of a temporal millennium.]

Jones, Henry. *Compend of Parallel and Explanatory Scripture References on Christ's Second Advent at Hand, With Synopsis and Principles of Interpretation.* New York: Piercy and Reed, June 1, 1843. 24 pp. (The Bible Reader, No. I.) [A series of parallel Old and New Testament references on the second advent, plus a summary of the doctrine and twenty-four principles of interpretation.]

————. *Modern Phenomena of the Heavens, or Prophetic "Great Signs" of the Special Near Approach of "The End of All Things."* New York: Piercy and Reed, July 1, 1843. 48 pp. (The Bible Reader, No. II.) [Discusses aurora borealis, dark day of May 19, 1780, falling stars of Nov. 13, 1833, the great comet of 1843, and other heavenly phenomena, as fulfilling Christ's forecast of "fearful sights and great signs" as warnings of His second advent. In this pamphlet, which was not published by J. V. Himes, Jones takes a dogmatic position not generally accepted by the Millerites, as references to the principal Millerite papers reveal. Miller did not even dogmatize regarding those most spectacular phenomena, the dark day and the falling stars, as signs of the advent.]

————. *"The Seven Churches in Asia," Figurative; and the Millennial Thousand Years, So Called, Coming Next After Rather Than Before the End of the World: Vindicated in Four Lectures.* Montpelier, Vt.: Knapp & Jewett, 1834. 69 pp.

Litch, Josiah. *An Address to the Public, and Especially the Clergy, on the Near Approach of the Glorious, Everlasting Kingdom of God on Earth, as Indicated by the Word of God, the History of the World, and Signs of the Present Times.* Boston: J. V. Himes, Jan. 29, 1842. 132 pp. (Second Advent Library, No. V.) [A prefatory chapter entitled "Address to the Clergy" is in the form of a letter, and appeals to them to give serious consideration to the prophetic view that the end is near. He expresses his belief that the advent "will be between the fall of the Ottoman Empire, which will probably take place this year [1840], and the termination of 1843."—*Page 13.* At the close of the letter is this line: "Millennial Grove, May 10, 1840."—*Page 17.* The remainder of the work sets forth an exposition of prophecy which Litch believes supports his view of the nearness of the advent. The preface is dated "Boston, July, 1841," and declares, "More than one year has now passed since this work was first given to the public."—*Page vi.*]

————. *Dialogue on the Nature of Man, His State in Death, and the Final Doom of the Wicked.* Philadelphia: J. Litch [no date]. 54 pp. [This pamphlet cannot be earlier than January, 1844, because it advertises *The Advent Herald.* Seeks to prove that man is an immortal spirit.]

————. *Judaism Overthrown: or, the Kingdom Restored to the True Israel, With the Scripture Evidence of the Epoch of the Kingdom in 1843.* Boston: J. V. Himes, February 22, 1843. (Second Advent Library, No. XXVIII.) 38 pp. [An argument against the doctrine of the literal return of the Jews.]

————. *Prophetic Expositions: or a Connected View of the Testimony of the Prophets Concerning the Kingdom of God and the Time of Its Establishment.* Boston: Joshua V. Himes, 1842. Vol. I, Nov. 21, 1842 (Second Advent Library, No. XIX), is 207 pp. Vol. II, Dec. 26, 1842 (Second Advent Library, No. XX), is 247 pp. [Exclusively theological discussion of Millerite teachings.]

————. *Refutation of "Dowling's Reply to Miller," on the Second Coming of Christ in 1843.* Boston: J. V. Himes, March 12, 1842. 90 pp. (Second Advent Library, No. XI.) [Dowling was one of Miller's most vigorous opponents, whose work was widely circulated and much quoted. At the time this refutation was written, Dowling's work had "been before the public something over a year."—*Page 7.* Dowling's various arguments are quoted at length throughout the refutation. A polemical work of prime value in clarifying the theological views of the Millerites.]

Millennial Harp, or Second Advent Melodies; Designed for Meetings on the Second Coming of Christ. Edited by Joshua V. Himes. Part Second. Boston: J. V. Himes, July 15, 1843.

71 pp. (Second Advent Library, No. XXXVII.) [A collection of second advent hymns with music.]

Miller, William. *Apology and Defence.* Boston: Joshua V. Himes, August, 1845. 36 pp. [Miller recounts his experience in coming to his conclusions on prophecy and in preaching them. A formal statement.]

——————. *Dissertation on the True Inheritance of the Saints and the Twelve Hundred and Sixty Days of Daniel and John.* Boston: Joshua V. Himes [Preface says Jan. 1], 1842. 72 pp. (Second Advent Library, No. VI.)

——————. *Evidences From Scripture & History of the Second Coming of Christ About the Year* A. D. *1843, and of His Personal Reign of 1,000 Years.* Brandon, Vt.: *Vermont Telegraph* Office, 1833. 64 pp. [This is the first printed work by Miller, except for a series of articles by him that had appeared in 1832 in the *Vermont Telegraph.* Reference to the manuscript of this pamphlet reveals a parenthetical note interpolated in the text, instructing the printer to insert at that point certain matter that had appeared as articles in the *Telegraph.* This matter occupies pages 43 to 61 in the pamphlet. The other material in the pamphlet bears a certain resemblance in places to the first articles Miller wrote for the *Telegraph* in 1832, but is patently not a reprint. The pamphlet could not have been published before March 12, 1833, because there is included in it an article that appeared in the *Telegraph* on that date, that is, an article from Vol. V, No. 25 of the *Telegraph.* The introduction opens thus: "The writer does not claim the title of a theologian, nor of infallibility, and only presents himself in common with other writers on the same, or other subjects of like import, to be tried by the infallible touchstone of divine truth."—*Page 3.* See *Signs of the Times,* April 1, 1841, where same introduction is given to a series by Miller. This pamphlet is very rare. We have found a copy only in the library of the Vermont Historical Society.]

——————. *A Familiar Exposition of the Twenty-fourth Chapter of Matthew, and the Fifth and Sixth Chapters of Hosea, to Which Are Added an Address to the General Conference on the Advent, and a Scene of the Last Day.* Boston: Joshua V. Himes, Jan. 15, 1842. 125 pp. (Second Advent Library, No. III.) [There is an addendum consisting of an Extract From Dr. Cotton Mather's "Famous Latin Preface" on the second coming of Christ.]

——————. *The Kingdom of God.* Boston: J. V. Himes, Oct. 25, 1842. 24 pp. (Second Advent Library, No. XXI.)

——————. *A Lecture on the Typical Sabbaths and Great Jubilee.* Boston: J. V. Himes, April 2, 1842. 34 pp. (Second Advent Library, No. XIV.)

——————. *Letter to Joshua V. Himes on the Cleansing of the Sanctuary.* Boston: Joshua V. Himes, Feb. 26, 1842. 16 pp. (Second Advent Library, No. IX.) [Here is found Miller's most precise statement on the subject.]

——————. *Remarks on Revelation Thirteenth, Seventeenth and Eighteenth.* Boston: Joshua V. Himes, Sept. 10, 1844. 74 pp. (Second Advent Library, No. XLVII.) [A brief discussion of the meaning of the symbols in these apocalyptic chapters of the Revelation.]

——————. *Reply to Stuart's "Hints on the Interpretation of Prophecy," in Three Letters, Addressed to Joshua V. Himes.* Boston: J. V. Himes, Dec. 1, 1842. 75 pp. (Second Advent Library, No. XXII.) [In a publisher's note, Himes states that the letters, which constitute most of this pamphlet, were originally prepared for publication in the *Signs of the Times.* The three letters discuss Stuart's views on prophecy with which Miller disagrees only in part. Pages 63 to 75 consist of an appendix which presents Miller's comments on Stuart's second edition of his work, etc.]

——————. *Review of a Discourse Delivered in the North Church. Newburyport, on the Last Evening of the Year 1841, by L. F. Dimmick, Pastor of the Church.* Boston: J. V. Himes, March 26, 1842. 36 pp. (Second Advent Library, No. XIII.)

——————. *Synopsis of Miller's Views.* Boston: Joshua V. Himes, 1843. 32 pp. [Sets forth 16 main points of belief concerning the advent. At the close is the name "William Miller" and "Low Hampton, Jan. 1, 1843."]

Mitchell, W. H. *History of the Second Advent Church in Portland, Maine.* Kennebunk Port, Maine: The Author, 1886. 24 pp. [An address delivered in Union Hall, July 4, 1886.]

Proceedings of the Mutual Conference of Adventists, Held in the City of Albany, the 29th and 30th of April, and 1st of May, 1845. New York: J. V. Himes [no date]. 32 pp.

BIBLIOGRAPHY

[Lists those in attendance, proceedings by sessions, resolutions, "Declaration of Principles," and finally, names those "approving of the doings of the Albany Conference." On pages 30 to 32 are found the resolutions passed at the New York Conference that began May 6.]

Return of the Jews, to Their Ancient City Jerusalem, and the Second Advent of Our Lord, to This World in Glory, Proved to Be Scriptural Doctrines, The. By a Citizen of Baltimore, 2d ed. Trenton: D. & F. Fenton, 1817. 72 pp. [Significant as indicating the range of interest in the subject of the second advent in the early part of the nineteenth century.]

Richardson, Edward Adams. *The Community, Groton, Mass., The Story of a Neighborhood.* Ayer, Mass.: H. S. Turner, 1911. 15 pp. [Gives a brief and rambling account of Groton and makes various references to the Millerites.]

Sabine, James. *The Appearing and Kingdom of Our Lord Jesus Christ: In Four Letters to an Unbeliever.* Boston: Joshua V. Himes, Sept. 15, 1842. 72 pp. (Second Advent Library, No. XVIII.) [The author is "rector of Christ church, Bethel, Vermont." A general presentation of the doctrine of the personal coming of Christ. In the preface he says: "The great doctrine of the second advent (the subject of the following letters) has been upon the mind of the writer for about nine years. His attention was called up to consider this very interesting question through the means of sermons received from the Old World, particularly some able discourses from the pen and pulpit of English preachers, clergymen of the Church of England. . . . At the time of the writer's embracing these views, he was not aware that any in this New World had paid the least attention to the subject."]

Second Advent Hymns: Designed to Be Used in Prayer and Camp Meetings. Published by J. V. Himes, 1842. 32 pp. [Page size about 2 by 4 inches. Words without music.]

Second Advent Hymns: Designed to Be Used in Prayer and Camp Meetings. 3d ed., with an addition of 23 new hymns. Concord, N. H.: John F. Brown, 1843. 64 pp. [Small book of hymns, 2½ by 4 inches. Words without music.]

Second Advent Library. This is the general title of a series of pamphlets published by Joshua V. Himes in Boston. In this library are found productions from the pens of most of the leading Millerites. In a few instances the writings of others who had written on the subject of the advent, were printed. Each pamphlet carries a specific number and date; for example, "Miller's Reply to Stuart's 'Hints on the Interpretation of Prophecy,'" is No. XXII, December 1, 1842. However, if two pamphlets have the same date of publication they sometimes have the same number. These pamphlets contained anywhere from a few pages, up to more than 200 pages. They were paper bound. Some numbers were also brought out in clothbound editions. Page size about 6½ by 4½ inches. Unfortunately, the date and Second Advent Library number are often found only on the outer cover. Hence when these pamphlets have been bound into volumes, with the covers removed, it is not always possible to say whether the pamphlet is a part of the Second Advent Library series. No complete file of this library is known to exist. For the purposes of this bibliography all pamphlets in this library, irrespective of number of pages, are listed under the section, Pamphlets. They may rightly be described as tracts for the times.

Second Advent Tracts. [An undated series consisting of at least twelve. Nos. 1 to 12 have been examined in the New York Public Library. This series of tracts is advertised in the 1842 edition of *The First Report of the General Conference of Christians Expecting the Advent of the Lord Jesus Christ. Held in Boston, Oct. 14, 15, 1840.* Reference to this report will show that the first seven of the twelve are reprints of the proceedings and the papers read at this first conference. The subjects of the twelve are as follows:

No. 1. *Proceedings of the Conference on the Second Coming of Our Lord Jesus Christ, Held in Boston, Mass., Oct. 14, 15, 1840.* 18 pp.

No. 2. *A Dissertation on the Second Advent.* By Josiah Litch. 16 pp.

No. 3. *A Dissertation on the Chronology of Prophecy.* By Josiah Litch. 18 pp.

No. 4. *Dissertation on the Restitution of Israel.* By Henry Jones. 24 pp.

No. 5. *A Dissertation on Prophetic Chronology.* By William Miller. 12 pp.

No. 6. *A Dissertation on the Judgment.* By William Miller. 12 pp.

No. 7. *History and Doctrine of the Millennium.* By Henry Dana Ward. (Discourse at second advent conference. Boston, Oct. 14, 1840.) 74 pp.

No. 8. *Proceedings of the Second Session of the General Conference of Christians Expecting the Advent of Our Lord Jesus Christ.* (Lowell, Mass., June 15-17, 1841.) 12 pp.

No. 9. *Dissertation on the Nature and Manner of Christ's Second Coming.* By Henry Jones. (Delivered at Second General Conference.) 38 pp.

No. 10. *Dissertation on the Glorified Kingdom of God on Earth at Hand.* By Josiah Litch. (Delivered at Second General Conference.) 16 pp.

No. 11. *Dissertation on the Fall of the Ottoman Empire, the 11th of August, 1840.* By Josiah Litch. (Delivered at Second General Conference.) 15 pp.

No. 12. *The Doctrine of the Millennium. The Order of the Resurrection and Order of the Judgment.* By Josiah Litch. (Delivered at Second General Conference.) 14 pp.

Spalding, Joshua. *Sentiments Concerning the Coming and Kingdom of Christ. . . . In Nine Lectures.* Boston: Joshua V. Himes [Pref., Oct. 1], 1841. 258 pp. (Second Advent Library, No. IV.) [Spalding is listed on the title page as "minister of the gospel at the Tabernacle in Salem." Editors' preface says of this work: "It was first published in Salem, Mass., in 1796. But with its author it passed away, and has long been, except by a few, forgotten. We look upon this publication as the day-star of returning light to the American churches on the subject of the near coming and kingdom of our Lord Jesus Christ."]

Sprague, John Francis. *Piscataquis, Biography and Fragment.* Bangor, Maine: C. H. Glass & Co., 1899. 102 pp. [Historical items of Piscataquis County, including references to Millerites.]

Starkweather, John. *A Narrative of Conversion to the Faith of the Premillennial Advent of Christ in 1843. With Suggestions and References Designed to Aid Serious Inquirers After Truth.* Boston: J. V. Himes, March 15, 1843. 48 pp. (Second Advent Library, No. XXXI.)

————. *The Reasonings of True Faith Respecting the 2300 Days in Daniel 8:14.* Boston: A. J. Wright, February, 1844. 18 pp. (The True Believer, No. 2.)

————. *A Scriptural Test of Saving Grace Exhibited in an Exposition of Daniel 12:10.* Boston: A. J. Wright, January, 1844. 35 pp. (The True Believer, No. 1.)

Storrs, George. *The Bible Examiner: Containing Various Prophetic Expositions.* Boston: J. V. Himes, May 1, 1843. 133 pp. (Second Advent Library, No. XXXIII.) [Most of this material first appeared in *The Midnight Cry.* A discussion of major prophecies, such as Daniel 2, 7, and 8. Also a refutation of the idea that the Jews will return to Palestine. This *Bible Examiner* is probably the forerunner of the journal by that name, which Storrs published.]

"*Surely I Come Quickly.*" *A Letter to Everybody.* By an English Author. From the fifth London edition, 1835, revised and abridged by J. V. Himes. Boston: J. V. Himes, March 5, 1842. 18 pp. (Second Advent Library, No. X.) [An exhortation to readiness for the advent because it will come unexpectedly as did destruction on Sodom.]

Thomas, Abel C. *Analysis and Confutation of Miller's Theory of the End of the World in 1843.* Montpelier, Vt.: Eli Ballou, 1843. 32 pp. [In his preface he says, "My principal reason for reviewing Mr. Miller's Theory is that it is productive of evil."]

Trial of Elder J. V. Himes Before the Chardon Street Church Together With a Vindication of the Course Taken by Prof. J. P. Weethee and Elder George Needham Relative to the Late Difficulties. (Published by Order of the Church.) Boston: Damrell & Moore, 1850. 135 pp. [See Appendix C for comments on this pamphlet.]

Voice in New Hampshire, A, or, Reflections on Rev. J. Ward's "Brief Remarks on Miller's Lectures." By a Female. Exeter: A. R. Brown, Nov. 24, 1842. 44 pp. (Social Library, No. 1.) The publisher states that "the authoress is a pious and intelligent lady of ——— with whom I am acquainted and who is highly esteemed in the church."—Page iii. [A reply to theological arguments against Miller's principal prophetic views.]

Ward, Henry Dana. *Israel and the Holy Land: "The Promised Land." In Which an Attempt Is Made to Show That the Old and New Testaments Accord in Their Testimony to Christ and His Celestial Kingdom, and in Their Testimony to His People, Israel, and Also to the Promised Holy Land.* Boston: J. V. Himes, Jan. 2, 1843. 57 pp. (Second Advent Library, No. XXIV.) Theological arguments against the doctrine of the return to Palestine of the literal Jews, and evidence in behalf of the view that the true Israel includes all who are Christ's.]

Weethee, J. P., and Needham, George. See *Trial of Elder J. V. Himes Before the Chardon Street Church Together With a Vindication of the Course Taken by Prof. J. P. Weethee and Elder George Needham Relative to the Late Difficulties.*

White, Ellen G. *A Sketch of the Christian Experience and Views of Ellen G. White.* Saratoga Springs, N. Y.: James White, 1851. 64 pp. [This pamphlet is largely devoted to the theological aspects of Millerism and the days immediately following. Contains also a few historical statements of value to those who are students of the early history of Seventh-day Adventism. Ellen G. White was one of the first leaders of this religious body.]

————. *A Sketch of the Christian Experience and Views of Mrs. E. G. White.* 2d ed. Battle Creek, Mich.: Review and Herald, 1882. Oakland, Calif.: Pacific Press, 1882. 71 plus 40 pp. [This pamphlet is substantially the same in text matter as the 1851 and 1854 pamphlets. The material of the 1851 pamphlet constitutes 71 pages, and the 1854 pamphlet has an additional 40 pages separately numbered. This was later republished as a part of a book called *Early Writings of Mrs. White,* which is currently in print.]

————. *Supplement to the Christian Experience and Views of Ellen G. White.* Rochester, N. Y.: James White, 1854. 48 pp. [As the name suggests, this is a supplement to the 1851 pamphlet of the same name. It clarifies certain statements in the original pamphlet and adds further material.]

Whiting, N. N. *Origin, Nature, and Influence of Neology.* Boston: J. V. Himes, March 1, 1844. 51 pp. (Second Advent Library, No. XLII.) [A discussion and condemnation of German Rationalism.]

————. *Prophetic View of the Condition of the Nations Which Is Immediately to Precede the Second Advent.* Boston: J. V. Himes, 1854. 31 pp.

Word of Warning. Boston: J. V. Himes [no date]. [A series of two-page leaflets dealing with main points of Millerite belief. Series runs up at least to No. 36.]

BOOKS

Adams, James Truslow, and Vannest, Charles G. *The Record of America.* New York: Charles Scribner's Sons [1940]. 966 pp.

Bates, Joseph. *The Autobiography of Elder Joseph Bates; Embracing a Long Life on Shipboard, With Sketches of Voyages on the Atlantic and Pacific Oceans, the Baltic and Mediterranean Seas; Also Impressment and Service on Board British War Ships, Long Confinement in Dartmoor Prison, Early Experience in Reformatory Movements; Travels in Various Parts of the World; and a Brief Account of the Great Advent Movement of 1840-44.* Battle Creek, Mich.: Seventh-day Adventist Publishing Assn., 1868. 318 pp. [The scope of this work is revealed in the title. A book of some value because of the fact that Bates had a prominent part in the Millerite movement.]

Beardsley, Frank Grenville. *A History of American Revivals.* 3d ed. New York: American Tract Society, 1912. 352 pp. [This work is a straightforward history of revivals during the period of American national life. There are occasional side lights that show the fervency of the revivals and the opposition that was sometimes generated against them by some ministers. Brief mention of Millerism, which sets forth the usual distorted picture, including ascension robes.]

Bliss, Sylvester. *Memoirs of William Miller, Generally Known as a Lecturer on the Prophecies, and the Second Coming of Christ.* Boston: J. V. Himes, 1853. 426 pp. [This is the only real biography of Miller that has ever been written. Other so-called biographies exist, but they are largely condensations or adaptations of Bliss' work. Bliss had most excellent opportunity to know the subject of his sketch. He was also in possession of much of Miller's correspondence, from which he quoted freely. All who write on Miller or Millerism are beholden to Bliss on some historical items. However, most of the letters and other manuscripts from which Bliss drew have been preserved and are now in the library of Aurora College, Illinois. For long years this material lay almost forgotten. Bliss wrote with excellent restraint, though he was a close friend of Miller's in the movement. An examination, today, of the principal sources from which he drew reveals that he quoted fairly and judiciously to paint a proper picture of Miller.]

Boudinot, Elias. *The Second Advent, or Coming of the Messiah in Glory, Shown to Be a Scripture Doctrine, and Taught by Divine Revelation, From the Beginning of the World.*

By an American Layman. Trenton, N. J.: D. Fenton & S. Hutchinson, 1815. 578 pp. [An exhaustive discussion of the theme of the second advent.]

Boutelle, Luther. *Sketch of the Life and Religious Experience of Elder Luther Boutelle.* Boston: Advent Christian Publication Society, 1891. 208 pp. [This work has some value inasmuch as Boutelle was active in the Millerite movement. However, he held a rather minor place. Only a small part of this work is devoted to the movement. The remainder deals with his life before and after his connection with Millerism. The reminiscences of an old man.]

Brief History of William Miller the Great Pioneer in Adventual Faith, A. 2d ed. Boston: Advent Christian Publication Society, 1910. 387 pp. [The preface states the sources of this work: "This 'Brief History of William Miller,' which is herewith presented to the public, is made up from various sources, such as his *Lectures*, the writings of Elders A. Hale, I. C. Wellcome, J. V. Himes and S. Bliss, more particularly the latter from his *Memoirs of William Miller;* together with some important additional facts and illustrations obtained by Elder E. D. Gibbs from an old record book which Mr. Miller kept from 1839 to 1843, and especially from a visit to his old home, and a personal interview with his youngest daughter, Mrs. Lucy Ann Bartholomew, who is now in her seventieth year."—*Page iii.* Because of the fact that this work draws heavily on Bliss, it is of limited value to those who have access to Bliss.]

Buckley, James M. *A History of Methodists in the United States.* Vol. V, of The American Church History Series, edited by Philip Schaff, *et al.* New York: The Christian Literature Co., 1896. 714 pp. [See pp. 298, 299, for discussion of physical manifestations at early camp meetings.]

Burrage, Henry S. *History of the Baptists in Maine.* Portland, Maine: Marks Printing House, 1904. 497 pp. [See pp. 197-201 for a restrained, if not sympathetic, summary of Miller's activities in Maine. Author states that Miller's teachings were carried to "almost every town and hamlet in Maine," and these teachings are given at least partial credit for the nearly 10,000 accessions to Baptist churches in Maine from 1840 to 1845.]

Bury, J. B. *The Idea of Progress. An Inquiry Into Its Origin and Growth.* New York: Macmillan Company, 1932. 352 pp. [Bury was Regius Professor of Modern History, and Fellow of King's College, in the University of Cambridge, a generation ago. The 1932 edition by Macmillan Company is described in a prefatory note as simply "the American edition." Professor Bury traces the history of the idea of progress through the centuries. His thesis is that the idea never began to have vogue until modern times. He declares that it was in the first quarter of the seventeenth century that the "soil was being prepared in which the idea of progress could germinate."—*Introduction, p. 36.* This work is significant as a historical and philosophical commentary on the idea of the moral and spiritual improvement of man in this present world, which began to receive well-defined support in theological circles in the eighteenth century.]

Campbell, David. *Illustrations of Prophecy; Particularly the Evening and Morning Visions of Daniel and the Apocalyptical Visions of John.* 2d ed. Boston: Geo. W. Light, 1841. 432 pp. [The book notices on the first edition, which are printed on pages 1 to 4, indicate that this work was widely endorsed by the religious press. The author speaks of Miller by name and argues against his views in certain instances. He holds to the postmillennial coming of Christ, preceded by the return of the Jews and the conversion of the world. However, he believes that great events and changes are impending for the world. In the preface to the second edition he says: "During the year since this work was issued (c. 1839), the affairs of the world have assumed an aspect of increasing interest. They confirm in no small degree, the general views of the author in relation to the apprehended changes of this period. . . . As the 'shooting of the fig tree' betokens the coming of summer, so do these signs the predicted changes that await our world." He then refers to prophetic signs which he believes fulfilling, and adds that we may "look for some great overturn speedily following these indications."—*Page 7.* In his Introductory Remarks he declares: "From the prophecies, as well as from other indications in the rapid advances of society, we have reason to suppose that we are approaching times of very peculiar interest." *Pages 20, 21.* He argues that prophecy can and should be understood by Christians.]

Chase, Irah. *Remarks on the Book of Daniel in Regard to the Four Kingdoms, Especially the Fourth; the '2300 Days;' the Seventy Weeks; and the Events Predicted in the Last Three Chapters.* Boston: Gould, Kendall and Lincoln, 1844. 84 pp. [Chase is listed on the title page as professor of ecclesiastical history in the Newton Theological Institution.

BIBLIOGRAPHY 539

The Preface opens thus: "The following essay was first published as an article in the *Christian Review*, for March, 1842."—Page iii. Preface reveals that it was written because of Millerite preaching.]

Corpus Juris, Being a Complete and Systematic Statement of the Whole Body of the Law as Embodied in and Developed by All Reported Decisions. Edited by William Mack and William Benjamin Hale. New York: The American Law Book Co., 1914-1935. 71 Vols. [This is the outstanding reference work which jurists consult.]

Cosmopolite, A. See *Miller Overthrown.*

Crocker, Henry. *History of the Baptists in Vermont.* Bellows Falls, Vt.: P. H. Gobie Press, 1913. 700 pp. [Makes a number of references to Miller and his preaching in giving the history of Baptist churches in different cities. Generally speaks of Millerism in derogation, and declares that it was one of the causes of the decline in Baptist Church in years following 1844.]

Crump, C. G. *History and Historical Research.* London: George Routledge & Sons, Ltd., 1928. 178 pp. [A delightful treatise on the difficulties involved in trying to write history impartially, and the techniques of collecting data, making notes, etc., involved in research work. The author was educated at Balliol College, Oxford.]

Cyclopaedia of American Biography. (New enlarged ed. of *Appleton's Cyclopaedia of American Biography.*) New York: Press Association Compilers, Inc., 1915-31. 12 vols.

Devens, R. M. *The Great Events of Our Past Century.* Chicago: Hugh Heron, 1881. 720 pp. [Under the author's name on title page is this: "Assisted by our most eminent authors, artists, scientists, statesmen, military and other officials." The preface explains that this work is designed "to preserve and perpetuate those special events in the first century of our nation's existence, which have had a controlling influence in shaping the destiny and molding the present greatness and glory of the American Republic—those events that have called forth the most intense interest, curiosity, admiration or terror on the part of the people; and also illustrate and bring into striking relief, the prevailing spirit or excitement of the period marked by their occurrence."—*Page 7.* For an excellent, dispassionate sketch of Millerism, see pages 307-314.]

Dick, Everett. *Founders of the Message.* Washington, D. C.: Review and Herald Publishing Assn., 1938. 333 pp. [Very readable and historically accurate sketches of William Miller, Joshua V. Himes, Joseph Bates, James White, Ellen G. White, J. N. Loughborough, and John Nevins Andrews. With the exception of the first two, this group were prominent in the early years of the Seventh-day Adventist Church.]

Dictionary of American Biography. New York: Charles Scribner's Sons, 1943. 21 vols.

Dowling, John. *An Exposition of the Prophecies, Supposed by William Miller to Predict the Second Coming of Christ, in 1843.* Providence: Geo. P. Daniels, 1840. 232 pp. [Dowling is listed on title page as "Pastor of the Pine-Street Baptist Church, Providence, R. I." This was one of the most widely quoted works written against Millerism. Sets forth postmillennial view.]

Edwards, Jonathan. *Thoughts on the Revival of Religion in New England, 1740. In Which Is Prefixed a Narrative of the Surprising Work of God in Northampton, Mass., 1735.* New York: American Tract Society [no date]. 446 pp. ["This edition is reprinted from the Worcester edition of President Edwards' works." The work discusses broadly the subject of revivals. The part that is significant in connection with a study of Millerism is the section devoted to the so-called excesses of revivals. Edwards endorses "outcries, faintings, and other bodily effects," and declares: "To rejoice that the work of God is carried on calmly without much ado, is in effect to rejoice that it is carried on with less power, or that there is not so much of the influence of God's Spirit; for though the degree of the influence of the Spirit of God on *particular persons* is by no means to be judged of by the degree of external appearances, because of the different constitution, tempers, and circumstances of men; yet if there be a very powerful influence of the Spirit of God on a mixed multitude, it will cause, some way or other, a great visible commotion."—*Page 259.*]

Emerson, Ralph Waldo. *The Complete Writings of Ralph Waldo Emerson.* New York: Wm. H. Wise & Co., 1929. 2 vols. [Subtitle reads, "Containing All of His Inspiring Essays, Lectures, Poems, Addresses, Studies, Biographical Sketches, and Miscellaneous Works."]

Encyclopaedia Britannica, The. 9th ed. New York: The Encyclopaedia Britannica Company, 1875-89. 25 vols. 11th ed. New York: The Encyclopaedia Britannica Company, 1910-11. 29 vols.

Fassett, O. R. *The Biography of Mrs. L. E. Fassett.* Boston: Advent Christian Publication Society, 1885. 168 pp. [The author, who was the husband of Mrs. L. E. Fassett, was a minister in the movement. He gives a number of very interesting side lights on Millerism. Most of the work deals with the years after 1844.]

Finney, Charles G. *Memoirs of Rev. Charles G. Finney.* New York: A. S. Barnes & Co., 1876. 477 pp. [Chapter 27 describes his interview with Miller. He had a low estimate of the Millerites' theology and dismissed them as wild with excitement.]

First Report of the General Conference of Christians Expecting the Advent of the Lord Jesus Christ, The, Held in Boston, Oct. 14, 15, 1840. Boston: J. V. Himes, 1842. [As the title indicates this is a conference report. The edition we have is 1842. There was an 1841 edition. Certain of the principal addresses are reproduced along with conference proceedings. Important as indicating the theological character of the movement when it was first taking definite shape.]

Fish, Carl Russell. *The Rise of the Common Man, 1830-1850.* (Vol. VI of *A History of American Life.*) New York: Macmillan Company, 1937. 391 pp. [This book gives a panoramic sketch of social, political, moral, religious, etc., conditions in the period 1830-50. Chapter IX, pp. 179-199, is entitled "The Religious Scene." Of value in creating a picture of the kind of world in which Millerites lived.]

Gaddis, Maxwell Pierson. *Footprints of an Itinerant.* Cincinnati: Methodist Book Concern, 1856. 546 pp. [Gaddis is described on the title page as "of the Cincinnati Conference." This is an autobiographical work giving the high lights of a Methodist preacher's life in the first half of the nineteenth century. He labored in the State of Ohio. A very good, firsthand account of Methodist camp meetings and revivals and the religious state of the people at that time.]

[Garrison, Wendell Phillips, and Garrison, Francis Jackson.] *William Lloyd Garrison, The Story of His Life Told by His Children.* New York: Century Co., 1885-89. 4 vols. [The title page does not carry authors' names, but the preface is signed by the two sons Wendell Phillips and Francis Jackson. The material in this biography is drawn from the files of Garrison's *Liberator,* from letters, and from other sources. This work is easily the best on the life of the founder of abolitionism.]

Gorham, B. W. *Camp Meeting Manual.* Boston: H. V. Degen, 1854. 168 pp. [A brief defense of camp meetings by a Methodist minister. He answers various charges brought against camp meetings, such as that they lead to disorder.]

Grob, Jean. *Life of Ulric Zwingli.* New York: Funk and Wagnalls, 1883. 200 pp.

Hale, Ezekiel, Junior, Versus Ezekiel J. M. Hale. See United States Circuit Court of the United States.

Hare, G. Emlen. *Christ to Return. A Practical Exposition of the Prophecy Recorded in the 24th and 25th Chapters of the Gospel According to St. Matthew.* Philadelphia: Herman Hooker, 1840. 132 pp. [Author seeks to show that there will be a second advent and that it will be sudden, unexpected. Apparently not related to Millerism, either pro or con.]

Hemenway, Abby Maria, editor. *Vermont Historical Gazetteer.* Vol. III. Claremont, N. H.: Claremont Manufacturing Co., 1877. Vol. IV, Montpelier, Vt.: Vermont Watchman and State Journal Press, 1882. Vol. V, Brandon, Vt.: Mrs. Carrie E. H. Page, 1891. [The *Gazetteer* was published in five bulky volumes, providing a very complete history of the towns in Vermont. See references to Millerism in: Vol. III, p. 718; Vol. IV, p. 846; Vol. V, p. 427. Originally published as a quarterly.]

Henshaw, John P. K. *An Inquiry Into the Meaning of the Prophecies Relating to the Second Advent of Our Lord Jesus Christ.* Baltimore: Daniel Brunner, 1842. 228 pp.

H[odge], O. J. *Reminiscences* by O. J. H. Cleveland, Ohio: The Imperial Press, 1902. 247 pp. [Pages 30-32 give reminiscences regarding the Millerites in Cleveland, among others that "many made themselves ascension robes, and some of the more deluded were seen wearing them in the streets."—*Pages 31, 32.* He remembers "a story being told" of a Millerite's climbing on top of a haystack in his robe and falling asleep, of boys' setting fire to the haystack, and of his crying out that he was in the middle of hell, "just as my wife has long predicted."—*Page 32.* Compare with interesting fire legends in Sears' collection of letters.]

Hurst, John Fletcher. *The History of Methodism.* New York: Eaton & Mains, 1902-04. 7 vols. Vol. V was published in 1903. [See Vol. V, pp. 522-538, for a discussion of early camp meetings and physical phenomena.]

Jackson, George Pullen. *White and Negro Spirituals, Their Life Span and Kinship.* New York: J. J. Augustin, 1943. 349 pp. [See chapter: "Farmer William Miller Dates the World's End," pp. 100-104. This chapter retells some of the idle stories of insanity, robes, etc.]

Johnson, Albert C. *Advent Christian History.* Boston: Advent Christian Publication Society, 1918. 598 pp. [The first part of this work gives a concise history of the 1844 period from the viewpoint of an Advent Christian minister. Of real value to the student of Millerism.]

Johnson, Allen. *The Historian and Historical Evidence.* New York: Charles Scribner's Sons, 1934. 179 pp. [This work is a text for the guidance of the man who wishes to write history. It deals with the basic problems of historical research and the evaluation of evidence, etc. Johnson is listed on the title page as "Professor American History, Yale University."]

Jones, Henry. *American Views of Christ's Second Advent. Selected and in Part Given by Henry Jones.* New York: Saxton & Miles, 1842. 252 pp. [As the title page reveals, this work consists "mostly of lectures delivered before late general conventions, in the cities of Boston, Lowell and New York; vindicating the Lord's personal and glorious appearing on earth, to judge the world, 'at hand,' without fixing the time; without a previous millennium; or return of the Jews to Palestine."]

————. *The Scriptures Searched: or Christ's Second Coming anl Kingdom at Hand.* New York: Gould, Newman & Saxton, 1839. 240 pp. [Jones is identified on title page as "Author of 'Principles of Interpreting the Prophecies.'" The Testimonials in the forepart from ministers of various sects, reveal that Jones had been preaching in their churches on the second advent at least as early as the first half of 1838. The "Author's Apology" is dated, "New York, Sept. 27, 1839." The author gives first a brief summary of 24 rules of interpretation. The book is devoted to a presentation of the premillennial view and an examination of counterviews.]

Litch, Josiah. *Christ Yet to Come: a Review of Dr. I. P. Warren's "Parousia of Christ."* Boston: American Millennial Assn., 1880. 192 pp. [This work is cited simply to show that Litch was active at this late date and still preaching the personal second coming. At the close of the Preface is the line: "42 Prairie Ave. Providence, R. I., April 28, 1880."]

————. *The Probability of the Second Coming of Christ About A. D. 1843.* Boston: David H. Ela, 1838. 204 pp. [An exposition of some of the main prophetic features of the Millerite beliefs. The author says in his preface: "The writer would here acknowledge himself indebted to Mr. William Miller's valuable lectures, for the leading ideas of the following pages. . . . The principal reason of its publication is, the scarceness of Mr. Miller's books, together with the importance of the subject." The work is significant as being the first book of exposition of Millerite teachings by any of those who were soon to be associated with Miller as leaders in the movement.]

Longfellow, Henry Wadsworth. *Kavanagh, a Tale.* Boston: Ticknor, Reed, and Fields, 1849. 188 pp.

Loughborough, J. N. *The Great Second Advent Movement: Its Rise and Progress.* Washington, D. C.: Review and Herald Publishing Assn., 1905. 480 pp. [Approximately the first 200 pages devoted to the period before 1845. Written long after the events. Should therefore be checked against the original sources whenever possible. The preface declares: "Having been familiar with the advent movement in 1843 and 1844, and having, since Jan. 2, 1849, proclaimed the doctrine, first as an Adventist, and since 1852 as a Seventh-day Adventist, I esteem it a pleasure to 'speak the things I have seen and heard.'"]

————. *Rise and Progress of the Seventh-day Adventists With Tokens of God's Hand in the Movement and a Brief Sketch of the Advent Cause From 1831 to 1844.* Battle Creek, Mich.: General Conference Association of the Seventh-day Adventists, 1892.

392 pp. [Only a small portion of this work is devoted to Millerism. Has a certain value because the author was personally acquainted with some who were leaders in Millerism.]

McMaster, John B. *A History of the People of the United States*. New York: D. Appleton & Co., 1883-1913. 8 vols. [Vol. VII, pp. 134-141, discusses Millerism. This volume was published in 1910. McMaster's work quotes very freely from newspapers of the day. This gives to it a certain unique value. But if the remainder of the work is as uncritical in its use of newspaper clippings as is the section devoted to Millerism, we must conclude that the history is of doubtful value. Every idle story published in the obviously rumor-filled newspapers of the 1840's, is woven into the sketch on Millerism. There is nothing to suggest to the reader that these newspaper items are highly undependable. Instead, the "It is said," or "It is reported," with which the newspapers of a hundred years ago introduced most of their stories about Millerism, are missing from McMaster's sketch. Glaring errors like these are set down as sober facts: the newspaper hoax date, April 23, 1843, for the end of the world; the two dead children at an encampment near Philadelphia (Phoenixville); the 26 Millerites in a Vermont asylum; a robed Millerite jumping from a tree and breaking his neck. These stories, embalmed in a serious history, have provided a source of misinformation for certain widely published articles on Millerism in more recent years.]

Merz, John Theodore. *A History of European Thought in the Nineteenth Century*. Vol. I, 2d unaltered ed. Edinburgh: William Blackwood and Sons, 1904-14. 4 vols. [This erudite work seeks to trace the history of thought in the areas of science, philosophy, and religion in the nineteenth century. The preface is dated 1896.]

Millennial Harp. Designed for Meetings on the Second Coming of Christ. Improved ed., three parts in one volume, compiled by Joshua V. Himes. Boston: [J. V. Himes] 1843. [Part I, words and music, 72 pp.; Part II, words and music, 72 pp.; Part III, words without music, 144 pp.; Supplement to the Harp, words with music, 36 pp. The preface of the *Millennial Harp* states, "The Harp, in its present form, embraces nearly all the hymns contained in our well-known works,—the 'Millennial Harp,' 'Musings,' and 'Melodies.' "]

Miller Overthrown: or the False Prophet Confounded. By a Cosmopolite. Boston: Abel Tompkins, 1840. 132 pp. [Under "General Remarks" the author says, "This is the day of strange things. We have phrenology, animal magnetism, sleeping preaching, political crisises [sic], and the end of the world."—*Page 4*.]

Miller, William. *Evidence From Scripture and History of the Second Coming of Christ, About the Year 1843: Exhibited in a Course of Lectures*. Troy: Printed for the Publishers by Kemble & Hooper, 1836. 223 pp. [The Introduction opens thus: "In presenting this pamphlet to the public, the writer is only complying with the solicitations of some of his friends, who have requested that his views on the prophecies of Daniel and John, might be made public." This 1836 edition contains sixteen lectures.

In 1838 an edition was published in Troy, N. Y., by Elias Gates. Tuttle, Belcher and Burton, Printers. The Introduction is the same, except the first phrase, which reads, "In presenting these lectures to the public." The 1838 edition contains eighteen lectures. The two added are "Daniel 9:24" as Lecture IV, and "Solomon's Song viii, 5" as Lecture XVII. This 1838 edition contains 280 pages.

In 1840 an edition of this work was published in Boston by B. B. Mussey. This contains 19 lectures, the new lecture being inserted as "Lecture XVII," "On the Punishment of the People of God Seven Times for Their Sins." This 1840 edition contains 300 pages.

In 1841 an edition was published in Boston by Moses A. Dow. This contains the same number of pages as the 1840 edition, plus a 4-page supplement, "Exposition of Miller's Chart." There is tipped in beside page 205, a "Chronological Chart of the World."

In 1842 an edition was published in Boston by Joshua V. Himes. This appears to be identical with the 1841 edition.]

Minnigerode, Meade. *The Fabulous Forties*. New York: Garden City Publishing Co., Inc., 1924. 345 pp. [A discussion of the temper of the times of 1840-50. Drawn largely from the newspapers of that period. First three pages give lurid picture of Millerism.]

Munger, Hiram. *The Life and Religious Experience of Hiram Munger, Including Many Singular Circumstances Connected With Camp-Meetings and Revivals*. 3d ed. Boston:

BIBLIOGRAPHY 543

The Advent Christian Publication Society, 1885. 195 pp. [A delightful story of one man's experiences in connection with the Millerite movement and in the years following. He might be described as in the militant succession of Nehemiah and Ezra. He had charge of the pitching of the camp at certain of the Millerite camp meetings. In this way he made his first contact with them. Of value to the student of Millerism because of the author's firsthand knowledge of certain events. However, he wrote long after the events.]

Mussey, Mrs. Abigail. *Life Sketches and Experiences.* Cambridge: Dakin & Metcalf, 1865. 227 pp. [The author was born in 1811 and had intimate acquaintance with the Millerite movement, having accepted Miller's teachings. This work contains a few valuable side lights on the movement, though only a small part of the work is devoted to the 1840's.]

National Cyclopaedia of American Biography, The. New York: James T. White and Company, 1893-1943. 30 vols.

New English Dictionary on Historical Principles (The Oxford Dictionary). Oxford: The Clarendon Press, 1888-

Newton, Sir Isaac. *Observations Upon the Prophecies of Daniel and the Apocalypse of St. John.* In Two Parts. London: J. Darby and T. Browne, 1733. 323 pp. [The versatility of Sir Isaac is revealed by this work on theology. The "Two Parts" are bound as one book, the first part dealing with Daniel, the second with the Apocalypse.]

Ogg, Frederic Austin. *Builders of the Republic,* Vol. VIII of *The Pageant of America, a Pictorial History of the United States.* Edited by Ralph Henry Gabriel. New Haven: Yale University Press, 1925-29. 15 vols. [This is one volume of a 15-volume work that presents the history of America largely in terms of contemporary pictures, cartoons, documents, etc. There is a running text that gives sequence to the record. The material is terse and very readable.]

[Porter, James.] *An Essay on Camp-Meetings.* By the author of *The True Evangelist.* New York: Lane & Scott, 1849. 86 pp. [A defense of camp meetings, seeking to show their value and answer objections raised against them. Porter was a member of the Methodist General Conference. This essay was first given as an address at a camp meeting. He declares, "As Methodists, we need these great occasions for *all* the people."—*Page 18.* In the chapter devoted to objections the author reveals that the camp meetings were often troubled by rowdies and drunks, and that the worshipers sometimes became too fervent and noisy in their religion.]

———. *Revivals of Religion.* Rev. ed. New York: Nelson & Phillips, 1877. 285 pp. [A discussion and defense of revivals.]

Richardson, Robert. *Memoirs of Alexander Campbell.* Philadelphia: J. B. Lippincott and Co., 1868, 1870. 2 vols.

Schaff, Philip. *The Creeds of Christendom, With a History and Critical Notes.* 4th ed., revised and enlarged. New York: Harper & Brothers, 1919. 3 vols. [In the preface of the first volume is this explanation of the field covered by each volume: "The first volume has expanded into a doctrinal history of the church, so far as it is embodied in public standards of faith. . . . The second volume contains the Scripture Confessions, the ante-Nicene Rules of Faith, the Ecumenical, the Greek, and the Latin Creeds, from the Confession of Peter down to the Vatican Decrees. It includes also the best Russian Catechism and the recent Old Catholic Union Propositions of the Bonn Conferences. The third volume is devoted to the Lutheran, Anglican, Calvinistic, and the later Protestant Confessions of Faith."—*Page v.*]

Scharf, John Thomas, and Westcott, Thompson. *History of Philadelphia. 1609-1884.* Philadelphia: L. H. Everts and Co., 1884. 3 vols. [Considered a standard work even today.]

Sears, Clara Endicott. *Days of Delusion.* Boston: Houghton Mifflin Company, 1924. 264 pp. [A very readable, much-quoted book on Millerism. Author gives great weight to anecdotes provided in letters written in response to a notice in New England newspapers asking for Millerite anecdotes. See Chapter 27 and Appendix I for a more extended discussion of this work.]

Simpson, Matthew. *Cyclopaedia of Methodism.* Philadelphia: L. H. Everts & Stewart, 1878. 1027 pp. [Simpson was a Methodist Episcopal bishop. Speaking of revivals he says, "There have, however, been some remarkable seasons, such as that between 1840 and 1844, which is alluded to by the bishops in their address to the General Conference

when they say, 'No period of our denominational existence has been more signally distinguished by more extensive revivals of the work of God and the increase of the church."
—*Pages 752, 753, Article, "Revivals."*]

Simpson, Samuel. *Life of Ulrich Zwingli.* New York: Baker and Taylor, 1902, 297 pp.

Skinner, Otis A. *The Theory of William Miller, Concerning the End of the World in 1843, Utterly Exploded.* Boston: Thomas Whittemore, 1840. 210 pp. [Preface explains that Miller gave a series of lectures in Cambridgeport at the Baptist meetinghouse and that Skinner was urged to deliver a series against him. This book consists of these lectures. Skinner is listed as pastor of the Fifth Universalist Society in Boston.]

Spalding, Arthur Whitefield. *Pioneer Stories of the Second Advent Message.* Rev. ed. Nashville, Tenn.: Southern Publishing Association, 1942. [Delightful human-interest stories of certain leaders in the advent movement of the 1840's. Historically accurate.]

Spurgeon, C. H. *John Ploughman's Talks.* Abridged ed. Washington, D. C.: Review and Herald Publishing Association, 1918. 74 pp. [A series of talks for common people on the homely virtues to be cultivated and the prevalent vices to be spurned.]

Stevens, Abel. *History of the Methodist Episcopal Church in the United States of America.* New York: Eaton and Mains [no date]. 4 vols. [See Vol. IV, pp. 432-434 for discussion of fanaticism at early camp meetings.]

Stuart, M[oses]. *Hints on the Interpretation of Prophecy.* Andover: Allen, Morrill & Wardwell, 1842. 146 pp. [This work was apparently written on account of the Millerite discussion of prophecy. It is examined at length in Millerite publications. Stuart is described on the title page as "Professor in Andover Theological Seminary."]

Sweet, William Warren. *The Story of Religion in America.* New York: Harper & Brothers, 1939. 656 pp. [First published under the title, "The Story of Religions in America." Sketches briefly the history of religious bodies in this country. Very readable and rather generally dispassionate. However, the author gives the usual picture of Millerism as a fanatical movement.]

Teggart, Frederick J. *Theory and Processes of History.* Berkeley: University of California Press, 1941. 323 pp. [The author explains in the preface: "Of the two books included in this volume, the first, entitled *Theory of History*, was originally published by the Yale University Press in 1925; the second, *The Processes of History*, was likewise issued by the Yale University Press, but in 1918."—*Page v.* The section on the *Theory of History* seeks to show "the relation of history to literature, philosophy, and science," and "to other fields of humanistic interest."—*Ibid.* "The Processes of History was designed to exhibit a program of research."—*Page vi.* At the time of writing this work the author was a professor emeritus of the University of California.]

Tennyson, Alfred Lord. *The Poetic and Dramatic Works of Alfred Lord Tennyson.* Cambridge ed. Boston: Houghton Mifflin Co., 1898. 887 pp.

Tyerman, L. *The Life and Times of the Rev. John Wesley, M. A., Founder of the Methodists.* 3d ed. London: Hodder and Stoughton, 1876. New York: Harper Brothers, 1872. 3 vols. [See Vol. I, p. 395, and Vol. II, p. 433, for discussion of fanaticism.]

Tyler, Alice Felt. *Freedom's Ferment.* Minneapolis: The University of Minnesota Press, 1944. 608 pp. [The subtitle indicates the scope of this work: "Phases of American Social History to 1860." This work is divided into three parts: "The Faith of the Young Republic," "Cults and Utopias," and "Humanitarian Crusades." For the reader who wishes to make a brief survey of the social history of America, this work will prove of great value. An extended bibliography suggests further sources of information. Pages 70 to 78 are devoted to Millerism. This sketch contains rather less than the usual number of historical errors as to dates and events than are found in brief sketches in other works. However, the usual ascension-robes, insanity, and suicide stories are mentioned. The author explains that "the examples of millennial frenzy are taken from McMaster."—*Page 560.* Thus rumor and gossip are seriously passed on to the present generation. We would refer the reader to the bibliographical note on McMaster.]

Tyso, Joseph. *A Defence of the Personal Reign of Christ.* London: Jackson & Walford, 1841. 152 pp. [This is a stricture on several works that teach merely a spiritual coming of Christ and a postmillennial advent. Tyso argues for the personal, premillennial advent, but believes He will reign on earth and that the Jews will be converted.]

Vincent, Henry. *A History of the Wesleyan Grove, Martha's Vineyard, Camp Meeting.* Boston: Geo. C. Rand & Avery, 1858. 203 pp. [A rather routine record of camp meetings from 1835 to 1858. Throws some light on the revival techniques of earlier days.]

Ward, Henry Dana. *Glad Tidings.* New York: Daniel Appleton, 1838. 190 pp. [In his introduction he refers to his earlier work against Freemasonry, which appeared anonymously in 1828, but which is listed in libraries under Ward. In the present volume he seeks to prove the literal soon coming of Christ and refute various heresies about the spiritual coming of Christ.]

Weems, Mason Locke. *A History of the Life and Death, Virtues and Exploits, of General George Washington.* Number 2 of An American Bookshelf. New York: Macy-Masius, 1927. 373 pp. [Reprinted from a later edition. The editor, Mark van Doren, believes that the hatchet story was invented and added, among other things, to the 1806 edition, by Weems, who was "neither 'parson' nor 'formerly rector of Mount Vernon Parish,' but a professional writer of tracts and biographies."—Page 5. The hatchet story appears on pages 23 and 24.]

Wellcome, Isaac C. *History of the Second Advent Message and Mission, Doctrine and People.* Yarmouth, Maine: I. C. Wellcome, 1874. 707 pp. [The first part deals with the history of the Millerite movement. The latter part of this work is devoted to the history, doctrines, and development of the Advent Christian Church. Particularly valuable because of biographical sketches of various men who participated in the movement. "In 1842 he read Mr. Miller's lectures and heard several sermons" on the advent. Finally severed his church connections September, 1844. "He now associated fully with the advent believers."—*Pages 568, 569.*]

Wesley, John. *The Journal of the Rev. John Wesley.* Edited by Nehemiah Curnock. New York: Eaton & Mains, 1909-16. 8 vols. [Vol. II covers from Sept. 20, 1738, to Oct. 27, 1743. See pp. 131, 147, 181, 182, 203, 204 for discussion of physical manifestations.]

――――――. *The Letters of the Rev. John Wesley.* Edited by John Telford. London: The Epworth Press, 1931. 8 vols. [See Vol. II, p. 346, and Vol. IV, pp. 338-384 for discussion of fanaticism.]

White, Ellen G. *Early Writings.* Latest ed. Washington, D. C.: Review and Herald Publishing Assn., 1938. 316 pp. [First issued in 1882 as a compilation of the two pamphlets *A Sketch of the Christian Experience and Views of Ellen G. White* (1851) and *Supplement to the Christian Experience and Views of Ellen G. White* (1854), together with the book *Spiritual Gifts, Vol. I, The Great Controversy Between Christ and His Angels, and Satan and His Angels* (1858). The first part deals with her personal experiences in the Miller movement.]

――――――. *The Great Controversy Between Christ and Satan. The Conflict of the Ages in the Christian Dispensation.* Washington, D. C.: Review and Herald Publishing Assn., 1911. 718 pp. [This religious work deals with the conflict between good and evil in the Christian Era in terms of the religious history of those centuries. Chapters 18 to 24 are of value in the study of Millerism in that they give the author's views regarding the religious significance of Miller and the relation of Millerism to Seventh-day Adventism.]

――――――. *Life Sketches of Ellen G. White.* Mountain View, Calif.: Pacific Press Publishing Assn., 1915. 480 pp. [The first 254 pages are from the pen of Ellen G. White and are an adaptation of her 1860 volume *My Christian Experience, Views and Labors,* plus certain additional material to round out the record of her life up to the date of the death of her husband, James White, in 1881. From page 255 on to the close of the book "her life story is continued by C. C. Crisler, . . . with the assistance of her son, W. C. White, and D. E. Robinson."—*Preface, p. 6.* This part of the book weaves her life story in with various historical developments of the Seventh-day Adventist denomination up to the time of her death in 1915.]

――――――. *My Christian Experience, Views and Labors in Connection With the Rise and Progress of the Third Angel's Message.* (Spiritual Gifts, Vol. II.) Battle Creek, Mich.: James White, 1860. 304 pp. [This volume deals with historical incidents from 1844 to 1860 in the life of Ellen G. White and her husband, James White. This is the most complete of any early work by Seventh-day Adventists on the history of the denomination up to 1860. However, the book does not profess to be a history, but rather the record of a series of incidents. The reader receives a picture of numerous conferences held with advent groups, hardships and much sickness endured, and fanaticism rebuked.]

White, James. *Life Incidents, in Connection With the Great Advent Movement, as Illustrated by the Three Angels of Revelation XIV.* Battle Creek, Mich.: Steam Press of the Seventh-day Adventist Publishing Assn., 1868. 373 pp. [This work consists of a discussion of Miller's preaching, the author's activities as a Millerite preacher, a sketch of certain high points in Millerite history, a sketch of the beginnings of the Seventh-day Adventist Church, and a discussion of certain doctrines distinctive to that church.]

————. *Life Sketches, Ancestry, Early Life, Christian Experience, and Extensive Labors of Elder James White, and His Wife, Mrs. Ellen G. White.* Battle Creek, Mich.: Steam Press of the Seventh-day Adventist Publishing Assn., 1880. 416 pp. [The first 125 pages are essentially the same material as is found in the first 191 pages of James White's *Life Incidents* published in 1868. Pages 126 to 324 are a reproduction, almost wholly in quotation marks, from the work by Ellen G. White, *My Christian Experience, Views and Labors,* published in 1860. The remainder of the work deals briefly with certain theological views and with a sketch of the development of the Seventh-day Adventist denomination up to the time the work was written. An 1888 edition by the same publishers contains 453 pages. The first 350 pages give the life of James and Ellen White as it is given in the 1880 edition. The remainder of the book, prepared by an unidentified author, describes the last illness and death of James White and also sketches further development of the work of the Seventh-day Adventists.]

————. *Sketches of the Christian Life and Public Labors of William Miller, Gathered From His Memoir by the Late Sylvester Bliss, and From Other Sources.* Battle Creek, Mich.: Steam Press of the Seventh-day Adventist Publishing Assn., 1875. 416 pp. [This is very largely Bliss material and hence contains little of value to those who have access to Bliss.]

Whittier, John Greenleaf. *Prose Works. Vol. I (The Writings of John Greenleaf Whittier,* Vol. V), Riverside ed. Boston & New York: Houghton, Mifflin & Co., 1889. [Contains chapter entitled "The World's End," which is a description of Millerite camp meetings.]

Williams, C. S. *Descendants of Captain Joseph Miller of West Springfield, Mass., 1698-1908.* New York: Tobias A. Wright, 1908. 39 pp. [One of several genealogical works that throw light on the Miller family. The data it contains agrees in large part with that of other genealogies.]

PUBLIC DOCUMENTS

U. S. Bureau of the Census. *Religious Bodies: 1926.* Washington: United States Government Printing Office, 1930. 2 vols. [Volume I, summary and detailed tables. Volume II contains discussion of separate denominations: statistics, history, doctrine, organization, and work. The statements of history, policy, and doctrines of the various bodies are generally from the offices of the various bodies, and hence authoritative.]

U. S. Bureau of the Census. *Religious Bodies: 1936.* Washington: United States Government Printing Office, 1941. 2 vols. [This 1936 census report follows the same style as the 1926 report, except that Volume II is really two volumes, being printed as Part I and Part II.]

United States. Bureau of Labor Statistics. Bulletin of Bureau of Labor Statistics, No. 604. *History of Wages in the United States From Colonial Times to 1928.* Washington: United States Government Printing Office, 1934. 574 pp. [As the title indicates, this work traces the history of wages. Of value to the student of Millerism when he seeks to discover comparisons between the prevailing wage rates of those times and the contributions by the Millerites to their work in the 1840's.]

United States. Circuit Court of United States. Massachusetts District. *In Equity, Ezekiel Hale, Junior, Versus Ezekiel J. M. Hale.* Boston: Mudge and Corliss, 1849. 591 pp. [This is a report of the legal action instituted in 1845 by Ezekiel Hale, Jr., against his son, Ezekiel J. M. Hale, to recover property given to the son at the time when the father, a Millerite, thought the world would end in 1844. This legal work consists largely of the depositions of 79 persons who were acquainted with the plaintiff. These depositions made in 1849, describe the life, beliefs, and actions of the plaintiff. A most revealing volume. We believe a copy of this is to be found only in the Public Library, Haverhill, Mass.]

BIBLIOGRAPHY

ANNUAL REPORTS

ASYLUM REPORTS

[Almost all these annual asylum reports were published as paper-bound documents. Dates indicate the particular years' reports examined in detail.]

California: *Insanity and Insane Asylums,* Report of E. T. Wilkins, M. D., Commissioner in Lunacy for the State of California, Dec. 2, 1871.

Connecticut: *Annual Reports of the Officers of the Retreat for the Insane.* (Hartford) 1840-47.

Maine: *Annual Reports of the Directors of the Maine Insane Hospital.* (Augusta) 1840-47.

Maryland: *Report of the President and Board of Visitors of the Maryland Hospital, and Resident Physician's Report.* (Baltimore) 1843-47. [From 1838 onward this hospital accepted only mental cases. No reports published previous to 1843.]

Massachusetts: *Annual Reports of the Board of Trustees of the Massachusetts General Hospital.* (Boston) 1840-47. [The annual reports of the McLean Asylum are a section of these reports, for McLean is a subsidiary of Massachusetts General Hospital.]

——. *Annual Reports of the Trustees of the State Lunatic Hospital at Worcester.* 1840-47.

——. *Report of the Superintendent of the Boston Lunatic Hospital and Physician of the Public Institutions at South Boston.* 1840-47.

New Hampshire: *Reports of the Board of Visitors, of the Trustees, and of the Superintendent of the New Hampshire Asylum for the Insane.* (Concord) 1842-47. [Opened Oct. 29, 1842.]

New York: *Annual Reports of the Managers of the State Lunatic Asylum.* (Utica) 1843-47. [Opened Jan. 16, 1843.]

Ohio: *Annual Reports of the Directors and Superintendents of the Ohio Lunatic Hospital.* (Columbus) 1840-47.

Pennsylvania: *Report of the Pennsylvania Hospital for the Insane.* (Philadelphia) 1841-47. [The Pennsylvania Hospital, a private institution, was founded in 1752, and up to 1841 received insane patients along with others in its main buildings. In that year the insane were moved to a separate building outside the city, which unit began to be known as the Pennsylvania Hospital for the Insane, for which separate reports were issued.]
Annual Reports on the State of the Asylum for the Relief of Persons Deprived of the Use of Their Reason. (Near Philadelphia) 1840-47. [A Quaker institution, also known as The Friends' Asylum for the Insane.]

Vermont: *Annual Reports of the Trustees of the Vermont Asylum for the Insane.* (Brattleboro) 1840-47.

OTHER REPORTS

Boston, Mass. City Directory. See Stimpson's Boston Directory.

Lancaster County [Pa.] Historical Society. *Papers.* Vol. IX., No. 3. Lancaster, Pa., 1905. [This volume consists of papers read before the society Nov. 4, 1904. Includes paper by David Bachman Landis entitled "The Second Adventists, or Millerites." Contains very little of value. Describes Millerite preachers as frauds. Says of Millerites: "More than one person was specially robed ready for the final flight." The whole paper is very superficial.]

Ohio Church History Society. *Papers.* Oberlin: Printed for the Society, 1890-1901. [In Vol. VI (1895) is an article entitled "A Stormy Epoch, 1825-1850," by Mrs. L. A. M. Bosworth, which devotes about two pages to Millerism. Of small value.]

Seventh-day Adventists. *Year Book of the Seventh-day Adventist Denomination, 1944.* Washington, D. C.: Review and Herald Publishing Assn., 1944. 407 pp.

Stimpson's Boston Directory, Containing Names of the Inhabitants, Their Occupations, Places of Business, and Dwelling Houses, and the City Register, With Lists of the Streets, Lanes, and Wharves, the City Officers, Public Offices, and Banks, and Other Useful Information. Boston: Stimpson and Clapp, 1831.

MISCELLANEOUS

ALMANAC

"The Great Western Almanac for 1844." Philadelphia: Jos. McDowell [1843?]. 36 pp. Library of Congress.

BROADSIDES

"End of the World in 1843." (25x31 in.) American Antiquarian Society, and library of Review and Herald Publishing Assn. [Published previous to May 10, 1843. Not a Millerite production. Anonymous. Pirated entire, except illustration of second coming of Christ, from Millerite publications. Exposed by the Millerites as a non-Millerite publication. See *Signs of the Times*, May 10, 1843, p. 76. The statement that this broadside is anonymous is based on the fact that no identifying statement is found on the broadside in our possession, which is an original, and which is identical with another original in the library of the American Antiquarian Society. But an original in the New York Public Library carries this identifying line at the bottom of the broadside: "Boston. Published by E. Leland, for the Proprietor, Washington St., Wm. White & H. P. Lewis, Printers." Whether the broadside first appeared with this identifying line, and later without it, or whether the reverse was the case, cannot now be known.]

"End of the World, Oct. 22, 1844." (22x33 in.) American Antiquarian Society, and library of Review and Herald Publishing Assn. [Internal evidence indicates publication between Oct. 12 and 19, 1844. Not a Millerite production. Anonymous. Same illustration as in "End of the World in 1843." One scurrilous article added to pirated Millerite text.]

"Grand Ascension of the Miller Tabernacle." (22x33 in.) American Antiquarian Society. [Anonymous. Scurrilous. Upper half, filled with cartoon, lower half with ridiculous stories. Internal evidence indicates publication between Oct. 16 and 22, 1844, probably at Boston.]

"The Great High Priest of Millerism Unmasked," etc. (Approximately 14x19 in.) 2d ed. Rockport, Mass.: Sylvanus Brown, Oct. 15, 1842. Essex Institute, Salem, Mass. [Six columns; scurrilous. First two columns, and note "2d edition" at bottom of last two columns, an attack on Himes. The remainder is attack on other denominations.]

"In Honor of the King of Kings." (11x15 in.) [n.p.] C. R. Gorgas, Oct. 7, 1844. American Antiquarian Society. [Filled with display lines setting forth the alleged vision of Gorgas as to the hour of the advent.]

"Millennial Song." Tune, "Rosin the Bow." (7½x7½ in.) [Notation in Vermont Historical Society record that it is by A. H. Mills, Middlebury, Vt., 1842. Consists of eight stanzas of eight lines each. Skit on Millerism.]

CHART

[Fitch, Charles, and Hale, Apollos.] A Chronological Chart of the Visions of Daniel and John. (39x56 in.) 14 Devonshire St. [Boston]: J. V. Himes [1842?]. (B. W. Thayer and Co., Lithography, Boston.) Advent Source Collection. [This chart was widely used in the public meetings of the Millerites to illustrate their exposition of prophecy. Authorized by the general conference held in Boston in May, 1842. Showed 1843 as the final terminus of prophecies.]

MAPS (Library of Congress)

"Map of the Circuit of Ten Miles Around the City of Philadelphia. From Original Surveys by J. C. Sidney, C. E." Philadelphia: Robert P. Smith, 1847.

"Map of the New England States." Boston: Nathan Hale, 1826.

"Map of Washington County, N. Y. From Actual Surveys by Morris Levey." Philadelphia: James D. Scott and Robert Pearsell Smith, 1853.

"New Topographical Atlas of Washington County, N. Y., From Actual Surveys Especially for This Atlas." Philadelphia: Stone and Stewart, 1866.

Index

Abbott, Lyman, editor of *Outlook* 409, 413
Abolitionism 54, 175, 176, 178, 181, 182, 260, 301
Abusive stories in the papers re Millerism 73, 128, 129
"Address to the Public," November, 1844 261-265
"Address to Advent Believers," by Miller (December, 1844) 272
"Address to the Brethren Scattered Abroad" 280, 281
Advent awakening simultaneous in various lands 9, 156, 157, 470
Advent Christian Church, development of 454-456
Advent, first, fulfilled spring types 229n
Advent Herald, The (see also *Signs of the Times*) 138, 161, 162, 164, 165, 167,169, 171, 172, 207-210, 213, 214, 216, 221, 230, 243, 261, 267-272, 281, 282, 309, 316, 318, 319, 384, 396, 397, 434, 440, 447, 448, 479, 480, 483, 500, 502, 513
Advent, second (see also Miller—Theology, and Time), churches hostile to 148, 164, 165, 264, 265
 doctrine in Bible and Christian history 83, 428-436
 expected at end of 2300 days 33, 34, 39, 273n
 fulfills autumn types 229n
Advent Review and Sabbath Herald 214, 403, 404
Advent Shield and Review, The 127n, 152, 188, 189, 204, 383, 500
Adventist, name, adopted as distinctive term 206, 207, 434
Adventists, English (not Millerites) 156
Advertisements, burlesques on Millerism 128
Albany conference 280-283
Albany Evening Journal (N. Y.) 343, 387
American Mercury 330n, 504, 513
American Newspaper Rate-Book 405
Annihilation, preached by Storrs and Fitch 283, 284
Apollo Hall, New York City, Miller preaches in 100
Apology and Defence, by William Miller 24, 27, 29-31, 33-36, 41-43, 73, 204, 283-285
Appleton's Cyclopedia of American Biography 414
April 23, 1843, rumor about 126, 140, 156, 380, 416
Artaxerxes Longimanus 506
Asbury, Bishop 294
Ascension robes 370-426, 496-503
Ascension-robes affidavit 496-498
Asylums, insane 337-369, 488-495
 annual reports of—California 364; Maine (1842) 352, 355, 356, 360, 366, 368; Maryland (1844) 350n; Massachusetts: Boston Lunatic Hospital (1844) 353, (1845) 361, 362; McLean Asylum (Mass. General Hospital) (1841) 353, 361; State Lunatic Hospital (Worcester) (1843) 355, (1844) 365, (1846) 351, 353, (1851) 364; New Hampshire (1843) 351-355, (1844) 351, (1846) 352, (1848) 353, (1852) 357-359, 362-368; Pennsylvania (1841) 354; Ohio (1842) 354, (1851) 364
 case histories 341-348, 361, 488-495
Atonement, day of, antitypical 229n; Karaite, Oct. 22, 1844, 213
Attendance at Millerite meetings 105, 106, 111, 118, 119, 130, 145, 160, 161, 183, 210, 219, 226, 245
Autumnal types, significance 229
Autobiography, by Joseph Bates 180-184, 247

Babylon. See second angel's message
Bangor, Maine, advent conference at 112
Barbour, Philander, letter to William Miller 260
Barnes, S., letter to J. V. Himes 141, 142
Barry, Thomas F., letter to William Miller 76
Bates, Joseph, biographical data 180-185; at Exeter camp meeting 214, 215; at general conferences 81, 101, 102; comment on October 22 247; endorses new sanctuary view 459; pioneer Seventh-day Adventist 457
 Autobiography 180-184, 247
 Second Advent Way Marks and High Heaps 103, 215
Bay State Democrat (quoted) 371
Baxter, letter from William Miller 258, 259
Bellows, C. C., re ascension robes 405, 406
Bible Examiner 191, 192
Bibles, Miller family 150
Bibles, Millerism increased sale of 78, 146
Bicycle, Millerism illustrated by 275, 276
Bliss, Sylvester 230, 479, 481
 letter from William Miller 270, 271
 Memoirs of William Miller 19, 20, 38, 43n, 45, 46n, 52, 68, 72, 81, 171, 228, 229, 309, 403, 478, 499-501, 506, 507
Bolton, Sarah T., letter in *The Midnight Cry* 382
Boston, conferences in 81, 95, 96, 171, 172; Himes' activities in 174, 175; Miller in (1839-1840) 71-75; mob disturbance in 220-223
Boston Daily Bee 240, 257, 299, 347
Boston Daily Courier 335n, 386
Boston Daily Mail 221n, 227, 257n, 300, 513
Boston Herald 504
Boston Investigator 107, 195, 279, 280, 375, 376, 473
Boston Post 240, 255-258, 299n, 300, 339, 395
Boutelle, Luther, *Life and Religious Experience* 249, 501, 502

550   THE MIDNIGHT CRY

Bowery store window sign, "Muslin for Ascension Robes" 386-388, 391, 414
Bridegroom, parable of, applied 124
Brinegar, W. C. M. D., letter to F. D. Nichol 369
Broadsides, scurrilus 152, 153, 240, 242, 287, 420
Brook Farm 291, 292
Brother Jonathan 130
Brownlee, Doctor, opposes Miller 119, 451
Brownson, Dr. O. A. 298
Buckley, James M., *A History of Methodism in the United States* 295
Burlesques of Millerism 128, 131, 395, 503
Bury, J. B., *The Idea of Progress* 435n
Bush, Rev. George, opponent of Miller, on Bible prophecy 439, 440, 445, 447-452
Reasons for Rejecting Mr. Miller's Views on the Advent, With Mr. Miller's Reply 440, 448

Caledonian 253
Camp Meeting Manual, by B. W. Gorham 279n
Camp meetings, Millerite 104-106, 109-111, 114, 115, 117-122, 143, 145, 146n, 156, 209, 212-218, 316-318, 346
non-Millerite 106, 117, 118, 294, 295-297
Campbell, Alexander 508, 509
"The Coming of the Lord," *Millennial Harbinger* 153
Canada, Millerism in 111, 141
Canfield, Edward, letter to Himes and Litch 116
Caricature prints (see also Broadsides) 152, 153, 381, 382
Cartoons 152, 153
Casco Street Christian Church 75-77
Catholics, violence against 298
Century Magazine 194, 195, 407, 408
Certain Cases in the New Hampshire State Asylum, Oct. 29, 1842, to Feb. 25, 1843, 488-492
Chandler, S. C., letter to William Miller 169
Chardon Street Chapel 71, 81, 95, 96, 174-176, 308, 309, 480, 481
Charges against Miller and Millerism, general 73, 89, 254, 257; adventurers 89; ascension robes 370-426; 496-498; demoralizing influence, embezzlement 323, 327; emotionalism 303, 314; encouraging idleness 263; false date of April 23, 1843, 140; fanaticism 217-227, 303-336; insanity 89, 131, 226, 259, 303, 338-369, 488-492; murder 89, 338, 340-344, 516; neglect of business, family, property 263, 335; personal profit 121, 128, 252, 253; suicide 259, 338-348; swindling 115, 253
refutation of 73, 74, 75, 89, 90, 120, 250, 254-259, 470-474
Charts, 102, 103, 109, 110, 120, 121, 129, 134, 151, 155, 185, 201
Chase, Irah, *Remarks on the Book of Daniel* 440, 445

Chestnut Street M. E. Church of Portland, Maine, *Records of Stewards and Leaders* 457n
Chicago Express 343
Child, Mrs. 335, 386, 387
Chinese Museum, Philadelphia, Miller lectures in 130
Christ, priestly work of 229n, 458, 459
Christian Herald 138
Christian Palladium 97, 193, 194
Christian Watchman 173, 315
Chronology in Millerite interpretations 160n, 169, 173, 206-208, 213, 268, 272, 273, 284-286, 454
Church membership, question of, in 1843 87, 147
Churches, attitude toward Millerism 119, 147, 264, 265
Churchill, Winston S., "Shall We All Commit Suicide?" *Hearst's International* 512
Cincinnati, October 22 meeting at 244, 245, 513
Cincinnati Chronicle 245, 391
Cincinnati Miscellany 245
Clemons, Mrs. E. C., letter to Miller 230n, 478-480
Cleveland Herald 244
Closing of stores 238, 239, 336
Collins, L. C., letter to Himes and Litch 103, 312
Cole, Timothy, letter to Miller 67, 68
"Come Out of Her, My People," by Charles Fitch 148, 149
Comet of 1843 135, 379
Commentaries not used by Miller 150
Common fund of Millerites 70, 249
Communal societies in 1840's 291
Communion service, interdenominational 93
Complete Writings of Ralph Waldo Emerson, The 291, 292
Concord Freeman 298
Concord, N. H., great tent first used at 114
Conferences, second advent 83, 85-87, 93-96, 100-103, 112, 141, 160, 171, 172
Concordance, Miller's use of 30, 52, 150
Connecticut Courant 129, 132
Controversy, religious, bitter in 1840's 89, 90, 93, 116, 122, 123, 255, 298
examples of, in history 276
within Millerism after October 22 277-279
Conversions—of gamblers 75, 76; of Miller 28-30; of opposers 63; of skeptics 96, 107; of world (see Millennium)
Cook, J. B., letter from William Miller 283n
Cook, Rev. Parsons 74
Corpus Juris 401, 418
Cox, G. F., letter to Miller, Litch, and Himes 268, 269
Credulity in 1840's 299, 300, 320
of Millerites 319, 320, 471
Creeds, and formulas feared by Miller 279
church, on advent 431-436
Creeds of Christendom, The, by Philip Schaff 431-433, 436
Crops abandoned 213
Crosier, O. R. L., on the sanctuary 458, 459
Cruden's Concordance used by Miller 31, 150

INDEX   551

Crump, C. G., *History and Historical Research* 11, 13
Cyclopaedia of American Biography 414n
Cyclopaedia of Methodism, by Matthew Simpson 297

Daily Cincinnati Atlas 329n
Daily Eastern Argus 222
Daily Evening Transcript (Boston) 143, 221n, 302, 338, 371
Daily Morning Post (Pittsburgh) 293
Daily National Intelligencer (Washington) 168, 225, 335n, 387
Day Dawn, The 459, 460
Day for a year. See Year-day principle
Day-Star, The 249n, 459n
Day set for the end of the world 365, 370
Days of Delusion, by Clara Endicott Sears 416-426, 498-502, 513-515
Dead, state of. See Mortality
"Dear Brother" (unknown), letter from William Miller 285
Debts, paid before end 239, 240
Defence of Elder Joshua V. Himes 481
Defense, summary 470-474
Deist, Miller a 21, 22, 24-27, 30
Descendants of Captain Joseph Miller, C. S. Williams 477
Destitute, care of after October 22 251, 252
Devens, R. M., *The Great Events of Our Past Century* 286, 333n
Denomination, Millerism not a 80, 147, 211, 266, 269, 275, 281, 282
Dial, The 291
Dictionary of American Biography 414
Diet, reforms in 233, 293
Disappointment, first (spring) 163, 169-173, 208, 209
 the great (October 22) 246-269; effect on Millerism 274-276; effect on Millerites (false) 250, (true) 261-273; explained by light on the sanctuary 458; new explanations of, opposed by Miller 283; permitted by God 261, 262, 266, 267, 281; softened by possible error in chronology 273
Diversity of beliefs among Millerites 83, 90, 92-94
Dixon, J. T., ascension-robe offer 405
Dowling, John, *An Exposition of the Prophecies, Supposed by William Miller to Predict the Second Coming of Christ, in 1843* 443-451
 refutes Miller 133
Dresden, Miller's first preaching at 42, 43
Druggist dispenses tracts with drugs 116

Early Writings, by Ellen G. White 163n
East Kingston, N. H., first Millerite camp meeting in U. S. at 104
Editors admonished by Miller after October 22 278, 279
Edson, Hiram, describes disappointment of October 22 247, 248; explanation of sanctuary 457-459; manuscript on his life and experience 248, 458-460

1843 (see also Time of second advent), end of 158, 160n
"1843 chart" 102, 103
1844, prophetic periods extended into (Miller) 160n; (Snow) 207, 208, 213
Elections, national 254, 263, 264, 289, 290
Elliott, George A., *M. D.* 369
 letter to F. D. Nichol 494
Emancipator, Southard acting editor 192
Emerson, Ralph Waldo, "Life and Letters in New England" 291, 292
 "New England Reformers" 291
Emotionalism, common in the 1840's 83, 84, 219, 220, 254, 293-298, 315, 316, 482
 in Millerite meetings 219, 222, 314-319
Employment, abandoning, advised against 86, 87, 132, 133, 139, 235, 236
 advised by some 252, 263
 during closing days 213, 236-240, 251, 252, 263
 urged during Presidential campaign 263, 264
Emmons, H., letter in *The Day-Star* 249n
Encyclopaedia Britannica 415
End of the world (see also Advent, and Time of second advent), scientist lecture on 168; basic idea of Millerism 33, 428
"End of the World" broadsides 241
England, Adventist periodicals from 91; Himes' plans for work in 209, 210; Millerism in 142, 155, 156
Evangelism, lay 86, 134, 235, 236, 238
 methods of, used by Millerites 86; Bible classes 121; camp meetings 114; discussion with ministers 121; libraries 87, 88, 91; literature circulation 92, 121; prayer meetings 78, 86; prophetic stationery 134; temporary local papers 124, 125, 144; tracts 157
Evening Mirror (New York) 293
Evening Mercantile Journal 264, 290
Evening Post (Rochester, N. Y.) 143
Evening Post for the Country 219, 335n
Exeter, N. H., camp meeting at 213-216, 316
Exposition of the Prophecies, Supposed by William Miller to Predict the Second Coming of Christ, in 1843, An, by John Dowling 443, 444n, 446, 449
Extremes (see also Fanaticism), leaders seek to avoid 236, 237, 265, 266

Fairhaven Antislavery Society 182
Fairhaven Temperance Society organized 181
"Faith in Scotland," in *The Midnight Cry* 125
Fanatic, definition of 307
Fanaticism (see also Charges, Miller, and Millerites), definition of 310n
 in Christian history 305
 in Methodism 305-307
 in Millerism 146, 217, 218, 242, 249, 303-336; discountenanced by Millerite leaders 127, 139, 159, 222, 236, 237, 265, 266, 271, 309-313, 481-488
Few Evidences of the Time of the Second

Coming of Christ, to Elder Andrus by William Miller, A 39, 442
Finance, Millerite, methods of 95, 96, 101, 115, 120, 134
First angel's message recognized by Miller 284; used by S. D. A.'s 461, 462
First Report of the General Conference of Christians Expecting the Advent of Our Lord Jesus Christ, The 82, 83
Fitch, Charles, biographical data 63, 64, 95, 185-188, 231
  Millerite activities—at Oberlin College 111, 186, 187; in Haverhill (1842) 201; preaches unconsciousness of dead and annihilation 283, 284; presents chart 102; prominent Millerite leader 95, 126, 148, 185; sermon on Babylon 148, 149; slow to accept October 22 231
  letter in *Signs of the Times* 78
  letters to—"Brother and Sister [W. C.] Palmer" 187; William Miller 63
  Letter to Rev. J. Litch on the Second Coming of Christ 116, 186
  Slaveholding Weighed in the Balance of Truth and Its Comparative Guilt 185
Fleming, L. D., letter to William Miller 76
Foreign countries, Millerism in 112, 125, 155-157, 209, 210
Footprints of an Itinerant, by Maxwell Pierson Gaddis 246, 295, 296, 337
Fosdick, Raymond B., *The Rockefeller Foundation, a Review for 1943* 512
457 B. C. begins 2300 days and 70 weeks 33, 160n, 273, 443, 444, 506
Freedom of discussion among Millerites 74, 75, 93-95, 120, 192n, 279
Freedom of religion desired by Miller 279
French, Calvin, fanaticism of 308
"Friend Robins," letter from William Miller 23, 24
Froom, L. E., on prophetic interpretation 507

"Gabriel, Blow That Horn!" by Regis Canevin Toomey 513-518
Gaddis, Maxwell Pierson, *The Footprints of an Itinerant* 246, 295, 296, 337
Galusha, Elon 151, 152, 164, 167
  letter in *The Advent Herald* 483
Galusha, Jonas, 22, 152n
Garrison, Wendell Phillips, *William Lloyd Garrison. The Story of His Life Told by His Children* 182
Garrison, William Lloyd 175, 176, 292
Gates, I. R., arrest and release 253, 254
  letter in *The Midnight Cry* 254
Genius of Christianity 220
Geology, arguments against Millerism 128, 168
Gilman, Henry Hale, *The Mill and the Millerite* 203n, 400n
Glad Tidings, The (Rochester) 144
Godey's Lady's Book 425
Gorgas, Doctor, leader of a fanatical movement in Philadelphia 324, 325, 392, 484-488
Gorham, B. W., *Camp Meeting Manual* 297n

Gospel Banner 345
Graham, Sylvester 201, 203, 293
"Grand Ascension of the Miller Tabernacle!" broadside 241, 242, 420
Graveyards 334, 377, 383, 390
Great Controversy, The by Ellen G. White 462
Great Events of Our Past Century, The, by R. M. Devens 286, 333n
Great Western Almanac for 1844, The 422n
Grigg, George 326-328
Grove meetings 145, 146
Guardians for Millerites 335, 517, 518
Gunn, Lewis C. 325, 326, 448

Hale, Apollos 102, 103, 126, 481
Hale, Ezekiel, Jr. 104, 199-203, 399
Hale, Ezekiel, Jr., vs. E. J. M. Hale, Suit in equity 201, 202
Hahn, F. B. 458, 459
Hampshire Gazette 129
Harding, Dr. George T. 369
Harmon, Ellen. See White, Ellen G.
Harmon family expelled from Methodist Church 457n
Harper's Magazine 410, 411
Hatley, Canada, first Millerite camp meeting in America 111
Haverhill Gazette (Mass.) 302, 377, 492
Hawley, Silas 126, 138, 147, 183, 444, 505
  letter in *The Midnight Cry* 145-147
Healing by prayer, five cases, reported in *The Midnight Cry* 320
Hearst's International 511, 512
Heavenly phenomena 135-137
Hell-fire stories, trio of 421
Hellweg, Capt. J. F., letter to F. D. Nichol 135n
Hempstead Inquirer 145
Hendryx, Truman, letters from Miller 43-49, 51-53, 55-62, 64, 83
Herald (New York) 225, 243, 244
Hereditary and Periodical Insanity in Relation to So-Called Religion-Induced Insanity 493-495
Hewitt, C. H., letter to F. D. Nichol 455
Higgins, Mrs., fanaticism of 325n, 484, 486
Himes, Joshua V., biographical data 71, 81, 174-176, 479, 480
  character of, promoter and leader 71, 72, 74
  charges against, and replies—ascension robes 410-412; "Disturbances at the Tabernacle" 221, 222; embezzlement after October 22 253; fraud after October 22 253; insanity and suicide 339, 395; keeping the record clear 222; profit from members 252, 253; trial and defense of 480, 481
  letters from—S. Barnes 141, 142; Edward Canfield 116; L. C. Collins and G. F. Cox 268, 269; Miller 78, 79, 112, 129, 140, 169, 229, 266-268, 270, 271, 278, 282n
  letters in—*The Midnight Cry* 211, 212, 383; *Signs of the Times* 112, 312, 373
  letters to—editor of *Outlook,* Oct. 29, 1894,

on robes 410, 411; Litch (*Signs of the Times*) 100; Miller 87, 88, 231n, 480
Millerite activities—at conferences 81, 94, 95, 112; comment on Gorgas incident 484-488; devotes himself to Miller's work 71, 72; discountenances fanaticism 222, 309; endorses separation from churches 211, 212; establishes *Signs of the Times* 73, 74; invites calls for lecturers 111; in New York City 100; in New York State (July, 1844) 209; in Ohio (August, 1844) 209; in Philadelphia (July, 1844) 208; in Washington 161, 162; mission to Europe canceled 230; on western tour (1844) 208-211; preaches on shipboard 112, 113; prominence of 94, 126; publishing work 73, 74, 88, 91, 99, 100; slow to accept October 22 216, 230; stops Gorgas' chart 324, 325; with Miller at death 286; work after 1844 283
post-Millerite activities 410
Views of the Prophecies and Prophetic Chronology, Selected From Manuscripts of William Miller, With a Memoir of His Life 77, 78
Hingham Patriot (Mass.) 380
Histories, inaccuracy of, re Millerism (see also Hoaxes) 330-333, 415, 416, 513, 518
History and Historical Research, by C. G. Crump 11, 13
History of Methodism, The, by John Fletcher Hurst 294, 295
History of Methodism in the United States, A, by James M. Buckley 295
History of Philadelphia, by Scharf and Westcott 331, 332, 407
History of the People of the United States, A, by John B. McMaster 330n 415, 416, 513
History of the Second Advent Church in Portland, Maine, by W. H. Mitchell 76
History of the Second Advent Message, by Isaac C. Wellcome 101, 192
History of the Wesleyan Grove, Martha's Vineyard, Camp Meeting, A, by H. Vincent 297
History, impartial, reasons for not writing 10-12
Hoaxes, historical 503-505; of Miller's supposed lecture at Washington 127, 128; of 1,000-year error and ascension robes 373, 374
Holiness, false idea of, warned against 139
Holy of holies 229n, 459
Housetops, Millerites on 383
House, Millerism illustrated by 428, 429, 436
Hudson River boat, Miller preaches on 52
Hurst, John Fletcher, *The History of Methodism* 294, 295
Hymns, advent 113, 115, 183, 199, 217

Idea of gradual world improvement heavenly discounted today 511, 512
Idea of Progress, The, by J. B. Bury 435n

"In Honor of the King of Kings," broadside 324
Incomes in the 1840's 95
Independent (New York) 405, 406
Infidel editor commends Miller 280
letter from William Miller 473
Inquirer, Hempstead 145
Insanity, attributed to Millerism (see also Charges) 337-369, 488-495
charged against non-Millerite revivals 337; causes of, supposed 350-359; hereditary and periodical 493-495
Intelligencer (Harrisburg, Pa.) 485
Investigator. See *Boston Investigator*
Islands, Millerism reaches 134, 155, 156

Jewelry, contribution of 211
Jewish (sacred) year, spring beginning of 126, 135, 158, 159, 163
Jonah, comparison with 262, 271
Jones, Henry, 50, 94, 95, 177-180, 433n, 478
letters to William Miller 46n, 50, 177-179
Jones, I. E. 478n; letters to Miller 192n, 277, 278
Josiah Allen's Wife, "The Last Day," *Ladies' Home Journal* 408
Journal (Napa, Calif.) 505
Journal of Commerce (New York) 373, 374
Journal of the Rev. John Wesley, The 306
Judaism Overthrown, pamphlet by J. Litch, reviewed in *Spirit of the XIX Century* 441

Karaite Jews, reckoning of 163, 213n, 229
"Kavanagh," by Longfellow, reference to robes 402
Kennebec Journal (Augusta, Maine) 129, 136, 347n

Ladies' Home Journal 408
Lafayette, Marquis de, visit of 37, 38
Lecturers, calls for, handled by Himes 111
Lecturers, examined and recommended by committee 91, 92
Legal controversy between Ezekiel Hale, Jr., and his son 400
Letter to Rev. J. Litch on the Second Coming of Christ, by Charles Fitch 186
Letters of John Wesley, The 307
Letters, how sent in 1840's 91
to and from Miller 151
to Clara Endicott Sears 416-426
"Liars' Department" 115, 116, 372, 373
Liberator, The 175
"Life and Letters in New England," *The Complete Writings of Ralph Waldo Emerson* 291, 292
Life and Religious Experience, by Luther Boutelle 249, 501
Life and Times of the Rev. John Wesley, The, by L. Tyerman 305, 306
Life Incidents, by James White 197, 198, 214, 317, 462
Lighthouse keepers, literature to 111
Litch, Josiah, biographical data 68, 88, 188-

190; Millerite activities—as "general agent" 88; at Newark camp 117; at Hatley camp meeting 111; comment on October 22 247; prominence of 88, 94, 126; slow to accept Oct. 22 231; unable to prevent Philadelphia encampment 324n
letters from—Edward Canfield 116; G. F. Cox 268, 269; Himes 100
letter in *The Midnight Cry* 154, 268, 310, 311
letter to William Miller 247, 483
"Address to the Clergy" 450
Judaism Overthrown, reviewed in *Spirit of the XIX Century* 441
The Probability of the Second Coming of Christ About 1843 189
"The Rise and Progress of Adventism" 383
Literature, Millerite, circulation of 52, 60, 61, 85-88, 92, 99, 100, 111, 112, 116, 124, 125, 144, 155, 156, 211, 234
Littel's Living Age 286, 474
Loughborough, J. N., on Snow's arrival at Exeter camp 214n
Louisville, tent in 218, 219
Louisville Morning Courier 219
Low Hampton, N. Y., home of Miller 17, 26, 93, 94, 150, 228, 229, 250, 272, 286
Lowell Advertiser 292
Lowell Courier 131, 292
Luther, controversy with Zwingli 276

McMaster, John B., *A History of the People of the United States* 330n, 415, 416, 513
Magazine of Christian Literature 123, 408
Maine Inquirer 131, 164, 343-345, 371, 379, 380
Maine Wesleyan Journal 77
"Map of the Circuit of Ten Miles Around the City of Philadelphia," 326n
Marsh, Joseph, accepts Millerism 97, 98, 193-195
letter from Miller 484, to Miller 98
Note in *Signs of the Times* 193
Marsh, Sarah M., letter to Miller 97
Martha Wood, schooner, Himes preaches aboard 112
Martha's Vineyard, camp meetings at 296, 297
Massachusetts Spy (Worcester) 122, 138, 299n
Matthewson, Ann 319, 320, 471n
Mattison, Elder, accepts Miller's teaching 62
"Memoir," *Bible Examiner* 191
Memoirs of Alexander Campbell, by Robert Richardson 509
Memoirs of William Miller, by Sylvester Bliss 20, 38, 52, 68, 72, 81, 171, 228, 229, 252, 309, 403, 478, 499-501, 506, 507
Mencken, H. L. 504, 505; letter to F. D. Nichol 505
Mesmerism, Storrs attributes seventh-month movement to 270
Methodist Church, some fanaticism in 305-307
Michigan, Millerites from 210
Millerism in 141, 142

Midnight Cry, The 23, 26-28, 99, 121, 123-125, 127n, 134, 137, 139, 145-147, 149, 151, 154-157, 161, 163, 164, 166, 171, 172, 194, 196, 208, 212, 219, 220, 222, 223, 229-233, 235-239, 252, 254, 261-268, 270, 273, 309n, 310, 311, 319, 320, 324-328, 330, 335, 338, 344, 374, 375, 377, 382, 383, 395, 396, 410, 411, 437n, 445, 452, 484, 485, 487, 488, 499, 500
Midnight cry (term) 155; at Exeter camp meeting 213-216
Mill and the Millerite, The by Henry Hale Gilman 203n, 400n
Millennial Harbinger 153, 509
Millennial Harp, The 113
Millennial Musings 113
Millennium (see also World, gradual betterment of), Millerite view 434, 436, 450, 506-508
temporal, at end of 2300 days 447-450; popular belief in 434-436
"Miller, or the End of the World," play 131
Miller, William
Biographical data—ancestry 477, 478; early life 17-20; marriage 20; civil and military service 22-25; deism and conversion 21, 25-30; preparation for preaching 30-40; spare-time preaching 41-56; preaching tours (1831) 43, 44, (1833) 52, 53, (1834) 56, (1835) 57-59, (1836) 59-61, (1837) 62, (1838) 64, 66, (1839) 66, 67, 69, (1834-39) 57, 69; activities (1840) 75-83; (1841) 85, 93; (1842) 98, 100, 101, 106, 111, 112, 115, 117-122; (1843) 126-131, 140, 151, 154; (1831-43 summary) 160; (early 1844) 158, 160-162; reaction to first disappointment 169-173; (summer, 1844) 208-212, 228; acceptance of October 22 228, 229; reaction to great disappointment 250, 266-268, 270-272, 283-286; work after 1844 283; declining days 285, 286; ill-health 60, 67, 80, 81, 85, 122, 123, 140, 160, 228, 285; home and family 42, 65, 66, 129, 149-151, 477, 478

Characteristics—analytical mind 29, 271, 272; common sense 122; conservatism 29, 32, 34-36, 212, 228, 482; courage 51, 260; forceful preaching 47, 49, 62, 63, 75, 77, 78, 83, 84, 122, 123, 129, 132, 482; faith 112, 171, 207, 266, 279, 280; homely speech 62, 123; humility 51, 55, 57, 60, 65, 112; humor 39, 40, 51, 98, 99; knowledge of Bible 122, of church history 127, 278, 279, of history 122, of human nature 123, 127, 278, 279; leadership in his community 19, 20, 22, 24, 38; limited education 77, 122, 123, 131; logical reasoning 29-31, 33, 63, 131, 188; methodical habits 19, 31, 38n; militancy 54, 83, 84, 89, 90, 122, 258, 259; moderation 159, 160, 271, 313, 482; open-mindedness 65, 93; orthodoxy 32, 36, 37, 427; outspokenness

77, 122, 123, 129; personal descriptions 67, 77, 122, 123; reading habit 19-21, 122, 150, 151, 437n; self-criticism, 34, 35, 64, 65, 112, 266, 267; sincerity 118, 122, 286; sense of duty 35, 41, 42, 78, 79, 160; tolerance 93, 279
Letters, collection of 151
Letters from—"Bah!" 140; Philander Barbour 260; Thomas F. Barry 76; S. C. Chandler 169; Mrs. E. C. Clemons 230n, 478-480; Timothy Cole 68; G. F. Cox 268, 269; Elias Fasset 23n; Charles Fitch 63; L. D. Fleming 76; Elon Galusha and 60 others 151; Himes 87, 88, 231n, 480; Henry Jones 46n, 50, 177-179; I. E. Jones 192n, 277, 278; Josiah Litch 247, 483; Joseph Marsh 98, 193; Sarah M. Marsh 97; "R. D." 129; H. P. Stebbins 115; Charles W. Stewart 97; Henry Dana Ward 90; Isaac Wescott 57, 58, 69; N. N. Whiting 250, 251, 269, 270, 483, 485, 486
Letters in—The Midnight Cry 154; Signs of the Times 313
Letters to—Elisha Ashley 37; Joseph and Anna Attwood 40; "Brother Baxter" 258, 259; J. B. Cook 283n; "Dear Brother" (unknown) 285; editor of Boston Investigator 279, 280, 473; Elon Galusha 167; Truman Hendryx 43n-49, 51-62, 64, 65; Joshua V. Himes 78, 79, 112, 129, 140, 169, 229n, 266-268, 270, 271, 278, 279, 282n; Joseph Marsh 484; William S. Miller 65, 66, 75, 129; Dr. I. O. Orr 250, 267; "Friend Robins" 23, 24; "second advent believers" (January, 1844) 158-160; Elder Smith of Poultney, published in Vermont Telegraph 45; John Stanley 25; recommends to 3d general conference examining committee 91, 92
Theology
Difference from contemporary theology 207, 434, 435, 445-453
Position on: advent, nature of 428, 429, 446, 447, time of 33, 126, 127, 229 (see also Time of second advent); Bible 28, 30-32, 47, 77; disappointment, explanation of 272, 273, 283, 284, 286, 454, God's hand in 271, 284, no new reckoning after 267, 271; first angel's message (recognized) 284; Jews, return of 435, 506, 507; millennium 434, 446, 506-508; nature of man 27, 29, 283, 284; prophecies 32, 33, 77, 505-510; resurrection 39, 506, 507; salvation 29, 30, 112, 271; sanctuary 33, 39, 229, 441, 442, 454; second angel's message 166-168, 266, 267, 271, 272; types, spring and autumn 229
Supported by: Bible 120, 428-430; church creeds 431-433; theologies 285, 436-441, 444, 445, 505-508
Writings
"Address to Second Advent Believers," January, 1844 158-160

"Address to Advent Believers," December, 1844 272
Apology and Defence 24, 27, 29-31, 33-36, 41-43, 73, 204, 283-285
Arithmetic notebook 18
Articles in Vermont Telegraph 45, 46, 48, 50
Boyhood Diary 19
"Dissertation on Calumny" 21
Evidence From Scripture and History of the Second Coming of Christ, About the Year 1843: Exhibited in a Course of Lectures (book)—1st ed. (1836) 59, 61, rev. ed. (1838) 59n, sale of 66, new edition (1840) 75
Evidences From Scripture & History of the Second Coming of Christ About the Year A. D. 1843, and of His Personal Reign of 1,000 Years (pamphlet)—published (1833) 51, second edition (1835) 57, 58, pirated 59
A Few Evidences of the Time of the Second Coming of Christ, to Elder Andrus by William Miller, MS. 39, 442
Lectures (book). See Evidence From Scripture . . . in a Course of Lectures
"New Year's Address" (1843) 127
"New Year's Address," MS. (1844) 160n
Reply to Rev. George Bush, "Reasons for Rejecting Mr. Miller's Views on the Advent" 440, 448
Statement of belief (MS.) 36, 37
General:
Accusation of Fanaticism 271, 481-484
Aim, to proclaim good news of Bible 279, 280
Charges against 46, 50, 62, 78, 79, 118, 121, 129, 131, 259
Confession of error (spring, 1844) 171, 173, 209, (fall, 1844) 284
Criticism of the movement 271, 481-484
Error—chronology suspected 206-208, 213, 268, 272, 273; event, not time 173, 456, 458, 472, 510
Finances 121, 129
Lectures (book). See Miller—Writings
Not a fanatic 29, 46, 272
Not a prophet 128
Not an emotionalist 29, 31, 84, 482
Not a self-seeker 34, 129, 160, 167, 168
Miller's Interpretation of Major Prophecies 505
Miller's Secondary Proofs for the 1843 Date 507
Miller, William S., Miller's eldest son 65, 66, 150
letters from William Miller 65, 66, 75, 129; from Isaac Wescott 69
Miller family Bibles 150
Miller family genealogy 477
Miller Family Magazine, The 478
Millerism, attacks on, to be discounted (see also Charges) 288, 300, 301
burlesques of 128, 131, 395, 503

caricatures on 152, 153, 381, 382
defense of, summarized 470-474
definition of, Miller's 473, 474
denominations arising from 266, 454-464
extent of 79, 125, 134, 142, 154-157
fanaticism exceptional in. See Fanaticism
growth of 154, 212
illustrated by—a bicycle 275, 276; an edifice 428, 429, 436; a river 139, 274, 282, 283, 304
interdenominational character of 60, 92, 93, 103, 108, 109, 115, 124, 133, 142, 146, 147, 204, 211, 266, 275, 427, 428
more than mere time 95, 154, 172, 207, 428, 433, 434, 446
period after great disappointment 262, 263, 274-279, 282
results of—Bible reading increased 161, Bible sales increased 78, 146, churches built up 70, 72, 78, 79, debts paid 239, 240, lives reformed 70, 72, 75, 76, murder confessed 143, prayer meetings organized (businessmen) 78, restitution 132, singing and praying 161, wrongs righted 240
"Millerism and Insanity," editorial in *New York Daily Tribune* 344, 367, 378
Millerite (name) 45, 206, 207
Millerite leaders, charges against (see Charges)
condemn Philadelphia encampment 330
described 174-205
final advice of 231-238
last to embrace Oct. 22 215, 216, 228-231
moderation of 136, 137, 139, 140, 231-235, 237, 265, 266, 482
not illiterate (Parker) 195
on ascension robes 372-376, 382-384, 394-398, 402, 403
rebuke fanaticism 307-313, 481-488
restraint of 136, 137
sincerity of 120, 121
Millerites, attitude toward attacks (see also Charges, refutation of) 255
characterized by—cheerfulness 198, 199, 245; courage 175, 176, 204; decorum 130, 217, 219, 245, 246, 316; faithfulness 219; freedom of opinion 74, 75, 93-95, 120, 192n, 279; independence of conventions 191, 203, 204; interest in new ideas 203; less interest in ordinary pursuits 202, 203; little fanaticism. See Fanaticism; moderation 234; self-denial 178-182; sense of urgency 102-105, 114, 158, 199; sensible sermons 219; sincerity 219, 245; singing 199; tolerance. See Freedom of discussion; 192n; unanimity 92; unselfishness 219; zeal for reforms 203, 204
from all classes 217-219, 226, 304, 470
number of 154, 204, 205, 513
regarded as (see also Charges)—credulous 201; fanatical 382, 383; ignorant 226; intelligent 217, 226, 227; monsters 100; orderly 245; peculiar 118, 119, 184, 194; pious 153, 217; respectable 226, 227; sincere 226, 245

Ministers, attitude of toward Millerism 46, 49-51, 56, 62, 70, 72, 76, 86, 89, 107, 108, 119, 129, 144, 147
Minor, Mrs. C. S. 324n, 326
Mission stations reached by Millerite papers 134, 155, 156
Mitchell, W. H., *History of the Second Advent Church in Portland, Maine* 76
Mobs, at Boston 220, 221
at Philadelphia 223, 224
cause closing of meetings 220-225, 243, 250, 251
disturbances by, frequent in closing weeks 224, 225
"Monitory wafers," use of by Millerites 91
Morning Watch, The 270, 273, 484
Morse, Washington, "Remembrance of Former Days," *The Advent Review and Sabbath Herald* 248
Mortality of man, incorporated into Advent Christian doctrine 455
Fitch on 283, 284
Litch on 192n
Millerite leaders on 192n, 283, 284
Storrs on 192
Most holy place 229n, 458, 459
Mountaintops, Millerites on 334, 377, 390
Mourners, demonstrations of at Louisville 219
Mourners' bench not used by Miller 84
Murderer, repentant, confesses 143
Muslin for ascension robes 414
Mutual Conference of Adventists (1845) 280-282

National Aegis (Worcester, Mass.) 335n, 387
National Cyclopaedia of America Biography 414
National Institute Convention, address at 168
National Intelligencer 375
Neal's Saturday Gazette (Philadelphia) 240, 385
New England Puritan 396
"New England Reformers," by Ralph Waldo Emerson 291
New English Dictionary on Historical Principles, A (*Oxford Dictionary*) 397
New Hampshire Baptist Register 396
New Hampshire Statesman 253
"New Year's Address, A," by Miller (1843) 127
"New Year's Address" (1844 MS.) 160n
New York City, association formed in 101; conference at (1844) 165; convention at (1844) 161; difficulties in 100; Miller in 79; Miller and Himes in 100; mobs at 250, 251
New York Daily Tribune 129, 133, 344, 345n, 367, 378
New York Evangelist 298, 393
New York Express 325n
New York Herald Extra, on Newark camp meeting 117, 122
New York Observer 298, 299, 374, 377, 378
New York Plebeian 131
New York Spectator 225, 239, 253, 384
Newark Daily Advertiser 225, 310, 335n, 342

INDEX 557

Newark, N. J., camp meeting at 117-122
Newburyport Daily Herald (Mass.) 325n
Newspaper reporting in the 1840's 225
Newspapers. See Press
Newton, Sir Isaac 437
Observations Upon the Prophecies 444n, 467, 468
Niles National Register 380, 517
Non-resistance 175, 201
North American (Philadelphia) 226
Norway, Millerism known in 155

Oberlin College, Fitch lectures at 111, 186, 187
Observations Upon the Prophecies, by Sir Isaac Newton 444n, 467, 468
October 22 spent by Millerites in churches 243-246; in homes 249; not in graveyards 249
Olive Branch 396
Olsen, Dr. Alfred B. 369
Opposition to Millerism (see also Charges, Controversy), early 46, 48, 49, 51; in churches 87, 146, 147, 163-165, 228, 229; increase of (1841) 89; logic little used 79, 90, 171, 243, 263; only verbal until late 1841 96; strain on Miller's patience 112; types of (see also Broadsides and Caricatures)—abusive stories 73, 128, 129; anonymous letters 129, 258; editorials 243, 385; falsehoods 263; fireworks 384; mob disturbance of meetings 169, 220-225; newspaper extra 133; noise 130, 385; press reports 100; scurrilous attacks 131; sermons 89, 118, 119; signed statement 89; "slang" 79, 397; threats of personal attack 115, 183, 184, 96; violence, at Nashua, N. H. 96
Organization, lack of 79, 80, 91, 92, 172, 274-276, 281, 282; separate, not the object of Adventists 80; step toward 269, 281; through general conferences 80, 82, 83, 91, 92, 94
Orr, I. O., letter from Miller 250, 267
Orthodoxy of Millerite views. See Miller—Theology
Osgood, A. M. 164
Outlook 409-411
Oxford Dictionary. A New English Dictionary on Historical Principles 397

Parker, Jane Marsh, on ascension robes 407-409
reminiscences of her father 194, 195, of William Miller 123
"A Little Millerite," *Century Magazine* 194, 195, 407, 408
"A Spiritual Cyclone: The Millerite Delusion," *Magazine of Christian Literature* 123, 408
"Did the Millerites Wear Ascension Robes?" *Outlook* 409-411
Pennsylvania Inquirer (Philadelphia) 122, 123, 322, 325n, 329, 485
Pennsylvanian (Philadelphia) 257, 326n, 516

Phelps, Philip M. M. 22, 150, 477
letter to F. D. Nichol 496, 497
Phenomena in the heavens 135-137
Philadelphia encampment 242n, 321-334, 406, 407, 484, 485, 487
Philadelphia, Miller's lectures in 129, 130
mob disturbance at 223, 224
Philadelphia Alarm, 13 numbers of, in 1843 124, 125
Philadelphia Public Ledger 130, 223-226, 239, 310, 322, 332, 335n, 371, 372, 379, 387
Phrenologist examines Miller 98, 99
Pioneer spirit of 1840's 290, 291
Pittsfield Sun 310
Plattsburg, Battle of 24, 25
Play, "Miller, or the End of the World" 131
Poetic and Dramatic Works of Alfred Lord Tennyson, The 428
Polk, campaign of 254, 263, 289, 290
Porter, James, *Revivals of Religion* 337, 368
Portland, Maine 75, 76, 91-93
Portland Bulletin (Maine) 302, 315, 335, 337, 346, 377, 518
Portland Daily Advertiser (Maine) 223, 336, 340
Portland Daily American (Maine) 221n
Portsmouth Journal 224, 347, 371
Possessions, disposal of 230, 251-254, 335, 336, 339
Poultney, Miller moves to 20
Prayer meetings 78, 86
Preble, T. M., letter in *Signs of the Times* 96
Presbyterian, The 394
Presidential election of 1840's 288-290, 329
Press, credulity of 301, 396, 397
eyewitness account of Newark camp meeting 117-122
eyewitness account of a Millerite meeting in Cincinnati, Ohio, on October 22, 1844 390, 391
inaccuracy of 130, 222, 223, 257, 258, 329-331, 382, 383, 513
reporting in the 1840's 225, 382
reports on ascension robes 371, 372, 374-376, 379-382, 384-390, 392-395, 400, 405, 406n
unreliability of as a witness 117n, 256-258, 340
use of rumor and hearsay 117n, 225, 256, 371, 372
Press comment, favorable 117-122, 131, 132, 143, 145, 153, 154, 217-220, 223, 224, 226, 245, 257, 286, 336, 344
foreign 155
on October 22 activities 243-245
unfavorable 73, 100, 129, 133, 153, 219, 222, 223, 256, 303, 314, 315n, 322, 323, 327-334, 337-339, 344
Prints, caricature 152, 153
Probability of the Second Coming of Christ About 1843, The, by Josiah Litch 189
Profits not made by leaders 120, 121, 129
Prophecies. See Miller—Theology
Protracted meetings 295, 296
Providence Daily Journal 123, 253

Publications, Millerite (see also Literature)
—extra issues in October, 1844 231; depots for 134, 144, 154; policy re attacks 79, 115, 116, 335, 372, 373, 382; printed in England 142; published differing views 74, 75, 94, 192n; *Second Advent Library* 85; sent abroad 134; temporary local papers 124, 125, 144; tracts 157; treatment of charges 79, 115, 116, 335, 372, 373, 382, 499, 500

Rail, riding on, Bates threatened with 183,
"R. D.," letter to William Miller 129
Reader's Digest 330n, 513
Reasons for Rejecting Mr. Miller's Views on the Advent, by Rev. George Bush, With Mr. Miller's Reply 440, 448
Reform movements, Millerite spokesmen drawn from 175-185, 200-202
 prevalent in 1840's 290, 291
Reformation, doctrine of advent 83, 431, 432
Reformers quoted by Millerites 83
Religious Bodies: 1936, United States, Bureau of the Census 455-457
Remarks on the Book of Daniel, by Irah Chase 440, 445
Reminiscences, unreliability of 400-402, 423, 424
Republican Herald 340
Resurrection 39, 506, 507
Revival, result of Millerite camp meetings (East Kingston) 107, 108
 stimulated by Miller's preaching 70, 76
Revival methods, prevalent, not used by Miller 83, 84, 482
Revivals, emotionalism in 219, 220, 482
 defense of, by Methodists 337
 mourners at, 219, 220, 482
"Revivals and Excitement," *Zion's Banner* 315
Revivals of Religion, by James Porter 368
Rewards offered for ascension-robe proof 382, 403-406
Rhodes, S. W., pioneer Seventh-day Adventist 457
Richardson, Robert, *Memoirs of Alexander Campbell* 509
Ridicule, Fitch afraid of 186
 following disappointment 249, 250, 268
 of Millerite children 195
Riker, Abraham, shoe dealer, false report of suicide 335, 336, 339, 517, 518
"Rise and Progress of Adventism, The," *The Advent Shield and Review* 383
River, Millerism compared to 139, 274, 282, 283, 304
Robes, ascension. See Ascension robes
Robins, letter from Miller 23, 24
Rockefeller Foundation, The, A Review for 1943, by Raymond B. Fosdick 512
Rules, judicial 13-15, 258n, 400-402, 418, 424, 496, 497
Rumors, growth of 68, 218n; in press reporting 117n, 225, 256, 371, 372, used as evidence against Millerism 14

Sabbath, message of 460-463

Salem Register (Mass.) 379
Sanctification, false ideas of 139, 159, 308, 313; Fitch believes in 187
Sandy Hill *Herald* 131, 132
Sanctuary, doctrine, steps in development of—on earth, 33, 39, 273n 441, 442; in heaven, Christ leaving most holy on October 22, 229n, 458; Christ entering most holy on October 22, 229n, 458-460.
Schaff, Philip, *The Creeds of Christendom* 431-433, 436
Scharf, Thomas, and Westcott, Thompson, *History of Philadelphia* 331, 332, 407
Scoffers (see also Opposition), column for, in *Signs of the Times* 79
 reaction to passing of October 22 250, 268
Scotland, preparing for advent in 1843 125
Sears, Clara Endicott, collection of letters re robes 416-426; *Days of Delusion* 416-426, 498-502, 513-515
Second advent. See Advent, second
Second Advent of Christ, The (periodical) 148
Second advent libraries (organizations) 87, 88, 91, 144
Second Advent Library (pamphlet series) 85, 91, 150
Second Advent Way Marks and High Heaps, by Joseph Bates 103, 215
Second angel's message developed 146-149, 163-168, 179; not endorsed by Miller 166-168, 212, 228, 266, 271, 272, 281; used by S. D. A.'s 461, 462
Second coming of Christ. See Advent, second
Sectarian differences submerged among Millerites 93, 109, 115, 139, 271, 272
"Separation From the Churches," by Himes 211, 212
Seventh-day Adventists, development of 456-465
 efforts of, to trace robes 403, 404
 message of 465-469
Seventh-day Sabbath Message 460-463
Seventh-month movement criticized by some 213n, 215, 217, 229, 270, 277. See also Time of second advent, day.
Seventy weeks interlocked with 2300 days 273n, 286, 442-445, 506, 507
Shoemaker in New York, story of 335
Shortridge, Mr. 377-379, 415, 416, 422, 423
Shryock, Harold, *M. D.* 369
Signs in the heavens 135-137
Signs of the Times 74, 78, 79, 80, 85, 87, 88, 90, 91, 94-96, 99, 100, 101, 103, 105-107, 111-116, 125-134, 136-138, 140-144, 146, 153-155, 156, 158, 160, 164, 190, 193, 199, 241, 308, 312-314, 340, 341, 373, 381, 450, 499, 500, 505, 506, 510, 513
Simpson, Matthew, *Cyclopaedia of Methodism* 297
Simpson, Samuel, *Life of Ulrich Zwingli* 276n
Skeptics converted 96, 107
Slaveholding Weighed in the Balance of Truth and Its Comparative Guilt, by Charles Fitch 185

INDEX 559

Slavery 54, 175-179, 181-185, 191, 192, 201, 260, 301
Smith, Lucy, marriage to William Miller 20
Smith, Elder, letters of Miller to, published in *Vermont Telegraph* 45
Snow, Samuel S., biographical data 195, 196
  letter in *The Midnight Cry* 208
  "true midnight cry" given by 207, 208, 213-216, 229n
Southard, Nathaniel 141, 149-151, 154, 192, 229, 230, 325n, 420, 437n
Spalding, A. W., *Pioneer Stories* 43n
Spaulding, A., letter in *The Midnight Cry* 151
Spaulding, Joel, letter to *Signs of the Times* 199
Spirit of the Times 239
Spirit of the XIX Century, 441
Springfield (Mass.) *Democrat* 115, 116
Stanley, John, letter from Miller 25
State Banner (Bennington, Vt.) 122
"Statement and Protest," in *The Advent Herald* 318
Stationery bearing chart 134
Starkweather, John, fanaticism of 308, 309
Stebbins, H. P., letter to Miller 115
Sterne, Lawrence, *Life of Tristram Shandy* 396
Stevens, Brother, description of, by Sarah T. Bolton 382, 383
Stewart, Charles W., letter to Miller 97
Stockman, L. S., disciplined by church 163, 164
Stone wall, Miller's 259
Stories, false about Himes 253, 256
  about Miller—mistake of 1,000 years 68, 371; new stone wall in 1843 150, 259; no more rain 89; no more marriages 89; general—April 23, 1843 140, 156; arrests of leaders 253, 254; ascension robes 370-426, 496-503 *passim*; Boston tabernacle 130, 137; falling away after spring disappointment 206; girl with strapped trunk 218n; insanity, murder, suicide 336-369, 488-495 *passim*; "orgies" at Philadelphia 130; throwing away money 240
"tall," believed in 1840's 299, 300
Storm, alleged, on Oct. 22, 1844, 331, 332
Storrs, George, biographical data 126, 191, 192, 252, 270, 330; letter in *The Midnight Cry* 270; on man's mortality 192, 283, 284
Storrs, Hattie, "Memoir" in *Bible Examiner* 191
Stuart, Moses, *Hints on the Interpretation of Prophecy* 438, 439
Sun (Baltimore) 222, 227, 240, 244, 322, 323, 337, 338, 347, 504, 505
Suicide, attributed to Millerism 336, 338. See also Charges; of the race 511, 512
Suit in equity, *Ezekiel Hale, Jr., vs. E. J. M. Hale* 201, 202

Tabernacle, Boston 137-139, 220, 221
Tarrying time 158, 159, 162, 163, 169, 267
Teeterboard, illustration of 12
Temperance reform in 1840's 177, 180, 181, 200-202, 292
Tennyson, *The Poetic and Dramatic Works of Alfred Lord Tennyson* 428
Tent, great 108, 114, 117, 121, 142-144, 201, 218, 219
Tenth day of the seventh month 213n, 215, 229. See also Time of second advent
"Text Book," earliest, notes on sermons heard 38
"Text Book," 1839-1844 57, 61, 69n
Theology, Millerite (see also Miller—Theology), based on Scriptures, history, and logic 120; diversity in Millerite 83, 90, 92, 93; nature of prophetic fulfillment more distinctive than the time 207; unanimity of remarkable, 92; warnings against extremes 139
Third angel's message 461-463
Three angels' messages. See First, Second, Third, etc.
Time of second advent, 1843 (Jewish year)—
  "about the year 1843" 33, 37, 126, 443; between March 21, 1843, and March 21, 1844, 126, 127n, 158, 370; cause of opposition 90; elasticity in reckoning 169-173; increasing emphasis on in 1842 101; Miller not dogmatic about 162, 163; no day set in 1843 by Millerite leaders 125-127, 380; not accepted by all Adventists 83, 90, 93-95, 121; passing of (see Disappointment, first) 1844 (day)—advanced to October 22 accepted by almost all Millerites 269, 270; arrived at by Snow 213; at first generally opposed 216; calculated by Karaite calendar 213n, 229; leaders late to embrace 215, 216, 228-231; Miller slow to accept 228, 229; mistake in, admitted 262, 263; mistake in, permitted for good 266, 267, 269; movement within the movement 215; not accepted by Cox 268, 269, Whiting 269, some Millerite ministers 268; October 22, 1844, 370, 443; papers accept late 216, 229, 230; passing of (see Disappointment, great), preaching of, a test 261, 262; preaching of, blessed by God 271; seemed the work of God 216; swept all before it 216; "true midnight cry" 213-216
1853 or 1854 set by group 454
exact hour, Gorgas' alleged revelation of 324, 327, 328
expectation after first disappointment 158, 159, 162, 163, 169, 209, 210, 267
expectation after great disappointment 263, 267-269, 454
Miller's views after October 22 267, 268, 271-273
not accepted by all Adventists 101, 172
not only teaching of Millerism 95
not the main question 207
possible error in chronology 169, 272, 273, 284, 286, 454
Toomey, R. C., "Gabriel, Blow That Horn!" 513-518; letter to F. D. Nichol 514

Trial and defense of Joshua V. Himes 480, 481
Tribune 345
Trumpet 78, 79
Twenty-three hundred days, believed to reach to temporal millennium 447-450, to second advent 33, 34, 39, 273n; end of, explained by Edson and associates 457-459; equal 2300 years 39; extended into 1844 (Miller) 160n, (Snow) 207, 208, 213; extended past 1844 273n, 454, 455; heart of Miller's teaching 441, 443; interlocked with 70 weeks 273n, 286, 444, 445, 506, 507; near end believed by many 445, 447; possible error in chronology of 268, 272
Tyerman, L., *The Life and Times of the Rev. John Wesley* 305, 306
Tyler, campaign of 289, 290
Tyson, F. C., *M. D.*, letter to F. D. Nichol 341, 368, 369

United States, Bureau of the Census, *Religious Bodies* 455-457
United States Gazette 225
United States Saturday Post (Philadelphia) 245, 323, 329, 385, 386, 391
Universalism opposed by Miller 77

Vermont Chronicle 173
Vermont Phoenix 290
Vermont Telegraph, Miller's articles in 45
Vermont Watchman and State Journal (Montpelier) 338
Views of the Prophecies and Prophetic Chronology, Selected From Manuscripts of William Miller, With a Memoir of His Life, edited by Joshua V. Himes 77, 78
Vincent, H., *A History of the Wesleyan Grove, Martha's Vineyard, Camp Meeting* 297
Violence—attacks on meetings at Nashua, N. H. 96; in 1840's 293, 294; threats of, to Himes 115, to mayor of Albany 115
Virgins, ten, parable of 213, 458
Visions, not used by Miller 159; professed by Gorgas
Voice of Truth and Glad Tidings, The 282, 407, 484, 500, 503
Volcanoes 168

Wages in the 1840's 95
War of 1812, Miller's experience in 22-25
Ward, Henry Dana 90, 94, 192, 193; letter in *Signs of the Times* 94; letter to William Miller 90
Washington, George, and cherry tree 503, 504
Washington, D. C., hoax of Miller's appearance in 127, 128; Miller lectures in 161, 162
  National Institute Convention 168

Washington, N. H., group of Adventists begin observing the seventh-day Sabbath 457
Watertown, fanatics from, at Exeter 215, 316-318
Weems, Parson, on Washington and the cherry tree 503, 504
Weethee, J. P. 164, 480, 481
Wellcome, Isaac C., *History of the Second Advent Message* 101, 192
Wescott, Isaac, letter to Miller 57, 58, 69
Wesley, John, deals with fanaticism 305-307
  meetings disturbed by mobs 96
  The Journal of the Rev. John Wesley 306
  Letters of John Wesley 307
West, Elder, attacks Miller's views 64
West, Millerism in 141, 144, 154, 210
Wheeler, Frederick 457
Wheeler, Jacob, affidavit of 496-498
White, Ellen G., consults Stockman 163n; endorses new sanctuary view 460n; expelled from Methodist Church 457n; pioneer Seventh-day Adventist 457; testimony of relation of Seventh-day Adventism to Millerism 462
  Early Writings 163n
  The Great Controversy 462
White, James 196-198, 457, 459; offers robe reward 403, 404
  letter in *Signs of the Times* 199
  Life Incidents 197, 198, 214, 317, 462
Whiting, N. N. 172, 193, 324, 325n, 483
  letter to William Miller 250, 251, 269, 270, 483, 485, 486
Whittier, John Greenleaf, describes Derry camp meeting (September, 1844) 217, 218; description of East Kingston camp meeting 110; on end of the world 429; repeats trunk story 218, 514
  Prose Works 110, 218, 429n, 514
Wilkins, Mary E., "A New England Prophet," *Harper's Magazine* 409-411
William Lloyd Garrison, The Story of His Life, as Told by His Children 182
Williams, C. S., *Descendants of Captain Joseph Miller* 477
Wings, little Negro with 422
Winter, Robert, in England 142, 155, 156
  letter in *The Midnight Cry* 155, 156
Wisconsin, Millerism in 141, 210
Wolff, Joseph, in Asia 156
World, destruction of—Millerites not positive on 448
  rational and Scriptural 512
  end of. See End of the World
  gradual betterment of 434, 435, 448, 449, 511, 512

Year-day principle in interpretation of prophecy 33, 438, 441, 444, 506
Yom Kippur, day of judgment to the Jews 459
Youth's Cabinet, Southard edits 192

Zion's Banner 315, 316
Zion's Herald 154

We invite you to view the complete
selection of titles we publish at:

www.TEACHServices.com

Scan with your mobile
device to go directly
to our website.

Please write or email us your praises, reactions, or
thoughts about this or any other book we publish at:

P.O. Box 954
Ringgold, GA 30736

info@TEACHServices.com

TEACH Services, Inc., titles may be purchased in bulk for
educational, business, fund-raising, or sales promotional use.
For information, please e-mail:

BulkSales@TEACHServices.com

Finally, if you are interested in seeing
your own book in print, please contact us at

publishing@TEACHServices.com

We would be happy to review your manuscript for free.

www.ingramcontent.com/pod-product-compliance
Lightning Source LLC
Chambersburg PA
CBHW060219230426
43664CB00011B/1477